SOMETHING ABOUT THE AUTHOR

SOMETHING ABOUT THE AUTHOR

Facts and Pictures about Authors
and Illustrators of Books for Young People

ANNE COMMIRE

VOLUME 25

GALE RESEARCH COMPANY
BOOK TOWER
DETROIT, MICHIGAN
48226

Editor: Anne Commire

Associate Editors: Agnes Garrett, Helga P. McCue

Assistant Editors: Dianne H. Anderson, Susette A. Balogh, Kathryn T. Floch,
Mary F. Glahn, Susan Miller Harig, D. Jayne Higo,
Melissa Renck, Linda Shedd, Susan L. Stetler

Consultant: Adele Sarkissian

Sketchwriters: Rosemary DeAngelis Bridges, Eunice L. Petrini

Research Assistant: Kathleen Betsko

Editorial Assistants: Lisa Bryon, Susan Pfanner, Elisa Ann Sawchuk

Production Supervisor: Carol Blanchard

Text Layout: Vivian Tannenbaum

Cover Design: Arthur Chartow

Special acknowledgment is due to the members of the *Contemporary Authors* staff
who assisted in the preparation of this volume.

Also Published by Gale

CONTEMPORARY AUTHORS

*A Bio-Bibliographical Guide to Current Writers in
Fiction, General Nonfiction, Poetry, Journalism,
Drama, Motion Pictures, Television,
and Other Fields*

(Now Covers More Than 60,000 Authors)

Library of Congress Catalog Card Number 72-27107

Copyright © 1981 by Gale Research Company. All rights reserved.

ISBN 0-8103-0087-7

ISSN 0276-816X

Table of Contents

Introduction   9

Forthcoming Authors   13

Author Index   239

Acknowledgments   15

Illustrations Index   225

A

Aronin, Ben 1904-1980
Obituary Notice 21

Augarde, Steve 1950- 21

B

Bagnold, Enid 1889-1981 23

Batten, H. Mortimer
1888-1958 34

Beatty, John 1922-1975
Obituary Notice 35

Beeby, Betty 1923- 37

Benchley, Nathaniel 1915- 39

Bennett, Russell H. 1896- 45

Bentley, Phyllis 1894-1977
Obituary Notice 45

Beresford, Elisabeth 45

Berry, Erick
see Best, Allena Champlin
Obituary Notice 48

Best, Allena Champlin 1892-1974
Obituary Notice 48

Black, Irma S. 1906-1972
Obituary Notice 48

Blyton, Enid 1897-1968 48

Bobbe, Dorothie 1905-1975
Obituary Notice 61

Brecht, Edith 1895-1975
Obituary Notice 61

Briggs, Katharine Mary 1898-1980
Obituary Notice 62

Broadhead, Helen Cross
1913- 62

Buck, Pearl S. 1892-1973 63

C

Callahan, Philip S. 1923- 77

Cameron, Eleanor 1912- 78

Chaundler, Christine 1887-1972
Obituary Notice 83

Chenery, Janet 1923- 84

Childs, Fay 1890-1971
Obituary Notice 84

Collins, Hunt
see Hunter, Evan 153

Colman, Morris 1899(?)-1981
Obituary Notice 85

Connelly, Marc 1890-1980
Obituary Notice 85

Cottam, Clarence 1899-1974 85

Cox, Wally 1924-1973 86

Cronin, A. J. 1896-1981
Obituary Notice 89

Cross, Helen Reeder
see Broadhead, Helen Cross 62

Cuffari, Richard 1925-1978
Obituary Notice 89

D

Davis, Louise Littleton
1921- 89

Denney, Diana 1910- 90

De Roo, Anne Louise 1931- 91

Domjan, Joseph 1907- 92

Downer, Marion
1892(?)-1971 93

Duggan, Alfred Leo
1903-1964 95

Duncombe, Frances 1900- 97

E

Edey, Maitland A. 1910- 98

Edwards, Cecile 1916- 99

Ehrlich, Amy 1942- 100

Emerson, William K. 1925- 101

Enright, D. J. 1920- 102

Ernst, Kathryn 1942- 103

F

Farber, Norma 1909- 104

Fax, Elton Clay 1909- 106

Finder, Martin
  see Salzmann, Siegmund 207

Fisher, Aileen 1906- 108

Fisk, Nicholas 1923- 111

Floherty, John Joseph
  1882-1964 113

Fodor, Ronald V. 1944- 115

Francois, André 1915- 116

Freeman, Mae 1907- 117

Fuller, Margaret
  see Ossoli, Sarah Margaret
  marchesa d' 186

G

Garrison, Webb B. 1919- 119

Gluck, Felix 1924(?)-1981
  Obituary Notice 120

Goble, Paul 1933- 120

Goldberg, Herbert S. 1926- 122

Grant, Bruce 1893-1977
  Obituary Notice 122

Grant, Gordon 1875-1962 123

Green, Hannah
  see Greenberg, Joanne 127

Greenberg, Joanne 1932- 127

Gri
  see Denney, Diana 90

Gringhuis, Dirk
  see Gringhuis, Richard H.
  Obituary Notice 128

Gringhuis, Richard H. 1918-1974
  Obituary Notice 128

Groch, Judith 1929- 128

Gutman, Naham 1899(?)-1981
  Obituary Notice 129

H

Hardy, Thomas 1840-1928 129

Harris, Sherwood 1932- 139

Helps, Racey 1913-1971
  Obituary Notice 139

Hersey, John 1914- 139

Hogner, Nils 1893-1970 142

Housman, Laurence
  1865-1959 144

Hughes, Richard 1900-1976
  Obituary Notice 153

Hunter, Evan 1926- 153

J

Jacobs, Joseph 1854-1916 159

Janes, Edward C. 1908- 167

Jennings, S. M.
  see Meyer, Jerome Sydney
  Obituary Notice 181

Jensen, Niels 1927- 168

Jumpp, Hugo
  see MacPeek, Walter G.
  Obituary Notice 177

K

Kemp, Gene 1926- 169

Kennell, Ruth E. 1893-1977
  Obituary Notice 170

Knotts, Howard 1922- 170

Komoda, Beverly 1939- 171

L

A Lady of Quality
  see Bagnold, Enid 23

Lambert, Janet 1894-1973 172

Langley, Noel 1911-1980
  Obituary Notice 173

Larrecq, John M. 1926-1980
  Obituary Notice 173

Luther, Frank 1905-1980
  Obituary Notice 173

M

Mac
  see MacManus, Seumas 175

Macdonald, Shelagh 1937- 174

MacManus, James
  see MacManus, Seumas 175

MacManus, Seumas
  1869-1960 175

MacPeek, Walter G. 1902-1973
  Obituary Notice 177

Maitland, Antony 1935- 177

Marsten, Richard
  see Hunter, Evan .153

Martin, Peter
  see Chaundler, Christine
  Obituary Notice 83

Maxon, Anne
  see Best, Allena Champlin
  Obituary Notice 48

McBain, Ed
  see Hunter, Evan .153

McGregor, Iona 1929- 179

McNeely, Jeannette 1918- 180

Means, Florence Crannell
  1891-1980
  Obituary Notice 181

Meyer, Jerome Sydney 1895-1975
  Obituary Notice 181

Milgrom, Harry 1912- 181

Moon, Carl 1879-1948 182

Moon, Grace 1877(?)-1947 185

O

Olds, Helen Diehl 1895-1981
  Obituary Notice 186

Ossoli, Sarah Margaret marchesa d'
  1810-1850 186

P

Park, Ruth 190

Pease, Howard 1894-1974
  Obituary Notice 191

Perrault, Charles
  1628-1703 192

Pollock, Mary
  see Blyton, Enid 48

Price, Susan 1955- .206

R

Radley, Gail 1951- .206

Ritts, Paul 1920(?)-1980
  Obituary Notice 207

Ross, Diana
  see Denney, Diana 90

S

Salten, Felix
  see Salzmann, Siegmund 207

Salzmann, Siegmund
  1869-1945 207

Sedges, John
  see Buck, Pearl S. 63

Stevenson, Burton E.
  1872-1962 213

Sutherland, Efua 1924- 215

T

Teale, Edwin Way 1899-1980
  Obituary Notice 215

V

Verner, Gerald 1897(?)-1980
  Obituary Notice 216

W

Webster, Gary
  see Garrison, Webb B. 119

Whitney, Thomas P. 1917- 216

Woodford, Peggy 1937- 218

Wymer, Norman George
  1911- 219

Introduction

As the only ongoing reference series that deals with the life and work of authors and illustrators of children's books, *Something about the Author* provides young readers with a unique source of information for their library research projects or book reports as well as a personal introduction to the authors they are reading. *SATA* is equally valuable to their teachers and librarians. The *SATA* editors aim to include not only well-known authors and illustrators whose books are most widely read, but also those less prominent people whose works are just coming to be known. *SATA* is often the only readily available information source for the less well-known writers and artists.

Scope Expanded

Although *SATA*'s basic aim has not changed during its publication life, the series itself has changed considerably, in both obvious and subtle ways. For example, in Volumes 1 through 14 *SATA* included only contemporary figures who were alive in 1960 and later. With Volume 15 we dropped this somewhat arbitrary criterion at the suggestion of our readers and expanded *SATA*'s scope to include the full time-range of children's literature. At the same time, the *Yesterday's Authors of Books for Children* series, which dealt exclusively with people deceased before 1960, was discontinued after two volumes. Both of these volumes are kept in print and their entries have been added to the cumulative indexes of *SATA*. Major figures formerly slated for the *YABC* series now appear in *SATA*. As available information has allowed, the Sidelights sections for both historical and contemporary figures in *SATA* have been expanded to the lengthier and more informative "chronolog" format in which the highlights of the person's life and work are chronologically arranged and drawn, as far as possible, from personal writings like autobiographies, reminiscences, diaries, letters, and the like.

For the added convenience of our readers, Volume 15 also inaugurated a Table of Contents, which has since progressed through several stylistic changes until the present format, the most practical and readable to date, was adopted in Volume 23. The catch-word device, using the biographee's name at the outer corners of each page, was introduced in Volume 13 to help readers locate a particular listee more easily.

Obituaries Added

In Volume 20 *SATA* included obituaries for the first time. Not simply a death notice, a *SATA* obituary is a kind of capsule sketch, providing brief but up-to-date information. Obituaries are written for: 1) recently deceased persons who are already listed in *SATA* as well as those who have not yet been included in the series; and 2) persons who died in the past but were never listed in *SATA* or who were listed before their deaths occurred. A special effort has been made to write "retrospective" obituaries on all persons listed in *SATA* to date who are known to have died before the practice of providing obituary notices was begun in Volume 20. The first of these retrospective obituaries appeared in Volume 24 and the remainder continue in Volumes 25 through 27.

One of the most obvious changes in the *SATA* series occurred in Volume 21. The time seemed right for a face lift and *SATA*'s traditional look gave way to its present bright blue cover. Now that time enough has passed for everyone to become accustomed to the change (and even to shelve Volumes 20 and 21 side-by-side!), most users seem very pleased with the new look, and we hope that the more distinctive cover has achieved its objective of catching the eye of new users.

Forthcoming Authors Cited

A Forthcoming Authors list became a regular feature of *SATA* with Volume 21. Although many hundreds of authors and illustrators are always under consideration for future volumes, this published Forthcoming Authors list attempts to cite only those people that are most interest-worthy in the estimation of the editors. We invite you to send us the names of writers or artists that you would like to see in the series but who are not on the Forthcoming Authors list.

In Volume 24 birth and death dates, as reflected in the series' sketches and obituaries, were added to the Cumulative Author Index and will be regularly included in all additions to the Author Index. All known dates were also added to the Forthcoming Authors list in this volume. Though dates may seem a relatively minor item of information, they often provide the quick bit of data that places the person in a particular time-frame or sets him or her apart from others with a similar name.

Revised Sketches Added

In Volume 25 *SATA* is publishing the first revised sketches on persons who appeared in early volumes of the series: Enid Bagnold, Nathaniel Benchley, Pearl Buck, Eleanor Cameron, and Aileen Fisher. Every succeeding volume will contain additional revised sketches. Revision will not be done systematically on every sketch in a particular original *SATA* volume. Rather, the editors will select from all of the early volumes those authors and illustrators who are of interest to today's readers and who have been active enough to require extensive updating of their original sketches. No artificial time-limit will be set between publication of the original and revised sketches for a given author. A sketch may be revised as often as there is significant and substantial change to be made in the sketch. Each revision will feature a thorough updating of all its sections as well as a particular effort to include new and informative Sidelights.

Highlights of This Volume

These are some of the people in Volume 25 that we hope you'll find particularly interesting:

ENID BAGNOLD......who once described herself as a "writer from the age of nine." You may know her best as the author of *National Velvet,* which became a classic motion picture starring a child actress named Elizabeth Taylor. Bagnold also wrote the critically-acclaimed play, "The Chalk Garden."

NATHANIEL BENCHLEY......a celebrity in his own right and a member of the famous family that includes his late father Robert, the humorist and writer, and his son Peter, the author of *Jaws.* Nathaniel Benchley adapted the movie "The Russians Are Coming! The Russians Are Coming!" from his novel *The Off-Islanders.* His novel *Bright Candles* was named one of the Best Books for Young Adults by the American Library Association.

PEARL S. BUCK......the eminent humanitarian and author. The daughter of Presbyterian missionaries, Buck grew up in China and taught in universities there until the Communist government forced foreigners out of the country. Winner of the Pulitzer Prize in fiction and the Nobel Prize for literature, Buck wrote more than 85 books, including numerous work of fiction for children. Some of her best known books became equally popular motion pictures—"The Good Earth," "Dragon Seed," and "China Sky."

WALLY COX......perhaps best remembered as the meek Mr. Peepers of the long-running TV series or even as the real-life roommate of actor Marlon Brando. But you may not have known that he wrote the children's book, *The Tenth Life of Osiris Oaks.*

PAUL GOBLE......the English author/illustrator with what seems to be an unlikely fascination with American Indians. But, as he explains, he grew up on the writings of Grey Owl and Ernest Thompson Seton, and now he carries on in their tradition. Goble won the 1979 Caldecott Medal for *The Girl Who Loved Wild Horses.*

JOANNE GREENBERG......better known as the "Hannah Green" who wrote the enormously-popular young adult novel, *I Never Promised You a Rose Garden.*

LAURENCE HOUSMAN......whose long and prolific career as a playwright, novelist, and essayist began with his writing and illustrating for children in books like *The House of Joy* and *The Rat-Catcher's Daughter.*

EVAN HUNTER......whose *Blackboard Jungle* was a landmark in the literature that deals realistically with problem teenagers. You may also know him as the "Ed McBain" who writes the popular "87th Precinct" detective series, or as the creator of the 1976 TV mini-series, "The Chisholms."

CHARLES PERRAULT......the 17th-century lawyer-poet-critic and member of the prestigious French Academy who is remembered today for his spare-time work—rewriting in the style of his day the already half-forgotten folk tales that we now call *Little Red Riding Hood, Sleeping Beauty, Cinderella,* among many more.

SIEGMUND SALZMANN......the Viennese journalist who, as "Felix Salten," gave us Bambi, later to be immortalized by Walt Disney in his animated feature film.

Among the other authors and illustrators in Volume 25, you'll find an impressive list that includes Pulitzer Prize-winner John Hersey and National Book Award-winners Eleanor Cameron and Norma Farber, as well as Antony Maitland, who won the Kate Greenaway Medal for distinguished British book illustration, and André Francois, who has had four books included among the New York Times' Choice of Best Illustrated Books of the Year.

We hope you find these and all the sketches in *SATA* both interesting and useful. Please write and tell us if we can make *SATA* even more helpful for you.

A Partial List of Authors and Illustrators
Who Will Appear in Forthcoming Volumes of
Something about the Author

Adrian, Mary
Ahlberg, Allan
Ahlberg, Janet
Allard, Harry
Allen, Agnes B.   1898-1959
Allen, Jack   1899-
Anastasio, Dina   1941-
Ashley, Bernard   1935-
Atwater, Richard   1892-1948
Ayme, Marcel   1902-1967
Bach, Alice H.   1942-
Baskin, Leonard   1922-
Becker, May Lamberton   1873-1958
Beim, Jerrold   1910-1957
Beim, Lorraine   1909-1951
Bell, Robert S. W.   1871-1921
Bennet, Jay   1912-
Bernheim, Evelyne   1935-
Blos, Joan W.
Boase, Wendy
Boegehold, Betty   1913-
Boning, Richard A.
Bowden, Joan C.   1925-
Brady, Lillian
Brewton, Sara W.
Broger, Achim   1944-
Bronin, Andrew   1947-
Bronson, Wilfrid   1894-
Brookins, Dana   1931-
Bruna, Dick   1927-
Burchard, Marshall
Burgess, Gelett   1866-1951
Burke, David   1927-
Burstein, Chaya
Butler, Hal   1913-
Carey, M. V.   1925-
Carrick, Malcolm   1945-
Carroll, Ruth R.   1899-
Chesterton, G. K.   1874-1936
Choate, Judith
Christopher, John   1922-
Clarke, Joan B.
Clements, Bruce   1931-
Cohen, Joel H.
Cohen, Miriam
Cole, Joanna
Collodi, Carlo   1826-1890
Cooper, Elizabeth Keyser   1910-
Craik, Dinah M.   1826-1887
Crews, Donald
Dabcovich, Lydia
Danziger, Paula   1944-
Dasent, Sir George Webbe   1817-1896

D'Aulnoy, Marie-Catherine   1650(?)-1705
DeGoscinny, Rene
Delessert, Etienne   1941-
Disney, Walt   1901-1966
Ditmars, Raymond   1876-1942
Donovan, John   1928-
Doty, Jean Slaughter   1929-
Dumas, Philippe   1940-
Eckert, Allan W.   1931-
Elwood, Roger   1943-
Erickson, Russell E.   1932-
Erwin, Betty K.
Etter, Les   1904-
Everett-Green, Evelyn   1856-1932
Falkner, John Meade   1858-1932
Falls, C. B.   1874-1960
Farmer, Penelope   1939-
Fischer, Hans Erich   1909-1958
Forest, Antonia
Freeman, Barbara C.   1906-
Freschet, Berniece   1927-
Fujikawa, Gyo
Gackenbach, Dick
Gans, Roma   1894-
Gardam, Jane   1928-
Gardner, John C.   1933-
Gatty, Margaret   1809-1873
Gauch, Patricia L.   1934-
Gault, Clare   1925-
Gault, Frank   1926-
Gelman, Rita G.   1937-
Gemme, Leila Boyle   1942-
Goble, Dorothy
Gorey, Edward St. John   1925-
Gould, Chester   1900-
Grabianski, Janusz   1929(?)-1976
Gregor, Arthur S.
Gregorian, Joyce
Gridley, Marion E.   1906-1974
Gross, Ruth B.
Gruelle, Johnny   1880(?)-1938
Gutman, Bill
Gwynne, Fred   1926-
Halacy, Daniel S., Jr.   1919-
Hale, Lucretia P.   1820-1900
Haley, Gail E.   1939-
Hayes, Geoffrey R.   1947-
Hazen, Barbara S.   1930-
Heide, Florence Parry   1919-
Hentoff, Nat   1925-
Henty, George Alfred   1832-1902
Hicks, Clifford B.   1920-

Highwater, Jamake
Hirshberg, Albert S.   1909-1973
Hood, Thomas   1779-1845
Hughes, Ted   1930-
Hunt, Clara Whitehill   1871-1958
Ingelow, Jean   1820-1897
Isadora, Rachel
Jacques, Robin   1920-
Jameson, Cynthia
Jeschke, Susan   1942-
Jewell, Nancy   1940-
Johnston, Norma
Jones, Hettie   1934-
Judson, Clara Ingram   1879-1960
Kahl, Virginia   1919-
Kahn, Joan   1914-
Kalan, Robert
Kantrowitz, Mildred
Kasuya, Masahiro   1937-
Keith, Eros   1942-
Kessler, Ethel
Ketcham, Hank   1920-
Klein, Aaron E.   1930-
Koehn, Ilse
Kraske, Robert
Leach, Maria   1892-1977
Leckie, Robert   1920-
Levoy, Myron
Levy, Elizabeth   1942-
Lewis, Naomi
Lines, Kathleen
Little, Mary E.   1916-
Livermore, Elaine
Longsworth, Polly   1933-
Lubin, Leonard
Macaulay, David   1946-
MacDonald, George   1824-1905
MacGregor, Ellen   1906-1954
MacKinstry, Elizabeth A.   d. 1956
Manley, Deborah   1932-
Marryat, Frederick   1792-1848
McKee, David   1935-
McKillip, Patricia A.   1948-
McNaught, Harry   1897-1967
McPhail, David   1940-
Mendoza, George   1934-
Miller, Edna   1920-
Mohn, Peter Burnet   1934-
Molesworth, Maria L.   1839(?)-1921
Molly, Anne S.   1907
Momaday, N. Scott   1934-
Moore, Lilian
Moore, Patrick   1923-

Morgenroth, Barbara
Murphy, Shirley Rousseau   1928-
Myers, Elisabeth P.   1918-
Myers, Walter Dean   1937-
Nordlicht, Lillian
Oakley, Graham   1929-
O'Brien, Robert C.   1918-1973
O'Hanlon, Jacklyn
Orr, Frank   1936-
Orton, Helen Fuller   1872-1955
Overbeck, Cynthia
Packard, Edward   1931-
Pearson, Susan   1946-
Perkins, Lucy Fitch   1865-1937
Peterson, Jeanne Whitehouse   1939-
Plotz, Helen   1913-
Pogany, Willy   1882-1955
Pope, Elizabeth M.   1917-
Porter, Eleanor Hodgman   1868-1920
Poulsson, Emilie   1853-1939
Prather, Ray
Pursell, Margaret S.
Pursell, Thomas F.
Pyle, Katharine   1863-1938
Rae, Gwynedd   1892-
Raynor, Dorka
Rees, David   1936-
Reynolds, Marjorie   1903-
Ribbons, Ian   1924-
Richler, Mordecai   1931-
Roberts, Elizabeth Madox   1886-1941
Rock, Gail
Rockwell, Anne   1934-

Rockwell, Harlow
Rose, Elizabeth   1933-
Rose, Gerald   1935-
Ross, Diana   1910-
Ross, Frank, Jr.   1916-
Ross, Wilda   1915-
Roy, Cal
Sabin, Francene
Sabin, Louis   1930-
Schellie, Don   1932-
Schick, Alice   1946-
Schneider, Leo   1916-
Seaman, Augusta   1879-1950
Sendak, Jack
Sewall, Helen   1881-
Sewell, Marcia   1935-
Shapiro, Milton J.   1926-
Shearer, John   1947-
Silverstein, Shel   1932-
Simon, Hilda   1921-
Smith, Doris Buchanan   1934-
Steiner, Charlotte
Stevens, Leonard A.   1920-
Stevenson, James
Stong, Phil   1899-1957
Sutton, Felix   1910(?)-
Tallon, Robert   1940-
Taylor, Ann   1782-1866
Taylor, Jane   1783-1824
Taylor, Mark
Tenniel, Sir John   1820-1914
Todd, Ruthven   1914-
Tomalin, Ruth

Tomes, Margot   1917-
Tourneur, Dina K.   1934-
Tripp, Wallace   1940-
Tunis, John R.   1889-1975
Turska, Krystyna   1933-
Van Iterson, S. R.
Varga, Judy
Villiard, Paul   1910-1974
Waber, Bernard   1924-
Wagner, Jenny
Walters, Hugh   1910-
Watson, Nancy D.
Watts, Franklin   1904-1978
Welber, Robert
Welles, Winifred   1893-1939
Wellman, Alice   1900-
Wild, Jocelyn
Wild, Robin
Willard, Nancy   1936-
William-Ellis, Amabel
Wilson, Gahan   1930-
Windsor, Patricia   1938-
Winn, Marie
Winterfeld, Henry   1901-
Wolde, Gunilla
Wolf, Bernard
Wolitzer, Hilma   1930-
Wong, Herbert H.
Wood, Phyllis Anderson   1923-
Wyss, Johann David   1743-1818
Yeoman, John   1934-
Zollinger, Gulielma   1856-1917

In the interest of making *Something about the Author* as responsive as possible to the needs of its readers, the editor welcomes your suggestions for additional authors and illustrators to be included in the series.

GRATEFUL ACKNOWLEDGMENT

is made to the following publishers, authors, and artists,
for their kind permission to reproduce copyrighted material.

ADDISON-WESLEY PUBLISHING CO., INC. Illustration by Lydia Dabcovich from *There Once Was a Woman Who Married a Man* by Norma Farber. Text copyright © 1978 by Norma Farber. Illustrations copyright © 1978 by Lydia Dabcovich. Reprinted by permission of Addison-Wesley Publishing Co., Inc.

ARTEMIS VERLAGS AG. Illustration by Hans Fischer from *Puss in Boots,* adapted from Charles Perrault by Hans Fischer. Reprinted by permission of Artemis Verlags AG.

ASSOCIATED BOOK PUBLISHERS LTD. Jacket design by Graham Humphreys from *Days of Courage* by Niels Jensen. Copyright © 1971 by Niels Jensen. Reprinted by permission of Associated Book Publishers Ltd.

ATHENEUM PUBLISHERS. Illustration by Julia Noonan from *The Rat-Catcher's Daughter: A Collection of Stories* by Laurence Housman. Copyright © 1974 by Atheneum Publishers. Afterword copyright © 1974 by Ellin Greene. Reprinted by permission of Atheneum Publishers.

THE BOBBS-MERRILL CO., INC. Photograph from *The Unexpected Years* by Laurence Housman. Copyright 1936 by Laurence Housman./ Illustration by Diana Thorne from *Renni the Rescuer* by Felix Salten. Copyright 1940 by The Bobbs-Merrill Co. Both reprinted by permission of The Bobbs-Merrill Co., Inc.

THE BODLEY HEAD LTD. Illustration by Philippe Jullian from *The Fairy Tales of Charles Perrault,* translated by Norman Denny. Copyright 1950 by The Bodley Head Ltd. Reprinted by permission of The Bodley Head Ltd.

BRADBURY PRESS, INC. Illustration by Paul Goble from *The Girl Who Loved Wild Horses* by Paul Goble. Text and illustrations copyright © 1978 by Paul Goble./ Illustration by Susan Jeffers from *The Buried Moon* by Joseph Jacobs. Copyright © 1969 by Susan Jeffers./ Illustration by Errol Le Cain from *Cinderella; or, The Little Glass Slipper* by Charles Perrault, translated and adapted by Errol Le Cain. Text copyright © 1972 by Faber & Faber Ltd. Illustrations copyright © by Errol Le Cain. All reprinted by permission of Bradbury Press, Inc.

CHILDRENS PRESS. Illustration by Tom Dunnington from *The Secret Seven and the Old Fort Adventure* by Enid Blyton. Copyright © 1972 by Regensteiner Publishing Enterprises, Inc. Reprinted by permission of Childrens Press.

CLARENDON PRESS. Sidelight excerpts from *The Collected Letters of Thomas Hardy, Volume Two, 1893-1901,* edited by Richard Little Purdy and Michael Millgate. Reprinted by permission of Clarendon Press.

COLBY COLLEGE PRESS. Sidelight excerpts from *The Letters of Thomas Hardy,* edited by Carl J. Weber. Reprinted by permission of Colby College Press.

COLLIER-MACMILLAN. Illustration by Robert Jones from *The Little Fox in the Middle* by Pearl S. Buck. Copyright © 1966 by Pearl S. Buck. Copyright © 1966 by The Macmillan Co. Reprinted by permission of Collier-Macmillan.

CONCORDIA PUBLISHING HOUSE. Illustration by Aline Cunningham from *Led By a Star: The Wise Men for Beginning Readers* by Jeannette McNeely. Copyright © 1977 by Concordia Publishing House. Reprinted by permission of Concordia Publishing House.

CONSTABLE & CO. LTD. Illustration by W. Heath Robinson from "Old Time Stories," by Charles Perrault. Reprinted by permission of Constable & Co. Ltd.

COWARD, McCANN & GEOGHEGAN, INC. Illustration by Margot Tomes from *A Curiosity for the Curious* by Helen Reeder Cross. Text copyright © 1978 by Helen Reeder Cross.

15

Illustrations copyright © 1978 by Margot Tomes. Reprinted by permission of Coward, McCann & Geoghegan, Inc.

THOMAS Y. CROWELL CO. PUBLISHERS. Illustration by Ben Shecter from *Clean as a Whistle* by Aileen Fisher. Copyright © 1969 by Aileen Fisher. Illustrations copyright © 1969 by Ben Shecter. Reprinted by permission of Thomas Y. Crowell Co. Publishers.

D. V. PUBLICATIONS LTD. Illustration by Beek from *Noddy Goes to Toyland* by Enid Blyton. Text copyright 1949 by Enid Blyton. Artwork copyright 1949 by Sampson Low, Marston & Co. Ltd. Reprinted by permission of D. V. Publications Ltd.

DELACORTE PRESS. Sidelight excerpts and photographs from *Margaret Fuller: From Transcendentalism to Revolution* by Paula Blanchard. Copyright © 1978 by Paula B. Blanchard. Both reprinted by permission of Delacorte Press.

DELPIRE EDITEUR. Illustration by André Francois from *Crocodile Tears* by André Francois. Reprinted by permission of Delpire Editeur.

ANDRÉ DEUTSCH LTD. Illustration by Steve Augarde from *Barnaby Shrew, Black Dan and . . . the Mighty Wedgewood* by Steve Augarde. Copyright © 1979 by Steve Augarde./ Jacket illustration by Meg Rutherford from *No End to Yesterday* by Shelagh Macdonald. Copyright © 1977 by Shelagh Macdonald. Both reprinted by permission of André Deutsch Ltd.

THE DEVIN-ADAIR CO., INC. Illustration by Richard Bennett from "Conaleen and Donaleen," in *The Well o' the World's End,* retold by Seumas MacManus. Copyright 1939 by Seumas MacManus. Reprinted by permission of The Devin-Adair Co., Inc.

THE DIAL PRESS. Illustration by Martha Alexander from *The Everyday Train* by Amy Ehrlich. Text copyright © 1977 by Amy Ehrlich. Pictures copyright © 1977 by Martha Alexander. Reprinted by permission of The Dial Press.

DODD, MEAD & CO. Illustration by Elton C. Fax from *Contemporary Black Leaders* by Elton C. Fax. Copyright © 1970 by Elton C. Fax. Reprinted by permission of Dodd, Mead & Co.

DOUBLEDAY & CO., INC. Illustration by Robert Binks from *Cotton-Wooleena* by Laurence Housman. Text copyright © 1967 by Jonathan Cape Ltd. Illustrations copyright © 1974 by Doubleday & Co., Inc./ Illustrations by Carl Moon from *Solita* by Grace Moon. Copyright 1938 by Grace Moon. Both reprinted by permission of Doubleday & Co., Inc.

WILLIAM B. EERDMANS PUBLISHING CO. Illustration by Betty Beeby from *Potawatomi Indian Summer* by E. William Oldenburg. Copyright © 1975 by William B. Eerdmans Publishing Co. Reprinted by permission of William B. Eerdmans Publishing Co.

ELSEVIER-DUTTON PUBLISHING CO., INC. Illustration by Gail Owens from *Julia and the Hand of God* by Eleanor Cameron. Copyright © 1977 by Eleanor Cameron./ Illustration from *One for the Money* by Janet Lambert. Copyright 1946 by E. P. Dutton & Co., Inc./ Illustration by Giulio Maestro from *Egg-Ventures* by Harry Milgrom. Text copyright © 1974 by Harry Milgrom. Illustrations copyright © 1974 by Giulio Maestro./ Jacket illustration by Trina Schart Hyman from *The Court of the Stone Children* by Eleanor Cameron. All reprinted by permission of Elsevier-Dutton Publishing Co., Inc.

FABER & FABER LTD. Illustration by Gri from *The Golden Hen and Other Stories* by Gri./ Illustration by C. Walter Hodges from *Growing Up in Thirteenth Century England* by Alfred Duggan. Copyright © 1962 by Alfred Duggan./ Illustration by Carol Dinan from *Tamworth Pig and the Litter* by Gene Kemp. Copyright © 1975 by Gene Kemp. All reprinted by permission of Faber & Faber Ltd.

FARRAR, STRAUS & GIROUX, INC. Illustration by Jay Chollick from "The King of Araby's Daughter," in *The Bold Heroes of Hungry Hill* by Seumas MacManus. Copyright 1951 by Seumas MacManus. Copyright renewed © 1979 by Patricia MacManus and Mariquita MacManus Mullan./ Illustration by Antony Maitland from *Idle Jack,* retold by Antony Maitland. Copyright © 1977 by Antony Maitland. Both reprinted by permission of Farrar, Straus & Giroux, Inc.

GREENWILLOW BOOKS. Jacket design by Lynn Sweat from *The Devil's Piper* by Susan Price. Copyright © 1973 by Susan Price. Reprinted by permission of Greenwillow Books.

GROSSET & DUNLAP, INC. Illustration by Kurt Wiese from *Bambi* by Felix Salten. Copyright 1929 by Simon & Schuster, Inc. Reprinted by permission of Grosset & Dunlap, Inc.

HAMISH HAMILTON LTD. Illustration by Nicholas Fisk from *Look at Aircraft* by Philip Joubert. Reprinted by permission of Hamish Hamilton Ltd.

HARCOURT BRACE JOVANOVICH, INC. Illustration by Hans Fischer from *Puss in Boots,* adapted from Charles Perrault by Hans Fischer. Reprinted by permission of Harcourt Brace Jovanovich, Inc.

HARPER & ROW, PUBLISHERS. Illustration by Mel Furukawa from *The Magic Sled* by Nathaniel Benchley. Text copyright © 1972 by Nathaniel Benchley. Pictures copyright © 1972 by Mel Furukawa./ Sidelight excerpts from *Pearl S. Buck: A Biography* by Theodore F. Harris. Copyright © 1969 by The John Day Co., Inc./ Sidelight excerpts from *For Spacious Skies: Journey in Dialogue* by Pearl S. Buck with Theodore F. Harris. Copyright © 1966 by The Pearl S. Buck Foundation, Inc./ Sidelight excerpts from *My Several Worlds* by Pearl S. Buck. Copyright 1954 by Pearl S. Buck./ Illustration by Howard Knotts from *A Day in the Country* by Willis Barnstone. Text copyright © 1971 by Willis Barnstone. Pictures copyright © 1971 by Howard Knotts./ Illustration by Arnold Lobel from *Red Fox and His Canoe* by Nathaniel Benchley. Text copyright © 1964 by Nathaniel Benchley. Pictures copyright © 1964 by Arnold Lobel./ Illustration by Arnold Lobel from *The Strange Disappearance of Arthur Cluck* by Nathaniel Benchley. Text copyright © 1967 by Nathaniel Benchley. Pictures copyright © 1967 by Arnold Lobel./ Portrait sketch from *Pearl S. Buck: A Biography* by Theodore F. Harris in consultation with Pearl S. Buck. Copyright © 1971 by Creativity, Inc./ Prints by Hiroshige and Hokusai from *The Big Wave* by Pearl S. Buck. Copyright 1947 by the Curtis Publishing Co. Copyright 1948 by Pearl S. Buck./ Illustration by William Arthur Smith from *The Water-Buffalo Children* by Pearl S. Buck. Copyright 1943 by Pearl S. Buck./ Illustration by Esther Brock Bird from *The Dragon Fish* by Pearl S. Buck. Copyright 1944 by Pearl S. Buck./ Illustration by Regina Shekerjian from *The Chinese Story Teller* by Pearl S. Buck. Text copyright © 1971 by Pearl S. Buck. Illustration copyright © 1971 by The John Day Co., Inc. All reprinted by permission of Harper & Row, Publishers.

HAWTHORN HOUSE, INC. Illustration by Margaret Fuller from *The Complete History of the Deluge* by Margaret Fuller. Copyright 1936 by Margaret Fuller. Reprinted by permission of Hawthorn House, Inc.

WILLIAM HEINEMANN LTD. Illustration by Antony Maitland from *The Ghost of Thomas Kempe* by Penelope Lively. Copyright © 1973 by Penelope Lively. Illustrations copyright © 1973 by William Heinemann Ltd./ Sidelight excerpts for Efua Sutherland from *Reader's Guide to African Literature.*/ Illustration by Paul Brown from *National Velvet* by Enid Bagnold. Copyright 1935 by Enid Bagnold Jones. Copyright 1949 by William Morrow & Co., Inc./ Illustration by Laurian Jones from *National Velvet* by Enid Bagnold. Copyright 1935 by Enid Bagnold. All reprinted by permission of William Heinemann Ltd.

HODDER & STOUGHTON LTD. Sidelight excerpts from *Enid Blyton: A Biography* by Barbara Stoney./ Illustration by Edmund Dulac from *Stories from the Arabian Nights,* retold by Laurence Housman. Both reprinted by permission of Hodder & Stoughton Ltd.

HOLIDAY HOUSE, INC. Photograph by Philip S. Callahan from *The Magnificent Birds of Prey* by Philip S. Callahan. Copyright © 1974 by Philip S. Callahan. Reprinted by permission of Holiday House, Inc.

HOLT, RINEHART & WINSTON. Illustration by Willy Pogany from *The Home Book of Verse for Young Folks,* selected and arranged by Burton Egbert Stevenson. Copyright 1915 by Henry Holt & Co. Copyright 1929 by Henry Holt & Co., Inc. Reprinted by permission of Holt, Rinehart & Winston.

THE HORN BOOK, INC. Sidelight excerpts from *Illustrators of Children's Books: 1744-1945,* compiled by Bertha E. Mahony and others. Copyright 1947; copyright renewed © 1974 by The Horn Book, Inc./ Sidelight excerpts from *Illustrators of Children's Books: 1957-1966,* compiled by Lee Kingman and others. Copyright © 1968 by The Horn Book, Inc. Both reprinted by permission of The Horn Book, Inc.

KESTREL BOOKS. Illustration by Gunvor Edwards from *Snuffle to the Rescue* by Elisabeth Beresford. Text copyright © 1975 by Elisabeth Beresford. Illustrations copyright © 1975 by Gunvor Edwards. Reprinted by permission of Kestrel Books.

ALFRED A. KNOPF, INC. Illustration by Laurian Jones from *Alice and Thomas and Jane* by Enid Bagnold. Copyright 1930, 1931 by Alfred A. Knopf, Inc. Reprinted by permission of Alfred A. Knopf, Inc.

THE LIMITED EDITIONS CLUB. Aquatint by William Sharp from *The Wall* by John Hersey. Copyright © 1958 by John Hersey. This edition by special arrangement with Alfred Knopf. Special contents of this edition copyright © 1957 by The George Macy Co. Reprinted by permission of The Limited Editions Club.

J. B. LIPPINCOTT CO. Jacket illustration by Glo Coalson from *Me and Mr. Stenner* by Evan Hunter. Copyright © 1976 by Hui Corporation./ Illustration by Carl Moon from *Lost Indian Magic* by Grace and Carl Moon. Copyright 1918 by Frederick A. Stokes Co. Both reprinted by permission of J. B. Lippincott Co.

LITTLE, BROWN & CO. Illustration by Leonard Shortall from *A Mystery for Mr. Bass* by Eleanor Cameron. Copyright © 1960 by Eleanor Cameron./ Illustration by Trina Schart Hyman from *A Room Made of Windows* by Eleanor Cameron. Copyright © 1971 by Eleanor Cameron./ Illustration by Robert Henneberger from *The Wonderful Flight to the Mushroom Planet* by Eleanor Cameron. Copyright 1954 by Eleanor Cameron./ Illustration by Sheilah Beckett from *Cinderella,* adapted by John Fowles. Translation copyright © 1974 by John Fowles. Illustrations copyright © 1974 by Sheilah Beckett. All reprinted by permission of Little, Brown & Co.

LOTHROP, LEE & SHEPARD BOOKS. Photographs by Frank J. Miller from *Kites: How to Make and Fly Them* by Marion Downer. Copyright © 1959 by Lothrop, Lee & Shepard Co., Inc. Reprinted by permission of Lothrop, Lee & Shepard Books.

MACMILLAN, INC. Illustration by Stuart Tresilian from *The Circus of Adventure* by Enid Blyton./ Wood engraving by Clare Leighton from *The Pinnacled Tower: Selected Poems* by Thomas Hardy, edited by Helen Plotz. Copyright © 1975 by Helen Plotz. Copyright © 1975 by Macmillan Publishing Co./ Illustration by Nonny Hogrogian from *Vasilisa the Beautiful,* translated by Thomas P. Whitney. Text copyright © 1970 by Thomas P. Whitney. Illustrations copyright © 1970 by Nonny Hogrogian. All reprinted by permission of Macmillan, Inc.

WILLIAM MORROW & CO., INC. Illustration by Gordon Grant from *The Secret Voyage* by Gordon Grant. Copyright 1942 by Gordon Grant. Reprinted by permission of William Morrow & Co., Inc.

FREDERICK MULLER LTD. Illustration by Harry Toothill from *With Mackenzie in Canada* by Norman Wymer. Copyright © 1963 by Norman Wymer. Reprinted by permission of Frederick Muller Ltd.

OXFORD UNIVERSITY PRESS, INC. Sidelight excerpts from *The Collected Letters of Thomas Hardy, Volume One, 1840-1892,* edited by Richard Little Purdy and Michael Millgate./ Illustration by John Lawrence from *Our Exploits at West Poley* by Thomas Hardy. Illustrations copyright © 1978 by Oxford University Press. Both reprinted by permission of Oxford University Press, Inc.

PENGUIN BOOKS. Illustration by Gunvor Edwards from *Snuffle to the Rescue* by Elisabeth Beresford. Copyright © 1975 by Elisabeth Beresford. Illustrations copyright © 1975 by Gunvor Edwards. Reprinted by permission of Penguin Books.

PRENTICE-HALL, INC. Illustration by Tomie de Paola from *Danny and His Thumb* by Kathryn F. Ernst. Copyright © 1973 by Kathryn F. Ernst. Illustrations copyright © 1973 by Tomie de Paola./ Illustration by Ray Abel from *Why Didn't I Think That?* by Webb Garrison. Copyright © 1977 by Webb Garrison. Illustrations copyright © 1977 by Ray Abel. Both reprinted by permission of Prentice-Hall, Inc.

G. P. PUTNAM'S SONS. Illustration by Richard Cuffari from *Summer of the Burning* by Frances Duncombe. Copyright © 1976 by Frances Duncombe. Reprinted by permission of G. P. Putnam's Sons.

RANDOM HOUSE, INC. Sidelight excerpts from *Children for Adoption* by Pearl S. Buck. Copyright © 1964 by Random House, Inc./ Illustration by Robert Patterson from *You Will Go to the Moon* by Mae and Ira Freeman. Copyright © 1959 by Mae and Ira Freeman. Both reprinted by permission of Random House, Inc.

RICHARDS PRESS LTD. Illustrations by Beek from *The Big Noddy Book* by Enid Blyton. Text copyright © 1968 by Enid Blyton. Illustrations copyright © 1968 by Sampson Low, Marston & Co. Ltd. Reprinted by permission of Richards Press Ltd.

ST. MARTIN'S PRESS, INC. Photographs from *Thomas Hardy: An Illustrated Biography* by Timothy O'Sullivan. Copyright © 1975 by Timothy O'Sullivan. Reprinted by permission of St. Martin's Press, Inc.

SAMPSON LOW. Illustrations by Beek from *The Big Noddy Book* by Enid Blyton. Text copyright © 1968 by Enid Blyton. Illustrations copyright © 1968 by Sampson Low, Marston & Co. Ltd./ Illustration by Beek from *Noddy Goes to Toyland* by Enid Blyton. Text copyright 1949 by Enid Blyton. Artwork copyright 1949 by Sampson Low, Marston & Co. Ltd. Both reprinted by permission of Sampson Low.

SCHOLASTIC BOOK SERVICES. Illustration by Kilmeny and Deborah Niland from *The Gigantic Balloon* by Ruth Park. Text copyright © 1975 by Ruth Park. Illustrations copyright © 1975 by Kilmeny and Deborah Niland. Reprinted by permission of Scholastic Book Services.

CHARLES SCRIBNER'S SONS. Illustration by Feodor Rojankovsky from "Cracker Time," in *Cricket in a Thicket* by Aileen Fisher. Text copyright © 1963 by Aileen Fisher. Illustrations copyright © 1963 by Feodor Rojankovsky./ Illustration by Ernest H. Shepard from "Possession," a play, in *The Golden Sovereign* by Laurence Housman. Copyright 1937 by Laurence Housman./ Illustration by Marcia Brown from *Cinderella; or, The Little Glass Slipper*, a free translation from the French of Charles Perrault. Copyright 1954 by Marcia Brown. All reprinted by permission of Charles Scribner's Sons.

SIMON & SCHUSTER, INC. Illustration by F. A. Fitzgerald from *The Tenth Life of Osiris Oaks* by Wally Cox and Everett Greenbaum. Text copyright © 1972 by Wally Cox and Everett Greenbaum. Illustrations copyright © 1972 by F. A. Fitzgerald./ Illustration by Barbara Cooney from *Bambi: A Life in the Woods* by Felix Salten. Text copyright 1928, 1956 by Simon & Schuster, Inc. Illustrations copyright © 1970 by Barbara Cooney Porter. Both reprinted by permission of Simon & Schuster, Inc.

THE VIKING PRESS. Illustration by Lilian Obligado from *Pickles and Jake* by Janet Chenery. Text copyright © 1975 by Janet Dai Chenery. Illustrations copyright © 1975 by Lilian Obligado de Vajav. Reprinted by permission of The Viking Press.

HENRY Z. WALCK, INC. Illustration by Nils Hogner from *Molly the Black Mare* by Nils Hogner. Copyright © 1962 by Nils Hogner./ Illustration by Margery Gill from *Jack and the Beanstalk* by Joseph Jacobs. Copyright © 1975 by Margery Gill. Both reprinted by permission of Henry Z. Walck, Inc. (a division of David McKay Co., Inc.).

WATSON-GUPTILL PUBLICATIONS. Drawings by Gordon Grant from *Gordon Grant Sketchbook*. Copyright © 1960 by Watson-Guptill Publications, Inc. Reprinted by permission of Watson-Guptill Publications.

FRANKLIN WATTS, INC. Illustration by Rod Slater from *Camping* by E. C. Janes. Copyright © 1963, 1977 by Franklin Watts, Inc./ Illustration by Charles Mozley from "Ricky with a Tuft" in *Famous Fairy Tales* by Charles Perrault. Copyright © 1959 by Franklin Watts, Inc. Both reprinted by permission of Franklin Watts, Inc.

Sidelight excerpts from an article, "Gordon Grant Stresses Drawing for Watercolorists," September, 1960, in *American Artist*. Reprinted by permission of *American Artist*./ Photograph from *Meteorites: Stones from the Sky* by R. V. Fodor. Copyright © 1976 by Ronald V. Fodor. Reprinted by permission of the American Meteorite Laboratory./ Photograph from *Wonders of Starfish* by Morris K. Jacobson and William K. Emerson. Copyright © 1977 by Morris K. Jacobson and William K. Emerson. Reprinted by permission of the American Museum of Natural History./ Sidelight excerpts and photographs from *The Story of My Life* by Enid Blyton. Reprinted by permission of the Estate of Enid Blyton./ Sidelight excerpts and photographs from *Enid Bagnold's Autobiography* by Enid Bagnold. Copyright © 1969 by Enid Bagnold. Reprinted by permission of Brandt & Brandt Literary Agents, Inc./ Illustration by Paul Brown from *National Velvet* by Enid Bagnold. Copyright 1935, 1949 by Enid Bagnold Jones. Reprinted by permission of Brandt & Brandt Literary Agents, Inc./ Sidelight excerpts from an article, "Wally Cox and Mr. Peepers," by Tim Taylor, April, 1955, in *Coronet*. Reprinted by permission of *Coronet*./ Photograph from *Lost World of the Aegean* by Maitland A. Edey. Copyright © 1975 by Time, Inc. Reprinted by permission of Deutsches Archäologisches Institut, Athens.

Sidelight excerpts from *The Early Life of Thomas Hardy, 1840-1891* by Florence Emily Hardy. Copyright 1928 by Florence Emily Hardy. Reprinted by permission of the Trustees of the late Miss E. A. Dugdale./ Sidelight excerpts from *The Later Years of Thomas Hardy, 1892-1928* by Florence Emily Hardy. Copyright 1930 by Florence Emily Hardy. Reprinted by permission of the Trustees of the late Miss E. A. Dugdale./ Sidelight excerpts from an article, "An Interview with Nathaniel Benchley," by Paul Janeczko, September, 1976, in *English Journal*. Reprinted by permission of *English Journal*./ Sidelight excerpts from an article, "One Thumping Lie Only," by Nicholas Fisk, edited by Edward Blishen, in *The Thorny Paradise*. Reprinted by permission of Nicholas Fisk./ Illustration by John Freas from *Fifteen Rabbits* by Felix Salten. Copyright 1929 by Paul Zsolnay Verlag. Text copyright 1930 by Simon & Schuster, Inc; copyright renewed © 1958 by Simon & Schuster, Inc. New illustrations copyright © 1976 by John Freas. Reprinted by permission of John Freas./ Sidelight excerpts from an article, "Caldecott Acceptance Speech," by Paul Goble, August, 1979, in *Horn Book* magazine. Reprinted by permission of Paul Goble./ Sidelight excerpts from *Robert Benchley* by Nathaniel

Benchley. Reprinted by permission of International Creative Management./ Sidelight excerpts from *For Spacious Skies: Journey in Dialogue* by Pearl S. Buck with Theodore F. Harris. Copyright © 1966 by The Pearl S. Buck Foundation, Inc. Reprinted by permission of Harold Ober Associates, Inc./ Sidelight excerpts from *My Several Worlds* by Pearl S. Buck. Copyright 1954 by Pearl S. Buck. Reprinted by permission of Harold Ober Associates, Inc.

Sidelight excerpts from an article, "Thomas P. Whitney Loses Nothing in the Translation," by Phillip M. Perry, July, 1974 in *Writer's Digest*. Reprinted by permission of Phillip M. Perry./ Sidelight excerpts from an article, "My Life as a Small Boy," by Wally Cox, November, 1961, in *Good Housekeeping*. Copyright © 1961 by Wally Cox. Reprinted by permission of Gloria Safier./ Sidelight excerpts from an article, "The Other Mr. Peepers," by Elise Morrow, April 16, 1955, in the *Saturday Evening Post*. Reprinted by permission of the *Saturday Evening Post*./ Sidelight excerpts from an article, "Novels and Nights to Remember," March 19, 1966, in *Saturday Review*. Copyright © 1966 by *Saturday Review*. Reprinted by permission of *Saturday Review*./ Illustration by Gordon Grant from *Penrod* by Booth Tarkington. Copyright 1914 by Doubleday, Page & Co. Reprinted by permission of Grant Shaw, Douglas Shaw, Bernard H. D. Reinold, and Campbell Grant./ Illustration by Gordon Grant from *Penrod Jashber* by Booth Tarkington. Copyright 1929 by Doubleday, Doran & Co., Inc. Copyright 1915, 1917, 1918 by International Publications, Inc. Reprinted by permission of Grant Shaw, Douglas Shaw, Bernard H. D. Reinold, and Campbell Grant./ Sidelight excerpts from an article, "Joanne Greenberg," April, 1972, in *Top of the News*. Reprinted by permission of the American Library Association from *Top of the News*./ Sidelight excerpts from an article, "An Interview with Evan Hunter—Ed McBain," by Evan Hunter, April, 1969, in *The Writer*. Reprinted by permission of The Writer, Inc./ Sidelight excerpts from an article, "An Exclusive Re-Visit with Evan Hunter," by Fran Krajewski, April, 1971, in *Writer's Digest*. Reprinted by permission of *Writer's Digest*.

PHOTOGRAPH CREDITS

Nathaniel Benchley: Deidra G. Allan; Helen Cross Broadhead: William Russ; Philip S. Callahan: Kevin Callahan; Marion Downer: Yolla Niclas; Norma Farber: Babette S. Whipple; Nicholas Fisk: Heath Studios; André Francois: André Martin; John Hersey: Constance Brewster; Howard Knotts: Ilse-Margret Vogel; Janet Lambert: Henry Ries; Peggy Woodford: Andra Nelki.

something about the author

ARONIN, Ben 1904-1980

OBITUARY NOTICE: Born 1904; died August 26, 1980, in Chicago, Ill. Author, Hebrew scholar, and lawyer. Aronin, a Chicago lawyer for more than fifty years, was known as Uncle Ben on the children's television program "Magic Door," which he created. In 1962 he received a Chicago Emmy Award for the show. For many years Aronin taught Hebrew and Bible classes at the College of Jewish Studies. He was the author of a Hebrew epic entitled *The Abramiad* and numerous children's books, including *The New Mother Goose Book, Mother Goose and Father Gander,* and *Daily Prayers for Children.* He also wrote books of fantasy, including *Cavern of Destiny, The Moor's Gold,* and *The Lost Tribe: Being the Strange Adventures of Raphael Drale in Search of the Lost Tribes of Israel. For More Information See: Science Fiction and Fantasy Literature,* Volume 1, Gale, 1979. *Obituaries: Chicago Tribune,* August 28, 1980; *Contemporary Authors,* Volume 102, Gale, 1981.

STEVE AUGARDE

AUGARDE, Steve 1950-

PERSONAL: Given name Stephen Andre Augarde; born October 3, 1950, in Birmingham, England; son of Eric Claude (a builder, interior decorator) and Grace Olive (Eveson) Augarde; *Education:* Attended Yoevil School of Art, Somerset College of Art, and Rolle Teacher Training College. *Home and office:* 16 Ridge Rd., Hornsey, London N. 8, England.

"... This tortoise is so ... so ... *strong* that he can crush *four* walnuts all at once! Whether he's in the mood or not!" ■ (From *Barnaby Shrew, Black Dan and ... the Mighty Wedgewood* by Steve Augarde. Illustrated by the author.)

CAREER: Author and illustrator of children's books. Worked for a time as a gardener for the National Trust at Montacute House, England. Also a semi-professional musician.

WRITINGS—All the children; all self-illustrated: *A Lazy Day,* Fabbri & Partners, 1974; *The River That Disappeared,* Fabbri & Partners. 1974; *The Willow Tree,* Fabbri & Partners, 1974; *Pig,* Deutsch, 1976, Bradbury 1977; *Barnaby Shrew Goes to Sea,* Deutsch, 1978; *Barnaby Shrew, Black Dan and the Mighty Wedgwood,* Deutsch, 1979; *Mr. Mick,* Deutsch, 1980; *January Jo,* Deutsch, 1981. Also illustrator of *Septimus Fry,* Deutsch, 1980.

SIDELIGHTS: "I wrote and illustrated my first children's book when I was ten years old. It was called something like 'The Fantastic Four' or maybe even 'The Famous Four,' at any rate it relied fairly heavily, I suspect, on Enid Blyton, Malcolm Saville and Anthony Buckeridge for style and inspiration. It was fairly racy stuff though, being about a gang of desperate drug smugglers who went around stuffing things into fish at one end of a river, to be netted by their accomplices down at the other end. Lord knows why, 'The Fantastic Four,' as brave a bunch of lads as you'd wish to find, and obviously Special Branch material, managed to foil these desperadoes with the sort of ease that would make you think they were born doing it. 'The Fantastic Four,' I have no doubt, would have gone on from strength to strength—striding up and down the land in their flannel shorts and wellie-boots smiting criminals about the ears and generally earning the wonder and admiration of all. ('Who *were* those four fine boys?' 'That, my friend, was "The Fantastic Four."' 'Well I bet their mothers are proud of them.' 'Aye, and their country.')

"All this glory was, sadly, not to be. There were more important things to be doing, like taking exams and 'choosing a career.' It's never too early to start thinking about 'it' seemed to be the consensus of opinion. All those years of tests, exams, 'O' levels, 'A' levels, colleges. The sole purpose seeming to be to set one up for a good career. I could have skipped the lot! I should have started my career at ten with 'The Fantastic Four!' They would have been knighted by know, at least. Every home would have a set. Right next to the encyclopaedias, 'The Fantastic Four Push the Boat Out,' 'Four to the Fore,' 'The Fantastic Four on Safari,' 'The Fantastic Four Rule the Cosmos.' Oh, those four lads would have been the very backbone of the Western World by now. Actually, I think it might have been three of them and a dog.

"Writing stories and drawing pictures was all I was ever any good at. All I can say here about that decade of secondary and further education is that that's how long it took before it occurred to me that I might make some sort of living out of what I was doing in the first place.

"Of course 'The Fantastic Four' are now way past the point where they might have achieved their fame and just rewards. One of them writes kids books, short stories and plays a bit of jazz. Another drives a lorry for his dad, the other works in a helicopter factory, I think. The dog's buried at the bottom of the garden."

BAGNOLD, Enid 1889-1981
(Pseudonym: A Lady of Quality)

PERSONAL: Born October 27, 1889, in Rochester, England; died March 31, 1981, in St. John's Wood, London; daughter of Arthur Henry (a colonel, Royal Engineers) and Ethel (Alger) Bagnold; married Sir Roderick Jones (chairman, Reuters Agency), July 8, 1920 (died, 1962); children: Laurienne (wife of Comte Pierre d'Harcourt), Timothy, Richard, Dominick. *Education:* Attended Priors Field in Godalming, England, and schools in Paris, France, Switzerland, and Marburg, Germany; studied drawing and painting with Walter Sickert. *Home:* Rottingdean, Sussex, England; 29 Hyde Park Gate, London

S.W.7, England. *Agent:* Harold Freedman, Brandt & Brandt, 101 Park Ave., New York, N. Y. 10017.

CAREER: As summarized by author, who was Lady Jones in private life, "Simply writing. From the age of nine." During World War I served in English hospital for two years, then as driver attached to French Army. *Awards, honors:* Arts Theater Prize for "Poor Judas," 1951; Award of Merit Medal and $1,000 prize of American Academy of Arts and Letters for play, "The Chalk Garden," 1956.

*WRITINGS—*For children: *Alice and Thomas and Jane* (illustrated by daughter, Laurienne Jones), Heinemann, 1930, Knopf, 1931; *National Velvet* (illustrated by Jones), Morrow, 1935, reprinted, Pan books, 1978; [other editions include those illustrated by Paul Brown, Morrow, 1949; Earle B. Winslow, Junior Deluxe Editions, 1958; and an abridged edition illustrated by Al Brulé, Grossett, 1961].

For adults: *A Diary without Dates,* Heinemann, 1918, Morrow, 1935, reprinted, Virago, 1978; *The Sailing Ships, and Other Poems,* Heinemann, 1918; *The Happy Foreigner* (novel), Century, 1920; (under pseudonym A Lady of Quality) *Serena Blandish; or, The Difficulty of Getting Married,* Heinemann, 1924, Doran, 1925, reprinted, Curtis Books, 1972; (translator) Princess M. L. Bibesco, *Alexander of Asia,* Heinemann, 1935; *The Door of Life* (novel), Morrow, 1938 (published in England as *The Squire,* Heinemann, 1938); *The Loved and Envied* (novel), Doubleday, 1951; *The Girl's Journey: The Happy Foreigner*

(From the movie "National Velvet," starring Elizabeth Taylor and Mickey Rooney. Copyright 1944 by Loew's, Inc.)

Bagnold, at about age twenty.

[and] *The Squire,* Doubleday, 1954; *Enid Bagnold's Autobiography,* Heinemann, 1969, Little, Brown, 1970; *Poems,* Heinemann, 1978.

Plays: *Lottie Dundass* (three-act; first produced in London at Wimbledon Theatre, 1942), Heinemann, 1941, revised (two-act; first produced on the West End at Vaudeville Theater, July 21, 1943), Samuel French, 1944; *Two Plays* (contains "Lottie Dundass" and "Poor Judas"), Heinemann, 1944, published as *Theatre,* Doubleday, 1951; *National Velvet* (three-act; first produced in London at Embassy Theatre, April 20, 1946), Dramatists Play Service, 1961; "Poor Judas," first produced in London at Arts Theatre Club, July 18, 1951; "Gertie," first produced on Broadway at Plymouth Theatre, January 30, 1952, produced on the West End as "The Little Idiot" at Queen's Theatre, November 10, 1953; *The Chalk Garden* (three-act; first produced on Broadway at Ethel Barrymore Theatre, October 26, 1955, produced on the West End at Haymarket Theatre, April 12, 1956), Random House, 1956; "The Last Joke," first produced on the West End at Phoenix Theatre, 1960; *The Chinese Prime Minister* (three-act; first produced on Broadway at Royale Theatre, January 2, 1964, produced on the West End at Globe Theatre, May 20, 1965), Random House, 1964; *Four Plays* (contains "The Chalk Garden," "The Chinese Prime

Minister," "The Last Joke," and "Call Me Jacky"), Little, Brown, 1970; *A Matter of Gravity* (three-act; first produced on Broadway at Broadhurst Theatre, 1976), Samuel French, 1978.

ADAPTATIONS—Motion pictures: "National Velvet," starring Elizabeth Taylor, Metro-Goldwyn-Mayer, 1944; "The Chalk Garden," starring Deborah Kerr, Universal, 1964; "International Velvet," starring Tatum O'Neal, copyright © 1978 by United Artists.

Television: *National Velvet,* NBC-TV, September 18, 1960, to September 10, 1962.

Plays: S. H. Behrmann, *Three Plays* (includes "Serena Blandish"; first produced on Broadway at Morosco Theatre, January 23, 1929), Farrar, Straus, 1934; Vera Beringer, *Alice, Thomas, and Jane* (two-act; for children), Samuel French, 1934; "National Velvet" (radio play), Theatre Guild on the Air, 1950. "Lottie Dundass" (radio play), Theatre Guild on the Air, 1950.

SIDELIGHTS: **October 27, 1889.** Born in Rochester, England. Bagnold's father, Arthur Henry, was a colonel with the Royal Engineers and the family frequently moved because of his career. "My father was a clever man. If I asked some questions he would answer. If I asked too many he told me to stop. He knew the difference between curiosity and trying for attention.

"National Velvet"

by

ENID BAGNOLD

DRAWINGS BY LAURIAN JONES

WILLIAM MORROW AND COMPANY
New York • 1935

(From *National Velvet* by Enid Bagnold. Illustrated by her daughter, Laurian Jones.)

"He was the rooftree and knew everything. He knew why one was ill; and the cure. Tapeworm, ringworm, the taking out of thorns, the laying down of drains (privies were once the basic business of the Royal Engineers).

"No one corrected me except Daddy (I must call him what I called him), and though he whipped me three times I knew he thought I was a miracle. He was severe. I didn't get to know him. He wouldn't have minded that. He wanted obedience." [Enid Bagnold, *Enid Bagnold's Autobiography*, Little, Brown, 1969.[1]]

1895. ". . .When I was six . . . my brother Ralph was born. Of course there had been mystery. I had thought it was a bicycle. I was led into the room, and told to walk on tiptoe and there lay the baby—a disappointment. He was to become an explorer, a Fellow of the Royal Society, and the greatest living expert on the flow of sand (by wind to form sand dunes and by water in rivers and under the sea), but oh I would have exchanged him that day for a bicycle."[1]

1898. Family moved to Jamaica after father's appointment there. "When I was nine and Ralph was three, my father sailed ahead to prepare a house. We followed—my mother, the baby, Miss Evans and I—in an old fruit ship called the *Don*. It rolled like a whale.

"Miss Evans was to be my governess. . . .

Bagnold, just before her marriage.

"The day we neared Jamaica an inner life began. It must have, for I never remember anything earlier—of ecstasy, of admiration for nature. Beauty never hit me until I was nine. But when we landed, the lack of mist, flowers higher than I was, emerald leaves of black leather, the shine of black people, their thrush's eyes, the zigzagging quiver of air hit by heat, the tropic leap into the spangled night—this was the first page of my life as someone who can 'see.' It was like a man idly staring at a field suddenly finding he had Picasso's eyes. In the most startling way I never felt young again. I remember myself then just as I feel myself now."[1]

Spring, 1902. "My father's command was up. We sailed for England on the 28th of March . . . and into Plymouth Sound on the 12th of April. In the ship love came into my life. Little girls of twelve are fascinated by love. They may mock it but they long to watch it. Faces of lovers, notes, trembling hands—the beautiful and secret disease they have just heard of. In the ship there was a rich young lady—Miss Daisy Epps of Epps Cocoa. I carried her love-letters to the ship's doctor. She had swimming-blue eyes and wrote on a pad on her lap. I hung around. She would look up and hand me the stuck-down envelope and I sped off. Once or twice I scribbled ardent messages of my own on the back. 'Don't despair,' and 'She loves you.'

"On landing, we went to the dreariest of places. Lodgings in Ryde, in the Isle of Wight. No love, no excitement. It was like being dragged out of a theatre. I had to carry on. So *I* wrote love-letters. There was a mahogany sideboard in the horrible sitting-room, with a coarse lace cover. Under this, hearing my father's step on the stairs, I poked a half-finished letter.

(From the television series "National Velvet," starring Lori Martin. Presented on NBC-TV, 1960-62.)

As she drew up she saw the little man was done, stretched up unnaturally on its neck. He took a year falling. ■ (From *National Velvet* by Enid Bagnold. Illustrated by Paul Brown.)

"'What's that?' said my father, too close behind me. 'Give it to me.' It was so unlike him that I think he must have found something before. He carried the letter to the window to read. (What dreadful twelve-year-old heat and passion simmered across that page?) He called my mother.

"'Come here and look at this.' They read it together. I began to scream. There was no way out except screaming. I couldn't bear to wait for the first question.

"Shaking me, my father said:

"'*Who is this man?*'

"'*Nobody-nobody*-NOBODY!'

"'*Enid—I don't believe you.*'

"'Nobody-nobody-nobody.'

"'*I want his name.*'

"'There isn't anybody . . . ANYBODY . . .'—yelling and running up to my bedroom.

"Unaware of being followed I fell on my knees in the room.

"'Oh GOD . . . ' I howled at Him. 'God God God they don't believe me!' I bawled at Him. I was tropically overdeveloped and there might have been a man. But I suppose there really are accents of truth in a voice. I suppose mine had them. I was believed.

"I was then to go to boarding school (and needed it). But suddenly I was said to have a patch on my lung. I spent that winter with an unremembered governess (in sleeping bags with hot water bottles) doing lessons in the garden. Even in 1902 my father was up to date with Davos.

"It was because of this, and after this, that Daddy said:

"'Find her a school on sandy soil.'

"And by this remark, this divine frail accident, my life was altered. Theirs too perhaps. But everything alters one's life."[1]

1903. Attended Priors Field School in Godalming, England. "The school on sandy soil was near Godalming, and it was Mrs. Huxley's. And Mrs. Huxley was the mother of Julian, Trev and Aldous.

"How difficult it must be to send your darling to boarding school. I was agog. It never occurred to me what Mummie felt. But Daddy was determined I should have a good education. It was as though he was living now among the 'A's' and 'O's.' What did he think I was going to do or be? Surely he assumed I was bound for marriage? Or did Mummie's trouble with adding-up affect him? ('She *must* learn mathematics.') But as Prior's Field was above all a literary school they didn't lay stress on mathematics. Or I was unable to consume them.

"I was rough and difficult to snub, and gay. I was clever enough but of that I took no notice. Clever enough not to show up as a 'show-off-er' but I managed very well as a card. Being fat (the result of Jamaica) I was cut out for clowning. To make them laugh one had to spend oneself without counting the esteem-cost. That was not a bad lesson. Often I got it wrong and looked a fool. But that I had to bear, and soon I got the timing. . . .''[1]

1906-1907. Left Mrs. Huxley's school and went abroad for further study. "Paris was a dream of happiness. I stayed a year.

"It was a large and expensive school at Neuilly called the Villa Léona, owned by a Madame Yeatman, who was quite famous in her day. She had retired (I never saw her) and was succeeded by Miss Eastman.

"There was the opera (which I couldn't bear) but there was Sarah Bernhardt. This is what I remember. It was *L'Aiglon.*

"On Thursdays we went out in small groups to museums and when possible I slipped across a particular road to chalk 'Vive Sarah!' on the wall of the Boulevard Péréire.

"There was also Mounet Sully. And there was Coquelin. I suppose no one falls in love with Napoleon now. Hitler has seen to that. But I did. Recollecting that golden fire I can hardly separate Napoleon, Rostand, Madame Sarah's white-uniformed youth (at sixty), Coquelin's back against a tree ('*Ce sont les cadets de Gascoigne!*')—and Napoleon. On Napoleon's death-day I borrowed a black dress from a girl called Edith Jordan, who was in mourning, and with the stretched back fastened together with chains of safety pins came ponderously down to Morning Prayers.

"Miss Eastman fixed the shimmer of her pince-nez on me from where she stood.

"'Turn around, Enid Bagnold.'

"The broad white vertical band of petticoat from neck to hem was displayed to the rostrum.

(From *Alice and Thomas and Jane* by Enid Bagnold. Illustrated by her daughter, Laurian Jones.)

"'And why is this?'

"'It is the day Napoleon died,' I said in the ringing tones of Hyde Park Corner.

"'There is no need to make Napoleon absurd,' she said. 'Go to your room and change.'

"It was a radiant year, fighting to conquer the French language—poems, plays—entering French literature. . . . The Paris year was over. I was 'finished, burnished, ready.'"[1]

1907. "And now we have the parents with the great gosling come home. Awkward, clever, bubbling, in touch with life but not with graces, mad about herself, furious with her face, not well dressed, unable to dance, suddenly shocked, struggling, imprisoned by strange standards.

"Dear and beloved Warren Wood. It was from there I rose like a dragon-fly to my adventures. Always returning.

"It was from there I went to my Chelsea life, and from there, later, to my high society. But always to come back and tell and tell. Not the whole truth. And how my mother listened.

She always remained as she was: she never grew older: adoring, amused, delighted. Whatever wrong I was doing I couldn't do wrong.

"There was so much love in the house, such gaiety at my return, such pride in presenting me, such beauty in the garden. It wasn't that my mother was so good with flowers—not as good as I am. It was the garden itself, its extraordinary position, as it hung, hidden (query existing? Was it real?) at the edge of the Old Dover Road, on the crown of Shooter's Hill, traffic pouring from London, not a sound reaching in. Eight miles from London Bridge and in May the bluebells were solid; in June the bracken. The ancient trees grew there since Henry the Eighth (whose Shoot it had been). Our garden had two and a half acres. The rest of the forty acres of the old Shoot went with Falconwood next door, a Palladian house come down in the world that belonged to nobody in particular.

"Dear and beloved Warren Wood (in winter ice cold), each room marvellously important. Each room different, very personal, the whole enclosed in a 'Gothic' villa with a turret, built (Daddy said) in a bad period, and sinking a little at one side."[1]

(From the stage production "A Matter of Gravity," starring Katharine Hepburn. First produced at the Broadhurst Theatre, February 3, 1976.)

1912. Moved to London and began writing. "It wasn't long before the seventy-five pounds a year began to pinch. I loved to buy things. I had rather buy things and go hungry. (After all, there was the fat to melt.) There was a small restaurant down the road on the Embankment called 'The Good Intent,' and when I ate there I stole a roll from the folds of the pleated napkin on the next table. That saved on breakfast. It was mock-hunger and mock-poverty because I could always have gone home, and Daddy would have given me more if I had seriously asked. But one had pride; and a job was the answer. With whom? Under whom? To work for whom?"[1]

Worked as a journalist for Frank Harris, then editor of *Hearth and Home.* "He had just become editor of *Hearth and Home.* He needed to staff it cheap. There and then he offered me a nebulous job at thirty-five shillings a week (more than doubling my seventy-five pounds a year). I took it. I became a sort of journalist.

"Our little group, expanding, had made friends with (or slightly included) Katherine Mansfield and Middleton Murry. They joined us in the shock of the spell of Frank Harris. But soon they were dusting their knees and sneaking off. Katherine

Mansfield was the first to go. Murray lasted a little longer. . . . I hardly noticed that only I was left.

"Imagine . . . to be courted by this ugly, famous, and glamorously misunderstood man. How could I escape? I didn't want to escape. I tripped eagerly after him on his detonating trail, hand-grenades exploding. It was life all right.

"Soon Frank Harris had slipped out of his editorship of *Hearth and Home* and bought a tainted little property called *Modern Society.* This had a scandal-page with a newly-invented spice, called 'What a Little Bird wants to know.' Now I was really and truly a journalist. I was up to my neck in it.

". . . I did the bulk of the work. I faked things. Or plagiarized. I stole. I rewrote stories from Maupassant and signed them myself (needless to say, at my chief's suggestion): I drew, or traced, legs and girls from *La Vie Parisienne:* I lifted cookery articles from foreign papers.

"I had no conscience. 'I obeyed my Chief.' That was the answer I heard years later from a Basuto in the dock in a tent in Basutoland, accused of ritual murder. 'I cut off his lips and

(From the movie "The Chalk Garden," starring Deborah Kerr and Hayley Mills. Released by Universal Pictures Co., 1963.)

his tongue. I did it for my Chief.' If I had been sent shoplifting, I would have been off—flags flying.

"The thirty-five shillings never grew any larger. I had to ask for it every week. If I hadn't I shouldn't have got it. But I never thought of asking for more. Half the paper was under my control. I was as happy as a lark."[1]

At the end of nine months of journalism under Frank Harris, Bagnold returned home to Warren Wood. "I began to write a novel (about Frank Harris). But the prose had a Germanic and smelly texture. The shadow cast by his form of thought wouldn't let me succeed.

"I never finished it, because I found I really didn't know my subject.

"My father ('You can't write all day!') gave me bookbinding tools and a wooden frame to sew the pages. I was nimble with my large hands, as he was. Bookbinding did quite well instead of Frank Harris.

"I had my Tower Room (my gas for glue) coloured inks for drawing on my letters—fun for the hands when the words wouldn't come. There was an ozone in the Gothic pinnacle.

"And so began my second life at home, never to leave it wholly until I married."[1]

1914. During World War I, served in an English hospital for two years and later, as a driver attached to the French Army. "Everyone, trained or not, was rushed into the great military hospital, the Royal Herbert Hospital, at the foot of the Hill, to fetch and carry. Operations went on without stopping. I saw legs in buckets outside the theatre doors. No such trainloads came in the second war. The men at the beginning of that first war were simply picked off the battlefields. That was the difference: in the first war one was closer to suffering.

"The Royal Herbert Hospital, when I was first there was staffed by old-time Sisters in scarlet capes, who inherited from peace the idea that men in bed were malingerers. At the opening of the war men lived on meat and died on the gravy: there was no light diet.

"When a man died his bed was emptied, his mattress taken away to be disinfected. No attempt was made to see that the visiting parents didn't arrive to behold the empty wire of the bed. This attitude and these things shocked me more than the plight of the men themselves. I kept a diary of such shocks."[1]

1918. First book, the diary written during her wartime service, *A Diary without Dates,* was published.

1918-1919. "Round about twenty-nine I got engaged to a gentleman-farmer-squire. I might have married him but we quarrelled at night on a heath. All his four tyres had punctured because he had that day taken his car out of storage where it had been all through the war. I was going to his home to meet his parents. It was a sweet-smelling summer night. I suggested we stuff the outer covers with hay so that we could roll on gently to a garage. But he hadn't a jack. He had those useless writer's fingers. . . . But he didn't write. Out of this situation the quarrel flared and the bully rose in me. Our characters caught fire and smoked. We were not for each other. I couldn't go through the week-end: but walked three miles and got a train home.

"I had, just before this, met Roderick.

"These 'successes with men' . . . were spread over ten years, if you start at nineteen. I was a very slow starter but later a little momentum was gained. To attract—I saw—was a kind of trick. I became more expert. I lost this expertise when I married and never quite got it back."[1]

July 8, 1920. Married Sir Roderick Jones, chairman of Reuters Agency. "I married him because he made me. I watched myself. It was like a new and wildly-interesting job. And in a way I had no choice. He was an irrevocable man and what he wanted went.

". . .We went on our honeymoon, two extraordinary strangers. But the man who could take the cornfield so easily couldn't take lesser things.

"The honeymoon of these two strangers was a journey with a hundred editors to the Imperial Press Conference at Montreal (or perhaps Ottawa). . . . When we landed there were two trains waiting to carry us across Canada—two trains—our home. Restaurant cars, shaded lamps, polished brass, polished waiters (oh lost world of wonderful trains). As we travelled we took on the fruits of the countryside, river-trout, game, eggs, butter cream. Each night we stopped for some vast dinner at some hotel where speeches on Empire were made by us, and to us from the Canadian Press. We dressed for dinner on the train—a hundred men and women—shuffling and passing each other to the luggage van and dragging from piled trunks and suitcases evening dresses, petticoats, stockings, shoes. The speeches went on till nearly midnight and then back to sleep on the train, which would sometimes be stationary or sometimes moving off to the next halt.

"I had never in my life done anything like this. Never had a duty. Never had to behave myself. Never heard anything so mockworthy as all this hot air. The only fun was to laugh at it and I never doubted but that Roderick would laugh too.

"Back in London.

"Back with the trunks and boxes settling into Roderick's flat in South Street. Back to be waited on (and hated by) his personal cat-valet. He was a green-eyed man with fangs who made faces at me behind my back. He was observed in the mirror. He had to go.

"When the excitement and deference to a bride and congratulations and settling-in and temporary adjustments of two strangers—when all this sank shallowly into place—then the real deep maladjustments showed up.

"He trained me as he trained his men at Reuters. He praised and blamed and watched and insisted. I fought and forgot and cried and lost my temper. In the morning he left me lists. I put them down as soon as he had gone to the office. We had different ideals and different standards. I considered myself an uppish intellectual. Which indeed I wasn't.

"In that South Street flat I felt sick, which was odd. I hadn't felt sick in the Chelsea flat. Later on I knew why I was sick. I was having a baby.

"Pass over all that—pass over the night of her birth (temporarily back at Warren Wood) and there I was with a cradle beside me.

(From the stage production "The Chalk Garden," starring Gladys Cooper and Betsy von Furstenberg. First produced at the Barrymore Theatre, October 26, 1955.)

(From the movie "International Velvet," starring Tatum O'Neal. Copyright © 1978 by United Artists.)

"Motherhood is a tarnished old word and is used to convey any sentimentality. I didn't feel it for two days. But after that there swept over me the same savage delight in a job which I had had when I married Roderick. 'She'll be astonishing! She'll be the light of the world. Oh—the *next* generation! It's here in my hands.' Is that motherhood? It's what I felt. She had a lousy start. The midwife . . . stayed in her bedroom and wouldn't appear. The doctor managed alone. The baby had a spot of blood in its eye. It gave me the horrors to try to breast-feed her, but I conquered it.

"The responsibilities grew, the possessions grew, and good God I was founding a family."[1]

1920-1930. As Bagnold's family grew to three sons and a daughter, she continued to write—three novels and a children's book. "When I was engaged to Roderick—that brief time—I had told him that I wrote. That was a statement he ought to have heeded, but he was too much in love to bother. It meant that in my married life three hours would be taken out of each day. I was to rule a household with three hours short. By the nature of my first thirty years of living I wasn't a ruler. I wasn't used to having authority and I hated it. When I had to face a human being with rebuke I trembled. When something like courage came it was too violent and too late. After my wobbling

socialism and my loving-to-be-liked I had to find out that there was some mystique in being a ruler.

"We *were* rich. Or we lived richly. I knew Roderick wasn't personally rich as people thought he was, because I knew that he had borrowed half a million from the Bank of Scotland to buy out the then Chairman and Board of Reuters when he first took over—and this had to be paid back.

"For a woman who is mink-rich or Ritz-rich it's different. But I was the wife of a man who intended, for the sake of his job, to keep up his position. Things had to be run and I had to run them."[1]

1935. Wrote best known novel, *National Velvet*, based upon her family's equestrian interests. "I started *National Velvet* as a study in a girl's relationship with her pony. But it turned immediately and by itself into a story. All our gay life and its details, dogs, canaries, emotions of children, everything jumped into my hands. I had only to snatch and type on and all our full life was on the page. All the fantastic joy and fun."[1]

1940. "I won't talk of the war; it was everybody's war. All England, and every countryside has its stories. All I prayed and hoped was that it wouldn't come near Timothy, the son who was nearest it. But it did. And it took off his leg. He wrote to me as soon as it was: 'I never liked walking. And now I shan't have to.' But he was wrong. He re-learnt everything, walking, riding, dancing. If he has managed again to ski he has hidden it from me; but I shouldn't be surprised.''[1]

1941. ''There had come a day . . . when Roderick resigned from Reuters. It has been . . . said that he was 'pressed to resign.' Well, in a way he was. He was pressed by his own temperament and by a self control which though of iron had got to melting point. Every successful man is surrounded by ambitious men. So was he. There were men around him waiting to misinterpret a letter or a slip of speech. He was not democratic. Far from it. Nor was Churchill. Nor was Lord Reith. You can't abate a man who has learnt through twenty-five years to run the immensely complicated machine which is Reuters. The 'slowness' of democracy (of constant consultation) doesn't suit it. I have no doubt my husband sometimes stung his Board.''[1]

1945. Went to America for the Broadway production of her second play, which failed after three performances. ''I flew with my little talent locked like a goldfish in my breast, for that was my part, my offering to the hard work to come and the reason for my going.

''I had brought him with me but he had never been out in the open. Whenever I faced him up to the icy water of rewriting he began to turn on his back and show his pale belly.

''My director was a man of great experience, great integrity, kindness and rage. Just before the first rehearsal he made me a striking speech. 'I want to tell you,' he said 'though I shall hate it to happen, that you and I will end in dreadful battle, that you may leave America loathing me.'

''Why?

''Because from tomorrow. . . . But you'll see.' I saw—in time. He was right about the battle, but not right about my leaving America loathing him.

''We opened in New York on a Wednesday and came off on the Saturday.

''I came back here (after *Gertie*) to Rottingdean and continued a play I had long begun. One doesn't start one play after another, as it may seem. There is so much pain, wasted life, time lost after the written word CURTAIN, and while the script, clean as laundry, goes out to seek its fortune. The only sanity is to be half-armed at least, with the roots or seeds of another to have something up one's sleeve against the coming agony. There's the agony of being refused. I've had that from London, but there has always been New York. There's the agony of being taken, and mangled. In my plays there is something that always seduces the director, star or management into turning author.

''I was well on, I thought, with *The Chalk Garden*. It took all the same three more years.''[1]

October, 1956. On the eve of her sixty-sixth birthday Bagnold attended the successful Broadway opening of *The Chalk Garden*. ''Oddly enough no flowers, no parties. We sailed for England. In the months following I was given the Award of Merit for Drama by the American Academy of Arts and Letters for *The Chalk Garden*. A thousand dollars went with it and I built the little canal that crosses my garden.''[1]

Autumn, 1961. Husband's health grew increasingly frail. ''We made the autumn move up to London. There we spent our mornings as we had always done, I buried with my typewriter: he drowsily, reading the newspaper, growing older. We met at lunch—each with our minds full to bursting with separate interests—flared a little in the old way on meeting—subsided, melted, grew always closer.

''Now began the long flight of the little illnesses which seem to have nothing to do with each other, and which precede death. One thing after another gets tired of its function. Each slight Unworking is a surprise.

''There is no adding up. Not at first.

''It's hard to describe a man with whom one fights for three parts of forty-two years and explain that one so loves him. And that with his exactions, his insistence, his domination, his infuriating habits, not one of which would he change, that he had for me total loyalty, total admiration, and that while he was angry with me he too, like my father thought me the Seventh Wonder.

''. . . His clothes grew old. He wouldn't buy new ones. The little contrivances in his room broke, I was always mending them.

''And so we live after forty-two years, till everything drops away, and the hooks of friends slip, and, two in a boat, there are only we who understand each other.''[1]

Winter, 1962. Husband died.

Spring, 1962. Resumed work on her latest play. ''I swore to myself when Roderick died that I'd manage non-responsibility. It's not so easy after a lifetime. I said I would live like a watchful hermit; watching myself, flowers, a dog; things that don't ask questions. That I would get out of bed (dress or dressing-gown) carrying my 'perception' undamaged into the day. Freshness and solitude are vital. I must have written a lot of this into *The Chinese Prime Minister* in the long period after Roderick died and before it was produced; for this 'resolve' comes into it constantly. . . .

''But habit is strong. Like an idiot I fabricate duties. And then too there has to be someone to look after me; the least possible. The house, not me. And a human being in the house takes something; a fraction, hardly noticeable. But noticeable! I have to give; pour something into a cup held out. It's a little wine, taken from myself. I mustn't grudge it. And then (the habit of a woman) indignation for work not done must be suppressed. It's a destroyer—indignation! So we live. With the minimum of battle. Plus that little glass of wine.

''I catch myself talking like a young poet; not an old woman.

''Why not? At present I imagine myself timeless.''[1]

1969. Wrote her autobiography. ''You might think that a woman of seventy-eight, glancing at a house where she was once in love, would be full of regrets. The extraordinary thing about age is that you don't regret love.

''Even in the looking glass there's nothing to be done. The golden veil has blown off the face.

''How many years have I been writing plays, the hours so happy as the pages come together. To me it's an ascent of hard and grinding joy till I reach the peak and come out into the open. Then comes the destruction!

"There are as many ways of writing a play or a book (or one's life) as there are flowers in the field. But only one tickles your fancy. The first and the lightest decision is the only originality. Forsake that and the governess-intellect begins sorting again.

"I get sick of how well I write (like one's face in the glass). I get sick of those two voices—the one that speaks first and the one that (instantaneous, overlapping) suggests the improvement. Fling him out! He's the devil! What a vigil!

"After this sort of battle, conducted alone, I approach the theatre. It is as though one had to stoop to go in at a doorway.

"Half dazed at first by the gaiety and welcome, relieved, ready to be espoused and assisted, yet once again, as I have said before, what I have done isn't understood *in time*. I explain, but it is not words that are needed, but a more Chinese approach as though the talk were a ritual, and quite other than the essence. My extravagances of language should be taken as the common air of the Characters, allowed to float by unnoticed. They are not meant to be played to be applauded. All I expect is a little hum which though not quite catching the meaning yet catches it backwards. If I hear that, I know how unselfishly the players have played.

"But instead hints are blown up. Talks open with the awkwardness of a beginning: no one behaves as though they had known each other well.

"Things don't work out that way. But how *how* to work in double harness?

"I would be prepared now to print and never by played.

"Perhaps I cannot bear again the non-communication. What hard and vigilant work!"[1]

1970-1979. Continued to live in London and Sussex. "I don't know what evaporates in age. Movement and speed, of course. But one adapts oneself. Appearance? Well yes: but one should look new in age. There should be a sirensuit of exquisite comfort; zipped, so that one single movement frees you from the melancholy of a hundred thousand dressings and undressings. The things I feared to lose is not gone. The tactile surprises, the sensual love of the garden. Bare feet on grass, the heat of the cobbles after shade, the cold pool behind the fuchsia hedge where I bathe naked. I have more time. I am not pushed and hurried off a sensation. . . .

"I once asked a very old gentleman (and he was deaf) across a luncheon table what it was like to very old.

"'Routine,' he twinkled, 'Just as good as love.'

"But only a man can install routine.

"Much alone and independent—very slowly I may become a man."[1]

March 31, 1981. Died in St. John's Wood in north London. "Theatergoers want more than a story or a slice of life. They want a flavor, an aroma up the nostrils—that's what they'll remember five years on." [*New York Times*, April 1, 1981.[2]]

ENID BAGNOLD

FOR MORE INFORMATION SEE: Books, May 17, 1931, April 28, 1935; *New York Herald Tribune,* April 26, 1935, December 30, 1951, December 29, 1963; *New York Times,* May 5, 1935, December 29, 1963; *New Yorker,* January 19, 1952, February 16, 1976; *Atlantic,* October, 1952; Kenneth Tynan, *Curtains,* Atheneum, 1961; *Theatre Arts,* January, 1964; Enid Bagnold, *Enid Bagnold's Autobiography,* Heinemann, 1969, Little, Brown, 1970; *Times Literary Supplement,* December 4, 1969, February 1, 1979; *Punch,* July 10, 1978; *Drama: Theatre Quarterly Review,* Winter, 1979.

OBITUARIES: Chicago Tribune, April 1, 1981; *New York Times,* April 1, 1981; *Washington Post,* April 3, 1981; *Newsweek,* April 13, 1981; *Time,* April 13, 1981; *Publishers Weekly,* April 24, 1981; *School Library Journal,* May, 1981.

BATTEN, H(arry) Mortimer   1888-1958

PERSONAL: Born February 4, 1888, in Otley, Yorkshire, England (some sources cite Singapore); died January 3, 1958, in Vancouver, Canada; son of William Townsend (a civil engineer) and Sarah (Barker) Batten; married Ivy Kathleen Godfrey, September, 1918; children: one son, two daughters. *Education:* Educated at Oakham School, Rutlandshire, England; studied natural history and game preservation in Canada. *Religion:* Protestant. *Home:* Le Jeune Lodge, Box 8 Kamloops, British Columbia, Canada. *Agent:* Charles Lavell Ltd., 176 Wardour St., London WIV 3AA, England.

CAREER: Author of books on natural history, wild animals, and birds; lecturer. Began writing about 1912; in early 1920s began broadcasting on BBC radio, and travelled throughout Canada working as a prospector, forest ranger, and surveyor;

later turned to fur-trapping and running a motorboat service on the Mattagami River; also served with the Canadian Police Force. Lectured extensively in England and Ireland, using films and slides of animals to illustrate his lectures. *Military service:* Served in World War I, 1914-18, and World War II; was a dispatch rider, served with French Army (received Croix de Guerre), and in Royal Air Force. *Member:* Caledonian United Service Club, New Club (Edinburgh).

WRITINGS: Jim and the Wolves, Warwick Brothers & Rutter (Toronto), 1912; *The Red Man of the Northland,* Warwick Brothers & Rutter, 1914; *In the Grip of the Yukon: A True Story,* Warwick Brothers & Rutter, 1916; *Ka-ka-kee, the Sioux: A Tale of a Prairie Feud,* Warwick Brothers & Rutter, 1917; *Who Are the ''Forest Rangers''?,* Warwick Brothers & Rutter, 1918; *Tommy and the Timber Wolves: A Story of Canadian Life,* Warwick Brothers & Rutter, 1919.

Forest Fire: A Terror of the Canadian Bush, Warwick Brothers & Rutter, 1920; *Habits and Characters of British Wild Animals* (illustrated by Warwick Reynolds), W. & R. Chambers, 1929; *Tracks and Tracking: A Book for Boy Scouts,* W. & R. Chambers, 1920; *Romances of the Wild* (illustrated by Reynolds), Blackie & Son, 1922, reprinted, Transatlantic, 1977; *Woodlore for Young Sportsmen,* Heath Cranton (London), 1922; *Many Trails* (illustrated by Morgan Stinemetz), H. Holt & Co., 1921; *The Badger Afield and Underground,* H. F. & G. Witherby, 1923; *Inland Birds: Northern Observations by a Sportsman,* Hutchinson, 1923; (editor) *W. and A. K. Johnston's Tracks of British Animals,* W. & A. K. Johnston (Edinburgh), 1923; (editor) *W. & A. K. Johnston's Tracks of British Birds,* W. & A. K. Johnson, 1923; *British Wild Animals: Their Tracks, Characteristics, Habits, Etc.,* C. Arthur Pearson, 1924; *Dramas of the Wild Folk* (illustrated by Harry Rountree), S. W. Partridge (London), 1924; *Prints from Many Trails,* Jenkins, 1924, reprinted, Ettrick Press, 1947; *Nature from the Highways,* Jenkins, 1925; *Nature Jottings of a Motorist,* Jenkins, 1926; *Patrol Calls and Signs: The ABC of All the Patrol Creatures, Their Habits and Characteristics,* C. A. Pearson, 1926; *The Golden Book of Animal Stories,* Blackie & Son, 1927, reissued (illustrated by Ernest Aris), 1958.

Some British Wild Animals (adapted from *Habits and Characters of British Wild Animals*), W. & R. Chambers, 1930; *Birds of Our Gardens: How to Feed and Encourage Them,* privately printed, 1931; *Tales of the Wild* (adapted from stories in *The Golden Book of Animal Stories*), Collins, 1934; *Jock and Old November, and Other Motoring and Fishing Stories of the Highlands,* Highway Press (Edinburgh), 1932; *2LO Animal Stories,* Grant & Murray (Edinburgh), 1931; *Woodland Stories,* Collins, 1932; *How to Feed and Attract the Wild Birds,* Grant & Murray, 1933; *Wild Life Stories,* Collins, 1933; (editor and compiler) *Among Wild Beasts,* Collins, 1934; *The Animal Picture Book,* Thomas Nelson, 1934; *Go Back: The Life Story of an Alsatian Wolfhound,* Moray Press (London), 1934; *Our Garden Birds: Their Food, Habits and Appearances,* Thomas Nelson, 1934; *Our Country's Wild Animals,* Thomas Nelson, 1935; *Muskwa the Trail Maker,* Moray Press, 1936; *Starlight,* D. Appleton-Century 1936; *Tameless and Swift: A Book of Animal Stories,* W. & R. Chambers, 1936; *Red Ruff: The Life Story of a Fox,* W. & R. Chambers, 1937, Penguin, 1947; *The Romantic Story of the Country-Side,* Hutchinson, 1937; *Sentinels of the Wild* (illustrated by Kathleen Nixon), George Newnes, 1938; *Electricity and the Camera: Nature, Big Game, and Home Photography Simplified,* Moray Press, 1939; *Wild Animals at Home,* Longmans & Co. (London), 1939.

Tales of Wild Bird Life (illustrated by Len Fullerton), Blackie & Son, 1948, reprinted, Transatlantic, 1977; *Yellowface* (illustrated by Jack Matthew), Evans Brothers, 1948; (contributor) *The Wonder Book of Comics,* Odhams, 1949; *British Wild Animals: An Authoritative Description Based on a Lifetime's Study and Observations of the Habits and Characteristics of Britain's Wild Animals,* Odhams, 1952; *Ray of the Rainbows* (illustrated by Vernon Stokes), Hollis & Carter, 1952, Roy, c. 1955; *The Singing Forest* (illustrated by Maurice Wilson), W. Blackwood, 1955, Penguin, 1958, Farrar, Straus, 1964; *Whispers of the Wilderness: Tales of Wild Life in the Canadian Forests* (illustrated by Nixon), Blackie & Son, 1960; *The Children's Book of Tracks and Tracking: A Book for Boy Scouts, Girl Scouts and Every Lover of Woodcraft,* W.& R. Chambers, 1961; *Wild and Free: Stories of Canadian Animals* (illustrated by Stuart Tresilian), Blackie & Son, 1961.

Contributor of stories and articles to periodicals, including *Cornhill, Discovery, Natural History, Boy's Own Paper, Blackwood's, Scout, Chambers', Captain, Illustrated London News, British Boy,* and others.

HOBBIES AND OTHER INTERESTS: Fishing, shooting, motoring, wildlife photography.

SIDELIGHTS: Batten was born in Singapore and educated at Oakham. As a young man he traveled throughout Canada where he worked at various jobs—as a forest ranger, a prospector, and a surveyor. At one time he was a fur trapper and ran a boat service on the Mattagami River.

About 1912 he began writing professionally. Batten was especially known as a writer of moving and memorable animal stories. His special interests were motoring and natural history. He became a frequent broadcaster on radio programs for the BBC.

FOR MORE INFORMATION SEE: Brian Doyle, *The Who's Who of Children's Literature,* Schocken Books, 1968.

BEATTY, John (Louis) 1922-1975

OBITUARY NOTICE—See sketch in *SATA* Volume 6: Born January 24, 1922, in Portland, Ore.; died March 23, 1975, in California. Historian, educator, author, and editor. Beatty was a professor of history at the University of California, where he specialized in English history of the sixteenth, seventeenth, and eighteenth centuries. As a hobby, he co-authored many historical books for young people with his wife, Patricia. Two of their award-winning titles are *The Royal Dirk* and *Campion Towers. For More Information See: Contemporary Authors,* Volumes 5-8, revised, Gale 1969; *Third Book of Junior Authors,* Wilson, 1972; *Twentieth Century Children's Writers,* St. Martin's, 1978. *Obituaries: Publishers Weekly,* April 28, 1975; *Contemporary Authors,* Volumes 57-60, Gale, 1976.

Some books are to be tasted, others to be swallowed, and some few to be chewed and digested: that is, some books are to be read only in parts, others to be read, but not curiously, and some few to be read wholly, and with diligence and attention.

—Francis Bacon

"Surrender!" Andy said, stepping out from behind the fallen tree and fitting another arrow to the string of the magic bow. He was a bit annoyed that his voice happened to squeak just as he gave the command, so that it didn't come out sounding nearly so heroic as he thought it should.
■ (From *Potawatomi Indian Summer* by E. William Oldenburg. Illustrated by Betty Beeby.)

BEEBY, Betty 1923-

PERSONAL: Born March 26, 1923, in Detroit, Mich.; daughter of Norton Harris (an elementary school principal) and Dorothy (Waite; a parlimentarian; civilian defense director for women) Pearl; married James Addison Beeby (a pharmacist), March 29, 1944; children: James Addison, Jr., Jane Joann, John A., Josephine Jean. *Education:* Pratt Institute, Brooklyn, N. Y., diploma, 1943. *Home:* Eastport, Mich. 49627. *Office:* Box 226, Eastport, Mich. 49627.

CAREER: Architectural Forum and Time/Life, Inc., New York, N. Y., cover and layout artist, 1943-45; Bahlman Art Studio, Kalamazoo, Mich., artist and designer, 1956; Kalamazoo Vegetable Parchment Co., Parchment, Mich. package designer. 1957-58; *Sequoia Press,* Kalamazoo, Mich., illustrator 1960-65. Freelance illustrator, painter, work has included a 50-foot mural at Fort Michilimackinac, Mackinaw City, Mich., 1975 and art for a children's program on CBS, 1977. Child Guidance Circle (president, 1957), Kalamazoo, Mich.; Kalamazoo Citizen's Committee, Kalamazoo, Mich., 1960; Upper Torch Lake Association, 1977; Artist's North and Crooked Tree Arts Council, 1977. *Exhibitions:* Kalamazoo Civic Center (one-man show), Kalamazoo, Mich., 1956; Kalamazoo Institute of Arts, Kalamazoo, Mich., 1975. *Member:* Kalamazoo Institute of Arts, Kalamazoo Professional Artists (secretary, 1965), Kal Art League. *Awards, honors:* Booth Scholarship to Pratt Institute, 1940; Chicago Book Clinic Awards for *Just Josie,* 1960, *Whistle Up the Bay,* 1966, and *Potawatomi Indian Summer,* 1975.

WRITINGS—Self-illustrated: Just Josie, Reilly & Lee, 1960.

Illustrator: Carol Dornfeld Stevenson, *Stubborn Binder,* Reilly & Lee, 1961; Nancy Stone, *Whistle Up the Bay,* Eerdmans, 1966; Catherine Vos, *Child's Story Bible,* Eerdmans, 1977; Owen Barfield, *The Silver Trumpet,* Eerdmans, 1968; Louise Jean Walker, *Daisy: The Story of a Horse;* Eerdmans, 1970; Nancy Stone, *The Wooden River,* Eerdmans, 1973; E. William Oldenburg, *Potawatomi Indian Summer,* Eerdmans, 1975. Illustrator of Larry Smith's *The Peterboro Letters.* Has also illustrated stories and children's text books for Lyons & Carnahan and Scott, Foresman.

(With Al Balkin) "Reaching and Teaching Through Music," volume 1 (six filmstrips; six cassettes; teacher's guide) for Oak Woods Media.

WORK IN PROGRESS: Pasajes, six college level Spanish text books for Random House.

SIDELIGHTS: "My sisters and I used to perform stunts and feats of daring on a swing that hung between our dining room and living room for whatever company that came to visit our home in Detroit, where I grew up.

"At mealtimes we delved into weighty problems: 'How did people first make laws?.' 'What is straight up and down?,' 'Why was money invented?.' 'Why do people live in groups?,' 'What do you need to stay alive?,' 'What makes a good leader?,' 'What does it take to make you happy?,' 'How do people learn?' . . . and the like.

"I recall never having enough paper to draw on. To this day I covet the stuff in memory of those days when I had only the backs of printed forms or salvaged scrap.

"People were my favorite subjects, but I remember a frustrated 'tree' period in which I tried again and again, yet never succeeding to bring a tree to a conclusion. This may say something about my nature.

"Fortunately I was encouraged to go to Cass Technical High School. The long street-car rides to and from Cass gave me plenty of opportunity to study and draw people. Above all, a very special teacher there provided the ingredients that every student should be privy to at least once in their lifetime.

"The first summer out of Cass I worked as a waitress on the Georgian Bay Boat Line and missed my own graduation. But a diploma came by mail and word that I'd received the Booth Scholarship to study that fall at Pratt Institute in Brooklyn.

"As a 'green horn' eighteen years old in Grand Central Station, my first day in New York City, I was pegged for a wallet heist . . . mine! So I lost my hard-earned summer's earnings. I scrimped along on a meager diet in a Brooklyn brownstone that first year at Pratt. My last year I worked as a part-time assistant to Jean Carlu, the famous French poster artist.

"Three of us at Pratt got jobs in the city after graduation and rented an apartment at '#12 Fifth Avenue. Those were heady days . . . being paid for work we loved to do. I was hired at *Time/Life* Magazines. A year or so later, by sheer chance, I met and fell in love with a handsome Navy officer. We were married not long after that.

"Eventually, while he was in the South Pacific, I went back to stay at my parents' home where our first baby was born in Detroit. When my husband returned from overseas, we moved to Marquette, Michigan (for six years) and later to Kalamazoo (for twenty years).

"Though I never stopped drawing and painting, it seemed a whole new way of life as a mother would end my career. I seemed, however, only to be gestating, in more ways than one. We had four children in fairly rapid succession. It was while I played with them and did the chores that I began making children's books.

"I was slow at growing up and never took a liking to housework. To lessen its sting, I practiced evasion and invention. Even my ironing board cover became a medium of expression. I'd ironed so many colored patches over its holes it looked like 'art,' so I sewed it down on a bright cloth with tassels and flew it as my banner.

"Adept as I was at playing, it was only natural we would make puppets and stage productions . . . some of the plays were: 'Ma Perkins in Outer Space,' 'The Chuckleberry Tales,' 'Six Fingered Fanny,' or the 'Marvelous Mystery of the Missing Sock' . . . and variations on Sherlock Holmes' mysteries.

"The kids had a 'Full Moon Museum Society' in a small building at the back of the lot where all sorts of wonders are displayed: exotic papier mâché animals in a reptile room, shells, skulls, nests and even Cleopatra's cosmetic dishes. People came from miles around to see their museum.

"I've made a wooden painted story 'Box of Hours' to celebrate those lovely years when our children were small.

"In those days I made so many mock-ups of illustrated children's books that one day I began to send them out to pub-

Betty Beeby, working on a fifty foot mural.

lishers. As I gathered rejection slips and my library of unpublished works increased, the day came after ten years when I finally sold one.

"It was just a small thirty-two page, two color, line-drawn edition, but what an elation it was!

"After that I was asked to illustrate other books, most of which were done in pen and ink. The full color illustrated books that I've done were in felt pen colors and water color. I sometimes combine mediums using everything from collage to painting over dried starch on paper for certain effects.

"On the side, I have a need to paint for myself—I work in oils, acrylics, water colors, etchings and lithographs.

"The attitude most valuable to an artist, I would guess, is curiosity. It's hard to handle. It means letting many things

claim ones attention, but that is how it's aroused. I find it natural to believe in most everything.

"While I draw, doors open and let me see . . . and yet, mercifully, lets what I see be. I have often discovered a spade is seldom a spade. If I set myself at odds with my memory and shut out past reference, I usually draw better.

"I'm inspired by writers who paint words that sway, swish slam, stalk and string with power and thought. They, like the great painters, have been inspiration and sustenance to me.

"I was also influenced by Mary L. Davis at Cass Technical High School and Will Burtin at Pratt Institute."

FOR MORE INFORMATION SEE: Kalamazoo Gazette, February 1, 1959, March 13, 1960, March 11, 1973, January 12, 1975; *Battle Creek Enquirer and News,* February 17, 1960; *Petoskey News Review,* July 18, 1975; *Grand Rapids Press,* August 31, 1975; *Detroit News,* September 11, 1975.

BENCHLEY, Nathaniel (Goddard) 1915-

PERSONAL: Born November 13, 1915, in Newton, Mass; son of Robert (a writer) and Gertrude (Darling) Benchley; married Marjorie Bradford, May 19, 1939; children: Peter Bradford, Nathaniel Robert. *Education:* Harvard University, B. S., 1938. *Politics:* Democrat. *Home:* Box 244, Siasconset, Mass. 02564. *Agent:* Roberta Pryor, International Creative Management, 40 West 57th St., New York, N.Y. 10019.

CAREER: New York Herald Tribune, New York, N. Y., city reporter, 1939-41; *Newsweek,* New York, N. Y., assistant drama editor, 1946-47; free-lance writer and artist. *Member:* Coffee House and Century Association (both New York), Pacific Club (Nantucket, Mass.).

WRITING—For children; all published by Harper except as noted: *Sinbad the Sailor,* Random House, 1960; *Red Fox and His Canoe* (illustrated by Arnold Lobel), 1964; *Oscar Otter* (illustrated by Lobel), 1966; *The Strange Disappearance of Arthur Cluck* (illustrated by Lobel), 1967; *A Ghost Named Fred* (illustrated by Ben Shecter), 1968; *Sam the Minuteman* (illustrated by Lobel), 1969; *The Several Tricks of Edgar Dolphin* (illustrated by Mamoru Funai), 1970; *The Flying Lesson of Gerald Pelican* (illustrated by Funai), 1970; *Feldman Field-*

NATHANIEL BENCHLEY

mouse, 1971; *Gone and Back,* 1971; *The Magic Sled* (illustrated by Mel Furakawa), 1972; *Only Earth and Sky Last Forever,* 1972; *Small Wolf* (illustrated by Joan Sanden), 1972; *The Deep Dives of Stanley Whale* (illustrated by Mischa Richter), 1973; *Bright Candles: A Novel of the Danish Resistance,* (ALA Notable Book), 1974; *Beyond the Mists,* 1975; *A Necessary End: A Novel of World War Two,* 1976; *Snorri and the Strangers* (illustrated by Don Bolognese), 1976; *George the Drummer Boy* (illustrated by Bolognese), 1977; *Kilroy and the Gull* (illustrated by John Schoenherr), 1977; *Running Owl the Hunter* (illustrated by Funai), 1979; *Walter, the Homing Pigeon* (illustrated by Whitney Darrow, Jr.), 1981; *Snip* (illustrated by Irene Trivas), Doubleday, 1981.

For adults: *Side Street,* Harcourt, 1950; (editor) *The Benchley Roundup,* Harper, 1954; *Robert Benchley,* McGraw, 1955; *One to Grow On,* McGraw, 1958; *Sail a Crooked Ship,* McGraw, 1960; *The Off-Islanders,* McGraw, 1961; *Catch a Falling Spy,* McGraw, 1963; *A Winter's Tale,* McGraw, 1964; *A Firm Word or Two,* McGraw, 1965; *The Visitors,* McGraw, 1965; *The Monument,* McGraw, 1966; *Welcome to Xanadu,* Atheneum, 1968; *The Wake of the Icarus,* Atheneum, 1969; *Lassiter's Folly,* Atheneum, 1971; *The Hunter's Moon,* Little, Brown, 1972; *Humphrey Bogart,* Little, Brown, 1975; *Portrait of a Scoundrel,* Doubleday, 1979; *Sweet Anarchy,* Doubleday, 1979.

Also author of "The Frogs of Spring" (play), 1953, and the screenplay for "The Great American Pastime," Metro-Goldwyn-Mayer, 1956; contributor of articles and short stories to *New Yorker, Holiday, Esquire, McCall's, Ladies' Home Journal, Cosmopolitan, Playboy, Collier's, Redbook, This Week, Vogue, Argosy, Harper's Bazaar, Nugget,* and other national magazines.

**"What chicken?" Gus replied.
"I only steal things, not chickens."**

■ (From *The Strange Disappearance of Arthur Cluck* by Nathaniel Benchley. Illustrated by Arnold Lobel.)

(From the movie "Sail a Crooked Ship," starring Robert Wagner and Ernie Kovacs. Released by Columbia Pictures Corp., 1961.)

ADAPTATIONS—Movies and filmstrips: "Sail a Crooked Ship," starring Ernie Kovacs, Columbia Pictures Corp., 1961; "The Russians Are Coming, the Russians Are Coming" (motion picture), adaptation of *The Off-Islanders,* starring Carl Reiner, Eva Marie Saint, Alan Arkin, Brian Keith, and Jonathan Winters, United Artists, 1966; "The Spirit Is Willing" (motion picture), adaptation of *The Visitors,* starring Sid Caesar and Vera Miles, Paramount Pictures, 1966; "A Ghost Named Fred" (filmstrip; with teacher's guide and multimedia kit), Harper & Row, 1974; "The Strange Disappearance of Arthur Cluck" (filmstrip; with teacher's guide and multimedia kit), Harper & Row, 1974; "Oscar Otter" (filmstrip; with teacher's guide and multimedia kit), Harper & Row, 1976.

SIDELIGHTS: **November 13, 1915.** Born in Newton, Massachusetts. Father, Robert Benchley, was a well known humorist ". . . [I] weighed in at 6 pounds 1 ounce and was conceded by everybody to be extremely plain, was named Nathaniel Goddard Benchley, after Robert's great-grandfather, Nathaniel Goddard, who had been a deacon in Millbury, Massachusetts. No matter how you looked at it, there was family mixed in it

somehow, and no matter how you pronounced it, it was a long name for a small child. They decided to call [me] Petey Dink, or more formally Mr. Dink. At the end of the day that had seemed like a week, [my father] splurged on a steak-and-onion dinner at the Harvard Club, and then went back to the quiet and lonely apartment, and to sleep on the cot." [Nathaniel Benchley, *Robert Benchley,* McGraw-Hill, 1955.[1]]

1938. After being educated at Phillip Exeter Academy, Benchley graduated from Harvard University.

1939. Married Marjorie Bradford. Much of Benchley's adult life was spent in New York City, where he was a reporter on the New York *Herald Tribune* and, later, as assistant drama editor for *Newsweek* Magazine. ". . .I got married and moved to New York. On an average of three nights a week, when [my father] was in town, he would call and suggest that my wife and I have dinner with him. These dinners would follow a precise, almost ritualistic pattern. Marjorie or I would accept the invitation, and then, because we would always have been

(From the movie "The Russians Are Coming! The Russians Are Coming!," starring Brian Keith and Alan Arkin, based on the novel *The Off-Islanders* by Nathaniel Benchley. Released by United Artists, 1966.)

"All polar bears can swim," the Mayor announced.

"Not me! I was born in the zoo, and I never learned!" ■ (From *The Magic Sled* by Nathaniel Benchley. Illustrated by Mel Furukawa.)

to '21' the time before, he would say that we ought to try someplace new, just for sake of variety. We would think of several places, all of which would be discarded for one reason or another, and then he would say, 'The hell with it. I'll meet you at "21."' It seldom varied, although the places we went to afterward varied widely. But no matter where we went, it always got late, because there seemed no rational reason to go to bed when staying up with him was so much more pleasant. Also, both he and I shared the fear that we might miss something good if we went to bed. He once explained why he was always the last to leave a party by saying, 'I can't seem to bring myself to say, "Well, I guess I'll be toddling along." . . . It isn't that I *can't* toddle. It's that I can't *guess* I'll toddle.' And that was the way it was when we were together—until sleep was an absolute necessity, if not an accomplished fact, nobody could guess they'd toddle along. And he had immediately won Marjorie's heart by introducing her as 'my daughter' instead of 'my daughter-in-law,' so she didn't care if she never went to bed.

"It was at '21,' one night after we had finished dinner that we saw Humphrey Bogart standing at the bar. At the time, Bogart had played nothing but gangster roles; I had never met him, and knew about him only through his pictures, so I was somewhat surprised when Gramps [his father] said, 'Watch this,' and left the table and moved quietly in behind Bogart. He tapped him on the shoulder. 'All right,' he said. 'Finish your drink and get out. We don't want your kind in here.'

"Bogart turned and looked at him, then dropped his cigarette on the floor, spat out a thin stream of smoke, and reached slowly into an inner pocket. Two customers next to him sidled away nervously, and the bartender began to grope under the bar for a weapon. 'Who's going to make me, pal?' Bogart asked, moving in closer.

"'Don't you worry about that,' said my father, coldly. 'Just get going.' He put one finger on Bogart's chest, and gave a small push. I thought he had gone crazy.

"'If that's the way you want to play, O. K.,' Bogart said, showing his fangs. There was a quick flurry; a woman screamed, and then Bogart began to laugh. 'That face,' he said, doubling over. 'I can't look at that face without laughing.'

"I later found out that they had staged some fairly spectacular mock fights, but that they always wound up with Bogart helpless with laughter. That face, trying to look like a gangster was more than he could bear.''[1]

1941-1945. Aside from service in the Navy during World War II, Benchley spent most of his life in New York City until, in

And all three bears caught fish while Red Fox paddled. How could he get rid of the bears?
■ (From *Red Fox and His Canoe* by Nathaniel Benchley. Illustrated by Arnold Lobel.)

1969, he and his wife took up permanent residence on Nantucket Island. "I got back from the Pacific on November 15, 1945, and those of us who were headed for East Coast separation centers were put in barracks in Oceanside, California, until transportation could be found. . . .

"Two days later, we boarded a train for Los Angeles where, we were told, a special train was waiting to take us East. We reached Los Angeles about noon, and for some reason the whole place looked different from the last time I had been there; it was drab and dirty in the harsh November sunshine, and there was a kind of flat shabbiness about it that was faintly depressing. We waited in line for about eight hours to get on the special train, and when we got aboard we found that thirty of us were assigned to an observation car with space for twenty. Lieutenant commanders and above slept alone in upper berths; the rest doubled up in the lowers. Since everybody had colds, it didn't much matter who slept where.

"The trip took five days. There was no diner so three times a day the train stopped and everybody raced into whatever the town was and swarmed through the lunchrooms and cafeterias and saloons, and then the engineer blew the whistle and, like a movie film being run backwards, the town was emptied of running figures and the train filled up and moved on. By the time we reached the home stretch, between Pittsburgh and New York, the train had been shunted and switched around so often that the observation car was just behind the tender, and the coal that blew off the tender was piled knee-deep on the observation platform.

"The train's ultimate destination was Boston, but I got off at Pennsylvania Station, in New York, at 2 A. M. November 22. The station was dark and empty; the escalators had stopped running, and I carried my luggage up the long, echoing staircases into the high-domed concourse. One faint light burned by a telephone booth, and I slid my bags along the floor and then, panting, dropped into the booth and called Marjorie. She answered after one ring.

"'I suppose you've heard the news,' she said.

"I stared at the holes in the telephone mouthpiece, and knew exactly what she was going to say. 'No,' I said. 'What?'

"'Gramps died this morning,' she said. 'Or yesterday morning, I mean.'

"He had had a series of nosebleeds, each more severe than the one before, and then, about four days previously, he had had one that wouldn't stop. He was taken to the hospital, but the hemorrhaging had become general and finally he had gone into a coma and, at 6 A. M. November 21, had died of, technically, a cerebral hemorrhage. There had been a quick, frantic calling and scurrying among his friends; forty people volunteered to give blood, and he had eight transfusions, but the whole thing happened so quickly that many people didn't even hear about it until it was on the radio.

"He took with him to the hospital a book of philosophical essays called *The Practical Cogitator, or, The Thinker's Anthology,* and he made marginal notations on the five pages that he read. The last essay he read was called 'Am I Thinking?' by James Harvey Robinson, and the marginal notation beside the title reads: 'NO. (and supposing you were?)'"[1]

1950-1960. Wrote novels and biographies. Benchley has two sons. ". . . [My] first son, christened Bradford, was called

Pete so much that his name was legally changed. Before he was called Pete, Bradford was called Paddington Station. [My] second son, Nathaniel Robert, was known as Whistle Stop. For some reason, no Benchley ever seems to come by his right name easily."[1]

1960-1975. Continued to free-lance as a writer. Besides adult books, Benchley wrote children's stories, articles and short stories for magazines, and plays. "I've found that every time I sound off about writing (and it isn't often that people ask me), something rises up out of the ground and hits me in the back of the head, sort of as a warning against hubris. As far as I'm concerned, this business breeds as much superstition as the theatre and parachute jumping, and what may work for one person will be of no possible use for another. You ask 'from what experience you derive your material,' and to that I think I can safely reply that you derive your material from everything you do, see, or hear, but beyond that I can't be of much help . . .''

"I write every morning. I see if I can get a thousand words down. Every morning, summer and winter, seven days a week. The winter, of course, is the best time to work here, but in the summer I have a place across the street from my home on the other end of the island [Nantucket]. There's a garage over there where I do my writing. The main thing during the summer is to duck all the people who are here on vacation. They can't seem to understand that you are not on vacation. July and August are murder here. If you wanted to, you could go to about three cocktail parties a day. That's murder. You'd never get anything done. So my wife and I don't go to any. It's harder to work in the summer only because of those distractions. When you live in a place like Nantucket, you don't do so much of the sailing and the golfing because there are all those things to do around the house.

"I do a first draft on the typewriter, and then, to vary the routine, I go back and rewrite each chapter as I get it done. But the matter of rewriting and retyping is such a grinding bore that it's better to break it up and do a chapter at a time rather than the whole bloody thing at the end. I've done it both ways, but this seems to work best. At one time, however, I was working on an adult book and had to retype forty pages a day. When you're doing that much, you have a tendency to make mistakes.

"Generally, I write from nine to twelve, but it depends really on how long it takes me to get my thousand words done. I didn't quite get a thousand done yesterday because our summer place was broken into. Sometimes, if it's going well, you just run over. But the main thing is to leave a so-called window into the next day's work. Never stop at a block or at the end of anything. Always leave . . . maybe even half a sentence, so you have something to get you going again." [Paul Janeczko, "An Interview with Nathaniel Benchley," *English Journal,* September, 1976.[2]]

The ingredients of the perfect children's book according to Benchley are ". . . that you don't talk down to [children]. Beyond that, they like humor, again not talking down to them. Also, they like suspense. You need a 'page turner.' Each right-hand page has to have a what-will-happen-next to it.

"I would say that the ideal children's book would be something like *Charlotte's Web.* Adults can appreciate that book as well as children.

"A lot of people believe that you should not have the so-called teen-age novel. They feel that you go straight from Tom Swift and the Hardy Boys to *Madame Bovary*. I don't think that's necessarily true, especially since there are so many kids now with, shall we say, limited reading ability. In the days when there was nothing to do but read, then people started on the 'classics' earlier. Nowadays, young people need a certain amount of help to show them what is possible."[2]

Benchley calls himself an amateur-professional painter. "That is," he explains, "I do landscape paintings of amateur quality which people for some reason seem to buy at professional prices."

FOR MORE INFORMATION SEE: Saturday Review, December 10, 1955; *New York Times Book Review,* June 25, 1967, October 12, 1969, May 2, 1971, November 7, 1971, February 8, 1976, December 16, 1979; *Publishers Weekly,* October 2, 1972; *Esquire,* July, 1974; *Christian Science Monitor,* July 7, 1975, September 12, 1979; *English Journal,* September, 1976; *Best Sellers,* October 1976; Doris de Montreville and Elizabeth D. Crawford, editors, *Fourth Book of Junior Authors & Illustrators,* H. W. Wilson, 1978; *America,* September 18, 1979.

BENNETT, Russell H(oradley) 1896-

PERSONAL: Born November 30, 1896, in Minneapolis, Minn. son of Russell Meridan and Helen (Harrison) Bennett; married Miriam Fletcher, May 13, 1924; children: Winslow W., Helen H. (Mrs. W. J. Beus), Miriam (Mrs. D. S. Leslie, Jr.), Fletcher, Meridan, David T., Noel F. *Education:* Graduated from Phillips Academy, 1915; Yale University, A. B., 1920; graduate study at Columbia University, 1920-21. *Politics:* Republican. *Religion:* Methodist. *Home:* 2217 E. Lake of Isles Blvd., Minneapolis, Minn. 55405. *Office:* Bennett Office, Inc., 1210 Baker Building, Minneapolis, Minn. 55402.

CAREER: Mining engineer, author. Bennett Office, Inc., Minneapolis, Minn., owner, 1919—; Shoderee Ranch, Pincher Creek, Alberta, owner/operator, 1932-1972; Electro Manganese Corp., Knoxville Tenn., chairman 1941-56; has also been chairman, Placer Development Ltd.; director, Meridan Iron Co., Minneapolis, Minn. and Sargent Land Co. Minneapolis commissioner, Metropolitan Drainage Commission, 1927-31; chairman of the board of trustees, Dunwoody Industrial Institute, 1937-81. *Member:* American Institute of Mining and Metallurgical Engineers, Century Association (New York City), Explorers' Club, Minneapolis Club.

WRITINGS: The Compleat Rancher (illustrated by Ross Santee), Rinehart, 1946, revised edition, T. S. Denison, 1965; *Quest for Ore* (forward by Herbert Hoover), T. S. Denison, 1963. Contributor of articles to professional journals.

A good book is the precious life-blood of a master spirit, embalmed and treasured up on purpose to life beyond life.

—John Milton

BENTLEY, Phyllis (Eleanor) 1894-1977

OBITUARY NOTICE—See sketch in *SATA* Volume 6: Born November 19, 1894 in Halifax, England; died June 27, 1977. Author and lecturer. Bentley was fascinated with the history and people of her native Yorkshire, a locale which figured largely in her writing. *Inheritance,* her best-known novel, deals with the effects of the industrial revolution there. Bentley's regional novels for children include *The Adventures of Tom Leigh* and *Sheep May Safely Graze.* In addition, Bentley wrote several books about the Brontes, also natives of Yorkshire, and in the mystery genre she created the character Miss Marian Phipps, an elderly detective. For her contributions to literature, Bentley was awarded the Order of the British Empire in 1970. *For More Information See: Twentieth Century Authors,* first supplement, Wilson, 1955; Phyllis Bentley, *O Dreams, O Destinations,* Gollancz, 1962; *Contemporary Authors,* Volumes 1-4, revised, Gale 1967; *Longman Companion to Twentieth Century Literature,* Longman, 1970; *Encyclopedia of Mystery and Detection,* McGraw, 1976. *Obituaries: London Times,* June 29, 1977.

BERESFORD, Elisabeth

PERSONAL: Born in Paris, France; daughter of J. D. (a novelist) and Evelyn (Roskams) Beresford; married Maxwell Robertson (a broadcaster), 1949; children: one daughter, one son. *Education:* Attended schools in Brighton, Sussex, England. *Agent:* A. M. Heath Ltd., 40-42 William IV St., London WC2N 4DD, England and David Higham Assoc., 5 Lower John St., London W.1, England.

CAREER: Writer; free-lance journalist, beginning 1948; radio broadcaster. *Wartime service:* Radio operator in Women's Naval Service during World War II.

WRITINGS—For children: *The Television Mystery,* Parrish, 1957; *Flying Doctor Mystery,* Parrish, 1958; *Trouble at Tullington Castle,* Parrish 1958; *Cocky and the Missing Castle* (illustrated by Jennifer Miles), Constable, 1959; *Gappy Goes West,* Parrish, 1959; *Tullington Film-Makers,* Parrish, 1960; *Two Gold Dolphins* (illustrated by Peggy Fortnum), Constable, 1961, Bobbs-Merrill (illustrated by Janina Domanska), 1963; *Danger on the Old Pull'n Push,* Parrish, 1962, White Lion Publishers, 1976; *Strange Hiding Place,* Parrish, 1962; *Diana in Television,* Collins, 1963; *The Missing Formula Mystery,* Parrish, 1963; *The Mulberry Street Team* (illustrated by Juliet Pannett), Friday Press, 1963 (also see below); *Awkward Magic* (illustrated by Judith Valpy), Hart-Davis, 1964, Granada Publishing, 1978; *The Flying Doctor to the Rescue,* Parrish, 1964; *Holiday for Slippy* (illustrated by Pat Williams), Friday Press, 1964 (also see below); *The Magic World* (illustrated by J. Domanska), Bobbs-Merrill, 1964.

Game, Set and Match, Parrish, 1965; *The Hidden Mill* (illustrated by Margery Gill), Benn, 1965 (also see below), Meredith Press, 1967; *Knights of the Cardboard Castle* (illustrated by C. R. Evans), Methuen, 1965, revised edition (illustrated by Reginald Gray), 1976; *Travelling Magic* (illustrated by J. Valpy), Hart-Davis, 1965, published as *The Vanishing Garden,* Funk, 1967, Granada Publishing, 1977; *Peter Climbs a Tree* (illustrated by M. Gill), Benn, 1966; *The Black Mountain Mystery,* Parrish, 1967; *Fashion Girl,* Collins, 1967; *Looking for a Friend* (illustrated by M. Gill), Benn, 1967; *More Adventure Stories* (contains "The Mulberry Street Team," "Hol-

ELISABETH BERESFORD

iday for Slippy,'' and ''The Hidden Mill''), Benn, 1967; *The Island Bus* (illustrated by Robert Hodgson), Methuen, 1968, revised edition (illustrated by Gavin Rowe), 1977; *Sea-Green Magic,* Hart-Davis, 1968, revised edition (illustrated by Ann Tout), 1976; *The Wombles,* Benn, 1968, revised edition (illustrated by Margaret Gordon), Meredith Press, 1969 (also see below); *David Goes Fishing* (illustrated by Imre Hofbauer), Benn, 1969.

Gordon's Go-Kart (illustrated by M. Gill), McGraw, 1970; *Stephen and the Shaggy Dog* (illustrated by Robert Hales), Methuen, 1970; *Vanishing Magic* (illustrated by A. Tout), Hart-Davis, 1970; *The Wandering Wombles* (illustrated by Oliver Chadwick), Benn, 1970 (also see below); *Dangerous Magic* (illustrated by O. Chadwick), Hart-Davis, 1972; *The Invisible Womble and Other Stories* (illustrated by Ivor Wood), Benn, 1973; *The Secret Railway* (illustrated by James Hunt), Methuen, 1973; *The Wombles at Work* (illustrated by M. Gordon), Benn, 1973, revised edition (illustrated by B. Leith), 1976 (also see below); *The Wombles in Danger,* Benn, 1973; *Invisible Magic* (illustrated by R. Gray), Hart-Davis, 1974; *The Wombles Go to the Seaside,* World Distributors, 1974; *The Wombles to the Rescue* (illustrated by M. Gordon), Benn, 1974 (also see below).

Orinoco Runs Away (illustrated by M. Gordon), Benn, 1975; *The Snow Womble* (illustrated by M. Gordon), Benn, 1975; *Snuffle to the Rescue* (illustrated by Gunvor Edwards), Harmondsworth, 1975; *Tomsk and The Tired Tree* (illustrated by M. Gordon), Benn, 1975; *Wellington and the Blue Balloon*

(illustrated by M. Gordon), Benn, 1975; *The Wombles Book* (contains ''The Wombles'' and ''The Wondering Wombles''), Benn, 1975; *The Wombles Gift Book* (illustrated by M. Gordon and Derek Collard), Benn, 1975; *The Wombles Make a Clean Sweep,* Benn, 1975; *Bungo Knows Best* (illustrated by M. Gordon), Benn, 1976; *The MacWombles' Pipe Band* (illustrated by M. Gordon), Benn, 1976; *Madame Cholet's Picnic Party* (illustrated by M. Gordon), Benn, 1976; *Tobermory's Big Surprise* (illustrated by M. Gordon), Benn, 1976; *The Wombles Go Round the World* (illustrated by M. Gordon), Benn, 1976; *The Wombles of Wimbledon* (contains ''The Wombles at Work'' and ''The Wombles to the Rescue''), Benn, 1976; *The World of the Wombles* (illustrated by Edgar Hodges), World Distributors, 1976; *The Wombles Annual, 1975 to 1978,* four volumes, World Distributors, 1974-77; *Beginning to Read Storybook,* Benn, 1977; *Secret Magic* (illustrated by Caroline Sharpe), Hart-Davis, 1978; *Toby's Luck* (illustrated by Doreen Caldwell), Methuen, 1978; *Wombling Free* (illustrated by E. Hodges), Benn, 1978; *The Happy Ghost* (illustrated by J. Carey), Methuen, 1979; *The Treasure Hunters,* Elsevier-Nelson, 1980; *Curious Magic,* Elsevier-Nelson, 1980; *The Four of Us,* Hutchinson, 1981; *The Battle of Ballig Fort,* Methuen, in press.

For adults; all novels; all published by Hale, except as noted: *Paradise Island,* 1963; *Escape to Happiness,* 1964; *Roses Round the Door,* 1965; *Islands of Shadows,* 1966; *Veronica,* 1967; *A Tropical Affair,* 1968, Dell, 1978; *Saturday's Child,* 1969; *Love Remembered,* 1970; *Love and the S. S. Beatrice,* 1972; *Pandora,* 1974; *Thunder of Her Heart,* Dale Books, 1978; *The Steadfast Lover,* Hale, 1980; *The Silver Chain,* Hale, 1980.

Plays: ''The Wombles,'' produced in London, England, 1974; (with Nick Renton) ''Road to Albutal,'' produced in Edinburgh, Scotland, 1976. Also author of screenplay, ''The Wombles,'' 1977, and more than sixty ''Womble'' television scripts. Contributor of short feature stories to magazines.

WORK IN PROGRESS: Weavers Deep, a family saga for adults; *The Survivors,* a history of magical creatures.

SIDELIGHTS: ''Having a novelist for a father and two brothers who were successful writers I was brought up in a world of books so it seemed natural that I should become a writer too. I started off as a journalist and eventually became a radio and television reporter for the BBC, a job which has taken me from the Outback in Australia to the jungles of South America which, of course, all make wonderful backgrounds for books. I've also met some extraordinary and unusual people from gold-miners to royalty, from Dukes to derelicts. Children (and adults) write to me from all over the world and quite often they seem to know more about my books than I do. I particularly like listening to children, because—fortunately—they still go on believing that anything is possible and that all kinds of adventures are just around the next corner. And when I put something funny into a story and it makes me laugh I know it will make a lot of children laugh. And there's no better sound in the world than children laughing.

''Now I've been asked to write a big family saga (adult) and am looking forward to it—but with some trepidation as it's a completely new field for me. I particularly enjoy writing for children and meeting them and getting their letters from all over the world—even one from China. Quite often they tell me my plots and they seem to know more about my characters than I do. One of the many wonderful things about children

"What a pretty little kitten you are," said Mr. Beak.

"I will sell you for lots of money."

■ (From *Snuffle to the Rescue* by Elisabeth Beresford. Illustrated by Gunvor Edwards.)

is that *they* still live in a world where anything is possible and the words 'once upon a time' can make it all happen.''

Beresford achieved her greatest success as a writer through the creation of her ''Womble'' series for children. These tales, which number over twenty-five explore the fantasy world of the Womble family.

The family consists of numerous hard working, but fun loving creatures such as Bungo and Wellington. The Orinoco film puppets were designed by Ivor Wood. All the books are colorfully illustrated to depict Wood's originations.

The enduring Wombles uphold old-fashioned virtues. They are also concerned with conservation, and constantly seek other uses of worn-out items. The family motto is ''make good use of bad rubbish.''

The Wombles have become somewhat of a legend in children's literature. The stories have been translated into various other media and twenty languages.

Some of Beresford's other publications for children are set in a fantasy world. Several of these stories, including *Secret Magic*, tell of characters journeying through time. The main character of *Secret Magic* is a talking cat who is actually an ancient sphinx. In *Invisible Magic* a young boy encounters a princess from another era while bicycling in a park. A girl and her younger brother befriend a magician from ancient Britain in *Traveling Magic*.

HOBBIES AND OTHER INTERESTS: ''Reading, photography, surfing, gardening, and not working, if at all possible.''

BEST, (Evangel) Allena Champlin 1892-1974
(Erick Berry, Anne Maxon)

OBITUARY NOTICE—See sketch in *SATA* Volume 2: Born January 4, 1892, in New Bedford, Mass.; died in February, 1974. Prolific author and illustrator of children's books, mostly under the pseudonym Erick Berry. Although she began her career as an illustrator, Best became an author as well when she discovered that publishers welcomed stories about the people and places she visited in her extensive foreign travels. During a trip to Africa, she met and married children's author Herbert Best, with whom she collaborated on several books, and many of whose books she illustrated. *For More Information See: Junior Book of Authors*, 2nd edition, Wilson, 1951; *Illustrators of Children's Books, 1946-1956*, Horn Book, 1958.

BLACK, Irma S(imonton) 1906-1972

OBITUARY NOTICE—See sketch in *SATA* Volume 2: Born June 6, 1906, in Paterson, N. J.; died June 18, 1972, in New York, N. Y. Children's author and editor, educator. Black devoted much of her life to the field of children's literature through teaching, research, and writing. A faculty member for forty years at the Bank Street College of Education, she was especially noted for creating the Bank Street Readers. As editor of and contributor to this basic reading series, Black departed from the use of traditional Dick and Jane models by employing urban children as central characters. In addition, Black was the author of helpful guides for the parents of young children and of numerous children's stories, both fictional and nonfictional. In recognition of Black's contributions to literature, Bank Street College of Education has given the Irma Simonton Black Award since 1973. *For More Information See: Contemporary Authors*, Volumes 1-4, revised, Gale, 1967; *Authors of Books for Young People*, Scarecrow, 1971. *Obituaries: New York Times*, June 19, 1972; *AB Bookman's Weekly*, July 17-31, 1972; *Contemporary Authors*, Volumes 37-40, revised, Gale, 1973.

BLYTON, Enid (Mary) 1897-1968
(Mary Pollock)

PERSONAL: Born August 11, 1897, in East Dulwich, London, England; died November 28, 1968; daughter of Thomas Carey and Theresa Mary (Harrison) Blyton; married Major Hugh Alexander Pollock (an editor), 1924 (divorced, 1942); married Kenneth F. Darrell Waters (a surgeon), 1943 (died, 1967); children: Gillian, Imogen. *Education:* Attended Guildhall School of Music, 1916; National Froebel Union teaching school, Ipswich (first class passes), 1918. *Residence:* "Green Hedges," Beaconsfield, Buckinghamshire, England.

CAREER: Teacher at a boys' preparatory school in Kent, England, 1919; private tutor to a family in Surbiton, Surrey, England, 1920; formed Darrell Waters Ltd. with her second husband, Kenneth F. Darrell Waters, to handle business contracts with publishers, 1950; author and editor of poems, stories, and educational articles. Shaftesbury Society Babies Home, Beaconsfield, committee member, 1948, later chairman, 1954-67; also sponsored children's clubs to support other

charitable organizations for children and animals. *Awards, honors:* The island of Jersey, U.K., paid tribute to Blyton's 'Noddy' characters by portraying them on a 1970 commemorative stamp.

WRITINGS—All for children: *Child Whispers* (poems), J. Saville, 1922; *Real Fairies* (poems), J. Saville, 1923; *Responsive Singing Games*, J. Saville, 1923; *The Enid Blyton Book of Fairies*, George Newnes, 1924, reissued, 1964; *Songs of Gladness* (music by Alec Rowley), J. Saville, 1924; *The Zoo Book*, George Newnes, 1924; *The Enid Blyton Book of Bunnies*, George Newnes, 1925; *Silver and Gold* (poems; illustrated by Lewis Baumer), Thomas Nelson, 1925; *The Bird Book* (illustrated by Ronald Green), George Newnes, 1926; *The Enid Blyton Book of Brownies*, George Newnes, 1926, reissued, 1964; *Tales Half Told*, Thomas Nelson, 1926; *The Animal Book*, George Newnes, 1927, reissued, 1954; *Let's Pretend* (illustrated by I. Bennington Angrave), Thomas Nelson, 1928; *Nature Lessons*, Evans Brothers, 1929; *Tarrydiddle Town*, Thomas Nelson, 1929.

Tales of Ancient Greece, George Newnes, 1930, reissued, Latimer House, 1951; *Tales of Robin Hood*, George Newnes, 1930; *Cheerio! A Book for Boys and Girls*, Birn Brothers, 1933; *Five Minute Tales*, Methuen, 1933; *Let's Read*, Birn Brothers, 1933; *My First Reading Book*, Birn Brothers, 1933; *Read to Us*, Birn Brothers, 1933; *The Enid Blyton Poetry Book*, Methuen, 1934; *The Old Thatch Series*, 8 volumes, W. & A. K. Johnston, 1934-35, a second series, 8 volumes, W. & A. K. Johnston, 1938-39; *The Red Pixie Book*, George Newnes, 1934; *Round the Year with Enid Blyton*, Evans Brothers, 1934, reissued, 1950; *Ten Minute Tales*, Methuen, 1934; *The Children's Garden*, George Newnes, 1935; *The Green Goblin Book*, George Newnes, 1935 [abridged edition published as *Feefo, Tuppeny and Jinks*, Staples Press, 1951]; *Hedgerow Tales*, Methuen, 1935; *Hop, Skip and Jump*, J. Coker, 1935; *The Tale of Mr. Wumble*, J. Coker, 1935.

The Famous Jimmy (illustrated by Benjamin Rabier), Muller, 1936, Dutton, 1937; *Fifteen Minute Tales*, Methuen, 1936; *The Yellow Fairy Book*, George Newnes, 1936; *Adventures of the Wishing Chair* (illustrated by Hilda McGavin), George Newnes, 1937; *Enid Blyton's Sunny Stories*, George Newnes, 1937-52; *The Adventures of Binkle and Flip* (illustrated by Kathleen Nixon), George Newnes, 1938; *Billy-Bob Tales* (illustrated by May Smith), Methuen, 1938; *Mr. Galliano's Circus*, George Newnes, 1938, reissued, May Fair Books, 1962; *Boys' and Girls' Circus Book*, News Chronicle, 1939; *The Enchanted Wood*, George Newnes, 1939; *Hurrah for the Circus!* (illustrated by E. H. Davie), George Newnes, 1939, reissued, May Fair Books, 1962; *Naughty Amelia Jane*, George Newnes, 1939.

Birds of Our Garden (illustrated by R. Green and Ernest Aris), George Newnes, 1940; *Boys' and Girls' Story Book*, George Newnes, 1940; *The Children of Cherry Tree Farm* (illustrated by Harry Rountree), Country Life, 1940; *Mister Meddle's Mischief* (illustrated by Joyce Mercer and Rosalind M. Turvey), George Newnes, 1940; *The Naughtiest Girl in the School*, George Newnes, 1940; *Tales of Betsy-May* (illustrated by F. Gale Thomas), Methuen, 1940; *The Treasure Hunters* (illustrated by E. Wilson and Joyce Davies), George Newnes, 1940; *Twenty Minute Tales*, Methuen, 1940; *The Adventures of Mr. Pink-Whistle*, George Newnes, 1941; *The Adventurous Four*, George Newnes, 1941; (reteller) Jean de Brunhoff, *The Babar Story Book*, Methuen, 1941 [excerpt published separately as *Tales of Babar*, Methuen, 1942]; *A Calendar for Children*, George Newnes, 1941; *Enid Blyton's Book of the Year*, Evans

Blyton in a quiet corner of her garden.

Brothers, 1941, revised edition, 1950; *Five O'Clock Tales*, Methuen, 1941.

The Children of Willow Farm (illustrated by H. Rountree), Country Life, 1942; *Circus Days Again*, George Newnes, 1942, reissued, May Fair Books, 1962; *Enid Blyton Happy Story Book*, Hodder & Stoughton, 1942; *Enid Blyton Readers*, Books 1-3, Macmillan, 1942, Books 4-6, 1944, Book 7, 1948, Books 10-12, 1950; *Enid Blyton's Little Books* (first of a series), Evans Brothers, 1942; *Hello, Mr. Twiddle!* (illustrated by H. McGavin), George Newnes, 1942; *I'll Tell You a Story* (illustrated by Eileen A. Soper), Macmillan, 1942; *I'll Tell You Another Story*, Macmillan, 1942; *John Jolly at Christmas Time*, Evans Brothers, 1942; *Land of Far-Beyond*, Methuen, 1942; *More Adventures of Willow Farm*, Country Life, 1942; *Naughtiest Girl Again*, George Newnes, 1942, reissued, May Fair Books, 1962; *The O'Sullivan Twins*, Methuen, 1942; *Shadow, the Sheep Dog*, George Newnes, 1942; *Six O'Clock Tales* (illustrated by Dorothy M. Wheeler), Methuen, 1942.

Bimbo and Topsy (illustrated by Lucy Gee), George Newnes, 1943; *The Children's Life of Christ*, Methuen, 1943; *Dame Slap and Her School* (illustrated by D. M. Wheeler), George Newnes, 1943; *John Jolly by the Sea*, Evans Brothers, 1943; *John Jolly on the Farm*, Evans Brothers, 1943; *The Magic Faraway Tree* (illustrated by D. M. Wheeler), George Newnes, 1943; *Merry Story Book* (illustrated by E. A. Soper), Hodder & Stoughton, 1943; *Polly Piglet* (illustrated by E. A. Soper), Brockhampton Press, 1943; *Seven O'Clock Tales*, Methuen, 1943; *The Toys Come to Life* (illustrated by E. A. Soper), Brockhampton Press, 1943.

At Appletree Farm, Brockhampton Press, 1944; *Billy and Betty at the Seaside*, Valentine & Sons, 1944; *A Book of Naughty Children*, Methuen, 1944; *The Boy Next Door* (illustrated by A. E. Bestall), George Newnes, 1944; *The Christmas Book* (illustrated by Treyer Evans), Macmillan, 1944; *Come to the Circus* (illustrated by E. A. Soper), Brockhampton Press, 1944; *The Dog That Went to Fairyland*, Brockhampton Press, 1944; *Eight O'Clock Tales* (illustrated by D. M. Wheeler), Methuen, 1944; *Enid Blyton's Nature Lover's Books* (illustrated by Donia Nachshen and Noel Hopking), Evans Brothers, 1944; *Jolly Little Jumbo*, Brockhampton Press, 1944; *Jolly Story Book* (illustrated by E. A. Soper), Hodder & Stoughton, 1944; *Rainy Day Stories* (illustrated by Nora S. Unwin), Evans Brothers, 1944; *Tales from the Bible* (illustrated by E. A. Soper), Methuen, 1944; *Tales of Toyland* (illustrated by H. McGavin), George Newnes, 1944, reissued, Dean, 1963; *The Three Golliwogs*, George Newnes, 1944.

The Blue Story Book (illustrated by E. A. Soper), Methuen, 1945, reissued, Atlantic Book, 1966; *The Brown Family* (illustrated by E. and R. Buhler), News Chronicle, 1945; *The Conjuring Wizard and Other Stories* (illustrated by E. A. Soper), Macmillan, 1945; *Enid Blyton Nature Readers*, Macmillan, Numbers 1-20, 1945, Numbers 21-30, 1946; *The Family at Red Roofs* (illustrated by W. Spence), Lutterworth, 1945; *The First Christmas* (photographs by Paul Henning), Methuen, 1945; *Hollow Tree House* (illustrated by Elizabeth Wall), Lutterworth, 1945, reissued, May Fair Books, 1966; *John Jolly at the Circus*, Evans Brothers, 1945; *The Naughtiest Girl Is a Monitor*, George Newnes, 1945; *Round the Clock Stories* (illustrated by N. S. Unwin), National Magazine, 1945, reissued, Dean, 1963; *The Runaway Kitten* (illustrated by E. A. Soper), Brockhampton Press, 1945; *Sunny Story Book*, Hodder & Stoughton, 1945; *The Teddy Bear's Party* (illustrated by E. A. Soper), Brockhampton Press, 1945; *The Twins Go to Nurs-*

ery Rhyme Land (illustrated by E. A. Soper), Brockhampton Press, 1945.

Amelia Jane Again, George Newnes, 1946; *The Bad Little Monkey* (illustrated by E. A. Soper), Brockhampton Press, 1946; *The Children at Happy House* (illustrated by Kathleen Gell), Basil Blackwell, 1946; *Chimney Corner Stories* (illustrated by Pat Harrison), National Magazine, 1946, reissued, Dean, 1963; *The Enid Blyton Holiday Book* (series of twelve books), Low, 1946; *The Folk of the Faraway Tree* (illustrated by D. M. Wheeler), George Newnes, 1946; *Gay Story Book* (illustrated by E. A. Soper), Hodder & Stoughton, 1946; *Little White Duck and Other Stories* (illustrated by E. A. Soper), Macmillan, 1946; *The Put-Em-Rights* (illustrated by E. Wall), Lutterworth, 1946; *The Red Story Book*, Methuen, 1946; *The Surprising Caravan* (illustrated by E. A. Soper), Brockhampton Press, 1946; *Tales of Green Hedges* (illustrated by Gwen White), National Magazine, 1946, reissued, World Distributors, 1961; *The Train That Lost Its Way* (illustrated by E. A. Soper), Brockhampton Press, 1946; *The Adventurous Four Again*, George Newnes, 1946.

At Seaside Cottage (illustrated by E. A. Soper), Brockhampton Press, 1947; *Before I Go to Sleep: A Book of Bible Stories and Prayers for Children at Night*, Latimer House, 1947; *Enid Blyton's Treasury*, Evans Brothers, 1947; *The Green Story Book* (illustrated by E. A. Soper), Methuen, 1947; *The Happy House Children Again* (illustrated by K. Gell), Basil Blackwell, 1947; *House-at-the-Corner* (illustrated by Elsie Walker), Lutterworth, 1947; *Jinky Nature Books*, four parts, E. J. Arnold, 1947; *Little Green Duck and Other Stories*, Brockhampton Press, 1947; *Lucky Story Book* (illustrated by E. A. Soper), Hodder & Stoughton, 1947; *Rambles with Uncle Nat* (illustrated by N. S. Unwin), National Magazine, 1947; *A Second Book of Naughty Children* (illustrated by K. Gell), Methuen, 1947; *The Smith Family*, Books 1-3, E. J. Arnold, 1947; *The Very Clever Rabbit* (illustrated by E. A. Soper), Brockhampton Press, 1947.

The Adventures of Pip, Sampson Low, 1948, reissued, Dean, 1965; *The Boy with the Loaves and Fishes* (illustrated by E. Walker), Lutterworth, 1948; *Enid Blyton's Bedtime Series*, two parts, Brockhampton Press, 1948; *Children of Other Lands*, J. Coker, 1948; *Come to the Circus!* (illustrated by Joyce M. Johnson; not the same as the 1944 book published under the same title), George Newnes, 1948; *Just Time for a Story* (illustrated by Grace Lodge), Macmillan, 1948; *Jolly Tales*, Johnston, 1948; *Let's Garden* (illustrated by William McLaren), Latimer House, 1948; *Let's Have a Story* (illustrated by George Bowe), Pitkin, 1948; *The Little Girl at Capernaum* (illustrated by E. Walker), Lutterworth, 1948; *Mister Icy-Cold*, Shakespeare Head Press, 1948; *More Adventures of Pip*, Sampson Low, 1948; *Nature Tales*, Johnston, 1948; *Now for a Story* (illustrated by Frank Varty), Harold Hill, 1948, reissued, World Distributors, 1961; *The Red-Spotted Handkerchief and Other Stories* (illustrated by K. Gell), Brockhampton Press, 1948; *The Little Button-Elves*, J. Coker, 1948; *The Secret of the Old Mill* (illustrated by E. A. Soper), Brockhampton Press, 1948; *Six Cousins at Mistletoe Farm* (illustrated by Peter Beigel), Evans Brothers, 1948, reissued, 1966; *Tales after Tea*, Laurie, 1948; *Tales of the Twins* (illustrated by E. A. Soper), Brockhampton Press, 1948; *They Ran Away Together* (illustrated by Jeanne Farrar), Brockhampton Press, 1948; *We Want a Story* (illustrated by G. Bowe), Pitkin, 1948.

The Bluebell Story Book, Gifford, 1949; *Bumpy and His Bus* (illustrated by D. M. Wheeler), George Newnes, 1949; *A Cat*

He's a little wooden man, and his head nod-nod-nods all the time. He even nods his head when he wants to say "No." I expect you can guess why he is called Noddy. ■ (From *The Big Noddy Book* by Enid Blyton. Illustrated by Beek.)

in Fairyland, Pitkin, 1949; *Chuff the Chimney Sweep*, Pitkin, 1949; *The Circus Book*, Latimer House, 1949; *The Dear Old Snow Man*, Brockhampton Press, 1949; *Don't Be Silly, Mr. Twiddle*, George Newnes, 1949; *The Enchanted Sea*, Pitkin, 1949; *Enid Blyton Bible Pictures, Old Testament* (illustrated by John Turner), Macmillan, 1949; *The Enid Blyton Bible Stories, Old Testament*, Macmillan, 1949; *Enid Blyton's Daffodil Story Book*, Gifford, 1949; *Enid Blyton's Good Morning Book* (illustrated by Don and Ann Goring), National Magazine, 1949, reissued, World Distributors, 1963; *Humpty Dumpty and Belinda*, Collins, 1949; *Jinky's Joke and Other Stories* (illustrated by K. Gell), Brockhampton Press, 1949; *Mr. Tumpy and His Caravan* (illustrated by D. M. Wheeler), Sidgwick & Jackson, 1949; *My Enid Blyton Bedside Book* (series of 12 books), Arthur Barker, beginning 1949; *Oh, What a Lovely Time*, Brockhampton Press, 1949; *Robin Hood Book*, Latimer House, 1949; *A Story Party at Green Hedges* (illustrated by G. Lodge), Hodder & Stoughton, 1949; *The Strange Umbrella*, Pitkin, 1949; *Tales after Supper*, Laurie, 1949; *Those Dreadful Children* (illustrated by G. Lodge), Lutterworth, 1949; *Tiny Tales*, Littlebury, 1949.

The Astonishing Ladder and Other Stories (illustrated by E. A. Soper), Macmillan, 1950; *A Book of Magic*, J. Coker, 1950; *The Enid Blyton Pennant Series*, 30 parts, Macmillan, 1950; *The Magic Knitting Needles and Other Stories*, Macmillan, 1950; *Mister Meddle's Muddles* (illustrated by R. M. Turvey

and J. Mercer), George Newnes, 1950; *Mr. Pink-Whistle Interferes* (illustrated by D. M. Wheeler), George Newnes, 1950; *The Poppy Story Book*, Gifford, 1950; *Round the Year Stories*, J. Coker, 1950; *Rubbalong Tales* (illustrated by Norman Meredith), Macmillan, 1950; *Six Cousins Again* (illustrated by Maurice Tulloch), Evans Brothers, 1950, reissued, May Fair Books, 1967; *Tales about Toys*, Brockhampton Press, 1950; *The Three Naughty Children and Other Stories* (illustrated by E. A. Soper), Macmillan, 1950; *Tricky the Goblin and Other Stories* (illustrated by E. A. Soper), Macmillan, 1950; *What an Adventure*, Brockhampton Press, 1950; *The Wishing Chair Again*, George Newnes, 1950; *Yellow Story Book* (illustrated by K. Gell), Methuen, 1950, reissued, Atlantic Book, 1967.

Benny and the Princess and Other Stories, Pitkin, 1951; *Buttercup Story Book*, Gifford, 1951; *Down at the Farm*, Sampson Low, 1951; *Father Christmas and Belinda*, Collins, 1951; *The Flying Goat and Other Stories*, Pitkin, 1951; *Gay Street Book* (illustrated by G. Lodge), Latimer House, 1951; *Hello Twins*, Brockhampton Press, 1951; *Let's Go to the Circus*, Odhams, 1951; *The Little Spinning Mouse and Other Stories*, Pitkin, 1951; *The Magic Snow-Bird and Other Stories*, Pitkin, 1951; *A Picnic Party with Enid Blyton* (illustrated by G. Lodge), Hodder & Stoughton, 1951; *Pippy and the Gnome and Other Stories*, Pitkin, 1951; *The Proud Golliwog*, Brockhampton Press, 1951; *The Runaway Teddy Bear and Other Stories*, Pitkin, 1951; *The Six Bad Boys* (illustrated by Mary Gernat),

Green Hedges.

Lutterworth, 1951; *'Too-Wise' the Wonderful Wizard and Other Stories,* Pitkin, 1951; *Up the Faraway Tree* (illustrated by D. M. Wheeler), George Newnes, 1951.

Bright Story Book (illustrated by E. A. Soper), Brockhampton Press, 1952; (with W. E. Johns and others) *The Children's Jolly Book,* Odhams, 1952; *Bible Pictures, New Testament,* Macmillan, 1952; *Come Along Twins,* Brockhampton Press, 1952; *Enid Blyton Tiny Strip Books* (series), Sampson Low, 1952; *Enid Blyton's Animal Lover's Book,* Evans Brothers, 1952; *Enid Blyton's Colour Strip Books,* Sampson Low, 1952; *Enid Blyton's Omnibus* (illustrated by Jessie Land), George Newnes, 1952; *The Mad Teapot,* Brockhampton Press, 1952; *Mandy, Mops and Cubby Again,* Sampson Low, 1952; *Mandy, Mops and Cubby Find a House,* Sampson Low, 1952; *Mr. Tumpy Plays a Trick on Saucepan,* Sampson Low, 1952; *My First Enid Blyton Book* (followed by the second and third *Enid Blyton Books*), Latimer House, 1952; *My First Nature Book* (illustrated by E. A. Soper; followed by the second and third *Nature Books*), Macmillan, 1952; *The Queer Adventure* (illustrated by N. Meredith), Staples Press, 1952; *Snowdrop Story Book,* Gifford, 1952; *The Story of My Life* (autobiography), Pitkin, 1952; *The Very Big Secret* (illustrated by R. Gervis), Lutterworth, 1952.

Clicky the Clockwork Clown, Brockhampton Press, 1953; *The Enid Blyton Bible Stories, New Testament,* 14 books, Macmillan, 1953; *Enid Blyton's Christmas Story* (illustrated by Fritz Wegner), Hamish Hamilton, 1953; *Gobo and Mr. Fierce,*

Sampson Low, 1953; *Here Come the Twins,* Brockhampton Press, 1953; (translator) *Little Gift Books* (illustrated by Pierre Probst), Hackett, 1953; *Mandy Makes Cubby a Hat,* Sampson Low, 1953; *Mr. Tumpy in the Land of Wishes,* Sampson Low, 1953; *My Enid Blyton Story Book* (illustrated by Willy Schermele), Juvenile Productions, 1953; *Snowball the Pony* (illustrated by Iris Gillespie), Lutterworth, 1953; *The Story of Our Queen* (illustrated by F. Stocks May), Muller, 1953; *Visitors in the Night,* Brockhampton Press, 1953; *Well, Really, Mr. Twiddle!* (illustrated by H. McGavin), George Newnes, 1953.

The Adventure of the Secret Necklace (illustrated by Isabel Veevers), Lutterworth, 1954; *The Castle without a Door and Other Stories,* Pitkin, 1954; *The Children at Green Meadows* (illustrated by G. Lodge), Lutterworth, 1954; *Enid Blyton's Friendly Story Book* (illustrated by E. A. Soper), Brockhampton Press, 1954; *Enid Blyton's Marigold Story Book,* Gifford, 1954; *The Greatest Book in the World* (illustrated by Mabel Peacock), British & Foreign Bible Society, 1954; *Little Strip Picture Books* (series), Sampson Low, 1954; *The Little Toy Farm and Other Stories,* Pitkin, 1954; *Merry Mister Meddle!* (illustrated by R. M. Turvey and J. Mercer), George Newnes, 1954; *More about Amelia Jane* (illustrated by Sylvia I. Venus), George Newnes, 1954.

Away Goes Sooty (illustrated by P. Probst), Collins, 1955; *Benjy and the Others* (illustrated by K. Gell), Latimer House, 1955; *Bible Stories from the Old Testament* (illustrated by G. Lodge), Muller, 1955; *Bible Stories from the New Testament* (illustrated by G. Lodge), Muller, 1955; *Bimbo and Blackie Go Camping* (illustrated by P. Probst), Collins, 1955; *Bobs* (illustrated by P. Probst), Collins, 1955; *Christmas with Scamp and Bimbo,* Collins, 1955; *Enid Blyton's Little Bedtime Books,* eight books, Sampson Low, 1955; *Neddy the Little Donkey* (illustrated by Romain Simon), Collins, 1955; *Enid Blyton's Sooty* (illustrated by P. Probst), Collins, 1955; *Enid Blyton's What Shall I Be?* (illustrated by P. Probst), Collins, 1955; *Foxglove Story Book,* Gifford, 1955; *Gobbo in the Land of Dreams,* Sampson Low, 1955; *Golliwog Grumbled,* Brockhampton Press, 1955; *Holiday House* (illustrated by G. Lodge), Evans Brothers, 1955; *Laughing Kitten* (photographs by Paul Kaye), Harvill, 1955; *Mandy, Mops and Cubby and the Whitewash,* Sampson Low, 1955; *Mischief Again* (photographs by P. Kaye), Harvill, 1955; *Mr. Pink-Whistle's Party* (illustrated by D. M. Wheeler), George Newnes, 1955, reissued, 1966; *Mr. Tumpy in the Land of Boys and Girls,* Sampson Low, 1955; *More Chimney Corner Stories* (illustrated by P. Harrison), Latimer House, 1955; *Playing at Home* (illustrated by Sabine Schweitzer), Methuen, 1955; *Run-about's Holiday* (illustrated by Lilian Chivers), Lutterworth, 1955; *The Troublesome Three* (illustrated by Leo), Sampson Low, 1955.

The Clever Little Donkey (illustrated by R. Simon), Collins, 1956; *Colin the Cow-Boy* (illustrated by R. Caille), Collins, 1956; *Enid Blyton's Animal Tales* (illustrated by R. Simon), Collins, 1956; *Four in a Family* (illustrated by Tom Kerr), Lutterworth, 1956; *Let's Have a Party* (photographs by P. Kaye), Harvill, 1956; *Scamp at School* (illustrated by P. Probst), Collins, 1956; *Story Book of Jesus* (illustrated by E. Walker), Macmillan, 1956; (contributor) *Children's Own Wonder Book,* Odhams, 1956; *New Testament Picture Books 1-2,* Macmillan, 1957; *Birthday Kitten* (illustrated by G. Lodge), Lutterworth, 1958; *Clicky Gets into Trouble* (illustrated by Molly Brett), Brockhampton Press, 1958; *Mr. Pink-Whistle's Big Book,* Evans Brothers, 1958; *My Big-Ears Picture Book,* Sampson Low, 1958; *Rumble and Chuff* (illustrated by David Walsh), Juvenile Productions, 1958; (with others) *The School*

Companion, New Educational Press, 1958, reissued, Grolier Society, 1969.

Adventure of the Strange Ruby, Brockhampton Press, 1960; *Adventure Stories*, Collins, 1960; *Clicky and Tiptoe* (illustrated by M. Brett), Brockhampton Press, 1960; *Happy Day Stories* (illustrated by Marcia Lane Foster), Evans Brothers, 1960; *Mystery Stories*, Collins, 1960; *Old Testament Picture Books*, Macmillan, 1960; *Tales at Bedtime* (illustrated by H. Mc-Gavin), Collins, 1960; *Will the Fiddle* (illustrated by G. Lodge), Instructive Arts, 1960; *The Big Enid Blyton Book* (selections), Hamlyn, 1961; *Happy Holiday, Clicky* (illustrated by M. Brett), Brockhampton Press, 1961; *The Four Cousins* (illustrated by Joan Thompson), Lutterworth, 1962; *Stories for Monday*, Oliphants, 1962; *Stories for Tuesday*, Oliphants, 1962; *The Boy Who Wanted a Dog* (illustrated by Sally Michel), Lutterworth, 1963; *Enid Blyton's Sunshine Picture Story Book* (first of a series), World Distributors, 1964; *Happy Hours Story Book*, Dean, 1964; *Story Book for Fives to Sevens* (illustrated by Dorothy Hall and Grace Shelton), Parrish, 1964; *Storytime Book*, Dean, 1964; *Tell-a-Story Books*, World Distributors, 1964.

Trouble for the Twins, Brockhampton Press, 1965; *The Boy Who Came Back* (illustrated by E. Walker), Lutterworth, 1965; *Easy Reader* (first of a series), Collins, 1965; *Enid Blyton's Sunshine Book*, Dean, 1965; *Enid Blyton's Treasure Box*, Sampson Low, 1965; *The Man Who Stopped to Help* (illustrated by E. Walker), Lutterworth, 1965; *Enid Blyton's Playbook* (first of a series), Collins, 1966; *The Fairy Folk Story Book*, Collins, 1966; *Enid Blyton's Fireside Tales*, Collins, 1966; *Gift Book* (illustrated by W. Schermele), Purnell, 1966; *The Happy House Children*, Collins, 1966; *John and Mary* (illustrated by Fromont; series of nine books), Brockhampton Press, 1966-68; *Pixie Tales*, Collins, 1966; *Pixieland Story Books*, Collins, 1966; *Stories for Bedtime*, Dean, 1966; *Stories for You*, Dean, 1966; *Holiday Annual Stories*, Sampson Low, 1967; *Holiday Magic Stories*, Sampson Low, 1967; *Holiday Pixie Stories*, Sampson Low, 1967; *Holiday Toy Stories*, Sampson Low, 1967; *The Playtime Story Book*, Numbers 1-4, World Distributors, 1967; *Adventures on Willow Farm*, Collins, 1967; *Brownie Tales*, Collins, 1968; *The Playtime Books*, Numbers 9-12, World Distributors, 1968; *Once Upon a Time*, Collins, 1968.

Enid Blyton's A Shock for Sheila, and Other Stories, Dean, 1976; *Enid Blyton's Julia Saves Up, and Other Stories*, Dent, 1976; *Enid Blyton's The Story That Came True, and Other Stories*, Dean, 1976; *Enid Blyton's Sunnyside Stories*, Purnell, 1976; *Enid Blyton's The Train That Went to Fairyland, and Other Stories*, Dent, 1976; *Enid Blyton's Twilight Tales*, Purnell, 1976.

"Secret" series; all originally published by Basil Blackwell: *The Secret Island*, 1938, reissued, May Fair Books, 1965; *The Secret of Spiggy Holes*, 1940, reissued, May Fair Books, 1965; *The Secret Mountain*, 1941, reissued, May Fair Books, 1965; *The Secret of Killimooin*, 1943, reissued, May Fair Books, 1965; *The Secret of Moon Castle*, 1953, reissued, May Fair Books, 1966.

"St. Clare's" series; all originally published by Methuen: *The Twins at St. Clare's*, 1941, reissued, May Fair Books, 1963; *Summer Term at St. Clare's*, 1943, reissued, May Fair Books, 1963; *Claudine at St. Clare's*, 1944; *The Second Form at St. Clare's* (illustrated by W. Lindsay Cable), 1944, reissued, May Fair Books, 1963; *Fifth Formers at St. Clare's* (illustrated by W. L. Cable), 1945.

They came up to the bears' van, their heels clicking sharply. Their loud voices angered the three bears, and they growled and flung themselves at the bars. ∎ (From *The Circus of Adventure* by Enid Blyton. Illustrated by Stuart Tresilian.)

"Five" series; all originally published by Hodder & Stoughton: *Five on a Treasure Island*, 1942, reissued, Atheneum, 1972; *Five Go Adventuring Again*, 1943, reissued as *Five Find a Secret Way*, Atheneum, 1972; *Five Run Away Together* (illustrated by E. A. Soper), 1944, reissued as *Five Run Away to Danger*, Atheneum, 1972; *Five Go to Smugglers' Top*, 1945, reissued, Atheneum, 1972; *Five Go off in a Caravan* (illustrated by E. A. Soper), 1946; *Five on Kirrin Island Again*, 1947, reissued as *Five Guard a Hidden Discovery*, Atheneum, 1972; *Five Go off to Camp*, 1948, reissued as *Five on the Track of a Spook Train*, Atheneum, 1972; *Five Get into Trouble* (illustrated by E. A. Soper), 1949, new edition published as *Five Caught in a Treacherous Plot* (illustrated by Betty Maxey), Atheneum, 1972; *Five Fall into Adventure* (illustrated by E. A. Soper), 1950, new edition illustrated by B. Maxey, Atheneum, 1972; *Five on a Hike Together* (illustrated by E. A. Soper), 1951; *Five Have a Wonderful Time* (illustrated by E. A. Soper), 1952; *Five Go Down to the Sea* (illustrated by E. A. Soper), 1953; *Five Go to Mystery Moor*, 1954; *Five Have Plenty of Fun*, 1955; *Five on a Secret Trail* (illustrated by E. A. Soper), 1956; *Five Go to Billycock Hill* (illustrated by E. A. Soper), 1956; *Five Get into a Fix* (illustrated by E. A. Soper), 1958; *Five on Finniston Farm* (illustrated by E. A.

Soper), 1960; *Five Go to Demon's Rocks* (illustrated by E. A. Soper), 1961; *Five Have a Mystery to Solve* (illustrated by E. A. Soper), 1962; *Five Are Together Again* (illustrated by E. A. Soper), 1963; *Fabulous Famous Five* (illustrated by B. Maxey), 1974 (contains *Five Get into Trouble, Five Fall into Adventure,* and *Five on a Hike Together*).

"Mary Mouse" series; all published by Brockhampton Press: *Mary Mouse and the Doll's House,* 1942; *More Adventures of Mary Mouse,* 1943; *Little Mary Mouse Again,* 1944; *Hallo, Little Mary Mouse* (illustrated by Olive F. Openshaw), 1945; *Mary Mouse and Her Family* (illustrated by O. F. Openshaw), 1946; *Here Comes Mary Mouse Again,* 1947; *How Do You Do, Mary Mouse,* 1948; *We Do Love Mary Mouse,* 1950; *Welcome Mary Mouse* (illustrated by O. F. Openshaw), 1950; *Hurrah for Mary Mouse,* 1951; *A Prize for Mary Mouse,* 1951; *Mary Mouse and Her Bicycle* (illustrated by O. F. Openshaw), 1952; *Mary Mouse and the Noah's Ark* (illustrated by O. F. Openshaw), 1953; *Mary Mouse to the Rescue,* 1954; *Mary Mouse in Nursery Rhyme Land,* 1955; *A Day with Mary Mouse* (illustrated by Frederick White), 1956; *Mary Mouse and the Garden Party* (illustrated by F. White), 1957; *Mary Mouse Goes to the Fair* (illustrated by F. White), 1958; *Mary Mouse Has a Wonderful Idea* (illustrated by F. White), 1959; *Mary Mouse Goes to Sea* (illustrated by F. White), 1960; *Mary Mouse Goes Out for the Day* (illustrated by F. White), 1961; *Fun with Mary Mouse* (illustrated by R. Paul-Hoeye), 1962; *Mary Mouse and the Little Donkey* (illustrated by R. Paul-Hoeye), 1964.

"Mystery" series; all originally published by Methuen: *The Mystery of the Burnt Cottage* (illustrated by J. Abbey), 1943, reissued, British Book Center, 1973; *The Mystery of the Disappearing Cat* (illustrated by J. Abbey), 1944, reissued, British Book Center, 1973; *Mystery of the Secret Room,* 1945, reissued, British Book Center, 1975; *Mystery of the Spiteful Letters* (illustrated by J. Abbey), 1946, reissued, British Book Center, 1976; *The Mystery of the Missing Necklace,* 1947, reissued, British Book Center, 1975; *The Mystery of the Hidden House* (illustrated by J. Abbey), 1948, reissued, British Book Center, 1973; *The Mystery of the Pantomime Cat,* 1949, reissued, May Fair Books, 1963; *The Mystery of the Invisible Thief,* 1950, reissued, British Book Center, 1973; *The Mystery of the Vanished Prince* (illustrated by T. Evans), 1951, reissued, British Book Center, 1974; *The Mystery of the Strange Bundle* (illustrated by T. Evans), 1952, reissued, British Book Center, 1974; *The Mystery of Holly Lane* (illustrated by T. Evans), 1953, reissued, British Book Center, 1976; *The Mystery of Tally-Ho Cottage* (illustrated by T. Evans), 1954, reissued, British Book Center, 1975; *Mystery of the Missing Man* (illustrated by Lilian Buchanan), 1956, reissued, British Book Center, 1974; *Mystery of the Strange Messages* (illustrated by L. Buchanan), 1957, reissued, British Book Center, 1975; *The Mystery of Banshee Towers* (illustrated by L. Buchanan), 1961, reissued, British Book Center, 1974; *The Mystery That Never Was* (illustrated by Gilbert Dunlop), 1961.

"Mystery" series; all originally published by Collins: *The Rockingdown Mystery* (illustrated by G. Dunlop), 1949, reissued, Collins, 1965; *The Rilloby Fair Mystery* (illustrated by G. Dunlop), 1950, reissued, May Fair Books, 1967; *The Rubadub Mystery* (illustrated by G. Dunlop), 1952, reissued, Collins, 1965; *Ring O' Bells Mystery,* 1955, reissued, Collins, 1967; *Rat-a-Tat Mystery,* 1956; *Ragamuffin Mystery,* 1959, reissued, Collins, 1966.

"Adventure" series; all originally published by Macmillan: *The Island of Adventure* (illustrated by Stuart Tresilian), 1944,

reissued, Thames Publishing, 1960, published in America as *Mystery Island,* Macmillan, 1945; *The Castle of Adventure* (illustrated by S. Tresilian), 1946; *The Valley of Adventure* (illustrated by S. Tresilian), 1947; *The Sea Adventure* (illustrated by S. Tresilian), 1948; *The Mountain of Adventure,* 1949; *The Ship of Adventure* (illustrated by S. Tresilian), 1950; *The Circus of Adventure* (illustrated by S. Tresilian), 1952; *River of Adventure* (illustrated by S. Tresilian), 1955, reissued, St. Martin's, 1966.

"Family" series; all published by Lutterworth; all illustrated by Ruth Gervis, except as noted: *The Caravan Family* (illustrated by William Fyffe), 1945; *The Saucy Jane Family,* 1947; *The Pole Star Family,* 1950; *The Seaside Family,* 1950; *The Buttercup Farm Family,* 1951; *The Queen Elizabeth Family,* 1951.

"Malory Towers" series; all originally published by Methuen: *First Term at Malory Towers,* 1946, reissued, May Fair Books, 1963; *The Second Form at Malory Towers,* 1947, reissued, May Fair Books, 1963; *Third Year at Malory Towers* (illustrated by Stanley Lloyd), 1948, reissued, May Fair Books, 1963; *The Upper Fourth at Malory Towers,* 1949, reissued, May Fair Books, 1963; *In the Fifth at Malory Towers* (illustrated by S. Lloyd), 1950, reissued, Atlantic Book, 1967; *Last Term at Malory Towers* (illustrated by S. Lloyd), 1951.

"Noddy" series; all originally published by Sampson Low: *Little Noddy Goes to Toyland* (illustrated by Harmsen Van Der Beek), 1949; *Hurrah for Little Noddy,* 1950, reissued, British Book Center, 1974; *The Big Noddy Book* (illustrated by H. Van Der Beek; series of eight books), 1951, reissued, Purnell, 1975; *Here Comes Noddy Again,* 1951, reissued, British Book Center, 1974; *Noddy and Big Ears Have a Picnic,* 1951; *Noddy and His Car,* 1951, reissued, Dobson, 1974; *Noddy Goes to the Seaside,* 1951; *Noddy Has More Adventures,* 1951; *Noddy Has a Shock,* 1951; *Noddy off to Rocking Horse Land,* 1951; *A Tale of Little Noddy,* 1951; *Enid Blyton's Noddy's Ark of Books,* 1952; *Noddy and Big Ears,* 1952, reissued, Sampson Low, 1967; *Noddy and the Witch's Wand,* 1952; *Noddy's Car Gets a Squeak,* 1952; *Noddy Colour Strip Book* (illustrated by H. Van Der Beek), 1952; *Noddy Goes to School,* 1952, reissued, British Book Center, 1974; *Noddy's Penny Wheel Car,* 1952; *Well Done, Noddy,* 1952, reissued, British Book Center, 1974; *New Noddy Colour Strip Book,* 1953; *The New Big Noddy Book,* 1953, reissued as *Enid Blyton's Big Noddy Book,* Purnell, 1976; *Noddy and the Cuckoo's Nest,* 1953; *Noddy at the Seaside,* 1953, reissued, British Book Center, 1974; *Noddy Cut-Out Model Book,* 1953; *Noddy Gets Captured,* 1953; *Noddy Is Very Silly,* 1953; *Noddy's Garage of Books* (illustrated by H. Van Der Beek; five books), 1953; *Enid Blyton's Noddy Giant Painting Book,* 1954; *Enid Blyton's Noddy Pop-Up Book,* 1954; *How Funny You Are, Noddy!,* 1954; *Noddy Gets into Trouble,* 1954, reissued, Purnell, 1976; *Noddy and the Magic Rubber,* 1954, reissued, British Book Center, 1974; *Noddy's Castle of Books* (illustrated by H. Van Der Beek; five parts), 1954.

Noddy in Toyland, 1955; *Noddy Meets Father Christmas,* Sampson Low, 1955, reissued, British Book Center, 1974; *You Funny Little Noddy!,* 1955, reissued, Purnell, 1976; *Be Brave Little Noddy!,* 1956, reissued, British Book Center, 1974; *A Day with Noddy,* 1956; *Enid Blyton's Noddy Playday Painting Book,* 1956; *Noddy and His Friends,* 1956, reissued, Sampson Low, 1965; *Noddy and Tessie Bear,* 1956, reissued, Purnell, 1976; *Noddy Nursery Rhymes,* 1956; *The Noddy Toy Station Books,* Numbers 1-5, 1956; *Do Look Out, Noddy!,* 1956, reissued, British Book Center, 1974; *Noddy and Bumpy Dog,*

1. One day Noddy drove down the streets of Toyland in his dear little car.

2. And he met two other little cars. One was driven by a little boy-doll and the other by a smart golliwog.

3. "Hallo!" said the doll, hooting loudly. "Let's have a look at your car, Noddy."

4. Noddy stopped. "It's not much of a car," said the golliwog. "It can't go very fast, can it?"

5. Noddy was cross. "Good gracious, it can go at sixty miles an hour!" he said; and look, he's whizzing up the street!

6. "Can it go backwards?" asked the doll. "Mine can—but not very fast—look!"

(From *The Big Noddy Book* by Enid Blyton. Illustrated by Beek.)

1957, reissued, British Book Center, 1974; *Noddy's New Big Book*, 1957; *My Noddy Picture Book*, 1958; *Noddy Has an Adventure*, 1958, reissued, Dobson, 1976; *The Noddy Shop Book*, Numbers 1-5, 1958; *Noddy's Own Nursery Rhymes*, 1958; *You're a Good Friend, Noddy!*, 1958, reissued, British Book Center, 1974; *A.B.C. with Noddy*, 1959; *Noddy and Bunkey*, 1959, reissued, British Book Center, 1974; *Noddy Goes to Sea*, 1959, reissued, Dobson, 1976; *Noddy's Car Picture Book*, 1959.

Cheer Up, Little Noddy!, 1960, reissued, British Book Center, 1974; *Noddy Goes to the Fair*, 1960, reissued, British Book Center, 1974; *Noddy's One, Two, Three Book*, 1960; *Noddy's Tall Blue Book* (also *Green, Orange, Pink, Red,* and *Yellow Books;* six books in all), 1960; *Mr. Plod and Little Noddy*, 1961, reissued, Purnell, 1976; *Noddy's Toyland Train Picture Book*, 1961; *A Day at School with Noddy*, 1962, reissued, Purnell, 1974; *Noddy and the Tootles*, 1962, reissued, British Book Center, 1974; *Noddy and the Aeroplane*, 1964, reissued, Purnell, 1976; *Learn to Count with Noddy*, 1965; *Learn to Go Shopping with Noddy*, 1965; *Learn to Read about Animals with Noddy*, 1965; *Learn to Tell the Time with Noddy*, 1965; *Noddy and His Friends: A Nursery Picture Book*, 1965; *Noddy Treasure Box*, 1965; *Noddy and His Passengers*, 1967; *Noddy and the Magic Boots* [and] *Noddy's Funny Kite*, 1967; *Noddy and the Noah's Ark Adventure Picture Book*, 1967; *Noddy in Toyland Picture Book*, 1967; *Noddy Toyland ABC Picture Book*, 1967; *Noddy's Aeroplane Picture Book*, 1967.

"Secret Seven" series; all originally published by Brockhampton Press: *The Secret Seven* (illustrated by George Brook), 1949, new edition published as *The Secret Seven and the Mystery of the Empty House* (illustrated by Tom Dunnington; edited by M. Hughes Miller), Childrens Press, 1972; *The Secret Seven Adventure* (illustrated by G. Brook), 1950, new edition published as *The Secret Seven and the Circus Adventure* (illustrated by T. Dunnington; edited by M. H. Miller), Childrens Press, 1972; *Well Done, Secret Seven* (illustrated by G. Brook), 1951, new edition published as *The Secret Seven and the Tree House Adventure* (illustrated by T. Dunnington; edited by M. H. Miller), Childrens Press, 1972; *Secret Seven on the Trail* (illustrated by G. Brook), 1952, new edition published as *The Secret Seven and the Railroad Mystery* (illustrated by T. Dunnington; edited by M. H. Miller), Childrens Press, 1972; *Go Ahead Secret Seven* (illustrated by Bruno Kay), 1953, new edition published as *The Secret Seven Get Their Man* (illustrated by T. Dunnington; edited by M. H. Miller), Childrens Press, 1972; *Good Work, Secret Seven* (illustrated by B. Kay), 1954, new edition published as *The Secret Seven and the Case of the Stolen Car* (illustrated by T. Dunnington; edited by M. H. Miller), Childrens Press, 1972.

Secret Seven Win Through (illustrated by B. Kay), 1955, new edition published as *The Secret Seven and the Hidden Cave Adventure* (illustrated by T. Dunnington; edited by M. H. Miller), Childrens Press, 1972; *Three Cheers Secret Seven* (illustrated by Burgess Sharrocks), 1956, new edition published as *The Secret Seven and the Grim Secret* (illustrated by T. Dunnington; edited by H. M. Miller), Childrens Press, 1972; *Secret Seven Mystery* (illustrated by B. Sharrocks), 1957, new edition published as *The Secret Seven and the Missing Girl Mystery* (illustrated by T. Dunnington; edited by M. H. Miller), Childrens Press, 1972; *Puzzle for the Secret Seven* (illustrated by B. Sharrocks), 1958, new edition published as *The Secret Seven and the Case of the Music Lover* (illustrated by T. Dunnington; edited by M. H. Miller), Childrens Press, 1972; *Secret Seven Fireworks* (illustrated by B. Sharrocks), 1959, new edition published as *The Secret Seven and the Bonfire Adven-*

ture (illustrated by T. Dunnington; edited by M. H. Miller), Childrens Press, 1972.

Good Old Secret Seven (illustrated by B. Sharrocks), 1960, new edition published as *The Secret Seven and the Old Fort Adventure* (illustrated by T. Dunnington; edited by M. H. Miller), Childrens Press, 1972; *Shock for the Secret Seven* (illustrated by B. Sharrocks), 1961, new edition published as *The Secret Seven and the Case of the Dog Lover* (illustrated by T. Dunnington; edited by M. H. Miller), Childrens Press, 1972; *Look Out Secret Seven* (illustrated by B. Sharrocks), 1962, new edition published as *The Secret Seven and the Case of Missing Medals* (illustrated by T. Dunnington; edited by M. H. Miller), Childrens Press, 1972; *Fun for the Secret Seven* (illustrated by B. Sharrocks), 1963, new edition published as *The Secret Seven and the Case of the Old Horse* (illustrated by T. Dunnington; edited by M. H. Miller), Childrens Press, 1972.

"Josie, Click, and Bun" series; all illustrated by D. M. Wheeler and published by George Newnes: *The Little Tree House: Being the Adventures of Josie, Click and Bun*, 1940, reissued as *Josie, Click and Bun and the Little Tree House*, 1951; *The Further Adventures of Josie, Click and Bun*, 1941; *Josie, Click and Bun Again*, 1946; *More about Josie, Click and Bun*, 1947; *Welcome Josie, Click and Bun*, 1952.

"Bom" series; all published by Brockhampton Press, except as noted: *Bom and His Magic Drumstick*, 1956; *Bom the Little Toy Drummer*, 1956; *Enid Blyton's Bom Painting Book*, Dean, 1956; *Bom Goes Adventuring* (illustrated by R. Paul-Hoeye), 1958; *Bom and the Clown*, 1959; *Bom and the Rainbow*, 1959; *Hullo Bom and Wuffy Dog* (illustrated by R. Paul-Hoeye), 1959; *Bom Goes to Magic Town*, 1960; *Here Comes Bom* (illustrated by R. Paul-Hoeye), 1960; *Bom at the Seaside* (illustrated by R. Paul-Hoeye), 1961; *Bom Goes to the Circus* (illustrated by R. Paul-Hoeye), 1961.

Under pseudonym Mary Pollock; all published by George Newnes, except as noted: *Children of Kidillin*, 1940; *Three Boys and a Circus*, 1940; *Adventures of Scamp*, 1943; the latter two books were reissued together under the author's real name as *Dog Stories*, Collins, 1959; *The Secret of Cliff Castle*, 1943; *Smuggler Ben*, 1943; *Mischief at St. Rollo's*, 1947.

Plays: *A Book of Little Plays*, Thomas Nelson, 1927; *The Play's the Thing* (music by A. Rowley), Home Library Book Co., 1927, reissued in two volumes as *Plays for the Older Children* [and] *Plays for Younger Children*, George Newnes, 1940; *Six Enid Blyton Plays*, Methuen, 1935; *The Blyton-Sharman Musical Plays for Juniors*, six parts, A. Wheaton, 1939; George H. Holroyd, editor, *Cameo Plays* (only Book 4 by Blyton), E. J. Arnold, 1939; *How the Flowers Grow, and Other Musical Plays*, A. Wheaton, 1939; *School Plays: Six Plays for School*, Basil Blackwell, 1939; *The Wishing Bean and Other Plays*, Basil Blackwell, 1939; *Finding the Tickets*, Evans Brothers, 1955; *Mr. Sly-One and Cats*, Evans Brothers, 1955; *Mother's Meeting*, Evans Brothers, 1955; *Who Will Hold the Giant?*, Evans Brothers, 1955; *Enid Blyton's Book of the Famous Play Noddy in Toyland*, Sampson Low, 1956.

Reteller: *Aesop's Fables*, Thomas Nelson, 1928; *Old English Stories*, Thomas Nelson, 1928; *Pinkity's Pranks and Other Nature Fairy Stories*, Thomas Nelson, 1928; Joel C. Harris, *Tales of Brer Rabbit*, Thomas Nelson, 1928; *The Knights of the Round Table*, George Newnes, 1930, reissued, 1950; *Tales from the Arabian Nights*, George Newnes, 1930, reissued, 1951; *The Adventures of Odysseus: Stories from World History,*

Evans Brothers, 1934; *The Story of the Siege of Troy: Stories from World History*, Evans Brothers, 1934; *Tales of the Ancient Greeks and Persians: Stories from World History*, Evans Brothers, 1934; *Tales of the Romans: Stories from World History*, Evans Brothers, 1934; J. C. Harris, *Heyo, Brer Rabbit!*, George Newnes, 1938; J. C. Harris, *The Further Adventures of Brer Rabbit*, George Newnes, 1942; J. C. Harris, *Brer Rabbit and His Friends*, J. Coker, 1948; *Brer Rabbit Book* (series of eight books), Latimer House, 1948; *The Two Sillies and Other Stories*, J. Coker, 1952; J. C. Harris, *Brer Rabbit Again*, Dean, 1963; *Tales of Brave Adventure*, Dean, 1963; J. C. Harris, *Enid Blyton's Brer Rabbit's a Rascal*, Dean, 1965; *Tales of Long Ago* (selections from *Tales of Ancient Greece* and *Tales from the Arabian Nights*), Dean, 1965.

Editor: *The Teacher's Treasury*, three volumes, George Newnes, 1926; *Sunny Stories for Little Folks*, George Newnes, 1926-36; *Modern Teaching in the Infant School*, four volumes, George Newnes, 1932; *Modern Teaching: Practical Suggestions for Junior and Senior Schools*, six volumes, George Newnes, 1928; (and contributor) *Pictorial Knowledge*, 10 volumes, George Newnes, 1930; *Treasure Trove Readers* (junior series), A. Wheaton, 1934; *Nature Observation Pictures*, Warne, 1935; Thomas A. Coward, *Birds of the Wayside and Woodland*, Warne, 1936; *The Children's Book of Prayers*, Muller, 1963; *Enid Blyton's Favourite Book of Fables from the Tales of La Fontaine*, Collins, 1955.

Also author and editor of several periodicals and annuals, including *Enid Blyton's Magazine*, [London], beginning 1953; *Playways Annual*, Lutterworth, 1953; *Enid Blyton's Magazine Annual* (first of a series), Evans Brothers, 1954; *Sunny Stories Annual*, [London], 1954; *Enid Blyton's Annual* [London], beginning 1957; *Enid Blyton's Bom Annual*, [London], 1957; *Enid Blyton's Bedtime Annual*, [Manchester], 1966; *The Big Enid Blyton Story Annual*, Purnell, 1973-76.

SIDELIGHTS: **August 11, 1897.** Born in East Dulwich, London, England. "Well, I was quite an ordinary little girl. I am perfectly certain that not one of the grown-ups round me then ever guessed for one moment that I was going to be [a] storyteller when I grew up.

"I had two brothers and no sisters, though I always longed for one. I went to school, of course, to a kindergarten that I loved. I remember everything about it—the room, the garden, the pictures on the wall, the little chairs, the dog there, and the lovely smells that used to creep out from the kitchen into our classroom when we sat doing dictation. I remember how we used to take biscuits for our mid-morning lunch and 'swap' them with one another—and how we used to dislike one small boy who was clever at swapping a small biscuit for a big one.

"I was lucky enough to have an excellent memory, . . . what a real blessing it is. It means that you can learn a list of 'spelling' or a poem in a quarter of the time that others can. When I was eight or nine I could read down a page once, then shut my eyes and repeat it word for word. I never forgot what I had read. I can still shut my eyes and see a page of my geography book—'Manufactures: Macclesfield for silk. Luton for hats. Leeds for woollen goods. Sheffield for steel goods . . .' and so on.

". . . I often wish I had learnt more poetry then—it is the easiest time in your life to memorise things, and you never forget them—it means that you have a store of lovely quotations to draw on for the rest of your life.

"I loved school, every minute of it. I loved learning. Nothing was ever dull to me, not even sums which I was not good at doing. I hadn't the right kind of brain for figures and I used to look on in awe when I saw other boys and girls doing the most complicated sums. How clever they were, I thought!

"'So long as I get to the top in something else I'll be all right,' I used to think. And what did I get to the top in? Yes—essay and composition and story-writing.

"The things I liked best of all at school when I was at the kindergarten were the things I have liked best all my life—stories—music—nature—and games. . . .

"What did I read? I read *Alice in Wonderland, Alice Through the Looking-Glass, The Water-Babies* (and skipped the part where all those long and extraordinary words come), *Black Beauty*, which I *loved*, though some of it was too sad, and, of course, *Little Women*, which I read again and again. Those children were real children. . . . 'When I grow up *I* will write books about real children,' I thought. 'That's the kind of books I like best. That's the kind of book I would know how to write.'

"I read every single old myth and legend I could get hold of—the old Norse myths, the old Greek myths, which I thought were beautiful, but rather cruel. I still think that. I read every old folk tale I could find, from countries all over the world.

"I read the *Children's Encyclopaedia* from end to end, and then read it all over again. . . . It gave me my thirst for knowledge of all kinds, and taught me as much as ever I learnt at school. It sent me questing through my father's vast array of book-cases for other books—books on astronomy, nature, poetry, history, old legends. There were many volumes above my head that I found and read because I *had* to know more about the things I read in the *Children's Encyclopaedia*.

"My father had hundreds of books of all kinds on every subject under the sun that interested him. He read, he wrote, he painted, he played the piano endlessly (and the banjo, which I and my brothers loved!), and he was a very fine naturalist. He was an amateur astronomer too, and had a large telescope. So, . . . there was no end to the reading I was able to have in my childhood—books on every conceivable subject." [Enid Blyton, *The Story of My Life*, Pitkins, 1952.[1]]

When asked how she began writing books, Blyton replied: ". . . I meant to be a writer from the time I could read and write, even before that, I think. . . .

". . . I didn't know that I had the gift, of course, I only knew that I liked making up stories better than I liked doing anything else.

"I was an ordinary child. . . . I did the things that all children do, I had the same fears, the same likes and dislikes. . . .

"But I was different in one way. . . .

"When I went to bed I used to lie still and wait for my 'thoughts.' I didn't know what else to call them then. I suppose now I would say that I waited for my 'imagination' to set to work.

"In a minute or two my 'thoughts' would come flooding into my mind. I distinguished them easily from my ordinary thinking. In my ordinary thinking I thought what I wanted to think—

but in these 'thoughts' I wasn't thinking as usual at all. They seemed to come from somewhere else, not myself.

"They were stories, of course. They came then as they do now, out of nowhere—out of my imagination, or from my 'sub-conscious'. . . .

"Before I could write I used to *tell* my brothers my stories. After I could write I found just as much pleasure in writing them down—more, I think, because I began to find I liked handling words.

"I kept a diary regularly, every single day. But I didn't only write down my daily doings, I wrote down anything interesting that I thought or that I had read. Year after year I kept my diary, and never missed a day. . . .

"I wrote letters. I wrote letters to anyone I thought wouldn't mind having one. I also wrote letters to imaginary people. My family thought this was silly and I suppose it did seem a silly thing to do—to write endless letters—but letter-writing is something that all true writers love. . . .

". . . They [family] didn't even know that I *wanted* to write, nor did they know that I could. . . .

"What made it all more difficult for me was the fact that my family thought I had another gift, not the gift for writing at all. They thought that my gift, quite definitely, was music.

"Music is in my family. I have an aunt who has always been a brilliant musician and is still. I was continually told that I resembled this aunt in looks, and that I had her gift for music.

"For some time I had been writing all kinds of things, hoping to get them printed. I felt that if only I could get something printed perhaps it might be possible to go to my parents and say: 'See—I have something printed already. Need I go on with music?'"[1]

1911. "When I was about fourteen a famous writer for children, called Arthur Mee . . . ran a poem competition for children in one of his magazines. I loved writing poetry, so I sent in a poem. To my utter amazement and delight, I had a letter back from the great man himself. He liked my poem. He would print it. But more than that, he told me that he liked the letter I had sent with it. 'You can write,' he said. 'Send in other things to our page. Perhaps one day you will *really* write.'

"All through my teens I wrote and wrote and wrote—everything I could think of! Poems, stories, articles, even a novel. I couldn't stop writing and I loved every minute of it.

"But alas—except for one unexpected acceptance of a poem by a magazine, then called *Nash's Magazine* nothing was successful. Day after day the manuscripts came back, and slid through the letter-box with a thud I came to know only too well.

". . . My family thought it was a great waste of money on my part to go on buying paper and big envelopes, and stamps to send out things that always came back. I had to put a stamp on the addressed envelope for the return of the story or poem, of course, and I hadn't much money in those days. Children then were not allowed as much pocket money as they are now, and my father didn't approve of us having very much to spend.

"I was often in despair. Was I too young? Was my writing foolish and worthless? Was music really my gift and *not* writing?

"I *was* too young, of course. You need experience of many kinds before you can really write anything worth while. Nevertheless it was all good practice for me.

". . . I had no success at all at the beginning. I had at least five hundred things sent back to me, and on only one of them was there even a personal note. This one was a humorous poem (or so I thought!) and I had absurdly and boldly sent it to *Punch* (aiming at the moon, you see!).

"The usual self-addressed envelope came back. I opened it. There was my poem—but written at the side was a sentence or two in a small, neat handwriting.

"'Idea good. Spoilt by wrong accent in line 10, and bad rhyme in line 12. Try again sometime.'

"And did I 'try again' as he advised me to? Yes, of course I did, but not for a long time did I get anything accepted by *Punch*.

"But alas! I had no definite success in my writing that I could show to my parents, saying: 'Look! This is what I want to do! Let me write, don't make me take up music, now that I am leaving school.'

"It looked as if I had 'shot at the moon' but hadn't even hit a tree! . . ."[1]

1916. "It was the summer holidays. My father had entered me for the Guildhall of Music for the following September. I was working for the exam called L.R.A.M., and the last year had been filled with piano practice, study of harmony, and singing.

"I went to spend part of the holiday on a farm. There, every Sunday, I went off to teach in the Sunday-school with a trained kindergarten teacher with whose family I was staying.

"I told stories—Bible stories—to a class of wide-eyed, listening children. I loved it. I loved the children, of course, but I loved the teaching too, and the telling of stories in my own way. I drew and painted big pictures for the Sunday-school wall. I helped in the hand-work the children often did in that well-run and interesting Sunday-school.

"And then, quite suddenly, I knew what I ought to do. I knew it without a single doubt. I wanted to be a writer for children, I knew that very well—but I wasn't getting anywhere in my writing. There was no training for that either, because I had made enquiries. I was up against a blank wall—I must get to my goal in some other way.

". . . Suddenly knew the way to go. I must train as a kindergarten teacher, of course! I would then be with children all day long, I would hear them talk, see the things they did, find out exactly what they liked and disliked, what they feared, what they longed for. I would see naughty children and good children, I would learn what the children wanted to read and also what they *ought* to read!

"I could write all the time I was training! I could try out my stories and poems and plays on the children themselves. They should be my critics."[1]

1918. Entered Froebel Union teaching school. "... I took up my training. I loved every minute of it. I was a round peg in a round hole. I taught, I told stories, I played for the children to sing, I prepared their hand-work, I listened to all they said, I was as close to them as I could be.

"I wrote all the time. . . ."[1]

1920. Governess to the children of Horace and Gertrude Thompson in Surbiton, Surrey. "I have in my care a young, serious, and most profound philosopher. His mind grinds slowly, but it grinds exceedingly small, and he reduces everything and everyone to their lowest common factors. Consequently he occasionally utters observations which, while on the surface appearing superficial, betray a perception and a reasoning which are astonishing. . . ." [Barbara Stoney, *Enid Blyton: A Biography*, Hodder & Stoughton, 1974.[2]]

1921. First humorous essay published in the *Saturday Westminster Review* entitled: *On the Popular Fallacy that to the Pure all Things are Pure*. "... I find that those to whom all things are pure must be either extremely undiscerning or hypocritical. This is a very grave decision, as I myself possess several relatives who profess to trust everybody, and to find no fault with anything. 'Everything,' according to them 'has some good in it,' and 'Evil cannot touch those who do not believe in it.' Of course there really is something in that—but it may lead to Christian Science, which is quite all right outside the family, but very uncomfortable in. Aunt Maria did not believe in measles herself, even when she had it, so that I thought it most unkind of her to pass it on to people who did believe in it. However, she could never see my point—she may do now that I am in 'Really Good People' set."[2]

1922. Published book of verse, *Child Whispers*. "The children of nowadays are different in many of their likes and dislikes, from the children of ten years ago. This change of attitude is noticeable as much in the world of children's poetry as it is in other things. In my experience of teaching I have found the children delight in two distinct types of verses. These are the humorous type and the imaginative poetical type—but the humour must be from the child's point of view and not from the 'grown up's'—a very different thing. And the imagination in the second type of poem must be clear and whimsical, otherwise the appeal fails and the child does not respond.

"As I found a lack of suitable poems of the types I wanted, I began to write them myself for the children under my supervision, taking, in many cases, the ideas, humorous or whimsical, of the children themselves, as the theme of the poems! Finding them to be successful, I continued until the suggestion was made to me that many children other than those in my own school, might enjoy hearing and learning the poems. Accordingly this collection of verses is put forward in the hope that it will be a source of sincere enjoyment to the little people of the world."[2]

1923. Met Hugh Pollock, an editor with the George Newnes publishing firm. "Pollock wrote and asked if I'd collaborate with him. It was a lovely letter.

"[He] wanted to know if I'd do a child's book of the Zoo. He asked me to meet him at Victoria tomorrow . . . I said I would."[2]

1924. Pollock divorced his wife to marry Blyton. "Hugh phoned at 6.15 to say he was coming down to see me and bringing two rings for me to choose from. He came and we

They had a very good tea. Noddy was hungry and so was Big-Ears. Through the side window they could see the little house they had built. Noddy began to feel very, very happy. ■ (From *Noddy Goes to Toyland* by Enid Blyton. Illustrated by Beek.)

looked at them in the summer house. They were lovely but the one I've chosen is adorable! [a three-tiered diamond and emerald, set in gold] Hugh was such a dear and I do love him so. . . . It will be lovely to be really engaged. . . ."[2] The couple wed on August 28 of that year.

1925. Deluged with correspondence from both children and adults in response to an article on "happy people." She replied through her *Teacher's World* column: "I've been looking for it [happiness] straight ahead all my life and I've always found it. I don't mean content—though that is a very lovely thing—but real, proper, exultant happiness that makes you want to sing, and gives that lift of the heart which is so well-known in childhood at the thought of some delightful treat! . . . Happiness is simply an interest in and a keen appreciation of everything in life. A sense of humour doubles the ability to appreciate it."[2]

When asked by her readers what she disliked, Blyton wrote: "... I'm quite willing to relate a few of the things I don't like, for it would be nice to find a few fellow-sufferers.

"Well, to begin with, of course, I hate going to the dentist. I dream about it for nights beforehand. In vain I say to myself,

'Don't be silly. The dentist is a very nice man. Think of how nice and bright and shining all his dear little instruments are. Think how nice it is to sit in a chair that goes up and down, and backwards and forwards at any moment.' There always comes a moment when Myself answers back and says, 'Uugh! Don't talk such rubbish. I HATE going to the dentist.'

"Then another thing I really dislike is walking in a crowd. I always have disliked it from a child, because it makes me feel I am in a dream, and not properly myself. It was only the other day I discovered why I got the dream illusion. When you walk in a crowd you can't hear your own footsteps—and you don't hear them in a dream either. Time after time in dreams have I gone down the street like a wraith, hearing never a footfall. Think of your own dreams—you never hear your feet walking, do you? And that, I think, is why I get the queer dream-feeling in crowds, and dislike it so much.

"I don't like doing anything that makes people stare at me. I have a remarkable habit of getting into a bus which is going in the wrong direction. When I give the conductor my penny and say, "Charing Cross, please," and he says, 'Aw, you're going the wrong way,' and rings the bell with a jerk, I go as red as a penny stamp, and feel dreadful inside. Even when I get out of the 'bus, I feel as if everyone in the street must be saying, 'Look! Look! There's the girl who got in the wrong 'bus!' And I determine fiercely never to do it again. But I did it yesterday, alas!—and I shall quite probably do it to-morrow.

"The next thing I'm going to say is a very silly thing—but I don't like thinking about eternity. You think about time, and the end of time, and then you think what's beyond the end of time, and it gives you a sort of gasping-for-breath feeling. Lots of people never think these sorts of things at all, for I've asked them but *I* do sometimes, and I don't like it, it's too big and overwhelming.

"I don't like hearing sad stories if I can't help to put things right. I can't bear to hear stories of the war. I once heard a Scotsman tell of a mortally wounded Turk whom he found two days after a battle, and to whom he gave some water. He couldn't get a doctor to him, but managed to visit him again after a further two days. He was still alive. The next time, the poor wretch was asleep. The Scotsman shot him out of pity. That story haunted me for weeks, and still does—and other stories too. The feeling of impotence that comes when a story of suffering is related, is one of the hardest things to bear, that I know. If you could go straight off and put things right, it wouldn't matter—but you can't in ninety-nine cases out of a hundred.

"Oh, there are lots and lots of things I dislike a little or dislike a lot. But the reason I write so much more about the things I love is because love or liking is positive, and dislike is negative, and I give *my* vote to the positive things of life."

"Deep down in me I have an arrogant spirit that makes me a bit scornful of other people, if I think they are stupid or led by the nose,or at the mercy of their upbringing and environment—unable to think for themselves. I keep it under because I want to be charitable, but I have at times been horrid and contemptuous—really I have. I am usually the one who puts forth my opinion in most company I meet with and I am listened to, which is very bad for me. . . . In my mind I like to *dominate* even though I don't appear to be doing so! . . ."[2]

July 15, 1931. "Gillian was born at 6.30 this a.m.—8¾ lbs., in weight, 21½ inches in length, a lovely child. Hugh is de-

lighted. A very easy confinement all over in five hours. Dr. Poles delivered baby and Dr. Bailey gave chloroform. I came round about 7 feeling very hungry and comfortable. Baby sucked as soon as she was put to the breast. Hugh went up to town in afternoon."[2]

October 27, 1935. Imogen Mary born.

December, 1942. Divorced Pollock.

1943. Married Kenneth Darrell Waters, a surgeon.

Of her family, Blyton wrote: "There are four of us in the family—my husband, whose name is Kenneth Darrell Waters, and my two Girls, Gillian and Imogen. . . .

"We all have a sense of humour. We are all (thank goodness!) good tempered. Nobody sulks, nobody complains, nobody is unkind. But that, of course, is largely a matter of upbringing. Spoilt children are selfish, complaining and often conceited. But whose fault is that? It is the mother, always the mother, that makes the home. The father does his share, he holds the reins too—but it is the mother who makes a happy, contented home. She is the centre of it. She should always be there to welcome the children home, to see to them and listen to them."[1]

Blyton lived in "Green Hedges" with her family.

"'PAX HUIC DOMUI'

". . . 'Peace be to this house.' Those words were carved on the beam long before I came to Green Hedges, but I liked them so much that I left them there. All homes should be happy, peaceful places, especially where there are children."[1]

October 12, 1947. ". . . My little girl, Imogen, has developed infantile paralysis—yesterday. I had a specialist down and we took her up to Great Ormond Street Hospital late last night, poor child. She was very good and brave but it was heartrending. There is paralysis of the left leg so far, but I am praying that it will not spread any more. . . . I do feel a bit knocked over at the moment—it's so awful to see one's own child attacked liked this—though I am hoping it will be one of the milder attacks and that it has been diagnosed early enough for us to prevent any desperate damage. . . ."[2] Imogen made a good recovery after spending many months in a hospital.

March 21, 1949. In a letter to her editor: ". . . I have finished the first two 'Little Noddy' books, and here they are. I have written them with a view to giving Van Beek [illustrator for the books] all the scope possible for his particular genius—toys, pixies, goblins, Toyland, brick-houses, doll houses, toadstool houses, market-places—he'll really enjoy himself! I don't want to tell him how to interpret anything because he'll do it much better if he has a perfectly free hand—but as Noddy (the little nodding man) Big Ears the Pixie, and Mr. and Mrs. Tubby (the teddy bears) will probably feature in any further books, and will be 'important' characters as far as these books are concerned, I'd be very glad if he could sketch out these characters and let me see roughs. (He said he would do this for me.)

"Now about the general title—at the moment this is 'All Aboard for Toyland,' and I imagine we might have as a 'motif' a toy train rushing along crowded with passengers—going all round the jacket top, sides and bottom or something like that—to give the books a 'series' look. The specific titles (which will all be different of course) will each contain the name 'Noddy.' In the end, if they are very successful, they'll probably be referred to and ordered as the 'Noddy' books. . . .''[2]

1955. At the close of the play, *Noddy in Toyland,* Blyton wrote: ''. . . I have had a play for children put on at the Stoll Theatre in London. (It was a great success I am thankful to say!). For the first two days I endeavoured to use the same process of writing as I use for my books—finding characters and settings and then using the 'cinema screen' in my mind, on which the whole story seems to be projected from beginning to end without any active volition from me. This method was a *complete* failure for the writing of the play. It was very odd. I stumbled over the writing. I laboured, I could not draw on my imagination at all. Then like a flash I seemed to discard the old way of writing, and instead of needing to see characters in their story setting and using the 'cinema screen,' into my mind came the stage itself, all set with scenery. And then in came the characters on this stage, singing, talking, dancing—and once again something went 'click' and the whole writing of the play went out of my hands and was taken over by my imagination again. I no longer stumbled, puzzled, tried to invent. There

"Let me see!" said Binkie, and glued her eye to the eyepiece of the telescope. "Yes! There is a light. It's somewhere on the ground floor—is it shining out of the entrance?" ■ (From *The Secret Seven and the Old Fort Adventure* by Enid Blyton. Illustrated by Tom Dunnington.)

were the characters, all dressed for their parts, there were their houses and their 'props' (car, bicycle, etc.) and on they came, talking, dancing, singing. . . .''[2]

November 28, 1968. Died in London.

Psychologist, Michael Woods who attempted an analysis of Blyton from her works, stated: ''She was a child, she thought as a child and she wrote as a child. . . .''[2]

Blyton's books were banned in seven of London's libraries. Blyton explained the reason for the ban, ''children badger the library assistants all day for a Blyton book and will not go away without one.'' [*New York Times,* November 29, 1968.[3]]

Blyton had more than 400 books published and her work was translated into 93 languages.

HOBBIES AND OTHER INTERESTS: Gardening, reading, bridge, and golf.

FOR MORE INFORMATION SEE: Springfield Republican, March 11, 1945; *Weekly Book Review,* March 11, 1945; *New York Times,* September 15, 1946; *Saturday Review of Literature,* September 28, 1946; Enid Mary Blyton, *Story of My Life* (autobiography), Pitkin, 1952; Brian Doyle, editor, *Who's Who of Children's Literature,* Schocken, 1968; Barbara Stoney, *Enid Blyton: A Biography,* Hodder & Stoughton, 1974; Obituaries—*New York Times,* November 29, 1968; *Time,* December 6, 1968; *Publishers Weekly,* December 30, 1968.

BOBBE, Dorothie   1905-1975

OBITUARY NOTICE—See sketch in *SATA* Volume 1: Born March 1, 1905, in London, England; died March 19, 1975, in New York, N. Y. Author of American historical biographies for adults and children. Among the subjects of her children's books are Abigail Adams, DeWitt Clinton, and Anne Mac-Vicar. Bobbe also contributed to *American Heritage* and the *New York Times Magazine. For More Information See: Contemporary Authors Permanent Series,* Volume 2, Gale, 1978. *Obituaries: New York Times,* March 20, 1975; *AB Bookman's Weekly,* April 21, 1975; *Contemporary Authors,* Volumes 57-60, Gale, 1976.

BRECHT, Edith   1895-1975

OBITUARY NOTICE—See Sketch in *SATA* Volume 6: Born April 7, 1895, in Lancaster City, Pa.; died August 16, 1975. Author of children's books. A long-time resident of suburban Philadelphia, Brecht later returned to her native Lancaster County, Pennsylvania. This locale and its predominantly Amish population influenced much of her writing, providing setting and character. Deeply interested in their unique culture, Brecht chose to write about her Amish and Mennonite neighbors in such books as *Benjy's Luck* and *The Little Fox.* Other of Brecht's stories for young people drawn from her Lancaster County experiences include *Timothy's Hawk* and *The Mystery of the Old Forge. For More Information See: Contemporary Authors, Permanent Series,* Volume 2, Gale 1978.

BRIGGS, Katharine Mary   1898-1980

OBITUARY NOTICE: Born November 8, 1898, in London, England; died October 15, 1980, in Kent, England. Free-lance writer best known as a scholar of folklore. Her books on folklore include *The Anatomy of Puck, Folktales of England, The Fairies in English Tradition and Literature,* and *A Dictionary of British Folktales in the English Language.* Briggs also wrote several plays and novels. *For More Information See: Contemporary Authors,* Volumes 9-12, revised, Gale 1974; *Who's Who in the World,* 4th edition, Marquis, 1978. *Obituaries: London Times,* October 25, 1980; *Publishers Weekly,* November 7, 1980; *Contemporary Authors,* Volume 102, Gale, 1981.

BROADHEAD, Helen Cross   1913-
(Helen Reeder Cross)

PERSONAL: Born August 26, 1913, in Wilmington, N. C.; daughter of Arthur Maurice and Helen (Newbold) Cross; married Edward Hall Broadhead, June 5, 1936 (divorced, 1961); children: David Edward, Cynthia Newbold (Mrs. Phillip M. Joseph). *Education:* Duke University, A. B., 1935; Trinity College, M. A., 1958. *Politics:* Independent. *Religion:* Presbyterian. *Home:* Larchmont Palmer House, 1299 Palmer Ave., Apt. 209, Larchmont, N. Y. 10538. *Agent:* Dorothy Markinko, McIntosh & Otis, 475 Fifth Ave., New York, N. Y. 10017.

CAREER: University of Hartford, Hartford, Conn., instructor in English, 1958-61; St. Margaret's School, Waterbury, Conn., English department head, 1961-67; Master's School, Dobbs Ferry, N. Y., English teacher, 1967-78; Westchester Community College, Valhalla, N. Y., adjunct professor, 1968—.

WRITINGS—All under name Helen Reeder Cross; all for children: *Life in Lincoln's America,* Random House, 1964; *A Curiosity for the Curious* (illustrated by Margot Tomes), Coward, 1978; *The Real Tom Thumb* (illustrated by Stephen Gammell), Four Winds, 1980.

Contributor of stories and articles to such periodicals as the *New York Times, Gourmet, History Today, English Journal,* and *New England Galaxy.*

WORK IN PROGRESS: "*Isabella Mine*—a semi-autobiographical book about an eleven-year-old girl's life in the Tennessee mountains in the late 1920's, to be published by Lothrop, Lee & Shepard Co."

SIDELIGHTS: "My 'semi-retired' days are filled with reading and writing, with friends with whom I enjoy concerts, plays and art shows in New York, with family, gourmet cooking, entertaining—and with one or two courses to teach at the community college."

What a curiosity! A dozen boys trailed behind Old Bet. Some turned cartwheels. ■ (From *A Curiosity for the Curious* by Helen Reeder Cross. Illustrated by Margot Tomes.)

HELEN CROSS BROADHEAD

BUCK, Pearl S(ydenstricker) 1892-1973 (John Sedges)

PERSONAL: Born July 26, 1892 in Hillsboro, W. Va.; died March 6, 1973, in Danby, Vermont; daughter of Absalom and Caroline (Stulting) Sydenstricker (Presbyterian missionaries); married John Losing Buck (agricultural instructor), March 13, 1917 (divorced, 1935); married Richard John Walsh (president, John Day Co., publishers), June 11, 1935; children: (first marriage) Carol; (adopted) Richard, John, Edgar, Jean C., Henriette. *Education:* Attended boarding school in Shanghai, China, 1907-09; Randolph-Macon College, B. A., 1914; Cornell University, M. A., 1926. *Home and office address:* R.D.1., Box 164, Perkasie, Pa.

CAREER: Pearl S. Buck was a teacher in China and the United States before she began writing in earnest. She taught psychology at Randolph-Macon College in Virginia for one semester following her graduation from that school in 1914 and later taught English literature in China at the University of Nanking, Southeastern University, 1925-27, and at Chung Yang University, 1928-30. Along with the writing that brought her the Nobel Prize for Literature in 1938 and many other honors, she was active in promoting better understanding be-

tween peoples, and in child welfare work. She and her second husband published *Asia* Magazine during the years 1941-46, and for a decade she headed the East and West Association, which she had founded in 1941. In 1949 she also founded Welcome House, Inc., an adoption agency for Asian-American children and, in 1964, organized the Pearl S. Buck Foundation. She was a leader, too, in developing interest in retarded children. In 1966, she was elected to the board of directors of Weather Engineering Corp. of America in Manchester, N. H. In 1968 she was elected trustee of Windham College.

MEMBER: National Institute of Arts and Letters, American Academy of Arts and Letters, Phi Beta Kappa. *Awards, honors:* Pulitzer Prize in Fiction, 1932, Howells Medal for the most distinguished work of American fiction published in the period 1930-35, both for *The Good Earth;* Nobel Prize for Literature, 1938; honorary M. A., Yale University, 1933; D. Litt., University of West Virginia, 1940, St. Lawrence University, 1942, Delaware Valley College, 1965; LL. D., Howard University, 1942; L.H.D., Lincoln University, 1953, Woman's Medical College of Philadelphia, 1954; D.H.L., University of Pittsburgh 1960, Hahnemann Hospital, 1966; D. Mus., Combs College of Music, 1962; D. H., West Virginia State College, 1963; D.H.L., Bethany College, Bethany, W. Va., 1963; LL. D., Muhlenberg College, 1966. President's Committee on Employment of Physically Handicapped, citation, 1958; Big Brothers of America, citation, 1962.

PEARL S. BUCK, 1938

WRITINGS—Fiction for children; all published by John Day, except as indicated: *The Young Revolutionist,* Friendship Press, 1932; *Stories for Little Children* (illustrated by Weda Yap), 1940; *The Chinese Children Next Door,* 1942; *The Water-Buffalo Children* (also see below; illustrated by William Smith), 1943; *The Dragon Fish* (also see below; illustrated by Esther Bird), 1944; *Yu Lan: Flying Boy of China* (illustrated by George Hartmann), 1945; *The Big Wave* (illustrated by Kazue Mizamura), 1948, reprinted, 1973; *One Bright Day,* 1950 (published by England as *One Bright Day and Other Stories for Children,* Methuen, 1952); *Johnny Jack and His Beginnings* (also see below; illustrated by Kurt Werth), 1954; *The Beech Tree* (also see below; illustrated by Werth), 1954; *Christmas Miniature* (illustrated by Anna Magnana), 1957 (published in England as *The Christmas Mouse,* Methuen, 1958); *The Christmas Ghost* (illustrated by Magnana), 1960; (editor) *Fairy Tales of the Orient* (illustrated by Jeanyee Wong), Simon & Schuster, 1965; *The Big Fight* (illustrated by Mamoru Funai), 1965; *The Little Fox in the Middle* (illustrated by Robert Jones), Collier Books, 1966; *The Water-Buffalo Children* [and] *The Dragon Fish,* Dell, 1966; *The Beech Tree* [and] *Johnny Jack and His Beginnings,* Dell, 1967; *Matthew, Mark, Luke, and John* (illustrated by Funai), 1967; *The Chinese Story Teller* (illustrated by Regina Shekerjian), 1971; *A Gift for the Children,* 1973; *Mrs. Starling's Problem* (illustrated by Leslie Merrill), 1973.

Nonfiction for children: *When Fun Begins,* Methuen, 1941; *The Man Who Changed China: The Story of Sun Yet-sen* (illustrated by Fred Castellon), Random House, 1953; *Welcome Child* (photographs by Alan Haas), John Day, 1964; *The Story Bible,* Bartholomew House, 1971.

Adult fiction; all published by John Day, except as indicated: *East Wind: West Wind,* 1930, reprinted, 1967; *The Good Earth* (also see below), 1931 reprinted, Pocket Books, 1975; *Sons* (also see below), 1932, reprinted, Pocket Books, 1975; (translator) Shui-hu Chüan, *All Men Are Brothers,* 1933, reprinted, 1968; *The First Wife and Other Stories* (also see below), 1933, reprinted, Methuen, 1963; *The Mother,* 1934, reprinted, 1973; *A House Divided,* Reynal & Hitchcock, 1935, reprinted, Pocket Books, 1975; *House of Earth* (contains *The Good Earth* and *Sons*), Reynal & Hitchcock, 1935; *This Proud Heart,* Reynal & Hitchcock, 1938, reprinted, John Day, 1965; *The Patriot,* 1939.

Other Gods: An American Legend, 1940, reprinted Severn House, 1976; *Today and Forever: Stories of China* (also see below), 1941; *Dragon Seed,* 1942, reprinted, Pocket Books, 1972; *China Sky,* Triangle Books, 1942; *Twenty-Seven Stories,* Sun Dial Press, 1943; *The Promise,* 1943; *The Story of Dragon Seed,* 1944, (under pseudonym John Sedges) *The Townsman,* 1945, reprinted, Pocket Books, 1975, published under real name as *The Townsman: A "John Sedges" Novel,* John Day, 1967; *Portrait of a Marriage,* 1945, reprinted, Pocket Books, 1975; *China Flight,* Triangle Books, 1945; *Pavilion of Women,* 1946, reprinted, Pocket Books, 1978; *Far and Near: Stories of Japan, China, and America,* 1947 (published in England as *Far and Near: Stories of East and West,* Methuen, 1949); (under pseudonym John Sedges) *The Angry Wife,* 1947, reprinted under real name, Pocket Books, 1975; *Peony,* 1948, reprinted, Pocket Books, 1978 (published in England as *The Bondmaid,* Methuen, 1949); (under pseudonym John Sedges) *The Long Love,* 1949, reprinted under real name, Pocket Books, 1975; *Kinfolk,* 1949, reprinted, Pocket Books, 1978.

God's Men, 1951, reprinted, Pocket Books, 1978; *The Hidden Flower,* 1952; (under pseudonym John Sedges) *Bright Procession,* 1952; *Come, My Beloved,* 1953, reprinted, Pocket Books,

1975; (under pseudonym John Sedges) *Voices in the House,* 1953, reprinted, White Lion Publishers, 1977; *Imperial Woman,* 1956, reprinted, White Lion Publishers, 1977; *Letter from Peking,* 1957, reprinted, Pocket Books, 1975; *American Triptych: Three "John Sedges" Novels,* 1958; *Command the Morning,* 1959, reprinted, Pocket Books, 1975.

Fourteen Stories, 1961, reprinted, Pocket Books, 1976 (published in England as *With a Delicate Air and Other Stories,* Methuen, 1962); *Satan Never Sleeps,* Pocket Books, 1962; *Hearts Come Home and Other Stories,* Pocket Books, 1962; *The Living Reed,* 1963, reprinted, Pocket Books, 1979; *Stories of China* (contains contents of *The First Wife and Other Stories* and *Today and Forever*), 1964; *Escape at Midnight and Other Stories,* Dragonfly Books, 1964; *Death in the Castle,* 1965; *The Time Is Noon,* 1967; *The New Year,* 1968; *The Three Daughters of Madame Liang,* 1969; *The Good Deed and Other Stories of Asia, Past and Present,* 1969.

Mandala, 1970; *Once Upon a Christmas,* 1972; *The Goddess Abides,* 1972; *A Gift for the Children,* 1973; *Mrs. Starling's Problem,* 1973; *All under Heaven,* 1973; *Words of Love* (poetry), 1974; *The Rainbow,* 1974; *East and West: Stories,* 1975; *Secrets of the Heart: Stories,* 1976; *The Lovers and Other Stories,* 1977; *Mrs. Stoner and the Sea and Other Works,* Ace Books, 1978; *The Woman Who Was Changed and Other Stories,* Crowell, 1979.

Nonfiction; all published by John Day, except as indicated: *East and West and the Novel: Sources of the Early Chinese Novel,* College of Chinese Studies (Peking), 1932; *Is There a Case for Foreign Missions?* (pamphlet), North China Language School, 1932; *The Exile* (biography of author's mother; also see below), Reynal & Hitchcock, 1936, reprinted, Pocket Books, 1976; *Fighting Angel: Portrait of a Soul* (biography of author's father; also see below), Reynal & Hitchcock, 1936, reprinted, Pocket Books, 1976; *The Chinese Novel* (lecture), 1939.

Of Men and Women, 1941, reprinted, 1971; *American Unity and Asia,* 1942, reprinted, Books for Libraries, 1970 (published in England as *Asia and Democracy,* Macmillan 1943); *Pearl Buck Speaks for Democracy,* New York City Common Council for Unity, 1942; *What America Means to Me,* 1943, reprinted, Books for Libraries, 1971; *The Spirit and the Flesh* (contains *Fighting Angel* and *The Exile*), 1944; (compiler) *China in Black and White: An Album of Woodcuts,* 1945; *Tell the People: Mass Education in China,* Institute of Pacific Relations, 1945, published as *Tell the People: Talks with James Yen about the Mass Education Movement,* John Day, 1945; *Talk about Russia with Masha Scott,* 1945; (with Erna von Pustau) *How It Happens: Talk about the German People, 1914-1933,* 1947; (with Eslanda Goode Robeson) *American Argument,* 1949.

The Child Who Never Grew, 1950; *My Several Worlds: A Personal Record,* 1954, reprinted Pocket Books, 1975; *Friend to Friend: A Candid Exchange between Pearl S. Buck and Carlos P. Romulo,* 1958; *The Delights of Learning,* University of Pittsburgh Press, 1960; *A Bridge for Passing* (autobiography), 1962; *The Joy of Children,* 1964; (with Gweneth T. Zarfoss) *The Gifts They Bring: Our Debts to the Mentally Retarded,* 1965; *Children for Adoption,* Ramdom House, 1965; (with others) *My Mother's House,* Appalachia Press, 1966; *The People of Japan,* Simon & Schuster, 1966; (with Theodore F. Harris) *For Spacious Skies: Journey in Dialogue,* 1966; *To My Daughters, with Love,* 1967.

Da Lobo gave a great squeaky bellow and threw up her head and ran. How she ran! She ran through the pampas grass down the hill, over the rough places and over the smooth, and we clung to each other . . . . ■ (From *The Water-Buffalo Children* by Pearl S. Buck. Illustrated by William Arthur Smith.)

The Kennedy Women: A Personal Appraisal, Cowles Book Co., 1970; *China as I See It,* 1970; *Pearl Buck's America,* Bartholomew House, 1971; *Pearl S. Buck's Oriental Cookbook,* Simon & Schuster, 1972; *China Past and Present,* 1972; *A Community Success Story: The Founding of the Pearl Buck Center,* 1972; (editor) *Pearl Buck's Book of Christmas,* Simon & Schuster, 1974.

Plays: "Flight into China," produced in New York, 1939; *Sun Yat Sen: A Play, Preceded by a Lecture by Dr. Hu-Shih,* Universal Distributors, 1944; "The First Wife," produced in New York, 1945; "A Desert Incident," produced in New York, 1959; "Christine," produced in New York, 1960; "The Guide" (adaptation of novel by N. K. Narayan), produced on Broadway at Lincoln Art Theater, 1965. Also author of a television drama, "The Big Wave," produced by the National Broadcasting Co., 1956. Contributor of articles and stories to numerous magazines. Co-editor, *Asia,* 1941-46.

ADAPTATIONS—Movies and filmstrips: "The Good Earth" (motion picture), starring Paul Muni, Metro-Goldwyn-Mayer,

1937 (movie excerpts have been adapted into educational films of the same name by Teaching Film Custodians, 1943, 1946, and into a filmstrip by Ealing Films, 1977); "The Good Earth" (filmstrips), Popular Science Publishing Co., 1969, Educational Dimensions, 1972; "Dragon Seed" (motion picture), starring Agnes Moorehead, Metro-Goldwyn-Mayer, 1944; "China Sky" (motion picture), starring Anthony Quinn, RKO Radio Pictures, 1945; "The Big Wave" (motion picture), Stratton Productions, 1962; "Satan Never Sleeps" (motion picture), starring William Holden, Twentieth Century-Fox, 1962; "The Chinese Children Next Door" (filmstrip), narrated by Pearl Buck, H. M. Stone, 1976.

Recordings: "Sun Yat-sen: The Man Who Saved China," Enrichment Records, 1967.

SIDELIGHTS: **July 26, 1892.** Born in Hillsboro, West Virginia; the daughter of Presbyterian missionaries stationed in Chinkiang, China. "I remember when I was born. I am sure I remember. How else can I account for the intimate knowledge I have always had of my mother's house? I have never lived

"We'll bury the dragon fish," Lan-may said, "right here by these blue flowers. Then we'll remember where it is. When we come here again we'll dig it up and play with it . . . ." ■ (From *The Dragon Fish* by Pearl S. Buck. Illustrated by Esther Brock Bird.)

there for more than a few weeks at a time, and not many times. The first time I walked into it on my own feet I was already nine years old. Yet already I knew every room that I was to see. I knew how the grapevine grew over the portico. I knew when I entered the door that the parlor was to the left and the library to the right. . . .

"I cannot account for the birth of memories, but they are in me and they center about the room where I was born. I distinctly see my mother as she looked when I first saw her. I feel myself in her arms, looking up into her dark eyes. She had a vivid, pretty face.

"That is the face I saw when I was born. I like to know, as I do know, that she rejoiced at my arrival. Three children she had lost before I was born, all small, the eldest four, the youngest six months. All are buried in the hot Chinese earth. It was because of their deaths that I was given the privilege of being born in my own country. It was a privilege I treasure,

for I am the only one among my brothers and sisters who is so born. Yes, she was happy to see me. I know, for we exchanged looks, I remember her cheek against mine. She was a brown woman, her skin a soft brunette cream. I suppose this came from her Dutch ancestry and the French Huguenot strain through her mother, my grandmother. I did not inherit her brown looks. Instead I have the fair skin, light hair and blue eyes of my father's ancestry. What I inherited from my mother is inside me. I love people too easily, as she did. But then my first memory is of love. To be able to think back, as I can, to feel one's way back to the first moment of the new life outside the womb and to remember, as I do, nothing but love, overwhelming love, provides the atmosphere for one's whole life. So loved for one's self, one loves in return, easily and richly—and sometimes too often and too faithfully. For this gift of loving, I thank my beloved mother." [Theodore F. Harris, *Pearl S. Buck: A Biography,* John Day, 1969.[1]]

September, 1892. "The day came, a day in late September, when my parents decided that we must leave my mother's house and set forth on the long journey to China. My eldest brother, a lad of twelve, was with us, and we made a little party of four. Knowing my father, I am sure that he rejoiced to be on his way back to his work. I have a secret conviction that my mother's family, too, were not sorrowful at his departure. He was not a person who accommodated himself. Wherever he was he remained the tall slim figure of a scholar, intent upon his own study and research. I know he absented himself often from my mother's house on errands connected with delving into ancient languages as well as preaching in neighboring churches. When he came back no one was quite as much at ease as we were in his absence. I think he felt this and was sometimes a little sad. Yet he must have known, too, how much he was respected in my mother's house, and with him his ancestral family."[1]

1896-1900. Spent her earliest years in a small bungalow overlooking the Yangtze River in the port of Chinkiang. "I knew vaguely, of course, that my family was different from those around us in more ways that the one of gods. We ate different food, for one thing, though I preferred Chinese food, and liked chopsticks better than a knife and fork. If I very often wore Chinese clothes, especially padded gowns in winter to keep me warm in unheated houses, still I knew my 'real' clothes were not these gowns but my dresses and coat and hat and little aprons. And of course the English I spoke to my parents was my language, even though I spoke Chinese first and more easily.

"But nobody put the matter into definite words for me until one day when, just before a Chinese New Year, Wang Amah [her nurse] was trying on my new cap. It fitted my head closely and covered my ears and curved into my neck, and a heavy silver chain, transferred from cap to cap as I wore them out, secured it under my chin. Wang Amah grumbled as she pushed my yellow curls into my cap.

"'Ah, this strange hair! It is getting so long that a cap won't hide it anymore.'

"'Why must we hide it?' I asked.

"'Because it doesn't look like proper hair, that's why,' she complained. 'It doesn't look human, this hair!'

"I felt the burden of my misfortune. 'Wang Amah, why do I have this hair instead of nice straight black hair?' I asked sadly.

"'Because you come from an outer country, poor child,' she said.

"'Is America an outer country?' I inquired.

"'Every country except China is an outer country,' she said. Then she took pity on me and enfolded me in her arms and smelled my cheeks, which was the Chinese way of kissing. 'Never mind,' she said 'you cannot help it. I will hide it all under the cap and no one will see it. . . . Alas, there are your eyes! I cannot hide them.'

"'Why do you want to hide them, Wang Amah?' I asked in fresh dismay.

"'They are so blue,' she said, 'and everyone should have black eyes.'

"'Why are my eyes blue?'

"'Who knows?' she replied. 'I only know that sometimes Americans have blue eyes.' She thought of something else. 'Ah, your poor mother!'

"'Why is my mother poor?'

"Wang Amah looked solemn and she pursed her full underlip. 'I have been with her for the births of all you six children, yet never once did she know what color your eyes would be when you were born, or what your hair. Four of you had blue eyes, poor souls, like your father's, and only two brown, like hers.' She smelled my cheek again. 'But you all have lovely white and red skin. When people talk to me about your eyes and hair I tell them to look at your skin, like white jade, and your lips and cheeks red as this satin.'

"Thus I knew that I was American and I never forgot it. I had a country somewhere of my own, where children were like me.'"[1]

1900. Family forced to flee to Shanghai during Boxer Rebellion. ". . .My world changed as a result of an imperial edict sent forth by the Empress, in which she ordered the death of every white man, woman and child.

"Our Chinese home was no longer a shelter and place of safety. Anxiety pervaded the atmosphere and my parents tried to decide whether we should leave for Shanghai and the protection of our own government officials there or stay with our Chinese friends. For our friends, too, were in peril. The imperial edict included all Chinese Christians as traitors and persons worthy of death. . . .

"It was a confusing time for a small child. My whole life was changed. I was no longer allowed to wander beyond the compound walls. My favorite place in the long pampas grass outside the gate was forbidden. Snakes I had been warned against, yet the danger now was not from snakes but from angry people. For suddenly we were all changed, it seemed. We were not the friendly American family we thought we had been, living in a friendly Chinese community. Even my father's friends no longer came to the house. No one came to the house. Our servants remained faithful but they were afraid, too, of what might happen to them and to their families. We were responsible for 'slicing China up like a melon,' as the old Empress put it, and for the exploitation of the Chinese people. . . .

. . . He found his mother and his two brothers and his two sisters waiting for him. ■ (From *The Little Fox in the Middle* by Pearl S. Buck. Illustrated by Robert Jones.)

"'Let us go home to your house in America,' I begged my mother.

"She shook her head. 'Not yet.'

"We did go to Shanghai, however, and stayed there, my mother and baby sister and our Chinese nurse and I, while my father remained alone in our Chinese home. There in that city we lived for nearly a year and there my mother had time to tell me stories of her home and her people, who were also mine, it seemed, although I did not know them.

"During that year the siege of Peking took place. The old Empress Dowager fled with her court, and did not come back again until the imperial forces had been defeated and the Boxers proved charlatans. New treaties were made, the Chinese subdued but resentful, and after the next summer we went back to our Chinese home. But it was never the same again, never secure, never safe. One never knew when the resentment would break forth in some new explosion.'"[1]

1902. Returned to her home in Chinkiang. "Those were strange conflicting days when in the morning I sat over American schoolbooks and learned the lessons assigned to me by my mother, who faithfully followed the Calvert system in my education, while in the afternoon I studied under the wholly different tutelage of Mr. Kung. I became mentally bifocal, and so I learned early to understand that there is no such condition in human affairs as absolute truth. There is only truth as people see it, and truth, even in fact, may be kaleidoscopic in its variety. The damage such perception did to me I have felt ever since, although damage may be too dark a word, for it merely meant that I could never belong entirely to one side of any question. To be a Communist would be absurd to me, as absurd as to be entirely anything and equally impossible. I straddled the globe too young." [Pearl S. Buck, *My Several Worlds*, John Day, 1954.[2]]

1907-1909. Attended a boarding school in Shanghai. "Miss Jewell's School was established in buildings of somber and indestructible grey brick. Never have I seen, except in London, such buildings, shaped, it seemed, for eternal life. Upon the ground floor by the front door was the parlor and there on the day upon which I was to be received my mother and I sat waiting for Miss Jewell. Shades of *Nicholas Nickleby* enveloped me as I looked around that dreary parlor. The windows were partly sunken beneath the pavement of the street outside and they were heavily barred against thieves, a reasonable condition but one which added something dreadful to my impression of the room. Texts from the Bible, framed in dark oak, hung upon the pallid walls, and the furniture was nondescript and mixed. In a small English grate beneath a black wooden mantel an economical fire smoked up the chimney, a handful of coals carefully arranged to smoulder and not to burn."[2]

1910-1914. Educated at Randolph-Macon College in Virginia. "Arrived at Lynchburg, Virginia, I found my college to be a collection of red brick buildings, still new enough to look raw, at least to my eyes accustomed to years of the finest and most cultivated scenery in the world, which certainly the best Chinese landscapes are. Within those buildings there was no beauty to be found, and the minimum even of comfort. I can

measure how long ago that was when I return now occasionally to visit my college and find it mellowed with beauty everywhere and a place already enriched by tradition. In my day, however, it was stark, and it was hard to have no beauty to look at as I came and went along the wide halls down which the only carpeting was a strip of dull brown linoleum, thick as leather. But other promises were fulfilled. We were soundly taught and the curriculum carried no hint that we were young women and not young men. We were not corrupted by home economics or dressmaking or cookery or any such soft substitute for hard thinking. We were compelled to take sciences whether we liked them or not, and mathematics and Latin were emphasized and excellently administered. Each year the student body petitioned for a course in home economics, for in that day no girl thought it possible that she might not marry, and each year the faculty sternly refused to yield to the request. The theory was, and I think it entirely correct, that any educated woman can read a cookbook or follow a dress pattern. It is the brain that needs education and it can teach the hands. . . .

"By my junior year I was sufficiently American to be elected president of my class, and then I had really to identify myself with my college mates in fairness to them. That was the best year of my college life and I enjoyed it. Other honors came my way, I do not remember them all now, but they had their

(From the movie "Dragon Seed," starring Katharine Hepburn and Turhan Bey. Copyright 1944 by Loew's, Inc.)

part in my happiness and I was too innocent or young or unconcerned to realize that many honors do not make one better loved. Such revelation and premonition of the future came in my senior year, when needing some extra money, I competed for prizes for the best short story and the best poem of the year and won them both. I was glad for the cash and not, I think, unduly impressed by the honor, since I had written stories and poems equally badly, I am sure, as long as I could remember. But what astonished and wounded me was that in the congratulations of my fellows I discerned a slight hostility, a hint of complaint that one person had been given the two best prizes. Upon reflection, I felt the justice of this, and yet what could I say?''[2]

June, 1914. Received a B. A. degree from Randolph-Macon College and accepted an assistantship at the college. Began to teach, but soon returned to China to nurse her ill mother. ''So I came to the end of college and took my place in the long procession of graduates. I received my diploma, lonely to know that my parents were not in the chapel crowded with other parents, although by then I was used to loneliness of that sort, at least. Summing it up, I am amazed at how little I learned in college. No one except myself was to blame for this, I am sure. College was an incident in my life and out of its main stream, an experience which remains incidental. My attempt,

successful enough in its own way, to be like other American girls, was not permanent, I fear, and after my graduation I was faced with my two worlds again. Which should I choose? Should I stay to become permanently American or should I go home again to China?

''All during the days of packing and farewells, I pondered this choice. I wanted to stay, that I knew. Between the two countries my heart chose my own, for I was beginning not to understand that beyond the college walls was a whole country I still did not know, although it was mine and I was born to it. I had my living to earn but that was no problem and I felt secure enough in myself. I could choose among several teaching jobs, including one to remain on in the college as an assistant in psychology with the professor under whom I had majored. Already during my senior year I had been a minor assistant to the extent of helping him correct freshman papers and examinations. Yet my conscience moved me to return to my parents. I did not want to be a missionary, for I knew I could never preach or persuade people to change their religion. I had seen enough of that dangerous business in years gone by. Moreover, I had not the spiritual attitudes which could make it possible for me to proclaim my religion superior to all others. I had seen too many good people who were not Christian, and, as my father used to remark, it took the arrogance out of anybody

(From the movie "The Good Earth," starring Luise Rainer. Copyright 1937 by Metro-Goldwyn-Mayer Corp.)

to have to acknowledge that the best Christian coverts were always good people anyway, the best Buddhists or Mohammedans or Taoists or what not, even before their conversion to Christianity.

"One day a letter came from my father that my dearly loved mother had been taken with sprue, a tropical disease which at that time no physician knew how to cure and scarcely to treat. Yet it was a slowly fatal disease, robbing the blood of its red corpuscles until in the end the victim died of a deadly anemia. My mind was made up on the instant. I wrote to the Presbyterian Board of Foreign Missions under whom my parents worked and asked to be sent to China as a teacher, and I packed my bags and prepared to sail as soon as I could get passage. I did not think of my return as permanent, but only until my mother was well again, or if she did not get well, then until—but that end I could not face."[2]

November, 1914. Returned to China. "My own life now was divided again. My daily duty, besides teaching in the new boys' school, and supervising seventeen to twenty young Chinese women who were being trained for various types of work in other schools, was to care for my mother. I took over the management of the house in order to relieve her, and in her place I carried on the work among women for which she was responsible. I could not and would not lead religious meetings, but my mother did not do much of this sort of thing herself. She was too sensitive to impress upon others directly the advantages even of the religion in which she still fervently believed. Her meetings were usually friendly gatherings where the women told of their difficulties and problems and opportunities and needs, and my mother endeavored as best she could to fulfill each demand. I was too young to take her place, but I could listen and promise to get her advice for the next meeting. It was an invaluable experience thus to hear Chinese women open their hearts because of their faith in my mother and I was always touched and moved at their acceptance of me in her place.

"Beyond this I made a fierce and determined attack upon the disease which threatened my mother, working with the doctors to learn all I could about it. Nothing but diet was then tried as a cure, and we experimented with all the known foods to find the one most suitable to her. . . ."[2]

May 13, 1917. Married John Losing Buck, an American agricultural specialist. "The time had come for marriage, as it comes in the life of every man and woman, and we chose each other without knowing how limited the choice was, and particularly for me who had grown up far from my own country

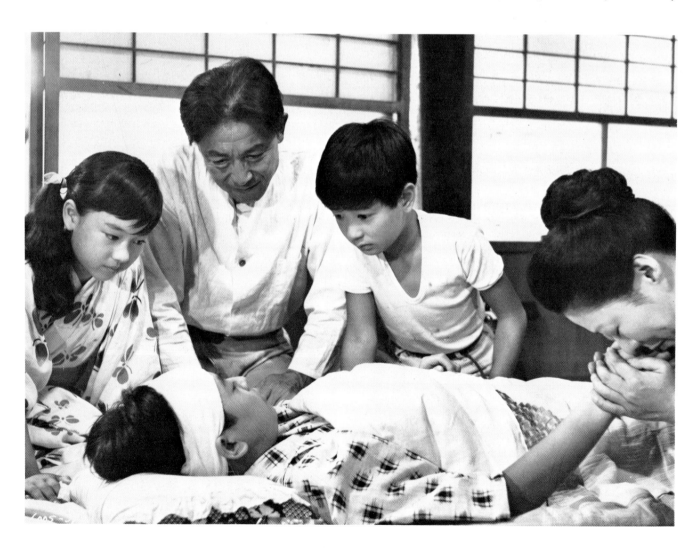

(From the movie "The Big Wave," starring Sessue Hayakawa. Released by Allied Artists Corp., 1961.)

(From *The Big Wave* by Pearl S. Buck. Illustrated with prints by Hiroshige and Hokusai.)

and my own people. I have no interest now in the personal aspects of that marriage, which continued for seventeen years in its dogged fashion, but I do remember as freshly as though it were yesterday the world into which it transported me, a world as distant from the one I was living in as though it had been centuries ago. It was the world of the Chinese peasant.''[2]

Moved to northern China, where Buck became head of a girls' school. ''It was a lovely little Chinese house. We had a lawn and a flower garden, enclosed in a compound wall. Beyond our wall was the city wall, and we lived in its shelter. There were only four rooms, but what pleasure it was to arrange the furniture, hang the curtains, paint a few pictures for the walls, to hang the Chinese scrolls! I was happy and busy. When all was finished—well, what next? I took over the girls' school, I invited a girlhood friend, a young Chinese woman, to be my assistant—alas, she wouldn't stay because she missed the rice she had always eaten in the South and she did not like the wheaten bread of the North. Well, I found someone else, and I made new friends.''[1]

1921. Moved to Nanking, where her husband taught agricultural theory at the university. ''My child was born the first year in Nanking . . . and after that I was not so free to come and go as I had been. I did not mind, for to have a child was a miracle to me and I did not dream of the dark future in store for us both. Mercifully I was to have nearly four years of happy ignorance about her. During that same year my mother died,

not suddenly, but slowly and unwillingly, and I am glad that she never knew what lay ahead for me. . . . ''[2]

1922. First article published. Taught English literature at the University of Nanking.

1925. Came to America, where Buck hopelessly tried to find a cure for her retarded daughter, Carol, who had been born with the metabolic inability to assimilate proteins, phenylketonuria. ''I don't know of any blow in all my life that was as rending. It was as if my very flesh were torn. It was beyond belief, and yet I knew I had to believe it, and shape my life around the fact.[1]

''. . .When I was told of the hopelessness of her case, I felt it wise to plunge into some sort of absorbing mental effort that would leave me no time to think of myself. The child's father had also been granted a year's leave of absence and he decided to spend it at Cornell University. Thither we went, the three of us. We found a small house, very cheap, and I, too, decided to study, and for my Master's degree.''[2]

July, 1925. Adopted her first child. ''I was sure that there must be a baby somewhere who needed me. I found her in a small orphanage in upstate New York. A friendly Presbyterian minister took me there and the director led me into the nursery. There were twenty babies in their cribs.

"'Take your choice,' the director said.

"Was there ever such a choice presented to a young mother? I went from crib to crib. At last I came to one where a very small, very pale little girl lay, her eyes closed. She seemed scarcely to breathe.

"'How old is she?' I asked.

"'Three months,' the director said, 'and she has never gained since birth. She weighs only seven pounds. She will not eat.'

"'I want her,' I said.

"He argued against it immediately. Why should I take a child doomed to death? But I insisted. I felt a strange instant love for the exquisite dying child. I took her in my arms and carried her away. The very next day she began to eat. In a fortnight one wouldn't have known her. She was actually plump. My husband and I finished our work for our master's degrees [1926] and took our two daughters back to China with us."[1]

1927. Barely escaped with her family during a revolutionary attack on Nanking. "It was the most sudden event imaginable. We heard at the breakfast table that the revolutionists were marching into the city, and were glad, because the days of fighting had been tense ones, and also because we, as a group of foreign university teachers, were heartily in sympathy with the national aims.

"Then in fifteen minutes we were fleeing for our lives. Our faithful servants came running to tell us that the Nationalists were killing foreigners, and they helped us to hide. It was true, for our vice-president, Dr. Williams, had already been killed—shot instantly when he did not give up his watch to a band of soldiers. We hid all day—thirteen hours to be exact—in a tiny hovel where a poor woman, whom I had helped, lived. We could not make a sound, since the soldiers were all around us—and 'we' includes two babies under two and my seven-year-old. But they were very good. All day we listened to the most hideous shouting and crashing in of gates and doors. Our servants crept in to tell us that the soldiers were urging the common people in to take out things, since now everything was to be in common, and there was to be no more private property.[1]

". . .We stayed there that night and all the next day, still not knowing whether we were to be released or held for an unknown purpose, but there was nothing lonely about our imprisonment. One by one through the night and the next day the few remaining white people who had not yet been found were brought to join our number. We knew now the dead. . . .

". . . Late in the afternoon of that second day, however, we were told to gather ourselves together and come out of the building. We were to march to the Bund, there to be taken off on the warships. When we reached the gate we found that several broken-down carriages had been provided for the old people and women with little children, and so I with other

(From the movie "Satan Never Sleeps," starring Nancy Kwan and William Holden. Released by Twentieth Century-Fox Film Corp., 1962.)

mothers climbed in and drove off down the familiar streets. . . . The streets were lined with watching silent people, but the scene, so familiar, had changed overnight. Would I ever see the city again? I did not know, and yet I could not imagine never coming back.''[2]

After a stay in Japan, Buck and her family resumed their lives in China.

1929. ''In the midst of these years I made a swift journey to the United States to put my invalid child into a permanent school. The decision had been hastened because I foresaw a future in China so uncertain in terms of wars and revolutions that the only safety for a helpless child was in a life shelter. It was during those few months in the United States . . . that I heard my first novel, *East Wind: West Wind,* had been accepted for publication. I had sent that slender manuscript off to David Lloyd in New York a year before, and then so much had happened that I had all but forgotten it. I was visiting in a friend's house in Buffalo when a cablegram from David Lloyd reached me, forwarded from China, and telling me that the book had been taken by the John Day Company, and that I was asked to come to the company office to discuss some revisions. This news came one morning when I was feeling very desolate at the prospect of a future of separation from my child, and while it did not compensate, nevertheless it brightened life in its own way. I am told that both agency and publisher were astounded at the calmness with which I replied, and at the fact that I waited weeks before going to New York. I suppose my habitual casualness about time is the result of having lived so long in a timeless country. . . . Almost immediately I returned to China.''[2]

1929-1931. ''The house in Nanking was empty without my little elder daughter and not all the friends and family could fill it. This, I decided, was the time to begin really to write. So one morning I put my attic room in order and faced my big Chinese desk to the mountain, and there each morning when the household was in running order for the day I sat myself down to my typewriter and began to write *The Good Earth.* My story had long been clear in my mind. Indeed, it had shaped itself firmly and swiftly from the events of my life, and its energy was the anger I felt for the sake of the peasants and the common folk of China, whom I loved and admired, and still do. For the scene of my book I chose the north country, and for the rich southern City, Nanking. My material was therefore close at hand, and the people I knew as I knew myself.

''How long the days were, in the separation from my child, although I crammed them full! In the afternoon I taught my classes in the new government university, and when I came home at four o'clock there were always guests for tea, young Chinese intellectuals, old Chinese friends, young Americans and English from the Language School which had been opened in Nanking by cooperating mission boards. Still the days were too long, for there were the evenings and the weekends and the long hot summers when schools were closed. . . . In the summers I had even more time, for my father always spent the two hottest months of summer with my sister's family in the mountains, and the house was emptier than ever. It was then that I decided to begin my translation of the great Chinese novel *Shui Hu Chüan,* which later I called *All Men Are Brothers.*

''Meanwhile I was writing *The Good Earth.* This I did in three months, typing the manuscripts twice myself in that time. . . .

Susan was coming back with the glass of water in both hands....■ (From *The Chinese Story Teller* by Pearl S. Buck. Illustrated by Regina Shekerjian.)

''My mind could not rest after I had finished *The Good Earth* and almost immediately I began to write another novel, *The Mother,* in which I portrayed the life of a Chinese peasant woman, but more than that, I hoped, it was the life of such a woman anywhere, who has been given no fulfillment except her own experience and understanding. . . .''[2]

1931. ''The year . . . was a monumental one in many ways for me. In that year my dear old father died in the eightieth year of his life. In that year the Yangtse River swelled with unusual rains and flooded our whole countryside, a sight no

Portrait sketch of Pearl S. Buck.

one living had ever seen before, and in that year the Japanese empire builders seized Manchuria, and all thinking Chinese and a few white people comprehended the full portent of this act of aggression. Mr. Lung, the old Chinese scholar who was working with me on my translation of *Shui Hu Chüan,* said to me often and anxiously, 'Can it be possible that the Americans and the English do not understand what it means that Japan has taken Manchuria? There will be a Second World War.'

"I said that neither English or Americans could understand this.

"For me, of course, the most moving event was my father's death. . . . During the last two years his tall ascetic frame had grown more and more frail, his nature more completely the saint, and I feared, observing these changes, that he had not many more years to live. . . .

"I could not even get to his funeral, for the river was flooding at a frightening speed and all ships were delayed. With my father's death the last of my childhood life was gone, and I was from then on living in the new world of struggle and confusion. His steady faith that all things work together for good was removed from my house."[2]

Late 1932. *The Good Earth* was awarded the Pulitzer Prize for the best novel of the year.

1934. Left China and her failing marriage and took up permanent residence in the United States. "There were personal reasons . . . why I should return to my own country. It is not necessary to recount them, for in the huge events that were changing my world, the personal was all but negligible. My invalid child, nevertheless, had become ill after I left, and it was obvious that for her sake I should live near enough to be with her from time to time. The grey house, too, had ceased to be a home for family life, in spite of my efforts, for the distances between the man and the woman there had long ago become insufferable. There were no differences—only a difference so vast that communication was impossible, in spite of honest effort over many years. It was the deep difference which my parents had perceived long before I did, and which had made my mother try to persuade me against the marriage. I had not heeded her and although sadly soon I had known her right, I had been too proud to reveal myself wrong. Now the difference had come to include the child who could not grow and what should be done for her, and there was no bridge left to build between. It was time for me to leave China."[2]

Summer, 1934. Bought an old stone house in Pennsylvania. "My first summer I spent in New York, and the result of it was that I learned that I could never understand my country unless I became part of it somewhere else and not merely a city visitor. This meant a home, and home meant a house, and where does one live when there is a vast country from which to choose? The choice may be merely geographical, and I saw many places delightful enough in which to remain, the bare beauty of Western deserts, the enchanted high plains of Kansas, the mountainous states of the Rockies, the close hills of New England. I set aside the Deep South. I could not live where the colonial atmosphere prevailed, and where I would have always to look at signs to see where I belonged in railroad stations and restaurants. Besides, I planned at last for more children, for here, I thought, was a safe country for children, and I did not want the responsibility of having them instilled with color prejudices which I knew would be dangerous to us in the world of the near future.

"After some musing and travelling, I decided on a region where the landscapes were varied, where farm and industry lived side by side, where sea was near at hand, mountains not far away, and city and countryside were not enemies, a big rich state, a slice of the nation—Pennsylvania. . . ."[2]

June 11, 1935. Divorced John Buck and married Richard J. Walsh, president of the John Day Company (publishers). "Then came the decision to go to Reno. It was a difficult decision because . . . I wasn't convinced—I never had been convinced—about marriage. I question very much whether marriage is a good relationship for me. I believe in relationships and I don't think people can do without them, but I don't know whether the demands of marriage are very wise for a person like myself to undertake. I enjoy housekeeping. I don't do any of the work myself, but I enjoy having a house—but then one can have that anyway without marriage. I think perhaps the inconvenience of not being married in our society made me realize that I'd better get the legalities over with for, difficult as it was, it was the only practical way of living.

"In short, after we had decided that we would be happier together, the only sensible thing to do was to get married. . . . We were married that same afternoon the divorce was granted.

"After the trip to Lake Tahoe, we started home. We went by train, because Richard had left the car somewhere near New

York, and then we drove to the house I had bought, and we made it into our home. . . .''[1]

1936-1937. Adopted three boys and a girl. A family eventually grew to include eight adopted children of culturally and racially mixed backgrounds and her own retarded daughter.

1938. Awarded the Nobel Prize for Literature—the only American woman so honored. ''Then suddenly there came the most unexpected event of my life. How well I remember that day! It was in the autumn. . . . I was sitting in my study in the big apartment in New York before we had moved to the country. I remember the very morning—indeed, the hour. It was ten o'clock, the children were out on the terrace with the nurse, and I was at work. Suddenly the telephone rang. I took up the receiver and heard my secretary's excited voice.

'''You've been awarded the Nobel Prize!'

''I didn't believe her, of course, but before I could say, 'I don't believe you,' another telephone rang, and I heard my husband saying, 'You've won the Nobel Prize, it's in the papers today!'

''Of course I still didn't believe it. 'I think it's reporters' talk,' I said, 'and I shan't believe it until you have called Sweden by long distance and inquired.'

''Well, it was true. The award came to me at exactly the right moment, and exactly as Alfred Nobel had planned. For he had directed that the prize for literature was not to be given to long-established, old and successful writers, and I was still young, as writers go. In fact, I was the next-to-the-youngest person ever to get the Nobel Prize for literature. I believe Rudyard Kipling was a little younger than I. At any rate, to receive it at that moment gave me back the confidence I was beginning to lose. I was swept up into all the old publicity again. Incidentally, the prize was given for my work as a whole, which up to that time had been Chinese, and special mention was made of the two biographies [of her mother and father].''[1]

1941. Wrote prolifically during the war years. ''The war years we all know too well for them to be retold again. My task was to keep the children as free from fear as possible, to continue my work, to maintain what is called an even keel. It was a familiar atmosphere, but one I had never expected in my own country. As in China, however, I determined not to allow the war to shadow my existence, nor to prevent me from getting the most possible out of my daily life.''[2]

1941-1946. With her husband, published *Asia* magazine and established the East and West Association, a forerunner of the present People-to-People program. ''There was no other magazine in the United States which carried full and authentic information about Asian life. At that moment it seemed folly to end the last means of informing our people and providing the knowledge essential to their own safety and welfare. It was as near a missionary impulse as I ever had, and my husband shared it. We were given the magazine and all its assets in the hope . . . that it could be saved. Suffice it to say that we did keep it going for another five years, until events after the end of the war made it impossible. There was, as a matter of fact, an increase in American interest in Asia during the war years, and had there been enough paper available, the magazine might have become self-supporting.''[2]

1949. Established an adoption agency, Welcome House, Inc., dedicated to finding homes for American-Asian children in

PEARL S. BUCK

Bucks County, Pennsylvania. ''Once we found that people did want to adopt the mixed-blood babies and once we took the firm stand that parents must not be rejected on grounds of non-matching race and religion, the rest was easy. A group of our citizens formed a board of directors and we made a formal application to the State of Pennsylvania to set up a private adoption agency. We found the officials sympathetic and circumspect. Were we sure there were enough such children born in the United States to warrant an agency especially for them? We asked them to make their own investigation. They wrote to all state agencies to inquire. The replies showed that while there were not mixed-blood children in great numbers, nevertheless they constituted the chief problem for adoption agencies. There were simply no prospective parents for such children.

''We were granted our charter at once after that. It was a charter like none other, perhaps, in the world, for it permits Welcome House, Inc., to receive and place for adoption children from any state in the Union, born in the United States but of Asian or part-Asian ancestry. We set up a modest office, employed two social workers of experience and warm heart, and two other workers equally devoted, to carry on the business of Welcome House, Inc. From then on there were no more problems—no big ones, that is. There are always problems with adoption, generally speaking. Our laws are confused and contradictory, and often it is as difficult to place a child for adoption in another state as though it were another country.'' [Pearl S. Buck, *Children for Adoption,* Random House, 1964.[3]]

1951. Elected to the National Institute of Arts and Letters.

May 28, 1960. Husband died after a seven year illness. ". . . Our life was organized casually around work and children and we lived deeply. Our pleasures were in music and people and children and books and the world of woods and mountain and sea. [Pearl S. Buck, *A Bridge for Passing*, John Day, 1961. [4]]

1964. Organized the Pearl S. Buck Foundation for the welfare of the Asian-American children destined to live in the country in which they were born. ". . .This is the only agency to which I have ever given, or will ever give, my own name. I have done so because, after fifteen years of observation and experience in the field of lost and needy children, I am compelled to the conclusion that the most needy in the world in our present age are the children born in Asia, whose mothers are Asian but whose fathers are American. [Pearl S. Buck and Theodore F. Harris, *For Spacious Skies: Journey in Dialogue*, John Day, 1966. [5]]

June 11, 1967. Dedicated the Opportunity Center of the Pearl S. Buck Foundation in Korea. "You may ask, as I am often asked, why a writer concerns herself with such activities. I have asked myself the same question and upon examining my own reasons I have come to the conclusion that they are artistic rather than humanitarian. I have an artist's love of order— order in the cosmic sense. It is disorderly to have children without families, disorderly to permit human beings to be lost. Disorder is destructive, the very composition is unhappy. Perhaps composition is the accurate word rather than order. Children with nowhere to go, no one to belong to, break the composition of human life. It seems necessary for me to try to restore order and therefore composition, whether it be of a room or a life. This is happiness."[5]

March 6, 1973. Died at her vacation home in Danby, Vermont. Buck wrote more than eighty-five books and was one of the most widely translated authors in American literature. She had been working simultaneously on several books, as was her habit, at the time of her death. Shortly before her death Buck had relinquished all but five of her literary works to Wolper Productions, Inc. for radio, television and movie adaptations with the stipulation that the proceeds from their use would go to the Buck Foundation.

"It seems good, sometimes, to think of simply *not being*. Why people want immortal life I cannot imagine. I hope to be mortal."[1]

FOR MORE INFORMATION SEE—Books: Pearl Buck, *The Child Who Never Grew*, John Day, 1950; Buck, *My Several Worlds*, John Day, 1954; Paul Doyle, *Pearl Buck*, Twayne, 1965; Betsy Edgar, *Our House*, McClain, 1965; Eve Parshalle, *Kashmir Bridge-Women*, Oxford University Press, 1965; Buck, *For Spacious Skies*, John Day, 1966; D. W. Thompson, *Pearl Buck*, University of Oklahoma Press, 1968; Theodore Harris, *Pearl S. Buck: A Biography*, John Day, Volume I, 1969, Volume II, 1971; *Authors in the News*, Volume 1, Gale, 1976; *Contemporary Literary Criticism*, Gale, Volume 7, 1977, Volume 9, 1979; *Contemporary Authors, New Revisions Series*, Volume 1, Gale, 1980.

Periodicals: *Books*, March 1, 1931, September 25, 1932, January 20, 1935, February 9, 1936, November 29, 1936; *New York Times*, March 15, 1931, September 25, 1932, January 20, 1935, February 9, 1936, November 29, 1936, September 10, 1969; *Outlook*, March 18, 1931; *Saturday Review of Literature*, March 21, 1931, September 24, 1932, February 8,

1936, December 5, 1936; *Bookman*, May, 1931, October, 1932; *Spectator*, May 2, 1931; *Nation*, May 13, 1931, November 16, 1932, February 6, 1935; *New Statesman and Nation*, May 16, 1931, December 3, 1932; *Saturday Review*, May 16, 1931, November 5, 1932, March 31, 1956, November 22, 1958, July 12, 1969; *Christian Century*, May 20, 1931, October 5, 1932, March 13, 1935, February 5, 1936, April 7, 1937, December 9, 1970; *New Republic*, July 1, 1931, October 26, 1932, January 23, 1935, December 9, 1936; *Chicago Daily Tribune*, September 24, 1932; *Times Literary Supplement*, October 6, 1932, January 24, 1935, February 15, 1936, October 19, 1967, March 21, 1980; *New York Herald Tribune*, January 21, 1935; *Forum*, March, 1935; *Christian Science Monitor*, February 7, 1936, December 1, 1936, December 24, 1958, July 10, 1969; *Commonweal*, December 11, 1936; *Atlantic*, March, 1937, July, 1969; *Best Sellers*, February 1, 1965, April 1, 1968, April 1, 1969, June 1, 1970, November 1, 1970; *National Observer*, April 29, 1968; *New York Times Book Review*, February 23, 1969, March 11, 1979; *Time*, July 25, 1969; *Detroit News*, January 16, 1972, November 20, 1979; *Saturday Evening Post*, Spring, 1972; *English Journal*, April, 1980.

For Children: Pearl Buck, *My Several Worlds* (abridged for younger readers), John Day, 1957; Celin Schoen, *Pearl Buck: Famed Author of Oriental Stories*, Sam-Har Press, 1972; Irvin Block, *The Lives of Pearl Buck*, Crowell, 1973; Elizabeth Myers, *Pearl S. Buck: Literary Girl*, Bobbs-Merrill, 1974.

Movies and filmstrips: "Pearl S. Buck" (motion picture), National Broadcasting Company, 1960; "Reading Out Loud: Pearl S. Buck" (motion picture), Stratton Productions, 1962; "Pearl S. Buck: An American from China" (filmstrip), Society for Visual Education, 1974; "Pearl Buck: The Woman, the Word, and Two Good Earths" (motion picture), with Hugh Downs, Comco Productions, 1978.

OBITUARIES: London Times, March 7, 1973; *New York Times*, March 7, 1973, March 10, 1973; *Washington Post*, March 7, 1973; *Publishers Weekly*, March 12, 1973; *Antiquarian Bookman*, March 19, 1973; *Newsweek*, March 19, 1973; *Time*, March 19, 1973; *New Republic*, March 24, 1973; *Christianity Today*, March 30, 1973; *Good Housekeeping*, June, 1973.

Know you what it is to be a child? It is to be something very different from the man of today. It is to have a spirit yet streaming from the waters of baptism; it is to believe in love, to believe in loveliness, to believe in belief; it is to be so little that the elves can reach to whisper in your ear; it is to turn pumpkins into coaches, and mice into horses, lowness into loftiness, and nothing into everything, for each child has its fairy godmother in its soul.

—Francis Thompson

Grown-ups never understand anything for themselves, and it is tiresome for children to be always and forever explaining things to them.

—Antoine de Saint-Exupéry

CALLAHAN, Philip S(erna) 1923-

PERSONAL: Born August 29, 1923, in Fort Benning, Ga.; son of Eugene C. (an army colonial) and Enid (Ainsa) Callahan; married Winnie McGee, August 27, 1949; children: Cathy, Peggy, Kevin, and Colette. *Education:* University of Arkansas, B. A., M. S., 1953; Kansas State University, Ph. D., 1956. *Religion:* Roman Catholic. Office: USDA Insect Attractant, Behavior and Basic Biology Laboratory and Entomology Department, University of Florida, Gainesville, Fla. 32604.

CAREER: Louisana State University, Baton Rouge, 1956-63, began as assistant professor, became associate professor of entomology; University of Georgia, Athens, professor of entomology, 1963-69; Southern Grain Insects Research Lab, Agricultural Research Service, Tifton, Ga., entomologist, 1962-69; University of Florida, U. S. Department of Agriculture Insect Attractant, Behavior and Basic Biology Research Lab, Gainsville, Fla., entomologist, research biophysicist, 1969—. *Member:* Entomologist Society of America, American Ornithological Union, New York Academy of Sciences, Explorers Club, North American Falconers Association.

WRITINGS—Nonfiction: *Insect Behavior* (juvenile; self-illustrated), Four Winds, 1970; *Insects and How They Function* (juvenile; self-illustrated), Holiday House, 1971; *The Evolution of Insects* (juvenile; self-illustrated), Holiday House, 1972; *The Magnificent Birds of Prey* (juvenile), Holiday House, 1974; *Bird Behavior* (juvenile), Four Winds, 1975; *Tuning In to Na-*

PHILIP S. CALLAHAN

ture: Solar Energy, Infrared Radiation & the Insect Communication, Devin-Adair, 1975; *Birds and How They Function* (juvenile), Holiday House, 1979; *Soul of the Ghost Moth* (autobiography), Devin-Adair, 1980.

Also author of scientific reports for governmental agencies and national organizations, including *Insect Molecular Bioelectronics,* for Entomological Society of America, 1967.

WORK IN PROGRESS: "I have two books in progress—one called *Exploring the Spectrum* for young adults and another entitled *The Mysterious Round Towers of Ireland.*"

SIDELIGHTS: "I am a member of the famous Explorers Club and tend to write about my own experiences in science and travel. After World War II, I hiked and hitch-hiked around the world and became intrigued by the *form* of living organisms and religious structures.

"After I became an insect biophysicist, I began extensive research which led to my discovery that insect antenna really are tuned to infrared, coherent waves from the molecules they detect and that many religious structures, round towers in Ireland, fairy rings, church steeples, and pyramids are, in reality, *stove antenna* that resonate to the cosmic paramagnetic and electromagnetic forces of nature.

"My books for young adults are written to acquaint them with the elegance of the interaction of nature and low-energy electromagnetic energy. This is the subject of my book, *Tuning In to Nature. The Soul of the Ghost Moth* is my autobiography and tells how my many travels led to my scientific discoveries.

Banding birds is painless, despite the protesting look of the nestling in front. ■ (From *The Magnificent Birds of Prey* by Philip S. Callahan. Photograph by the author.)

"My second love is birds and the training of falcons in the ancient sport of falconry. I take all my own photographs and love to paint (watercolor) wild life—thus, I illustrated all my own books."

FOR MORE INFORMATION SEE: Horn Book, June 6, 1973.

CAMERON, Eleanor (Butler)   1912-

PERSONAL: Born March 23, 1912, in Canada; daughter of Henry and Florence (Vaughan) Butler; married Ian Stuart Cameron, 1934; children: David Gordon. *Education:* University of California, Los Angeles, student, two years; Art Center School, Los Angeles, student, one year. *Home:* Pebble Beach, Calif.

CAREER: Public Library, Los Angeles, Calif., clerk, 1930-36; Board of Education Library, Los Angeles, Calif., clerk, 1936-42; Foote, Cone & Belding (advertising), Los Angeles, Calif., research librarian, 1943-44; Honig, Cooper & Harrington (advertising), Los Angeles, Calif., research librarian, 1956-58. Member of the editorial board, *Cricket Magazine,* and of the advisory board of the Center for the Study of Children's Literature, Simmons College, Boston, Mass.; gave the annual Gertrude Clark Whittall Lecture at the Library of Congress, 1977; judge in the children's category for the National Book Awards, 1980. *Member:* P.E.N., Save-the-Redwoods League.

ELEANOR CAMERON

Now Mr. Bass settled himself at his desk and turned on the lamp. In this room his homemade telescope stood, pointing up to the domed ridged roof. ■ (From *A Mystery for Mr. Bass* by Eleanor Cameron. Illustrated by Leonard Shortall.)

Awards, honors: Hawaiian Children's Choice Nene Award, 1960, for *Wonderful Flight to the Mushroom Planet;* Commonwealth Award and Mystery Writers of America Award, 1964, for *A Spell Is Cast;* Southern California Council on Literature for Children and Young People, 1965, Annual Award, for Distinguished Contribution to the Field of Children's Literature; Commonwealth Award, 1969, for *The Green and Burning Tree: On the Writing and Enjoyment of Children's Books;* Globe-Horn Book Award, 1971, for *A Room Made of Windows;* National Book Award, 1974, for *The Court of the Stone Children;* finalist for the National Book Award, 1976, for *To the Green Mountains.*

WRITINGS—All published by Atlantic-Little, Brown; except as noted: *The Unheard Music* (adult novel), 1950; *The Wonderful Flight to the Mushroom Planet* (Junior Literary Guild selection), 1954; *Stowaway to the Mushroom Planet* (Junior Literary Guild selection), 1956; *Mr. Bass's Planetoid* (Junior Literary Guild selection), 1958; *The Terrible Churnadryne* (Junior Literary Guild selection), 1959; *A Mystery for Mr. Bass,* 1960; *The Mysterious Christmas Shell* (Junior Literary Guild selection), 1961; *The Beast with the Magical Horn,* 1963; *A Spell Is Cast* (Horn Book honor list; Junior Literary Guild selection), 1964; *Time and Mr. Bass,* 1967; *The Green and Burning Tree: On the Writing and Enjoyment of Children's Books* (adult), 1969.

A Room Made of Windows (ALA Notable Book; *Horn Book* honor list), 1971; *The Court of the Stone Children* (ALA Notable Book; Junior Literary Guild selection), Dutton, 1973; *To the Green Mountains* (ALA Notable Book; *Horn Book* honor list), Dutton, 1975; *Julia and the Hand of God* (ALA Notable Book; *Horn Book* honor list; Junior Literary Guild selection),

Dutton, 1977; *Beyond Silence,* Dutton, 1980. Contributor to *Horn Book, Wilson Library Bulletin,* and other periodicals. Contributor of tape, "A Branch of the Tree: Children's Literature as a Part of World Literature," *Prelude: Mini-Seminars on Using Books Creatively,* Series 4, Children's Book Council.

SIDELIGHTS: "When David, my son, was seven-almost-eight, he loved the *Doctor Dolittle* books so much that he almost lived in them. One day, having finished the whole series for perhaps the fourth or fifth time, he asked me if I would write a story for him about two boys his own age who would build a little space ship and fly away to discover a planet just the right size to explore in a day or two. 'And let it be a magical story,' he went on, not even listening to me when I protested that I was writing a book for grown-ups. 'And be sure the other boy in it is Chuck, because naturally my best friend has to go along with me.'

"I told him that I doubted I would ever have even the shred of an idea for this adventure of his, but the next morning I discovered that overnight a personality—the personality of the slight, quick, gay, wise little man, whose name I found later to be Tyco Mycetes Bass—had taken shape in my imagination as well as the central idea of the *The Wonderful Flight to the Mushroom Planet.*

"After I had finished, David informed me that of course there would have to be another adventure and I had grown so fond of Mr. Bass by this time that I agreed. Besides, I had already begun to picture his cousin, Mr. Theodosius Bass and I knew that he had to be in the story. Then I came across a limerick about a certain young lady named Bright, who could travel far faster than light, and at once the idea for *Stowaway to the Mushroom Planet* came to me, weaving itself around the character of Mr. Theo."

"When *Stowaway* was finished, I began thinking about meteors and meteorites, and I grew so fascinated by the subject that I made *Mr. Bass's Planetoid* twice as long as it should have been. David said, 'What if the boys got in their space ship and flew out into space and landed on a big meteor going around the earth about a thousand miles out—' Yes, and for an extremely important reason, I thought, and then began to see Mr. Prewytt Brumblydge, that surprising little man who was at the bottom of the reason.

"As for *The Terrible Churnadryne,* it grew partly out of that word churn-a-dryne and partly out of my love of the Big Sur country. This coastland is about one hundred miles south of San Francisco, and I have loved it ever since I was a child. In this country, there are steep cliffs plunging into the sea, and pines and cypress and redwoods. And the fog comes winding and curling in around the tops of the hills, then muffles up the coast in white veils, the way it did when Tom and Jennifer saw the churnadryne."

For several years, as I became more and more deeply involved in the world of children's literature and talked about it to teachers and parents and librarians, the idea of a book of critical essays on the subject had been taking shape. I had no desire to write anything textbookish, but something purely personal which would not only express my delight in the finest children's books I had read, but would combine my own experiences of writing with those principles of the art I could divine at work in books that had given me pleasure as a critical adult. Though *The Green and Burning Tree* is a very personal expression on the subject, a section of references relating to the text has been included, as well as a lengthy bibliography and a detailed index in the hope that these will be of use to all of those involved in bringing books to children and to those who are about to enter the field.

It was awful always to have to use words you weren't sure about, to have to use them in front of people and not just in your own head, and see everybody tickled inside themselves. Felony Franklinburg she'd named her doll. . . . But when she told it to a roomful of her mother's and father's friends, their mouths opened in round black pockets of laughter. ■ (From *A Room Made of Windows* by Eleanor Cameron. Illustrated by Trina Schart Hyman.)

"*The Green and Burning Tree* has seemed to divide my work in two so decidedly that some have told me they were surprised to find it was the same Cameron who wrote the early books as the later ones. It appears that *Tree* taught me something; as if I learned, in the process of writing about other people's work, much that could better my own. However, I want to say that I am still fond of *Wonderful Flight, Time and Mr. Bass, The Terrible Churnadryne,* and *A Spell is Cast.*

"What has happened since *Tree* is that I have been basing (but only basing) these later novels on childhood experience, using actual situations as the takeoff into events that never happened in real life, whereas the earlier books were wholly imaginative. However, both *Julia and the Hand of God* and *A Room Made of Windows* are somewhat autobiographical. *Room,* concerning Julia at the age of twelve, is situated in my own childhood experience of wanting to become a writer and of having a mother who wanted to marry again much against my wishes. There is a brother, which is not autobiographical, and why I needed him in the novel I don't know—but I turned my son David (of the 'Mushroom Planet' books, but grown older) into my brother Greg, where he found his place as if he had always belonged there. But these are true facts: the writing, and the resentment of a prospective new father, that I had a room almost literally made of windows, and a big desk, and that I lived in a brown bungalow with a white roof, in a two-story apartment at the back. In this novel I apparently evoked the Berkeley of my childhood so strongly that some who grew up in the city at that time have written to tell me of their intense emotional reactions.

"*Julia and the Hand of God* was written later, but concerns Julia at the age of eleven, trying to write and not succeeding as she does succeed in *Room.* Because of the pleasure I had in returning to that world of Berkeley I'd known as a child, I was suddenly struck with a desire to return to it again. This desire came to me with great force while I was reading a book of short stories, *A Few Fair Days,* by the English writer Jane Gardam about a small girl who I'm sure must have been Jane as a child. The reading of that book inexplicably brought certain Berkeley scenes and moments crowding into my mind, and set going incidents woven around a younger Julia that I thought would become a book of short stories. But the stories would not stay separate. As time passed, I began to see the connection between them, and that they were lacing themselves into a novel. *Julia and the Hand of God* is far less autobiographical than *Room.* But I *was* invariably overwhelmed with a kind of horrified fascination at the idea of another earthquake every time we crossed by ferry over to San Francisco; I *did* have a friend named Maisie; and there *was* a fire that almost wiped out Berkeley.

"As for *The Court of the Stone Children,* I have always been fascinated by museums, and the furnished rooms often displayed in them, since I was first taken at the age of six to the De Young Museum in Golden Gate Park in San Francisco. However, it was the restored rooms in the Los Angeles County Museum with paneling, fireplaces, and furniture from a French château that gave me my first dim glimmering of *Court.* I thought how cold they seemed with no books lying about as though just put down, no small personal objects to make them seem lived in, deserted only for a moment. 'What if a child came here alone and began to feel that someone, someone near her own age. . . . ' And so it all began.

"One of the great pleasures of my life as a child was to cross the bay from Berkeley and go to the museum. Since then I have explored many museums, both here and in the British Isles. But in *Court,* which takes place in the present, I was writing about a boy and girl of around thirteen or fourteen, the age I myself was when I was deep in books and becoming more and more engrossed with the idea of the past, more and more sensitively aware of the life that had gone on in those De Young Museum rooms. Therefore I could put my novel nowhere but in the city I had loved all those years ago with its stunning views, its blue bay, steep hills, and idiosyncratic architecture.

"*To the Green Mountains* comes out of my very early years, between three and six, when I lived in a small town in Ohio. I had thought of it for a long time as an adult novel, but slowly I began to see its events (none of which actually happened) through the eyes of thirteen-year-old Kath, rather than through the eyes of her mother, and I can't explain why. All this slow changing went on over a period of thirty years, and the reason I put off writing was because I was afraid I could not do sufficient justice to the two black characters, Grant and his wife Tissie. But they became so real to me that finally, when I realized that I need not be afraid because, after all, I was going to see them through Kath's eyes, I knew I could set to work. But first I thought I must go to that little town in Ohio, and actually started to make arrangements at the airport ticket desk, at a time when I had to go east to New York. But something told me I must not stop off in Ohio on the way back. 'Trust to the aesthetic impulse.' Those were the words that suddenly came to mind, very commandingly. And I obeyed them, knowing that it would be far better to evoke a poetic picture of reality than to spoil what I had once known with facts of the present day, because these would bear little relation to my childhood. And what astounded me in the writing was the vividness of the sights and sounds and smells that came back: the smell of the thick summer dust, the sound of the pony's hooves in it, insects singing in the breathless heat, the smells inside certain houses, the looks of the big, cool, cave of a dining room at the hotel. And strangely enough, though I could get back to Grant, the headwaiter, only through my mother's words, and Tissie was purely imagined, they emerge with the same intensity. They give each other life, and I felt this strongly as I wrote. Strangely, too, though I wrote the book just as I had written all the others, from inside the perceptions of the child protagonist, *Mountains* seems for an older audience than the others.

"And so does *Beyond Silence.* But then this novel, a time fantasy like *The Court of the Stone Children,* is about a fifteen-year-old boy told in the first person by his twenty-one-year-old self looking back six years to a summer when he goes to Scotland with his father to escape the unhappiness the death of his older brother has brought on him. The big house in which they stay was once called 'Cames Castle' where his father had spent blissful vacations as a boy, but it is now a hotel. Here Andrew undergoes an opening up of the past through extra-sensory experiences which bring him to an understanding of his own unhappiness and pervading sense of guilt.

"My husband is a Scot and so it was with great pleasure that I went to Scotland with him and became acquainted with the country in his company. On that first visit we stayed in just such a huge old house as 'Cames' (called in reality by another name) on the shore of a loch. There, the idea of the book first came to me, but changed almost out of recognition over the nine years between then and the writing of it. Some agree that the book is a time fantasy, some look on it as psychological science fiction, while others see it as a study of a disturbed

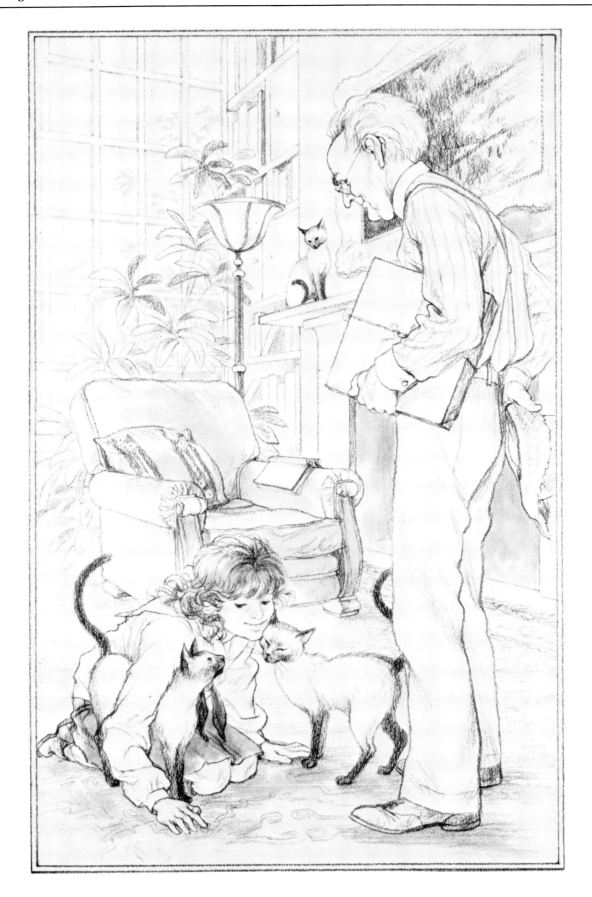

Julia knelt down and put her cheek against Timka's, and got strenuously rubbed and pushed against, while Sookie came nosing in under Julia's arm. ■ (From *Julia and the Hand of God* by Eleanor Cameron. Illustrated by Gail Owens.)

boy. I wrote it as fantasy, but an English reader (Phyllis Parrott, together with Eileen Colwell, the organizer of the Loughborough Conferences on Children's Literature) writes me, 'For me it is true "realism," because through Andrew and in the way he comes to terms with himself and with truth, you make the reader face reality, face situations, which *could* happen to any of us. Beyond materialism you take the reader, too, into an appreciation of spiritual values.'"

"I have always been aware of the work of the unconscious in my writing, as explained in a lecture given at the Library of Congress, 'Into Something Rich and Strange: Of Dreams, Art, and the Unconscious.' And it was interestingly revealed in *Silence* by the fact that I began the novel in the first person, changed my mind a fourth of the way through and went back and wrote the whole thing in the third person, only to have my editor tell me that she felt something was wrong; she felt at a distance from Andrew, a formality. I knew at once what the trouble was; I had gone against the direction I had been given in the beginning, and therefore went back and rewrote the whole novel in the first person as I knew it should have been in the first place. Why this particular novel demanded to be written in this way, I know not. Also, I did not know that an experience I had had between sleeping and waking, and which I gave to Andrew, was called hypnagogic until my husband brought me an article on the subject and I recognized what had happened to me. But what is most interesting is the way the unconscious weaves its materials, in great complexity as in the case of *Court* and *Silence,* so that when the novel is finished, the writer realizes he could never have *thought* it all out in all its minute and astonishing interlacings as the unconscious has given it. To me, it is invariably something of a miracle.

"Also, I have known for some time that for me place is of the first importance in bringing my novels into being. Place creates characters and therefore story. Stories form because of characters reacting to one another within a world that means something special to me and that makes the characters possible, as real as life and known in every facet. I wait until that unmistakable moment when I feel a novel urgently wanting to be

(From *The Court of the Stone Children* by Eleanor Cameron. Jacket illustrated by Trina Schart Hyman.)

. . . Ta drew from around his neck the beautiful necklace of stones and flung it up to them—and as it came slithering and swerving upward through the green air, it seemed almost like something alive. ∎ (From *The Wonderful Flight to the Mushroom Planet* by Eleanor Cameron. Illustrated by Robert Henneberger.)

written, which is when the folder full of conversations, and the illuminations they have been giving me, becomes fact. And I never force anything.

"Concerning my own books for children, I should like to say that my instinctive desire seems always to instill into them, if not outright. magic, then the feeling of magic, of wonder in the everyday world, a sense of something indefinable but precious to the child which hovers behind what the unperceiving, often uncaring adult regards as simple fact, if it is to be regarded at all. To me this is a very necessary element in any book which will mean something special to children and which will make them want to read it more than once.

"Basic also in my philosophy of writing for children is a great respect for their eager imaginations and hungry minds. I feel that aside from their love of a good story, they appreciate, more than most adults realize, writing that is pictorially alive, that makes them aware in all their senses of mood and atmosphere and place that are, or should be, inseparable from the story. To the extent that the writer himself is aware in all *his* senses of every element of the story, and is able to communicate

his awareness, to that extent the child will feel to the depths the impact of what he is reading. From the letters I have received, I know that all of this is true. I know that many children are quite consciously aware of the ambience of a story, of the depth of characterizations, of the intensity that makes them as readers a living part of the book so that they want to go back and live it again, and of the difference between muscular, evoking writing that has a special tone, and the awkward, flat one-dimensional prose that cares nothing for a child's aesthetic sense, that indeed insults it.

"As for awareness of audience, because I am living in a child's world as I write and because I am hoping that children will enjoy my story, to that extent only am I 'writing for children.' But I have never written for age level, nor chosen words according to some preconceived notion of what certain age levels can handle. For I believe that the only possible way to write a story is to put it down in words and sentences that best convey its essence. Words find their place in a sentence as much because of the rhythm and flow of that sentence as because of meaning. Sound enhances meaning; brings the poetic overtone I am always listening for. If I write, then rewrite, and then again rewrite, it is not only for my own satisfaction (certainly it is chiefly for that) but because I believe that with the help of perceptive parents and teachers and librarians, the child himself can be helped to perceive the difference between careless writing and good, between the book that holds nothing but story and the book that in all its elements has been created with devotion by its author."

HOBBIES AND OTHER INTERESTS: Astronomy, anthropology, art, poetry, and literary criticism.

FOR MORE INFORMATION SEE: Wilson Library Bulletin, October, 1962; *Horn Book,* October, 1964, February, 1966; *Young Readers' Review,* April, 1967; *Christian Science Monitor,* May 4, 1967; Eleanor Cameron, *The Green and Burning Tree: On Writing and Enjoyment of Children's Books,* Atlantic, Little-Brown, 1969; Doris de Montreville and Donna Hill, editors, *Third Book of Junior Authors,* H. W. Wilson, 1972; *Cricket Magazine,* June, 1975; *The Quarterly Journal of the Library of Congress,* April, 1978; Daniel Kirkpatrick, editor, *Twentieth Century Children's Writers,* St. Martin's, 1978; *The Openhearted Audience: Ten Authors Talk About Writing for Children,* Library of Congress, 1980; *Children's Literature Association Quarterly,* Winter, 1980, 1981.

CHAUNDLER, Christine 1887-1972 (Peter Martin)

OBITUARY NOTICE—See sketch in *SATA* Volume 1: Born September 5, 1887, in Biggleswade, Bedfordshire, England; died in December, 1972. Children's author, editor. Though Chaundler was, at various times in her career, an editor for *Little Folks,* a children's editor for Nisbet & Co., and a reviewer of children's books for *Quiver,* she is most remembered for her numerous girl's school stories. At the height of her popularity in the 1920s and 1930s she wrote such books as *The Fourth Form Detectives* and *Sally Sticks It Out.* Later she turned to writing and collecting legends and folklore. *A Year-Book of Fairy Tales, A Year-Book of Customs,* and *The Blue Book of Saints' Stories, Retold,* are several of the thirteen in this vein written during the 1950s and 1960s. *For More Information See: The Who's Who of Children's Literature,* Schocken, 1968; *Contemporary Authors, Permanent Series,* Volume 2, Gale, 1978. *Obituaries: London Times,* December 22, 1972.

He lay down on the ground to show Pickles how. Pickles lay down too and nuzzled Charlie . . . . "You can't lie down with him at the pet show," said Emily. ■ (From *Pickles and Jake* by Janet Chenery. Illustrated by Lilian Obligado.

CHENERY, Janet (Dai) 1923-

PERSONAL: Born April 10, 1923, in New Rochelle, N.Y.; daughter of William Ludlow and Margaret Elizabeth (Miller) Chenery; married French H. Conway, January 30, 1943 (marriage ended, 1954). *Education:* Attended Sweet Briar College, University of Chicago, and University of North Carolina. *Home:* Winston Dr., Washington Depot, Conn. 06794.

CAREER: Western Publishing Co., New York City, editor, 1957-63; Harper & Row Publishers, Inc., New York City, senior editor, 1963-67; Simon & Schuster, Inc., New York City, editor-in-chief, 1967-73; Doubleday & Co., New York City, editorial director, 1973-79. *Member:* Children's Book Council (treasurer), Women's National Book Association.

WRITINGS—All for young people: *The Golden Book of Lost Worlds: Great Civilizations of the Past* (adapted for young readers from Leonard Cottrell's *The Horizon Book of Lost Worlds*), Golden Press, 1963; *The Toad Hunt* (illustrated by Ben Shecter), Harper, 1967; *Wolfie* (illustrated by Marc Simont), Harper, 1969; *Pickles & Jake* (illustrated by Lillian Obligado), Viking, 1975.

WORK IN PROGRESS: Length, Time, and Mass: A Guide to Usual and Unusual Measurements (adult reference), various freelance articles, and a novel for children.

CHILDS, (Halla) Fay (Cochrane) 1890-1971

OBITUARY NOTICE—See sketch in *SATA* Volume 1: Born August 31, 1890, in Chambers, Neb.; died in October, 1971. Teacher, children's author. Childs was born in a sod shanty, and her first teaching experience was in a one-room schoolhouse in Lenawee County, Michigan. Although over the years she took pleasure in telling stories to groups of children, it wasn't until age seventy, after taking a course in creative writing at Pasadena College, that Childs wrote her first work for publication. Uprisings in Kenya and the Congo led to an interest in and an urge to write about the problems of African children. The resulting short stories appeared in such children's magazines as *Jack and Jill, Junior Scholastic,* and *Junior Red Cross Journal.* Two of her stories "The Baboon Tree" and "The Strange Animal," were adapted as talking books for the blind. *For More Information See: Contemporary Authors, Permanent Series,* Volume 1, Gale, 1975.

Give a little love to a child, and you get a great deal back.

—John Ruskin

COLMAN, Morris   1899(?)-1981

OBITUARY NOTICE: Born about 1899; died March 5, 1981, in Croton, N.Y. Book designer and art director. Colman worked as a newspaperman and in the manufacturing departments of various publishers before he joined Viking Press in 1942. Three years later he was promoted to book designer, and in 1960 he became art director. Primarily in charge of the designs for Viking Junior Books, Coleman worked with such noted authors as William Pene du Bois, Ezra Jack Keats, Tasha Tudor, and Janina Domanska. He also designed a number of adult books. *Obituaries: Publishers Weekly,* April 10, 1981.

CONNELLY, Marc(us Cook)   1890-1980

OBITUARY NOTICE: Born December 13, 1890, in McKeesport, Pa.; died December 21, 1980, in New York, N.Y. Playwright, producer, director, and actor, best known for his Pulitzer Prize-winning play "The Green Pastures." Connelly was a prolific writer of lightly satirical plays for the stage, screen, and radio. He wrote dozens of plays, often collaborating with the eminent playwright George S. Kaufman. On his ninetieth birthday, Connelly was presented with a certificate of appreciation for his contributions to the theatre by New York mayor Edward Koch. Connelly's plays include "Dulcy," "Merton of the Movies," and "Helen of Troy, New York." Among his screenplays are "The Cradle Song," "Captains Courageous," and "I Married a Witch." *For More Information See:* Marc Connelly, *Voices Offstage,* Holt, 1968; *Current Biography,* Wilson, 1969; *Contemporary Literary Criticism,* Volume 7, Gale, 1977; *Contemporary Authors,* Volumes 85-88, Gale, 1980. *Obituaries: New York Times,* December 21, 1980; *Washington Post,* December 23, 1980; *London Times,* December 23, 1980; *Chicago Tribune,* December 23, 1980; *Newsweek,* January 5, 1981; *Publishers Weekly,* January 9, 1981; *Time,* January 12, 1981; *Contemporary Authors,* Volume 102, Gale, 1981.

COTTAM, Clarence   1899-1974

PERSONAL: Born January 1, 1899, in St. George, Utah; died March 30, 1974, in Corpus Christi, Tex., buried in Orem, Utah; son of Thomas P. and Emmaline (Jarvis) Cottam; married Margery Brown, May 20, 1920; children: Glenna Clair (Mrs. Ivan L. Sanderson), Margery B. (Mrs. Grant Osborn), Josephine (Mrs. Douglas F. Day), Carolyn (Mrs. Dwayne Stevenson). *Education:* Attended Dixie College, 1919-20, University of Utah, summer, 1923; Brigham Young University, A.B., 1926, M.S., 1927; attended American University, 1931; George Washington University, Ph.D., 1936. *Religion:* Church of Jesus Christ of Latter-day Saints. *Office:* Welder Wildlife Foundation, P.O. Box 1400, Sinton, Tex. 78387.

CAREER: Biologist and conservationist. Consolidated schools, Alamo, Nev., principal, 1922-25; Brigham Young University, Provo, Utah, instructor in biology, 1927-29; U.S. Fish and Wildlife Service (formerly U.S. Biological Survey), Washington, D.C., junior biologist, 1929-31, assistant biologist, 1931-35, senior biologist in charge of food habits research section, 1935-42, in charge of economics, wildlife investigations, 1942-44, assistant to director, 1944-46, chief of division on wildlife research, 1945-46, assistant director of Fish and Wildlife Service, 1946-54; Brigham Young University, professor of biology and dean of the College of Biological and Agricultural Sciences, 1954-58; Robert and Bessie Welder Wildlife Foun-

dation, Sinton, Tex., director, 1955-74. Consultant to Department of the Interior and other governmental agencies.

MEMBER: Wildlife Society of America (president, 1949-50), National Parks Association (president or chairman of the board, 1960-74), American Institute of Biological Sciences, National Audubon Society, Outdoor Writers Association of America, Ecological Society of America, Wildlife Management Institute, American Ornithologists' Union (fellow), Izaak Walton League of America, Soil Conservation Society of America, International Association of Game, Fish and Conservation Commissioners, American Forestry Association, American Fisheries Society, Limnology Society of America, International Platform Association, Society for Range Management, National Academy of Sciences, Texas Academy of Sciences, Texas Ornithological Society (president, 1957), Wilson Ornithological Society, Cooper Ornithological Society, Sigma Xi. *Awards, honors:* Aldo Leopold Memorial medal, Wildlife Society of America, 1955, for recognition of outstanding achievement in the wildlife and natural resources conservation field; Audubon Medal, National Audubon Society, 1961, to honor distinguished individual service to conservation; Poage Humanitarian award, Society for Animal Protection, 1962; Frances K. Hutchenson medal, Garden Clubs of America, 1962; James E. Talmage Scientific Achievement award, Brigham Young University, 1971.

WRITINGS: Food Habits of North American Diving Ducks, U.S. Government Printing Office, 1939; (with Herbert S. Zim) *Insects: A Guide to Familiar American Insects* (illustrated by James Gordon Irving), Simon & Schuster, 1951, revised edition, 1956; (co-editor with James B. Trefethen) George B. Saunders and others, *Whitewings: The Life History, Status, and Management of the White-winged Dove* (illustrated by Bob Hines), Van Nostrand, 1968. Also author of scientific monographs and contributor of articles to periodicals, including *Audubon Magazine, National Parks Magazine, Living Wilderness,* and *Saturday Evening Post.*

SIDELIGHTS: Cottam had a life-long dedication to the fields of biology and conservation. His endeavors to preserve America's national resources won him the honor of inclusion in the select group of conservationists to be awarded the Audubon Medal.

Cottam's interest in conservation involved him in several important "causes." In 1969, he campaigned against the application of a highly toxic pesticide in Texas. The pesticide, called dieldrin, would be destructive to the Gulf Coast bays, Cottam contended. Cottam was also active in the research on the long-range effects of DDT, a similar pesticide. In addition, Cottam was involved in the creation of the Padre Island National Seashore and the expansion of the Arkansas Wildlife Refuge.

Cottam published several books and numerous articles related to biology and conservation. One of his books for the general reader, *Insects,* remains in print almost thirty years after its first publication. *Insects* is a beginner's guide to 225 species of American insects, explaining how to recognize and control them, as well as how to study and collect them. The handbook has also been translated into French.

FOR MORE INFORMATION SEE: Saturday Evening Post, November 10, 1945; *Audubon Magazine,* January-February, 1962. Obituaries: *New York Times,* April 3, 1974; *National Parks Magazine,* June, 1974.

COX, Wally 1924-1973

PERSONAL: Christened Wallace Maynard Cox; born December 6, 1924, in Royal Oak, Mich.; died February 15, 1973, in Los Angeles, Calif.; son of George Wallace (an advertising copywriter) and Eleanor Frances (an author of mystery stories; maiden name, Atkinson) Cox; married Marilyn Gennaro, June 7, 1954 (divorced); married Patricia Tiernan; children: two daughters. *Education:* Attended City College of New York (now of the City University of New York), about 1942. *Home:* New York City.

CAREER: Actor, author. Worked as a shoe-weaver, silversmith, and puppeteer apprentice before making his debut as a comedian at the Village Vanguard, 1948; appeared at a number of night clubs in New York including the Blue Angel, 1948-50; gained critical acclaim for his performance in "Dance Me a Song" at the Royale Theatre in New York, 1950; entertained at the Persian Room of New York's Plaza Hotel and appeared on a number of television programs such as "The Ed Sullivan Show," and "The Gary Moore Show," 1950-52; entertained the radio audience of WNEW as the "discless disc jockey," 1951; following his appearance in the television production of "The Copper," Cox became the bumbling, ingenuous hero of the popular situation-comedy series, "Mr. Peepers," NBC-TV, 1952-55; acted in the summer stock revival of "Three Men on a Horse," 1953; held the title role in "Adventures of Hiram Holiday," NBC-TV, 1956-57; appeared in a number of motion pictures including "Spencer's Mountain," 1963, "Morituri," 1965, "The Cockeyed Cowboys of Calico County," 1970, and "The Barefoot Executive," 1971; made regular guest appearances on the television game show "Hollywood Squares," 1966-73; wrote a number of short stories, plays, and four books. *Military service:* Drafted into the U.S. Army, 1942; served only four months before being honorably discharged. *Awards, honors:* Peabody award for "Mr. Peepers," 1953.

WRITINGS: (With William Redfield) *Mr. Peepers: A Sort of Novel,* Simon & Schuster, 1955; *My Life as a Small Boy* (self-illustrated), Simon & Schuster, 1961; *Ralph Makes Good,* Simon & Schuster, 1966; (with Everett Greenbaum) *The Tenth Life of Osiris Oaks* (for children; illustrated by F. A. Fitzgerald), Simon & Schuster, 1972.

SIDELIGHTS: **December 6, 1924.** "I was born in Royal Oak, Michigan. When I was four months old, mother had something to do, so she parked me with an aunt in Hollywood, California. She came back for me when I was ten months old. I had long curls and I was supposed to have screamed all the way back to Michigan. From then on, in order, Northport, Michigan; Grosse Ile, Michigan; Wyandotte, Michigan—that was where I set fire to a barn—then Chicago.

". . .After Chicago, Omena, Michigan. Then Evanston, Illinois; back to Omena. Then we moved east, to Tomkins Cove, New York; New York City; New City, New York. Back to Detroit, where I finished high school, and then back again to New York City, where I've been, more or less, ever since." [Elise Morrow, "The Other Mr. Peepers," *Saturday Evening Post,* April 16, 1955.[1]]

1928. Father, an advertising copywriter and mother, an author of mystery stories, were divorced. Cox and his sister remained with their mother. "The three of us moved around a good deal. We lived in nine towns in twelve years, and I had a miserable time in every one of them except Northport, Michigan. There were only two bullies there." [Tim Taylor, "Wally Cox and Mr. Peepers," *Coronet,* April, 1955.[2]]

"I come from many places, but the only place I like to think of myself as coming from is a northerly part of Michigan, itself a northerly state, where snow that fell in the middle of winter fell upon snow that was already there, so that the depth of it merely varied and never ended until spring showed up.

"I dare say the snow is piled very high there in the middle of winter to this very day, but it was certainly twice as high when I was a lad, because I was a great deal shorter then than I am now. We lived on a gravel side road in which the county had not much interest, but the farmer farther up the road, in fits of friendliness or necessity, would attach a V-shaped wooden plow to the front of his crawler tractor and plow a groove one car wide past our place into the village. As I remember, a total of four families used that road in the wintertime, and I do not recall an incident in which one car met another on it when snow held sway, and it's just as well, as one of the parties would have had a mess of backing to do.

"The winds that carried the snow usually left a bare avenue right next to the house and used the surplus snow to build a high drift in the back with quite a steep face. Sometimes these drifts would rise to three or four feet, in which case they seemed to ask that caves be dug into them. No such cries went unheeded. Lacking shovels or disdaining them, we sons of the raw northland would delve into the banks of snow with our

Roger wondered if the people would get sore at him if they knew he could hear their thoughts. They all seemed pretty nice now. Maybe it was the warm purring that came with the voices that made them seem kind. ■ (From *The Tenth Life of Osiris Oaks* by Wally Cox and Everett Greenbaum. Illustrated by F. A. Fitzgerald.)

WALLY COX

very hands, scooping out enormous caves that you could get two whole boys into if you doubled them up. Mighty cozy in there.

"To this day, I find it depressing to walk down a city street in December and see bunches of Christmas trees bound and gagged, awaiting sale into slavery. I used to walk through the woods with a pail and a hatchet, knocking snow from little wild Christmas trees to see what they looked like, and end up with what I thought was the most perfect tree in the land. I can't help feeling that Christmas trees should be free for the picking. But then I feel the same way about cherries, apples, swimming and a host of other things that country lads have, so you can see I'm just maladjusted." [Wally Cox, *My Life as a Small Boy,*" excerpts taken from an article in *Good Housekeeping,* November, 1961.[3]]

After graduation from high school, Cox and his mother and sister settled in New York City. In school he got straight A's, but not without effort. "I got good marks in my subjects because I was afraid not to. What's more, I soon learned that the only way I could avoid abrasions and contusions from rubber-propelled paper clips when I got up to recite was to act the clown. If my fellow students could laugh at me while I answered the teachers' questions, they no longer seemed to object that I answered them correctly." [2]

1942. Enrolled in City College in New York where he majored in botany. His studies were interrupted when his mother was stricken with paralysis and he was forced to become the family breadwinner. Worked as a shoe-weaver, and as a silversmith and puppeteer apprentice until drafted into the Army. After four months in the Army he received an honorable discharge.

1946. Met and roomed with Marlon Brando who introduced Cox to the world of actors, playwrights, and ballet dancers. At social gatherings Cox became an informal entertainer. When Cox joined the American Creative Theater Group, the director advised him to develop his monologues into a night club act. "The thought of getting up in front of a roomful of people gave me the shakes. Then I remembered my experiences as a classroom cutup. I did the imitation, everybody laughed, and I discovered that the sound of applause can be extremely pleasant." [2]

1948. First engagement at the Village Vanguard in New York City brought him instant recognition as a comic.

July 3, 1952 Made his television debut as Robinson J. Peepers in the situation comedy series, "Mr. Peepers." The program, a summer replacement, became a popular series on NBC-TV with 10,000,000 viewers. "I like being Peepers, and I'll be happy to play him for as long as people want to see him. Of course, there is always the possibility that the public will grow tired of both of us, and if that happens, then I'll have to find something else to do." [2]

1955. First book was published.

1972. Co-authored his book for children, *The Tenth Life of Osiris Oaks.* Besides being a comedian, Cox also acted in several motion pictures, made regular guest appearances on the game show "Hollywood Squares," and wrote a number of

The television wedding of "Mr. Peepers" stirred nation-wide interest. The weekly series starring Wally Cox, Pat Benoit, and Tony Randall was presented on NBC-TV, 1952-55.

short stories, plays, and four books. "I act because that's how I make my living, but I write because I like to. Writing gives me a real sense of accomplishment. You can write what you want; an actor does what the job calls for. If you're not called for *Hamlet*, you never play *Hamlet*, but a writer can do anything. . . .

"Acting to some people is more a necessity than to others. Some politicians, salesman, lawyers are very good at representing themselves as something they don't particularly feel. As a kid I learned to act a cold into a two-week illness. Especially on Sunday afternoon with school coming up the next morning. Then I would act a cold into a relapse. With that kind of self-training behind me, I didn't bother to go to acting school when I started out." ["Novels and Nights to Remember," *Saturday Review*, March 19, 1966.[4]]

February 15, 1973. Died at the age of forty-eight of a heart attack at his home in Los Angeles, California.

FOR MORE INFORMATION SEE: "Mr. Peepers Emerges," *Life*, July 7, 1952; J. Poling, "Wally Cox is Mr. Peepers," *Collier's*, January 3, 1953; "Mr. Peepers Grows Bold," *Look*, May 5, 1953; R. Gehman, "Wally Cox, the Man Behind Mr. Peepers," *Cosmopolitan*, October, 1953; J. Long, "Love Life of Mr. Peepers," *American Magazine*, October, 1953; "Peep at Peepers," *Good Housekeeping*, November, 1953; F. Marshall, "Mr. Peepers Does His Homework," *Popular Mechanics*, February, 1954; *Current Biography Yearbook 1954*; E. Morrow, "Other Mr. Peepers," *Saturday Evening Post*, April 16, 1955; T. Taylor, "Wally Cox and Mr. Peepers," *Coronet*, April, 1955; Steve Allen, *Funny Men*, Simon & Schuster, 1956; Wally Cox, "My Life as a Small Boy," *Good Housekeeping*, November, 1961; Wally Cox, *My Life as a Small Boy*, Simon & Schuster, 1961, H. Frankel, "Novels and Nights to Remember," *Saturday Review*, March 19, 1966.

Obituaries: *New York Times*, February 16, 1973; *Newsweek*, February 26, 1973; *Time*, February 26, 1973; *Contemporary Authors*, Volume 41-44, Gale, 1974; *Current Biography Yearbook 1974*.

CRONIN, A(rchibald) J(oseph) 1896-1981

OBITUARY NOTICE: Born July 19, 1896, in Dumbarton, Scotland; died of bronchitis, January 6, 1981, in Glion, Switzerland. Surgeon and novelist. Cronin turned from a successful medical practice to writing best selling novels in 1931. Among his novels are *Hatter's Castle*, *The Stars Look Down*, *The Keys of the Kingdom*, *The Citadel*, and *Shannon's Way*. One of his more recent books, *Dr. Finlay's Casebook*, was adapted for television in England, where it became a long-running series. *For More Information See: Current Biography*, Wilson, 1942; A. J. Cronin, *Adventures in Two Worlds*, Little, Brown, 1956; *Contemporary Authors*, Volumes 1-4, revised, Gale, 1967; *Contemporary Novelists*, 2nd edition, St. Martin's, 1976. *Obituaries: Chicago Tribune*, January 10, 1981; *New York Times*, January 10, 1981; *Washington Post*, January 10, 1981; *Newsweek*, January 19, 1981; *Time*, January 19, 1981; *Publishers Weekly*, January 23, 1981; *AB Bookman's Weekly*, January 26, 1981; *Contemporary Authors*, Volume 102, Gale, 1981.

CUFFARI, Richard 1925-1978

OBITUARY NOTICE—See sketch in *SATA* Volume 6: Born March 2, 1925, in Brooklyn, N.Y.; died October 10, 1978, in Brooklyn, N.Y. Illustrator and painter. Cuffari worked for various art studios before turning to free-lance illustration in 1968. Kenneth Grahame's *The Wind in the Willows*, Jacqueline Jackson and William Perlmutter's *The Endless Pavement*, Lee Kingman's *Escape from the Evil Prophecy*, and Elizabeth Marie Pope's *The Perilous Gard* are only a few of the nearly two hundred children's books which he illustrated. Cuffari's work was featured in an American Institute of Graphic Arts children's book show and in a Children's Book Showcase of the Children's Book Council. He was honored with two Society of Illustrators Citations of Merit. Regarding his career, Cuffari once stated, "I think that working with or for children in any way is a privilege." *For More Information See: Illustrators of Books for Young People*, Scarecrow, 1975; *Illustrators of Children's Books, 1967-1976*, Horn Book, 1978. *Obituaries: School Library Journal*, December, 1978.

DAVIS, Louise Littleton 1921-

PERSONAL: Born September 7, 1921, in Paris, Tenn.; daughter of Grover C. (an army officer) and LaRue L. (a music teacher; maiden name, Littleton) Davis. *Education:* Attended Washington Univeristy, St. Louis, Mo.; Murray State Uni-

LOUISE LITTLETON DAVIS

versity, A.B.; Vanderbilt University, M.A.; further study at University of North Carolina. *Religion:* Episcopal. *Home:* 2118 Ashwood Ave., Nashville, Tenn. 37212. *Office:* 1100 Broadway, Nashville, Tenn. 37202.

CAREER: The Tennessean (newspaper), Nashville, Tenn., feature writer, 1950—. Member of Board of Editorial Advisors of *Tennessee Historical Quarterly,* 1975—. *Member:* Tennessee Press Association, Metropolitan Historical Commission, Ladies Hermitage Association, Tennessee Historical Society (vice-president), Nashville Symphony Association, Blount Mansion Association, Association for the Preservation of Virginia Antiquities, Tennessee Botanical Gardens and Fine Arts Center. *Awards, honors:* Chosen woman of the year, Nashville, Tenn., 1953; Historical Achievement Award, Metropolitan Nashville and Davidson County Historical Commission, 1974.

WRITINGS: Snowball Fight in the White House, Westminster Press, 1974; *Frontier Tales of Tennessee,* Pelican, 1976; *More Tales of Tennessee,* Pelican, 1978; (with John Egerton) *Nashville: The Faces of Two Centuries, 1780-1980,* Plus Media, 1979. Also author of the short histories, *Children's Museum of Nashville,* 1973, and *The First Seventy-Five,* 1978.

WORK IN PROGRESS: Stories of Nashville history.

SIDELIGHTS: "I have travelled through most of Europe on newspaper assignments or on international relations. I'm interested in Tennessee business and influence abroad.

"I am also enthusiastic about the Latin language and its influence on French and English languages. I have the greatest fascination with the English language and European and American history."

The wedding of Miss Pussy. ■ (From *The Golden Hen and Other Stories* by Gri. Illustrated by the author.)

DENNEY, Diana   1910-
(Gri, Diana Ross)

PERSONAL: Born July 8, 1910, in Valetta, Malta; daughter of William Jones (a commander in the Royal Navy) and Margery (maiden name, Grenfell) Ross; married Antony Denney, 1939 (divorced, 1948); children: twin daughters, Sarah and Teresa, and one son, Timothy. *Education:* Girton College, Cambridge, B.A. (with honors), 1931; attended Central School of Art, London, 1932-34. *Home:* Minster House, Shaw, Melksham, Wiltshire, England.

CAREER: Author and illustrator of books for children. Worked as an art teacher, 1930-34.

WRITINGS: Under maiden name Diana Ross, except as noted: *The World at Work,* Country Life, 1939; *The Story of the Beetle Who Lived Alone,* Faber, 1941; (with Antony Denney) *Uncle Anty's Album,* Faber, 1941; *The Golden Hen and Other Stories* (self-illustrated under pseudonym, Gri), Faber, 1942; *The Little Red Engine Gets a Name,* Faber, 1942; *The Wild Cherry* (self-illustrated under pseudonym, Gri), Faber, 1943; *Nursery Tales,* Faber, 1944; *The Story of Louisa,* Penguin, 1945; *The Story of the Little Red Engine,* Faber, 1945, reprinted, Harmondsworth, 1976; *The Little Red Engine Goes to Market,* Faber, 1945; *Whoo, Whoo, the Wind Blew,* Faber, 1946.

The Enormous Apple Pie and Other Miss Pussy Stories, Lutterworth Press, 1951; *The Tooter and Other Nursery Tales,* Faber, 1951; *The Bridal Gown and Other Stories* (self-illus-

trated under pseudonym, Gri), Faber, 1952; *The Little Red Engine Goes to Town,* Faber, 1952; *Ebenezer the Big Balloon,* Faber, 1952; *The Bran Tub* (self-illustrated under pseudonym, Gri), Lutterworth Press, 1954; *The Little Red Engine Goes Travelling,* Faber, 1955; *The Little Red Engine and the Rocket,* Faber, 1956; *William and the Lorry,* Faber, 1956; *Child of Air* (self-illustrated under pseudonym, Gri), Lutterworth Press, 1957; *The Little Red Engine Goes Home,* Faber, 1958; *The Dreadful Boy,* Hamish Hamilton, 1959.

The Merry-Go-Round, Lutterworth Press, 1963; *Old Perisher,* Faber, 1965; *The Little Red Engine Goes to Be Mended,* Faber, 1966; *Nothing to Do,* Hamish Hamilton, 1966; *The Little Red Engine and the Taddlecombe Outing,* Transatlantic, 1969; *The Little Red Engine Goes Carolling,* Transatlantic, 1971; *I Love My Love With an A: Where Is He?,* Merrimack, 1972.

WORK IN PROGRESS: Poetry, painting and sculpture.

SIDELIGHTS: "I always told stories from early childhood to my brother and sister. I began to write down my stories when I was teaching—to start the class off. I read my stories, then they read theirs. The 'Red Engine' series began as a goodnight story for my nephew John Scott who lived in a house above a railway cutting on a very branch line. Most of the nursery tale and 'true' type of story were based on incidents from family life. The ones I have most enjoyed writing have been the fairy stories written for myself—and most of all the 'Miss

Pussy' and old 'Jackanapes' stories. Gri—who illustrated some of my books when I could persuade publishers of his merits—was in fact my cat who would sit on top of my drawings as I worked on them.'' [*Twentieth Century Children's Writers*, St. Martin's Press, 1978.]

Denney has produced two kinds of stories—nursery tales for young children and magical tales for everyone—over a period of thirty years. During the 1950's when children's radio and television programs were expanding, she was a pioneer contributor.

FOR MORE INFORMATION SEE: Horn Book, January-December, 1947.

De ROO, Anne Louise   1931-

PERSONAL: Born 1931 in Gore, New Zealand; daughter of William Fredrick de Roo (a health inspector) and Amy Louisa (Hayton) de Roo. *Education:* University of Canterbury, Christchurch, New Zealand, B.A., 1952. *Home:* 38 Joseph St., Palmerston North, New Zealand. *Agent:* A.P. Watt & Son, 26-28 Bedford Row, London WC1R 4HL, England.

CAREER: Dunedin Public Library, Dunedin, New Zealand, library assistant, 1956; Dunedin Teacher's College, Dunedin, librarian, 1957-59; governess and part-time gardener in Church Preen, Shropshire, England, 1962-68; secretary in Barkway, Hertfordshire, England, 1969-73; medical typist in Palmerston North, New Zealand, 1974-78; full-time writer, 1978—.

WRITINGS—All juvenile fiction: *The Gold Dog*, Hart-Davis, 1969; *Moa Valley*, Hart-Davis, 1969; *Boy and the Sea Beast*, Hart-Davis, 1971, Scholastic Book Services, 1974; *Cinnamon and Nutmeg*, Nelson, 1974; *Mick's Country Cousins*, Macmillan (London), 1974; *Scrub Fire*, Heinemann, 1977, Atheneum, 1980; *Traveller*, Heinemann, 1979; *Because of Rosie*, Heinemann, 1980.

Plays: (With John Schwabe) *The Dragon Master* (children's musical, first produced in Palmerston North, New Zealand, 1978.)

WORK IN PROGRESS: The second of two books dealing with the rebellion of the Maori chief Hone Heke in 1844-45, for children; a second children's musical in collaboration with John Schwabe.

SIDELIGHTS: Realizing that the fiction of Europe and North America presents setting unnatural to a New Zealand child, Anne de Roo's goal is to create good stories with settings familiar to the children of her native land. de Roo characterizes herself as ''a New Zealand writer, principally concerned with the building up in a young country of a children's literature through which children can identify themselves and their roots, whether European or Maori.'' An added purpose of de Roo's writing is to expose children of other parts of the world to New Zealand culture. ''I do delight in having this additional usefulness as well, although I will always feel that my chief responsibility is to young New Zealanders.''

De Roo spent twelve years in England where her first five books were written. She regards those years as a period of growth ''which enabled me to return with a new perspective and a new and deeper appreciation of the natural beauty of

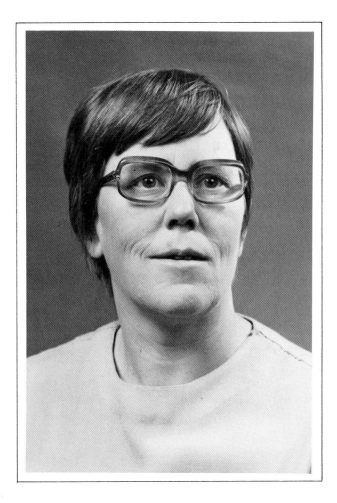

ANNE LOUISE DE ROO

New Zealand's forests, mountains and sea. It has also given me the opportunity to concentrate in the last few years on historical stories, for which I now have the material available for research.''

De Roo feels the need to ''branch out from time to time into the realms of fantasy and fairy tale'' as an escape from what she terms her ''basically European reading and education.'' She has done this primarily through musical theatre for children. ''The theatre is a lifelong love and much of my spare time is devoted to amateur theatre, which is particularly strong in a small country with little scope for professional theatre. The spoken word, its sounds and possibilities, has always fascinated me, from youthful poetry writing onwards and even in books the dialogue is the part in which I always feel most at home.''

Read not to contradict and confute, nor yet to believe and take for granted, nor to find talk and discourse, but to weigh and consider.

—Francis Bacon

DOMJAN, Joseph 1907-

PERSONAL: Born March 15, 1907, in Budapest, Hungary; naturalized American citizen since 1962; married Evelyn (a graphic artist), March 13, 1944; children: Alma, Michael Paul, Daniel George. *Education:* Attended Royal Academy of Fine Arts, Budapest, Hungary, Master Diploma, 1935-42. *Home:* Tuxedo Park, N.Y. 10987.

CAREER: Artist. Hungarian Royal Academy of Fine Arts, Budapest, Hungary, assistant professor of fine arts, 1941-42; self-employed woodcut artist in Budapest, Hungary, 1942-56, in Switzerland, 1956-57, in United States, 1957—. Work exhibited at one-man shows in Scandinavia, 1948, fifteen one-man shows in China, 1955, in Geneva, Switzerland, 1956, and in America at one-man shows at museums, libraries, and universities, including Cincinnati Art Museum, Georgia Museum of Art Works, mostly color woodcuts, in permanent collections of more than a hundred museums on three continents, among them Victoria and Albert Museum, Metropolitan Museum of Art, Bibliotheque National, Smithsonian Institution, Library of Congress. Lecturer and author.

MEMBER: Metropolitan Museum of Art (life fellow), Print Council of America, American Color Print Society, Silvermine Guild of Artists, Goetheanum (Switzerland), Society of Illustrators, Society of American Graphic Artists, Societe d'Encouragement au Progres (Paris), National Academy of Design, National Register of Prominent Americans. *Awards, honors:* National Salon prize, 1936; Fine Arts Hall prize, 1941; Nemes Mercell prize, 1942; purchase award, Johansen Abstract Collection, 1948; purchase award, International Color Woodcut Exhibition, Victoria and Albert Museum, 1950; purchase award, International Exhibition of Graphic Arts, and Mihaly Zichy Prize for Graphic Arts, 1952; Munkacsy Prize of Fine Arts and "Master of the Color Woodcut" (China), 1955; Kossuth Prize of Fine Arts, 1956; Rockefeller Foundation grant, 1957; Printmaker of 1961, Print Club of Albany, 1961; book awards from National Educational Society and American Institute of Graphic Arts, 1964; award of faithfulness, Washington-Kossuth Historical Society, 1966; Sonia Watter Award, American Color Print Society, and award of merit, Society of Illustrators, 1967; award of excellence, Society of Illustrators, 1968; silver medal and diploma, Societe d'Encouragement au Progres, 1969; medal of honor, Hungarian Helicon Society, George Washington award, American Hungarian Studies Foundation, and silver medal and diploma, International Academy of Literature, Arts and Science, 1970; Kasser Art Foundation fellowship, 1971; Chapelbrook Foundation grant, 1972; Rakoczi award, Sarospatak, Hungary, 1976; Rakoczi award, Toronto, 1980. *Exhibitions*—permanent collections: Domjan Museum, Sarospatak, Hungary; Domjan Gallery, Schweinfurt Memorial Art Center, Auburn, N.Y.

JOSEPH DOMJAN

Bell Eagle. ■ (From *Wing Beat,* a collection of eagle woodcuts by Joseph Domjan.)

in the river in a triple coffin of iron, silver, gold—it was my childhood fantasy to find his treasures. Magnificent Scythian archeological gold treasures of deer was a national heritage in Hungary. I did find the gold treasures; they became an inexhaustible source of inspiration with the clear source of folk art from which my art derived and came into blossoming. Remembrances of peasant villages and wood carved doors are still alive in my heart; as well as girls in ornate costumes crowned in beaded head-dresses in the folk art tradition of people blessed with talent and fantasy.

"I have written books of folk tales for children four to eight years old, like *The Proud Peacock, The Little Cock, I Went to the Market,* etc. Another world opened during my trip to China and Mongolia, my meeting with the venerable Master Chi-pai-shi in China. Chinese legends and stories are in my book *The Artist and the Legend* for eight to twelve years old. I was involved in tradition and history and [one of my last] books, *Pacatus, a Trademark from Antiquity,* is on the history of art and industry. It tells about Pacatus, the owner of a brick factory and the trademark—a running chicken—of industry in ancient Pompeii and air pollution, a problem of 2,000 years ago, up to the latest development of technical innovations that serve archeology and museology.

"The sound of the waterfall in the forest of Tuxedo Park plays the background music. Deer walk in the forest and eat my daylilies. . . . Art and nature, legends and beauty of the earth and beauty man created around the world will forever give me new ideas . . . but even more than words, my art, my woodcuts, my colors tell the stories, the pictures talk to children of all ages and to all young at heart. They speak to peoples of all languages, this is my message—images of joy and beauty. . . .''

FOR MORE INFORMATION SEE: Hans Vollmer, *Algemeines Lexicon den Bildenden Kunstler,* Volume I, 1953; John R. Biggs, *Woodcuts,* Bradford Press, 1958; *Library Journal,* March 15, 1970.

WRITINGS—Self-illustrated and designed: *Wildflowers,* Medimpex (Budapest), 1954; (fine arts editor) *Hunyadi* (album), [Budapest], 1956; *32 Color Woodcuts,* Corvina (Budapest), 1956; *Ungarische Legende,* Atlantis Verlag (Zurich), 1957; *Henry Hudson of the River,* Art Edge, 1959; *Janos Hunyadi: 10 Woodcuts,* Art Edge, 1960; *Hungarian Heroes and Legends,* Van Nostrand, 1963; *Peacock Festival,* Art Edge, 1964; *The Proud Peacock,* Holt, 1965; *The Little Princess Goodnight,* Holt, 1966; *Domjan the Woodcutter* (monograph) Art Edge, 1966; *The Fifteen Decisive Battles of the World,* Limited Editions Club, 1969; *The Little Cock,* Lippincott, 1969; *Hungarian Song,* American Hungarian Literary Guild, 1969; *Domjan Portfolio,* Art Edge, 1970; *I Went to the Market,* Holt, 1970; *Faraway Folk Tales,* Holt, 1972; *Domjan, In the Forest of the Golden Dragon,* Pierre Mornnand, 1973; *Domjan, Arte,* Ancona, 1973; *Bellringer* (poems by Ruth Laurene; woodcuts by Domjan), Opus, 1975; *The Artist . . . and the Legend: A Visit to China Is Remembered and the Legends Unfold. . .,* Domjan Studio, 1976; *Wing Beat* (eagle woodcuts by Domjan), Domjan Studio, 1976; *Pacatus, a Trademark from Antiquity,* [Paris], 1979; *Edge of Paradise,* Domjan Studio, 1979; *Sungates* (woodcuts by Domjan), Domjan Studio, 1980; *Toldi,* Helicon (Budapest), 1981.

SIDELIGHTS: "I grew up with folk tales, fairy tales, legends of the miraculous deer that lured the twin brothers, Hunor and Magor, westward in their hunt toward the Karpathian basin— that is how the legend tells about the migration of the peoples. Attila the Hun was drinking from a golden cup, he was buried

DOWNER, Marion   1892(?)-1971

PERSONAL: Born about 1892; died October 6, 1971. *Education:* Began her art training in her Spokane, Washington, high school under Josephine Guilbert; attended the Chicago Art Institute; continued her studies in London, New York, and Paris.

CAREER: Artist, illustrator, author of books for young people. Marion Downer wrote eleven books for children and illustrated several others. *Awards, honors:* Recipient of the Children's Spring Book Festival Award, older children's category, for *The Story of Design,* 1964.

WRITINGS—All for children: *Be an Artist* (self-illustrated), Lothrop, 1941; *My Room Is My Hobby* (self-illustrated), Lothrop, 1942; *Guess Who I Am,* Lothrop, 1944; *Discovering Design* (ALA Notable Book), Lothrop, 1947; *Paul Cezanne,* Lothrop, 1951; (with Yolla Niclas) *David and the Sea Gulls,* Lothrop, 1956; *Kites: How to Make and Fly Them* (photographs by Frank J. Miller), Lothrop, 1959; *The Story of Design* (ALA Notable Book), Lothrop, 1963; *Roofs over America* (ALA Notable Book), Lothrop, 1967; *Long Ago in Florence: The Story of the Della Robbia Sculpture* (illustrated by Mamoru Funai), Lothrop, 1968; *Children in the World's Art,* Lothrop, 1970.

. . . Just leave your kite in a tree for next year's birds to nest in . . . . ■ (From *Kites: How to Make and Fly Them* by Marion Downer. Photograph by Frank J. Miller.)

Illustrator: Helen E. Stiles, *Pottery of the Ancients*, Dutton, 1938; Frances Margaret Fox, *Little Mossback Amelia*, Dutton, 1939; H. E. Stiles, *Pottery of the American Indians*, Dutton, 1939; H. E. Stiles, *Pottery of the Europeans*, Dutton, 1940; Marian Johnston, *Snow House*, Dutton, 1940; H. E. Stiles, *Pottery of the United States*, Dutton, 1941; Edith L. Johnson, *Log Cabin Children*, Lothrop, 1942; Verna Hills, *Here's Suzy!*, Lothrop, 1948.

SIDELIGHTS: "The first time my drawing attracted attention, the result was mortifying. I was in the sixth grade and had made a poster which the teacher thought very fine. She sent me carrying it to other rooms, even the awesome eighth grade room, where I stood holding it, as I'd been told for all to see. What killed all the pride I might have had in the drawing, was a misspelled word in the lettering, which someone in each room pointed out. There was no 'e' on the word, 'come.'

"To this day, in writing books, I make frightful errors. By writing *Discovering Design*, I learned that the word 'rhythm' has two h's. By writing Paul Cézanne, I learned to spell 'easel.' It is not 'easle' as I had thought. The editors patiently correct me.

"The poster incident was embarrassing, but my first story writing experience was fun, for the class laughed heartily when the teacher read aloud a simple joke on myself which I had written. My story related how the boy next door had fooled me by pretending to take my picture while I has posed my prettiest with our fat black cat on my lap. The point was the silly prankster's confession next day that he had had no film in his camera and my scorn for all boys next door. The class enjoyed this tale but they laughed with more friendly fun at what happened next. The teacher asked me to rise but my skirt was caught in the folding seat and I was yanked back with a flop.

"I went to school out on the other side of the Rocky Mountains, in Spokane, Washington, where I was born. When I was finishing high school, the kind and understanding teachers put their heads together, as teachers do, and told me I must go to art school when I graduated for I had been all ears in art and English classes and hard to arouse from dreams in others.

"My mother said that New York was far too distant from the Pacific Coast for one so young and listless. Chicago became my goal. I arrived there alone and I forgot the name of the art school whose ad we had seen in a magazine because an enormous art school and museum towered in plain view on Michigan Boulevard. I climbed the steps and enrolled at one of the greatest art schools in the world, the Chicago Art Institute.

"To dare the far-away New York was an idea that seemed imperative after a few years. Here, I went to another great school, the Art Students' League, but only to evening classes because I was earning my every dollar by drawing advertising. Later I took myself to Paris and to London for study in schools but above all, to see the museums.

"Some day, I believe, great philosophers will make us all understand that the food the world most needs is to be found in the finest art and in the finest books."

Downer's works are included in the Kerlan Collection at the University of Minnesota.

FOR MORE INFORMATION SEE: Horn Book, January-December, 1947, June, 1959; *New York Herald Tribune,* December 16, 1951; *Christian Science Monitor,* January 16, 1964. Obituary: *Publishers Weekly,* November 8, 1971.

MARION DOWNER

DUGGAN, Alfred Leo   1903-1964

PERSONAL: Born in 1903, in Buenos Aires, Argentina; emigrated with his family to England in 1905; died April 4, 1964; son of Alfred Hubert and Grace (Hinds) Duggan; married Laura Hill, 1953; children: one son. *Education:* Attended Eton College and Balliol College, Oxford University. *Home:* Herefordshire, England.

CAREER: Author of historical fiction and books for young people. Collected specimens for the British National Museum, which took him all over the world. After 1941, and for the remainder of World War II, Duggan worked in an airplane factory. *Military service:* Served in the London Irish Rifles (T.A.) in Norway, 1938-41, until given a medical discharge. *Member:* St. James' Club.

WRITINGS—For children: *The Castle Book* (illustrated by Raymond Briggs), Pantheon, 1960 (published in England as *Look at Castles*, H. Hamilton, 1960); *Look at Churches* (illustrated by R. Briggs), H. Hamilton, 1961, published in America as *Arches and Spires: A Short History of English Churches from Anglo-Saxon Times,* Pantheon, 1962; *Growing Up in Thirteenth Century England* (ALA Notable Book; illustrated by C. W. Hodges), Pantheon, 1962 (published in England as *Growing Up in the Thirteenth Century,* Faber, 1962); *The Romans* (illustrated by Richard M. Powers), World Publishing, 1964; *Growing Up with the Norman Conquest* (illustrated by C. W. Hodges), Faber, 1965, Pantheon, 1966.

Historical fiction: *Knight with Armour,* Coward, 1950, reissued, New English Library, 1973; *Conscience of the King,* Coward, 1951, reprinted, Faber, 1962; *Thomas Becket of Canterbury,* Faber, 1952, published in America as *The Falcon and the Dove: A Life of Thomas Becket of Canterbury,* Pantheon, 1966; *The Little Emperors,* Coward, 1953, reprinted, Faber, 1963; *The Lady for Ransom,* Coward, 1953, reissued, New English Library, 1973; *Leopards and Lilies,* Coward, 1954, reissued, Chatto & Windus, 1971; *My Life for My Sheep,* Coward, 1955 [another edition illustrated by Georg Hartmann, Image Books, 1957; published in England as *God and My Right,* Faber, 1955, reprinted, 1963]; *Julius Ceasar: A Great Life in Brief,* Knopf, 1955, reprinted, 1966; *Winter Quarters,* Coward, 1956.

Devil's Brood (illustrated by G. Hartmann), Coward, 1957; *He Died Old: Mithradates Eupator, King of Pontus,* Faber, 1958, published in America as *King of Pontus: The Life of Mithradates Eupator,* Coward, 1959; *Three's Company,* Coward, 1958; *Children of the Wolf,* Coward, 1959 (published in England as *Founding Fathers,* Faber, 1959, reissued, P. Davies, 1972); *Family Favourites,* Faber, 1960, Pantheon, 1963, reissued, P. Davies, 1973; *The Cunning of the Dove,* Pantheon, 1960, reissued, Image Books, 1966; *The Right Line of Cerdic,* Pantheon, 1961 (published in England as *The King of Anthelney,* Faber, 1961); *Lord Geoffrey's Fancy,* Pantheon, 1962; *Besieger of Cities,* Pantheon, 1963 (published in England as *Elephants and Castles,* Faber, 1963); *The Story of the Crusades, 1097-1291* (illustrated by C. Walter Hodges), Faber, 1963, Pantheon, 1964; *Count Bohemond,* Faber, 1964, Pantheon, 1965.

Other: (Author of introduction) William A. Taylor, *Historical Fiction,* Cambridge University Press, 1957.

ALFRED LEO DUGGAN

Though peasants work hard, the Church provides them with generous holidays . . . . ■ (From *Growing Up in Thirteenth Century England* by Alfred Duggan. Illustrated by C. Walter Hodges.)

SIDELIGHTS: In 1924, Duggan sailed a 600-ton barquentine from England to the Galapagos Islands, becoming one of the few people to cross the Atlantic Ocean under sail.

Duggan began his writing career in 1950. The *New York Times* review of *Besieger of Cities* said, ''[The author] has combined wit and scholarship to provide his readers with an insight into a complex age through the re-creation of a character whom previous biographers had reduced to caricature. His Demetrius has the complexity of a credible cosmopolite. His third-century B.C. settings have the authenticity of controlled scho-larship. . . . His style has the urbanity of the age he is dramatizing, and his characters become intelligible as they lead the reader to understanding.''

Of *The Romans,* the *Christian Science Monitor* wrote, ''The author succeeds by giving 12's-on-up the bare bones of Roman history largely devoid of color and spectacle usually associated with that city. In its way this is all to the good for the reader gains a beginning understanding of the political movements and clashes of factions. . . .'' *Horn Book* commented that ''although the author's factual accuracy is beyond reproach, his style seems excessively chatty and informal, and his statements are occasionally moralistic.''

The Falcon and the Dove: A Life of Thomas Becket of Canterbury, published posthumously in America, was reviewed by a *Saturday Review* critic, who wrote, ''Always impressive by the extent to which he could simultaneously entertain and instruct, the late Mr. Duggan is again superb. His candid, percipient biography of Becket gives a marvelous picture of the intricacies of twelfth-century feudal society and of the complexity of the relations between Church and State.''

FOR MORE INFORMATION SEE: J. K. Hutchens, ''On an Author,'' *New York Herald Tribune Book Review*, January 17, 1954; ''Some Important Fall Authors Speak for Themselves,'' *New York Herald Tribune Book Review*, October 24, 1954; Stanley J. Kunitz, editor, *Twentieth Century Authors*, first supplement, H. W. Wilson, 1955; E. Waugh, ''Alfred Duggan: In Memoriam,'' *America*, October 24, 1964; ''Fiction of 1972: Alfred Duggan,'' *The Times Literary Supplement, 1969-1973*, Oxford University Press, 1970-74; Doris de Montreville and Elizabeth D. Crawford, editors, *Fourth Book of Junior Authors & Illustrators*, H. W. Wilson, 1978. Obituaries—*New York Times*, April 5, 1964; *History Today*, June, 1964; *London Spectator*, July 10, 1964.

Most of the basic material a writer works with is acquired before the age of fifteen.

—Willa Cather

DUNCOMBE, Frances (Riker) 1900-

PERSONAL: Born July 11, 1900; daughter of Chandler White (a lawyer) and Millie (Snyder) Riker; married Herbert S. Duncombe, Jr. (a lawyer), June 27, 1925; children: Herbert S. III, David, Cynthia Duncombe Caldwell. *Education:* Attended Miss Porter's School at Farmington, Ethel Walker School, Bryn Mawr College, New York School of Fine and Applied Arts, and Columbia University. *Home:* Mount Holly Rd., Cross River, N.Y. 10518.

CAREER: Writer, mainly of youth books.

WRITINGS: Hoo DeWitt, Holt; *High Hurdles*, Holt, 1941; *Clarinda*, Holt, 1944; *Eemi, the Story of a Clown*, Holt, 1946; *Ghost at Garnet Lodge*, Sloane, 1949; *Death of a Spinster*, Scribner, 1958; (with others) *Katonah: A History of a New York Village and Its People*, Katonah Village Improvement Society, 1961; *Cassie's Village*, Lothrop, 1965; *The Quetzal Feather*, Lothrop, 1967; *Summer of the Burning* (illustrated by Richard Cuffari), Putman, 1976.

FOR MORE INFORMATION SEE: Publishers Weekly, February 23, 1976.

Hannah sat beside Ma on the mattress. Everything that had been home all her life was going.
■ (From *Summer of the Burning* by Frances Duncombe. Illustrated by Richard Cuffari.)

MAITLAND A. EDEY

EDEY, Maitland A(rmstrong) 1910-

PERSONAL: Born February 13, 1910, in New York, N.Y.; son of Alfred (a stockbroker) and Marion (a writer; maiden name, Armstrong) Edey; married Helen Winthrop Kellogg (a physician), April 24, 1934; children: Maitland A., Jr., Winthrop K., Beatrice Edey Phear, Marion Edey. *Education:* Princeton University, A.B., 1932. *Politics:* Independent. *Religion:* None. *Home:* 1199 Park Ave., New York, N.Y. 10028.

CAREER: Messenger on Wall Street, 1932-33; clerk for book publishers in New York, 1933-41; *Life*, New York, N.Y., 1941-55, began as editor of "Speaking of Pictures" section, became assistant managing editor; free-lance writer, 1955-60; Time-Life Books, New York, N.Y., 1960-70, began as series editor, became editor-in-chief; free-lance writer, 1972—. Trustee, 1946-62, and mayor, 1958-62, of Incorporated Village of Upper Brookville, N.Y.; director of New York Philharmonic Symphony Society, 1950-75; trustee of Putney School 1958-74; chairman of advisory council of Old Westbury College, 1967-72; member of corporation of Woods Hole Oceanographic Institution, 1968-73; director of Conservation Foundation, Washington, D.C., 1969—; director of Scudder Special Fund (mutual fund), 1961—, trustee of Felix Neck Wildlife Trust, 1973—, and Sheriff's Meadow Foundation, 1978—.

Military service: U.S. Army Air Forces, Intelligence, 1942-46; became major; received Legion of Merit and presidential citation. *Member:* Century Club (New York), Coffee House Club (New York).

WRITINGS: American Songbirds, Random House, 1940; *American Waterbirds,* Random House, 1941; (with F. Clark Howell) *Early Man,* Time-Life, 1965; *The Cats of Africa,* Time-Life, 1968; *The Northeast Coast,* Time-Life, 1972; *The Missing Link,* Time-Life, 1973; *The Sea Traders,* Time-Life, 1974; *The Lost World of the Aegean,* Time-Life, 1975; *Great Photo Essays From Life,* New York Graphic, 1978; *Lucy: The Beginnings of Humankind,* Simon & Schuster, 1982.

WORK IN PROGRESS: "I am now planning a general work for the layman on the latest ideas and interpretations of Darwinian evolution."

SIDELIGHTS: "Never confident in my ability to earn a living as a writer, I went into the book publishing business instead, nearly starved there, and didn't really manage any kind of a respectable career in the writing or publishing world until I went to work for *Life* magazine in 1941. There I found myself writing short articles to go with picture stories every week, and occasionally longer ones. I enjoyed this and gained more confidence as a writer, but was escalated into managerial duties, so I resigned in 1955 to devote myself full-time to fiction. That was a disaster. I have several completed and partly complete novels in the back of my desk, plus a number of short stories. Some I wrote at that time, some later. None have been published.

"In 1960 I returned to Time Inc., this time as an editor of its newly-formed book division. Again I had opportunities to write, this time book-length works. I learned that any talent I had was for non-fiction—for explaining to others, in as interesting ways as I could, things that interested me. My fields of choice are natural history, archeology, and lately the emergence and evolution of man. I find that subject utterly fascinating, and its complexities a great challenge.

"If my experience has any lesson to offer, it is that a writer should stick to his last; learn what he is best at, polish that, and forget other forms that he has no talent for, whatever their allure to him.

"Having dealt for many years now, both as an editor and a writer, with subjects that are monitored by career professionals, I have learned that too often the professionals—particularly in the field of art—take an elitist view of their domains, and are scornful of efforts to make them accessible to the layman. There are notable exceptions, of course. One who comes to mind is the late Harlow Shapley, whose popular explanations of the cosmos are magnificent. Another is George Gaylord Simpson, whose writings about evolution, while not aimed at the layman, are accessible to him. Others are less cooperative with the public; some are downright hostile to it, and I find this shocking. I think that it is of critical importance, in a world increasingly dominated by the sciences, that public knowledge about it be made as readily available and as palatable as possible. I am happy that I have been able to find a congenial niche there. I believe that clarity is the writer's first responsibility, and take the position that anything I can comprehend I should be able to make comprehensible to the reader. The art—with which I struggle endlessly—comes in making interesting what you have made comprehensible."

HOBBIES AND OTHER INTERESTS: Ornithology, photography, reading, and music.

This Minoan wine press, from about 1600 B.C., was found in the service quarters of a villa at Vathy Petro in central Crete. ■ (From *Lost World of the Aegean* by Maitland A. Edey. Photograph courtesy of Deutsches Archäologisches Institut, Athens.)

EDWARDS, Cecile (Pepin)   1916-

PERSONAL: Born June 24, 1916, in Medfield, Mass.; daughter of Joseph Amedee (a freight agent) and Lauda (Southiere) Pepin; married Wilfred Carl Edwards (a textile finisher), December 28, 1941; married (second husband) Ernest L. Hyatt, July 20, 1974; children: (first marriage) Carl Normand, Johnathan Hayes, David Wayne, Gloria Marie. *Education:* Wheelock College, student, 1934-37; University of New Hampshire, library courses, summer, 1957; Keene State College, B.S. Ed., 1971; Franklin Pierce College, student in anthropology, 1969-70; completed writing masters program with the Institute of Children's Literature, 1980; private study of piano for fifteen years. *Address:* 318 Townsend Rd., Mason, N.H. 03048.

CAREER: Wrentham State School, Wrentham, Mass., teacher of retarded children, 1939-41; Norfolk Central School, Norfolk, Mass., first grade teacher, 1955-57; Walpole Public Library, Walpole, Mass., children's librarian, 1957-59; Vogel School, Wrentham, Mass., teacher, 1965-69; Rindge Memorial School, Rindge, N.H., elementary school teacher, 1971-79; free-lance writer. *Member:* New Hampshire Teacher's Association (retired member), National Education Association.

WRITINGS: Luck for the Jolly Gale, Abingdon, 1947; *Party for Suzanne,* Abingdon, 1952; *Champlain, Father of New France,* Abingdon, 1955; *Roger Williams, Defender of Free-*

dom, Abingdon, 1957; *Horace Mann, Sower of Learning,* Houghton, 1958; *King Philip, Loyal Indian,* Houghton, 1962; *Days of Radiance,* Golden Quill Press, 1964; *John Alden, Steadfast Pilgrim,* Houghton, 1965; *Origin of North American Indians* (first in a series of eight), National Educators for Creative Instruction. Contributor of articles, poems and stories to *Wee Wisdom, Christian Science Monitor, Highlights for Children, Parents, Horn Book, Catholic World,* and other periodicals.

WORK IN PROGRESS: Birds of Fire for Beta Books; two more books in the series, *Origins of North American Indians.*

SIDELIGHTS: "As a child, my overwhelming ambition was to become a great pianist, like Myra Hess. I practiced hours and hours. At Wheelock teacher's college I became interested in writing for children and have been writing ever since.

"I like to get at my writing early in the morning. Although I aim for at least four uninterrupted hours, it doesn't always work out that way. When there's a deadline to meet, though, it means staying with it until I have finished my quota. There is a great deal of research involved in the work I do, so I have to spend much time in libraries and museums.

"I hope my stories will help readers to see that children who lived long ago were very much like the children of today. They

CECILE EDWARDS

may have worn different clothes and had different problems to solve. But they used whatever resources they had in solving these problems. They laughed, cried, fought, failed, and won, just as do the children of today.''

HOBBIES AND OTHER INTERESTS: Music, gathering folk tales and stories about the Algonquin Indians, growing herbs and experimenting with them.

FOR MORE INFORMATION SEE: Horn Book, January-December, 1947.

There is no frigate like a book
To take us lands away,
Nor any coursers like a page
Of prancing poetry.

This traverse may the poorest take
Without oppress of toll;
How frugal is the chariot
That bears a human soul.

                                                    —Emily Dickinson

EHRLICH, Amy   1942-

PERSONAL: Born July 24, 1942, in New York, N.Y.; daughter of Max (an author) and Doris (Rubenstein) Ehrlich; children: One son, Joss. *Education:* Bennington College, student, 1960-62, 1963-65. *Address:* 379 6th St., Brooklyn, N.Y. 11215.

CAREER: Early jobs for short periods included teacher in day care center, fabric colorist, and hospital receptionist; Dial Press, New York, N.Y., children's book editor, 1978—.

*WRITINGS—*Juveniles: *Zeek Silver Moon,* Dial, 1972; (adapter) *Wounded Knee,* Holt, 1974; *The Everyday Train* (illustrated by Martha Alexander), Dial, 1976; (reteller) Hans Christian Andersen, *Tumbelina* (pictures by Susan Jeffers), Dial, 1979; (reteller) Hans Christian Andersen, *The Wild Swans* (pictures by Susan Jeffers), Dial, 1981; *Leo, Zack, and Emmie* (illustrated by Steven Kellogg), Dial, 1981.

WORK IN PROGRESS: ''I am working on a novel for nine-to-twelve year olds in the science fiction genre, and on a sports story for beginning readers, ages seven to nine.''

SIDELIGHTS: ''I am working on being a professional. Editing children's books is valuable experience in structure and style. And having a son of my own is valuable insight into the reality of today's children. The forms I am presently working in are fantasy and comedy. Children are very keyed into both, I think.''

FOR MORE INFORMATION SEE: Publishers Weekly, February 28, 1977.

If she was reading a book, she stopped in the middle. ∎
(From *The Everyday Train* by Amy Ehrlich. Illustrated by Martha Alexander.)

Starfish stranded at Orchard Beach, New York. Notice their trails in the sand and the specimen on the lower left trying to right itself. ■ (From *Wonders of Starfish* by Morris K. Jacobson and William K. Emerson. Photograph courtesy of American Museum of Natural History.)

EMERSON, William K(eith) 1925-

PERSONAL: Born May 1, 1925, in San Diego, Calif.; son of Horace Paine and Vera (Vaught) Emerson. *Education:* San Diego State College (now California State Univeristy), A.B., 1948; University of Southern California, M.S., 1950; University of California, Berkeley, Ph.D., 1956. *Home:* 10 East End Ave., New York, N.Y. 10021. *Office:* American Museum of National History, Central Park W. at 79th St., New York, N.Y. 10024.

CAREER: Malacologist. Univeristy of California, Museum of Paleontology, Berkeley, paleontologist, 1950-55; American Museum of Natural History, New York, N.Y., assistant curator, 1955-61, associate curator, 1961-66, curator of living vertebrates, 1966—, chairman of department, 1960-74; San Diego Museum of Natural History, research associate, 1962—. Leader of "Puritan" American Museum expedition to western Mexico, 1957; member of Belvedere expedition to Gulf of California, 1962.

WILLIAM K. EMERSON

MEMBER: American Association for the Advancement of Science (fellow), American Malacological Union (president, 1961-62), Society of Systematic Zoology (member of council, 1960-63), Paleontological Society, Western Society of Malacologists (president, 1969-70).

WRITINGS: (With M. K. Jacobson) *Shells of the New York City Area,* Argonaut Books, 1961, revised edition published as *Shells from Cape Cod to Cape May with Special Reference to the New York Area,* Dover, 1971; (with M. K. Jacobson) *Wonders of the World of Shells: Sea, Land, and Freshwater,* Dodd, 1971; (with Andreas Feininger, illustrator) *Shells,* Viking, 1972; (with Arnold Ross) *Wonders of Barnacles,* Dodd, 1974; (with M. K. Jacobson) *American Museum of Natural History: Guide to Shells, Land, Freshwater and Marine, from Nova Scotia to Florida,* Knopf, 1976; (with M. K. Jacobson) *Wonders of Starfish,* Dodd, 1977; (with G. D. Saunders) *Spotter's Guide to Shells,* Mayflower, 1979. Contributor to encyclopedias; contributor of articles and reviews to scientific journals.

WORK IN PROGRESS: A book on mollusks.

SIDELIGHTS: "I had the very good fortune of being introduced to the magical world of nature at an early age. My mother enrolled me in natural history classes at the San Diego Zoo and Natural History Museum. I became fascinated by the seemingly endless variety of the invertebrates, the animals without backbones. At first, I collected and raised butterflies and moths,

from the eggs to the adults, and later my interests became fixed on sea shells, when my grandmother gave me a collection of large and colorful specimens from the South Seas. My first job as a teenager was mounting butterflies at the San Diego Natural History Museum, for which I received twenty cents per hour. I helped the keeper of reptiles of the San Diego Zoo by trapping rodents to use for food for the snakes, and he in turn provided me with shedded snake skins for my collection.

"As museum scientist, I have long recognized the need to communicate the wonders of nature to the lay person. My popular books, juvenile and adult, hopefully have achieved this goal."

HOBBIES AND OTHER INTERESTS: New world archaeology and pre-Columbian artifacts.

FOR MORE INFORMATION SEE: Publishers Weekly, February 28, 1977; *Horn Book,* June, 1978.

ENRIGHT, D(ennis) J(oseph) 1920-

PERSONAL: Born on March 11, 1920, in Leamington, Warwickshire, England; son of George and Grace (Cleaver) Enright; married Madeleine Harders, 1949; children: Dominique (daughter). *Education:* Downing College, Cambridge Univer-

D. J. ENRIGHT

sity, B.A., 1944, M.A., 1946; University of Alexandria, D. Litt., 1949. *Agent:* Bolt & Watson Ltd., 8/12 Old Queen St., London, S.W.1, England.

CAREER: University of Alexandria, Alexandria, Egypt, assistant lecturer in English, 1947-50; University of Birmingham, Birmingham, England, extra-mural lecturer, 1950-53; Konan University, Kobe, Japan, visiting professor, 1953-56; Free University of Berlin, Berlin, Germany, visiting professor, 1956-57; Chulalongkorn University, Bangkok, Thailand, British Council Professor, 1957-59; University of Singapore, Singapore, professor of English, 1960-70. *Encounter,* joint editor, 1970-72; Chatto & Windus Ltd., Publishers, London, director, 1974—. *Member:* Royal Society of Literature (fellow; London).

WRITINGS: A Commentary on Goethe's "Faust", New Directions, 1949; *The Laughing Hyena and Other Poems,* Routledge & Kegan Paul, 1953; *Academic Year,* Secker & Warburg, 1955; *The World of Dew: Aspects of Living Japan,* Secker & Warburg, 1955; (editor) *Poets of the 1950's,* Kenkyusha (Tokyo), 1955; *Bread Rather than Blossoms,* Secker & Warburg, 1956; *Heaven Knows Where,* Secker & Warburg, 1957; *The Apothecary's Shop,* Secker & Warburg, 1957; (editor with T. Ninomiya) *The Poetry of Living Japan,* Grove, 1957; *Insufficient Poppy,* Chatto & Windus, 1960; *Some Men are Brothers,* Chatto & Windus, 1960; (editor with E. de Chickera) *English Critical Texts,* Oxford University Press, 1962; *Addictions,* Chatto & Windus, 1962; *Figures of Speech,* Heinemann, 1965; *The Old Adam,* Chatto & Windus, 1965; *Conspirators and Poets,* Chatto & Windus, 1966; *Unlawful Assembly,* Wesleyan University Press, 1968; *Selected Poems,* Chatto & Windus, 1969; *Memoirs of a Mendicant Professor,* Chatto & Windus, 1969; *Shakespeare and the Student,* Chatto & Windus, 1970, Schocken, 1971; *The Typewriter Revolution and Other Poems,* New York Library Press, 1971; *Daughters of Earth,* Chatto & Windus, 1972; *Foreign Devils,* Covent Gardens Press, 1972; *Man Is an Onion: Essays and Reviews,* Chatto & Windus, 1972, LaSalle, Illinois, Library Press, 1973; *The Terrible Shears: Scenes from a Twenties Childhood,* Chatto & Windus, 1973, Wesleyan University Press, 1974; *Rhymes Times Rhyme* (juvenile), Chatto & Windus, 1974; *Sad Ires and Others,* Chatto & Windus, 1975; (editor) *A Choice of Milton's Verse,* Faber, 1975; (editor) Samuel Johnson, *Rasselas,* Penguin, 1976; *The Joke Shop* (juvenile), McKay, 1976; *Paradise Illustrated,* Chatto & Windus, 1978; *Wild Ghost Chase* (juvenile), Chatto & Windus, 1978, Merrimack, 1980; *A Faust Book,* Oxford University Press, 1979; *Beyond Land's End* (juvenile), Chatto & Windus, 1979, Merrimack, 1980; (editor) *The Oxford Book of Contemporary Verse 1945-1980,* Oxford University Press, 1980; (editor) *Collected Poems,* Oxford University Press, 1981.

WORK IN PROGRESS: Currently compiling *The Oxford Book of Death,* for publication by Oxford University Press, publication expected in 1983.

SIDELIGHTS: "Three reasons why I began—and then continued—to write for children: (1) as a publisher I perceived that sales of children's books were healthier than those of adult books (at least the adult books I wrote myself); (2) as a writer I knew that the important thing for a writer is to *write,* no matter what; (3) I found that writing for children (or for my dream notion of children) permits a greater imaginative freedom than writing for adults, since children are more liberal as readers, or more versatile, and do not insist that the writer stays within the limits of a set genre."

Danny really liked to suck his thumb. ■ (From *Danny and His Thumb* by Kathryn F. Ernst. Illustrated by Tomie de Paola.)

ERNST, Kathryn (Fitzgerald) 1942-

PERSONAL: Born November 12, 1942, in New York, N.Y.; daughter of Joseph Michael (a physician) and Helen Ann (a social worker; maiden name, Dougherty) Fitzgerald; married John Lyman Ernst, December 11, 1971 (divorced, April, 1977). *Education:* Wells College, B.A., 1963; New York University, graduate study, 1963-64. *Residence:* New York, N.Y. *Office:* A. G. Becker, 55 Water St., New York, N.Y.

CAREER: Prentice-Hall, Inc., Englewood Cliffs, N.J., assistant editor, 1963-64, associate editor, 1964-65; Small Business Administration, Washington, D.C., confidential assistant for public affairs, 1965-66; Donaldson, Lufkin & Jenrette, New York City, portfolio analyst, 1966-67; Prentice-Hall, Inc., editor in Trade Division, 1968, director of children's books, 1969-74, assistant vice-president in Trade Division, 1974-75; Franklin Watts, Inc., New York City, vice-president and editorial director, 1975-77; International Telephone & Telegraph, New York City, staff operations executive, marketing manager, general manager, 1977-80; A. G. Becker, national institutional equity sales manager, 1980—.

AWARDS, HONORS: Outstanding achievement award from Small Business Administration, 1966; Christopher Award for Editorial Achievement from Christopher Brothers, 1972, for acquiring and publishing anonymously written *Go Ask Alice,*

Prentice-Hall, 1971; Outstanding Science Book from the National Science Teachers Association, for *Mr. Tamerin's Trees*, 1977; YWCA Academy of Achievers, 1979.

WRITINGS: Danny and His Thumb (juvenile; illustrated by Tomie de Paola), Prentice-Hall, 1973; *Mr. Tamarin's Trees* (juvenile; illustrated by Diane de Groat), Crown, 1976; *Owl's New Cards* (juvenile), Crown, 1977; *Charlie's Pets* (juvenile; illustrated by Arthur Cumings), Crown, 1978; *Indians: The First Americans* (juvenile; illustrated by Richard Smolinski), Watts, 1979; *The Complete Calorie Counter for Dining Out*, Jove, 1980; *The Complete Carbohydrate Counter for Dining Out*, Jove, 1980.

WORK IN PROGRESS: The Complete New York Apartment Guide.

SIDELIGHTS: "Bad poetry, murky short stories, and the first chapter of a thoroughly unfinished novel were all I'd written before finding children's books. Then, in 1970, two major life events coincided: I was director of children's books for Prentice-Hall and I met two very special children, Alexandra and Matthew Ernst (then six and four years old), who were destined to be my stepchildren. Being around Alex and Matt seemed to make it easy to write. They reminded me of so many childhood things and levels of emotion that I'd put away in order to try to grow up. They also helped me understand what books kids liked and why.

"Needless to say, this helped my publishing career enormously. Oddly though, when it comes to writing fiction, I work almost exclusively for myself. The scenes, characters, events have to delight me and I don't really know whether anyone else will respond to them. (I figure it's my editor's job to know whether my fiction deserves to be published.)

"With non-fiction the balance between me and the reader is reversed. While it's important to me to write in a fresh way and enjoy the results, 'the reader' is always in my mind and counts more than I in the final version. The primary thing in non-fiction, in my view, is to connect facts and insights with fun. The world is a spectacularly interesting place and to be dull about it writing for kids is a crime. If a child misses that connection between learning and excitement (through dull books or teachers) something very serious has been lost and may never be recovered. I suppose that's why children's books will always fascinate me, even if I never write another word. They're important in a way that adult books simply aren't and, by definition, they require a sense of responsibility, a level of craft, and a kind of insight and sparkle that other kinds of publishing don't require in order to survive."

FARBER, Norma   1909-

PERSONAL: Born August 6, 1909, in Boston, Mass.; daughter of G. Augustus and Augusta (Schon) Holzman; married Dr. Sidney Farber (deceased), July 3, 1928; children: Ellen, Stephen, Thomas, Miriam. *Education:* Wellesley College, A.B., 1931; Radcliffe College, M.A., 1932. *Home:* 1010 Memorial Dr., Cambridge, Mass. 02138.

CAREER: Musician, poet, author of picture books for children. Appeared as a soprano singer in solo recitals and with small ensemble groups and orchestras, 1940—. *Member:* Phi Beta Kappa. *Awards, honors:* Premier prix in singing from Jury

NORMA FARBER

Central des Etudes Musicales (Belgium), 1936; Children's Book Showcase award from Children's Book Council, 1976, for *As I was Crossing the Boston Common;* National Book Award from American Academy and Institute of Arts and Letters, 1976, for *As I was Crossing the Boston Common;* choice of best illustrated children's books of the year from *New York Times*, 1978, for *There Once Was a Woman Who Married a Man;* Golden Rose award from New England Poetry Club, for poetry; prizes for poetry from Poetry Society of America.

WRITINGS—For children: Did You Know It Was the Narwhale?, Atheneum, 1967; *As I Was Crossing the Boston Common* (illustrated by Arnold Lobel), Dutton, 1973; *I Found Them in the Yellow Pages* (illustrated by Marc Brown), Little, Brown, 1973; *Where's Gomer?* (illustrated by William Pene de Bois), Dutton, 1974; *This Is the Ambulance Leaving the Zoo* (illustrated by Tomie de Paola; Junior Literary Guild selection), Dutton, 1975; *A Ship in a Storm on the Way to Tarshish* (illustrated by Victoria Chess), Greenwillow Books, 1977; *Six Impossible Things Before Breakfast: Stories and Poems* (illustrated by T. de Paola), Addison-Wesley, 1977; *How the Left-Behind Beasts Built Ararat* (illustrated by Antonio Frasconi), Walker, 1978; *There Once Was a Woman Who Married a Man* (illustrated by Lydia Dabcovich), Addison-Wesely, 1978; *The Wanderers from Wapping* (illustrated by Charles Mikolaycak), Addison-Wesley, 1978; *How Does It Feel to be Old?* (illustrated by Trina S. Hyman), Dutton, 1979; *Never Say Ugh! to a Bug* (illustrated by Jose Aruego), Greenwillow Books, 1979; *There Goes Feathertop!* (illustrated by

He ate and he ate and he finished the stew.
He wiped his moustaches but never said Boo.

■ (From *There Once Was A Woman Who Married a Man* by Norma Farber. Illustrated by Lydia Dabcovich.)

M. Brown), Dutton, 1979; *Small Wonders* (illustrated by Kazue Mizumura), Coward, 1979; *Up the Down Elevator*, Addison-Wesley, 1979; *How the Hibernators Came to Bethlehem* (illustrated by Barbara Cooney), Walker, 1980.

Poetry collections: *The Hatch*, Scribner, 1955; *Look to the Rose*, privately printed, 1958; *A Desperate Thing: Marriage is a Desperate Thing*, Plowshare Press, 1973, also published as *A Desperate Thing: Marriage Poems*, Plowshare Press, 1973; (translator with Edith Helman) Pedro Salinas, *To Live in Pronouns: Selected Love Poems*, Norton, 1974; *Small Wonders: Poems*, Coward, 1979; *Something Further: Poems*, Kylix Press, 1979. Contributor of poetry to periodicals, including *America, Christian Century, Horn Book, Nation, New Catholic World, New Republic, New Yorker, Poetry*, and *Saturday Review*.

SIDELIGHTS: "I have composed verses since earliest childhood. My interest in poetry grew as I grew. It has never diminished—on the contrary. Though I do try now and again a bit of prose. Indeed, I have just completed a novel, my first, which will appear in the fall of 1982. It concerns a girl, age seventeen, who was 'cursed' of witchcraft by Cotton Mather in 1692-1693.

"It dawned on me a while ago that I have two obsessions: the alphabet, and Noah's Flood. My picture books *Did You Know It was the Norwhale?* and *Where's Gomer?* testify to the second preoccupation. Alphabet poems and stories enchant me because these twenty-six letters are the warp and woof, the living texture of our spoken and written communication. I just can't celebrate the English language loudly enough.

"In starting to write *This Is the Ambulance Leaving the Zoo*, I set myself the task of putting an alphabet into a story. I doubt if I knew who the occupant of the Ambulance was going to be until I arrived at Y, so rapidly did the strange ride narrate itself. I jumped for joy when X, that stickler, came to hand like a fawn. And when, at Z, the alphabet unexpectedly took off and reversed itself—my pleasure knew no bounds. I retraced myself hilariously!

"Oh, I have other interests besides alphabets and the Flood: ants, bees, crickets, doves, elevators, frogs, grubs, hibernators, icicles, Jonah, kites, ladybugs, maggots, narwhales, onions, penthouses, quarks, rhinoceroses, scarecrows, tornadoes, umbrellas, vending-machines, waterfalls, x's on peepers' backs, Yarrow, zircons. . . ."

Farber has published several types of books for children, including nonsense ballads and instructional alphabet and counting stories. Most of her books are written in rhyme, making them especially appropriate for reading aloud.

Farber's *As I Was Crossing the Boston Common*, for which she received the Children's Book Showcase and the National Book awards, is narrated by a turtle. He relates his experiences one day as he crossed the Boston Common, encountering beasts, fish, and fowl along the route. The unusual creatures parade before him in alphabetical order, from the angwantibo, boobook, and coypu to the zibet.

A number of Farber's story lines are taken from Biblical or classical tales. Such is the case in her fantasy ballad, *How the Left-Behind Beasts Built Ararat*, which is a spoof on the story of Noah and his ark. As the great flood is overtaking the land, Noah finds to his dismay that there is no more room on the ark and many animals will have to stay behind. A cow directs the left-behind animals as head of the "Committee for Staying Alive," and the group literally makes a mountain out of a molehill. All of the animals are on the peak just in time to avoid the waters and land the Ark.

Another of Farber's nonsense stories is *There Once Was a Woman Who Married a Man*. The man never said a word, although the woman made every attempt to break the silence. She tried nearly drowning him, jumping on the bed, and doing a fandango dance, but all to no avail. Finally, the town carnival solves her problem. As she and her silent husband go up the Loop-the-Loop roller coaster, she hears him mumble, "I'm sick."

FOR MORE INFORMATION SEE: Publishers Weekly, April 30, 1973; *Horn Book*, December, 1974, February, 1976, June, 1977, February, 1978, August, 1979, February, 1980. *Language Arts*, April, 1981.

FAX, Elton Clay 1909-

PERSONAL: Born October 9, 1909, in Baltimore, Md.; son of Mark Oakland (a clerk) and Willie Estelle (Smith) Fax; wife deceased; children: Betty Louise (Mrs. James Evans). *Education:* Attended Syracuse University. *Religion:* Protestant. *Home:* 51-29 30th Ave., Woodside, N.Y.

ELTON CLAY FAX

CAREER: Illustrator, with work exhibited at National Gallery of Art and Corcoran Gallery of Art, Washington, D.C., also illustrator of books; chalk-talk lecturer in high schools under management of School Assembly Service of Chicago, Ill., and Rochester, N.Y. U.S. Department of State specialist in South America and Caribbean, 1955, in East Africa, 1964; representative of American Society of African Culture on tour of Nigeria, 1963. *Member:* Authors Guild of America, International Platform Association.

WRITINGS: (Self-illustrated) *West Africa Vignettes,* American Society of African Culture, 1960, enlarged edition, 1963; *Contemporary Black Leaders,* Dodd, 1970; *Seventeen Black Artists,* Dodd, 1971; *Garvey: The Story of a Pioneer Black Nationalist,* Dodd, 1972; *Through Black Eyes,* Dodd, 1974; *Black Artist of the New Generation,* Dodd, 1977; *Hoshar* (self-illustrated), Progress Publishers of Moscow, 1980. Contributor to *Harlem, U.S.A.*

Illustrator: Robert N. McClean, *Tommy Two Wheels,* Friendship Press, 1943; Shirley Graham and George D. Lipscomb, *Dr. George Washington Carver,* Messner, 1944; Georgene Faulkner and John Becker, *Melindy's Medal,* Messner, 1945; Clifford B. Upton, *Upton Arithmetic-Grade 4,* American Book Co., 1945; Shannon Garst, *Sitting Bull,* Messner, 1946; *Story Parade Treasure Book* (includes: Aileen Fisher, *Susie's Story,* and Jane Flory, *The Haunted Skyscraper*), John C. Winston, 1946; Florence Hayes, *Skid,* Houghton, 1948; S. Garst, *Buffalo Bill,* Messner, 1948; G. Faulkner, *Melindy's Happy Summer,* Messner, 1949; Montgomery M. Atwater, *Avalanche Patrol,* Random House, 1951; Celeste Edell, *A Present from Rosita,* Messner, 1952; M. M. Atwater, *Rustlers on the High Range,* Random House, 1952; Eugene F. Moran, Sr., *Famous Harbours of the World,* Random House, 1953; Regina Woody, *Almena's Dogs,* Farrar, Straus, 1954; Clara Baldwin, *Cotton for Jim,* Abingdon, 1954; Harold Lamb, *Genghis Khan and the Mongol Horde,* Random House, 1954; Jeanette Eaton, *Trumpeter's Tale: The Story of Young Louis Armstrong,* Morrow, 1955; James H. Robinson, editor, *Love of This Land,* Christian Education Press, 1956; Harold Courlander, *Terrapin's Pot of Sense,* Holt, 1957; Ella Huff Kepple, *Mateo of Mexico,* Friendship Press, 1958; Verna Aardema, *Otwe,* Coward, 1960; V. Aardema, *The Na of Wa,* Coward, 1960; V. Aardema, *The Sky God Stories,* Coward, 1960; V. Aardema, *Tales from the Story Hat,* Coward, 1960; Letta Schatz, *Taiwo and Her Twin,* McGraw-Hill, 1964; V. Aardema, *More Tales from the Story Hat: African Folk Tales,* Coward, 1966; Joanna Johnston, *Paul Cuffee,* Dodd, 1970; Genevieve Gray, *The Seven Wishes of Joanna Peabody,* Lothrop, 1972.

SIDELIGHTS: "When I was growing up in Baltimore, Maryland, the only institution of public service that was not segregated was the Enoch Pratt Free Library. Because my mother had been a country school teacher who believed in the power of learning she instilled in my brother and me the need to read, and because we could not afford to own the many books she felt I should learn to read, we borrowed from the public library. Along with the standard classical fairy tales so beautifully illustrated in pen and ink and in color, I became enamoured of a series of travel books for children known as 'Our Little Cousins.'

"How I enjoyed reading about our little cousins from far off and often exotic lands—Armenia, Bolivia, Latvia, Georgia, Kenya, Argentina, Uruguay, Italy, Uganda, Ethiopia, Nigeria. . . . How little indeed did I ever dream I would not only visit such places but that I would be making drawings in them and later writing about them so that others could share what

(From *Contemporary Black Leaders* by Elton C. Fax. Illustrated by the author.)

I have seen and heard and felt. When I illustrated Verna Aardema's *Tales from the Story Hat* and *More Tales from the Story Hat* I had been to Ghana in West Africa and had seen the kinds of straw hats worn by the African story tellers. When I illustrated Harold Lamb's *Ghengis Khan and the Mongol Horde* for Random House I had never been to Central Asia to see the *steppes,* the *yurtas,* and the nomadic peoples of whom he wrote so compellingly. For my illustrations I had to use photographs and old prints. Since then I have been twice to Central Asia, have dined in a *yurta,* and have walked not only along the sandy steppes but have stood upon the spot where the Mongol leader, Ghengis Khan, not only lost a battle to the Turkmen tribesman but lost a son as well. That spot was in Nisa, a green and lovely and tranquil village of the Soviet Republic of Turkmenia.

"A few weeks later I was in Latvia at a lovely and restful residence for writers where I was the only foreign resident. There, facing the Baltic Sea I began the writing of my book, *Hoshar.* One day after dinner I sat down at my desk and proceeded with my narrative of what I had only recently seen and learned much farther south and east in Exotic Central Asia. Time passed quickly. The sun was still bright in the western sky and I looked at my watch. It was 11:15 p.m.! Immediately I recalled my reading as a child of our little cousins who lived in the Land of the Midnight Sun.

"If I were to offer any suggestions to the young who wish to have this kind of an experience they would be simple. First, be *willing* to learn. Then be willing to give of yourselves without *expecting* to be rewarded. Third, know that *all* peoples everywhere in this world are members of the *human* family."

AILEEN FISHER

FISHER, Aileen (Lucia) 1906-

PERSONAL: Born September 9, 1906; in Iron River, Mich.; daughter of Nelson E. and Lucia (Milker) Fisher. *Education:* University of Chicago, student, 1923-25; University of Missouri, B.J., 1927. *Home and Office:* 505 College Ave., Boulder, Colo. 80302.

CAREER: Women's National Journalistic Register, Chicago Ill., director, 1928-31; Labor Bureau of the Middle West, Chicago, Ill., research assistant 1931-32; free-lance writer, 1932—. *Member:* Theta Sigma Phi. *Awards, honors:* Silver Medal from U.S. Treasury Department, World War II; National Council of Teachers of English Award for poetry for children, 1978.

WRITINGS: The Coffee-Pot Face, McBride, 1933; *Inside a Little House,* McBride, 1938; *Guess Again!,* McBride, 1941; *That's Why,* Nelson, 1946; *Over the Hills to Nugget,* Aladdin, 1949; *Trapped by the Mountain Storm,* Aladdin, 1953; *Up the Windy Hill* (verse), Abelard, 1953; *Timber! Logging in Michigan,* Aladdin, 1955; *Off to the Gold Fields,* Nelson, 1955; *Cherokee Strip: The Race for Land,* Aladdin, 1956; *All on a Mountain Day,* Nelson, 1956; *A Lantern in the Window,* Nelson, 1957; *Runny Days, Sunny Days,* Abelard, 1958; *Skip,* Nelson, 1958; *Fisherman of Galilee,* Nelson, 1959.

Going Barefoot (illustrated by Adrienne Adams), Crowell, 1960; *Where Does Everyone Go?,* Crowell, 1961; *Summer of Little Rain,* Nelson, 1961; *I Wonder How, I Wonder Why,* Abelard, 1962; *Like Nothing at All,* Crowell, 1962; *My Cousin Abe,* Nelson, 1962; *I Like Weather* (illustrated by Feodor Rojankovsky), Crowell, 1963; *Cricket in a Thicket* (illustrated by Janina Domanska), Scribner, 1963; *Listen, Rabbit* (illustrated by Symeon Shimin), Crowell, 1964; *In the Middle of the Night,* Crowell, 1965; *Arbor Day,* Crowell, 1965; (with Olive Rabe)

We Dickinsons (Junior Literary Guild selection), Atheneum, 1965; *In the Woods, In the Meadow, In the Sky,* Scribner, 1965; *Best Little House,* Crowell, 1966; *Valley of the Smallest: The Life Story of A Shrew,* Crowell, 1966; (with Olive Rabe) *Human Rights Day,* Crowell, 1966; *Skip Around the Year,* Crowell, 1967; *My Mother and I* (illustrated by Kazue Mizumura), Crowell, 1967; *Up, Up the Mountain,* Crowell, 1968; *We Went Looking* (illustrated by Marie Angel), Crowell, 1968; (with Olive Rabe) *We Alcotts* (*Horn Book* honor list), Atheneum, 1968; *Easter* (illustrated by Ati Forberg), Holiday, 1968; *Sing, Little Mouse* (illustrated by S. Shimin), Crowell, 1969; *Clean as a Whistle,* Crowell, 1969; *In One Door and Out the Other* (illustrated by Lillian Hoban; poems), Crowell, 1969.

Jeanne d'Arc, Crowell, 1970; *But Ostriches,* Crowell, 1970; *The Ways of Animals,* ten volumes, Bowmar, 1973; *Do Bears Have Mothers Too?* (illustrated by Eric Carle), Crowell, 1973; *My Cat Has Eyes of Sapphire Blue* (illustrated by M. Angel), Crowell, 1973; *Once We Were on a Picnic,* Crowell, 1975; *The Ways of Plants,* ten volumes, Bowmar, 1977; *I Stood Upon a Mountain* (illustrated by Blair Lent), Crowell, 1979; *Feathered Ones & Furry* (illustrated by E. Carle; Junior Literary Guild selection), Crowell, 1979; *Like Nothing at All* (illustrated by Leonard Weisgard), Crowell, 1979; *Out in the Dark and Daylight* (illustrated by Gail Owens), Harper, 1980; *Anybody Home?* (illustrated by Susan Bonners), Crowell, 1980.

Plays: *Set the Stage for Christmas,* Row, Peterson & Co., 1948; *Health and Safety Plays and Programs,* Plays, 1953; *Holiday Programs for Boys and Girls,* Plays, 1953; (with Olive Rabe) *United Nations Plays and Programs,* Plays, 1954, 2nd edition, 1961; (with O. Rabe) *Patriotic Plays and Programs,* Plays, 1956; *Christmas Plays and Programs,* Plays, 1960; *Plays About Our Nation's Songs,* Plays, 1962; *Bicentennial Plays and Programs,* Plays, 1975. Contributor to *Story Parade, Jack and Jill, Child Life,* and other publications.

ADAPTATIONS—Filmstrips: "Going Places" (with record or with cassette), Bowmar-Nobel, 1973; "Animal Disguises" (with seven records or with cassette), Bowmar-Nobel, 1973; "Animal Houses" (with record or with cassette), Bowmar-Nobel, 1973; "Animal Jackets" (with record or with cassette), Bowmar-Nobel, 1973; "No Accounting for Tastes" (with record or with cassette), Bowmar-Nobel, 1973; "Now That Days Are Colder" (with record or with cassette), Bowmar-Nobel, 1973; "Sleepy Heads" (with record or with cassette), Bowmar-Nobel, 1973; "Tail Twisters" (with record or with cassette), Bowmar-Nobel, 1973; "Ways of Animals" (ten filmstrips with teacher's guide, with record or with cassette), Bowmar-Nobel, 1973; "You Don't Look Like Your Mother Said the Robin to the Fawn" (with record or with cassette), Bowmar-Nobel, 1973; "Filling the Bill" (with record or with cassette), Bowmar-Nobel, 1973.

SIDELIGHTS: "I was a lucky child. When I was four years old my father had a serious bout with pneumonia. This made him decide to give up his business in Iron River and more or less retire to the country. He bought forty acres near Iron River and built the big, square white house where I grew up. We called the place High Banks because it was on a high bank above the river, which was always red with water pumped from the iron mines. Still, the river was good to wade in, swim in, fish in, and skate on in winter. When I was young there was still quite a bit of logging nearby, and my brother and I used to follow the iced logging roads. There was a big landing for the logs on the railroad about a mile from our house. We had all kinds of pets—cows, horses, and chickens. And we had a

. . . **A little Mouse peeked**
out of a hole,
and up it streaked
to nibble at crumbs
from her fingers and thumbs.

■ (From *Clean as a Whistle* by Aileen Fisher. Illustrated by Ben Shecter.)

big garden in summer. I loved it. I have always loved the country.

"On my eighth birthday a sister was born. I took immediate charge of her because she was, after all, my birthday present. Six years later another sister came along, but by that time my brother and I were almost ready to go to college.

"I went to the University of Chicago for two years, then transferred to the school of journalism at the University of Missouri. After receiving my degree in 1927, I worked in a little theatre during the summer, then went back to Chicago to look for a job. I found one—as an assitant in a placement bureau for women journalists! That fall I sold my first poem to *Child Life* magazine, a nine-lined verse entitled 'Otherwise.'

"My aim in Chicago was to save every single cent I was able to so that I could escape back to the country life I loved and missed. I had to be economic so I took a cheap, dark, first floor room in a third-rate hotel on Chicago's south side. It had only one window and that opened onto a cement area that lead to an alley. Across the panes were bars to keep prowlers away!

"The room was furnished with a steel cot, a wardrobe badly in need of varnish, two chairs and a kitchen table I used for a desk.

"Coming in from work one evening I jotted down some lines I had thought about on the walk from the station. I then went out to dinner at a small, nearby restaurant where I could get a meal for sixty cents. When I got back to my room I liked the nine lines I hurriedly wrote and sent them off, along with several other verses, to Marjorie Barrows, then editor of *Child Life*.

"I always liked to write verse. My mother had quite a flair for versifying, and I was sort of brought up on it. Mother was an ex-kindergarten teacher, which was fortunate for her offspring."

Fisher's first book, a collection of verses, was published in 1933. Today, her writing habits are still quite methodical. "I try to be at my desk four hours a day, from 8:00 a.m. to noon. Ideas come to me out of experience and from reading and remembering. I usually do a first draft by hand. I can't imagine writing verse on a typewriter, and for years I wrote nothing but verse so I formed the habit of thinking with a pencil or pen in hand. I usually rework my material, sometimes more, sometimes less. I *never* try out my ideas on children, except on the child I used to know—me! Fortunately I remember pretty well what I used to like to read, think about, and do. I find, even today, that if I write something I like, children are pretty apt to like it too. I guess what it amounts to is that I never grew up." [Lee Bennett Hopkins, "Profile: Aileen Fisher," *Language Arts,* October, 1978. [1]]

"I write for children for a very simple reason. I enjoy it. And I usually write about nature for the same reason. Also I feel that children who live in cities, and so many of them do these days, have little chance to get acquainted with nature first hand. Books are the best substitute. As for me, my day is not complete unless I have a good walk on a mountain trail with the dogs.

"I live in Boulder, Colorado, at the edge of town on a dead-end street, close to Flagstaff Mt. The highlight of each day is a walk with my dog and a friend and her dog on one of the many trails nearby. This keeps me in touch with the weather, the wildlife, and the wonderful scenery in every direction."

Beetle, you look so little to be wandering off so far. ▪
(From "Cracker Time" in *Cricket in a Thicket* by Aileen Fisher. Illustrated by Feodor Rojankovsky.)

HOBBIES AND OTHER INTERESTS: Woodworking, hiking, mountain climbing.

FOR MORE INFORMATION SEE: Horn Book, June, 1963, December, 1963, June, 1964, December, 1965, June, 1966, December, 1966, December, 1968, February, 1970, June, 1970, October, 1970, October, 1971, February, 1974; *New Yorker,* December 14, 1968; Lee Bennett Hopkins, *Books Are By People,* Citation Press, 1969; Lee Bennett Hopkins, "Profile: Aileen Fisher," *Language Arts,* October, 1978.

Books should to one of these four ends conduce,
For wisdom, piety, delight, or use.
—John Denham

FISK, Nicholas 1923-

PERSONAL: Born October 14, 1923, in London, England; married Dorothy Antoinette, 1949; children: Moyra and Nicola (twins), Steven, Christopher. *Education:* Educated in private secondary school in Sussex, England. *Home:* 59 Elstree Rd., Bushey Heath, Hertfordshire WD2 3QX, England. *Agent:* Laura Cecil, 17 Alwyn Villas, Canonbury, London N1, England.

CAREER: Writer and illustrator. Lund Humphries Ltd. (printers/publishers), London, England, head of creative group. Has worked as actor, advertising creative director, publisher, and musician. *Military service:* Royal Air Force. *Member:* Saville Club.

WRITINGS: Look at Cars (self-illustrated juvenile), Hamish Hamilton, 1959, revised edition, Panther, 1970; *Look at Newspapers* (juvenile), Hamish Hamilton, 1962; *Cars,* Parrish, 1963; *The Young Man's Guide to Advertising,* Hamish Hamilton, 1963; *The Bouncers* (self-illustrated), Hamish Hamilton, 1964; *The Fast Green Car,* Hamish Hamilton, 1965; *There's Something on the Roof,* Hamish Hamilton, 1966; *Making Music,* Crescendo Publishing Co., 1966; *Space Hostages* (juvenile), Hamish Hamilton, 1967, Macmillan, 1969; *Richthofen the Red Baron,* Coward, 1968; *Lindbergh the Lone Flier* (juvenile), Coward, 1968.

Trillions (juvenile), Hamish Hamilton, 1971, Pantheon, 1973; *High Way Home,* Hamish Hamilton, 1973; *Der Ballon,* Junior Press (Germany), 1974; *Grinny* (juvenile science fiction), Heinemann, 1973, Thomas Nelson, 1974; (with Carol Barker) *Emma Borrows a Cup of Sugar* (juvenile), Heinemann, 1974; *Little Green Spacemen,* Heinemann, 1974; (contributor) Edward Blishen, editor, *The Thorny Paradise* (juvenile anthology), Kestrel, 1975; *The Witches of Wimmering,* Pelham Books, 1976; *Time Trap,* Gollancz, 1976; *Wheelie in the Stars,* Heinemann, 1976; (contributor) Puffin, "Take Part" series, Ward Lock, 1977; *Escape from Splatterbang,* Pelham, 1977, Macmillan, 1979; *Antigrav,* Kestrel, 1978; *Monster Maker,*

NICHOLAS FISK

(From *Look at Aircraft* by Philip Joubert. Illustrated by Nicholas Fisk.)

Macmillan, 1980; *The Starstormer Saga* (continuing series), Knight Books, 1980; *A Rag, a Bone and a Hank of Hair*, Kestrel, 1980.

Illustrator: Philip Joubert, *Look at Aircraft*, Hamish Hamilton, 1960; (contributor of photographs) Eric Fenby, *Menuhin's House of Music*, Praeger, 1970; W. Mayne, *Skiffy*, Hamish Hamilton, 1973. General editor of "Hamish Hamilton Monographs," Hamish Hamilton, 1964. Contributor to *Pears Junior Encyclopaedia*. Contributor of articles and science fiction stories to magazines.

WORK IN PROGRESS: Children's novels, for Pelham Books, Kestrel Books; self-illustrated short stories for Penguin; children's science fiction series for Hodder & Stoughton; volume of short stories for Kestrel Books; TV series for young children, *Read On!*, for BBC TV.

SIDELIGHTS: "I am principally a writer; but also an illustrator, designer, and photographer. I am an impresario of printed things in my office job, producing anything from more or less learned works to advertising brochures. I write for children because children have generous, wide minds; today, they seem separated from the adult race only by size, power, and experience. Television put an end to the nursery ghetto.

"I write science fiction because it is liberating. The writer is free to invent his own games, rules and players (but of course these must be made clear to the reader, and the need to explain can impede the narrative). I greatly regret the label 'SF,' incidentally. SF were better named IF—stories centred on an If, a possibility, a leap. Children take such leaps in their stride. Adults are more staid. They go by the label; 'Oh, it's science fiction . . . I never read that.' However, the genre is sweeping the world along with it and the future looks bright, even lurid."

In an article for *The Thorny Paradise*, Fisk goes on to explain that: ". . . Yesterday's children got what was good for them.

Today's children get what they want. One of the things they don't want very much is a book. Literacy itself is becoming yet another commodity in short supply.

"Which poses a problem for the children's writer. However much he loves his craft—the act of devising and writing stories—he must still send his product to market. A typescript is merely a pupa. There can be no real life for the creature until it has been released by the publisher. So the writer must consider his market. What is the children's-book market? It is almost entirely an adult business. Adults commission, condition, review and distribute the writer's work. The buyer is not very often a child. Children buy, or get someone else to buy for them, a particular toy: not many children buy books.

"Yet the child recipient of a book makes judgements that may be crucial. Certain children's writers succeed in the face of opposition from librarians and educationists. Other writers, producing work that deserves and gets high praise from adults, find that their work brings nothing more tangible than rose-coloured exhalations of esteem.

"What is the writer to do? Should he stubbornly and devotedly aim to satisfy only himself, or should he conduct a market survey and set himself to conform with its findings? Should he consult his peers—the adults who establish the children's-book market—or should he talk to the children themselves and hope to learn something from them?

"Whichever course he follows (and most probably he will try all of them at one time or another) he will find no certain answers. A book is not a Go/No-Go product. It cannot be balanced like columns of figures, or checked with ruler and setsquare, or made to resume ticking if it stops. So even if the writer is certain of the excellence of his work on Monday, he may think very differently on Tuesday. Again, if his market survey reveals a definite trend and demand, it may be that the publishers are seeking an innovation. Yet again, even the most expert and sympathetic of his peers have bees in their bonnets that buzz a note different from the writer's.

"This leaves the children themselves. They make unreliable and disturbing guides.

"Unreliable, because the tastes of the majority are bounded by what they already know. New ideas and possibilities are not necessarily attractive to them (the proof of the pudding is puddings: try adding sherry to the nursery trifle. Or if the nursery trifle has always had sherry in it, try serving it without). Disturbing, because the more children one meets, the more clearly the dedicated writer realizes how minutely small his audience is. Forty-nine children in fifty ask the obvious questions—for example, 'Do you have trouble finding titles?' One child in fifty asks the question that matters—'Have you ever found a title so good that you couldn't make the story fit it?' (This writer was asked the last question by a small coloured boy wearing large spectacles. Professional spoke to professional in that moment.)

"Despite the gap between writer and readership, there are still conclusions the writer must reach and hold to, right or wrong, if he is to produce anything at all. My conclusions are as follows.

"Book-reading children have changed. Once, the majority of child readers—the middle-class owners of Rackham's latest, say—were a separate tribe who, ideally, spoke when they were spoken to and did as they were bid. Today, the nurseryless child lives in the company of adults, occupying the same rooms, joining in the family conversations and (most important) watching many of the same TV programmes. No Christopher Robin, this child. He has a smattering of adult phrases and attitudes. He appears harder, tougher, more of the world. His teddy bear, if he has one, wears a space helmet. His sister's wardrobe is supplied by fashion houses. Both are, quite consciously, 'consumers.'

"A veneer? Not all of it. Just as your grownup son seems to have instinctive mastery over car engines and your eighteen-year-old daughter seems to acquire an immediate and esteemed place in commerce, so today's children have a flair for the world they live in—a world in whose spindle Communication, Acquisition and Technology are embedded like 'Brighton' in pink rock. The children are better informed than ever they were about what makes things tick, how many beans make five, the Wankel engine, the pre-teen brassiere and a host of concepts and articles that never entered the minds of the Rackham child. (Conversely, this same child may adopt Rackham in the late teens and early twenties.)

"This is not to say that the 'tender' attributes of childhood are lost. Children still on occasion trail clouds of glory. Their eyes remain large and wondering. Their minds still have room for fantasy and fanaticism, myth and romance. It is just that their range, experience and admiration for the tangible have increased disproportionately.

"What can one write for these children? Even if everything said in the preceding paragraph is untrue, it still provides a table capable of supporting a typewriter. Children are more technological, more hardware conscious? Then write about twentieth-century things. Children are more experienced in techniques of communication? Then write faster narratives and pay less attention to old devices thought necessary to link and clarify a story. Children are less literate than they were—less able to understand the words? Ignore their ignorance and insist that they keep pace with you, the writer. Adults, too, must be permitted to express themselves.

". . . I began, nervously, by writing childish little books for little children; my only security was provided by precedent and a well-stocked bookshelf. Watching my own children and their friends (and reading what I had written) obliged me to mend my ways. My child readers might, occasionally, be persuaded to share my nostalgias and fancies—even my childhood—but this was not to be relied on. Better to devise stories that belonged either to a period the reader would recognize—the period of *now;* or to go so far back, or so far forward, that the reader must simply take my word for it.

"*Now* had little to offer. As an adult, I cannot share my reader's experiences, nor have I the Dickensian skills needed to transmogrify the present—to make something large as life and twice as natural. And in any case, for myself alone, the present means nothing very much. Like the Deal faithhealer, on the whole I dislike what I fancy I feel. How much better to board an era liner and travel into new times, possibilities and situations! How much more exciting the microscope's or telescope's viewpoint than one's own! How much more interesting the possibility than the fact; the drawn conclusion than the stated premise; the freedom of fantasy than the chains of present circumstance!

". . . Though children's books are adult concoctions, one must still play fair by the child readers. It would be unfair, for example, to write a children's novel centred on the adventures

of a child who finds himself in an apparently endless corridor arranged as a Moebius strip—yet a first-rate 'science fiction' story was written, for adults, on this premise. You yourself may not know what a Moebius strip is, but you can easily find out. A child cannot.

". . . It is arguable that the highest expression of humankind takes the form of a child. It is very easy indeed to argue that the human mind is at its most agile, adventurous, generous and receptive stage during childhood. So the children's writer is mixing with and working for the Right People.

"It is even possible to persuade oneself that by writing for children, one is doing some good. All the clichés about rat races and consumer societies are true, just as it is always true that the country is going to the dogs. It is a wonderful thing to crash the grey barriers—and all the more worthwhile if you can take the children with you." [Nicholas Fisk, "One Thumping Lie Only," *The Thorny Paradise*, edited by Edward Blishen, Kestrel, 1975.]

FOR MORE INFORMATION SEE: Publishers Weekly, March 26, 1973; Edward Blishen, editor, *The Thorny Paradise*, Kestrel, 1975.

FLOHERTY, John Joseph   1882-1964

PERSONAL: Born April 28, 1882, in Ireland; died December 3, 1964, in Mineola, N.Y.; son of Patrick Vincent and Katherine (Flanagan) Floherty; married Lillian Bessie Hunt, June, 1905; children: John Joseph, Cynthia Hunt (Mrs. John Joseph Gaeta). *Education:* Studied at St. Flanaans College, Ireland, 1899-1902, and at the Art Students League in New York. *Religion:* Episcopalian. *Home:* Port Washington, New York.

CAREER: Author of books for children. Reporter for the Root Newspaper Association, 1905-07, and for United Publishers Corporation, 1907-20; president of his own publishing company, John J. Floherty, Inc., 1921-28, and of Floherty & Staff, 1929-38. *Military service:* Served with the Seventh Regiment of the New York National Guard, 1904-13. *Member:* Dutch Treat Club.

WRITINGS: Fire Fighters! How They Work, Doubleday, Doran, 1933; *'Board the Airliner: A Camera Trip with the Transport Planes*, Doubleday, Doran, 1934; *Moviemakers*, Doubleday, Doran, 1935; *Guardsmen of the Coast*, Doubleday, Doran, 1935; *Police!*, Doubleday, Doran, 1936; *On the Air: The Story of Radio*, Doubleday, Doran, 1937; *Youth at the Wheel*, Lippincott, 1937; *Your Daily Paper*, Lippincott, 1938; *Sons of the Hurricane*, Lippincott, 1938; *Make Way for the Mail*, Lippincott, 1939; *Men without Fear*, Lippincott, 1940; *Aviation from Shop to Sky*, Lippincott, 1941, revised as *Aviation from the Ground Up*, 1950, reissued, 1960; *Youth and the Sea: Our Merchant Marine Calls American Youth*, Lippincott, 1941; *The Courage and the Glory*, Lippincott, 1942; *Sentries of the Sea*, Lippincott, 1942; *Inside the F.B.I.* (forward by J. Edgar Hoover), Lippincott, 1943; *Money-Go-Round: The Strange Story of Money*, Lippincott, 1944, reissued, 1964; *Behind the Microphone*, Lippincott, 1944.

Flowing Gold: The Romance of Oil, Lippincott, 1945, revised edition, 1957; *Men against Crime*, Lippincott, 1946; *White Terror: Adventures with the Ice Patrol*, Lippincott, 1947; *Behind the Silver Shield*, Lippincott, 1948, revised edition, 1957; *Shooting the News: Careers of the Camera Men*, Lippincott,

JOHN JOSEPH FLOHERTY

1949; *Five Alarm: The Story of Fire Fighting*, Lippincott, 1949; *Watch Your Step*, Lippincott, 1950; *Television Story*, Lippincott, 1951, revised edition, 1957; *Our F.B.I.: An Inside Story*, Lippincott, 1951; *High, Wide, and Deep: Science and Adventure with the Coast and Geodetic Survey*, Lippincott, 1952; *Get That Story: Journalism, Its Lore and Thrills*, Lippincott, 1952, revised edition, 1964; *Search and Rescue at Sea*, Lippincott, 1953; *Deep Down Under*, Lippincott, 1953; *Men against Distance: The Story of Communication*, Lippincott, 1954; *Troopers All: Stories of State Police*, Lippincott, 1954; *Forest Ranger*, Lippincott, 1956.

(With Mike McGrady) *Youth and the F.B.I.* (foreword by J. Edgar Hoover), Lippincott, 1960; (with McGrady) *Whirling Wings: The Story of the Helicopter*, Lippincott, 1961; (with McGrady) *Skin-Diving Adventures*, Lippincott, 1962.

Contributor of numerous articles to various newspapers and magazines.

SIDELIGHTS: "When J. Edgar Hoover, the Director of Federal Bureau of Investigation, invited me to visit the F.B.I. and study its operation, I knew that the invitation was really extended to the youth of America whose reporter I happened to be in this particular case.

"Imagine, if you can, a great clinic in which thousands of trained specialists and scores of scientists work day and night to stem the spread of a deadly epidemic. Then imagine every man and woman employed there dedicated to the cause of humanity and having as their motto, 'Fidelity, Bravery, and Integrity,' and you have a picture of what the F.B.I. is like.

"During my extended visit to the F.B.I., I was shown every phase of the work in classrooms, in laboratories, and on the range in Quantico, where special agents, new and old, get more and better firearm instruction than in any army in the world. Here, too, the student special agents are taught self-defense through a combination of wrestling. jiujitsu, and strange holds that are based on physical laws. When a G-Man gets into grips with a criminal, it is indeed a one-sided affair. It should be remembered, however, that a gun is never drawn by a G-Man except in self-defense or to prevent the escape of a prisoner.

"In the laboratories I was spellbound for days. A speck of copper, smaller than the period at the end of this sentence, was found on a knife-blade owned by a suspect accused of cutting through a screen door and murdering his victim. The spectroscope identified the copper atom as having come from the copper screen on the door—and then the man confessed.

"I noticed one physical characteristic that marks every G-Man. The eyes of these men sparkle with a cold light like the eye of an eagle. They seem to bore right through you. Yet they are the eyes of friendly men noted for their calm gentleness as they go about their chief job—getting the facts that will prove a person guilty, or better still, innocent.

"It is the story of these men that I tell in *Inside the F.B.I.*"

Inside the F.B.I., illustrated with photographs, was published by J. B. Lippincott Company in 1943. In all of Floherty's books, one can find three basic ingredients—inside facts, human interest and accuracy. In tracking down information for his books, Floherty traveled the equivalent of twice around the world.

FOR MORE INFORMATION SEE: (For children) Stanley J. Kunitz and Howard Haycraft, editors, *Junior Book of Authors*, second revised edition, H. W. Wilson, 1951; Obituaries—*New York Times*, December 5, 1964; *Publishers Weekly*, December 28, 1964.

RONALD V. FODOR

A meteoriticist uses a metal detector. ■ (From *Meteorites: Stones from the Sky* by R. V. Fodor. Photograph courtesy of the American Meteorite Laboratory.)

FODOR, Ronald V(ictor) 1944-

PERSONAL: Born June 10, 1944, in Cleveland, Ohio; son of Alex V. (a laborer) and Helen (Majoros) Fodor; married Marilyn Komarc (a public school teacher), August 20, 1966; children: Germaine Victoria, John Victor. *Education:* Ohio University, B.S., 1966; Arizona State University, M.S., 1968; University of New Mexico, Ph.D., 1971. *Home:* 415 Hailey Dr., Raleigh, N.C. 27606. *Office:* Department of Geosciences, North Carolina State University, Raleigh, N.C. 27650.

CAREER: University of New Mexico, Albuquerque, research scientist in geology, 1971-77; North Carolina State University, Raleigh, assistant professor of geology, 1977—. *Member:* Geological Society of America, Meteoritical Society, American Geophysical Union.

WRITINGS: Meteorites: Stones from the Sky (juvenile), Dodd, 1976; *What Does a Geologist Do?* (juvenile), Dodd, 1977; *The Complete Handbook on Auto Repair and Maintenance,* Parker Publishing, 1977; *Competitive Weightlifting,* Sterling, 1978; *What to Eat and Why: The Science of Nutrition* (juvenile), Morrow, 1979; *Growing Up Strong,* Sterling, 1979; *Impact!* (novel), Norton, 1979; *Nickles, Dimes, and Dollars: How*

Currency Works, Morrow, 1980; *Angry Waters: Floods and Their Control,* Dodd, 1980; *Frozen Earth: Explaining the Ice Ages,* Enslow, 1981.

WORK IN PROGRESS: More books for children; adult fiction.

SIDELIGHTS: "I am writing science on a popular level as a scientist—that is, as a specialist on the subject—as opposed to most books of similar subject matter being written by professional writers who have only an interest in science." His current scientific work involves "the mineralogy, geochemistry, and petrology of volcanic rocks and meteorites." This research has taken him to South America, Africa, Europe, and Hawaii.

Books are the treasured wealth of the world and the fit inheritance of generations and nations . . . . Their authors are a natural and irresistible aristocracy in every society, and, more than kings or emperors, exert an influence on mankind.

—Henry David Thoreau

ANDRÉ FRANCOIS

FRANCOIS, André   1915-

PERSONAL: Original name, André Farkas; began using "Francois" when he became a French citizen in the mid-1930's; born November 9, 1915, in Timisoara, Rumania; son of Albert Farkas (a civil servant) and Olga (Plon) Farkas; married Margaret Edmunds; children: Pierre, Catherine. *Education:* Attended Ecole des Beaux-Arts; studied at Cassandre's School of Fine Arts and Poster Design, 1935-36. *Address:* 95810 Grisy-lesPlâtres, Seine-et-Oise, France.

CAREER: Author and illustrator, artist. Began career as commercial artist, doing advertising for, among others, Standard Oil, Olivetti, Perrier, and Dutch Master Cigars; other aspects of his career include work in the graphic arts; painting—with several one-man shows to his credit: Librairie La Hune, 1955, Club du Meilleur Livre, 1958; the design of sets and costumes for plays and the ballet, including the Roland Petit Ballet of Paris, 1956, Peter Hall, 1958, and Gene Kelly, 1960; and art work, covers and caricatures, and political cartoons for *Vogue, Holiday, Femina, The New Yorker, La Tribune des Nations* and *Punch; Fortune* published a magazine section of his ads entitled "Advertising—a Continental Touch." *Awards, honors: The Magic Currant Bun* was a *New York Times* Choice of Best Illustrated Children's Books of the Year, 1952, as was

Crocodile Tears in 1956, *Roland* in 1958 and *You Are Ri-di-cu-lous* in 1970; Gold Medal of the Art Directors Club of New York.

WRITINGS—For children; all self-illustrated: *Crocodile Tears,* Faber, 1955, Universe, 1956, revised edition, Universe, 1964; *You Are Ri-di-cu-lous,* Pantheon, 1970; *The Eggzercize Book,* Daily Bul Publishers [Belgium], 1979.

Other: *Double Bedside Book,* Deutsch, 1952, published in America as *The Tattooed Sailor, and Other Cartoons from France* (introduction by Walt Kelly), Knopf, 1953; *The Half-Naked Knight* (cartoons and drawings), Knopf, 1958; *Heikle Themen,* Diogenes, 1959; *The Biting Eye of André Francois* (caricature and comic art), Perpetua, 1960; *The Penguin André Francois* (collection), Penguin, 1964; *Les Rhumes,* Melisa, 1971; *Qui Est le Plus Marrant?,* L'Ecole des Loisirs, 1971; *Santoun,* S. E. R. G., 1972; *Toi et Moi,* L'Ecole des Loisirs, 1973; (with Roger McGough) *Mr. Noselighter,* Deutsch, 1977.

Illustrator; for children: John Symonds, *William Waste,* Sampson Low, 1946; Jacques LeMarchand, *L'Odyssee d'Ulysse,* Leprat, 1947, translation by E. M. Hatt published as *The Adventures of Ulysses,* Criterion, 1960; Isobel Harris, *Little Boy Brown* (ALA Notable Book), Lippincott, 1949; Symonds, *The Magic Currant Bun,* Lippincott, 1952; Symonds, *Travelers Three,* Lippincott, 1953; Nelly Stephane, *Roland,* Harcourt, 1958; Symonds, *The Story George Told Me,* Harrap, 1963, Pantheon, 1964; Symonds, *Tom and Tabby,* Universe, 1964; Symonds, *Grodge-Cat and the Window Cleaner,* Pantheon, 1965.

Other: Diderot, *Jacques le Fataliste,* Reunis, 1946; Jacques Prevert, *Lettres des Iles Baladar,* NRF, 1952, reissued, Gallimard, 1967; R. Vailland, *Beau Masque,* NRF, 1954; J. Anselme, *On Vous l'a Dit,* Delpire, 1955; Balzac, *Contes Drolatiques,* Diogenes, 1957; Alfred Jarry, *Ubu Roi* (five-act play), Le Club du Meilleur Livre, 1958.

SIDELIGHTS: Francois is renowned for his work in a variety of different art fields, from the graphic arts and advertising to set and costume design to cartoons. He has even received commissions from Simpson's of Piccadilly in London for a pack of playing cards and from UNICEF to draw a series of Christmas cards. He feels he has been influenced by the works of George Grosz and Paul Klee, and perhaps the strongest imprint on his career resulted from the time spent in the studio of Cassandre, noted French poster painter. His artwork has hung in museums in New York and throughout Europe.

His artistic ability serves him well when he turns his hand to the realm of children's books. His first book illustrations published in the United States were those for *Little Boy Brown* in 1949. Children's author and illustrator Marcia Brown says of his work, "Entering the spirit of the text completely, M. Francois has enriched it as he creates in pen and ink and warm brown wash the world that is so exciting to a child. So directly is he concerned with telling the story that artistic considerations seem to fall naturally into place. Each line is drawn with feeling and control of feeling. Little Boy Brown sometimes appears in different actions on the same page, the way a child draws. . . . Author and artist are so successful in effacing themselves that it is Little Boy Brown who tells his story. To almost any small child this is a most personal book, because it is a book about himself."

With *Crocodile Tears* André Francois becomes creator of the story as well as of the illustrations. *The New Yorker* wrote,

**Ils savent raconter de jolies histoires,
They can tell charming stories . . . .**

■ (From *Crocodile Tears* by André Francois. Illustrated by the author.)

"Knowing juveniles will think everything about this piece of absurdity by the French cartoonist is funny—from its size, three by ten inches, down to the carton it comes in." And the *New York Times* comments, "This jaunty excursion into fantasy is told by M. Francois in a very few words and in witty pictures. His invention is fresh and ingenious, his line is sophisticated."

FOR MORE INFORMATION SEE: Marcia Brown, "Artist's Choice: *Little Boy Brown*," *Horn Book*, January, 1950; *New York Times*, November 4, 1956; *The New Yorker*, November 24, 1956; Bertha Mahony Miller and others, compilers, *Illustrators of Children's Books, 1946-1956*, Horn Book, 1958; *Graphis*, March, 1958; *Graphis*, November, 1959; Lee Kingman and others, compilers, *Illustrators of Children's Books, 1957-1966*, Horn Book, 1968; Doris de Montreville and Donna Hill, *Third Book of Junior Authors*, H. W. Wilson, 1972; Donnarae McCann & Olga Richard, *The Child's First Books*, H. W. Wilson, 1973; Barbara Bader, *American Picturebooks*, Macmillan, 1976; *Graphis 205*, 1979-80.

FREEMAN, Mae (Blacker) 1907-

PERSONAL: Born in 1907; married Ira Maximilian Freeman, 1935; children: one son, and one daughter.

CAREER: Author and photographer.

WRITINGS: Fun with Cooking, Random House, 1947; *Fun with Ballet*, Random House, 1952; *The Story of Albert Einstein, The Scientist Who Searched Out the Secrets of the Universe*, Random House, 1958; *Stars and Stripes: The Story of the American Flag* (illustrated by Lorence Bjorklund), Random House, 1964; *A Book of Real Science* (illustrated by John Moodie), Four Winds, 1966; *The Book of Magnets* (illustrated by Norman Bridwell), Four Winds, 1967; *Finding Out about the Past*, Random House, 1967; *When Air Moves By*, McGraw, 1968; *Finding Out about Shapes* (illustrated by Bill Morrison), McGraw, 1969; *Do You Know about Water?* (illustrated by Ernest K. Barth), Random House, 1970; *Do You Know about*

Stars? (illustrated by George Solonovich), Random House, 1970; *Gravity and the Astronauts* (illustrated by Beatrice Darwin), Crown, 1970; *The Real Magnet Book*, Scholastic Book Services, 1970; *Space Base* (illustrated by Raul Mina Mora), F. Watts, 1972; *The Wonderful Looking-Through Glass*, Scholastic Book Services, 1972; *Undersea Base* (illustrated by John Mardon), F. Watts, 1974.

MAE FREEMAN

Now you can see where you are. ■ (From *You Will Go to the Moon* by Mae and Ira Freeman. Illustrated by Robert Patterson.)

With husband, Ira Maximilian Freeman: *Fun with Science,* Random House, 1943, revised edition, 1956; *Fun with Chemistry,* Random House, 1944, reissued, 1967; *Fun with Figures,* Random House, 1946, reissued, 1963; *Fun with Geometry,* Random House, 1946, reissued, Kaye & Ward, 1969; *Fun with Astronomy,* Random House, 1953; *Fun with Your Camera,* Random House, 1955; *Your Wonderful World of Science* (illustrated by Rene Martin), Random House, 1957; *You Will Go to the Moon* (illustrated by Robert Patterson), Random House, 1959, revised edition, 1971; *The Sun, the Moon, and the Stars* (illustrated by R. Martin), Random House, 1959, revised edition, 1979; *Fun with Scientific Experiments,* Random House, 1960; *The Story of the Atom* (illustrated by R. Martin), Random House, 1960; *The Story of Electricity* (illustrated by R. Martin), Random House, 1961; *The Story of Chemistry* (illustrated by Charles Goslin), Random House, 1962; *Fun with Photography* (edited by Gordon Catling), E. Ward, 1962; *Fun and Experiments with Light,* Random House, 1963, reissued as *Fun with Light,* Kaye & Ward, 1968, Soccer, 1971.

SIDELIGHTS: Freeman lived for a while in Princeton, New Jersey, where she became acquainted with Albert Einstein. A result of that friendship was her biography for young readers, *The Story of Albert Einstein.* It was met with mixed reviews

from critics. *Kirkus* called it ''A well-realized portrait of a man who was a legend in his own lifetime. . . . The story of Einstein is brought within the grasp of children through selected facets of his life. With today's emphasis on science, it is likely to interest youngsters and the tone is nontechnical.'' The *New York Times,* on the other hand, said, ''Mrs. Freeman's biography of Einstein is an interesting and important book, but it is a study of the individual rather than what he created. No attempt is made to explain his theories, and although this is probably understandable when one considers their complexities, still there may be many young people who will feel dissatisfied at not being given any explanations.''

Freeman is also a photographer, and took her own photographs for *Fun with Ballet,* using her ten-year old daughter for a model. *Library Journal* called it ''inexpensive and accurate.'' *Saturday Review* said, ''This is the very first book for girls who want to study the art of ballet dancing.''

FOR MORE INFORMATION SEE: Horn Book, Volume XXIII, January-December, 1947, Volume XXIV, January-December, 1948; *Saturday Review,* November 15, 1952; *Kirkus,* March 1, 1958; *New York Times,* September 14, 1958; Muriel Fuller, editor, *More Junior Authors,* H. W. Wilson, 1963.

WEBB B. GARRISON

GARRISON, Webb B(lack) 1919-
(Gary Webster)

PERSONAL: Born July 19, 1919, in Covington, Ga.; son of Pinkney Jefferson and Lorena (Black) Garrison; married Mary Elizabeth Thomson, 1938; children: Carol Patricia, Webb Black, Jr., William Thomson. *Education:* Emory University, Ph.B., 1940, B.D., 1949; McKendree College, D.D., 1957. *Home:* 1615 Deerfield Circle, Decatur, Ga. 30033.

CAREER: The Methodist Church, South Carolina Conference, Timmonsville, S.C., pastor, 1940-49; Emory University School of Theology, Atlanta, Ga., assistant dean, 1950-54; Methodist General Board of Education, Nashville, Tenn., staff member, 1955-57; McKendree College, Lebanon, Ill., president, 1957-60; Roberts Park Methodist Church, Indianapolis, Ind., pastor, 1960-63; Central Methodist Church, Evansville, Ind., pastor, 1963—. Lecturer on communication at Methodist pastors' schools in twenty-eight states.

WRITINGS—Juveniles; all under pseudonym Gary Webster, except where indicated: *Wonders of Science*, Sheed & Ward, 1956; *Wonders of Man*, Sheed & Ward, 1957; *The Man Who Found Out Why: The Story of Gregor Mendel*, Hawthorn, 1963; *Journey Into Light: The Story of Louis Braille*, Hawthorn, 1964; *Wonders of Earth*, Sheed & Ward, 1967; (under name

Webb Garrison) *How It Started*, Abingdon, 1972; (under name Webb Garrison) *Why Didn't I Think of That?*, Prentice-Hall, 1977.

Juveniles; all contributions to anthologies and compilations: *Builders for Freedom*, Beckley-Cardy, 1949; *Builders for Progress*, Beckley-Cardy, 1950; *Latin American Leaders*, Beckley-Cardy, 1951; *Leaders of the Frontier*, Beckley-Cardy, 1952; *John Kieran's Treasury of Great Nature Writing*, Hanover, 1957; *Illustrated Library of the Natural Sciences* (four volumes), Simon & Schuster, 1958; *The Bible Story Library*, Bobbs-Merrill, 1963; *Audubon Nature Library*, Simon & Schuster, 1969.

Other: *The Preacher and His Audience*, Revell, 1954; *Why You Say It*, Abingdon, 1955; *Improve Your Church Bulletins*, Revell, 1957; *Sermon Seeds from the Gospels*, Revell, 1958; (under pseudonym, Gary Webster) *Codfish, Cats, and Civilization*, Doubleday, 1959, Kennikat, 1968; *Creative Imagination in Preaching*, Abingdon, 1960; (under pseudonym Gary Webster) *Laughter in the Bible*, Bethany, 1960; *Women in the Life of Jesus*, Bobbs-Merrill, 1962; (contributor) *Reaching Beyond Your Pulpit*, Revell, 1962; *A Guide to Reading the Entire Bible in One Year*, Bobbs-Merrill, 1963; (contributor) *History of American Methodism*, Abingdon, 1963; *The Biblical Image of the Family*, Tidings, 1965; *What's in a Word?*, Abingdon, 1965; *Ten Paths to Peace and Power*, Abingdon, 1966; *Strange Bonds Between Animals and Men*, Ace Books, 1966; *Giving Wings to a Warm Heart*, Methodist Commission on Promotion and Cultivation, 1968; *Strange Facts About the Bible*, Abingdon, 1968; *The Ignorance Book*, Morrow, 1970;

At first drive-in movies only operated during the warm months, but the development of individual speakers and in-car heaters made them a year-round institution. ■ (From *Why Didn't I Think of That?* by Webb Garrison. Illustrated by Ray Abel.)

Disasters that Made History, Abingdon, 1973; *Sidelights on the American Revolution,* Abingdon, 1974; *Devotions for the Middle Years,* The Upper Room, 1974; (with Halford E. Luccock) *Endless Line of Splendor,* United Methodist Commission on Communications, 1975; *Lost Pages from American History,* Stackpole, 1976; *Strange Facts About the Bible,* Abingdon, 1976; *Strange Facts About Death,* Abingdon, 1978. Contributor to most annual volumes of *The Upper Room Companion* and *Upper Room Disciplines.*

Work has appeared in such magazines as *American Legion Magazine, Blue Book, Car Life, Catholic Digest, Columbia, Coronet, Elementary Electronics, Journal of Living, Ladies' Home Journal,* and many more.

SIDELIGHTS: ''Writing for children is in many ways more demanding than writing for adults. Boys and girls will not tolerate dull material! Any time an adult can achieve a viewpoint of a boy or girl, something fresh and vivid is likely to result.

''Now that I have nine grandchildren, I find myself often engaged in the only attempts I've ever made at fiction—bedtime stories that center about the exploits of Archibald, an apple-worm who lives in the Great Smoky Mountains. Invariably, his adventures just happen to involve the girls and boys who are included in the evening audience. None of these stories have yet been prepared for publication.''

GLUCK, Felix   1924(?)-1981

OBITUARY NOTICE: Born about 1924, in Germany; died February 22, 1981, in London, England. Founder and managing director of Felix Gluck Press. Gluck spent part of World War II in a German concentration camp. After his liberation he worked for the state publishing house in Hungary as art director, a position which he also filled at Aldus Books after his emigration to England in 1956. In 1971 Gluck founded the Felix Gluck Press, which became especially noted for its series of illustrated children's classics and facsimile editions of old and rare books. Gluck won the National Book League Design Award seven times, and won honors at three Bologna Children's Book Fairs. *Obituaries: Publishers Weekly,* April 10, 1981.

GOBLE, Paul   1933-

PERSONAL: Born September 17, 1933, in Surrey, England; son of harpsichord makers; married Dorothy Goble (a children's author and in the industrial design business), marriage ended; married second wife, Janet, 1978; children: a son and a daughter (first marriage); one son (second marriage). *Education:* Attended the Central School of Arts and Crafts, London, 1956-59. *Home:* Nemo Route 104Y, Black Hills, Deadwood, S.D.57732.

CAREER: Children's author and illustrator, industrial designer. Visiting lecturer in the industrial design department at the Central School of Arts and Crafts, London, 1960; with wife, Dorothy Goble, ran his own design practice for ten years (during which time they won prizes in three industrial design competitions); senior lecturer in three-dimension design, Ravensbourne College of Art and Design, London. His first book, *Red Hawk's Account of Custer's Last Battle,* was published

in 1969, and all following books have dealt with Indian life. *Military service:* Two years of service in Germany. *Awards, honors:* Caldecott Medal, 1979, for *The Girl Who Loved Wild Horses. Exhibitions:* Dahl Fine Art Museum, Rapid City, S.D., one-man show, 1977, and others.

WRITINGS—For children: (With first wife, Dorothy Goble) *Red Hawk's Account of Custer's Last Battle (Horn Book* honor list; ALA Notable Book), Pantheon, 1969; (with D. Goble) *Brave Eagle's Account of the Fetterman Fight, 21 December 1866* (illustrated by Paul Goble), Pantheon, 1972 (published in England as *The Hundred in the Hands: Brave Eagle's Account of the Fetterman Fight, 21st December 1866,* Macmillan, 1972); (with D. Goble) *Lone Bull's Horse Raid* (illustrated by P. Goble), Macmillan, 1973, Bradbury, 1973; (with D. Goble) *The Friendly Wolf* (illustrated by P. Goble), Bradbury, 1974; *The Girl Who Loved Wild Horses* (illustrated by P. Goble), Bradbury, 1978; *The Gift of the Sacred Dog* (illustrated by P. Goble), Bradbury, 1980.

Illustrator: Richard Erdoes, transcriber and editor, *The Sound of Flutes and Other Indian Legends* (ALA Notable Book), Pantheon, 1976.

ADAPTATIONS—Recordings: ''Red Hawk's Account of Custer's Last Battle,'' read by Authur S. Junaluska, Caedmon Records, 1972.

WORK IN PROGRESS: ''I am working on.a Paul Goble calendar for 1983, to be published by Bradbury Press.''

SIDELIGHTS: ''I have been interested in everything Indian since I can remember. The books of Grey Owl and Ernest Thompson Seton are well known in the United States. Before

PAUL GOBLE

(From _The Girl Who Loved Wild Horses_ by Paul Goble. Illustrated by the author.)

television days my mother read the complete works of these two authors to my brother and me. Many other books too, but I loved best Grey Owl and Ernest Thompson Seton because both wrote about Indians and both were true naturalists. The world they wrote about was so different from the crowded island where I lived. And yet perhaps growing up so far from this country sharpened my need to know more. Over many years I acquired a considerable library of the better books concerning Native Americans, and I really studied those books.

"In 1959, after I had finished three years of training in industrial design at the Central School of Art and Design in London, I was fortunate to be given a long summer visit to this country. I accompanied Frithjof Schuon, the eminent Swiss writer on comparative religion. He had contacts among Sioux and Crow Indians, and the summer was spent on reservations in South Dakota and Montana.

"Love of Indians and love of nature have always been my priorities, but they never seemed a combination likely to support a family. For the next eighteen years, from 1959 to 1977, I kept it as a serious hobby and put my main energies into industrial design, with the eighteen years about equally divided between practicing and teaching the subject. The hobby took over completely when I left England to live in the Black Hills as a painter.

"As a teacher in England I had long summer vacations, and in recent years I spent four summers in the United States. My son Richard came with me on most of those visits. We would bring a small tent, hire a car, and spend the summer with Sioux friends in South Dakota and Crow Indian friends in Montana. During those summers I was privileged to take part in ceremonies, to be present at their sacred Sun Dances. I have taken part in building the Sun Dance lodge and have helped to pitch tipis. Knowing that I loved their ways, my Indian friends have told me much about their folklore and beliefs. They have given me new perspectives, and really all my travels were spiritual journeys.

"I do not know what is a valid reason for writing a book. _The Friendly Wolf_ . . . came about because I was distressed at how wolves in Alaska were being hunted to extinction by helicopter. No Indian story I had ever read had anything but fine things to tell about wolves. The Indian understands the language of the birds and animals and seeks to learn their wisdom. He knows they were here long before we were and being older, deserve our respect. We have been subjected to Walt Disney and his many followers. I have a horror of the havoc they have created with literature, art, and the blunting of our attitudes towards nature. Children grow up with the idea that bears are huggable, woodpeckers are destructive, coyotes and tomcats mean; and that whales and dolphins are happiest when being made to clown in a marina. Respect and inspiration are not there at all.

"Similarly, in _The Girl Who Loved Wild Horses_ I tried to express and paint what I believe to be the Native American rapport with nature. The Indian does not feel afraid or alone in the forests and prairies; he knows many stories about ancestors who turned into the seven stars of the Big Dipper and others who became the Pleiades. Indians tell about a girl who married the Morning Star and of their son who, coming from the Sky but living on Earth, did many wonderful things. Knowledge of this relationship with the universe gives them confidence. They have no thought to reorganize nature in a way other than that in which the Great Spirit made it. Indeed, it would be sacrilegious to do so.

"*The Girl Who Loved Wild Horses* is not a retelling of any one legend but a synthesis of many. Psychological interpretations should not be read into it. Simply, the girl loves horses, and perhaps she becomes one. If we think about something long enough, maybe we will become like that thing. I believe children will easily understand this. By the time we are grown up we might think some thought-doors have been opened, but perhaps others have been closed.

"I hope that Native Americans will approve of the book and will feel sympathy for the illustrations. At an . . . autographing party in a small South Dakota community, it gave me great joy when an Indian gave me a beautiful feather in a fold of red felt. And there was a sixth-grade Sioux boy who, while having breakfast, heard on the radio that I was to be at the Rapid City library that day. He told his mother he was not going to school, and so it was we met. It gives me a warm feeling when Indians respond to my books. Some will speak no English, and yet the lively discussions amongst themselves which the illustrations provoke tell me they are happy that a white man has admiration for their culture." [Paul Goble, "Caldecott Acceptance Speech," *Horn Book*, August, 1979.]

FOR MORE INFORMATION SEE: New York Times Book Review, November 9, 1970, September 24, 1972, November 11, 1973; *Horn Book,* February, 1977, December, 1978, April, 1979, August, 1979; Doris de Montreville and Elizabeth D. Crawford, editors, *Fourth Book of Junior Authors and Illustrators,* H. W. Wilson, 1978.

GOLDBERG, Herbert S. 1926-

PERSONAL: Born July 23, 1926, in New York, N.Y.; son of Murray and Bella (Rubin) Goldberg; married, 1948; children: Jacquelyn, Sheryl. *Education:* St. John's University, B.S., 1948; University of Missouri, M.A., 1950; The Ohio State University, Ph.D., 1953; additional study at Oak Ridge Institute of Nuclear Studies, 1954, and National Institutes of Health, 1962. *Home:* 401 Hulen Dr., Columbia, Mo. *Agent:* McIntosh & Otis, Inc., 18 East 41st St., New York, N.Y. *Office:* University of Missouri, Columbia, Mo.

CAREER: The Ohio State University, Columbus, research assistant, 1950-53; University of Missouri, Columbia, 1953—, started as assistant professor, became professor, associate dean, school of medicine, 1967—. Visiting scientist at Cambridge University, 1960; visiting professor at Southern Illinois University, 1961. Diplomate, American Broad of Microbiology. World Health Organization, United Nations, expert committee member; Ad Hoc Antibiotic Advisory committee, Food and Drug Administration. *Military service:* U.S. Navy, 1944-46. *Member:* American, French, and British Societies of microbiology, Sigma Xi. *Awards, honors:* Wellcome Foundation (Great Britain), travel fellowship, 1960.

WRITINGS: Antibiotics: Their Chemistry and Non-medical Uses, Van Nostrand, 1959; *Great Medical Discoveries,* Dou-

HERBERT S. GOLDBERG

bleday, 1960; *Hippocrates,* Watts, 1963. Contributor of fifty articles to professional journals.

WORK IN PROGRESS: Microbes, a book for children; *Basic and Applied Microbiology for Nurses; A Day in the Life of the Health Professionals.*

SIDELIGHTS: "I am currently active in directing young people into the health professions and am returning to the writing of children's books after a considerable interval of writing professional articles in medical journals."

GRANT, Bruce 1893-1977

OBITUARY NOTICE—See sketch in *SATA* Volume 5: Born April 17, 1893, in Wichita Falls, Tex.; died of a self-inflicted gunshot wound, April 8, 1977, in Winnetka, Ill. Newspaperman and author. Grant served as rewrite man, city editor, and war correspondent for the *Chicago Times,* (predecessor of the *Chicago Sun-Times*), and as a feature writer and reporter for various other papers in Dallas, Louisville, New York City, and Buenos Aires, Argentina. In 1946 he became a free-lance author and eventually wrote more than fifty books. Many, including *Warpath: A Story of the Plains Indians, Longhorn: A Story of the Chisolm Trail,* and *Isaac Hull, Captain of Old Ironsides,* were historically-oriented works for children. *For More Information See: Contemporary Authors,* Volumes 1-4, revised, Gale, 1967. *Obituaries: New York Times,* April 10, 1977; *AB Bookman's Weekly,* May 9, 1977; *Contemporary Authors,* Volumes 69-72, Gale, 1978.

GORDON GRANT

GRANT, Gordon   1875-1962

PERSONAL: Born June 7, 1875, in San Francisco, Calif.; died May 6, 1962 in New York City; son of George (a bank officer) and Grace Adelaide (Griffin) Grant; married Violet Maude Goodall (an actress), February 19, 1901. *Education:* Attended Heatherly and Lambeth Art Schools, London, England. *Politics:* Republican. *Religion:* Presbyterian. *Residence:* New York, N.Y.

CAREER: Artist. *San Francisco Examiner,* San Francisco, Calif., staff artist, 1895; *New York World,* New York, N.Y., staff artist, 1896; artist on Boer War front for *Harper's Weekly,* 1899-1901; staff artist for *Puck,* 1901-09. Work exhibited in permanent collections at the Metropolitan Museum of Art, the White House, and numerous other museums and public buildings. *Military service:* U.S. National Guard, 1907-18, became captain; served on Mexican border. *Member:* American Society of Graphic Artists, American Watercolor Society, National Academy of Design, National Arts Club (life member), Allied Artists of America, Chicago Society of Etchers, Audubon Artists, St. Andrew's Society, Philadelphia Watercolor Society, Baltimore Watercolor Club, Washington Watercolor Club,

Ship Model Society (founder and former president), Salmagundi (life member), Dutch Treat, Amateur Comedy (former president and life member). *Awards, honors:* Ranger Purchase Award from National Academy of Design; Chauncey F. Ryder Prize from American Watercolor Society; Shaw Prize from Salmagundi, 1931 and 1936; award from Chicago Society of Etchers, 1936; Silver Medal for Etching from Paris Exposition, 1937; Anonymous Members' Prize from Allied Artists of America, 1943; United States Honor Certificate granted by President John F. Kennedy.

WRITINGS—Self-illustrated: *The Story of the Ship,* McLaughlin, 1919; *Sail Ho!—Life Aboard the Old Sailing Ships,* Payson, 1931; *Greasy Luck: A Whaling Sketch Book,* Payson, 1932, reprinted, Caravan Maritime Books, 1970; (with Harold Platt) *Ship Ahoy!,* Doubleday, 1934; *New Story of the Ship,* McLaughlin, 1936; *Ships Under Sail: An Outline of the Development of the Sailing Vessel,* Garden City Publishing Co., 1939; *The Secret Voyage,* Morrow, 1942; *Sketchbook,* Watson-Guptill, 1960; *Wilderness* (poems), Noel Young, 1965; *Journey* (poems), Capricorn, 1969.

At about ten of the clock Penrod emerged hastily from the kitchen door. ■ (From *Penrod* by Booth Tarkington. Illustrated by Gordon Grant.)

One of Gordon Grant's many marine drawings.

(From *The Secret Voyage* by Gordon Grant. Illustrated by the author.)

Illustrator: Willis J. Abbot, *Panama and the Canal in Picture and Prose,* Sydnicate Publishing, 1913; Booth Tarkington, *Penrod,* Doubleday, Page, 1914, school edition, Globe Book, 1954; Booth Tarkington, *Ramsey Milholland,* Doubleday, Page, 1919; Henry Brundage Culver, *The Book of Old Ships,* Doubleday, 1924; Booth Tarkington, *Penrod Jashber,* Doubleday, Doran, 1929; Booth Tarkington, *Penrod: His Complete Story,* Doubleday, 1931; Culver, *Forty Famous Ships,* Doubleday, 1936; Wilbert Snow, *Before the Wind* (poem), Gotham House, 1938; Arthur H. Baldwin, *Sou'wester Victorious,* Random House, 1939; Robert Carse, *There Go the Ships,* Morrow 1942; Alexander Kinnan Laing, *Sea Witch,* Farrar, Straus, 1944; William Martin Williamson, editor, *The Eternal Sea: An Anthology of Sea Poetry,* Coward, 1946; Bruce Grant, *Eagle of the Sea,* Rand McNally, 1949; Herman Wouk, *The City Boy,* Doubleday, 1952; Leonard Outhwaite, *Unrolling the Map: The Story of Exploration,* John Day, 1972.

SIDELIGHTS: Grant, noted painter of ships and the sea, was born of Scottish parentage in the busy port city of San Francisco. Grant's father, an officer with Wells Fargo Nevada National Bank, decided that his son should be educated in Scotland, and it was during this four-and-one-half month passage aboard a Glasgow sailing ship that images of the sea became firmly implanted in young Grant's imagination.

After receiving his early education at Kirkcaldy School in Tifeshire, Scotland, Grant studied art in London. He began his career by returning to San Francisco where he spent one year as staff artist for the *Examiner*. After working for several other publications, he joined the military. Following his discharge, he took up painting and etching as a full-time career.

Grant's pictures of ships, harbors, and the sea proved to be immensely popular with the public and critics as well. He gained respect not only for his artistic merit, but also for his technical knowledge. Grant's renderings of ships were regarded as so accurate that he was commissioned by Congress to do the official portrait of the U.S.S. *Constitution*. The original painting of "Old Ironsides" now hangs in the President's office, and over a quarter of a million prints were sold to finance the restoration of the ship. "Marine subjects fall broadly into three groups: the open sea, off-shore waters, and harbor scenes. In the first named, the painter's composition involves two elements: the sky and the sea, with perhaps a ship or boat for the middle ground. In harbors, many more objects present themselves—shore, wharves, ships, boats, and a multitude of other things—material for middle and foreground. It would seem rather obvious to remark that the place to study the movement of deep water is at sea, and fortunate is the painter who can make long voyages to observe the ocean in its measureless moods.

"In drawing the open sea (and I cannot lay too much stress on drawing), the first thing to realize is that the waves, activated by the prevailing wind, move in the same direction, though, on occasion, currents will react and produce cross movements. With in-shore water—surf and tide—the opposite is at once noticeable. Waves about to break on the shore are often deflected by subsurface rocks and bottom formations, as well as by retreating waves thrown back by a rocky shore. Thus surf painting presents a more complex problem to the painter than does the open sea.

"My best advice to the student who wishes to paint surf is to forget your color box for the time being, and arm yourself with a large paper pad and a 6B carpenter's pencil. Having picked

Gordon Grant, sitting in front of his painting of a full-rigged ship.

out the most comfortable rock which presents itself, sit and watch the heave and roll of the sea; watch it for hours on end.

"Then put the pencil to work, looking for the long line—the *short* lines will take care of themselves; never lose sight of the fact that we are seeking a design. All must balance: sky, sea, rocks. One wave moves on leaving a trough which, in turn, will rise and become a wave. The proper disposition of the foam pattern and broken water is most important. This procedure I heartily recommend for days on end before the painting is begun.

"At each point you will note how the reflection of the sky becomes darker until there is no reflection at all—just deep blue—the sea itself. The moving sea is nothing more than countless millions of reflectors, tipped at different angles to the light rays. The near side of the waves is dark because you are looking into them. The far side is light since it reflects the sky. In-shore water is light in color because it is shallow: the light is reflected from a sandy bottom, much foam aerates it and accounts for the various shades of green peculiar to surf.

"The observant student cannot fail to ask himself why the water is brown today, gray tomorrow, and blue the next day. All these questions he can answer for himself if he has eyes to see. Knowing the 'why' he is well on his way to the 'how.'

". . .Like most professional painters, I use the best tools the market affords—sable brushes, handmade papers, and the best quality tube pigments. I prefer all-rag, medium rough paper in weights consistent with the scale of my contemplated picture. Although I sometimes paint on full sheets (22x30), more often, in recent years, I have painted on half sheets working directly before my subject. My palette consists of cadmium red, light and medium, cadmium yellow, pale and deep, lemon yellow, cadmium orange, Winsor blue, cobalt blue, ultramarine blue, Winsor or emerald green, burnt and raw sienna, alizarin crim-

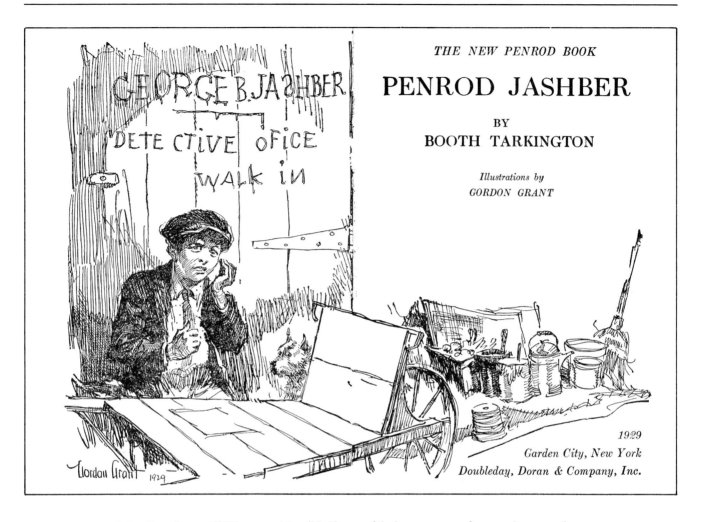

Meantime, Samuel Williams sped the gilded hours of the long summer afternoon by occupying himself in meritorious industry. ■ (From *Penrod Jashber* by Booth Tarkington. Illustrated by Gordon Grant.)

son and Payne's gray.'' [''Gordon Grant Stresses Drawing for Watercolorists,'' *American Artist,* September, 1960.]

Much of the appeal of Grant's paintings lies in the mysterious quality he managed to evoke through his use of light and shadow. Grant believed that the most important element of a work of art is that which exists in the mind of the viewer.

Grant's work began to be exhibited yearly in New York's Grand Central Gallery in 1928. It has since become part of collections in major museums and galleries throughout the country. His painting, ''Eternal Sea,'' the focal point of the Chapel of the Seaman's Church Institute in New York, is one of his better-known works.

Book illustration also comprised a major portion of Grant's career, and like all of his work, his illustrations grew out of continuous observation of ships, sailors, and the sea. *Sail Ho!,* for example, was the result of observations he made as a passenger on the *Star of Alaska. The Book of Old Ships* and *Forty Famous Ships,* both written with Henry B. Culver, contain accurate renderings of historic vessels, as does *Ship Ahoy!.* Grant died at his home in New York City on May 6, 1962.

HOBBIES AND OTHER INTERESTS: Model shipbuilding and amateur theater.

FOR MORE INFORMATION SEE: St. Nicholas, October, 1934; Bertha E. Mahony and others, compilers, *Illustrators of Children's Books: 1744-1945,* Horn Book, 1947; *Design,* September 11, 1953; B. M. Miller and others, compilers, *Illustrators of Children's Books: 1946-1956,* Horn Book, 1958; *American Artist,* September, 1960. Obituaries: *New York Times,* May 8, 1962; New York *Herald Tribune,* May 8, 1962; *Americana Annual,* 1963.

All that mankind has done, thought, gained or been: it is lying as in magic preservation in the pages of books.
—Thomas Carlyle

Books, like proverbs, receive their chief value from the stamp and esteem of ages through which they have passed.

—Sir William Temple

GREENBERG, Joanne (Goldenberg) 1932-
(Hannah Green)

PERSONAL: Born September 24, 1932, in Brooklyn, N.Y.; daughter of Julius Lester and Rosalie (Bernstein) Goldenberg; married Albert Greenberg, September 4, 1955; children: David, Alan. *Education:* American University, B.A. *Religion:* Jewish. *Address:* 29221 Rainbow Hills Rd., Golden, Colo. 80401. *Agent:* Lois Wallace, Wallace and Shell, 177 East 70th St., New York, N.Y. 10021, and William Morris Agency, 1350 Ave. of the Americas, New York, N.Y. 10019.

CAREER: Writer. Currently teacher's aide in rural school, teaching etymology; Lookout Mountain Fire Dept., Idledale Rescue Team, certified emergency medical technician. *Member:* Authors Guild, P.E.N., Colorado Authors' League, National Association of the Deaf. *Awards, honors:* Harry and Ethel Daroff Memorial Fiction Award, Jewish Book Council of America, 1963; Marcus L. Kenner award from the New York Association of the Deaf, 1971; The Christopher Award, from the Christophers, 1971, for *In This Sign;* Freida Fromm-Reichman Memorial award from the American Academy of Psychoanalysis, 1971; honorary D.L. from Western Maryland College, 1977 and from Gallaudet College, 1979.

WRITINGS—All published by Holt: *The King's Persons*, 1963; (under pseudonym, Hannah Green) *I Never Promised You a Rose Garden*, 1964; *The Monday Voices*, 1965; *Summering*, 1966; *In This Sign*, 1968; *Rites of Passage*, 1971; *Founder's Praise*, 1976; *High Crimes and Misdemeanors*, 1979; *A Season of Delight*, 1981. Magazine writings include a novella in *Hudson Review,* stories in *Virginia Quarterly, Chatelaine,* and *University of Kansas City Review,* and reviews in *Saturday Review.*

ADAPTATIONS—Movie: *I Never Promised You a Rose Garden* was made into a motion picture, starring Bibi Anderson and Kathleen Quinn, New World Pictures, 1977.

SIDELIGHTS: Greenberg's novel, *I Never Promised You a Rose Garden,* which has meant so much to young adult readers, was written under the pseudonym, Hannah Green. It concerned her own experience with mental problems. "*Rose Garden* which we call *INPYARG* at home, was written when my two sons were very small. I wanted the people at home near Golden, Colorado, some of whom are quite conservative, to look funny at my kids for what they do, not what their mother did. Also, we had taken a poll of my husband's hospital co-workers whenever they came up to the house. We'd ask them if they thought schizophrenia was curable or not. Most of them had said no, that there were only temporary remissions. I don't want to live that, to have people look at me, waiting. Sure I have anxiety about it—doesn't everybody? But I live a quiet life and I wanted to protect that.

"The rough thing really came when the kids got older. I'd wanted to tell them about all of this, but I couldn't find a way. They knew that I wrote a book under another name and that it was kind of a secret book. And then something happened to my older boy. One day at school a friend asked him if he was going to be as crazy as his mother was. He came home and said to me, 'Mom, were you crazy?' And I had to tell him

(From the movie "I Never Promised You a Rose Garden," starring Kathleen Quinlan and Bibi Andersson. Released by New World Pictures, 1977.)

JOANNE GREENBERG

'yes.' I hadn't expected him to learn of it just like that. I tried to catch him before he went away on me, because he's a defensive kid. I said, 'Wait a minute, insanity is not inherited. Are you worried about yourself? Because to the best of my knowledge, you are not and never will be.' And he said something like, 'When's supper?' And I said, 'I'm going to get you to hear me, no matter what.' Eventually he did.

". . .His brother Alan . . . reacted quite differently to the news. Alan said, 'Gee, that must have been awfully tough for you,' and he spent the rest of the summer opening car doors for me." ["Joanne Greenberg, " *Top of the News,* April, 1972.]

FOR MORE INFORMATION SEE: Top of the News, April, 1977.

GRINGHUIS, Richard H.   1918-1974
   (Dirk Gringhuis)

OBITUARY NOTICE—See sketch in *SATA* Volume 6: Born September 22, 1918, in Grand Rapids, Mich.; died March 31, 1974, in East Lansing, Mich. Educator, museum curator, author, and muralist. Gringhuis devoted most of his life to the preservation of Michigan history. Employed by Michigan State University as museum curator and associate professor of education, he also wrote, produced, and hosted a weekly edu-

cational television program for school children, "Open Door to Michigan." Gringhuis's interest in Michigan is also evident in his self-illustrated books for children, over half of which, including *Tuliptime* and *Open Door to the Great Lakes,* deal with some aspect of the state or its history. A muralist as well as an illustrator, Gringhuis painted scenes of Michigan history for display at such sites around the state as public libraries in East Lansing and Sturgis, and at Ft. Mackinac on Mackinac Island. *For More Information See: Contemporary Authors,* Volumes 1-4, revised, Gale, 1967. *Obituaries: Detroit Free Press,* April 3, 1974.

GROCH, Judith (Goldstein)   1929-

PERSONAL: Surname is pronounced Grosh; born May 14, 1929, in New York, N.Y.; daughter of Eli (a physician) and Caroline (an attorney; maiden name Kleppner) Goldstein; married Sigmund N. Groch (a physician), 1953 (died, 1961); married Wilbert Minowitz (a physicist), October 6, 1962; children: Deborah Susan, Emily Louise; Peter (stepson). *Education:* Vassar College, student, 1946-48; Columbia University, B.S., 1952. *Home:* 168 West 86th St., New York, N.Y. 10024. *Agent:* Marie Rodell-Frances Collin, 156 East 52nd St., New York, N.Y. 10022.

CAREER: Mayo Clinic, Department of Biophysics, Rochester, Minn., research technician, 1953-56; *Medical World News,* New York City, assistant managing editor, 1973—; free-lance writer. *Member:* Phi Beta Kappa, Authors Guild, Authors League of America, National Association of Science Writers.

JUDITH GROCH

Awards, honors: Winner of National Mass Media award, Thomas Alva Edison Foundation, 1963, for *You and Your Brain.*

WRITINGS—Juveniles, except as noted: *You and Your Brain,* Harper, 1963; *The Right to Create* (adult), Little, Brown, 1970; *Play the Bach, Dear!,* Doubleday, 1978. Contributor of articles and short stories to magazines, including *McCall's, Seventeen,* and *American Girl.*

HOBBIES AND OTHER INTERESTS: Painting, piano, ceramics, tennis.

FOR MORE INFORMATION SEE: Saturday Review, February 21, 1970; *Library Journal,* November 1, 1970.

GUTMAN, Naham   1899(?)-1981

OBITUARY NOTICE: Born about 1899; died in January, 1981, in Israel. A painter and sculptor, Gutman primarily wrote and illustrated children's books. *Path of the Orange Peels: Adventures in the Early Days of Tel Aviv,* written in Hebrew and later translated into English, is one of his better known books. *Obituaries: Contemporary Authors,* Volume 102, Gale, 1981; *AB Bookman's Weekly,* January 26, 1981.

HARDY, Thomas   1840-1928

PERSONAL: Born June 2, 1840, in Higher Brockhampton, Dorsetshire, England; died January 11, 1928, in Dorchester, England; ashes buried in Westminster Abbey; son of Thomas (a builder and stonemason) and Jamima Hardy; married Emma Lavinia Gifford, 1874 (died, 1912); married Florence Emily Dugdale, 1914 (died, 1937). *Education:* Attended local schools until the age of sixteen; later attended evening classes at King's College, London, 1862-67. *Home:* Max Gate, near Dorchester, England.

CAREER: Novelist and poet. Worked as an apprentice to John Hicks, an ecclesiastical architect, in Dorchester, 1856-62; employed as an architect in London, 1862-67. *Awards, honors:* Awarded a medal by the Royal Institute of British Architects, 1863; royal Order of Merit, 1910; gold medal of the Royal Society of Literature; honorary degrees from Oxford, Cambridge, St. Andrews, Bristol, and Aberdeen Universities.

WRITINGS—Of interest to young adults; all novels, except as noted: *Far from the Madding Crowd* (first published serially in *Cornhill Magazine,* 1874), Holt, 1874, new edition, Dodd, 1968; *The Return of the Native* (first published serially in *Belgravia,* 1878), Holt, 1878, new edition, Norton, 1969; *The Mayor of Casterbridge: The Life and Death of a Man of Character* (first published serially in *The Graphic,* 1886), Lovell, 1886, also published as *The Life and Death of the Mayor of Casterbridge: A Story of a Man of Character,* new edition, Houghton, 1969; *Tess of the D'Urbervilles: A Pure Woman Faithfully Presented* (various portions first published in *The Graphic, Fortnightly Review,* and *National Observer,* 1891), Osgood, McIlvaine, 1891, Harper, 1892, new edition, Norton, 1966; *Jude the Obscure* (first published serially in a modified form in *Harper's Magazine,* 1894-95), Harper, 1896, new edition, Houghton, 1965; *Our Exploits in West Poley* (first published serially in *Household,* 1892-93), later edition (edited

THOMAS HARDY

by Richard L. Purdy; illustrated by John Lawrence), Oxford University Press, 1978; *The Pinnacled Tower: Selected Poems of Thomas Hardy* (edited by Helen Plotz; wood engravings by Clare Leighton), Macmillan, 1975.

Other Novels: *Desperate Remedies,* privately printed (anonymously), 1871, later published under the author's name, Holt, 1874, new edition, St. Martin's, 1966; *Under the Greenwood Tree: A Rural Painting of the Dutch School,* Tinsley Brothers, 1872, Holt, 1873, new edition, St. Martin's, 1968; *A Pair of Blue Eyes* (first published serially in *Tinsley's Magazine,* 1872-73), Holt, 1973, St. Martin's, 1966; *The Hand of Ethelberta* (first published serially in *Cornhill Magazine,* 1875-76), Holt, 1876, new edition, St. Martin's 1958; *The Trumpet-Major* (first published serially in *Good Words,* 1880), Holt, 1880, new edition, St. Martin's, 1966; *A Laodicean; or, The Castle of the De Stancys* (first published serially in *Harper's Magazine,* European edition, 1880-81), Harper, 1881, new edition, St. Martin's, 1968; *Two on a Tower* (first published serially in *Atlantic Monthly,* 1882), Holt, 1882, new edition, St. Martin's, 1968; *The Romantic Adventures of a Milkmaid* (first published in *The Graphic,* 1883), Harper, 1884; *The Woodlanders* (first published serially in *Macmillan's Magazine,* 1886-87), Harper, 1887, new edition, St. Martin's 1967; *The Well-Beloved* (first published serially in the *Illustrated London News,* 1892, as *The Pursuit of the Well-Beloved*), Harper, 1897; *An Indiscretion in the Life of an Heiress* (first published serially in *New Quarterly Magazine,* 1878), privately printed, 1934, later edition (edited by Carl J. Weber), Johns Hopkins Press, 1935.

Selected short stories: *Wessex Tales: Strange, Lively and Commonplace,* Harper, 1888, new edition, St. Martin's, 1967 (con-

Past Things Retold

FRIENDS AND FAMILY

She showed us the spot where the maypole was yearly planted,
And where the bandsmen stood.

■ (From *The Pinnacled Tower: Selected Poems* by Thomas Hardy, edited by Helen Plotz. Wood engraving by Clare Leighton.)

tains *The Distracted Young Preacher, Fellow-Townsmen, The Three Strangers, Interlopers at the Knap,* and *The Withered Arm*); *A Group of Noble Dames* (published in a different form in *The Graphic,* 1890), Harper, 1891, new edition, St. Martin's, 1968; *Life's Little Ironies: A Set of Tales,* Harper, 1894, new edition, St. Martin's 1968; *A Changed Man, The Waiting Supper, and Other Tales,* Harper, 1913, new edition, St. Martin's, 1966; *The Short Stories of Thomas Hardy,* Macmillan, 1928 (contains *Wessex Tales, Life's Little Ironies, A Group of Noble Dames,* and *A Changed Man and Other Tales*).

Poems: *The Poetical Works of Thomas Hardy,* Macmillan, 1919-21, Volume I: *Collected Poems,* Volume II: *The Dynasts; Collected Poems of Thomas Hardy,* Macmillan, 1926; *Selected Poems* (edited by John Crowe Ransom), Macmillan, 1961; *Selected Shorter Poems of Thomas Hardy* (edited by John Wain), St. Martin's, 1966.

Separate poems—all privately printed, except as noted: *The Convergence of the Twain,* 1912; *Song of the Soldiers,* 1914; *Before Marching and After,* 1915; *The Oxen,* 1915; *In Time of the Breaking of Nations,* 1916; *To Shakespeare after Three*

Hundred Years, 1916; *When I Weekly Knew,* 1916; *A Call to National Service; An Appeal to America; Cry of the Homeless,* 1917; *The Fiddler's Story: A Jingle on the Times,* 1917; *Domicilium,* 1918; *Compassion,* 1924; *Yuletide in a Younger World* (illustrated by Albert Rutherston), Faber & Gwyer, 1927.

Plays: *The Three Wayfarers* (one-act; adapted from his story *The Three Strangers*), Harper, 1893, reprinted, Scholars Facsimiles & Reprints, 1940; *The Dynasts: A Drama of the Napoleonic Wars* (nineteen acts, in three parts), Macmillan, 1904-08, new edition, St. Martin's, 1965; *The Play of "Saint George,"* privately printed, 1921, later published in *Mumming and the Mummers' Play of St. George: Three Versions including that of Thomas Hardy* (edited by James Stevens Cox), Toucan Press, 1970; *The Famous Tragedy of the Queen of Cornwall at Tintagel in Lyonness* (one-act; produced, 1923), Macmillan, 1923.

Collections: *The Works of Thomas Hardy in Prose and Verse,* Wessex edition, 21 volumes, Macmillan, 1912-13, new Wessex edition, 1975; *The Works of Thomas Hardy,* Mellstock edition, 37 volumes, Macmillan, 1919-20; *The Life and Art of Thomas Hardy: Essays, Notes and Letters Collected for the First Time* (edited by Ernest Brennecke, Jr.), Greenberg, 1925, reprinted, Books for Libraries, 1968; *The Letters of Thomas Hardy* (edited by Carl J. Weber), Colby College Press, 1954, reprinted, Kraus, 1970; *Thomas Hardy's Personal Writings: Prefaces, Literary Opinions, Reminiscences* (edited by Harold Orel), Macmillan, 1967, University Press of Kansas, 1969.

Contributor of essays and criticism to *Chambers Journal, Longman's Magazine, New Review, Pall Mall Gazette, English Illustrated Magazine, Cornhill Magazine,* and *Book Monthly.*

ADAPTATIONS—Plays: *Tess in the Theatre* (two dramatizations of Tess of the D'Urbervilles; one by Thomas Hardy, one by Lorimer Stoddard; edited by Marguerite Roberts), University of Toronto Press, 1950.

Movies and filmstrips: "Tess of the D'Urbervilles" (motion picture), Metro-Goldwyn-Mayer, 1924; "Tess," starring Nastassia Kinski, directed by Roman Polansky based on *Tess of the D'Urbervilles,* Columbia Pictures, 1981; "The Greenwood Tree" (motion picture), British International Pictures, 1930; "August Heat" (motion picture), adaptation of *The Convergence of the Twain,* Department of Theater Arts, University of California, 1961; "Far from the Madding Crowd" (motion picture), starring Julie Christie and Terence Stamp, Vic Films/Metro-Goldwyn-Mayer, 1967; "The Return of the Native" (filmstrip), Popular Science Publishing, 1968; "Writers and Their Times (four filmstrips), Visual Publications, 1971; "A Hardy Summer" (filmstrip), Knight Film Distribution, 1972.

Recordings: "Thomas Hardy" (readings from his poems), Argo, 1968; "The English Poets: Thomas Hardy" (two records), Argo; "The Poetry of Thomas Hardy," read by Richard Burton (record or cassette), Caedmon.

SIDELIGHTS: **June 2, 1840.** Born in Higher Brockhampton, Dorsetshire, England, where he resided during his youthful years. ". . .My father is one of the last of the old 'master-masons' left—anywhere in England, I should think—the modern 'builders & contractors' having obliterated them. From time immemorial—I can speak from certain knowledge of four generations—my direct ancestors have all been master-masons, with a set of journeymen masons under them: though they have *never* risen above this level, they have *never* sunk below it. . . .''

''. . .As a child, [I was] brought up according to strict Church principles, [and] devoutly believed in the devil's pitchfork.'' [Richard Little Purdy and Michael Millgate, editors, *The Collected Letters of Thomas Hardy, Volume One, 1840-1892*, Oxford at the Clarendon Press, 1978.[1]]

1848. Began his studies at the village school.

Hardy loved to play the fiddle. At about the age of twelve he played at different functions for which his mother told him he should never take payment. On one occasion temptation was too strong and he accepted the pennies collected and bought *The Boys' Own Book*—a book which remained in his library all his life.

1856-1862. Apprenticed to John Hicks, an ecclesiastical architect. Hardy spent his mornings reading before going to work.

1862. Sojourned to London for advanced study in architecture. Worked as an assistant architect for Arthur Blomfield.

1865. Began to write verses—none were accepted for publication until later in his life when he reworked many of them. ''. . .The poetry of a scene varies with the minds of the perceivers. Indeed, it does not lie in the scene at all.'' [Florence Emily Hardy, *The Early Life of Thomas Hardy, 1840-1891*, Macmillan, 1928.[2]] One short story, ''How I Built Myself a House,'' was published.

1867. His first novel, *The Poor Man and the Lady*, was rejected by publishers, although they encouraged him to continue with his writing. The publisher, Macmillan, responded: ''[The novel was read] with care, and with much interest and admiration, but feeling at the same time that it has what seem to me drawbacks fatal to its success, and what I think, judging the writer from the book itself, you would feel even more strongly, to its truthfulness and justice.

''Much of the writing seems to me admirable. . . . You see I am writing to you as a writer who seems to me, at least potentially, of considerble mark, of power and purpose. If this is your first book I think you ought to go on. May I ask if it is, and—you are not a lady, so perhaps you will forgive the question—are you young?

''I have shown your MS. to one friend, whose judgment coincides with my own.''[2]

The opinion of that friend, Mr. John Morley was: ''If this man is young he has stuff and purpose in him.''[2]

1870. Met his future wife, Emma Lavinia Gifford, while working on a church restoration.

1872. Hardy wrote many of his novels in monthly installments for magazine publication, after which they were published as a novel. ''I am willing to supply to *Tinsley's* magazine the story [''A Pair of Blue Eyes''] I have in preparation. . . .

''The quantity to be about 20 pages of the magazine each month.

''Story to run about 12 months.

. . . I seem to hear the pattering of that mill-wheel when we walked by it, as well as if it were going now . . . . ■
(From *Our Exploits at West Poley* by Thomas Hardy. Illustrated by John Lawrence.)

''Publisher to have the right to publish a three volume edition of the novel for twelve months from the time of its appearance in this form. Afterwards all rights to revert to the author.''[1]

September 17, 1874. Married Gifford. ''I write a line to tell you all at home that the wedding took place yesterday, & that we are got as far as this on our way to Normandy & Paris. There were only Emma & I, her uncle who married us, & her brother, my landlady's daughter signed the book as one witness.

''I am going to Paris for materials for my next story. . . .''[1]

Hardy's novels concerned the places and people he was familiar with. ''. . .I find it a great advantage to be actually among the people described at the time of describing them.''[1]

Preferring to write poetry, Hardy noted: ''The truth is that I am willing, and indeed anxious, to give up any points which may be desirable in a story when read as a whole, for the sake of others which shall please those who read it in numbers. Perhaps I may have higher aims some day, and be a great stickler for the proper artistic balance of the completed work,

(From the seven-part drama "The Mayor of Casterbridge," starring Alan Bates and Anne Stallybrass. Presented on "Masterpiece Theatre," PBS-TV, beginning September 3, 1978.)

(From the movie "Far from the Madding Crowd," starring Julie Christie and Alan Bates. Released by Metro-Goldwyn-Mayer, 1967.)

(From the movie "Tess of the D'Urbervilles," starring Conrad Nagel and Blanche Sweet. Released by Metro-Goldwyn-Mayer, 1924.)

Tess Durbeyfield's experience was of this incapacitating kind. At last she had learned what to do; but who would now accept her doing? ■ (From the movie "Tess," based on the novel *Tess of the D'Urbervilles,* starring Nastassia Kinski. Copyright © 1980 by Columbia Pictures Industries, Inc.)

but for the present circumstances lead me to wish merely to be considered a good hand at a serial.''[2]

April 12, 1877. Hardy sent his manuscript of "The Return of the Native " to editor John Blackwood. "I have great pleasure in sending you the first 15 chapters of my new story—posted last night.

"Should you think the story to be of a kind which will suit readers of your magazine I will give any further particulars. The only point at all conditional in my offer of the MS. to you as editor, would have reference to the time at which, in the event of your liking it, the first part could appear, my wish being, if possible, to get the book issued complete not later than 1st May 1878.

"I will just add that, should there accidentally occur any word or reflection not in harmony with the general tone of the magazine, you would be quite at liberty to strike it out if you chose. I always mention this to my editors, as it simplifies matters. I do not, however, think you will meet with any such passage, as you will perceive that the story deals with a world almost isolated from civilization—moreover before beginning it I had resolved to write with a partial view to *Blackwood*.[1]

1878. Elected member to the Savile Club where me met many literary people.

December 3, 1880. Wrote to Henry Ponsonby, private secretary to Queen Victoria. "I have lately published in the pages of *Good Words* a serial story entitled 'The Trumpet-Major'— which is now complete, & has just been printed in the library edition.

"The action of the tale takes place at Weymouth, during the residence of His Majesty King George the Third in that borough, & several scenes illustrating the proceedings of the court, (collected from old people still living or recently deceased) are introduced into the narrative.

"For this reason it has occurred to me that it might not be deemed inappropriate to offer to Her Majesty a copy of the story. The honour of Her Majesty's acceptance of the same would, I need not say, give me the greatest pleasure. I therefore beg leave to request her gracious permission to send the volumes. . . .''[1]

Winter, 1880-1881. Suffered illness. ". . .My being ill. . . . The circumstances are that a cold I caught the other day left a troublesome local irritation behind it, making it advisable that I stay indoors for the present—though it does not affect my writing—indeed it gives me more leisure for the same.''[1]

". . .My third month in bed. Driving snow: fine, and so fast that individual flakes cannot be seen. In sheltered places they occasionally stop, and balance themselves in the air like hawks. . . . It creeps into the house, the window-plants being covered as if out-of-doors. Our passage (downstairs) is sole-deep, Em[ma] says, and feet leave tracks on it.''[2]

". . .I am getting on pretty fairly, but don't go out yet— passing my days over the fire, with my feet on the mantelpiece, & a pen in my hand, which does not write as often as it should. . . . I am doing the 12th number of my story, & the nearness of the end prevents my attaining to it quickly—the consciousness that it can be done at any time causing dilatoriness. I should probably have gone out by this time if it had

not been for the East wind. But patience is necessary. I am at home.''[1]

June 29, 1885. Moved to Max Gate outside Dorchester, into a house he designed himself. ". . .The leaves are approaching their finished summer shape, the evergreens wear new pale suits over the old deep attire. I watered the thirsty earth at Max Gate, which drank in the liquid with a swallowing noise. In the evening I entered Tayleure's Circus in Fordington Field for a short time during the performance. There is a dim haze in the tent, and the green grass in the middle, within the circular horsetrack, looks amazingly fresh in the artificial light. The damp orbits of the spectators' eyes gleam in its rays. The clowns, when 'off,' lounge and smoke cigarettes, and chat with serious cynicism, and as if the necessity of their occupation to society at large were not to be questioned, their true domestic expression being visible under the official expression given by the paint. This sub-expression is one of good-humoured pain.''[2]

"Our life here is quite rural, & you can do what you like." [Richard Little Purdy and Michael Millgate, editors, *The Collected Letters of Thomas Hardy, Volume Two, 1893-1901,* Clarendon Press, 1980.[3]]

". . .I was obligated to leave Town after a severe illness . . . some years ago—& the spot on which I live here is very lonely. However, I think that, though one does get a little rusty by living in remote places, one gains, on the other hand, freedom from those temporary currents of opinion by which town people are caught up & distracted out of their true courses.''[2]

1887. Asked to join the Folk-Lore Society. "My best thanks for your suggestion that I should become a member of the Folk-Lore Society.

"I will give the matter my consideration. But I regret to say that for the present I am unable to accept the invitation, my engagements in other directions putting it out of my power to enter into the aims of the Society—without which I should take no pleasure in being a member.''[1]

1891. Spent the season in London as Hardy and his wife did most every year. ". . .My plan . . .—make the country your headquarters, & take a place for a few weeks in London whenever you want to be there. . . .''[3]

Tess of the D'Urbervilles published. ". . .Read review of *Tess* in *The Quarterly.*. . . How strange that one may write a book without knowing what one puts into it—or rather, the reader reads into it. Well, if this sort of thing continues no more novel-writing for me. A man must be a fool to deliberately stand up to be shot at." [Florence Emily Hardy, *The Later Years of Thomas Hardy, 1892-1928,* Macmillan, 1930.[4]]

July 20, 1892. Father died. ". . .Mother described to-day the three Hardys as they used to appear passing over the brow of the hill to Stinsford Church on a Sunday morning, three or four years before my birth. They were always hurrying, being rather late, their fiddles and violoncello in green-baize bags under their left arms. They wore top hats, stick-up shirt-collars, dark blue coats with great collars and gilt buttons, deep cuffs and black silk 'stocks' or neckerchiefs. Had curly hair, and carried their heads to one side as they walked. My grandfather wore drab cloth breeches and buckled shoes, but his sons wore trousers and Wellington boots.''[4]

Hardy, dressed for the road.

1893. Rented a house in London for the spring season. "The worst of taking a furnished house is that the articles in the rooms are saturated with the thoughts and glances of others."[4]

1895. New edition of novels printed. "I am getting quite worn out with the unpleasant work of reading over the proofs of my old novels, the drudgery of hunting after printers' errors being anything but exhilarating—though sometimes a gleam of interest arises where one's past work seems fairly respectable."[3]

Hardy enjoyed bicycling. ". . .The advantage it has for literary people is that you can go out a long distance without coming in contact with another mind,—not even a horse's—& dissipating any little mental energy that has arisen in the course of a morning's application."[3]

December, 1898. First volume of poems published. ". . .Title: *Wessex Poems: With Sketches of Their Scenes by the Author*."[4]

"They [the sketches] are small pen-& ink drawings—much the worse from my years of unpractice. . . ."[3]

April, 1905. Received honorary degree of LL.D. from University of Aberdeen. "I am impressed by its coming from Aberdeen, for though a stranger to that part of Scotland to a culpable extent I have always observed with admiration the exceptional characteristics of the northern University, which in its fostering encouragement of mental effort seems to cast an eye over these islands that is unprejudiced, unbiased, and unsleeping."[4]

June 2, 1910. ". . .People of 70 seem much younger to me now-a-days than they did when I was a child—though, as I have confessed to some other friends, to be candid I think I felt rather more exhilarated by the birthday that was expressed by the 7 without the 0 than by that expressed with it. . . ." [Carl J. Weber, editor, *The Letters of Thomas Hardy*, Colby College Press, 1954.[5]]

July 19, 1910. Received the Royal Order of Merit.

Some of Hardy's fiction was adapted for the stage. "I am getting requests from music halls etc. for permission to perform that little melodramatic thing of mine written twenty years ago entitled 'The Three Wayfarers,'—In one act. I am willing to let anybody play it for a guinea a night, but I cannot possibly attend to the matter myself. . . ."[5]

June 1, 1912. Presented with the Gold Medal of the Royal Society of Literature.

November 27, 1912. Wife died.

February 10, 1914. Married Florence Emily Dugdale.

Hardy helped to raise money for the war [World War I] effort by sending manuscripts to the Red Cross sale and by contributing monies earned with the performance of one of his plays.

1919. Hardy was asked to make a speech at the opening of a war memorial, Brockhampton Reading-room. "I feel it an honour—and an honour of a very interesting kind—to have been asked by your President to open this Club as a memorial to the gallant men of this parish who fought in the last great war—a parish I know so well, and which is only about a mile from my own door.

"To come to my own recollections. From times immemorial the village contained several old Elizabethan houses, with mullioned windows and doors, of Ham Hill stone. They stood by the withy bed. I remember seeing some of them in process of being pulled down, but some were pulled down before I was born. To this attaches a story. Mr. Pitt, by whose orders it was done, came to look on, and asked one of the men several questions as to why he was doing it in such and such a way. Mr. Pitt was notorious for his shabby cloths, and the labourer, who did not know him, said at last, 'look here, old chap, don't you ask so many questions, and just go on. Anybody would think the house was yours!' Mr. Pitt obeyed orders, and meekly went on, murmuring, 'Well, 'Tis mine, after all!'

"Then there were the Poor-houses, I remember—just at the corner turning down to the dairy. These were the homes of the parish paupers before workhouses were built. In one of them lived an old man who was found one day rolling on the floor, with a lot of pence and halfpence scattered round him. They asked him what was the matter, and he said he had heard of people rolling in money, and he thought that for once in his life he would do it, to see what it was like.

"Then there used to be dancing parties at Christmas, and some weeks after. This kind of party was called a Jacob's Join, in which every guest contributed a certain sum to pay the expenses of the entertainment—it was mostly half-a-crown in this village. They were very lively parties I believe. The curious thing is that the man who used to give the house-room for the dances lived in a cottage which stood exactly where this Club-house stands now—so that when you dance here you will be simply carrying on the tradition on the spot."[4]

During this period Hardy destroyed many of his papers. ". . .I have not been doing much—mainly destroying papers of the last thirty or forty years." [Carl J. Weber, editor, *"Dearest Emmie" Thomas Hardy Letters to His First Wife*, St. Martin's Press, 1963.[6]]

June 2, 1920. On his eightieth birthday, Hardy wrote: "When, like the Psalmist, 'I call mine own ways to remembrance,' I find nothing in them that quite justifies this celebration.

"The value of old age depends upon the person who reaches it. To some men of early performance it is useless. To others, who are late to develop, it just enables them to complete their job."[4]

In Hardy's later years he demonstrated some interest in setting down facts of his life. ". . .I intend to write my autobiography through my good wife. . . . My idea . . . is to have the work appear after my death as a biography of myself written by my wife."[5]

July 21, 1927. Last public appearance. ". . . [I] laid the Commemoration Stone of the Dorchester Grammer School and delivered a short address on T[homas] H[ardy], the founder." [Evelyn Hardy, editor, *Thomas Hardy's Notebooks*, Hogarth Press, 1955.[7]]

January 11, 1928. Died at Max Gate after a short illness. Hardy continued to write poetry to the end. ". . .The glory of poetry lies in its largeness, admitting among its creators men of infinite variety. They must all be impractical in the conduct of their affairs; nay, they must almost, like Shelley or Marlowe, be drowned or done to death, or like Keats, die of consumption. They forget that in the ancient world no such necessity was recognized; that Homer sang as a blind old man, that Aeschylus

Max Gate.

Thomas Hardy, 1923. Portrait by Augustus John.

wrote his best up to his death at nearly seventy, that the best of Sophocles appeared between his fifty-fifth and ninetieth years, that Euripides wrote up to seventy."[4]

FOR MORE INFORMATION SEE: H. H. Child, *Thomas Hardy,* 1916, reprinted, Folcroft, 1974; Mary Ellen Chase, *Thomas Hardy: From Serial to Novel,* University of Minnesota Press, 1927; Arthur Symons, *A Study of Thomas Hardy,* C. J. Sawyer, 1927, reprinted, Haskell House, 1971; Jessie G. Sime, *Thomas Hardy of the Wessex Novels,* L. Carrier, 1928, reprinted, Folcroft, 1975; Carl J. Weber, *Hardy of Wessex: His Life and Literary Career,* Columbia University Press, 1940, revised edition, 1965; *Southern Review,* Thomas Hardy Centennial issue, Volume V, 1940; David Cecil, *Hardy the Novelist,* Bobbs-Merrill, 1946; C. J. Weber, *Hardy in America: A Study of Thomas Hardy and His American Readers,* Colby College Press, 1946, reprinted, Russell & Russell, 1966; Harvey C. Webster, *On a Darkling Plain: The Art and Thought of Thomas Hardy,* University of Chicago Press, 1947; Albert J. Guerard, *Thomas Hardy: The Novels and Stories,* Harvard University Press, 1949.

Rolfe A. Scott-James and C. S. Lewis, *Thomas Hardy,* Longmans, Green, 1921, revised edition, 1967; Douglas Brown, *Thomas Hardy,* Longmans, Green, 1954; Evelyn Hardy, *Thomas Hardy: A Critical Biography,* St. Martin's, 1954, reprinted, Russell & Russell, 1970; Richard L. Purdy, *Hardy: A Bibliographical Study,* Oxford University Press, 1954, 2nd edition, 1968; Florence E. Hardy, *The Life of Thomas Hardy, 1840-1928,* St. Martin's, 1962; Irving Howe, *Thomas Hardy,* Macmillan, 1967; R. G. Cox, editor, *Thomas Hardy: The Critical Heritage,* Barnes & Noble, 1970; Michael Millgate, *Thomas Hardy: His Career as a Novelist,* Random House, 1971; F. R. Southerington, *Hardy's Vision of Man,* Barnes & Noble, 1971; Donald Davies, *Thomas Hardy and British Poetry,* Routledge, 1973; Penelope Vigar, *The Novels of Thomas Hardy: Illusion and Reality,* Humanities Press, 1974; R. J. White, *Thomas Hardy and History,* Harper, 1974; D. Kramer, *Thomas Hardy: The Forms of Tragedy,* Wayne State University Press, 1975; G. Leeming, *Who's Who in Thomas Hardy,* Taplinger, 1975; Robert Gittings, *Thomas Hardy's Later Years,* Atlantic-Little, Brown, 1978.

For children: John and Helen Cournos, *Famous British Novelists,* Dodd, 1952; Dorothy J. Stirland, *Second Book of Great Writers,* Cassell, 1959; Nora Stirling, *Who Wrote the Classics?,* Volume II, Day, 1968.

HARRIS, Sherwood 1932-

PERSONAL: Born November 26, 1932, in New York, N.Y.; son of Sterling G. (in business) and Edna M. (Sell) Harris; married Lorna J. Briggs (a teacher's aide), September 11, 1953; children: Michael, Suzanne, Catherine, Margaret. *Education:* Princeton University, B.A., 1954. *Politics:* Democrat. *Home address:* Old Post Rd., Bedford, N.Y. 10506. *Agent:* Raines & Raines, 475 Fifth Ave., New York, N.Y. 10017. *Office: Reader's Digest,* Pleasantville, N.Y. 10570.

CAREER: Magazine and book editor. *Saturday Evening Post,* Philadelphia, Pa. and Washington, D.C., editorial assistant in Philadelphia and Washington, D.C., 1957-60; free-lance writer, 1960-64; *America Illustrated,* Washington, D.C., deputy editor, 1964-68; *Reader's Digest,* Pleasantville, N.Y., as-

sociate editor, 1968-71, senior editor, 1971—. *Military service:* U.S. Navy, 1954-57; pilot.

WRITINGS: The First to Fly, Simon & Schuster, 1970; *Great Flying Adventures,* Random House, 1973. Contributor to magazines, including *American Heritage* and *Saturday Evening Post.*

SIDELIGHTS: "In addition to my editing activities I teach flying part-time. Flying has been a lifelong interest—I learned to fly in the Navy, have written two books about it, and give flight instruction several hours a week at Connecticut Air Service in Danbury, Connecticut. I hold an Airline Transport Pilot's license plus my instructor ratings."

HELPS, Racey 1913-1971

OBITUARY NOTICE—See sketch in *SATA* Volume 2: Born February 2, 1913, in Bristol, England; died January 25, 1971, in Barnstaple, North Devon, England. Children's author and illustrator. Early in his career, Helps was an antiquarian bookseller, occasionally writing and illustrating stories for his daughter, Anne Rosemary. Beginning in 1946 he devoted himself full-time to writing for children. All of his books, which include *The Clean Sweep, Prickly Pie,* and *Two's Company,* are self-illustrated. *For More Information See: Contemporary Authors, Permanent Series,* Volume 2, Gale, 1978; *Authors of Books for Young People,* 2nd edition, supplement, Scarecrow, 1979. *Obituaries: Publishers Weekly,* March 29, 1971; *Contemporary Authors,* Volumes 29-32, revised, Gale, 1978.

HERSEY, John (Richard) 1914-

PERSONAL: Born June 17, 1914, in Tientsin, China; son of American citizens Roscoe Monroe (a Y.M.C.A. secretary in China) and Grace (a missionary; maiden name Baird) Hersey; married Frances Ann Cannon, April 27, 1940 (divorced February, 1958); married Barbara Day Addams Kaufman, June 2, 1958; children: (first marriage) Martin, John, Ann, Baird; (second marriage) Brook (daughter). *Education:* Yale University, B.A., 1936; attended Clare College, Cambridge, 1936-37. *Politics:* Democrat. *Home:* 420 Humphrey St., New Haven, Conn. 06511.

CAREER: Private secretary, driver, and factotum for Sinclair Lewis, summer, 1937; writer, editor, and correspondent, *Time* magazine, 1937-44, correspondent in China and Japan, 1939, covered South Pacific warfare, 1942, correspondent in Mediterranean theater, including Sicilian campaign, 1943, and in Moscow, 1944-45; editor and correspondent for *Life* magazine, 1944-45; writer for *New Yorker* and other magazines, intermittently, 1945—; made trip to China and Japan for *Life* and *New Yorker,* 1945-46; fellow, Berkeley College, Yale University, 1950-65; master, Pierson College, Yale University, 1965-70, fellow, 1965—; writer-in-residence, American Academy in Rome, 1970-71; lecturer, Yale University, 1971-76, professor, 1976—; visiting professor, Massachusetts Institute of Technology, 1975. Chairman, Connecticut Volunteers for Stevenson, 1952; member of Adlai Stevenson's campaign staff, 1956. Editor and director of writers' co-operative magazine, *'47.* Member of Westport (Conn.) School Study Council, 1945-50, of Westport Board of Education, 1950-52, of Yale Uni-

(From the movie "The War Lover," starring Robert Wagner. Released by Columbia Pictures Corp., 1962.)

(From the movie "A Bell for Adano," starring John Hodiak. Released by Twentieth Century-Fox Film Corp., 1945.)

versity Council Committee on the Humanities, 1951-56, of Fairfield (Conn.) Citizens School Study Council, 1952-56, of National Citizens' Commission for the Public Schools, 1954-56; consultant, Fund for the Advancement of Education, 1954-56; chairman, Connecticut Committee for the Gifted, 1954-57; member of Board of Trustees, Putney School, 1953-56; delegate to White House Conference on Education, 1955; trustee, National Citizens' Council for the Public Schools, 1956-58; member, visiting committee, Harvard Graduate School of Education, 1960-65, Loeb Drama Center, Harvard, 1980—; member, Yale University Council Committee on Yale College, 1959-64, chairman, 1964-69; trustee, National Committee for Support of the Public Schools, 1962-68; commissioner, National Commission on New Technological Uses of Copyrighted Works, 1975-78. *Member:* National Institute of Arts and Letters, American Academy of Arts and Letters (secretary, 1962-76), Authors League of America (member of council, 1946-70; vice-president, 1949-55, president, 1975-80), Authors Guild (member of council, 1946—), P.E.N. *Awards, honors:* Pulitzer Prize, 1945, for *A Bell for Adano;* Anisfield-Wolf Award, 1950, for *The Wall;* Daroff Memorial Fiction Award, Jewish Book Council of America, 1950, for *The Wall;* Sidney Hillman Foundation Award, 1951, for *The Wall;* Howland Medal, Yale University, 1952; National Association of Independent Schools Award, 1957, for *A Single Pebble;* Tuition Plan Award, 1961; Sarah Josepha Hale Award, 1963; named honorary fellow of Clare College, Cambridge University, 1967. Honorary degrees: M.A., Yale University, 1947; LL.D., Washington and Jefferson College, 1950; D.H.L., Dropsie College, 1950; Litt.D., Wesleyan University, 1954, Clarkson College of Technology, 1972.

WRITINGS—Of interest to young adults: *A Bell for Adano,* Knopf, 1944, with new foreward by Hersey, Modern Library, 1946; *Hiroshima* (first published in *New Yorker,* August 31, 1946), Knopf, 1946, school edition, Oxford Book Co., 1948; *The Wall,* Knopf, 1950; *A Single Pebble,* Knopf, 1956; *White Lotus,* Knopf, 1965; *My Petition for More Space,* Knopf, 1974.

Other writings; all published by Knopf, unless otherwise noted: *Men on Bataan,* 1942; *Into the Valley: A Skirmish of the Marines,* 1943; *The Marmot Drive,* 1953; *The War Lover,* 1959; *The Child Buyer,* 1960; *Here to Stay: Studies of Human Tenacity,* Hamish Hamilton, 1962, Knopf, 1963; *Too Far to Walk,* 1966; *Under the Eye of the Storm,* 1967; *The Algiers Motel Incident,* 1968; *Letter to the Alumni,* 1970; *The Conspiracy,* 1972; (editor) *The Writer's Craft,* 1974; (editor) *Ralph Ellison,* Prentice-Hall, 1974; *The President,* 1975; *The Walnut Door,* 1977; *Aspects of the Presidency,* Ticknor & Fields, 1980.

ADAPTATIONS: A Bell for Adano was adapted as a stage play by Paul Osborn, and opened at the Cort Theater in New York in December, 1944, and was made as a film by Twentieth Century-Fox in 1945; *The Wall* was dramatized by Millard Lampell and opened at the Billy Rose Theater in New York in December, 1960, and a film for television was produced by Time-Life and broadcast by CBS-TV in 1981; *The War Lover* was made into a film by Columbia Pictures in 1962; *The Child Buyer* was adapted as a stage play by Paul Shyre and opened at the University of Michigan Professional Theater Program, in Ann Arbor, in 1964.

WORK IN PROGRESS: A fictional biography of a missionary in China in the first half of the twentieth century.

SIDELIGHTS: "What should be the aims of a writer who undertakes a novel of contemporary history? . . .Above all,

(From *The Wall* by John Hersey. Aquatint by William Sharp.)

this kind of novel should make anyone who reads it better able to meet life in his generation—whenever that generation may be. . . . The task of this kind of novel, however, is not to illuminate events; it is to illuminate the human beings who are caught up in the events. . . . Journalism allows its readers to witness history; fiction gives its readers an opportunity to live it. . . . The novel of contemporary history is an established form. It has dignity, purpose, and separateness."

Hersey's earlier journalistic approaches emphasize these views. Lewis Gannett, in the *New York Herald Tribune Book Review,* said of *Hiroshima:* "John Hersey is a great reporter. He doesn't generalize and he doesn't write editorials. He knows that when headlines say a hundred thousand people are killed, whether in battle, by earthquake, flood or atom bomb, the human mind refuses to react to mathematics. The heart of the story—of any story—is the individual." *The New Yorker* devoted the entire editorial content of one issue to the publication of *Hiroshima* before it appeared in book form.

In a later article in the *Herald Tribune,* Milton Rugoff maintained that "clarity, authority and shining honesty . . . distinguish [Hersey's] work. We feel: this is the truth purged, as much as it can be, of bias and wish—and we believe. A quality that contributes such effects can hardly be dismissed. . . ."

JOHN HERSEY

Webster Schott summarized the import of Hersey's novels when he wrote: "His testings of the social possibilities of fiction run through eight novels. [Hersey has since written additional novels.] Good, bad, or indifferent, none covers the same territory, and all shout the ministerial exhortation: Shape up! For Hersey cares what humanity does to itself."

HOBBIES AND OTHER INTERESTS: Sailing, gardening, fishing, reading.

FOR MORE INFORMATION SEE: New York Times Book Review, February 6, 1944, February 26, 1950, June 10, 1956, September 25, 1960, January 19, 1965, February 28, 1966; *New York Herald Tribune Book Review,* August 29, 1946, March 5, 1950, August 20, 1950, June 3, 1956, September 25, 1960; *Saturday Review,* November 2, 1946, March 4, 1950, June 2, 1956, January 23, 1965; *Times Literary Supplement,* December 7, 1946; *Atlantic Monthly,* November, 1949, April, 1966; *Time,* June 4, 1956, January 29, 1965, March 25, 1966; *Newsweek,* January 25, 1965, June 7, 1965; *National Observer,* February 8, 1965; *Commonweal,* March 5, 1965; *Book Week,* September 26, 1965; *Life,* March 18, 1966; David Sanders, *John Hersey,* Twayne, 1967; Carolyn Riley, editor, *Contemporary Literary Criticism,* Gale, Volume I, 1973, Volume II, 1974.

HOGNER, Nils 1893-1970

PERSONAL: Born July 22, 1893, in Whitinsville, Mass.; died July 30, 1970, in Litchfield, Conn.; son of a doctor; married Dorothy Childs (an author), July 23, 1932. *Education:* Attended Rhodes Academy, Copenhagen, Denmark; Royal Academy of Arts, Stockholm, Sweden; Boston School of Painting; and the School of the Museum of Fine Arts, Boston.

CAREER: University of New Mexico, Albuquerque, art instructor, 1930-32; artist, illustrator, and mural painter. Member of board of directors, American Artists Professional League. *Military service:* Served in France with the American Expeditionary Force during the First World War. *Member:* National Society of Mural Painters (treasurer), Architectural League of New York (vice-president), Salmagundi Club.

WRITINGS—All self-illustrated, except as noted: (With Guy Scott) *Cartoon Guide of New York City,* J. J. Augustin, 1938; *The Lost Tugboat,* Abelard, 1952; *Boldy,* Abelard, 1953; *Dynamite, the Wild Stallion,* Aladdin Books, 1953; *Jean's Whale,* Abelard, 1955; *Sad Eye, the Clown,* Abelard, 1956; *Farm for Rent,* Abelard, 1958; *Jimmy's First Roundup,* Abelard, 1959; *Tanny,* Walck, 1960; *Molly the Black Mare,* Walck, 1962; *The*

Devil Stallion, Walck, 1967; *The Nosy Colt* (illustrated by Richard Lebenson), Walck, 1973.

Illustrator: Idella Purnell, *Pedro the Potter,* Thomas Nelson, 1935; Alice Gall and Fleming C. Crew, *Top of the World,* Oxford University Press, 1939; Glenn Balch, *Indian Paint: The Story of an Indian Pony,* Crowell, 1942, reissued, 1970; Marion Gill MacNeil, *Between Earth and Sky,* Oxford University Press, 1944; Lucile McDonald, *Bering's Potlatch,* Oxford University Press, 1944; Ralph Godwin De Voe, *Calling All Ducks,* Crowell, 1945; Edwin Burtis, editor, *All the Best Dog Poems,* Crowell, 1946; R. G. De Voe, *Adventures of Midgie,* Crowell, 1946; Frances Fullerton Neilson, *Ten Commandments in Today's World,* Thomas Nelson, 1946; A. Gall and F. H. Crew, *Winter Flight,* Oxford University Press, 1949; A. Gall and F. H. Crew, *Here and There and Everywhere,* Oxford University Press, 1950; Olga Townsend, *White-Tailed Deer,* Whittlesey, 1951; F. H. Crew, *More the Merrier,* Oxford University Press, 1952; Ruth Hepburn Protheroe, *Little Chief of the Gaspe,* Abelard, 1955; Ruth Hubbell Dudley, *Our American Trees,* Crowell, 1956; Helene Jamieson Jordan, *Seeds by Wind and Water,* Crowell, 1962.

Illustrator; all written by his wife, Dorothy Hogner: *Navajo Winter Nights,* Thomas Nelson, 1935; *Education of a Burro,* Thomas Nelson, 1936; *Little Esther,* Thomas Nelson, 1937; *Santa Fe Caravans,* Thomas Nelson, 1937; *Lady Bird,* Oxford University Press, 1938; *Westward, High, Low, and Dry,* Dutton, 1938; *Old Hank Weatherbee,* Oxford University Press, 1939; *Pancho,* Thomas Nelson, 1939; *Summer Roads to Gaspe,* Dutton, 1939; *Don't Blame the Puffins,* Oxford University Press, 1940; *Stormy, the First Mustang,* Oxford University Press, 1941 (published in England as *Stormy, the First American Mustang,* Hutchinson, 1944); *The Animal Book: American Mammals North of Mexico,* Oxford University Press, 1942; *Children of Mexico,* Heath, 1942; *The Bible Story,* Oxford University Press, 1943; *Our American Horse,* Thomas Nelson, 1944; *Reward for Brownie,* Oxford University Press, 1944; *Farm Animals and Working and Sporting Breeds of the United States and Canada,* Oxford University Press, 1945; *Unexpected Journey: The Story of a Dog,* Creative Age Press, 1945; *Winky, King of the Garden,* Oxford University Press, 1946; *Blue Swamp,* Oxford University Press, 1947; *Barnyard Family,* Oxford University Press, 1948; *Daisy: A Farm Fable,* Oxford University Press, 1949.

Dusty's Return, Oxford University Press, 1950; *The Wild Little Honker,* Oxford University Press, 1951; *Snowflake,* Oxford University Press, 1952; *Earthworms,* Crowell, 1953; *Herbs from the Garden to the Table,* Oxford University Press, 1953; *The Horse Family,* Oxford University Press, 1953; *The Dog Family,* Oxford University Press, 1954; *Wide River,* Lippincott, 1954; *Rufus,* Lippincott, 1955; *Spiders,* Crowell, 1955; *The Cat Family,* Oxford University Press, 1956; *Frogs and Polliwogs,* Crowell, 1956; *Conservation in America,* Lippincott, 1958; *Snails,* Crowell, 1958; *Grasshoppers and Crickets,* Crowell, 1960; *Water over the Dam,* Lippincott, 1960; *A Fresh Herb Platter,* Doubleday, 1961; *Butterflies,* Crowell, 1962; *Water Beetles,* Crowell, 1963; *Gardening and Cooking on Terrace and Patio,* Doubleday, 1964; *Moths,* Crowell, 1964; *A Book of Snakes,* Crowell, 1966; *Weeds,* Crowell, 1968; *Birds of Prey,* Crowell, 1969.

SIDELIGHTS: When Hogner was a young boy, his father wanted him to pursue a medical career, but his interest in art was so firm that he was sent instead to Europe to finish his training in art. Returning home, he continued his studies at the

NILS HOGNER

Boston School of Painting and at the Museum of Fine Arts School in New York.

After marrying author Dorothy Childs in 1932 he devoted himself to book illustration and mural painting. Hogner and his wife enjoyed the outdoors and frequently made camping trips throughout the United States, Canada, and Mexico. Their shared interest in wildlife and their combined skills in art and literature resulted in numerous books. One of their earlier books together was *Westward, High, Low, and Dry.* "Though the places Mr. and Mrs. Hogner visit are barren, the book is not. . . . To obtain the full essence of these places the Hogners not only give the reader their own experiences but the results of their reading in government bulletins, scholarly modern works, and narratives of the early explorers and travelers. . . . The result is a charming, simple account with no theatricals, no great descriptions, or philosophical analyses arising from the sights, but just what it is meant to be—a good, interesting travel book," commented a critic for *Saturday Review.* A reviewer for *Commonweal* noted, "The two-tone reproductions of Mr. Hogner's water colors give an added zest to a colorful tale of travel."

Before Hogner began to make black and white drawings for books, he used paintbrushes and oil paint. He particularly enjoyed painting murals, and exhibited widely.

The Hogners divided their time between their New York studio and their herb farm in Litchfield, Connecticut. Hogner was fond of birds, wild animals, such as chipmunks, squirrels, rabbits, and deer, and fish, and his books showed his enthusiasm for wildlife.

There, standing below him, the lion saw Molly, with the little black colt beside her, the lion crouched, ready to leap. ■ (From *Molly the Black Mare* by Nils Hogner. Illustrated by the author.)

Lost Tugboat was Hogner's first picture-book for which he supplied the text as well as the illustrations. A *New York Times* reviewer observed, ''Here is every detail of a tugboat's life. Little children will love both the story and the unusually lovely pictures. . . . You can almost smell the harbor.'' In reviewing the same book, a *Chicago Sunday Tribune* critic wrote, ''A rollicking, nautical tale for youngest readers.''

Hogner died on his farm in Litchfield, Connecticut, on July 30, 1970 at the age of seventy-two. Many of his books, including *Birds of Prey, Book of Snakes, Grasshoppers and Crickets,* and *Spiders* continue to be enjoyed by children.

HOBBIES AND OTHER INTERESTS: Gardening, fishing, and camping.

FOR MORE INFORMATION SEE: Saturdy Review of Literature, January 22, 1938; *Commonweal,* February 11, 1938; Stanley J. Kunitz, editor, *Junior Book of Authors,* second edition, H. W. Wilson, 1951; *Chicago Sunday Tribune,* July 13, 1952; *New York Times,* August 3, 1952; Lee Kingman, editor, *Illustrators of Children's Books,* 1957-1966, Horn Book, 1968.

Let nothing which is disgraceful to be spoken of, or to be seen, approach this place, where a child is.

—Juvenal

HOUSMAN, Laurence   1865-1959

PERSONAL: Born July 18, 1865, in Bromsgrove, England; died February 20, 1959, in Glastonbury, England; son of Edward (a lawyer) and Sarah Jane (Williams) Houseman; younger brother of the poet, A. E. Housman. *Education:* Received early education at Bromsgrove School, Worcestershire, England; studied art in London, England, at Lambeth School of Art, Natural Art Training College, and The Royal College of Art. *Politics:* Housman described himself as a ''rabid pacifist and internationalist.'' *Religion:* Roman Catholic. *Home:* Somerset, England.

CAREER: Author and illustrator. After studying art in London, Housman began his career as an illustrator; he gained prominence with his illustrations for the works of several eminent authors of the time; expanded his career to include authorship beginning with a number of fairy tales, legends, and poems, which he also illustrated, the first published in 1894; Housman eventually discontinued illustrating to devote his time to writing; he created a great stir in Britain and America with the anonymous publication of his first extensively popular work, *An Englishwoman's Love Letters* in 1900; in his more than sixty years of writing, Housman produced more than one hundred plays, novels, story collections, and other works, including an autobiography published in 1936; he is also the author of several essays and articles on subjects ranging from art and literature to morals and politics.

WRITINGS—For children: *A Farm in Fairyland* (self-illustrated), Dodd, Mead, 1894; *The House of Joy* (self-illustrated), K. Paul, Trench, Trubner, 1895, reprinted, Books for Libraries, 1969; *The Field of Clover* (engraved by Clemence Housman), K. Paul, Trench, Trubner, 1898; *The Blue Moon*, J. Murray, 1904; *The New Child's Guide to Knowledge: A Book of Poems and Moral Lessons for Old and Young*, Sidgwick & Jackson, 1911; *A Doorway in Fairyland*, J. Cape, 1922, Harcourt, 1923; *Moonshine and Clover* (engraved by Clemence Housman), Harcourt, 1923; *The Open Door*, B. Blackwell, 1925; *Puss in Boots*, B. Blackwell, 1926; *A Thing to Be Explained*, B. Blackwell, 1926; *Ethelrinda's Fairy*, B. Blackwell, 1928; *Wish to Goodness*, B. Blackwell, 1928; *Cotton-Wooleena*, B. Blackwell, 1930, reissued, Doubleday, 1974; *A Gander and His Geese, and the Promise of Beauty*, B. Blackwell, 1930; *Little and Good, and the Giant and the Pigmy*, B. Blackwell, 1930; *Turn Again Tales*, H. Holt, 1930; *What-O'Clock Tales* (illustrated by J. R. Monsell), B. Blackwell, 1932; *The Rat-Catcher's Daughter: A Collection of Stories* (selected by Ellin Greene; illustrated by Julia Noonan), Atheneum, 1974.

Fiction: *All-Fellows* (short stories), K. Paul, Trench, Trubner, 1896; *Gods and Their Makers* (novel), J. Lane, 1897; *An Englishwoman's Love Letters* (novel), Doubleday, Page, 1900; *A Modern Antaeus* (novel), Doubleday, Page, 1901; *Sabrina Warham: The Story of Her Youth* (novel), Macmillan, 1904; *The Cloak of Friendship* (short stories), J. Murray, 1905; *King John of Jingalo: The Story of a Monarch in Difficulties* (novel), H. Holt, 1912; *The Royal Runaway and Jingalo in Revolution: A Sequel to King John of Jingalo* (novel), Chapman & Holt, 1914; *The Sheepfold: The Story of a Shepherdess and Her Sheep and How She Lost Them* (novel), Duckworth, 1918; *Timblerigg: A Book of Revelation* (novel), J. Cape, 1924, A. & C. Boni, 1925, reprinted, Scholarly Press, 1971; *Odd Pairs: A Book of Tales* (short stories), J. Cape, 1925, reprinted, Books for Libraries, 1971; *Ironical Tales* (short stories), J. Cape, 1926, G. Doran, 1927; *Uncle Tom Pudd* (novel), J. Cape, 1927; *What Next? Provocative Tales of Faith and Morals* (short stories), J. Cape, 1938, reprinted, Books for Libraries, 1971; *Strange Ends and Discoveries: Tales of this World and the Next* (short stories), J. Cape, 1948; *The Kind and the Foolish: Short Tales of Myth, Magic, and Miracle* (short stories), J. Cape, 1952.

Plays: *Bethlehem: A Nativity Play* (privately produced in London, December 17, 1902), Macmillan, 1902; (with Harley Granville Barker) *Prunella* (first produced at the Court Theatre, 1906), Brentano's, 1906; *The Vicar of Wakefield* (three-act light opera based on Oliver Goldsmith's novel), Boorey, 1906; *The Chinese Lantern* (three-act), Brentano's, 1908; *Pains and Penalties: The Defense of Queen Caroline* (four-act), Sidgwick & Jackson, 1911; *Alice in Ganderland* (one-act), Woman's Press, 1911; *Bird in Hand* (one-act), S. French, 1916; *As Good as Gold* (one-act), S. French, 1916; *A Likely Story: A Roadside Comedy* (one-act), S. French, 1916; *The Lord of the Harvest: A Morality* (one-act), S. French, 1916; *Nazareth: A Morality* (one-act), S. French, 1916; *The Return of Alcestis* (one-act), S. French, 1916; *The Snow Man: A Morality* (one-act), S. French, 1916; *The Wheel* (three plays), Sidgwick & Jackson, 1919, S. French, 1920.

Angels and Ministers, J. Cape, 1921, Harcourt, 1922; *The Death of Orpheus*, Sidgwick & Jackson, 1921; *Little Plays of St. Francis*, S. Maynard, 1922, second series, Sidgwick & Jackson, 1931; *Dethronements: Imaginary Portraits of Political Characters*, J. Cape, 1922, Macmillan, 1923; *False Premises* (five one-act plays), B. Blackwell, 1922, Brentano's,

LAURENCE HOUSMAN

1923; *Followers of St. Francis: Four Plays of the Early Franciscan Legend*, Sidgwick & Jackson, 1923; *The Death of Socrates* (based on two of Plato's *Dialogues*), Sidgwick & Jackson, 1925; *The Comments of Juniper: Six Plays from the Life and Legend of St. Francis of Assisi*, Sidgwick & Jackson, 1926; *Ways and Means: Five one Act Plays of Village Characters*, Yearbook Press, 1928; *Cornered Poets: A Book of Dramatic Dialogues*, J. Cape, 1929.

The New Hangman (one-act), Putnam, 1930; *Palace Plays*, J. Cape, 1930; *Ye Fearful Saints! Plays of Creed, Custom, and Credulity*, Sidgwick & Jackson, 1932; *The Queen's Progress: Palace Plays* (second series), J. Cape, 1932; *Victoria and Albert: Palace Plays* (third series), J. Cape, 1933; *Nunc Dimittis: An Epilogue to "Little Plays of St. Francis"* (first produced by the University College London Dramatic Society, 1932), University of London, 1933; *Victoria Regina: A Dramatic Biography* (first produced privately at the Gate Theatre, 1935; produced at Lyric Theatre, June, 1937), J. Cape, 1934, Scribner, 1935; *Four Plays of St. Clare*, Sidgwick & Jackson, 1934; *The Golden Sovereign* (illustrated by Ernest H. Shepard), Scribner, 1937; *Gracious Majesty* (illustrated by E. H. Shepard), J. Cape, 1941, Scribner, 1942; *Palestine Plays*, J. Cape, 1942, Scribner, 1943; *Samuel: The King-Maker* (four-act), J. Cape, 1944; *Happy and Glorious: A Dramatic Biography* (illustrated by E. H. Shepard), J. Cape, 1945; *The Family Honour* (four-act comedy with epilogue), J. Cape, 1950; *Old Testament*

(From *Goblin Market* by Christina Rossetti. Illustrated by Laurence Housman.)

Plays, J. Cape, 1950; *Twenty Selected Little Plays of Saint Francis,* Sidgwick & Jackson, 1964.

Poetry: *Green Arras* (self-illustrated), Way & Williams, 1896; *Spikenard,* R. G. Badger, 1898; *The Little Land: With Songs from its Four Rivers,* G. Richards, 1899; *Rue,* At the Sign of the Unicorn (London), 1899; *Mendicant Rhymes,* [London], 1906; *Selected Poems by Laurence Housman,* Sidgwick & Jackson, 1908, reprinted, AMS Press, 1976; *The Heart of Peace,* W. Heinemann, 1918, Maynard, 1919; *The Love Concealed,* Sidgwick & Jackson, 1928; *The Collected Poems of Laurence Housman,* Sidgwick & Jackson, 1937.

Other works: (Translator) *Of Aucassin and Nicolette* (drawings by Paul Woodroffe), J. Murray, 1902, reprinted, Folcroft, 1974; (editor with W. Somerset Maugham) *The Venture: An Annual of Art Literature,* [London], 1903; *Arabian Nights: Five Stories Re-written by Laurence Housman* (illustrated by Edmund Dulac), Scribner, 1907; *Stories from the Arabian Nights Retold by Laurence Housman* (illustrated by E. Dulac), Doran, 1911; (translator) Aristophanes, *Lysistrata,* Woman's

Press, 1911; *Princess Badoura: A Tale from the Arabian Nights Retold by Laurence Housman,* Hodder & Stoughton, 1913; *St. Francis Poverello,* Sidgwick & Jackson, 1918; *Ploughshare and Pruning-Hook: Ten Lectures on Social Subjects,* Swarthmore Press, 1919; *Echo de Paris: A Study from Life,* J. Cape, 1923, D. Appleton, 1924; *Ten 'Litte Plays' Handbook,* Sidgwick & Jackson, 1927; (editor) *The Life of H. R. H. the Duke of Flamborough,* J. Cape, 1928, Dayson & Clarke, 1929; (editor) *War Letters of Fallen Englishmen,* Dutton, 1930; *The Unexpected Years,* Bobbs-Merrill, 1936; *A. E. H.: Some Poems, Some Letters, and a Personal Memoir by His Brother, Laurence Housman,* J. Cape, 1937; *My Brother, A. E. Housman,* Scribner, 1938, reprinted, Kennikat Press, 1969; (editor) *What Can We Believe? Letters Exchanged Between Dick Sheppard and Laurence Housman,* J. Cape, 1939; (with C. H. K. Marten) *The Long Journey,* B. Blackwell, 1943; *Back Words and Fore Words: An Author's Year-book, 1893-1945,* J. Cape, 1945.

Illustrator: George Meredith, *Jump-to-Glory Jane,* Swan Sonnenschein, 1892; Jonas Lauritz Idemil Lie, *Weird Tales from Northern Seas* (translated by R. N. Bain), Kegan Paul, 1893; Christina Georgina Rossetti, *Goblin Market,* Macmillan, 1893, reissued, Green Tiger Press, 1973; C. G. Rossetti, *Sing-Song: Speaking Likenesses: Goblin Market,* Garland Publishing, 1976; Jane Barlow, *The End of Elfintown,* Macmillan, 1894; Clemence Annie Housman, *The Were-Wolf,* J. Lane, 1896; Percy Bysshe Shelley, *The Sensitive Plant,* [London], 1898, Dutton, 1899, reissued, Haskell House, 1972.

ADAPTATIONS: "Prunella" (motion picture), Famous Players-Lasky Corp., 1918; "Victoria Regina" (motion picture for television), Compass, 1961.

SIDELIGHTS: **July 18, 1865.** Born in Bromsgrove, England, into a large Victorian family. "The life of our first parents began in a garden; so, during its short stage of innocence, did mine, though I was born in a house. The house, with its thick coat of ivy and its sham Gothic windows, had its share in the upbringing of the family of seven in which I came last but one. But I think the garden, as a protector of our liberties and a field for individual development, was of more moral importance. There—as could not so easily be done within doors—we were able to get out of sight and hearing of our elders, and do very much as we liked, and there were many things we liked doing, which we preferred that our elders should not know.

"We were seven in family almost as long as I can remember—not quite. My brother Herbert came three years after me; and the fact that his birthday was the day after mine always puzzled me; it presented a mathematical problem that I could not solve. I remember seeing him for the first time, lying in his cradle; and then a little later watching with distaste the screaming exposure of his gums during a paroxysm of teething. But one or two incidents in those first three years of my life, when I was sixth and last, came back to me like the momentary memories of a dream. Being lifted over a railing I could not climb, into a field of nurses and children, must, I think, have been one of them; rather later perhaps was an early attempt to drown in six inches of running water, from which I was rescued by my brother Robert. Of that I have memory of lying face downward in the brook, and seeing strange weeds swaying under me—not conscious that I was in any danger; and then of screaming violently when restored to dry land and the discomfort of feeling myself very wet." [Laurence Housman, *The Unexpected Years,* Bobbs-Merrill, 1936.[1]]

1867. "My second birthday I remember because of my first sight, on that day, of the birthday present which I then received, and kept thereafter as one of my dearest possessions—a cardboard box containing two tiny wax babes sunk in a bed of gold tissue, paper flowers, and silver leaves. I was told to go to a corner cupboard and look in; and crawling over the nursery floor, I pushed open the bottom door, and there found beauty awaiting me. Was it then that the love of doubtful art (which took twenty-five years to eradicate) was born in me? I know now that, for the next twelve at least, nearly every ornament and picture that I sincerely admired was not at all what it should be. In the church stained-glass windows, mostly rank bad; in the drawing room florid Victorian ornaments, heavy Victorian furniture, and gaudy gasoliers; in the nursery carpet, wallpaper, and pictures all ranged from indifferent to something much worse; and yet, from association, though their artistic merit was departed, I love them still; and one—a needlework landscape sweetly greyed by age, I still have and admire, and am powerless in the grip of association to regard as other than beautiful. So, even now, my education is not complete; nor do I wish it to be."[1]

1870. "I was about five years old when my mother died; and certain small incidents of the day have remained curiously distinct. It was a Sunday and we were faced without explanation with a strange disturbance in the usual arrangement of things; the midday meal was transferred from the dining to the drawing room. I asked why, and was told (an incident I should not otherwise have remembered) that it was because I was late in getting ready for church that morning. The answer was of course an absurd one, and I do not suppose that I believed it. The real reason—as I came to know later—was that in the large converted bedchamber next the dining room my mother lay dying, and did actually die a few minutes after the meal had ended.

"We were out on the front lawn, not playing. What my sisters were doing I do not remember; my baby brother Herbert was with them. I was walking with my nurse along the drive, by the grass-bordered flower beds. I saw our housekeeper cousin come out of the front door; she said something I could not hear. I saw my two sisters burst into tears, and throw themselves into her arms. The nurse seemed to take no notice; we walked on. 'What did she say?' I asked. Nurse (who had a defective palate) with a foolish scared look on her face, mumbled something which I did not catch. I asked again; she repeated it; this time I heard. Weeping was in the air. I turned, and rushed into the house, and threw myself sobbing on to the drawing-room sofa. As I lay and wept, I found that I had destroyed something which an hour before had been dear to me. A cover for quill pens, with a label lavishly embellished in gold and red had been given me for my amusement; and I had set it in a plate of water to soak off the label—a thing of beauty—from the cardboard which I did not want. Having got it off, I had laid it to dry on a piece of paper in the corner of the sofa; and there in my wild paroxysm of grief I had irretrievably crumbled it. Weeping for the loss of my mother, I wept for that too; and thus the day of her death has always had, incongruously attached to it, a red and gold label, with a white swan in the centre, advertising the virtue of quill pens."[1]

1871. Father remarried. "In the following years, when we had settled down into the new house my father brought home the bride who should have been mine. It was an evening in late July; we were all gathered in the entrance hall to greet them and when the greetings were over, my father gave me a roguish look, which meant, I suppose, "Cut you out, my boy!' I felt

(From *The Field of Clover* by Laurence Housman. Illustrated by the author.)

shy and embarrassed, and hung my head. But my heart was not broken.

"She told me afterwards, that over that first meeting with her adopted family she had felt very apprehensive and nervous; but I can remember no sign of it. She discussed with us that same evening what we were to call her. It was to be 'Mamma.' But as time went by we adopted the better word of 'Mater.' And in our grown-up years the other word fell into practical disuse. Certain names suit characters; and she was so very much more a 'Mater' than a 'Mamma,' perhaps because of a certain Roman touch, in her rule both over herself and others, but not Roman in the theological sense; quite the reverse."[1]

1876. Entered Bromsgrove school. "I went to school in my eleventh year, and there the easy days of childhood ended, and the more difficult ones of youth began. During my first term I was placed in a class with boys bigger than myself, who used to stick knives and pins into me if I dared to go above them. It was the old bad system; 'taking down' in class was the crude and lazy way which schoolmasters then employed for registering merit and progress. Quite naturally the older boys resented it, when in a manner humiliating to themselves a small junior was allowed to exhibit publicly so insignificant a thing in school life as mental superiority.

(From "Possession," a play, in *The Golden Sovereign* by Laurence Housman. Illustrated by Ernest H. Shepard.)

"But it was equally natural that, when for the moment I could do so, I should feel a certain enjoyment in pulling down the mighty from their seats, and exalting the humble and meek; for, outside the class, those bigger boys led me a terrible life, and inside, so far as discipline and decorum allowed—in that sort of League of Nations atmosphere which school hours established—they wished still to do the same, and bully the small nations.

"I use the political parallel because that was really my first training in politics; from it I had the sense to learn that physical force is not the basis of government as the materialists would have us believe. The basis of government is human nature. My human nature stuck it out, and the human nature of the bigger boys, being fundamentally decent, grew ashamed of itself, and they ceased to stick pins into me. In spite of my being the smaller and weaker, they allowed me at last to take them down. The small object-lesson of the limitations of physical force in a world where schoolboy honor (or the taboo that stands for it) allows no appeal to the higher authorities, helped to make me an idealist.

"Defenders of the Public School System—as it existed in my days, and as they would like it to continue—maintain that the bullying of small boys is good for them, and has a healthy and hardening effect on their characters. It may be so; but what of its effect on those who do the bullying? It seems to me a cowardly and despicable thing for the strong to afflict the weak; and I am inclined to think that the divine right of imperialism to swagger through the world, exploiting subject races for their supposed benefit has very largely had its origin in the bullying and fagging which have been countenanced in our public schools."[1]

1882. "These six years of rather unsatisfactory schooling for mind and morals were finished off by a piece of unexpected and, if I guess right, of undeserved success. My lack of classical attainment had made it quite evident that I was not going to be able to make my living by my brains in any scholarly sense; and as I had always shown an interest in colour and pattern, and was fond of drawing, it was decided—with little enough to show for it—that I had in me the makings of an artist; and so, a year before I left school, the thing was settled—I was to go to London and study art. But before that was to be allowed there was a ditch that I must cross; and I did not believe that I had the capacity for crossing it.

"My four brothers and I had all entered school on Foundation scholarships, and those ahead of me in years had on leaving passed an examination called the Higher Oxford and Cambridge Local which qualified for entry to the Universities. My father decided that, in order to round off the family record, I also must pass this perfectly unnecessary examination before leaving. It may only have been held over me as a threat, not seriously meant; but I took it to be real, and I entered for the examination with a sense of failure and the doom of another year's schooling lying ahead.

"The examiner who came to us that year was the famous Doctor Spooner, in whose name so many 'Spoonerisms' have been invented. I knew that I had done pretty badly in two at least of the papers that had been set, and when I entered his genial presence for my 'Viva,' I entered without hope. He put me on to a piece of Virgil over which I stumbled badly. Very soon he stopped me.

"'What' he inquired amiably, 'are you intending to do when you leave school?'

"'I am going to study art,' I said.

"'Then you are not going to the University?'

"'No, sir.'

"'Then why have you entered for this examination?'

"A flash of inspiration descended upon me. I told him the truth. 'Merely family pride, sir. My father says that if I don't pass it, I am to stay for another year.'

"He smiled a beautiful smile. 'Oh, indeed!' was all he said.

"A week later I had left school for good—very much for good. Doctor Spooner had passed me! And how I have loved him ever since!"[1]

Sent to London to study art with his older sister, Clemence. "It was, I suppose, at about this time that the pairing of our interests in art and literature became evident. Both in drawing and writing Clemence was then well ahead of me, and had already shown so much mental ability that my headmaster—though not one who favoured the claims of women to higher education—had said that he wished he had her in his sixth form. Eventually, when it was decided that to study art, I must go to London, Clemence was released from the Victorian bonds of home, for the sole reason that it was considered too risky for me to go alone without some one of more stable character to look after me. So when I left school we began studying together, first at the local art school; then, having each come into a small legacy upon the death of our grandmother, and Clemence into a somewhat larger one on her coming of age, we went up to London together—she to learn wood-engraving, and I to find out in the course of further study what particular line of art I was made for.

"I think now it was a very risky thing. It took me nearly seven years to find myself, to discover, that is to say, in what direction my individual interest and abilities were to find expression; and for some years the routine training of the art schools I attended did nothing to help me, leaving me with the depressed feeling that I should never do anything but pot-boiling. For though during that waiting period I had formed many enthusiasms, I was unable to give them an individual application; and though while at South Kensington I took a few prizes in the National Competition, I did not get near to having a style of my own."[1]

1893. Began writing and illustrating. "The personal kindness of my first publisher, Mr. Kegan Paul, came to me through the friendly interest of Alfred Pollard, to whom I owed most of my early introductions both to editors and publishers—and not introductions alone; he was a constant help to me in his criticism of my immature beginnings in verse and prose, and also in the loan of books for the bettering of my very haphazard knowledge of English literature, limited till then to the books which we had at home. Through him I received a commission from Kegan Paul to edit a selection of *The Writings of William Blake.* This was my first book; it was prentice-work, done at a time when Blake was far less known and appreciated than he is now; and Andrew Lang began his review of it with the words, 'To admire Blake is the mark of a clique.' It was true then, it is not true now. In the National Gallery of British Art, Blake has a room all to himself, and a floor paved with mosaics inspired by his design for the *Book of Job.*

The King got out the box, found the key, and gave it to the burglar.

"You can either open it yourself," he said, "or I will open it. And I can assure you that you are perfectly welcome to anything that it contains." ■ (From *Cotton-Wooleena* by Laurence Housman. Illustrated by Robert Binks.)

"After Blake, the firm of Kegan Paul published three books of my fairy stories, another of imaginary legends, called *All-Fellows,* which still has my heart, and a monograph on the work of Arthur Boyd Houghton. My illustrated tales they continued to publish, in spite of the protests of their head traveller, who, in his country rounds, not merely failed to find a market for them, but was met with derision when he offered them. My illustrations were not popular with the country booksellers; and to have his wares ridiculed hurt his sense of dignity, and also his standing with the trade. When I heard of it, I suggested that the right solution was for him to agree heartily with my detractors, but to say that just now they were 'the thing,' and that his firm had to publish them to meet a depraved taste. The idea was not my own; a friend had told me that she had heard two children discussing those same illustrations—one objecting to them, and the other saying that she must try to like them because now they were 'the thing.'

"The newspaper critics were similarly divided: the 'Thingummyites'—and the others. But these divided opinions did not much trouble me. . . .

"In the year before the appearance of my first fairy tales, an introduction from Pollard had secured me work both in illustration and writing from Harry Quilter, editor and proprietor of the *Universal Review.* In this case relations were not quite so friendly; but the work which I did for that boreal blast of a character, honest at least in his opinions, and uncompromising in the expression of them, led to a meeting which had a decisive effect upon my work. A story of mine called 'The Green Gaffer' with several illustrations, had appeared in the *Universal Review* and this, coupled with my attempt to obtain a copy of the first *Dial,* already out of print, brought me an invitation from Ricketts and Shannon to call at the 'Vale.' Within a month Ricketts had dragged me away from my timid preference for fuzzy chalk-drawings, as a means of concealing my bad draughtsmanship, and had set me to pen-work, with Rossetti and the other Pre-Raphaelites as my main guides both in composition and technique. From that time on, I felt set— I acquired a new confidence; I had found out at last what I wanted to do.

"My connection with the *Universal Review* brought me also another commission of special value and interest. Quilter, claiming the right to republish a book from a poem by George Meredith, called *Jump-to-Glory Jane,* set me to illustrate it. . . ."[1]

Despite continued offers from publishers for his illustrations or writings, Housman's first ten years in the field were financially lean. ". . .Such an income made it impossible for me to marry, had I wished it, in the class to which I was supposed to belong; I could not until I was well over forty, have run the risk of a family. But as the 'not impossible She' never came within the horizon of my waking dreams, that deprivation was more theoretical than real. Nevertheless there remains a large disproportion between the respectable reputation which I began to acquire in my early thirties, and the monetary return I got from it. And I wonder whether other authors—my superiors in quality and my equals in the favour of the critics—have had similar experiences; whether an author who does not aim at popularity must always have a hard time, unless his needs are as modest, and as unmatrimonial as were mine."[1]

1895. Housman worked as art critic on the *Manchester Guardian.* "I was still rather badly off, when, in my thirtieth year, the chance writing of a single article provided me with the basis of an income for several years to follow. The article itself only brought me five pounds; but it also resulted in a fixed stipend, so from that day I was sure of making a living. The circumstances were these. My friend, Alfred Pollard, had become the editor of a book-lovers' quarterly called *Bibliographica;* wishing for variety, and something less erudite than the exploration of mediaeval texts, and examples of early printing, he asked me for an article on any modern illustrator I chose to select. I chose Arthur Boyd Houghton, and my article was re-issued a year later in monograph form, with numerous illustrations, drawn mainly from Dalziel's *Arabian Nights* and the early numbers of the *Graphic.* Just then I chanced to meet R. A. M. Stevenson, who, wishing to give up his post as art critic to the *Manchester Guardian,* was looking round for a suitable successor to recommend.

"As I was both an illustrator and a writer, he thought that I might do; and having asked if I was willing, he sent in my name. But naturally, before appointing me, the editor wished to see a specimen of my work, and the only thing I had then written, in the way of art criticism, was my article on Houghton. I sent it along, and it secured me the job.

"To my connection with the *Manchester Guardian* and its wonderful editor, C. P. Scott, (a connection which lasted for sixteen years) I owe more than I can say. Not only did it relieve me during the first five years, from the fear of starvation, but it gave me confidence and a power of ready writing which till then I had lacked. Hitherto I had waited too much upon mood, and when dissatisfied with results would often put away a piece of writing and not look at it again for months—sometimes, indeed, never; for I still have by me a large pile of fragmentary stories and articles begun in the '90's, which I am now never likely to finish.

"But most of the press notices which I wrote for the *Manchester Guardian* had to be wired from the London office early the same evening; and though that is all in the ABC of journalism, it was for me a strange, and at first an unnerving experience. But even before I got the nerve, I found it was good for me; and my 'pot-boiling'—if so it must be regarded— has, I believe, enabled me to write better, and certainly to write more of the things I wished to write than would otherwise have been possible.

"While on the *Manchester Guardian,* I had a show of my own at the Fine Arts Society, Bond Street, a selection of my book illustrations up to date, to which, as far as I remember, my fellow critics were fairly kind, and the patrons of art more receptive than I had expected.

"In the event the show was rather a farewell to illustration, for after it I did little more, partly because my eyesight no longer served me for the very detailed style of drawing which was what most interested me, partly because I had found that I was more naturally cut out to be an author than an illustrator."[1]

1896. Besides writing and illustrating children's stories and fiction, Housman published his first book of poetry. His brother, A. E., author of *A Shropshire Lad,* gained more recognition than Housman, however. "It was in the year following the publication of *Green Arras* that the bright blow descended upon me. I had begun in a small way to make a reputation for myself; there were just about a thousand people who liked my books sufficiently to buy them—my prose books that is to say; my poems were only wanted by about half that number. But this meant that publishers were willing to take what I brought them, though royalties usually did not begin with first sales. But I was happy, and hopeful, and prolific; and having the *Manchester Guardian* as a standby was able to indulge in the luxury of writing poems and stories which did not bring me much profit.

"And then like a bolt from the blue out came *A Shropshire Lad,* and straightway, as an author with any individuality worth mentioning, I was wiped out. I became the brother of the *Shropshire Lad,* and for the next five years I laboured under the shadow of that bright cloud. . . .''[1]

1900. First successful book was published. "*An Englishwoman's Love Letters* gave me what I had never had before—financial elbow room, and apparent security for the future. The foolish fuss that was made about it seemed to suggest that its author might thereafter look forward to an assured income. Accustomed as I had been to live on less than

. . . And he went to the highest part of the palace, out onto the battlements of the great tower. ■ (From *The Rat-Catcher's Daughter: A Collection of Stories* by Laurence Housman. Illustrated by Julia Noonan.)

two hundred pounds a year, and with no wish to spend on a much larger scale, I found myself in possession of a bank balance of over two thousand pounds. So I could now do many small things which I wanted to do, and a few bigger things which then, for the first time, occurred to me as both desirable and possible."[1]

1904-1905. Co-authored his second play, "Prunella," which later became popular in the United States. "'Prunella' was produced in the winter . . . with 'Peter Pan' as its contemporary. . . . Both monetarily and with the critics the play failed. 'Quaint, but feeble,' I heard a lady say, as I came away from the first performance. The press damned it with faint praise; the general line taken by the critics was that the authors were ambitiously trying to produce a new *genre* which was scarcely worth while; Granville Barker and I were put severely in our places—in our anxiety to be original, we had merely been fantastic; most of the compliments went to Moorat's music.

"The one exception was a flaming and enthusiastic notice in the *St. James' Gazette. . . .* But one swallow in the press does

(From *Stories from the Arabian Nights,* retold by Laurence Housman. Illustrated by Edmund Dulac.)

not make a summer for theatrical management; the play trickled through three weeks, and retired on a heavy deficit. Subsequent revivals were symptomatic. In 1906 it paid its way and the critics became respectful. In 1907 it made a profit, and the critics were complimentary. In 1910, with the hearty assistance of the press, it was bringing its authors affluence when the death of King Edward brought the theatrical season to an untimely end. In 1916 it ran for a hundred nights in New York, and was put on the films.

"In my experience, the production of plays can provide an author with livelier satisfaction than the writing of books. It is pleasant to be told that one's books are appreciated; but it is not merely pleasant, it is thrilling, to see one's play, or its characters, brought to life by good production or good acting. I have had that great happiness even over plays which have not been a success."[1]

1916. First trip to America during World War I. "After two years of wartime employment without pay it became necessary for me to make a quick income. At that time the United States

was still good hunting-ground for indigent English authors who could put up readings or lectures. By good luck 'Prunella' had been produced at the Little Theatre, New York, in the spring of 1914 and had run for a hundred nights. On this windfall I was able to keep going till 1916. Then, on the supposition that New York might provide audiences for the part-author of a successful play, I fell in with the proposition made to me by [friends] . . . that I should go . . . and give lectures advocating what had not then been officially adopted in either country, the setting up of a League of Nations.

"New York is the most upstanding city in the world; it is also beautiful, so long as you look at it only from outside; but except at certain moments its beauty is hard as nails. My first sight of it was against sunset, its skyscrapers dark upon the west, till, as lights sprang stage by stage from basement to basement to roof, they became a pile of golden honeycombs—a melting loveliness of halfway lights and shades; then, character reasserting itself, they hardened into night, sharp-eyed and glittering amid their huge black walls, and once more the fairy palaces became prisons."[1]

1920. Second trip to America. "My second visit to America brought me more friends than money. In friends I came back rich, having picked them up all the way along. . . . But in pocket I should have fared badly, had it not been for two fortunate happenings which made things easier. The first was the starting at the very moment of my arrival of a new left-wing weekly called *The Freeman.* The editor, who, during my stay in Chicago was my part-time host, invited me to send him as many articles as I had time to write. And then, most opportunely to make writing easier, Brookwood Community School opened its friendly doors to me; and for some three weeks as a P. G. among students ranging in age from ten to twenty-three, I got all the peace and quiet I needed for literary work in place of the lecturing I had expected."[1]

1936. Published his autobiography at the age of seventy-one. "If a man intends or expects to live to the age of seventy, he should not publish his reminiscences before. Reminiscences, to be in their right place, should come—like grace after meat—at the end, not in the middle of the meal; still less should they be trotted out (as has happened too often of late years) as an apéritif for the career which is to follow. For who, indeed, knows till the meal is over how much he has to be thankful for? A dessert of sour grapes may spoil everything. So long as a man feels that he has still much waiting for him to do, or to endure, or is still adventurously inclined, he would do well to postpone not perhaps the writing but the publication of his reminiscences.

". . .I look back on a life which has not, in the ordinary sense, been adventurous. Even such domestic adventures as marriage, paternity, divorce, bitter bereavement, have stayed beyond the range of my experience; I have not had to face either the misery of poverty or the anxieties of wealth; I have escaped the penalties of the law, and the terrorizing influences of the theology which afflicted my youth. I have made and I have lost friends, with a residuum to the good. I have had pleasures and disappointments; but though the disappointments are perhaps more numerous and present to my recollection than the pleasures, I continue to find life worth having; its first ten years were the happiest, its next ten the least happy; after that, every decade has, so far as my personal experience is concerned, brought me increasing ease and contentment; and it seems to me now that if in age one can retain one's health, age is the likeliest time for getting on good terms with one's self and one's neighbours."[1]

February 20, 1959. Died at the age of ninety-four in Glastonbury, England. ". . .No life worth living can be isolated from the lives of others. Even the rebel forms part of the general scheme of things, and if the scheme becomes a bloody entanglement, he belongs to it all the more. And that, I think, is what makes life so interesting: whether one wills it or no, one has to belong."[1]

FOR MORE INFORMATION SEE: Stanley J. Kunitz and Howard Haycraft, editors, *Twentieth Century Authors,* Wilson, 1942; S. J. Kunitz, editor, *Twentieth Century Authors,* first supplement, Wilson, 1955; Ruth Z. Temple and Martin Tucker, editors, *Modern British Literature,* Volume two, Frederick Ungar Publishing Co., 1966.

Obituaries: *New York Times,* February 21, 1959; *Illustrated London News,* February 28, 1959; *Newsweek,* March 2, 1959; *Time,* March 2, 1959; *Wilson Library Bulletin,* April, 1959; *Drama,* Summer, 1959; *Americana Annual 1960; Britannica Book of the Year 1960.*

HUGHES, Richard (Arthur Warren) 1900-1976

OBITUARY NOTICE—See sketch in *SATA* Volume 8: Born April 19, 1900, in Weybridge, Surrey, England; died of leukemia, April 28, 1976, in Moredrin, Merionethshire, Wales. Novelist, poet, playwright. Hughes is best known for his 1929 novel *The Innocent Voyage,* which was published a year later as *A High Wind in Jamaica.* It has sold three million copies and remains a perennial favorite. Hughes wrote three other novels as well as plays, poetry, and children's stories. Most of his work achieved not only popular but critical success; his first drama, *The Sister's Tragedy,* was hailed by George Bernard Shaw as the finest one-act play ever written. At Oriel College, Oxford, Hughes became acquainted with Aldous Huxley, Robert Graves, Edmund Blunden, and T. E. Lawrence, and upon settling in Wales he became a close friend of Dylan Thomas. A self-confessed slow writer, he once jokingly called the enterprise "a race between the publisher and the undertaker." *For More Information See: Twentieth Century Authors,* Wilson, 1942; *The Who's Who of Children's Literature,* Schocken, 1968; *Contemporary Authors,* Volumes 5-8, revised, Gale, 1969; *Penguin Companion to English Literature,* McGraw-Hill, 1971; *Contemporary Literary Criticism,* Gale, Volume I, 1973, Volume II, 1979; *Twentieth Century Children's Writers,* St. Martin's, 1978. *Obituaries: London Times,* April 30, 1976; *New York Times,* April 30, 1976; *Washington Post,* April 30, 1976; *Newsweek,* May 10, 1976; *Time,* May 10, 1976; *AB Bookman's Weekly,* May 31, 1976; *Publishers Weekly,* May 31, 1976; *Contemporary Authors,* Volumes 65-68, Gale, 1977.

HUNTER, Evan   1926- (Hunt Collins, Richard Marsten, Ed McBain)

PERSONAL: Born October 15, 1926, in New York, N.Y.; son of Charles and Marie (Coppola) Lombino; Hunter legally changed his name; married Anita Melnick, October 17, 1949 (divorced); married Mary Vann Finley, 1973; children: (first marriage) Ted, Mark, Richard; Amanda Finley (stepdaughter). *Education:* Attended Art Students' League, New York City, and Cooper Union Art School; Hunter College, B.A., 1950. *Politics:* Democrat. *Agent:* William Morris Agency, 1350 Ave. of the Americas, New York, N.Y. 10019.

CAREER: Taught at two vocational high schools in New York for a short time, about 1950; held various jobs, including answering the telephone at night for American Automobile Association and selling lobsters for a wholesale lobster firm, both New York; worked for a literary agency, New York, for two years. Full-time writer. *Military service:* U.S. Navy, 1944-46. *Member:* Phi Beta Kappa. *Awards, honors:* Mystery Writers of America award, 1957, for short story, "The Last Spin," for screenplay, "The Birds," and for short story, "The Sardinian Incident."

WRITINGS: Find the Feathered Serpent, Winston, 1952; *Don't Crowd Me,* Popular Library, 1953; *The Blackboard Jungle,* Simon & Schuster, 1954; *Second Ending,* Simon & Schuster, 1956, reissued in paperback as *Quartet in "H",* Pocket Books, 1957, and then as *Second Ending,* Dell, 1967; *The Jungle Kids,* Pocket Books, 1956; (under pseudonym Hunt Collins) *Tomorrow and Tomorrow,* Pyramid, 1956; *Strangers When We*

(From the movie "The Birds," screenplay by Evan Hunter, starring Rod Taylor and Tippi Hedren, based on the novel by Daphne Du Maurier. Released by Universal Pictures Co., 1963.)

(From the movie "Blackboard Jungle," starring Glenn Ford and Sidney Poitier. Copyright 1955 by Loew's, Inc.)

Meet, Simon & Schuster, 1958; *A Matter of Conviction,* Simon & Schuster, 1959, reissued in paperback as *Young Savages,* Pocket Books, 1966.

The Remarkable Harry, Abelard, 1960; *The Wonderful Button,* Abelard, 1961; *Mothers and Daughters,* Simon & Schuster, 1961; *Happy New Year, Herbie and Other Stories,* Simon & Schuster, 1963; *Buddwing,* Simon & Schuster, 1964; (under pseudonym Ed McBain) *The Sentries,* Simon & Schuster, 1965; *The Paper Dragon,* Delacorte, 1966; *A Horse's Head,* Delacorte, 1967; *Last Summer,* Doubleday, 1968; *Sons,* Doubleday, 1969.

Nobody Knew They were There, Doubleday, 1971; *Every Little Crook and Nanny,* Doubleday, 1972; *The Easter Man,* Doubleday, 1972; *Seven,* Constable, 1972; *Come Winter,* Doubleday, 1974; *Streets of Gold,* Harper, 1974; (under pseudonym Ed McBain) *Where There's Smoke,* Random House, 1975; *The Chisholms,* Harper, 1976; (under pseudonym Ed McBain) *Guns,* Random House, 1976; *Me and Mr. Stenner* (juvenile), Lippincott, 1976; (under pseudonym Ed McBain), *Goldilocks,* Arbor House, 1978; *Love Dad,* Crown, 1981.

''87th Precinct Series,'' under pseudonym Ed McBain; all published by Simon & Schuster, except as indicated: *Cop Hater,* 1956; *The Mugger,* 1956; *The Pusher,* 1956; *The Con Man,* 1957; *Killer's Choice,* 1957; *Killer's Payoff,* 1958; *Lady Killer,* 1958; *Killer's Wedge,* 1959; *'Til Death,* 1959; *King's Ransom,* 1959; *Give the Boys a Great Big Hand,* 1960; *The Heckler,* 1960; *See Them Die,* 1960; *Lady, Lady, I Did It!,* 1961; *Like Love,* 1962; *The Empty Hours* (three novellas), 1962; *Ten Plus One,* 1963; *Ax,* 1964; *He Who Hesitates,* Delacorte, 1965; *Doll,* Delacorte, 1965; *Eighty Million Eyes,* Delacorte, 1966; *The 87th Precinct* (includes *Cop Hater, The Mugger, The Pusher, The Con Man),* Boardman, 1966; *Fuzz,* Doubleday, 1968; *Shotgun,* Doubleday, 1969; *Jigsaw,* Doubleday, 1970; *Hail, Hail, the Gang's All Here!,* Doubleday, 1971; *Sadie When She Died,* Doubleday, 1972; *Let's Hear it for the Deaf Man,* Doubleday, 1972; *Hail to the Chief,* Random House, 1973; *Bread,* Random House, 1974; *Blood Relatives,* Random House, 1975; *So Long as We Both Shall Live,* Random House, 1976; *Long Time No See,* Random House, 1977; *Calypso,* Viking, 1979; *Ghosts,* Viking, 1980.

Plays: ''The Easter Man,'' produced in Birmingham, England, at Birmingham Repertory Theatre, 1964, retitled ''A Race of Hairy Men!'' and produced on Broadway at Henry Miller's Theater, April, 1965; ''The Conjuror,'' produced at the University of Michigan, fall, 1969.

Screenplays: ''Strangers When We Meet,'' produced by Columbia, 1960; ''The Birds'' (based on Daphne du Maurier's story), produced by Alfred Hitchcock, Universal, 1963; ''Fuzz,'' produced by United Artists, 1972; ''Walk Proud,'' produced by Universal, 1979.

ADAPTATIONS—Movies: ''The Blackboard Jungle,'' Metro-Goldwyn-Mayer, 1955; ''Cop Hater,'' United Artists, 1958; ''The Muggers,'' based on *The Mugger,* United Artists, 1958; ''Strangers When We Meet,'' Columbia, 1959; ''The Pusher,'' United Artists, 1960; ''The Young Savages,'' based on *A Matter of Conviction,* United Artists, 1961; ''High and Low,'' based on *King's Ransom,* Toho International, 1963; ''Mr. Buddwing,'' based on *Buddwing,* Metro-Goldwyn-Mayer, 1967; ''Last Summer,'' Allied Artists, 1969; ''Without Apparent Motive,'' based on *Ten Plus One;* ''Blood Relatives.'' Hunter adapted his novel, *The Chisholms,* as a six-hour, mini-

The weekends I spent with my father made me happy, and they also made me sad. ■ (From *Me and Mr. Stenner* by Evan Hunter. Jacket illustrated by Glo Coalson.)

series for CBS-TV; ''87th Precinct'' was presented on NBC-TV from September 25, 1961 to September 10, 1962.

WORK IN PROGRESS: More 87th Precinct mysteries.

SIDELIGHTS: **October 15, 1926.** Born in New York City. Raised as the only child of parents of Italian descent, Hunter spent his first twelve years in a section of New York known as ''Italian harlem.'' ''. . . I lived in a slum for the first twelve years of my life. . . .'' [Evan Hunter, ''An Interview with Evan Hunter-Ed McBain,'' *The Writer,* April, 1969.[1]]

1938. Family moved to the Bronx, where Hunter was art editor of his high school literary magazine. Upon graduation from high school, Hunter attended the Art Students' League in New York City on a scholarship and, later, studied at the Cooper Union Art School. ''I fully intended to become an artist. While I was at Cooper—out of the isolated world of high school where I had been the top artist at the school—I was surrounded by people who were very serious about art and who were, frankly, much better than I was.

''It didn't take much perception to look around and see graphic representation of their talents as opposed to mine, and this shook me a bit. I had always written a little in high school, then I went in the Navy in 1944 and started writing. By the time I got out I decided that was what I wanted to do.'' [Fran

(From the movie "Fuzz," starring Burt Reynolds and Jack Weston. Screenplay by Evan Hunter.
Copyright © 1972 by United Artists Corp.)

Krajewski, "An Exclusive Re-Visit with Evan Hunter," *Writer's Digest,* April, 1971.[2]]

1944-1946. Stationed on a Navy destroyer in the Pacific during his military service.

October 17, 1949. Married Anita Melnick, a fellow classmate at Hunter College in New York. The couple had three sons.

1950. Received a B.A. degree in English (Phi Beta Kappa) from Hunter College.

1950-1954. Held a variety of jobs, including substitute teaching in New York vocational schools. "*The Blackboard Jungle* was based largely on my own brief experience as a substitute teacher, an example of the writer enlarging upon reality to cast himself as the hero fighting a battle against overwhelming odds. (*I* quit teaching; Richard Dadier stays on.) But certainly the characters, the setting, and the incidents were all firmly rooted in my memory before I sat down to write the book."[1]

1952. "I changed my name . . . while I was working for Scott [Scott Meredith Literary Agency]. Writing a lot of stories for the pulps by then, I used a lot of different names. I wrote so many, I'd have several stories in a single issue, and the editors who bought them didn't know. Charles Heckelmann, who was editor of Popular Library then, called up one day, since I was the agent who offered him a novel by someone named Evan

Hunter. He wanted to meet him. I asked Scott what to do, and he told me to go on up and see Heckelmann. When *I* explained I was Evan Hunter, Heckelmann was surprised, of course, but he wanted the book, and after I asked if I should put my real name on it, he said, 'I think "Evan Hunter" will sell a lot more tickets.' I became Evan Hunter.

Evan is shortened from Evander Childs High School, and the last name is appropriated from his college. "When I had put my own name on stories, they were rejected, and I think there's still a prejudice against writers with foreign names. If you're an Italian-American, you're not supposed to be a literate person." [Evan Hunter, "PW Interviews Evan Hunter," *Publishers Weekly,* April 3, 1981.[3]]

1954. After first successful novel, *The Blackboard Jungle,* became a full-time writer. "I think the first thing I had published was a science fiction short story in a pulp magazine for which I was paid $12. Everyone in America buys the overnight success legend, but actually I had had possibly one hundred short stories published and had written three or four novels before *The Blackboard Jungle.*"[2]

1956. First novel for the "87th Precinct series" under pseudonym, Ed McBain, was published. "I ended up using another name, Ed McBain, because the mystery writer is still considered a stepchild. But it's very easy for me to write the 87th

(From the movie "Walk Proud," screenplay by Evan Hunter. Copyright © 1979 by Universal City Studios, Inc.)

(From the television series "87th Precinct," starring Robert Lansing, Norman Fell, and Ron Harper. Presented on NBC-TV, 1961-62.)

Precinct mysteries, and I've kept going . . . because the series has been so well received. Besides, there's an ease with a mystery. You don't have the pressure to win mainstream approval. You don't have to worry if it will be reviewed or not."[3]

"I write the Ed McBain mysteries in a month. I write them very swiftly with very little revision. I try to keep them entertaining, suspenseful and exciting, but I have no intention in any of them of commenting on the society we live in, except as that society affects the cops. . . ."[2]

". . . A mystery should be exciting, believable, and entertaining. If you're lucky besides, it might just say a little something about crime and punishment."[1]

Hunter has written over thirty police mysteries and his "87th Precinct series" formed the basis of a popular television series.

1964. One of his favorite novels was published. "I loved *Buddwing*. I felt this was a real step forward for me in terms of technique and in terms of characterization. I don't know that it's my favorite novel. I think *Sons* [1969] really is my favorite because it says something very important, and I wish it would be read by everyone in America."[2]

1970—. Continues to write prolifically—besides novels, Hunter has written plays and screenplays. "I prefer the novel . . . as a means of communication. It seems to me it's the one thing that people do *alone* today. You can sit and read it and it's

absolutely private and personal; there's a one to one communication between you and the reader. So much more is demanded of the reader in a novel; he brings more of himself to it than he has to in entertainment media. You can savor it at your own pace."[2]

"I don't know why I've been attracted to writing about young people. I guess from 'Blackboard Jungle' it's been a situation that's always appealed to me, the idea of adults in conflict with the young. I think part of my fascination is with America as an adolescent nation and with our so-called adult responses that are sometimes adolescent.

"I think it hasn't yet been recognized in America that I write serious novels. The ease with which a reader can read my novels has been misinterpreted to mean that they're facile. I personally believe that hard-to-read novels are products of lazy novelists, unlike writers such as John Fowles or William Styron."[3]

Hunter lives with his second wife, Mary Vann, in Norwalk, Connecticut and in Sarasota, Florida, where he continues to write. When asked to give advice to an aspiring novelist, he responded: "I would tell him to write what he feels. This doesn't necessarily mean ['What he *knows*'] because he can always find out what he doesn't know. (People all over the world are dying to explain in detail exactly how they cut diamonds or fly airplanes or lead cavalry troops into battle. All anyone has to do is ask them.) I would also advise him to write whether he feels like it or not. If it's raining, and he's miserable and has outlined a happy party scene for that day, forget it and go on instead to the scene in which the hero's wife says she's running off with the butcher. The hardest part about writing is getting *something* down on paper. After that, it's all re-writing, which is infinitely easier."[1]

HOBBIES AND OTHER INTERESTS: Skiing, snorkling, and making home movies.

FOR MORE INFORMATION SEE: Kirkus Service, July 1, 1954; *Saturday Review,* October 9, 1954, January 7, 1956; *New York Times Book Review,* October 24, 1954, October 4, 1959, December 11, 1960; *Nation,* December 4, 1954; *Library Journal,* December 15, 1955, June 1, 1959, March 15, 1965; *New York Herald Tribune Book Review,* January 15, 1956, July 20, 1958, March 1, 1959, September 20, 1959; *Wilson Library Bulletin,* September, 1956; *Chicago Sunday Tribune,* June 8, 1958, June 19, 1966; *Catholic World,* August, 1958; *Times Literary Supplement,* November 21, 1958, November 25, 1959; *San Francisco Chronicle,* February 8, 1959, December 20, 1959; *New Statesman,* November 28, 1959; *New York Herald Tribune "Lively Arts,"* November 11, 1960; *Springfield Republican,* July 9, 1961; *Book Week,* May 17, 1964; Roy Newquist, *Conversations,* Rand McNally, 1967; *The Writer,* April, 1969, April, 1978; *Writer's Digest,* April, 1971; *Publishers Weekly,* April 3, 1981.

JOSEPH JACOBS

JACOBS, Joseph 1854-1916

PERSONAL: Born August 29, 1854, in Sydney, South Wales, Australia; emigrated to England in 1872, and to the United States in 1900; died January 30, 1916, in Yonkers, New York; son of John and Sarah Jacobs; married Georgina Horne; children: Philip, Sydney, May. *Education:* Attended the University of Sydney and the University of London; B.A., King's College, Cambridge University, 1876 (senior rank in moral sciences). *Religion:* Jewish. *Home:* Yonkers, New York.

CAREER: Historian, folklorist, and scholar. Editor, *Folk-Lore* (British journal), 1890-93; *Jewish Year-Book,* 1896-99; *Literary Year Book,* 1898-99; *Funk & Wagnall's Jewish Encyclopedia,* 1900; *American Hebrew* (magazine), 1908-16. Registrar and professor of English literature and rhetoric at the Jewish Theological Seminary of America, 1906-13. *Member:* Royal Academy of History (Madrid), Brooklyn Institute (corresponding member), Jewish Historical Society of England (president, 1898).

WRITINGS—For children; editor: *English Fairy Tales* (illustrated by John D. Batten), Putnam, 1890, reprinted, Dover, 1967; *Celtic Fairy Tales* (illustrated by J. D. Batten), Putnam, 1891, reprinted, Dover, 1968; *Indian Fairy Tales* (illustrated by J. D. Batten), Putnam, 1892, reprinted, Dover, 1969; *More English Fairy Tales* (illustrated by J. D. Batten), Putnam, 1893, reprinted, Schocken Books, 1968; *More Celtic Fairy Tales* (illustrated by J. D. Batten), Putnam, 1894, reprinted, Dover, 1968; *Aesop's Fables* (illustrated by R. Heighway), Macmillan, 1895, reprinted, B. Franklin, 1970; *The Book of Wonder Voyages* (illustrated by J. D. Batten), Macmillan, 1896, reprinted, University Microfilms, 1967; *Reynard the*

EVAN HUNTER

"Dear cousin, why are you thus heavy in spirit, and why is your countenance dejected? Grief is easy to carry when the burden is divided amongst friends; for the nature of a true friend is to behold and relieve that which anguish will not suffer the oppressed to see or suffer." ■ (From *The Most Delectable History of Reynard the Fox* by Joseph Jacobs. Illustrated by W. Frank Calderon.)

Fox, Burt, 1900, reissued, Abelard-Schuman, 1969; *Europa's Fairy Book* (illustrated by J. D. Batten), Putnam, 1916, reissued as *European Folk and Fairy Tales,* Putnam, 1967.

Selections: *Johnny-Cake* (illustrated by Emma L. Brock), Putnam, 1933, reissued, Viking, 1972; *Molly Whuppie: An Old English Fairy Tale* (illustrated by Pelagie Doane), Oxford University Press, 1939; *Deirdre: A Tale of Ancient Ireland in 45 Duans,* Ozark Guide Press, 1945; *The Pied Piper, and Other Fairy Tales* (illustrated by James Hill), Macmillan, 1963; *Hudden and Dudden and Donald O'Neary* (illustrated by Doris Burn), Coward-McCann, 1968; *The Buried Moon* (illustrated by Susan Jeffers), Bradbury Press, 1969; *Lazy Jack,* World Publishing, 1969; *The Magpie's Nest* (illustrated by William Stobbs), Follett, 1970; *Munachar & Munachar: An Irish Story* (illustrated by Anne Rockwell), Crowell, 1970; *The Crock of Gold* (illustrated by W. Stobbs), Follett, 1971; *Guleesh: A Picture Story from Ireland,* Follett, 1971; *Jack the Giant-Killer* (illustrated by Fritz Wegner), H. Z. Walck, 1971; *Master of All Masters* (illustrated by A. Rockwell), Grosset & Dunlap, 1972; *Hereafterthis* (illustrated by Paul Galdone), McGraw-Hill, 1973; *Jack and the Beanstalk* (illustrated by Margery Gill), H. Z. Walck, 1975.

Nonfiction: *Bibliotheca Anglo-Judaica,* [London], 1888; *Studies in Jewish Statistics, Social, Vital, and Anthropometric,* D. Nutt, 1891; *George Eliot, Matthew Arnold, Browning, Newman: Essays and Reviews from the 'Athenaeum',* D. Nutt, 1891; (editor and translator) *The Jews of Angevin England,* Putnam, 1893, reissued, Gregg International, 1969; *Studies in Biblical Archaeology,* D. Nutt, 1894; *An Inquiry into the Sources of the History of the Jews in Spain,* Macmillan, 1894; *As Others Saw Him: A Retrospect, A.D. 54,* Houghton, 1895, reprinted as *Jesus as Others Saw Him,* Arno, 1973; *Jewish Ideals, and Other Essays,* Macmillan, 1896, reprinted, Books for Libraries, 1972; *The Story of Geographical Discovery: How the World Became Known,* Appleton, 1899; (editor) *The Jewish Encyclopedia,* Funk & Wagnalls, 1906, reissued, Ktav Publishing, 1964; *Jewish Contributions to Civilization: An Estimate,* Jewish Publication Society of America, 1919.

Also author of *Tennyson and "In Memoriam": An Appreciation and a Study,* 1892; *Statistics of Jewish Population in London,* 1894; and *Literary Studies,* 1895. Also editor of *The*

A CROW, half-dead with thirst, came upon a Pitcher which had once been full of water; but when the Crow put its beak into the mouth of the Pitcher he found that only very little water was left in it, and that he could not reach far enough down to get at it. He tried, and he tried, but at last had to give up in despair. Then a thought came to him, and he took a pebble and dropped it into the Pitcher. ■ (From *The Fables of Aesop* by Joseph Jacobs. Illustrated by Richard Heighway.)

(From *More Celtic Fairy Tales,* selected and edited by Joseph Jacobs. Illustrated by John D. Batten.)

. . . He placed before them a grey sea instead of a green plain. The three heroes stripped and tied their clothes behind their heads, and Naois placed Deirdre on the top of his shoulder. ■ (From *Celtic Fairy Tales*, collected by Joseph Jacobs. Illustrated by John D. Batten.)

Palace of Pleasure, 1890; *Epistolae Ho-Elianae: The Familiar Letters of James Howell,* 1890; and *Barlaam and Josaphat: English Lives of Buddha,* 1896.

ADAPTATIONS—Filmstrips: "The Three Sillies" (with a teaching guide, script, and work sheet), Spoken Arts, 1967.

SIDELIGHTS: Jacobs was known as one of the great Jewish historians and researchers of the Victorian age. He was a prolific writer and wrote numerous books on sociology, history, literature and philosophy, as well as editing numerous other works.

He is especially remembered for his research into folk lore and, although his literary output was enormous, his most widely read books were (and still are) for children. His daughter, May Bradshaw Hays, gave the following biographical account of her father: "My father came from a very new country, Australia, in 1872, after he had received a degree from the University of Sydney. He planned to go on with his education at St. John's College, Cambridge, to become a lawyer, and then return to his native land to practise. But literature was in the air at Cambridge and, after matriculating, he decided to go to London and become a writer. There he met Miss Georgina Horne and married her, and as we children came along and the needs of his family grew, he had to turn his pen toward any source of income which offered. He told me once, with a rueful smile, that his first published book was a piece of ghost-writing he did for a dentist, titled *Dental Bridges and Crowns;* but in a few years his book reviews—which always presented a fresh and ingenious point of view—began to make literary London aware of him. . . .

"Joseph Jacobs could make friends with any child at once. He never used the trite questions, 'How old are you?' or 'Where do you go to school?' but began an absurd little quarrel with the child, on any subject which popped into his head. Then, when they were both stamping their feet at each other he would suddenly say, 'What's this in my pocket; have a look, will you?' and there was always some little present which made the child his friend for always. When he went out to dinner, the children in the family were waiting for him on the stairs, with cries, through the banisters, of 'Tell us about Tom Tit Tot, Uncle Joe!' or 'We want to hear "The King o' the Cats," Mr. Jacob!' In his white tie and tails, Father would sit among their little night-gowned figures until the tale was told, and then he would go and make apologies to his hostess for his lateness. He was always a Pied Piper. One look into his brilliant hazel eyes, and a child was his forever. He loved the nonsensical words which delight children—we had many in the family vocabulary, which would be sheer gibberish to an outsider. . . .

"Among my most vivid memories are the Sunday afternoons when Father would take me to Burne-Jones' studio, where pictures of great figures of angels and of beautiful drooping women in blue robes lined the walls. I would sit on William Morris' lap while he held his great handleless bowl of tea in one hand and stroked my pale-gold hair with the other. I didn't enjoy having my head patted, but was consoled by the knowledge that I had on my new green silk Kate Greenaway dress with the yellow smocking at the yoke. Scraps of the conversation going on round me penetrated my childish preoccupation with myself, however, and I remember particularly well one stormy argument between Joseph Jacobs and Andrew Lang. Mr. Lang said, 'You folklore people (Father was president of the Folk Lore Society at the time) would refuse to print any stories for children which haven't been handed down from granny to granny, and if you can't trace them right back to their beginnings among the rustic folk of every country.' To which my father mildly replied, 'Now, Andrew, do me justice, old man. In collecting the stories for my fairy-tale books I have had a cause at heart as sacred as our science of folklore—the filling of our children's imaginations with bright trains of images. If a story will advance that cause I have always used it whether I knew its derivation or not. I simply want to make children feel that reading is the greatest fun in the world; so that they will want to get to books for themselves at the earliest possible moment.' There spoke the young innovator from Australia, rebelling against folklore traditions!

"At the end of each of his fairy books, Dr. Jacobs always appended the sources and parallels for the stories, and his illustrator, John D. Batten, would draw a final picture warning little children not to read these notes or they would fall asleep an hundred years.' In these appendices, or in his prefaces, the author explained that he 'called them all fairy tales, although few of them speak of fairies . . . the words "fairy tales" must accordingly be taken to include tales in which occurs something "fairy," something extraordinary—fairies, giants, dwarfs, speaking animals. . . . Every collection of fairy tales is made up of folk tales proper, of legends, droll or comic anecdotes, cummulative stories, beast tales, or merely ingenious nonsense tales put together in such a form as to amuse children . . . and generally speaking it has been my ambition to write as a good old nurse will speak when she tells fairy tales.'

"Years spent in tracing the exact derivations of fairy tales convinced my father that many of the European folk tales have their source in India. He never felt, as other folklorists did, that the tales were brought to Europe by the Crusaders, but rather that they traveled in the most natural way, from father to son. In his notes appended to *Indian Fairy Tales* he tells how he has 'edited an English version of an Italian adaptation, of a Spanish translation of a Latin version, of a Hebrew translation of an Arabic translation of the Indian original!' He calculated that the original Indian tales have been translated into 38 languages, in 112 different versions. In one of the *Jatakas,* or Birth Stories of Buddha, he was of the opinion that he had traced in the story called 'The Demon with the Matted Hair' the source of the Tar-Baby incident in *Uncle Remus!*

"It was in 1896 that Dr. Jacobs was invited to come to America to deliver a series of lectures on 'English Style and Composition' at Johns Hopkins University. On his return he told us, 'I've found the country I want you children to grow up in.' And so, his library of 12,000 books was packed into strong wooden boxes and swung into the hold of a Cunarder and, at the turn of the century, we began life in a new country. Father put down strong roots at his second transplanting, and always loved the United States 'next to Australia.' He had a book-lined library overlooking the Hudson in his house in Yonkers in which he would contentedly play innumerable games of chess with my husband, David Hays. He never needed to look at the chessboard but would play 'blindfold,' as they call it, sitting on the other side of the room with not even a glance at the chessmen. Dave always said, 'He could beat me with both eyes tied behind his back.'

"Father fully intended to collect and re-tell the rich treasure-trove of the folk tales of New England, but this was a dream which never came true. However, when his granddaughter, Margaret Hays, was born, he said, 'Peggy must have a book of her own, just as you children have,' and so he set to work and gathered together the sixth and last volume—*Europa's Fairy Tales.* In his amazing, scholarly fashion he found and

And still the days went on, and the new Moon never came. Naturally the poor folk were strongly feared and mazed, and a lot of them went to the Wise Woman who dwelt in the old mill, and asked if so be she could find out where the Moon was gone.

"Well," said she, after looking in the brewpot, and in the mirror, and in the Book, "it be main queer, but I can't rightly tell ye what's happened to her. If ye hear of aught, come and tell me."

(From *The Buried Moon* by Joseph Jacobs. Illustrated by Susan Jeffers.)

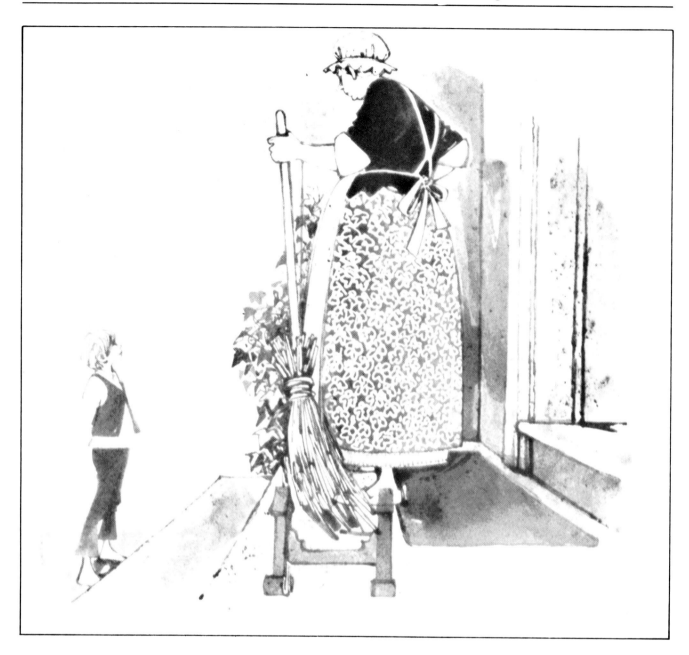

"My man is an ogre and there's nothing he likes better than boys broiled on toast. You'd better be moving on or he'll soon be coming." ■ (From *Jack and the Beanstalk* by Joseph Jacobs. Illustrated by Margery Gill.)

noted on the dedication page all the variants of the name Margaret, over twenty of them!

"People grow old in different ways. Some begin with a hardening at the heart which spreads outward until no trace of childhood is left. Others, the lucky ones, age only on the surface and keep the sensitive core of childhood within. In such a happy company did Joseph Jacobs belong.

"After his death, letters and tributes came to us from all over the world. Best of all, we liked the editorial which was headed,

'That fountain of fun frozen—impossible!' Those words described him exactly. My father was a fountain of fun which sparkled for all who knew him—young or old." [May Bradshaw Hays, "Memories of My Father, Joseph Jacobs," *Horn Book,* December, 1952.]

FOR MORE INFORMATION SEE: Alexander Marx, *Essays in Jewish Biography,* Jewish Publications, 1947; May B. Hays, "Memories of My Father, Joseph Jacobs," *Horn Book,* December, 1952; Brian Doyle, editor, *Who's Who of Children's Literature,* Schocken Books, 1968.

JANES, Edward C. 1908-

PERSONAL: Born in 1908, in Westfield, Massachusetts. *Education:* Studied at Deerfield Academy and Williams College.

CAREER: Author, editor. He has held a variety of journalistic positions with several magazines; once served as associate editor of *Outdoors Magazine;* travel editor of *Hunting and Fishing Magazine;* eastern field editor, *Outdoor Life;* he is the author of a number of books on the subjects of hunting and fishing.

WRITINGS—For children: (with Oliver H. P. Rodman) *The Boy's Complete Book of Fresh and Salt Water Fishing,* Little, Brown, 1949; *A Boy and His Gun,* A. S. Barnes, 1951; *Wilderness Warden* (illustrated by Raymond Abel), Longmans, Green, 1955; *A Boy and His Boat: An Introduction to Boating* (illustrated by Albert Michini), Macrae, 1963; *The First Book of Camping* (illustrated by Julio Granda), F. Watts, 1963, revised edition, 1977; *The Story of Knives,* Putnam, 1968; *When Men Panned Gold in the Klondike* (illustrated by William Hutchinson), Garrard, 1968; *When Cape Cod Men Saved Lives* (illustrated by W. Hutchinson), Garrard, 1968.

Other works: *Hunting Ducks and Geese,* Stackpole, 1954; *Trouble at Clear Lake,* Macrae, 1956; *Fresh-Water Fishing Complete,* Holt, 1961; *Nelson's Encyclopedia of Camping* (illustrated by Arno Maris), Nelson, 1963; *Westfield, Massachusetts, 1669-1969: The First Three Hundred Years,* Westfield Tri-Centennial Association, 1968; (editor), Ray Bergman, *Fishing with Ray Bergman,* Knopf, 1970; (editor), Lee Wulff, *Fishing with Lee Wulff,* Knopf, 1972; *Salmon Fishing in the*

EDWARD C. JANES

Northeast, Stone Wall Press, 1973; *I Remember Cape Cod* (illustrated by Robert MacLean), S. Greene Press, 1974; *Ringneck!: Pheasants and Pheasant Hunting,* Crown, 1975; editor of revised edition, Ray Bergman; *Trout,* Knopf, 1976.

SIDELIGHTS: Janes is an ardent hunting and fishing enthusiast who has written a number of informative books on these subjects. Most of his works have been highly recommended for their clarity and practical advice. *A Boy and His Boat,* for example, has been cited by the *New York Times* as "A well-written book of sound good sense. . . . There is even a chapter on water skiing and one on fishing from boats. Altogether one of the best of its kind around."

Janes has also written some fiction dealing with outdoor adventure themes. These efforts have also been fairly well-received. *Wilderness Warden,* the story of a young game warden's fight against a poaching ring, elicited this favorable comment from the *Saturday Review of Literature:* "The story is closely knit. It is also full of courage and suspense, of good characterizations, and of fast action; and in addition there are the feel and smell of the outdoors and appreciation for the magnificent forests of northern Maine. . . . This is an outstanding adventure story."

FOR MORE INFORMATION SEE: Saturday Review of Literature, November 12, 1955; *New York Times,* September 22, 1963.

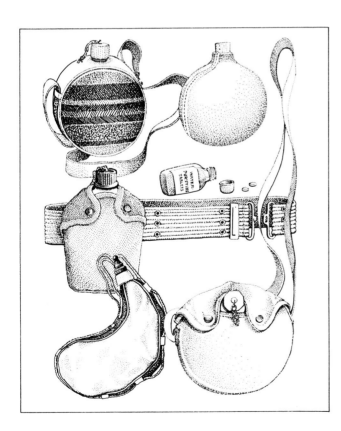

Old-fashioned canteens that are made of tin are likely to leak or rust. ■ (From *Camping* by E. C. Janes. Illustrated by Rod Slater.)

Dreams, books, are each a world; and books,
  we know,
Are a substantial world, both pure and good:
Round these, with tendrils strong as flesh and blood,
Our pastime and our happiness will grow.
          —William Wordsworth

JENSEN, Niels 1927-

PERSONAL: Born July 26, 1927, in Northern Schleswig, Denmark; son of Martin F. and Margretha Jensen; married Marie Raun, 1954; children: Martin, Karen, Lisbeth, Birgitte. *Education:* Ribe State Training College, graduate, 1954; Danish Post-Graduate Training College for Teachers, graduate study, 1970-71. *Home:* Vinkelvej 18, DK, 8410 Roende, Denmark.

CAREER: High school teacher in Roende, Denmark. *Awards, honors: Da landet laa oede* won Gyldendal's Anniversary Competition for the best book of fiction for children, 1970, and the Children's Book Prize from the Danish Ministry of Cultural Affairs, 1972.

WRITINGS: Da landet laa oede (title means "When the Land Lay Waste"), Gyldendal, 1971, translation by Oliver Stallybrass published as *Days of Courage: A Medieval Adventure,* Harcourt, 1973; *Kasper og krybskytten* (title means "Kasper and the Poacher"), Gyldendal, 1974; *Kasper og fogeden* (title means "Kasper and the Bailiff"), Gyldendal, 1974.

WORK IN PROGRESS: Further books in his fiction series for children, "Middelalderen" (title means "The Middle Ages").

SIDELIGHTS: "I was born in Northern Schleswig seven years after the province had become Danish according to the first voting for nationality in history. During my childhood there I experienced a living interest in political and historical facts.

NIELS JENSEN

History was always sensed as something of relevance which could influence one's everyday life with fatal consequences.

"As for my father, he had had to take part in the World War 1914-18. He took up reading intensely for the rest of his life, mainly in order to comprehend all the terrible things which had happened to him in his youth. My mother's bitterest experience of history was losing her fiancé on the battle-field of Flanders. All this gave me a real and true relation to history—a relationship which I later cultivated, partly through my teacher-education at Ribe State Training College and partly by self-studying." [Taken from the book jacket of *When the Land Lay Waste* by Neils Jensen, translated from the Danish by Oliver Stallybrass, Methuen, 1973.]

There he stood, a thin, scraggy boy with reddish hair that was long and matted. ■ (From *Days of Courage* by Niels Jensen. Jacket designed by Graham Humphreys.)

Multiplication is vexation,
Division is as bad;
The Rule of Three perplexes me,
And practice drives me mad.

—Anonymous

The piglets rushed forward in terror almost under the wheels of the approaching car. ■ (From *Tamworth Pig and the Litter* by Gene Kemp. Illustrated by Carol Dinan.)

KEMP, Gene 1926-

PERSONAL: Born December 27, 1926, in Wigginton, England; daughter of Albert (an electric meter reader) and Alice (Sutton) Rushton; married Norman Charles Pattison, August 20, 1949 (divorced, May, 1958); married Allan William George Kemp (a bus driver and union official), August 23, 1958; children: (first marriage) Judith Eve; (second marriage) Chantal Alice, Richard William. *Education:* University of Exeter, degree in English, with honors, 1945. *Politics:* Labour. *Religion:* Church of England. *Home:* 16 Waverley Ave., Exeter, Devonshire EX4 4NL, England. *Agent:* Gerald Pollinger, 18 Maddox St., Mayfair, London W1R 0EU, England. *Office:* Saint Sidwell's School, York Rd., Exeter, Devonshire, England.

GENE KEMP

CAREER: Teacher in private schools and in public secondary schools; Saint Sidwell's School, Exeter, England, teacher, 1963-77. Manager of Central School in Exeter; lecturer at Rolle College, 1974-75. Member of Council for the Advancement of State Education and of general management committee of Exeter Labour Party. *Member:* National Union of Teachers, National Association for the Teaching of English.

WRITINGS—Juveniles: *The Prime of Tamworth Pig*, Faber, 1972, Merrimack Book Service, 1979; *Tamworth Pig Saves the Trees*, Faber, 1973, Merrimack Book Service, 1978; *Tamworth Pig and the Litter*, Faber, 1975, Merrimack Book Service, 1978; *The Turbulent Term of Tyke Tiler*, Faber, 1977; *The Christmas of Tamworth Pig*, Faber, 1977; *Christmas With Tamworth Pig*, Faber, 1979; *Gowie Corby Plays Chicken*, Faber, 1979; *Ducks and Dragons* (a poetry anthology), Faber, 1980; *Dog Days and Cat Naps*, Faber, 1980; *The Clock Tower Ghost*, Faber, 1981.

Work anthologized in *Children's Literature in Education*, edited by Terry Jones and Geoff Fox. Contributor of poems to *Welsh Press*.

WORK IN PROGRESS: Research for a juvenile book on Saint Sidwell's School; a humorous book for adults; a book entitled *The Well*.

SIDELIGHTS: "*Tyke Tiler* is my most interesting book—I'd done a lot of research on language for it and used Peter and Iona Opie's *Language and Love of Schoolchildren.* . . .''

HOBBIES AND OTHER INTERESTS: Politics, reading folklore, myths, and adult literature ("I like Saul Bellow a lot."), amateur archaeology (visiting iron-age forts), gardening.

FOR MORE INFORMATION SEE: Times Literary Supplement, March 25, 1977.

KENNELL, Ruth E(pperson) 1893-1977

OBITUARY NOTICE—See sketch in *SATA* Volume 6: Born September 21, 1893, in Oklahoma City, Okla.; died March 5, 1977. Starting her career as a children's librarian in California, Kennell began a sojourn in Russia in 1922 which lasted more than five years and which influenced her life and writings. She went to Siberia as secretary and librarian for the American industrial colony at Kuzbas, a group giving technical aid to the post-revolutionary Soviet Union. While at Kuzbas, and later as a reference librarian at the International Library in Moscow, Kennell served as correspondent for *Nation*. The high point of her life in the Soviet Union came in 1927-28 when she acted as guide and secretary for Theodore Dreiser, with whom she maintained a twenty-year correspondence that inspired her to write *Theodore Dreiser and the Soviet Union 1927-1945: A Personal Chronicle*. Kennell's books for children also reflect her immersion in Russian culture. Her first, written upon her return to California, is the story of an orphan, *Vanya of the Streets*. Illustrated by Soviet artist Michael Perts, it was a critical success that one reviewer called "a sort of Russian Huck Finn." *For More Information See: Contemporary Authors, Permanent Series*, Volume 2, Gale, 1978.

KNOTTS, Howard (Clayton, Jr.) 1922-

PERSONAL: Born October 13, 1922, in Springfield, Ill., son of Howard Clayton (a lawyer) and Charlotte (Sterling) Knotts; married Ilse-Margaret Vogel (a writer and artist), June 1, 1959. *Education:* Knox College, student, 1940-43; Art Institute of Chicago, B.F.A. (honors), 1949. *Home and office address:* Duell Rd., Bangall, N.Y. 12506.

CAREER: Artist and writer. Paintings exhibited in major museums across the United States, and are in collections at Phillips Gallery and Joseph Hirshhorn Museum (both Washington, D.C.) and University Museum (Berkeley, Calif.). *Military service:* U.S. Army Air Forces, 1946-49. *Awards, honors: The Winter Cat* was named best juvenile book of the year by Friends of American Writers, 1972.

WRITINGS—Self-illustrated juveniles: *The Winter Cat*, Harper, 1972; *Follow the Brook*, Harper, 1975; *The Lost Christmas*, Harcourt, 1978; *Great-Grandfather, the Baby, and Me*, Atheneum, 1978; *The Summer Cat*, Harper, 1981.

(From *A Day in the Country* by Willis Barnstone. Illustrated by Howard Knotts.)

HOWARD KNOTTS

Illustrator: Willis Barnstone, *A Day in the Country,* Harper, 1971; May Sarton, *Punch's Secret,* Harper, 1974; Charlotte Zolotow, *When the Wind Stops,* Harper, 1975; Eve Bunting, *Winter's Coming,* Harcourt, 1977; Eve Bunting, *The Big Red Barn,* Harcourt, 1979; Eve Bunting, *Goose Dinner,* Harcourt, 1981.

SIDELIGHTS: "I am an artist (painter) who gradually became an author-illustrator of children's books because of my wife's activity in this field and because of an apparently natural enthusiasm and affinity for the genre."

KOMODA, Beverly 1939-

PERSONAL: Born November 26, 1939, in Seattle, Wash., daughter of Robert R. (a dentist) and Mary (Uno) Higashida; married Kiyoaki Komoda (an art director and free-lance illustrator), July, 1962; children: Paul, Daniel, Kurt. *Education:* Attended Chouinard Art Institute, 1957-61. *Religion:* Protestant. *Home:* 14 Maple Stream Rd., East Windsor, N.J.08520.

CAREER: Free-lance writer and illustrator, 1963—. *Member:* Authors Guild, Authors League of America.

WRITINGS—All children's books: *Simon's Soup* (self-illustrated; Junior Literary Guild selection), Parents' Magazine

Press, 1978; *The Lake Mess Monster* (self-illustrated) Parents' Magazine Press, 1980.

Illustrator—All children's books: Richard Jackson, *Douglas Saves the Day,* Macmillan, 1964; Carole Vetter, *The Wishing Night,* Macmillan, 1966; Carol G. Hogan, *Eighteen Cousins,* Parents' Magazine Press, 1968; Miriam Young, *Jelly Beans for Breakfast,* Parents' Magazine Press, 1968; Winifred E. Wise, *The Revolt of the Darumas,* Parent's Magazine Press, 1970; Mary Blount Christian, *The First Sign of Winter,* Parent's Magazine Press, 1973.

WORK IN PROGRESS: Picture books.

SIDELIGHTS: "I wish to depict truths via the humorous picture book story. In *Simon's Soup* the theme was the importance of perseverance to reach a goal. The story themes I use in *Simon's Soup* and in my works in progress are ones that I feel very strongly about in my own life. Portraying them humorously makes it fun.

"I have a large affection for the books that I read when young. My favorites became an integral part of me. I hope to give back in some small measure some of the enjoyment I experienced (and still do) as a 'bookworm,' through my work.

"Story ideas come while I am engaged in routine, dull occupations such as doing the laundry or weeding the garden.

BEVERLY KOMODA

The Lake Mess Monster appeared in my head one day in the shower—all that water may have been the inspiration.

"A humorous occurrence in daily life can be a spark to a story idea. One afternoon in Los Angeles, I was waiting for a bus by a busy intersection. A car approaching the red light lost a hub cap. The hub cap rolled across four lanes of heavy, fast-moving traffic without being touched, struck the opposite curb and rolled back through the same four lanes of traffic untouched, in time to be squashed flat by the car that lost it in the first place when the light turned green. I haven't written a story about this, but the zany quality of the event has led to other ideas.

"I particularly enjoy developing a story character—choosing his, her, or its name, deciding the physical appearance and all things related to the character, such as his dwelling, furniture, clothing, etc. I am often delighted to see a person nearly identical to the character I have in mind, walking down the street or next to me in a store.

"I work with a pen, sepia ink, and colored pencils on 2-ply smooth surface Bristol for the majority of my illustrations."

HOBBIES AND OTHER INTERESTS: "Interests include reading, films, the theater, making patchwork quilts, tennis, and hiking."

LAMBERT, Janet (Snyder)   1894-1973

PERSONAL: Born December 17, 1894, in Crawfordsville, Ind.; died March 16, 1973, in Brant Beach, Long Beach Island,

The horse leaned closer to meet her, and because Candy Kane's smile had a way of winning everything, from babies to mistreated and wary dogs and cats, he nuzzled against her shoulder.... ■ (From *One for the Money* by Janet Lambert.)

N.J.; daughter of Francis L. and Mabel Lee (Galey) Snyder; married Kent Craig Lambert (in the military) on January 1, 1918; children: Jeanne Ann. *Education:* Attended Ferry Hall, 1912; took drama lessons, was tutored in German and French in Indianapolis. *Politics:* Republican. *Religion:* Christian Scientist. *Home:* Brant Beach, Long Beach Island, N.J.

CAREER: Author of books for children, actress. Spent two-and-a-half years playing small parts on the stage in New York City and in Northampton, Mass., with a stock company. Lived on bases around the country as an army wife, and when stationed in New York City wrote her first book, *Star-Spangled Summer,* which was finished on a Thursday and bought by E. P. Dutton the following day.

WRITINGS—All for children; all published by Dutton: *Star-Spangled Summer* (illustrated by Sandra James), 1941; *Dreams of Glory,* 1942; *Candy Kane* (illustrated by Roberta Paflin), 1943; *Glory Be!,* 1943; *Whoa, Matilda!,* 1944; *Just Jenifer,* 1945; *One for the Money,* 1946; *Up Goes the Curtain,* 1946; *Friday's Child,* 1947; *Practically Perfect,* 1947; *Miss Tippy,* 1948; *Where the Heart Is,* 1948; *Little Miss Atlas,* 1949; *Treasure Trouble,* 1949; *Confusion—by Cupid,* 1950; *The Reluctant Heart,* 1950; *Miss America,* 1951; *Star Dream,* 1951; *Don't Cry, Little Girl,* 1952; *Summer for Seven,* 1952; *Rainbow after Rain,* 1953; *Welcome Home, Mrs. Jordan,* 1953; *Cinda,* 1954; *A Dream for Susan,* 1954; *High Hurdles,* 1955; *Love Traps*

JANET LAMBERT

Gently, 1955; *Fly Away, Cinda,* 1956; *A Song in Their Hearts,* 1956; *Myself and I,* 1957; *The Precious Days,* 1957; *Big Deal,* 1958; *We're Going Steady,* 1958; *Boy Wanted,* 1959; *For Each Other,* 1959; *Spring Fever,* 1960; *The Stars Hang High,* 1960; *Forever and Ever,* 1961; *Wedding Bells,* 1961; *Introducing Parri,* 1962; *Summer Madness,* 1962; *Extra Special,* 1963; *Five's a Crowd,* 1963; *On Her Own,* 1964; *That's My Girl,* 1964; *A Bright Tomorrow,* 1965; *Triple Trouble,* 1965; *First of All,* 1966; *Stagestruck Parri,* 1966; *Love to Spare,* 1967; *Sweet as Sugar,* 1967; *Hi, Neighbor,* 1968; *My Davy,* 1968; *Here's Marny,* 1969; *The Odd Ones,* 1969.

SIDELIGHTS: "I grew up in Crawfordsville, which was then known as the Athens of Indiana, and which is still proud of the number of authors it produces. General Lew Wallace was a friend of my father's and I spent many hours in his study and sitting with him under the beech tree, where he wrote *Ben Hur.*

"I was undecided whether to be an actress or a poet. and as I was sent once a week to Indianapolis to study 'elocution,' decided that I would be an actress and write my own plays. I chose Ferry Hall as a school because I thought I could go in to Chicago and could meet, or at least see the famous actresses, but I found myself in what I considered a penal institution. My writing, which had caused such a flurry in high school, was pronounced impossible, and my dramatic teacher said I had no ability. I tossed my clothes into a trunk and returned to the town dramatic club and the help of professors who taught in our own men's college, Wabash.

"My dream was to play with Walker Whiteside, and in 1915 when he was in Indianapolis I waylaid him in his hotel, told him his ingenue was poor and offered myself for the part. Strangely enough I got it. My mother was overcome but helpless, and as my father had died when I was twelve, I joined the company with an older sister for chaperon. Mr. Whiteside was both amazed and amused, and she did travel with us. The following winter I was offered a part in New York, and when the play closed I persuaded the chaperon my mother had burdened me with (a dean of women with a nervous breakdown) to put me in the Martha Washington Hotel. I wrote impossible stories all night, ranted Shakespeare all day until Jesse Bonstall sent me to Northampton, Mass., and the Northampton Players. The following winter, 1917, when I had at last outgrown the chaperons and had an apartment in New York with two girls, Colonel Lambert, who was then a captain and the boy from home, arrived in uniform and we were married.

"We chose New Year's day, 1918, as a perfect beginning for a new year—and three months later he was sent to France and I went home to wait the remaining eight months for our daughter. Six years of illness followed and twenty-three of living on army posts and writing endless stories for my little girl. There was always a serial chapter each night and while we lived in Poland (1930-32) I had to provide most of her reading matter."

FOR MORE INFORMATION SEE: Current Biography Yearbook, 1954, H. W. Wilson, 1954; Doris de Montreville and Donna Hill, editors, *Third Book of Junior Authors,* H. W. Wilson, 1972; (obituary) *Publishers Weekly,* April 9, 1973.

LANGLEY, Noel 1911-1980

OBITUARY NOTICE: Born December 25, 1911, in Durban, South Africa; died November 4, 1980, in Desert Hot Springs, Calif. Scriptwriter, playwright, director, and author. Langley wrote several screenplays including "The Wizard of Oz," "Tom Brown's Schooldays," "A Christmas Carol," and "Ivanhoe." Langley penned successful stage plays such as "Edward My Son," "Little Lambs Eat Ivy," and "Cage Me a Peacock." Among his books are *Tale of the Land of Green Ginger, Hocus Pocus, Edgar Cayce on Reincarnation,* and *A Dream of Dragonflies. For More Information See: Twentieth Century Writing: A Reader's Guide to Contemporary Literature,* Transatlantic, 1971; *The Filmgoer's Companion,* 4th edition, Hill & Wang, 1974; *Who's Who,* 126th edition, St. Martin's. 1974; *Contemporary Authors,* Volumes 13-61, revised, Gale, 1975; *Notable Names in the American Theatre,* James T. White, 1976; *International Motion Picture Almanac 1978,* Quigley, 1978. *Obituaries: London Times,* November 15, 1980; *Contemporary Authors,* Volume 102, Gale, 1981.

LARRECQ, John M(aurice) 1926-1980

OBITUARY NOTICE: Born April 10, 1926, in Santa Rosa, Calif., died October 4, 1980. Illustrator and graphic designer. Larrecq was staff illustrator for Kaiser Industries before he turned to free-lance work. He operated his own San Francisco studio and contributed award-winning illustrations and designs to national publications and exhibits. Various children's books which Larrecq illustrated appeared in the American Institute of Graphic Arts Children's Book Show, on the Horn Book Honor List, and as American Library Association Notable Books. *For More Information See: Illustrators of Books for Young People,* 2nd edition, Scarecrow, 1975; *Illustrators of Children's Books, 1967-1976,* Horn Book, 1978. *Obituaries: School Library Journal,* March, 1981; *Horn Book,* April, 1981.

LUTHER, Frank 1905-1980

OBITUARY NOTICE: Born Francis Luther Crow, August 4, 1905, near Lakin, Kansas; died November 16, 1980, in New York, N.Y. Singer, composer, and writer. Frank Luther recorded over 3000 tapes and records, and his recordings of classic nursery rhymes and fairy tales made his voice a familiar one to children. He was well known for his book *Americans and Their Songs,* which contains 125 songs representative of American musical style. His songwriting credits include "Barnacle Bill the Sailor" and "Christmas is a Comin'." He also composed a folk opera production of *Tom Sawyer,* which appeared on television in 1956. *For More Information See: American Authors and Books, 1640 to the Present Day,* 3rd edition, revised, Crown, 1972; *The Complete Encyclopedia of Popular Music and Jazz, 1900-1950,* Arlington House, 1974; *Who's Who in America,* 40th edition, Marquis, 1978. *Obituaries: New York Times,* November 20, 1980; *Publishers Weekly,* December 22-29, 1980; *Contemporary Authors,* Volume 102, Gale, 1981.

Life being very short, and the quiet hours of it few, we ought to waste none of them in reading valueless books.

—John Ruskin

Thanks to my friends for their care in my breeding,
Who taught me betimes to love working and reading.

—Isaac Watts

SHELAGH MACDONALD

MACDONALD, Shelagh 1937-

PERSONAL: Born December 20, 1937, in Hampshire, England; daughter of Frank and Marjory (Beale) Brookesmith; married Gilbert Macdonald (a chemist), June 21, 1968. *Education:* Attended grammar school in Blandford, England. *Home:* 99 Esmond Rd., Bedford Park, Chiswick, London W.4, England. *Agent:* Laura Cecil, 17 Alwyn Villas, Canonbury, London N.1, England. *Office:* Friedlander & Partners, Britannia Row, London N.1, England.

CAREER: Wellcome Foundation Ltd., London, England, medical copywriter, 1957-61; CPV International (advertising agency), London, copywriter, 1961-65; Young & Rubicam Ltd., London, senior copywriter, 1965-66; Papert, Koenig, Lois, London, creative group head, 1966-67; MacLaren Dunkley Friedlander, London, chief copywriter and associate director, 1967-69; Friedlander & Partners, London, creative director, 1976—. *Awards, honors:* Whitbread Literary Award from Whitbread & Company, 1977, for *No End to Yesterday.*

WRITINGS—Juveniles: A Circle of Stones, Deutsch, 1973; *Five From Me, Five From You,* Deutsch, 1974; *No End to Yesterday,* Deutsch, 1977.

Work represented in anthologies, including "The Island," in *Romance Stories,* edited by Elizabeth Bland, Octopus Books, 1979.

WORK IN PROGRESS: "Working on an adult novel—the title, as always, is unknown until the book is complete. The subject is a family—the relationships between children and parents,

how these are influenced by the parents' own relationships, and how the influences can last a lifetime."

SIDELIGHTS: "My first two novels are based in Greece—a country which I love and whose language I speak. Visits there undoubtedly inspired the idea behind those stories, which have mythological undertones while being set in modern Greece. My aim was not specifically to write for children, the ideas simply worked out that way. I try to write on different 'levels' so that adults might enjoy my books, too.

"The third book, *No End to Yesterday,* is based on my own mother's childhood, and is a story I wanted to write since I was ten years old. Finally I found the courage and stamina! That it was this book that won a major prize was to me a particular pleasure—it's a book in which I am, obviously, very involved emotionally. It is an 'odd' book in many respects, insofar as it's hard to categorize. It was published as a young adult's book, and as such it won a children's prize; strictly, it is not everyone's idea of a 'children's book,' although it is certainly about a child.

"Aside from saying 'I'll write your story someday' to my mother, and although I always enjoyed writing, I did not see myself growing up to *be* a writer. If anything, I thought I would be an artist."

HOBBIES AND OTHER INTERESTS: Reading, ornithology, theater, cinema, art, people, talk, good food and wine, travel, and drawing.

FOR MORE INFORMATION SEE: Junior Bookshelf, October, 1977.

(From *No End to Yesterday* by Shelagh Macdonald. Jacket illustrated by Meg Rutherford.)

MacMANUS, Seumas 1869-1960
(James MacManus, Mac)

PERSONAL: Given name listed in some sources as James; born in 1869, in Mountcharles, County Donegal, Ireland; died October 23, 1960, in New York, N.Y.; buried at Frosses, County Donegal, Ireland; married Anna Johnston (a poet under the pseudonym Ethna Carbery), 1901 (died, 1902); married Catalina Violante Paez, 1911; children: Mariquita, Patricia (second marriage). *Education:* Teachers' Training School, Enniskillen, Fermanagh, Ireland. *Residence:* New York, N.Y. and County Donegal, Ireland.

CAREER: Schoolmaster in Irish grammar schools; full-time writer and lecturer, circa 1895-1960; editor of the Irish weekly, *Chimney Corners*. *Awards, honors:* LL.D., Notre Dame University, 1917.

WRITINGS: The Humours of Donegal, Unwin, 1898; *A Lad of the O'Friels,* McClure, Phillips, 1903; *The Red Poocher,* Funk & Wagnalls, 1903; *Ballads of a Country-boy,* Gill, 1905; *Doctor Kilgannon,* Gill, 1907; *Yourself and the Neighbours* (illustrated by Thomas Fogarty), Devan-Adair, 1914; *Ireland's Case,* Irish Publishing, 1917; *Lo, and Behold, Ye!* (illustrated by Mabel Hatt), F. Stokes, 1919; *Top o' the Mornin',* F. Stokes, 1920; (with others) *The Story of the Irish Race,* Irish Publishing, 1921, revised edition, Devan-Adair, 1945; *The Donegal Wonder Book,* F. Stokes, 1926; *Bold Blades of Donegal,* F. Stokes, 1935; *The Rocky Road to Dublin,* Macmillan, 1938; *Heavy Hangs the Golden Grain,* Macmillan, 1950; *The Little Mistress of the Eskar Mor,* Gill, 1960.

(From "Conaleen and Donaleen," in *The Well o' the World's End,* retold by Seumas MacManus. Illustrated by Richard Bennett.)

Story collections: *The Bend of the Road,* Downey, 1898; *In Chimney Corners* (illustrated by Pamelia Colman Smith), Doubleday & McClure, 1899, reprinted, 1935; *Through the Turf Smoke: The Love, Lore, and Laughter of Old Ireland,* Doubleday & McClure, 1899, reprinted, Books for Libraries, 1969; *The Bewitched Fiddle and Other Irish Tales,* Doubleday & McClure, 1900; *Donegal Fairy Stories,* McClure, Phillips, 1900, reprinted (with illustrations by Frank Verbeck), Dover, 1968; *O, Do You Remember?,* Duffy, 1926; *Dark Patrick,* Macmillan, 1939, reprinted, Books for Libraries, 1971; *The Well o' the World's End* (illustrated by Richard Bennett), Macmillan, 1939; *Tales From Ireland* (illustrated by W. H. Conn), Evans, 1949; *The Bold Heroes of Hungry Hill and Other Irish Folk Tales* (illustrated by Jay Chollick), Pelegrini & Cudahy, 1951; *Hibernian Nights* (ALA Notable Book; introduction by Padraic Colum; illustrated by Paul Kennedy), Macmillan, 1963.

Other: (Editor) Anna MacManus, *The Four Winds of Eirinn,* Gill, 1902, reprinted, 1927; (author of introduction) Anna MacManus, *The Passionate Hearts,* Isbister, 1903; (editor) Mary Eva Kelly, *Poems,* Gill, 1909; (compiler with Alice Milligan), *We Sang for Ireland: Poems of Ethna Carbery,* Devin-Adair, 1950; "The Townland of Tamney" (one-act play, published together with "The Dream Physician" by Edward Martyn), De Paul University, 1972.

(From "The King of Araby's Daughter," in *The Bold Heroes of Hungry Hill* by Seumas MacManus. Illustrated by Jay Chollick.)

Also author of plays: "Bong Tong Come to Balriddery," "The Lad from Largymore," "The Leadin' Road to Donegal," "Nabby Harren's Matching," "Orange and Green," "The Resurrection of Dinny O'Dowd," "Rory Wins."

Author of prose and verse under name Mac. Contributor to magazines, including *Harper's, Century, Lippincott's,* and *McClure's.*

SIDELIGHTS: "I first opened my eyes in Donegal, Ireland's Northwest cornerstone. It is the wildest, most remote, most rugged and mountainous, the most barren and the most beautiful, as well as the most Irish territory in Ireland.

"I am of the mountain people. As a buachaill of a boy I herded on the hills, spaded on the farm, dallied to the mountain school where I got the daub of schooling that is mine. At night I moved from cottage to cottage, squatted in the groups that always surround the big, blazing turf-fires, hearkening to the women telling their fairy stories and the old men reciting ancient folk tales, singing the old songs, or chanting some thousand-year-old poem.

"Ere I crept out of childhood I was myself a shanachie—carried in mind and could tell a sheaf of the old tales, as I had learned them by a hundred firesides. I told the tales to the lads who companied me to the herding, the lads who with me scudded three miles over the hills to Mass on Sunday, to the lads who loitered with me to the little school. . . .

"During my boyhood, I devoured every book that was to be found within a six-mile radius, altogether as many as thirteen or fourteen or fifteen.

"At the age of sixteen I began verse-making—made songs while I herded or plied the spade on my father's hillside—chiefly, songs that dealt with Ireland's struggle for freedom, and with the heroes who had fought and died for love of Shiels Ni Gara. Within a year I was publishing prose and verse in the *Tir-Conaill Vindicator,* the little weekly paper of our country, published in Belashanny. I filled the columns of this paper every week—songs, sketches, stories, news-reports—written in school copybooks, on my knee, at the fireside after my day's work was finished. At the end of three years' contributing I got my first pay from good John MacAidan—a check for ten shillings, almost two and a half dollars. And I was indeed a proud man as well as a rich one. Then he printed for me my first book of poems, with the Irish title *Shuilers,* meaning Vagrants. Twelve hundred copies of it were bought at a shilling each—making me a millionaire.

"But to wealth I had now become no stranger, for I had been appointed master of our mountain school, teaching sixty to seventy boys in a room that was nearly thirty feet long by fifteen feet wide—for a great salary of three pounds, or fourteen dollars, a month, as well as a school penny which every scholar brought me each Monday morning.

"Now also *The Shamrock,* a penny weekly story paper in Dublin, ordered from me a series of nine stories at two and a half dollars each—which I did in nine days in school copybooks, on my knee, at my father's kitchen fireside at night.

"Hearing that American story papers would pay more than two and a half dollars a story, I wrote a bagful of them and, closing my school, with the bursting bag sailed for America in the steerage of a big liner. Arrived in New York I asked the names of magazines that would pay well for stories, and was told that *Harper's* and *The Century* were the wealthiest. I brought to *Harper's* seven of the copybooks, and kind old Mr. Alden, the editor, deeply interested in the mountain boy dressed in homespun, read the stories himself, and kept six of them. And to my dumbfounding, gave me one hundred dollars and upward for each of them.

"I went to *The Century* with ten stories, and they bought eight. With other stories, then, I tried the other seven or eight magazines that America knew at that time—and every one of them bought stories.

"I arrived in America in September, and sailed back to Donegal the following May, with a fortune—wherewith I bought a fairy hill of which I had always been enamored.

"I returned to America the next Fall, with a new bag of stories, and carried home in the following Spring three times as big a fortune as that of twelve months before. My Donegal neighbors, knowing that anyone who wished could shovel up bags full of such stories among our hills could hardly credit the gullibility of the American people.

"American publishers began putting out my books, not only folk-tale books, like *Donegal Fairy Stories . . . In Chimney-Corners . . . The Donegal Wonder-Book . . .* and *The Well o' the World's End . . .* but also novels like *A Lud of the O'Friels . . .* and original stories of Irish life, as well as Irish history, *The Story of the Irish Race. . . .*

"And I, who had never seen a college before I came to America, found a fruitful field lecturing and telling folk-tales to the big American universities, as well as to the big Clubs. This I have been doing for many, many winters. But for my summers I always go back to my own Donegal hills and my own Donegal people and my own Donegal fairies.

"Under the ocean, off the coast of Donegal, lies a fairy paradise, Tir na'n Og, the Land of Perpetual Youth, which on beautiful summer eves, is often seen by our fishermen rising over the waters, afar off. It is a special province of heaven set apart by the good Lord for His favorites, the Irish, whose bliss He desires and safeguards from the intrusion of Americans and other common peoples of earth—and there I hope to go when I die.

"That is, *if* I die." [Walter Romig, editor, *The Book of Catholic Authors,* Volume 5, Walter Romig & Co., 1942-(?).]

FOR MORE INFORMATION SEE: Stanley Kunitz and Howard Haycraft, editors, *Junior Book of Authors,* H. W. Wilson, 1934; Walter Romig, editor, *The Book of Catholic Authors,* Volume 5, Walter Romig & Co., 1942-(?); *New York Herald Tribune Review,* October 7, 1951. *Obituaries: Publishers Weekly,* November 7, 1960; *Horn Book,* December, 1962, February, 1963.

Matilda told such dreadful lies,
It made one gasp and stretch one's eyes;
Her aunt, who, from her earliest youth,
Had kept a strict regard for truth,
Attempted to believe Matilda:
The effort very nearly killed her.

—Hilaire Belloc

MacPEEK, Walter G. 1902-1973
(Hugo Jumpp)

OBITUARY NOTICE—See sketch in *SATA* Volume 4: Born March 14, 1902, in Stockton, Ill,; died January 31, 1973, in Seminole, Fla. Author and editor. MacPeek devoted forty-three years to the Boy Scouts, serving as professional troup leader, associate editor of *Scouting* magazine, and assistant to the director of editorial services of the Boy Scouts of America National Council. During this period he wrote five books among others, illustrating practical applications of Scouting ideals: *Celebrating Scout Week, The Scout Law in Action, The Scout Oath in Action, Scout Leaders in Action,* and *Resourceful Scouts in Action.* After his retirement in 1967, he became a consultant to the American Humanities Foundation, a columnist for *Boy's Life,* a contributing editor to *Quote,* and staff writer for the *New Brunswick News.* MacPeek contributed articles to various periodicals under the pseudonym Hugo Jumpp. *For More Information See: Who Was Who Among North American Authors, 1921-1939,* Gale, 1976; *Contemporary Authors, Permanent Series,* Volume 2, Gale, 1978. *Obituaries: Publishers Weekly,* February 26, 1973; *Contemporary Authors,* Volumes 41-44, revised, Gale, 1974.

MAITLAND, Antony (Jasper) 1935-

PERSONAL: Born June 17, 1935, in Andover, Somerset, England; son of Percy Eric (a career officer in the air force) and Alison Mary (Kettlewell) Maitland. *Education:* West of England College of Art, Bristol, National Diploma in Design, 1957. *Home:* 52b Warrington Crescent, London W9, England.

CAREER: Illustrator and designer. *Military service:* British Army, 1956-58. *Awards, honors:* Leverhulme research award, 1958-59; Kate Greenaway Award, British Library Association, 1961, for *Mrs. Cockle's Cat,* and commendation, 1973, for *The Ghost Downstairs;* Children's Spring Book Festival Award, Book World, 1963.

WRITINGS—All self-illustrated; all for young people: *The Secret of the Shed,* Constable, 1962, Duell, 1963; *Ben Goes to the City,* Longmans, Green, 1964, Delacorte, 1967; *James and the Roman Silver,* Constable, 1965; (reteller) *Idle Jack,* Farrar, Straus, 1977, reissued, 1979.

Illustrator: Philippa Pearce, *Mrs. Cockle's Cat,* Constable, 1961, Lippincott, 1962; P. Pearce, *A Dog So Small,* Constable, 1962, Lippincott, 1963; Emma Smith, *Out of Hand,* Macmillan (London), 1963; Anne Molloy, *Proper Place for Chip,* Hastings, 1963; Ruth Ainsworth, *The Ten Tales of Shellover,* Deutsch, 1963, Roy, 1968; Leon Garfield, *Jack Holborn,* Longmans, Green, 1964, Pantheon, 1965; Joan Clarke, *Happy Planet,* Lothrop, 1965; Elsie Locke, *Runaway Settlers,* Dutton, 1966, Penguin, 1971; L. Garfield, *Devil-in-the-Fog,* Pantheon, 1966; Ester Wier, *The Loner,* Constable, 1966; Richard Gavin Robinson, *Captain Sintar,* Deutsch, 1967, Dutton, 1969; Hanna Stephan, *The Long Way Home* (translated by Daphne Machin Goodall), Heinemann, 1967, also published as *The Quest,* Little, Brown, 1968; L. Garfield, *Smith,* Pantheon, 1967; L. Garfield, *Black Jack,* Longman Young Books, 1968, Pantheon, 1969; Ruth Ainsworth, *More Tales of Shellover,* Roy, 1968; Verne Davis, *Orphan of the Tundra,* Weybright, 1968; Barbara Willard, *To London! To London!,* Weybright, 1968; L. Garfield, *The Drummer Boy,* Pantheon, 1969; L.

Long ago there lived an old woman and her son, Jack. Now Jack was as stupid as he was large and as large as he was lazy . . . . ■ (From *Idle Jack,* retold and illustrated by Antony Maitland.)

. . . A tremendous gust of wind sent the starlings tumbling off the roofs—Mrs. Verity's dress ballooned around her.

"Gracious! What a gale! I'll have to go inside."

■ (From *The Ghost of Thomas Kempe* by Penelope Lively. Illustrated by Antony Maitland.)

Garfield, *Mr. Corbett's Ghost and Other Stories,* Longman Young Books, 1969, Penguin, 1972.

Peter Olney, *All Around You Assignment Cards,* Blond Educational, 1970; Penelope Lively, *Astercote,* Heinemann, 1970; Susan Dickinson, compiler, *The Restless Ghost, and Other Encounters and Experiences,* Collins, 1970, also published as *The Usurping Ghost, and Other Encounters and Experiences,* Dutton, 1971; R. Ainsworth, *The Phantom Cyclist and Other Stories,* Deutsch, 1971, Follett, 1974; Meta Mayne Reid, *Beyond the Wide World's End,* Lutterworth, 1972; L. Garfield, *Child o' War,* Holt, 1972; L. Garfield, *The Ghost Downstairs,* Pantheon, 1972; Elizabeth Goudge, *Henrietta's House,* Penguin, 1972; Margery Bianco, *Poor Cecco,* Deutsch, 1973; Aidan Chambers, *Aidan Chambers' Book of Ghosts and Other Hauntings,* Longman Young Books, 1973; P. Lively, *The Ghost of Thomas Kempe* (Junior Literary Guild selection), Dutton, 1973.

R. Ainsworth, *The Bear Who Liked Hugging People, and Other Stories,* Heinemann, 1976, C. Russak, 1978; Charles Causley, *Dick Whittington: A Story from England,* Puffin Books, 1976, Penguin, 1979; L. Garfield, *The Lamplighter's Funeral,* Heinemann, 1976; L. Garfield, *Mirror, Mirror,* Heinemann, 1976; Richard Arthur Warren Hughes, *The Wonder-Dog* (short stories), Greenwillow Books, 1977; Andrew Lang, compiler, *Green Fairy Book* (short stories; edited by Brian Alderson), Viking, 1978; *Forbidden Paths of Thual,* Kestrel, 1979.

SIDELIGHTS: "As one of six brothers I found that privacy was only possible by withdrawing into a world of imagination; it may be that I draw for children who feel the same way. I certainly draw on the memory of my own childhood when selecting what part of a story to illustrate and I frequently use a child's eye level when composing a drawing." [Lee Kingman and others, compilers, *Illustrators of Children's Books: 1957-1966,* Horn Book, 1968.[1]]

As an art student, Maitland was without any real ambition until a Leverhulme research award made a year of travel and study in Europe possible, "and I began to see and draw with real enthusiasm. For several years I made a living from illustrating and designing jackets only. *Mrs. Cockle's Cat* was almost my first illustrating work."[1] It won for him the 1961 Kate Greenaway Award.

Besides illustrating he now paints, designs, creates murals, and does graphic work for exhibitions and feels that "none of these things is more or less important than the other. This variety ensures that each job is approached as a fresh and individual problem. The changes of scale are exciting too—from designing a name plate for books to remodeling the facade of a building (Madame Tussaud's Wax Works). This is for me the only way to stay alive artistically."[1]

Maitland works either in black-and-white or full color. Both are used in *James and the Roman Silver* which he also wrote, taking the setting, various details and even the plot from childhood memories of Somerset. His illustrations are generally a combination of line and wash and he takes a special interest in the lettering for a jacket or title page since it can convey a feeling of period and mood.

Maitland divides his time between London and a cottage near the North Sea in the east of England. In addition to writing and illustrating children's books, he designs book jackets, furniture, and interiors, and creates wall murals. Maitland de-

signed the sets for an unreleased film based on the Grimms' fairy tale, *The Goose Girl.*

FOR MORE INFORMATION SEE: Bettina Hurlimann, *Picture-Book World,* Oxford University Press, 1968; Lee Kingman and others, compilers, *Illustrators of Children's Books: 1957-1966,* Horn Book, 1968; *Horn Book,* June 1973; Lee Kingman and others, compilers, *Illustrators of Children's Books: 1967-1976,* Horn Book, 1978.

McGREGOR, Iona   1929-

PERSONAL: Born February 7, 1929, in Aldership, Hampshire, England. *Education:* University of Bristol, B.A. (with honors), 1950. *Home:* 10 Belgrave Place, Edinburg EH4 34N, Scotland.

CAREER: Edinburgh University Press, Edinburgh, Scotland, sub-editor, 1951-57; classics teacher in English public schools, 1958-69; St. George's School for Girls, Edinburgh, Latin teacher, 1969—.

WRITINGS—Juvenile fiction; all published by Merrimack, except as noted: *An Edinburgh Reel,* 1968; *The Popinjay,* Faber, 1969; *The Burning Hill,* 1970; *The Tree of Liberty,* 1972; *The Snake and the Olive,* 1974; *Edinburgh and the Eastern Lowlands,* Faber, 1979.

Also author of radio play "A Kind of Glory," 1971.

WORK IN PROGRESS: "A juvenile novel set in early nineteenth century Edinburgh, centered 'round the notorious murderers, Burke and Hare."

SIDELIGHTS: McGregor's books for young people are characterized by vivid description and a stirring sense of action. Her characters interact with real figures and history, as she employs "the surface excitement of past events as a setting for perennial themes in human behaviour." *The Popinjay* and *The Edinburgh Reel,* like many of McGregor's stories, are set in her native Scotland. "Scotland is still full of ancient buildings that spur the imagination," she said.

In response to the characterization of herself as a historical novelist, McGregor further explained: "I would describe myself as a 'period' rather than a 'historical' novelist, since the setting is a focusing lens for the quirks and clashes of my characters, not an excuse for dramatizing the great public events in which they sometimes find themselves involved." Contending that she is more concerned with theme than with plot, McGregor continued: "The obvious difference between 'then' and 'now,' the dramatic irony of involving characters in events whose outcome is already known, are a great help to me in pointing up these themes. I also find that my social range is extended by going back in time . . . for whatever reasons, the distancing effect of a remoter period helps me pick out the pattern of circumstance and personality I wish to use."

Perhaps another reason McGregor sets her stories in the past is the fact that she feels more comfortable dealing with the objects and events of history. "Sixteenth century gunnery and medicine are within my scope; I doubt if I could say the same about their modern equivalents," she explained. "The minute detail found in research generates character and incident for me. Anyway, what is a historical novel? All novels are historical fiction, since they all modify and interpret past experience," McGregor concluded.

McNEELY, Jeannette 1918-
(Maron Mackie)

PERSONAL: Born December 12, 1918, in San Francisco, Calif.; daughter of Loren Goodell (a railway postal clerk) and Marjorie (Wood) Mackie; married William H. McNeely (a research organic chemist), August 9, 1940 (divorced, 1967); children: Craig Warren, Kathleen Bernice McNeely Walker, Loretta Jean, Linda Darlene. *Education:* University of California, Berkeley, A.B., 1940, San Diego State University, elementary teaching credential, 1961, U.S. International University, M.A., 1976. *Religion:* Protestant. *Home:* 5343 West Falls View Dr., San Diego, Calif. 92115.

CAREER: San Diego Unified School District, San Diego, Calif., teacher of the second grade, 1960—. *Member:* National Educational Association, Society of Children's Book Writers, California Teachers Association, San Diego Teachers Association, San Diego Professional Writers Workship, Pi Delta Phi.

WRITINGS: Where's Izzy? (juvenile picture book), Follett, 1972; (with Aline Cunningham) *Led by a Star: Matthew 2: 1-12 for Children,* Concordia, 1977; *Everybody Likes Me—But Me,* Oddo, in press. Contributor of juvenile fiction and adult non-fiction to *Christian Standard, Our Little Friend, One/Two, Young World, Pit,* and to other religious publications.

**Then the Wise Men left.
They went to their tents,
but they did not sleep well.**

■ (From *Led by a Star: The Wise Men for Beginning Readers* by Jeannette McNeely. Illustrated by Aline Cunningham.)

WORK IN PROGRESS—For young people: Under name Maron Mackie, *A Gift for Vivologo; Worm in a Cathedral; All for a Silly Thing Called Moop; Foggy Ideas.*

SIDELIGHTS: "Being shy as a child, I spent much time with books. Often I would be brought back to my surroundings with a start if someone spoke to me. I had been carried into the pages of the story as vividly as if I were one of the characters.

"The local newspaper printed a section of stories by children periodically. These stories and poems were given ratings called 'units,' which could be turned in for prizes when enough were accumulated. The relatively high ratings that my published stories received encouraged me to write for fun.

"However, it was not until late in life that I began to write seriously. My children had started school and I had begun to teach in the public schools. The incentive that pushed me then was a need I felt in the classroom. At that time there were few interesting stories that contained words in the limited reading vocabulary of beginning readers.

"I began to write for particular children in my own second grade classroom. They had been restless as they struggled with new skills while faced with an unappealing story. Their immediate interest upon being offered my stories spurred me later to write for publication.

"A few book ideas have been set aside waiting for vacation periods when I can work in bigger chunks of time. In the meanwhile I am writing short stories for periodicals."

JEANNETTE McNEELY

MEANS, Florence Crannell　1891-1980

OBITUARY NOTICE—See sketch in *SATA* Volume I: Born May 15, 1891, in Baldwinsville, N.Y.; died November 19, 1980, in Boulder, Colo. Author of children's books and adult biographies. The author of over forty books, Means was one of the earliest writers of children's literature to focus on minority groups. Concentrating her efforts on young readers because she felt they could be more easily reached by her message of racial equality, she lived among and extensively researched the American Indian, Black, Hispanic, and Oriental people she wrote about. Her Newbery honor book. *The Moved-Outers*, focused on the struggles of American-born Japanese during World War II. Other of her popular books included *Shuttered Windows*, 1938, and *Reach for a Star*, 1957, both still in print. *For More Information See: A Book of Children's Literature*, 3rd edition, Holt, 1966; *Contemporary Authors*, Volumes 1-4, revised, Gale, 1967; *Twentieth Century Children's Writers*, St. Martin's, 1978; *Who's Who in America*, 40th edition, Marquis, 1978. *Obituaries: Publishers Weekly*, February 27, 1981; *Horn Book*, April, 1981.

MEYER, Jerome Sydney　1895-1975
(S. M. Jennings)

OBITUARY NOTICE—See sketch in *SATA* Volume 2: Born January 14, 1895, in New York, N.Y.; died February 26, 1975, in New York, N.Y. Meyer worked in advertising before becoming an editor for Doubleday, Doran Company and later director of the mail order department of Crown Publishers. In 1927 he wrote *Advice and Care of Babies by a Bachelor Who Can't Bear Them*, the first of some sixty books he produced on a wide variety of subjects, including science, geography, mathematics, and, most notably, games and puzzles. Meyer, known as the "game book man," was the originator of the first radio-broadcast quiz-game, which he developed in connection with a client's advertising campaign. *For More Information See: Contemporary Authors*, Volumes 1-4, revised, Gale, 1967; *Author's and Writer's Who's Who*, sixth edition, Burke's Peerage, 1971; *Who's Who in World Jewry*, Pitman, 1972. *Obituaries: New York Times*, February 28, 1975; *AB Bookman's Weekly*, March 17, 1975; *Contemporary Authors*, Volumes 57-60, Gale, 1976.

MILGROM, Harry　1912-

PERSONAL: Born February 29, 1912, in New York, N.Y.; son of Samuel and Mary (Spector) Milgrom; married (second marriage) Betty Geltman Addison (an author and artist), June 26, 1969; children: (first marriage) Jeffrey, Paul. *Education:* The City College of New York, B.S., 1932; Columbia University, M.A., 1933.

CAREER: The City College of New York, New York, N.Y., physics instructor, 1947-49; Board of Education, New York, N.Y., physics, general science, radio teacher, 1935-53, assistant director of science for school system, 1953-69, director of science, 1969-70. Director, summer science institutes at Rutgers, The State University, 1957, Rochester University, 1958, New Mexico Highlands University, 1961, 1962; director, elementary science project, Manufacturing Chemists Association, 1959-60; director, science honors program for children, Columbia University School of Engineering, 1962—;

HARRY MILGROM

originator, Student Exposition on Energy Resources (SEER program), 1975; vice president for school programs, National Energy Foundation, 1977; science consultant to New York State Education Department and to Educational Testing Service. *Member:* National Science Supervisors Association, Physics Club of New York (treasurer, 1955-56), Elementary School Science Association (advisory board, 1960—), American Association for the Advancement of Science (fellow), National Science Teachers Association, National Association for Research in Science Teaching, New York Academy of Sciences, Phi Beta Kappa. *Awards, honors:* Named "Science Educator of the Year," by the Fordham University Chapter of Kappa Delta Pi, 1974; Recognition award from the Council for Elementary Science International, 1977.

WRITINGS: Golden Adventure Book of Weather, Golden Press, 1959; *Matter, Energy and Change*, Holt, 1960; *Explorations in Science*, Dutton, 1961; (with Hy Ruchlis) *The Science Book-Lab of Magnets*, Science Materials Center, 1961; (with H. Ruchlis) *The Science Book-Lab of Air Experiments*, Science Materials Center, 1961; (with H. Ruchlis) *The Science Book-Lab of Mathematical Shapes*, Science Materials Center, 1962; *Further Explorations in Science*, Dutton, 1963; *Adventures with a String*, Dutton, 1965; *Adventures with a Ball*, Dutton, 1965; *Experiments with Gravity*, Dutton, 1966; *Adventures with a Plastic Bag*, Dutton, 1967; *Adventures with a Straw* (illustrated by Leonard Kessler), Dutton, 1967; *Adventures with a Paper Cup*, Dutton, 1968; *Adventures with a Party Plate*, Dutton, 1968; *Understanding Weather* (illustrated by

(From *Egg-Ventures* by Harry Milgrom. Illustrated by Giulio Maestro.)

Lloyd Birmingham), Macmillan, 1970; *ABC Science Experiments* (illustrated by Donald Crews), Macmillan, 1970; *Adventures With a Cardboard Tube* (Junior Literary Guild selection; illustrated by Tom Funk), Dutton, 1972; *ABC of Ecology* (illustrated by D. Crews), Macmillan, 1972; *The Wonder of Change*, Ginn, 1972; *Egg-Ventures: First Science Experiments* (Junior Literary Guild selection; illustrated by Giulio Maestro), Dutton, 1974; *Paper Science* (illustrated by Daniel Nevins), Ginn, 1978. Also author of "Wonderworld of Science" (filmstrips), Bobbs-Merrill, 1957, 1959; "Adventure with Weather" (experiment kit), Capital Publishing Co., 1959; "Experiments in Science" (filmstrips), Bailey Film Associates. Editor, "Student Scientist" series, Rosen Press. Contributor to *Book of Popular Science, Compton's Pictured Encyclopedia,* and to professional journals. Contributing editor and columnist, *Elementary School Science Bulletin,* 1955-59.

SIDELIGHTS: "Before I was five years old my parents arranged for me to take violin lessons on the advice of a musician friend who told them I showed signs of talent. These lessons gave me early training in the orderly, systematic approach to the understanding and application of the basic principles of the discipline of music.

"Gradually, as I grew older, my interest spread to the field of science. At the age of ten I set up my own 'laboratory' in a closet about three by two feet square. There I spent many wonderful hours doing experiments, inventing simple gadgets and just exploring freely ideas that came to my mind.

"As an adult I set myself the goal of helping children bridge the gap between the *wonder* in their minds and the *wonders* in the world around them—wonders that can be found in the most commonplace things they encounter in their everyday lives. In my educational work with young people I try to get them to appreciate the joy and satisfaction that can stem from scientific understanding.

"The discovery experiments I feature in my books were developed, tried and tested in close association with my own children, with students in science classes, with youngsters in special science programs I conducted at the Columbia University School of Engineering, the Dalton School and the Hall of Science of the City of New York, and with my own grandchildren. An artist and author herself, my dear wife is ever ready to review my writing, to react to it and to make sure it is simple and understandable.

"I want to express my deep gratitude to my family and to my circle of students for pointing the way for me to become a writer of science books for children."

FOR MORE INFORMATION SEE: New York Herald Tribune, April 10, 1960; *New Yorker,* January, 1964; *Think,* May-June, 1964; *Horn Book,* February, 1975; *New York Post,* May 5, 1976.

MOON, Carl   1879-1948

PERSONAL: Born October 5, 1879, in Wilmington, Ohio; died June 24, 1948, in San Francisco, Calif.; son of Sylvester Bron-

CARL MOON

(From *Solita* by Grace Moon. Illustrated by Carl Moon.)

Beneath him dropped the great vertical cliffs over which a slip or a false move might cause him to plunge into the yawning depths below. ▪ (From *Lost Indian Magic* by Grace and Carl Moon. Illustrated by Carl Moon.)

ston (a physician) and Lacy (Gudgeon) Moon; married Grace Purdie (an author) June 5, 1911 (died September 6. 1947); children: Francis Maxwell, Mary Caryl. *Religion:* Christian Scientist. *Home:* Pasadena, Calif.

CAREER: Artist, author, and illustrator. Left his home in Ohio, armed with a camera, paints, and brushes, to pursue his dream of "hunting" American Indians, about 1902; began collecting paintings and photos of Indians, and operated his own art and photography studio in Albuquerque, N.M., 1904-07; compiled a large collection of Indian pictures for the firm of Fred Harvey at the Grand Canyon, Ariz., headquarters, 1907-14; has also compiled collections of American Indian photos, prints, and paintings for the Huntington Library, and for the American Museum of Natural History in New York; began writing books about Indians with his wife, Grace Moon, in 1918; contributed articles to magazines and newspapers regarding Indian rituals and customs; many examples of his work can be found in museums around the country including the Museum of Montclair, N.J., and the Smithsonian Institution in Washington, D.C. *Military service:* Member of the Ohio National Guard, 1896-97; California Reserves, 1917-18. *Member:* Pasadena Society of Artists; once served as a director of the California Writers Guild; honorary member of the Vagabonds.

WRITINGS—All self-illustrated: *The Flaming Arrow,* F. A. Stokes, 1927; *Painted Moccasin,* F. A. Stokes, 1931; *Tah-Kee, the Boy from Nowhere,* F. A. Stokes, 1932; *Indians of the Southwest,* privately printed, 1936.

Illustrator and co-author, with wife, Grace Moon: *Lost Indian Magic: A Mystery Story of the Red Man as He Lived before the White Men Came,* F. A. Stokes, 1918; *Wongo and the Wise Old Crow,* Reilly & Lee, 1923; *The Book of Nah-Wee,* Doubleday, Doran, 1932; *One Little Indian,* Whitman, 1950, new edition, 1967.

Illustrator: *Indian Legends in Rhyme,* F. A. Stokes, 1917; *Chi-Wee: The Adventures of a Little Indian Girl,* Doubleday, Page, 1925; *Chi-Wee and Loki of the Desert,* Doubleday, Page, 1926; *Nadita (Little Nothing),* Doubleday, Page, 1927, reissued under title *Nadita,* 1946; *The Runaway Papoose,* Doubleday, Doran, 1928; *The Magic Trail,* Doubleday, Doran, 1929; *The Missing Katchina,* Doubleday, Doran, 1930; *The Arrow of Tee-May,* Doubleday, Doran, 1931; *Far-Away Desert,* Doubleday, Doran, 1932; *Tita of Mexico,* F. A. Stokes, 1934; *Shanty Ann,* F. A. Stokes, 1935; *Singing Sands,* Doubleday, Doran, 1936; *White Indian,* Doubleday, Doran, 1937; *Solita,* Doubleday, Doran, 1938; *Daughter of Thunder,* Macmillan, 1942.

SIDELIGHTS: "My work dates from a boyhood interest in American Indians, probably the influence of James Fenimore Cooper. I worked in studios in Cincinnati, Ohio, Wheeling, West Virginia, and San Antonio, Texas, then moved to Albuquerque, New Mexico, in 1903, and bought a studio of my own. Began almost immediately to photograph, paint, and write about the Southwest Indians. Wrote for many magazines and a few newspapers mostly descriptive articles, illustrated by my own pictures.

"In 1906 exhibited my pictures at the White House, at the invitation of President Theodore Roosevelt. Exhibited the same year at National Gallery, by invitation of Dr. Holmes; and at Museum of Natural History in New York, by invitation of Dr. Henry Fairfield Osborn. In 1907 moved to Grand Canyon, Arizona, to begin collection of Indian pictures for Fred Harvey, and spent seven years completing this collection. In 1914 moved to Pasadena, California, to work independently again, and made collection of about three hundred prints and twenty-four oil paintings of Indians for Mr. Henry E. Huntington for the Huntington Library.

"In 1924 began publishing a four-volume set of pictorial books, *Indians of the Southwest,* containing twenty-five large prints per volume. These sets are owned by libraries and museums over the country. The Museum of Montclair, New Jersey, owns ten paintings of mine in oil. . . . I made the Florence Rand Lang collection of twenty-six oil paintings of Indians for the Smithsonian Institution at Washington, D.C. My paintings are in many private collections, schools, etc." [Bertha E. Mahony, and others, compilers, *Illustrators of Children's Books: 1744-1945,* Horn Book, 1947.]

FOR MORE INFORMATION SEE: Bertha E. Mahony, and others, compilers, *Illustrators of Children's Books, 1744-1945,* Horn Book, 1947; Stanley J. Kunitz and Howard Haycraft, editors, *Junior Book of Authors,* 2nd edition, Wilson, 1951; Martha E. Ward and D. A. Marquardt, *Authors of Books for Young People,* Scarecrow, 1964; (obituary) *New York Times,* June 26, 1948.

GRACE MOON

MOON, Grace   1877(?)-1947

PERSONAL: Born in 1877 (or, 1883 according to some sources), in Indianapolis, Ind.; died September 6, 1947; daughter of Francis Baillie and Mary Bragdon (Du Souchet) Purdie; married Carl Moon (an author and illustrator) June 5, 1911 (died June 24, 1948); children: Francis Maxwell, Mary Caryl. *Education:* Privately tutored; attended the University of Wisconsin and the Art Institute of Chicago. *Home:* Pasadena, Calif.

CAREER: Artist and author of books for children. With her husband, Carl, Grace Moon lived with various Indian tribes throughout the Southwest, collecting authentic material for her children's books; her first book was published in 1917; she produced a total of nineteen books in the course of her career; she also painted several portraits of Indian children which can be found in many private collections. *Member:* Daughters of the American Revolution, Pi Beta Phi, once served as a director of the California Writers Guild, president of the Pasadena Club of Zonta International, 1931-32. *Awards, honors:* Runner-up for the John Newbery Medal for *Runaway Papoose*, 1929.

WRITINGS—With husband, Carl Moon; all illustrated by Carl Moon: *Lost Indian Magic: A Mystery Story of the Red Man as He Lived before the White Men Came*, F. A. Stokes, 1918; *Wongo and the Wise Old Crow*, Reilly & Lee, 1923; *The Book of Nah-Wee*, Doubleday, Doran, 1932; *One Little Indian*, Whitman, 1950, new edition, 1967.

All illustrated by Carl Moon: *Indian Legends in Rhyme*, F. A. Stokes, 1917; *Chi-Wee: The Adventures of a Little Indian Girl*, Doubleday, Page, 1925; *Chi-Wee and Loki of the Desert*, Doubleday, Page, 1926; *Nadita (Little Nothing)*, Doubleday, Page,

1927, reissued under title *Nadita*, 1946; *The Runaway Papoose*, Doubleday, Doran, 1928; *The Magic Trail*, Doubleday, Doran, 1929; *The Missing Katchina*, Doubleday, Doran, 1930; *The Arrow of Tee-May*, Doubleday, Doran, 1931; *Far-Away Desert*, Doubleday, Doran, 1932; *Tita of Mexico*, F. A. Stokes, 1934; *Shanty Ann*, F. A. Stokes, 1935; *Singing Sands*, Doubleday, Doran, 1936; *White Indian*, Doubleday, Doran, 1937; *Solita*, Doubleday, Doran, 1938; *Daughter of Thunder*, Macmillan, 1942.

SIDELIGHTS: "When people ask me how I came to write about Indians, the answer is very simple. I have always liked Indians. When I was a little girl, I thought I really was an Indian because I was born in Indianapolis. Many years later I married Carl Moon, an artist who was interested in Indians, too, and we actually went down to the Southwest to the Indian Country to gather material for pictures he was making. Then it seemed like a dream come true.

"There simply isn't more glorious scenery anywhere than on the Painted Desert and through the land of the Hopis and the Navajos. And each hill and butte and canyon has a story, some of the stories true, and some of them only fairy tales, but all woven into the life of the people.

"Here is the tale of a queer-shaped rock just at the entrance to a canyon with steep, dark walls. It was told, they say, by a bald-headed eagle to a fat little Indian boy in the long ago.

Suddenly Rosa went down very fast. ■ (From *Solita* by Grace Moon. Illustrated by Carl Moon.)

The rock is very tall, and on its highest part there seems to be the nest of a bird.

"In the days when the world was young, an eagle had her nest in the canyon wall. When she came home one evening to feed her two downy eaglets, she found them talking to a coyote in the canyon below. The eagle knew very well that the coyote would like to have her little ones for his supper, but she did not fear him for her nest was high and the coyote had no wings. But even in those days the coyote was very sly, and he found a trail that led up to the eagle's nest. When it grew dark, he began to climb up that trail toward the nest of the eagle, and he laughed to himself as he climbed. But the eagle has always been a bird sacred to the gods and his feathers are used for prayer feathers; so when the coyote reached the edge of the nest and put out his sharp nose to snatch a tiny eaglet, there was a noise like thunder and the nest was not there!

"In the dark the coyote could not tell what had happened, but when it grew light he saw the tall rock standing as it is today with the eagle nest safe on top. It is always a lesson to teach that those who are good and live near to the gods in their thoughts are protected from evil.

"When I heard tales like this in the Indian country, I just had to get home and write as fast as I could to tell the tales to boys and girls everywhere. I wanted them to know about the little Indians like Yazhe and Kawani, as they are today, living a life that is free and true and filled to the brim with adventure. And so in *The Magic Trail*, *Chi-Wee*, *The Runaway Papoose*, and my other books I have written always about my little black-eyed Indian friends."

FOR MORE INFORMATION SEE: Stanley J. Kunitz and Howard Haycraft, editors, *Junior Book of Authors*, 2nd edition, Wilson, 1951; Martha E. Ward and D. A. Marquardt, editors, *Authors of Books for Young People*, Scarecrow, 1964. Obituaries—*New York Times*, September 8, 1947; *Publishers Weekly*, September 27, 1947; *Wilson Library Bulletin*, November, 1947.

OLDS, Helen Diehl 1895-1981

OBITUARY NOTICE—See sketch in *SATA* Volume 9: Born April 29, 1895, in Springfield, Ohio; died January 1, 1981, in Queens, N.Y. Author of books and magazine stories for children. Olds contributed books to the "Every Day Adventure Story" series published by Messner, and was the author of educational books which were often used in schools. Her final titles were a series of biographies about such persons as Christopher Columbus and Richard Nixon. In addition to being an author, Olds was a teacher of writing at Queens University and Hofstra University. *For More Information See*: *Contemporary Authors*, Volumes 1-4, revised, Gale, 1967; *Who's Who of American Women*, 7th edition, Marquis, 1972. *Obituaries*: *New York Times*, January 8, 1981; *School Library Journal*, February, 1981; *AB Bookman's Weekly*, March 9, 1981.

OSSOLI, Sarah Margaret (Fuller) marchesa d' 1810-1850 (Margaret Fuller)

PERSONAL: Born May 23, 1810, in Cambridgeport, Mass.; died June 19, 1850, in the wreck of the ship *Elizabeth* off the coast of Fire Island, New York; daughter of Timothy (a lawyer and congressman) and Margaret (Crane) Fuller; married Giovanni Angelo, Marquis d'Ossoli, December, 1847 (died June 19, 1850); children: Angelo (died June 19, 1850). *Education:* Privately tutored by her father. Her intensive education involved training in Latin, Greek, French, Italian, and other languages as well as English literature.

CAREER: After her father's sudden death in 1835, Margaret Fuller became a teacher at Bronson Alcott's school in Boston in order to support her younger brothers and sisters; moved to Providence, Rhode Island, and served as principal teacher in a private school, 1837-1839; returning to Boston, she instituted a series of "conversations" in which she instructed groups of women in social and philosophical subjects, 1839-1844; during this time, she acted as editor and contributor to *The Dial*, the Transcendentalist journal, July 1840-April 1844; served as the first literary critic of the *New York Tribune*, 1844-1846; in the spring of 1846, she sailed for Europe where she met several leading authors of the day and became involved with Giuseppe Mazzini and the fight for Italian liberation.

WRITINGS: Summer on the Lakes, in 1843, C. C. Little & J. Brown, 1844, reprinted, Haskell House, 1970, facsimile edition, B. de Graaf, 1972; *Woman in the Nineteenth Century*, Greeley & McElrath, 1845, reissued as *Woman in the Nineteenth Century, and Kindred Papers Relating to the Sphere, Condition and Duties of Woman*, Sheldon, Lamport, 1855, reprinted, Books for Libraries, 1972; *Papers on Literature and Art*, Wiley & Putnam, 1846, reprinted, AMS Press, 1972, reissued as *Literature and Art* (with an introduction by Horace Greeley), Fowlers & Wells, 1852, expanded edition published as *Art, Literature, and the Drama*, Roberts Brothers, 1889; *At Home and Abroad; or, Things and Thoughts in America and Europe*, Nichols & Co., 1856, reprinted, Kennikat Press, 1971; *Memoirs of Margaret Fuller Ossoli*, Phillips, Sampson, 1852, reprinted, B. Franklin, 1972; *Life Without and Life Within*, Brown, Taggard, 1859, reprinted, Literature House, 1970; *Love Letters of Margaret Fuller, 1845-1846*, D. Appleton, 1903, reprinted, AMS Press, 1970.

Selections: *Jottings from the Writings of Margaret Fuller* (edited by Edwin A. Studwell and R. A. Canby), H. M. Gardner, Jr., 1869; *The Writings of Margaret Fuller* (selected and edited by Mason Wade), Viking, 1941, reprinted, A. M. Kelley, 1973; *Margaret Fuller: American Romantic* (edited by Perry Miller), Doubleday, 1963.

Editor: *The Dial: A Magazine for Literature, Philosophy, and Religion*, Volumes 1-4, Russell & Russell, 1961.

Extensive collections of the author's manuscripts are held in the Boston Public Library and the Harvard College Library.

SIDELIGHTS: **May 23, 1810.** Born in Cambridgeport, Massachusetts.

1816. Studied Latin under her father's tutelage. "Trained to great dexterity in artificial methods, accurate, ready, with entire command of his resources, [my father] had no belief in minds that listen, wait, and receive. He had no conception of the subtle and indirect motions of imagination and feeling. His influence on me was great, and opposed to the natural unfolding of my character, which was fervent, of strong grasp, and disposed to infatuation, and self-forgetfulness." [Paula Blanchard, *Margaret Fuller: From Transcendentalism to Revolution*, Delacorte, 1978.[1]] From Latin, Fuller progressed to Greek and, by the age of eight, had discovered Shakespeare.

1821. Attended first school in Boston. Wrote to her mother: "Tell Papa that I do not believe I shall be happy if I leave school soon. Ask him mamma whether I shall not stay more than a year. Oh I hope I shall for I love the Dr [Parks] so much, and my companions seem so amiable that I long to stay. I talk about this too much perhaps but it is uppermost in my thoughts."[1]

1824-1826. Sent to Miss Prescott's School for Young Ladies in Groton, against her wishes. Wrote to her father: ". . . I shall willingly go to Groton for the summer, at your pleasure, though nothing else could in the least reconcile me to it. I shall entirely depend upon an immediate visit from you according to your promise. . . . How much I regret to leave this charming place, where I am beloved and go to one where I am an entire stranger and where I must behave entirely by rule. . . . I hope *you* are not quite so anxious to get rid of your *little* daughter."[1]

1826. Gained a reputation as a brilliant conversationalist. Returned to her family's home. "I rise a little before five, walk an hour, and then practise on the piano, till seven, when we breakfast. Next I read French,—Sismondi's Literature of the South of Europe,—till eight, then two or three lectures in Brown's Philosophy. About half-past nine I go to Mr. Perkins's school and study Greek till twelve, when, school being dismissed, I recite, go home, and practise again till dinner, at two. Sometimes, if the conversation is very agreeable, I lounge for half an hour over the dessert, though rarely so lavish of time. Then, when I can, I read two hours in Italian, but I am often interrupted. At six, I walk, or take a drive. Before going to bed, I play or sing, for half an hour or so, to make all sleepy, and, about eleven, retire to write a little while in my journal, exercises on what I have read, or a series of characteristics which I am filling up according to advice. Thus, you see, I am learning Greek, and making acquaintance with metaphysics, and French and Italian literature."[1]

November, 1834. With her father's encouragement, wrote an article which was printed in the *Daily Advertiser*. "It was responded to (I flatter myself by some big-wig) from Salem. He detected some ignorance in me. Nevertheless as he remarked that I wrote with 'ability' and seemed to *consider me* as an elderly gentleman *I considered* the affair as highly flattering. . . ."[1]

October 2, 1835. Father died—family responsibility rested heavily with Fuller. "My father's image follows me constantly, whenever I am in my room he seems to open the door and to look on me with a complacent tender smile. What would I not give to have it in my power, to make that heart beat once more with joy. . . ."[1]

Summer, 1836. Through the intercession of friends, met Ralph Waldo Emerson. Emerson recalled their first meeting: "I was, at that time, an eager scholar of ethics, and had tasted the sweets of solitude and stoicism, and I found something profane in the hours of amusing gossip into which she drew me, and, when I returned to my library, had much to think of the crackling of thorns under a pot."[1]

December, 1836. Began teaching at Bronson Alcott's Temple School in Boston. Three evenings a week Fuller gave lessons to women in her Boston apartment. One evening a week she translated, aloud, the works of de Wette and Herder for Dr. William Channing whose eyesight was failing. Fuller was plagued by headaches which were a handicap throughout her life. "It is but a bad head,—as bad as if I were a great man! I am not entitled to so bad a head by anything I have done."[1]

SARAH MARGARET MARCHESA D'OSSOLI

April, 1837. Accepted an offer to teach at the Greene Street School in Providence. "There is room here, if I mistake not, for a great move in the cause of education, but whether it is I who am to help move, I cannot yet tell. I sometimes think *yes,* because the plan is becoming so complete in my mind, ways and means are continually occurring to me, and so far as I have tried them, they seem to succeed."[1]

Spring, 1838. Wrote Emerson from Providence: "I have shut the door for a few days, and tried to do something; you have *really* been doing something. And that is why I write. I want to see you, and still more to hear you. I must kindle my torch again. Why have I not heard you this winter? I feel very humble just now, yet I have to say that the being lives not who would have received from your lectures as much as I should. There are noble books, but one wants the breath of life sometimes. And I see no divine person. I myself am more divine than any I see. I think that is enough to say about them. I know Dr. Wayland [president of Brown University] now, but I shall not care for him. He would never understand me, and, if I met him, it must be by those means of suppression and accommodation which I at present hate to my heart's core. I hate everything that is reasonable just now, 'wise limitations' and all. I have behaved much too well for some time past; it has spoiled my peace. What grieves me, too, is to find or fear that my theory is a cheat. I cannot serve two masters, and I fear all the hope of being a worldling and a literary existence also must be resigned. Isolation is necessary to me, as to others."[1]

December, 1838. Left her teaching position at Greene Street School. "I am wearied out. I have gabbled and simpered and given my mind to the public view these two years back, till there seems to be no good left in me."[1]

Spring, 1839. Translated Goethe's *Conversations With Eckerman.* "I find daily new materials and am at present almost burthened by my riches. I have found for instance all the Frankfort particulars in letters to Meyer. And Goethe's Darstellunggabe lends such beauty to the theme that I shall often translate, and string rather than melt my pears. I do not write steadily for the subject keeps fermenting and I feel that the hour of precipitation is not arrived. Often a study is suggested and I pass several days in the woods with it before I resume the pen. It would make quite a cultivated person of me, if I had four or five years to give to my task. But intend to content myself with doing it inadequately rather than risk living so long in the shadow of one mind.''[1]

Organized the Conversations—a series of informal female gatherings. By 1841 Fuller had decided to include men—such notables as Emerson and Bronson Alcott attended.

April, 1840. First editor of *The Dial,* the journal of the Transcendental Club, of which Fuller was a member. ''. . . I hope there will neither be a spirit of dogmatism nor of compromise. That this periodical will not aim at leading public opinion, but at stimulating each man to think for himself, to think more deeply and more nobly by letting them [*sic*] see how some minds are kept alive by a wise self-trust. . . . I am sure we cannot show high culture. And I doubt about vigorous thought. But I hope we shall show free action as far as it goes and a high aim. It were much if a periodical could be kept open to accomplish no outward object, but merely to afford an avenue for what of free and calm thought might be originated among us by the wants of individual minds.''[1]

July, 1842. Anxieties over her income, family, and her health compelled Fuller to relinquish the editorship of *The Dial.*

Summer, 1843. Toured what was then called the American northwest. Kept a journal which later became her book, *Summer on the Lakes.* ''I come to the West prepared for the distaste I must experience at its mushroom growth. I know that, where 'go ahead' is the only motto, the village cannot grow into the gentle proportions that successive lives and the gradations of experience involuntarily give. In older countries the house of the son grew from that of the father, as naturally as new joints on a bough, and the cathedral crowned the whole as naturally as the leafy summit the tree. This cannot be here. The march of peaceful is scarce less wanton than that of warlike invasion. The old landmarks are broken down, and the land, for a season, bears none, except of the rudeness of conquest and the needs of the day, whose bivouac-fires blacken the sweetest forest glades. I have come prepared to see all this, to dislike it, but not with stupid narrowness to distrust or defame. . . . I trust by reverent faith to woo the mighty meaning of the scene, perhaps to foresee the law by which a new order, a new poetry, is to be evoked from this chaos. . . .''[1]

September, 1844. Accepted Horace Greeley's offer to become the first woman journalist on the staff of the New York *Tribune.* Wrote *Woman in the Nineteenth Century,* a declaration of woman's rights. ''Woman has always power enough, if she choose to exert it, and is usually disposed to do so, in proportion to her ignorance and childish vanity. Unacquainted with the importance of life and its purposes, trained to a selfish coquetry and love of petty power, she does not look beyond the pleasure of making herself felt at the moment, and governments are shaken and commerce broken up to gratify the pique of a female favorite.

''. . . Men have, indeed, been, for more than a hundred years, rating women for countenancing vice. But, at the same time, they have carefully hid from them its nature, so that the preference often shown by women for bad men arises rather from a confused idea that they are bold and adventurous, acquainted

with regions which women are forbidden to explore, and the curiosity that ensues, then a corrupt heart in the woman. As to marriage, it has been inculcated on women, for centuries, that men have not only stronger passions than they, but of a sort that it would be shameful for them to share or even understand; that, therefore, they must 'confide in their husbands,' that is, submit implicitly to their will; that the least appearance of coldness or withdrawal, from whatever cause, in the wife is wicked, because liable to turn her husband's thoughts to illicit indulgence; for a man is so constituted that he must indulge his passions or die!''[1]

1845-1846. Left the Greeley home at Turtle Bay and took lodgings in New York City.

August, 1846. Sailed for Europe. Fuller's purpose in visiting Europe was threefold: she went as an ordinary tourist, as a literary pilgrim, and as a reporter for the *Tribune.* ''I do not look forward to seeing Europe now as so very important to me. My mind and character are too much formed. I shall not modify them much but only add to my stores of knowledge. Still, even in this sense, I wish much to go. It is important to me, almost needful in the career I am now engaged in. I feel that, if I persevere, there is nothing to hinder my having an important career even now. But it must be in the capacity of a journalist, and for that I need this new field of observation.''[1]

April, 1847. After touring Britain and France, arrived in Rome, where she met Giovanni Angelo Ossoli. ''All winter in Paris, although my life was rich in novelties of value, I was not well; the climate was too damp for me, and then I had too much intellectual excitement of the same kind as at home. I need a respite, a long leisure of enjoyment, a kind of spring time, to renovate my faculties. But Paris is the very focus of intellectual activity of Europe, there I found every topic intensified, clarified, reduced to portable dimensions: there is the cream of all the milk, but I am not strong enough to live on cream at present. I learned much, I suffered to leave Paris, but I find myself better here, where the climate is so enchanting, the people so indolently joyous, and the objects of contemplation so numerous and admirable, that one cannot pass the time better than by quietly *looking* one's fill. . . .

''The Italians sympathize with my character and understand my organization, as no other people ever did; they admire the ready eloquence of my nature, and highly prize my intelligent sympathy (such as they do not find often in foreigners) with their sufferings in the past and hopes for the future.''[1]

October, 1847. Settled into an apartment in Rome with Ossoli, who had become her lover. ''. . . My character is not now in what may be called the heroic phase. I have done, may do things that might invoke censure; but in the foundation of character,—in my aims, I am always the same and I believe you will always have confidence that I act as I ought and must, and will always value my sympathy.''[1]

February, 1848. Pregnant with Ossoli's child. ''I have known some happy hours, but they all lead to sorrow; and not only the cups of wine, but of milk, seem drugged with poison for me. It does not *seem* to be my fault, this Destiny; I do not court these things,—they come. I am a poor magnet, with power to be wounded by the bodies I attract. . . . With this year, I enter upon a sphere of my destiny so difficult, that I, at present, see no way out, except through the gate of death. It is useless to write of it . . . whether accident or angel will, I have no intimation. I have no reason to hope I shall not reap what I have sown, and do not. Yet how I shall endure it I cannot guess; it is all a dark, sad enigma. The beautiful forms of art charm no more, and a love, in which there is all fondness, but no help, flatters in vain.''[1]

May, 1848. As her pregnancy progressed, Fuller went into self-imposed seclusion in Aquila, a village fifty miles from Rome.

July, 1848. Moved to Rieti.

September 5, 1848. Son, Angelo Philip Eugene, born. Forced to leave her son with a wet nurse in Rieti while she returned with Ossoli to Rome. ''When I first took him in my arms he made no sound but leaned his head against my bosom, and staid so, he seemed to say how could you abandon me. . . . You speak of my being happy; all the solid happiness I have known has been at times when he went to sleep in my arms. . . . I do not look forward to his career and his manly life: it is *now* I want to be with him, before [illegible] care and bafflings begin. If I had a little money I should go with him into strict retirement for a year or two and live for him alone. This I cannot do; all life that has been or could be natural to me is invariably denied. . . .''[1]

1849. As a revolutionary partisan and a journalist for the *Tribune,* Fuller took an apartment in Rome, while awaiting its inevitable siege by the French. After a week of shelling by the French, Fuller wrote Emerson: ''Her glorious oaks,—her villas, haunts of sacred beauty, that seemed the possession of the world for ever,—the villa of Raphael, the villa of Albani, home of Winckelmann and the best expression of the ideal of modern Rome, and so many other sanctuaries of beauty,—all must perish, lest a foe should level a musket from their shelter. I could not, could not!

''I know not, dear friend, whether I shall ever get home across that great ocean, but here in Rome I shall no longer wish to live. O Rome, *my* country! could I imagine that the triumph of what I held dear was to heap such desolation on thy head.''[1]

April, 1849. During the siege of Rome, became a director of a Roman hospital. ''Since the 30th of April, I go almost daily to the hospitals, and though I have suffered, for I had no idea before how terrible gunshot wounds and wound-fevers are, yet I have taken pleasure, and great pleasure, in being with the men. There is scarcely one who is not moved by a noble spirit. Many, especially among the Lombards, are the flower of the Italian youth. When they begin to get better, I carry them books and flowers; they read, and we talk.

''The palace of the Pope, on the Quirinal, is now used for convalescents. In those beautiful gardens I walk with them, one with his sling, another with his crutch. The gardener plays off all his water-works for the defenders of the country, and gathers flowers for me, their friend.''[1]

July, 1849. Reunited with her son in Rieti where she found him suffering from malnutrition from which he eventually recovered. ''. . . He is so weak it seems to me he can scarcely ever revive to health. If he cannot, I do not wish him to live; life is hard enough for the strong, it is too much for the feeble. Only, if he died, I hope I shall, too. I was too fatigued before, and this last shipwreck of hopes would be more than I could bear.''[1]

Autumn, 1849. Wrote American friends and family, telling them that she was married and had a child. In Europe and America the news was received with shock and criticism. Fuller defied the scandalmongers. ''I feel a good deal of contempt

(From *The Complete History of the Deluge* by Margaret Fuller. Illustrated by the author.)

for those so easily disconcerted or reassured. I was not a child; I had lived in the midst of that New England society; in a way that entitled me to esteem, and a favorable interpretation, where there was doubt about my motives or actions. I pity those who are inclined to think ill, when they might as well have inclined the other way. However, let them go; there are many in the world who stand the test, enough to keep us from shivering to death.''[1]

October, 1849. Arrived in Florence with her son and Ossoli. The actual date of marriage to Ossoli was not certain, but the fact of their marriage is generally agreed upon.

March, 1850. Decided to return to America with her son and husband.

May 17, 1850. Sailed on the *Elizabeth.*

June 19, 1850. *Elizabeth* struck a sand bar off Fire Island, Long Island, New York at 3:30 a.m. Ossoli and Fuller's bodies were never found. The body of their son was washed ashore and brought for burial in Cambridge, Massachusetts. ''Say to those I leave behind that I was willing to die. I have suffered in life far more than I enjoyed, and I think quite out of proportion with the use my living here is . . . to others. I have wished to be natural and true, but the world was not in harmony with me—nothing came right for me. I think the spirit that governs the Universe must have in reserve for me a sphere where I can develop more freely, and be happier—on earth circumstances do not promise this before my forces shall be too much lavished to make a better path truly avail me.''[1]

1852. *Memoirs of Margaret Fuller Ossoli,* edited by Emerson, William Channing, and James Freeman Clarke published. Emerson wrote to Carlyle: ''The timorous said 'What shall she do?'. . . . But she had only to open her mouth and a triumphant success awaited her. She would fast enough have disposed of the circumstances and the bystanders. . . . Here were already mothers waiting tediously for her coming, for the education of their daughters.''[1]

FOR MORE INFORMATION SEE: Julia Ward Howe, *Margaret Fuller*, Roberts Brothers, 1883, reprinted, R. West, 1973; Thomas Wentworth Higginson, *Margaret Fuller Ossoli*, C. D. Warner, 1884, reissued, Haskell House, 1968; Frederick Augustus Braun, *Margaret Fuller and Goethe*, H. Holt, 1910, reissued, Folcroft, 1971; Katharine S. Anthony, *Margaret Fuller: A Psychological Biography*, Harcourt, 1921, reprinted, Scholarly Press, 1970; Margaret Bell, *Margaret Fuller*, A. & G. Boni, 1930, reprinted, Books for Libraries, 1971; Hugh Mason Wade, *Margaret Fuller, Whetstone of Genius*, Viking, 1940, reprinted, A. M. Kelley, 1973; Madeleine Bettina Stern, *Life of Margaret Fuller*, Dutton, 1942, reissued, Haskell House, 1968; Charles Allan Madison, *Critics and Crusaders: A Century of American Protest*, Holt, 1947; Mary Ormsbee Whitton, *These Were the Women, U.S.A. 1776-1860*, Hastings House, 1954; Faith Chipperfield, *In Quest of Love: The Life and Death of Margaret Fuller*, Coward, 1957; Dame Edith Sitwell, *English Eccentrics*, Vanguard, 1957.

Emily Taft Douglas, *Remember the Ladies*, Putnam, 1966; Gamaliel Bradford, *Portraits of American Women*, Books for Libraries, 1969; Joseph Jay Deiss, *Roman Years of Margaret Fuller: A Biography*, Crowell, 1969; Russell E. Durning, *Margaret Fuller, Citizen of the World*, C. Winter, 1969; Hope Stoddard, *Famous American Women*, Crowell, 1970; Miriam Gurko, *Ladies of Seneca Falls*, Macmillan, 1974; Bell G. Chevigny, *Woman and the Myth: Margaret Fuller's Life and Writings*, Feminist Press, 1977; Paula Blanchard, *Margaret Fuller: From Transcendentalism to Revolution*, Delacorte, 1978.

For children: Sarah Bolton, *Lives of Girls Who Became Famous*, Crowell, 1949; Caroline Horowitz and H. H. Horowitz, *Treasury of the World's Great Heroines*, Hart Publishing, 1951; Ellen Janet Cameron Wilson, *Margaret Fuller: Bluestocking, Romantic, Revolutionary*, Farrar, Straus, 1977; Abby Slater, *In Search of Margaret Fuller: A Biography*, Delacorte, 1978.

PARK, Ruth

PERSONAL: Born in Auckland, New Zealand; married D'Arcy Niland (a journalist and playwright), 1942 (died, 1967). *Education:* Attended St. Benedict's College, and University of Auckland. *Address:* ℅ Curtis Brown Ltd., P.O. Box 19, Paddington, NSW, Australia.

CAREER: Zealandia, Auckland, New Zealand, editor of children's page; *Auckland Star*, Auckland, children's editor; *Sydney Mirror*, Sydney, Australia, reporter; Twentieth Century-Fox, London, scriptwriter; free-lance writer and journalist; welfare worker in Auckland and in Sydney. *Awards, honors:* Monetary prize from *Sydney Morning Herald*, 1948, for *The Harp in the South;* runner-up in Australian Book of the Year award, 1975, for *Callie's Castle;* Miles Franklin Award, 1978; Children's Book of the Year Award, 1980, for *Playing Beatie Bow*.

WRITINGS—For children: The "Muddle-Headed Wombat" series; illustrated by Noela Young: *The Muddle-Headed Wombat*, Angus & Robertson, 1963; *The Muddle-Headed Wombat in the Tree-Tops*, Educational Press, 1965; *. . .at School*, Educational Press, 1966; *. . .in the Snow*, Educational Press,

1966; *. . .on a Rainy Day*, Angus & Robertson, 1969; *. . .in the Springtime*, Angus & Robertson, 1970; *. . .and the Bush Band*, Angus & Robertson, 1973; *. . .and the Invention*, Angus & Robertson, 1976; *. . .on Cleanup Day*, Angus & Robertson, 1976.

The Hole in the Hill (illustrated by Jennifer Murray), Ure Smith, 1961; *The Ship's Cat* (illustrated by Richard Kennedy), St. Martin's, 1961; *Tales of the South*, Macmillan (London), 1961; *The Road to Christmas* (illustrated by Young), St. Martin's, 1962; *The Road Under the Sea* (illustrated by J. Murray), Ure Smith, 1962; *The Shaky Island* (illustrated by Iris Millington), McKay, 1962; *Airlift for Grandee* (illustrated by Sheila Hawkins), St. Martin's, 1964; *Secret of the Maori Cave* (illustrated by Michael A. Hampshire), Doubleday, 1964; *Ring of the Sorcerer* (illustrated by William Stobbs), Horwitz, 1967; *The Sixpenny Island* (illustrated by David Cox), Ure Smith, 1968; *Ten-Cent Island* (illustrated by Robert Frankenberg), Doubleday, 1968; *Nuki and the Sea Serpent* (illustrated by Zelma Blakely), Longman, 1969; *Callie's Castle* (illustrated by Kilmeny Niland), Angus & Robertson, 1974; *The Gigantic Balloon* (illustrated by K. Niland and Deborah Niland), Collins, 1975, Parents' Magazine Press, 1976; *Merchant Campbell* (illustrated by Edwina Bell), Collins, 1976; *Roger Bandy* (illustrated by K. Niland and D. Niland), Rigby, 1977; *Playing Beatie Bow*, Thomas Nelson, 1980.

Novels: *The Harp in the South*, Houghton, 1948; *Poor Man's Orange*, Angus & Robertson, 1949, published as *12 ½ Plymouth Street*, Houghton, 1951; *The Witch's Thorn*, Angus & Robertson, 1951, Houghton, 1952; *A Power of Roses*, Angus & Robertson, 1953; *Pink Flannel* (illustrated by Phil Taylor), Angus & Robertson, 1955; *One-a-Pecker, Two-a-Pecker*, Angus & Robertson, 1957, published as *The Frost and the Fire*, Houghton, 1958; *The Good Looking Women*, Angus & Robertson, 1961; *Serpent's Delight*, Doubleday, 1962.

Other writings: (With husband, D'Arcy Niland) *The Drums Go Bang* (autobiography; illustrated by Phil Taylor), Angus & Robertson, 1956; *The Companion Guide to Sydney* (travel description), Collins, 1973; *Swords and Crowns and Rings*, Thomas Nelson, 1977, St. Martin's, 1978; *Come Danger, Come Darkness*, Hodder & Stoughton, 1978; *Flights of Angels*, Thomas Nelson, 1981. Also author of *When the Wind Changed*, Collins.

WORK IN PROGRESS: An adult novel, *Glimpses of True Love.*

SIDELIGHTS: "Although I am mostly known as an adult novelist, I have always written for children. I come of an isolated, storytelling family, Nordic Scots and Irish. Before my marriage I spent several years editing a large children's newspaper and there learned that what adults would like children to read, they simply don't. For this reason I have no interest in book awards, critiques, or scholarly dissertations from people who have never had any children and have never spent any time with them. My one criterion is whether children like to read my books; if they didn't, I'd stop writing them. Aside from having five children of my own, I always try out a children's story on a group . . . usually kindergarten.

"I have been published in the U.S.A. for many years. . . . Also I have written dozens of storybook texts for German, Nigerian and Scandinavian books. For the ABC Children's session I have written for close on twenty-five years. The best known of these many series is as *The Muddle-Headed Wombat*. About Wombat there are also eleven books available, published by Education Press. I also do educational books (supplementary

Peter Thin did all the dirty jobs other people in J. J. Jones's Gigantic Emporium didn't want to. He was often bullied and scolded, but Peter kept his heart light because he had a secret dream.
■ (From *The Gigantic Balloon* by Ruth Park. Illustrated by Kilmeny and Deborah Niland.)

readers) about some industry or aspect of Australian life. Lately I have done several adventure books for older age groups. They are all set in and around the Pacific, with which I am very familiar. *The Hole in the Hill, The Road Under the Sea, Ten-Cent Island* are some of these.

"I like children enormously and have spent much of my life with them, as teacher, children's editor and finally mother. I like interesting and amusing children and this is why I wrote children's books. Being a severely practical writer I write for children only, not publishers, adult buyers or adult critics. My idea of a successful children's book is not one that wins a prize, but one that gets worn out in all the libraries. Writing for children is different from writing for adults and much more difficult. Most adult writing is designed to expand the inner world of the reader. Children's writing is the reverse. For a child, all the doors of his imaginative vision open outwards; the content of the story is the marvellous world beyond these doors, the style is what opens them for boys and girls too small to reach the knobs."

FOR MORE INFORMATION SEE: New York Times, February 22, 1948, January 28, 1951, April 13, 1958; *New York Herald Tribune Weekly Book Review,* February 22, 1948; *Saturday*

Review of Literature, February 28, 1948; *Atlantic Monthly,* April, 1948; *New Statesman and Nation,* May 1, 1948; *Commonweal,* May 14, 1948, February 13, 1953; *New York Herald Tribune Book Review,* January 28, 1951, December 7, 1952, April 6, 1958; *Chicago Sunday Tribune,* February 11, 1951, December 28, 1952; *Catholic World,* April, 1951; *San Francisco Chronicle,* December 18, 1952; *Wall Street Review of Books,* December, 1975; *Times Literary Supplement,* April 2, 1976; *Observer,* September 24, 1978.

PEASE, Howard   1894-1974

OBITUARY NOTICE—See sketch in *SATA* Volume 2: Born September 6, 1894, in Stockton, Calif.; died April 14, 1974, in Mill Valley, Calif. Author of adventure stories for young people. Pease, during and after his student days at Stanford, was a merchant seaman, shipping out of San Francisco on various freighters. He later used his experiences at sea to give an authentic touch to many of his books, most notably the eleven titles in the "Tod Moran Mysteries" series, which includes the award-winning *Heart of Danger.* Early in his career, Pease was a teacher in California and an instructor in English in Vassar in order to supplement his income from writing. He gave up teaching altogether after the publication of his sixth book, *The Ship without a Crew,* to write full time. *For More Information See: Junior Book of Authors,* 2nd edition, Wilson, 1951; *Contemporary Authors,* Volumes 5-8, revised, Gale, 1969; *Twentieth Century Children's Writers,* St. Martin's, 1978. *Obituaries: Elementary English,* September, 1974.

PERRAULT, Charles 1628-1703

PERSONAL: Born January 12, 1628, in Paris, France; died May 16, 1703, in Paris, France; son of Pierre Perrault (a lawyer in Parliament); brother of Claude Perrault (a physician and architect), Nicolas Perrault (a Jansenist and poet), and Pierre Perrault (a translator and critic); children: three sons, one daughter. *Education:* Attended the college at Beauvais.

CAREER: Poet, critic, and writer of fairy tales. Called to the Bar, Paris, France, 1651, but practiced law only briefly; served as secretary to his brother, Claude; was appointed Controller of the Royal Buildings by Colbert, Minister of Finance under Louis XIV. Perrault is best known today for the fairy tales that he wrote in his spare time. Most critics agree that these stories were half-forgotten folk tales that Perrault rewrote in a modern, simple style. *Member:* French Academy (elected, 1671).

WRITINGS—For children: *Histoires; ou, Contes du Temps Passe,* [Paris], 1697 (the original edition was signed by Parrault's son, Pierre D'Armancour, but it is generally agreed that the tales were written by Perrault; also published in French as *Les Contes de Ma Mere L'Oye;* the original edition included the following fairy tales: *The Sleeping Beauty, Little Red Riding Hood, Blue-Beard, Puss in Boots, The Fairies, Cinderella, Riquet of the Tuft, Hop-o'-My-Thumb*), first translation by Robert Samber published in *Histories; or, Tales of Times Past,* J. Pote & R. Montagu, 1729, reprinted (edited by Alison Lurie and Justin G. Schiller; with a preface by Michael P. Hearn), Garland Publishing, 1977 [subsequent translations published under numerous titles, including *Perrault's Popular Tales* (edited by Andrew Lang), Clarendon Press, 1888, reprinted, Arno Press, 1977; *The Tales of Mother Goose* (translated by Charles Welsh; illustrated by D. J. Munro), D. C. Heath, 1901; *Fairy Tales* (illustrated by Charles Robinson), Dutton, 1913; *Old Time Stories* (translated by A. E. Johnson; illustrated by W. Heath Robinson), Constable, 1921, reissued as *Complete Fairy Tales,* Dodd, 1961; *French Fairy Tales* (edited by Louis Untermeyer; illustrated by Gustave Doré), Didier, 1945 (Doré's drawings originally appeared in the French edition published in 1867; his illustrations also appear in *All the French Fairy Tales* and in *More French Fairy Tales,* both published by Didier, 1946, and in A. E. Johnson's translation, *Perrault's Fairy Tales,* Dover, 1969); *The Fairy Tales of Charles Perrault* (foreward by Angela Carter; illustrated with etchings by Martin Ware), Gollancz, 1977].

Fairy tales published separately or as title stories of collections: *The Story of Blue Beard* ("La Barbe Bleue"; illustrated by Joseph E. Southall), Stone & Kimball, 1895; *The Whimsical History of Bluebeard* (translated by Arthur Quiller-Couch; illustrated by Hans Bendix), Limited Editions, 1952; *Bluebeard, and Other Fairy Tales* (translated by Richard Howard; illustrated by Saul Lambert), Macmillan, 1964; *The Story of Little Red Riding Hood* ("Le Petit Chaperin Rouge"; illustrated by Primrose, pseudonym of Primrose McPherson Robertson), Wilcox & Follett, 1946; *Little Red Riding Hood* (retold by Muriel W. Rothberg; illustrated by Pablo Ramirez), World

CHARLES PERRAULT, 1665

Publishing, 1965; *Little Red Riding Hood* (retold by Jane Carruth; illustrated by Elisabeth and Gerry Embleton), Hamlyn, 1973; *The Little Red Riding Hood* (illustrated by William Stobbs), Walck, 1972; *The Sleeping Beauty in the Wood* ("La Belle au Bois Dormant"), Limited Editions, 1949; *The Sleeping Beauty, and Other Tales* (retold by Shirley Goulden; illustrated by Benvenuti), Grosset, 1957; *My Book of the Sleeping Beauty* (illustrated by Maraja), Maxton, 1960; *The Sleeping Beauty* (translated and illustrated by David Walker), Heinemann, 1976, Crowell, 1977; *Sleeping Beauty* (translated by Fabio Coen; illustrated by Graham Percy), Knopf, 1980.

Puss in Boots ("Le Maistre Chat; ou, Le Chat Botté"; translated and illustrated by Marcia Brown; ALA Notable Book), Scribner, 1952; *Puss in Boots* (retold by Kathryn Jackson; illustrated by J. P. Miller), Simon & Schuster, 1952; *Puss in Boots* (retold by Hans Fischer), Harcourt, 1959; *My Book of Puss-in-Boots* (retold by J. Carruth; illustrated by Lupatelli), Follett, 1963; *Puss in Boots, The Sleeping Beauty, [and] Cinderella* (retold by Marianne Moore; illustrated by Eugene Karlin), Macmillan, 1963; *Puss in Boots [and] The Sleeping Beauty* (retold by Kathleen N. Daly; illustrated by Paul Durand), Golden Press, 1964; *Puss in Boots: Perrault's 'Maitre chat!* (retold and illustrated by William Stobbs), McGraw-Hill, 1975; *Puss in Boots* (translated by David Walker; illustrated by Jan Pienkowski), Crowell, 1978; *Puss in Boots* (translated by Fabio Coen; illustrated by G. Benvenuti), Knopf, 1979.

Cinderella; or, The Little Glass Slipper (''Cendrillon; ou, , a Petite Pantoufle de Verre''; translated and illustrated by M. Brown; ALA Notable Book), Scribner, 1954; *Cinderella, and Other Stories* (translated by Marie Ponsot; illustrated by J. L. Huens), Grosset, 1957; *My Book of Cinderella* (illustrated by Benvenuti), Maxton, 1960; *Cinderella* (retold by D. R. Miller; illustrated by P. Ramirez), World Publishing, 1965; *Cinderella* (retold by Janet Fulton), Golden Press, 1970; *Cinderella; or, The Little Glass Slipper* (illustrated by Shirley Hughes), H. Z. Walck, 1971; *Cinderella; or, The Little Glass Slipper* (illustrated by Errol Le Cain), Faber, 1972, Bradbury Press, 1973; *Cinderella* (retold by John Fowles; illustrated by Sheilah Beckett), Little, Brown, 1974; *Cinderella* (translated by David Walker; illustrated by Jan Pienkowski), Crowell, 1978; *Cinderella* (translated by Fabio Coen; illustrated by Serge Dutfoy), Knopf, 1980; *King Carlo of Capri* (''Riquet a la Houppe'' retold by Warren Miller; illustrated by Edward Sorel), Harcourt, 1958; *Tom Thumb* (''Petit Poucet''; retold by D. R. Miller; illustrated by Jose Correas), World Publishing, 1965; *Beauty and the Beast* (translated by Fabio Coen; illustrated by Serge Dutfoy), Knopf, 1980.

Poems: (With brothers Nicholas and Pierre Perrault) *Les Murs de Troie; ou, L'Origine du Burlesque,* [Paris], 1953; *Dialogue de l'Amour et de l'Amitie,* P. Bienfait, 1661; *Saint Paulin,* J. B. Coignard, 1686; *Le Siecle de Louis le Grand,* J. B. Coignard, 1687; *La Chasse,* [Paris], 1692; *Ode au Roy,* J. B. Coignard, 1693; *La Creation du Monde,* J. B. Coignard, 1692, also published as *Adam; ou, La Creation de l'Homme, Sa Chute, et Sa Reparation,* 1697.

Prose: *Paralelle des Anciens et des Modernes,* J. B. Coignard, 1688; *L'Apologie des Femmes,* J. B. Coignard, 1694, translated by Roland Grant as *The Vindication of Wives,* Rodale Press, 1954; *Les Hommes Illustres Qui Ont Paru en France pendant ce Siecle,* A. Dezallier, 1696-1700, translation by J. Ozell published as *Characters Historical and Panegyrical of the Greatest Men That Have Appeared in France during the Last Century,* B. Lintott, 1704-05; *Memoires de Charles Perrault,* Librarie des Bibliophiles (Paris), 1878; *Oeuvres Completes,* 3 volumes (edited by J. J. Pauvert and M. Soriano), [Paris], 1968-69.

Other: *A Concordance to Charles Perrault's Tales* (edited by Jacques Barchilon, E. E. Flinders, Jr., and J. Anne Foreman), Norwood Editions, 1977, reprinted, Folcroft, 1978.

ADAPTATIONS—Movies and filmstrips: ''Little Red Riding Hood'' (motion pictures), Thomas A. Edison, Inc. (eight minutes, silent, black & white), 1917, National Film Board of Canada (six minutes, sound, color), 1968; ''Little Red Riding Hood'' (filmstrips), Brunswick Productions (available in both Spanish and French teaching films), 1967, Cooper Films and Records (color, available with both phonodisc and phonotape, and with a teacher's guide), 1969; ''Puss in Boots'' (motion pictures), Thomas A. Edison, Inc., 1917, Encyclopaedia Britannica Films (15 minutes, sound, black & white, with a teacher's guide), 1958; ''The Story of Puss in Boots'' (filmstrip; color, with a phonodisc and a teacher's guide), Encyclopaedia Britannica Films, 1965, reissued (with a phonotape), 1974; ''Puss in Boots'' (filmstrips), Spoken Arts (color, with a phonodisc, teacher's guide, and reading script), 1968, H. M. Stone Productions (color, available with both phonodisc and phonotape, and with a teacher's guide), 1972, Educational Projections Corp. (color, with a teacher's manual), 1973, Urban Media Materials (color, available with both phonodisc and phonotape, and with a teacher's guide and duplicating masters), 1973.

First page of the original edition of ''Little Red Riding Hood.'' ■ (From *Contes de Perrault,* edited by Gilbert Rouger.)

''Le Petit Poucet'' (filmstrip), Editions Nouvelles, 1948, Gessler Publishing, 1950; ''Cinderella'' (motion pictures), Walt Disney Productions (74 minutes, sound, color), 1949, Miniature Opera Co. (37 minutes, color, sound), 1956, William Gernert, 1958; ''Cinderella; or, The Little Glass Slipper'' (filmstrip; color, available with both phonodisc and phonotape, and with teacher's notes), 1974; ''Sleeping Beauty'' (motion pictures), World Television Corp. (eight minutes, sound, black & white), 1952, Time, Inc. (15 minutes, sound, black & white), 1952, Walter Lantz Productions, 1958, Walt Disney Productions, 1958; ''The Glass Slipper'' (motion picture), adaptation of *Cinderella,* starring Leslie Caron and Michael Wilding, Metro-Goldwyn-Mayer, 1955; ''The Slipper and the Rose'' (motion picture), adaptation of *Cinderella,* starring Richard Chamberlain, Universal Pictures. ''Little Tom Thumb'' (motion picture), Importadora, 1958; ''The Fairies'' (filmstrip; color, with a phonodisc and a teaching guide, script, and work sheet), 1967.

SIDELIGHTS: **January 12, 1628.** ''I was born . . . one of twins (Francois was born several hours before me and died only six months later). I was called Charles by my brother,

(From "Old Time Stories," by Charles Perrault. Illustrated by W. Heath Robinson.)

"There," said the Fairy Godmother. "Now you can go to the Ball. Doesn't that make you happy?" ■ (From *Cinderella,* adapted by John Fowles. Illustrated by Sheilah Beckett.)

Receiver General of Finances, who acted as godfather together with my cousin Francoi Pepin as my godmother." [Charles Perrault, translation of *Memoires de Charles Perrault*, Librairie des Bibliophiles, 1878.[1]]

Perrault was the youngest son of an eminent Parisian lawyer. His parents took an active part in his and his brothers' early educations.

1637. Sent to school, where he was among the brightest in his class. "My mother took the trouble to teach me to read, after which I was sent to 'college' [private secondary school] in Beauvais at the age of eight and a half. I did all of my studies there, as (did) my brothers. My father took pains to make me repeat my lessons every evening after supper and made me tell him, in Latin, the substance of these lessons. This is a very good way to make students understand the mind of authors whose works they are memorizing.

"I was always among the top of my classes, outside of the elementary grades, because I was started at the sixth level when I didn't even know how to read well! I preferred poetry to prose and made up verses so well that my teachers often asked who had composed them for me. I noted that those of my companions who did well [in poetry] . . . continued to do so, so it is true that this talent is a natural one and is revealed from childhood on.

"I did particularly well in philosophy; often I needed only to listen to what my teacher said with no further need to study in order to know it. I got so much pleasure discussing in class that I loved school days as much as holidays. The ease which I had in discussion made me speak to my teacher with an extraordinary liberty which no other student dared to take.

"Since I was the youngest and one of the smartest in class, he [the tutor] wanted me to take oral exams for promotion to the next level at the end of two years; but my mother and father did not consent to this, due to the expense one incurs for this ceremony. The tutor was so chagrined at this, that he bade me be silent when I wanted to debate those preparing for this exam. I had the audacity to tell him that my arguments were better . . . because they were new . . . and their arguments were old and second-hand. I added that I would not apologize for speaking thus. . . . A second time he ordered me to be quiet, upon which I told him as I got up, that . . . since he would no longer let me say my lessons (for in those days philosophy students said their lessons *every* day like the other students and it is an error to have changed this); that no one argued against me any more; and that I was forbidden to argue against the others; that I was merely allowed to come to class. So saying, I bowed to him and all the students and exited from the classroom."[1]

1643. Left school and studied independently with a friend. "One of my friends named Beaurain, who was very fond of me, got up and followed me, he had sort of taken my side because all the class had let loose their feelings against him. We went to the Luxembourg gardens. After reflecting on the step we had just taken, we resolved *not* to return to class because we would gain nothing—except drill those who were allowed to answer. We started to study together.

"This 'folly' resulted in success, for had we completed our studies as usual . . . we would have wasted our time. We carried out our plan and for three or four years after that, M. Beaurain *came* almost *every day, twice a day,* to the house, mornings from 8:00-11:00 and afternoons from 3:00-5:00. If I learned something, I owe it particularly to those three or four

years of study. We read almost all the *Bible* and almost all Tertullien, *The History of France* by LaSerre and Devila; we translated the treatise by Tertullien about women's apparel; we read Virgil, Horace, Tacitus and the majority of the other classic authors, of whom we made resumes or extracts that I still have.

"The way we made these extracts was very useful to us. One of us read a chapter or certain number of lines and after reading it, dictated a summary of it in French, which we would write down, inserting the best lines in their original language. After one had read and dictated his, the other one did the same, which accustomed us to translate and summarize at the same time.

"In the summer, when 5:00 o'clock had struck, we used to go walking in the Luxembourg. Since M. Beaurain was more studious than I, he read further upon returning home. While we walked, he would tell me what he had read."[1]

Made his first literary attempts. Together with his friend, Beaurain, and his older brother Claude (a medical student), Perrault adapted the sixth book of the *Aeneid* into comic verse, which was then a popular literary fad. Later, he and his brothers collaborated on *Les Murs de Troie* ("The Walls of Troy"). "One day while [Beaurain and I] were working . . . , we started to laugh so loudly at the nonsense we were writing that my brother, the doctor, who had his study next to mine, came to find out what we were laughing about, started to work with us, and helped us very much. . . . He even worked more at it alone in his leisure time than all of us together. Thus the translation of the sixth book of the *Aeneid* was completed and, having put it together as well as I could, he drew for it two very beautiful sketches in China ink. This manuscript is among the books on the shelf where only those [written] by the family are kept. This work gave us the chance to work on *Walls of Troy,* of which the first book was done together and published; the second is only in manuscript form and was written by my brother, the doctor, alone."[1]

July 27, 1651. Admitted to the bar. "In the month of July . . . I went with two others, to take my bar exam at Orléans with M. Varet . . . and with M. Monjat. . . . It was not difficult at that time to receive one's degree, either in civil or canon law. The very evening that we arrived, we got the idea of being received right then. Having knocked at the door of the school at 10:00 p.m.; a servant, who came to the window to talk with us and, having ascertained what we wanted, asked us if our money was ready at hand. Upon being assured that we had it with us, he let us in and went to awaken the professors, who arrived all three with their night caps on under the square (pasteboard) hats. Looking at these three professors by the feeble light of the candle whose glow was diffused into the thick darkness of the vaulted ceilings, I could imagine ourselves before Minos, Aeacus and Rhadamante [judges in the ancient nether world] who had come to question the souls asking entrance before them. One of us was asked a question (which I now forget) and answered learnedly and at length with memorized Latin phrases. In reply to another question, he again answered with nothing of real substance. Nevertheless, these three professors later told us that during the last two years, they had examined no one as knowledgeable as we three were. I think that the sound of our money which was being counted behind us as we were being questioned, made our answers sound good also.

"The next day, having visited the church of St. Croix, the statue of Joan of Arc and other local points of interest, we set

For on the way he dropped the little white stones which he carried in his pocket all along the path. ■ (From "Little Tom Thumb" in *Perrault's Fairy Tales* by Charles Perrault. Illustrated by Gustave Doré.)

They broke more than twelve laces in pulling in their corsets to make their waists look smaller . . . . ▪ (From *Cinderella; or, The Little Glass Slipper* by Charles Perrault. Translated, adapted, and illustrated by Errol Le Cain.)

off again for Paris. On the 27th of that same month, all three of us were admitted to the bar.''[1]

However, Perrault soon became disillusioned with the practice of law, especially viewing the indifference to it of his brother and others of his friends. His brother abandoned law to purchase a post as Receiver General of Finances for the city of Paris and suggested that Perrault join him as his clerk. Perrault accepted and worked at this post for ten years, leaving it only to go to work for Colbert. ''I pleaded two cases with success not so much because I won both, (for the winning or losing of a case rarely comes from the worth of the lawyer) but because those who heard me plead my case testified they were much impressed, because greeting the judges and lawyers after the trial, they heaped praises upon me. Especially impressed was M. Daubray, civil lieutenant, who begged me to attach myself to the Châtelet [an important court in Paris] and promised me all the support that a lawyer could wish for.

''I would have done better perhaps to follow his advice, but my brothers were soured so on the profession of lawyer, that I began to feel the same way. My oldest brother, a very able lawyer with more spirit and eloquence than most of his peers, was doing nothing with his profession. I felt it would be the same with me and there is some proof that I was not mistaken.''[1]

1654-1664. Served as secretary to his brother, Claude. For ten years Perrault lived and worked with his older brother. In his spare time he began writing. ''My brother, having bought the post as Receiver General of Finances for the city of Paris, suggested . . . that I live with him and become his clerk. I accepted the job, seeing it as more pleasurable than wearing the garments of a lawyer. I was with him ten years, from the beginning of 1654 and left to go to work for M. Colbert in 1664. Since the job as collector did not take much of my time— I went back to my studies. The principal good luck was that my brother bought a very marvelous library. I had pleasure finding myself amid so many good books.

''I also began again to write poetry, the *Portrait of Iris,* being almost the first work I composed, followed by *Dialogue Between Love and Friendship,* which had several printings and was even translated into Italian.''[1]

1657. Mother died. Eldest brother inherited the family home at Viry. Perrault supervised the additions and other buildings to the estate. The skills which he acquired led, in part, to his position as supervisor of the Royal Buildings under the great minister, Colbert, who was Minister of Finance under King Louis XIV. ''My mother having died in 1657, my eldest brother was left the house at Viry. He had built there a body of buildings and since I had plenty of leisure, (my brother having employed another clerk as collector) I supervised the building. It is true that my brothers had a great hand in its design, but I supervised the workmen who had never built anything more complicated than cloister walls. I also made a rocky grotto there which was the finest ornament of this country home. When the workers showed off this grotto to neighbors, the latter were astonished at the skill they had shown.

"I report here the part I played in the building of the estate at Viry because the account of it reached the ears of M. Colbert and led to his thinking of me for the post of Superintendent of the Royal Buildings. . . ."[1]

February 3, 1663. Appointed by Colbert to an elite, small, advisory council that supervised the making of monuments, medals, and other works glorifying King Louis XIV. Soon the sketching of medals and creations of mottos and coats of arms were added to the work of the council, which was the seed of the future French Academy. Perrault became secretary of the "little council" and was taken into Colbert's confidence. Colbert shared many private and state secrets of the King with Perrault. "At that time the Swiss had just arrived to renew their alliance with France. It was necessary to make a medal on this subject, and our new-born Académie set itself to this work. M. l'abbé of Bourseis did the greatest part, for the verse engraved upon it was entirely his work.

"A few days later, M. Colbert asked for a standard for M. the Dauphin (future king) who was then only three or four years old. I had the honor of working up the one selected. . . . The body of it is a thunderbolt which emerges from the high cloud with these words: 'et ipso terret in ortu.' It was put on the standards of the Dauphin's regiment and on the helmets of his guards."[1]

When no special piece of work was commanded, the group edited poetic or prose works which glorified the king. Each member also worked independently on his own works praising royalty's accomplishments.

Later, Colbert decided to create a much larger *Académie* "for the advancement and perfection of all sciences," and had brought to him the names of all men in France or elsewhere who excelled in any field of knowledge. Among the names presented was Perrault's brother, Claude, who was reluctant

They ate with an appetite it did their parents good to see. ■ (From "Little Tom Thumb," in *Perrault's Fairy Tales* by Charles Perrault. Illustrated by Gustave Doré.)

(From the movie "The Slipper and the Rose: The Story of Cinderella," starring Richard Chamberlain. Produced by Universal Studios, 1976.)

(From the movie "The Glass Slipper," starring Michael Wilding and Leslie Caron, based on the fairy tale *Cinderella*. Copyright 1955 by Loew's, Inc.)

(From the animated film "Cinderella." Produced by Walt Disney Productions, 1949.)

(From the animated film "Sleeping Beauty." Copyright © 1958 by Walt Disney Productions.)

PERRAULT, 1696

to accept such a prestigious position. ''This modesty was sincere, although in him alone there were the talents of ten men. The family joined me and spent several days urging him but had difficulty in making up his mind.''[1]

January 1, 1664. When Colbert was appointed Superintendent of the Royal Buildings, Perrault was appointed his chief clerk. His brother's design for the Louvre was chosen at his suggestion: ''Monsieur Colbert being about to procure Designs for the fore front of the Louvre by the most celebrated architects of France and Italy, and Cavalier Bernino [the great Italian architect] being sent for to Paris, to the intent that this great man might himself execute his design; [my brother's] was preferred before all the others, and afterwards executed in the manner we see it. And it may be said,

'That in the single Front of the Louvre, there
'is as much beauty as Architecture, as in any of
'the Edifices of the Ancients.'

''When the draft of this Front was presented, it pleas'd extremely: That Area, those majestic Portico's, the Pillars whereof bear Architraves of 12 foot long, and square roofs of like breadth, surpriz'd the Eyes of those that are most accustom'd to fine things; but was believ'd that the execution of it was impossible, and that this design was more proper for picture, (because as yet the like had been seen only upon Cloth) than to serve as a Model for the frontispiece of a real Palace. Yet was it entirely executed, nor has there fail'd a single stone of that large roof, all flat and hung in the air. It was upon his

designs the Observatory was built; a work not only singular for its structure, whereof the plain and majestic Solidity hath no equal, but which may (of itself, without the help of any mathematical instrument) serve, by the form that is given in, for most part of astronomical observations. It is also upon his designs, that the great Model of the Triumphal Arch has been rais'd, and that a considerable part of this fame [sic] Arch is built after this pattern. So that he has had the advantage of having given the form of three [of] the finest pieces of architecture that ever was in the world.'' [Charles Perrault, *Characters Historical and Panegyrical of the Greatest Men That Have Appeared in France During the Last Century,* translated by S. Ozell, Bernard Lintott (London), 1704.[2]]

1671. Formally admitted to the French Academy. From time to time Perrault introduced many needful reforms in its management and customs.

1672. Made chancellor of the French Academy.

May 1, 1672. Married nineteen-year-old Marie Guichon. Perrault was forty-four. When Perrault decided to marry, he sought the approval of Colbert who asked several questions about the woman's dowry and background. ''It is too little,' he said to me, 'you can believe I am thinking of you. You see what I did for M. du Mets; certainly I will not do less for you. I will find you a girl, among the business families, who will bring you a much more worthwhile dowry. But,' he continued, 'is this a love match?'

''I replied, 'I saw the girl only once since she came out of the convent where she was put at the age of four; but I have known

Puss was allowed to swing on his trunk. ■ (From *Puss in Boots* by Hans Fischer, adapted from Charles Perrault. Illustrated by Hans Fischer.)

the mother and father for more than ten years. I know them and they know me, and I am assured that I will get along very well with them. That, sir, is the main reason I am getting into this. I would be very displeased to meet a father-in-law who would complain unceasingly that I was doing nothing, that would want that I plead with you all the time to think about me. I don't want at all to come to that. You give me a salary greater than I merit, but I do not profit from it. All the purchases that are made, I take no rebates from. There is more; the certificates you give for lodging and for various other privileges, I take nothing from that, but I and my clerk do our work painstakingly out of a respect I often do not show well. As for me, I am quite content that this go on, but there are some fathers-in-law that would not be at all pleased.'

"M. Colbert said to me, 'I believe you are right. Go about your business and be assured that I will take care of you.'

"I was very happy to have found the occasion to let this minister know clearly the way in which I served him and that I trusted in him completely to repay me for my work."[1]

When the gardens of the Tuilleries were completed and put into their present condition, Colbert was of the opinion they should be kept that way and barred to the public. Walking through them with Colbert, Perrault said: "You would not believe, Sir, the respect that everyone down to the smallest bourgeois has for this garden. Not only do the women and children warn each other never to pick a single flower and never to touch them; they walk here like thoughtful people. The gardeners, Sir, can bear witness to that. It would be distressful to the people not to be able to walk here, especially

First they tried it on princesses, then on duchesses and all the ladies of the court, but it was no use. ■ (From *Cinderella; or, The Little Glass Slipper,* a free translation from the French of Charles Perrault. Illustrated by Marcia Brown.)

"Beauty," proceeded riquet-with-the-tuft-of-hair, **"is so great a gift that it should be valued above all others. There is nothing, it seems to me, that can greatly afflict those who possess it."** ■ (From *The Fairy Tales of Charles Perrault,* translated by Norman Denny. Illustrated by Philippe Jullian.)

since they can no longer enter the Luxembourg gardens nor the Guise Palace."[1]

In response to Colbert's remark that only loafers came there, Perrault said: "People recovering from illnesses come here to enjoy the fresh air; they come, some do, to talk business; about marriage and everything that can be discussed more conveniently in a garden than in a church, where, one may sometime in the future have to meet."[1]

Colbert smiled at this and speaking to the assembled gardeners, and being reassured by them also, he decided not to close the gates to the public. Perrault was pleased he had influenced that decision, although the court would have preferred a restricted garden.

(From "Riquet with the Tuft," in *Fairy Tales* by Charles Perrault. Illustrated by Charles Robinson.)

May 25, 1675. First son, Charles Samuel, was baptized.

October 20, 1676. Second son baptized.

March 21, 1678. Third son, Peter, baptized.

October, 1678. Wife died. At fifty, Perrault was a widower with four young children to raise and educate. (One, a daughter, whose first name is not known.)

1681. Named director of the French Academy.

1682. Following a disagreement with Colbert, Perrault prepared to give up his direction of the Royal Buildings "without storm and strife."

1683. Upon the death of Colbert, Perrault was reimbursed for his post as head of the Royal Buildings program. Lost his position in the "little academy." Decided to devote himself to the education of his children and his writing. Settled in the Saint-Jacques district of Paris, which was close to schools. "Finding myself free, I thought that having worked steadily for twenty years and being over fifty years of age now, I could relax with decorum and devote myself to the education of my children.

"With this in mind, I went to live in the St. Jacques district, which being near to the schools, gave me the great facility to send my children there, having always thought that it was best for children to come home to sleep in their father's house when it was possible rather than sending them to board in the school where you are not too sure of the behavior. I gave them a tutor and I myself took great care to watch over their studies."[1]

1687. Gained prominence in the field of literature with his poem "Le Siècle of Louis XIV," which he read before the Academy, and in which he praised the superiority of modern letters. His statements aroused the anger of the classicists, especially Racine and Boileau. Between Boileau and Perrault arose the great literary quarrel concerning the merits of the ancients and the moderns, which lasted over a dozen years and did much to bring Perrault's name into prominence.

1697. *Les Contes de Ma Mère L'Oye* ("Tales of my mother, the goose") were published. The collection consisted of eighteen fairy tales, including: "Cinderella," "Sleeping Beauty," "Bluebeard," "Little Red Riding Hood," and "Puss in Boots." Besides borrowing from old French tales, Perrault, who knew Italian, borrowed ideas from Italian writers.

The book's dedication was signed 'Pierre D'Armancour,' who was Perrault's young son, and implied that he was the author of the tales. Scholars are divided over the authorship of the tales; one group believes that Pierre did write the tales, others claim the elder Perrault as the author, while a third group maintains that the two collaborated on the book. Nevertheless, Perrault was convinced that the tales were a genuine form of literature. ". . .The fables of old . . . furnish the most beautiful subjects and give more pleasure than more regularly carried out intrigues. These sorts of tales have the gift of pleasing all sorts of souls, pleasing great minds as well as lesser folk, the old as well as young folk; these idle fancies well presented amuse and lull reason, although contrary to this same reason, and can charm reason better than all imaginable probability." [Charles Perrault, *Contes,* with introduction by Gilbert Rouger, Editions Garnier Frères, 1967.[3]]

. . . **The King could not pull the shirt on, for his beautiful addlepated daughter had fitted the sleeve directly to the neckband, and securely sewed the two together!** ■ (From "Ricky with a Tuft," in *Famous Fairy Tales* by Charles Perrault. Illustrated by Charles Mozley.)

May 16, 1703. Died at his home in Paris at the age of seventy-five. Considered an upright, honest man even by his adversaries, Perrault was described by one of his contemporaries: "He possessed all the qualities which form the good and honest man: he was full of piety, probity and virtue; he was refined, modest, obliging, faithful to all the duties demanded by natural and acquired ties; and, in an important post under one of the greatest ministers which France has ever had and who honored him with his confidence, he never used his favor for his private fortune but always employed it for his friends." [Oscar Fay Adams, *Dear Old Story-Tellers,* Lothrop, Lee & Shepard, 1889.[4]]

FOR MORE INFORMATION SEE: Charles Perrault, *Memoires de Charles Perrault,* Librarie des Bibliophiles, 1878; *Perrault's Popular Tales,* edited by Andrew Lang, Clarendon Press, Oxford, 1888; Oscar Fay Adams, *Dear Old Story-Tellers,* Lothrop, Lee & Shepard, 1889; H. V. Velten, "The Influence of Charles Perrault's Contes de ma Mere L'Oye on German Folklore," *Germanic Review,* 1930; Elizabeth R. Montgomery, *Story Behind Great Stories,* McBride, 1947; Stanley J. Kunitz and Vineta Colby, editors, *European Authors, 1000-1900,* H. W. Wilson, 1967; Brian Doyle, editor, *Who's Who of Children's Literature,* Schocken Books, 1968; M. H. Arbuthnot, "Puss, the Perraults, and a Lost Manuscript," *Elementary English,* October, 1969; *Horn Book,* June, 1979.

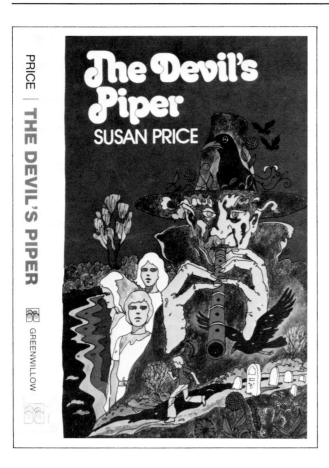

The tune finished on a long whistle—the whistle of a man, maybe, when he calls a dog on the hillside. It left the four townies staring breathlessly at grass and hawthorn that was greener than it had been a few minutes before. ■ (From *The Devil's Piper* by Susan Price. Jacket designed by Lynn Sweat.)

PRICE, Susan   1955-

PERSONAL: Born July 8, 1955, in Brades Row, Round's Green, Worcestershire, England; daughter of Alan (an electrical motor technician) and Jessie (Hanley) Price. *Education:* Educated in Tividale, England. *Home:* 77 Barncroft Rd., Tividale, Warley, Worcestershire, England. *Agent:* Osyth Leeston, A. M. Heath & Co., 40-42 William IV St., London WC2N 4DD, England.

CAREER: Writer of children's books. Supermarket assistant at Co-operative Society Grocery, 1973-75. *Awards, honors:* Other Award from Children's Rights Workshop, 1975, for *Twopence a Tub.*

WRITINGS—All for children: *The Devil's Piper,* Faber, 1973, Greenwillow Books, 1976; *Twopence a Tub,* Faber, 1975, Merrimack, 1978; *Sticks and Stones,* Faber, 1976, Merrimack, 1978; *Home From Home,* Faber, 1977, Merrimack, 1978. Also author of *Christopher Uptake* and *The Carpenter and Other Stories.*

WORK IN PROGRESS: An account of a young teacher during his probationary year.

SIDELIGHTS: "I was born in an industrial town and have never lived anywhere else. My family are working-class and have, for at least three generations, possessed intelligence and talent, but no property and no savings. If it had not been for the election of the Labour Party (Socialist) in 1948, I doubt if I would ever have received the education necessary to be an author; and I am aware that the education I was given was second-rate.

"I write for working-class kids. I think their parents have been conned all their lives and they will be conned unless they start thinking for themselves. Socialism and atheism are two tools towards that; cynicism a better one."

FOR MORE INFORMATION SEE: Publisher's Weekly, February 23, 1976; *Horn Book,* June, 1976.

RADLEY, Gail   1951-

PERSONAL: Born May 21, 1951, in Boston, Mass.; daughter of Earl Adrian (a government employee) and Bernice (a social worker; maiden name, Howell) Radley; married Joseph Killeen (director of a community corrections center), July 23, 1975; children: Anthony, Jana. *Education:* Attended Boston University, 1970-72, Kent State University, 1973, and College of Notre Dame of Maryland, 1978—. *Politics:* "Not aligned." *Religion:* Baha'i. *Home and office:* 4905 Roller Rd., Millers, Md. 21107.

CAREER: Arlington Hospital, Arlington, Va., electrocardiograph technician, 1974-75; Great Oaks Center, Silver Springs, Md., health assistant, 1975; Springfield Hospital Center, Sykesville, Md., rehabilitation therapy associate, 1976; writer, 1976—.

WRITINGS: The Night Stella Hid the Stars (juvenile), Crown, 1979; *Nothing Stays the Same Forever,* Crown, 1981; *Zahra's Journey,* Baha'i, 1981; *The Eagle's Wings,* Baha'i, 1981.

WORK IN PROGRESS—For children: *Megan's Darkest Secret;* a third novel; "subjects explored in these books include the remarriage of a parent, the imprisonment of a parent, and the romantic involvement between a teacher and a student."

SIDELIGHTS: "Two constants in my life have been writing and the Baha'i Faith. Since age eight or nine I have been interested in writing as a profession. At age fifteen I was introduced to and became a member of the Baha'i Faith.

"Rather than go directly to college after high school, I took a year to travel, work different jobs and experience living on my own. After two years of college, I drifted about until at age twenty-four, I married and also gained a six year old son. Two years later a daughter was born and we moved to rural Maryland.

"*The Writings of My Faith* have provided me with themes of hope and promise and have strengthened a sense of order and purpose in the world. I am currently working on novels for older children. I hope to provide readers with a sense of kinship with others, a belief that feelings can be viewed honestly and solutions found."

FOR MORE INFORMATION SEE: Booklist, December 15, 1978; *Sykesville Herald Record,* December 27, 1978, May 30, 1979.

GAIL RADLEY

RITTS, Paul 1920(?)-1980

OBITUARY NOTICE: Born about 1920; died of a heart attack, October 18, 1980, in Monroe, Mich. Producer, director, performer, and writer. Ritts was best known as a creator of children's television shows. He produced "The Big Top," a circus program, and with his wife, Mary, he created the Ritts Puppets for CBS-TV's "In the Park." The puppets achieved celebrity status by appearing regularly in two children's series and through appearances on the television variety shows of Ed Sullivan, Merv Griffin, Mike Douglas, and the "Tonight" shows. Ritts wrote scripts for ABC-TV's "Kid Power" and NBC-TV's "Muggsy" series and he wrote *The TV Jeebies*, a humorous book about television. His plays include, "The Quartet," "Oregon Bound," and "A Piece of Cake." *Obituaries: New York Times,* November 20, 1980; *Contemporary Authors,* Volume 102, Gale, 1981.

Monday's child is fair of face,
Tuesday's child is full of grace,
Wednesday's child is full of woe,
Thursday's child has far to go,
Friday's child is loving and giving,
Saturday's child has to work for its living,
But a child that's born on the Sabbath day
Is fair and wise and good and gay.

—Nursery rhyme

SALZMANN, Siegmund 1869-1945
(Martin Finder, Felix Salten)

PERSONAL: Born September 6, 1869, in Budapest, Hungary; died October 8, 1945, in Zurich, Switzerland; son of Philipp and Marie (Singer) Salzmann; married Ottilie Metzl (an actress), April 13, 1902. *Education:* Attended schools in Vienna, Austria, mostly self-taught. *Religion:* Jewish. *Home:* Wilfriedstrass 4, Zurich, Switzerland.

CAREER: Novelist, journalist, and theatre critic. Worked for a time at his cousin's insurance office; began writing at the age of seventeen; embarked on a journalism career around 1887; developed a long association with the Viennese newspaper, *Neue Freie Presse;* traveled extensively through Europe, the United States, and Egypt. *Member:* Vienna P.E.N. Club (honorary president until 1933).

WRITINGS—Fiction; under pseudonym Felix Salten: *Der Hund von Florenz,* Herz-verlag (Wien-Leipzig), 1923, translation by Huntley Paterson published as *The Hound of Florence: A Novel* (illustrated by Kurt Wiese), Simon & Schuster, 1930; *Bambi: Eine Lebensgeschichte aus dem Walde,* P. Zsolnay, 1926, translation by Whittaker Chambers published as *Bambi: A Life in the Woods* (foreword by John Galsworthy; illustrated by Kurt Wiese), Simon & Schuster, 1928, new edition, illustrated by Barbara Cooney, 1970 [another edition illustrated by Girard Goodenow, Junior Deluxe Editions, 1956; adaptations include *Walt Disney's Bambi,* edited by Idella Purnell, Heath, 1944; *Walt Disney's Bambi,* adapted by Bob Grant

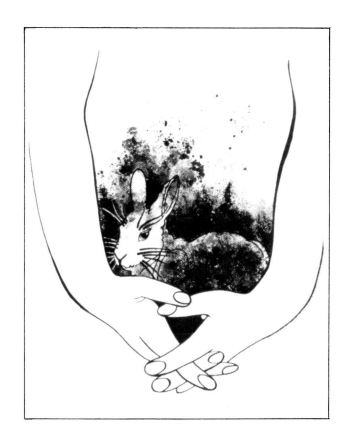

"Isn't he nice?" they cried. And the little girl declared, "I'm going to take him home." ■ (From *Fifteen Rabbits* by Felix Salten. Illustrated by John Freas.)

(From the movie "Perri." Copyright © 1957 by Walt Disney Productions.)

(From the movie "Florian," starring Robert Young and Helen Gilbert, based on the story "Florian, the Emperor's Stallion." Copyright 1940 by Loew's, Inc.)

(From the movie "The Shaggy D. A.," based on the story "Der Hund von Florenz." Copyright ©
1976 by Walt Disney Productions.)

(From the movie "The Shaggy Dog," starring Fred MacMurray, based on the story "Der Hund
von Florenz." Copyright © 1959 by Walt Disney Productions.)

(From the animated film "Bambi." Copyright 1942 by Walt Disney Productions.)

(From the animated film "Bambi." Copyright 1942 by Walt Disney Productions.)

from the Disney motion picture, Simon & Schuster, 1948; *Bambi's Fragrant Forest,* adapted by Disney Productions, Golden Press, 1975].

Simson: Das Schicksal eines Erwählten, P. Zsolnay, 1928, translation by W. Chambers published as *Sampson and Delilah: A Novel,* Simon & Schuster, 1931; *Fünfzehn Hasen: Schicksale im Wald und Feld,* P. Zsolnay, 1929, translation by W. Chambers published as *Fifteen Rabbits,* Simon & Schuster, 1930, reissued, Delacorte, 1976; *Gute Gesellschaft: Erlebnisse mit Tieren,* P. Zsolnay, 1930, translation by Paul R. Milton published as *Good Comrades* (illustrated by Bob Kuhn), Bobbs-Merrill, 1942; *Freunde aus Aller Welt: Roman eines Zoologischen Gartens,* P. Zsolnay, 1931, translation by W. Chambers published as *The City Jungle* (illustrated by K. Wiese), Simon & Schuster, 1932.

Florian: Das Pferd des Kaisers, P. Zsolnay, 1933, translation by Erich Posselt and Michael Kraike published as *Florian: The Emperor's Stallion,* Bobbs-Merrill, 1934, reissued as *Florian:*

The Lippizzaner, British Book Center, 1972; *Die Jugend des Eichörnchens Perri* (illustrated by Ludwig Heinrich Jungnickel), P. Zsolnay, 1938, translation by Barrows Mussey published as *Perri: The Youth of a Squirrel* (illustrated by L. H. Jungnickel), Bobbs-Merrill, 1938 [adaptations include *Walt Disney's Perri and Her Friends,* edited by Annie North Bedford (pseudonym of Jane Watson), Simon & Schuster, 1956; *Walt Disney's Perri* (illustrated by Dick Kelsey), edited by Emily Broun, Simon & Schuster, 1957].

Bambis Kinder: Eine Familie im Walde, 1939, translation by Barthold Fles published as *Bambi's Children: The Story of a Forest Family* (illustrated by Erna Pinner; edited by R. Sugden Tilley), Bobbs-Merrill, 1939, new edition, illustrated by William Bartlett, Grossett, 1969 [another edition illustrated by Phoebe Erickson (edited by Allen Chaffee), Random House, 1950]; *Renni der Retter: Das Leben eines Kriegshundes,* A. Mueller, 1941, translation by Kenneth C. Kaufman published as *Renni the Rescuer: A Dog of the Battlefield* (illustrated by Diana Thorne), Bobbs-Merrill, 1940; *A Forest World* (trans-

Felix Salten, with his children.

. . . **Bambi soon stopped being pleased with the snow, for it grew harder and harder to find food. He had to paw the snow away with endless labor before he could find one withered little blade of grass. The snow crust cut his legs and he was afraid of cutting his feet. ▪** (From _Bambi_ by Felix Salten. Illustrated by Kurt Wiese.)

lated from the German by P. R. Milton and Sanford J. Greenburger; illustrated by B. Kuhn), Bobbs-Merrill, 1942.

Djibi: Das Kaetzchen (illustrated by Walter Linsenmaier), A. Mueller, 1945, translation by Raya Levin published as _Jibby the Cat_ (illustrated by W. Linsenmaier), Pilot Press, 1946; (editor) _Fairy Tales from Near and Far_ (translated from the German by Clara Stillman; illustrated by Elice Johnson), Philosophical Library, 1945; _Kleine Welt_ (illustrated by Otto Betschmann), A. Mueller, 1944, translation published as _A Little World Apart,_ Pilot Press, 1947; (editor) _Felix Salten's Favorite Animal Stories_ (illustrated by Fritz Eichenberg), Messner, 1948.

Also author of the nonfiction works _Neue Menschen auf alter Erde_ ("New Men on the Old Earth") and _Fünf Minuten Amerika_ ("Five Minutes of America"); author of numerous plays produced in Europe. Contributor to the magazine _The Beautiful Blue Danube_ and other literary journals under the pseudonym Martin Finder.

ADAPTATIONS—Movies and filmstrips: "Florian" (motion picture), starring Robert Young and Charles Coburn, Metro-Goldwyn-Mayer, 1940; "Bambi" (motion picture), Walt Disney Productions, 1942; "Bambi Falls in Love" (motion picture; excerpts from the 1942 Disney movie), Walt Disney Home Movies, 1968; "Bambi" (filmstrips), Encyclopaedia Britannica Films, 1957, Eye Gate House (with teacher's guide), 1958, Walt Disney Productions (both captioned and sound versions, each with teacher's guide), 1970, Universal Education and Visual Arts, 1971.

"Perri" (motion picture), Walt Disney Productions, 1957; "Perri" (filmstrips; all produced by Encyclopaedia Britannica Films, 1957), "Perri: A Time of Adventure," "Perri: A Time of Danger," "Perri: A Time of Hunting," "Perri: A Time of Learning," "Perri: A Time of Preparing," "Perri: A Time of

Together"; "The Shaggy Dog" (motion picture), adaptation of _The Hound of Florence,_ starring Fred MacMurray and Tommy Kirk, Walt Disney Productions, 1959.

Recordings: "Bambi," adapted by Marianne Mantell, read by Glynis Johns, Caedmon Records, 1973.

SIDELIGHTS: Salzmann's childhood was a poor one and, according to his own account, he was largely self-taught. He was born in Budapest on September 6, 1869, but was moved to Vienna when he was only three weeks old. Most of his life was spent in that city.

At the age of seventeen he began to write stories, and was accepted as a journalist when several established writers, who recognized his talent, helped him to gain a place in literary magazines. Under the pseudonym Felix Salten, he wrote his most memorable and beloved story, _Bambi,_ which was translated and published in English in 1928. The original English version included a foreword by John Galsworthy who admitted that he did not like the method "which places human words in the mouths of dumb creatures," although he praised the author because "behind the conversation, one feels the real sensations of the creatures who speak."

Prior to the Nazi invasion of Austria, Salzmann had established a good literary reputation and was honorary president of the Vienna P.E.N. Club. Drawing upon the events of his childhood when he was poor and miserable, he wrote slowly and carefully with a yellow pencil. He kept pencils all over his house because he had a fear of having an idea and not having anything to jot it down with. He had a love for all animals and wrote frequently about horses, deer, and dogs.

Salzmann was forced from his homeland in 1939 and lived the remainder of his life in exile in Switzerland. He wrote the book for the popular movie version of _Bambi_ while in exile. He died after a long illness in Zurich on October 8, 1945. John Chamberlain said of him, "he has the gift of a tender, lucid style. His observation is next door to marvelous, and he invests the fruits of this observation with pure poetry."

FOR MORE INFORMATION SEE: Horatio Smith, editor, _Columbia Dictionary of Modern European Literature,_ Columbia University Press, 1947; (for children) Elizabeth Rider Montgomery, _Story behind Modern Books,_ Dodd, 1949; Frank N. Magill, editor, _Cyclopedia of World Authors,_ Harper, 1958. _Obituary: Publishers Weekly,_ October 20, 1945.

So ended the second day of maneuvers. ▪ (From _Renni the Rescuer_ by Felix Salten. Illustrated by Diana Thorne.)

STEVENSON, Burton E(gbert)   1872-1962

PERSONAL: Born November 9, 1872, in Chillicothe, Ohio; died May 13, 1962 in Chillicothe, Ohio; married Elizabeth Shepard Butler, June 12, 1895 (died, 1960). *Education:* Attended Princeton University, 1890-93.

CAREER: Correspondent for the United Press and *New York Tribune,* circa 1891-93; *Chillicothe Leader,* Chillicothe, Ohio, reporter, 1893-94; *Chillicothe Daily News,* Chillicothe, city editor, 1894-98; *Daily Advertiser,* Chillicothe, city editor, 1898-99; Chillicothe Public Library, Chillicothe, librarian, 1899-1957. Founder of American Library in Paris, France, 1918, director, 1918-20 and 1925-30. *Wartime service:* European director of American Library Association's Library War Service, 1918-25. *Member:* National Institute of Arts and Letters, Century Club (New York), Union Interalliee Club (Paris). *Awards, honors:* Ohioana grand medalist, Martha Kinney Cooper Ohioana Library Association, 1949; Litt.D., Marietta College, 1955.

WRITINGS—Juveniles: Tommy Remington's Battle, Century, 1902; *The Young Section-Hand,* L. C. Page, 1905; (compiler, with wife, Elizabeth Shepard Stevenson) *Days and Deeds: Book of Verse for Children's Reading and Speaking,* Baker & Taylor, 1906; (compiler, with E. S. Stevenson) *Days and Deeds: Prose for Children's Reading and Speaking,* Baker & Taylor, 1907; *The Young Train Dispatcher,* L. C. Page, 1907; *A Child's Guide to Biography: American Men of Action,* Baker & Taylor, 1909, published as *A Guide to Biography for Young Readers: American Men of Action,* 1910; *The Young Train Master,* L. C. Page, 1909; *A Guide to Biography for Young Readers: American Men of Mind,* Baker & Taylor, 1910; (compiler) *The Home Book of Verse for Young Folks,* Holt, 1915, revised, 1969; *A King in Babylon,* Maynard Small, 1917, published as *A King in Babylon: A Romantic Melodrama in Three Acts,* Baker & Taylor, 1955; *The Home Book of Modern Verse,* Holt, 1925, reprinted, 1953; (editor and compiler) *American History in Verse, for Boys and Girls,* Houghton, 1932; (compiler and editor) *My Country: Poems of History for Young Americans,* Houghton, 1932, reprinted, Books for Libraries, 1970.

Other: *At Odds With the Regent: A Story of the Cellamare Conspiracy* (historical novel), Lippincott, 1900; *A Soldier of Virginia: A Tale of Colonel Washington and Braddock's Defeat* (historical novel), Houghton, 1901; *The Heritage: A Story of Defeat and Victory,* Houghton, 1902; *The Holladay Case* (mystery novel), Holt, 1903; *Cadets of Gascony: Two Stories of Old France,* Lippincott, 1904; (editor) Henry Fielding, *The History of Tom Jones, a Foundling,* Holt, 1904; *The Marathon Mystery: A Story of Manhattan* (mystery novel), Holt, 1904; (editor) Theodore Winthrop, *Mr. Waddy's Return,* Holt, 1904; *Affairs of State,* Holt, 1906; *The Girl with the Blue Sailor,* Dodd, 1906; *That Affair at Elizabeth,* Holt, 1907; (editor) *Poems of American History,* Houghton, 1908, revised edition, Books for Libraries, 1970; *The Quest for the Rose of Sharon,* L. C. Page, 1909.

The Path of Honor: A Tale of the War in the Bocage, Lippincott, 1910; *Among Dutch Inns,* L. C. Page, 1911; (compiler) *Favorite Poems in English,* Holt, 1911; *The Spell of Holland: The Story of a Pilgrimage to the Land of Dykes and Windmills* (travel), L. C. Page, 1911; (compiler) *The Home Book of Verse, American and English, 1518-1920,* Holt, 1912; *The Mystery of the Boule Cabinet,* Dodd, 1912, reprinted, Arno, 1976; *The Young Apprentice,* L. C. Page, 1912; *The Destroyer: A Tale of International Intrigue,* Dodd, 1913; *The Gloved Hand: A*

She looked around with half-open lips, smiling, pleased as a child, seemingly quite unconscious of the many curious eyes centered upon her. ■ (From *The Marathon Mystery: A Story of Manhattan* by Burton E. Stevenson. Illustrated by Eliot Keen.)

Detective Story, Dodd, 1913; *The Charm of Ireland* (travel), Dodd, 1914; *Little Comrade: A Tale of the Great War,* Holt, 1915, published as *The Girl from Alsace: A Romance of the Great War,* Grosset, 1915 (published in England as *Little Comrade: The Romance of a Lady Spy in the Great War,* Hutchinson, 1915); *The Kingmakers,* Dodd, 1922; (editor) *Famous Single Poems, and the Controversies Which Have Raged Around Them,* Harcourt, 1923, reprinted, Books for Libraries, 1971; *The Storm-Center: A Romance,* Dodd, 1924; *The Coast of Enchantment,* Dodd, 1926.

The House Next Door: A Detective Story, Dodd, 1932, *Villa Aurelia: A Riviera Interlude,* Dodd, 1932 (published in England as *Mystery of Villa Aurelia,* Rich & Cowan, 1933); (compiler and editor) *Great Americans as Seen by the Poets: An Anthology,* Lippincott, 1933; (editor) *The Home Book of Quotations, Classical and Modern,* Dodd, 1934 (published in England as *Stevenson's Book of Quotations, Classical and Modern,* Cassell, 1958); (editor) *The Home Book of Shakespeare Quotations,* Scribner, 1937, reprinted, 1965 (published

**IV. Just Nonsense**

(From *The Home Book of Verse for Young Folks*, selected and arranged by Burton Egbert Stevenson. Illustrated by Willy Pogany.)

in England as *Stevenson's Book of Shakespeare Quotations*, Cassell, 1969); *The Red Carnation: An Antony Bigelow Story*, Dodd, 1939 (published in England as *Death Wears a Carnation*, Cassell, 1940).

(Editor) *The Home Book of Proverbs, Maxims and Familiar Phrases*, Macmillan, 1948, reprinted as *The Macmillan Book of Proverbs, Maxims, and Familiar Phrases*, Macmillan, 1965 (published in England as *Book of Proverbs, Maxims, and Familiar Phrases*, Routledge & Kegan Paul, 1949); (compiler) *The Home Book of Bible Quotations*, Harper, 1949, reprinted, 1977; (compiler) *The Standard Book of Shakespeare Quotations*, Funk & Wagnalls, 1953.

Contributor to periodicals, including *Bookman, Century, Delineator, Dial, Independent, Ladies' Home Journal, Lippincott's Magazine, McClure's Magazine, Munsey, Nation, Pictorial Review*, and *St. Nicholas*.

ADAPTATIONS—Films: "On Dangerous Ground," adaptation of *Little Comrade*, World Film Corporation, 1916; "In

the Next Room," adaptation of *The Mystery of the Boule Cabinet*, First National Pictures, 1930.

SIDELIGHTS: Stevenson published over 15,000 pages during the eighty-nine years of his life. He was as flexible a writer as he was prolific, writing a number of mystery and detective novels, children's books, travel books, historical novels, and anthologies.

From early childhood Stevenson wanted to be a writer. At the age of twelve he constructed a makeshift press and began publishing a monthly entitled *The Boys' Own*. The amateur publication was continued until Stevenson entered Princeton University at age seventeen.

Stevenson's literary interests were further developed during his college years. He supported himself as a typesetter and later as a correspondent for the *New York Tribune* and the United Press International. In addition, he was a member of the board of the college weekly, *The Tiger*.

During the summer vacation following his junior year, Stevenson was offered a reporter job by the editor of his hometown newspaper, the *Chillicothe Leader*. Deciding that the paper offered an education more attuned to his interests and goals, Stevenson accepted the position and dismissed plans to complete his degree.

In 1899 Stevenson was appointed librarian of the Chillicothe Public Library. It was a job that provided a suitable atmosphere and enough time for him to devote attention to his writing. His first book was published in 1900, and for the next fifty years Stevenson published at least one book nearly every year.

During World War I, Camp Sherman was built outside of Chillicothe. The servicemen expressed a desire for a library service. Stevenson initiated a statewide campaign for book donations and was appointed camp librarian. In the fall of 1917 he was called to Washington, D.C., to head a national campaign.

Stevenson's involvement in establishing libraries for servicemen led to his appointment as European Director of the American Library Association's Library War Service. In 1918 he and his wife left for Paris, where they lived intermittently for seven years. During that time Stevenson supervised the distribution of some two million books and at least twice as many magazines.

After the war Stevenson saw a need in Europe for a center that would provide accurate information on the United States. He converted his Paris office into The American Library and became its director. In 1920 Stevenson returned to his post as librarian of the Chillicothe Public Library.

As a writer, Stevenson is probably best known for his compilations of anthologies. His *Home Book of Proverbs, Maxims and Familiar Phrases*, published in 1948, took him nearly ten years to compile. When he was in his late seventies Stevenson decided he was dissatisfied with his original compilation of Shakespeare quotations, published in 1937. He undertook the task of rereading all of Shakespeare and compiling a book which he felt would have wider appeal. He believed the first compilation was most useful to students and reference libraries, with the second being intended for a more general audience.

FOR MORE INFORMATION SEE: *New York Times Book Review*, November 3, 1906, January 26, 1913, October 5, 1913,

March 21, 1913, November 17, 1913, December 9, 1934, November 7, 1948; *Literary Digest*, December 14, 1912; *Bookman*, March, 1913; *Times Literary Supplement*, July 31, 1924; *Outlook*, July 8, 1925; *New York Herald Tribune Books*, August 23, 1925, April 23, 1933, December 30, 1934, May 26, 1935, November 14, 1937; *International Book Review*, December, 1925; *New York Herald Tribune*, December 9, 1934; *Saturday Review of Literature*, December 15, 1934, November 27, 1937; *Christian Science Monitor*, July 3, 1935; *New York Herald Tribune Weekly Book Review*, December 5, 1948.

OBITUARIES: New York Times, May 15, 1962; *Time*, May 25, 1962; *Newsweek*, May 28, 1962; *Publishers Weekly*, May 28, 1962; *Library Journal*, July, 1962; *Wilson Library Bulletin*, September, 1962; *American Annual*, 1963.

SUTHERLAND, Efua (Theodora Morgue) 1924-

PERSONAL: Born June 27, 1924 in Cape Coast, Ghana. Married William Sutherland (an educator) in 1954; three children. *Education:* Earned B.A. from Homerton College, Cambridge; also attended School of Oriental and African Studies, London, and Ghana University. *Address:* % Longman Group, 74 Grosvenor St., London W1X OAS, England.

CAREER: Playwright, producer, director, and writer of children's stories. Teacher in Ghana, 1951-54. Founding director of Experimental Theatre Players (now Ghana Drama Studio), Accra, 1958—. Co-founder (with husband, William Sutherland) of school in Trans-Volta region of upper Ghana. Founder of Ghana Society of Writers (now University of Ghana Writers Workshop), Legon. Founding director of Kusum Agoromba (children's touring theatre group) at University of Ghana School of Drama, Legon.

WRITINGS—Plays for children: *Vulture! Vulture! and Tahinta: Two Rhythm Plays*, Ghana Publishing House, 1968, Pantheon, 1970; "Anase and the Dwarf Brigade" (based on *Alice and Wonderland*), first produced in Cleveland at Karamu House Theatre, February 5, 1971.

Poetry for children: *Playtime in Africa* (photographs by Willis E. Bell), Brown, Knight, & Truscott, 1960, Atheneum, 1962.

Adult plays: *Edufa* (based on the play, *Alcestis*, by Euripedes; produced in Accra in Ghana Drama Studio, 1962), Longmans, Green, 1967, published in *Plays from Black Africa*, edited by Fredric M. Litto, Hill & Wang, 1968; *Foriwa* (three-act; produced in Accra in Ghana Drama Studio, 1962), Ghana State Publishing Corporation, 1962, Panther House, 1970; *The Marriage of Anasewa: A Storytelling Drama* (one-act; first produced in Accra, Ghana, September, 1971), Longman, 1975.

Other: *The Roadmakers* (travel; photographs by W. E. Bell), Ghana Information Services, 1961; *The Original Bob: The Story of Bob Johnson, Ghana's Ace Comedian* (photographs by W. E. Bell), Educational Publications, 1970.

Also author of radio plays "Odasani" (based on *Everyman*), "The Pineapple Child" (a fantasy), "Nyamekye" (music and dance), and "Anansegoro: You Swore an Oath" (one-act). Contributor of poems and plays to various periodicals. Co-founder of *Okyeame* magazine, Accra, Ghana.

SIDELIGHTS: "I'm on a journey of discovery. I'm discovering my own people. I didn't grow up in rural Ghana—I grew up in Cape Coast with a Christian family. It's a fine family, but there are certain hidden areas of Ghanaian life—important areas of Ghanaian life, that I just wasn't in touch with; in the past four or five years I've made a very concentrated effort to make that untrue. And I feel I know my people now.

"Some of my writing for children is in both English and Akan; I am anxious that children are started off bilingually in the schools. This can't happen unless there is literature in support of it. So this is all part of my experimental programme—to find out what can be translated in both languages towards this end." [*Reader's Guide to African Literature*, Zell, 1971.[1]]

Growing up in the Ghanaian city of Cape Coast, Sutherland was isolated from the traditional folk culture of the rural areas. Her goal has since been to discover that which is uniquely Ghanaian and to convey it through her writing.

Sutherland's plays are heavily sight-and-sound-oriented and often are based on traditional African folklore. The use of rhyme, rhythm, music, dance, and audience participation makes them more suitable for stage or radio performance than for reading. Consequently, much of Sutherland's work is not represented in print.

Sutherland's objective has been to unify Ghana through the preservation of national art forms. She has designed an open-air theatre for the performance of traditional storytelling and contemporary drama, feeling that such a theatre would be more adaptable to these art forms than would the European proscenium stage. She found the Experimental Theatre and the Ghana Drama Studio in Accra. "The Drama Studio has really come as another expression of my desire to have more and more people interested in writing—primarily for children. But later on it turned out that not everyone is interested in writing for children, although there are a great many interested in writing. To give another reason why people would want to write I started to build a Drama Studio and develop the experimental theatre programme."[1]

FOR MORE INFORMATION SEE: Reader's Guide to African Literature, Zell, 1971; *African Authors*, Herdeck, 1974.

TEALE, Edwin Way   1899-1980

OBITUARY NOTICE—See sketch in *SATA* Volume 7: Born June 2, 1899, in Joliet, Ill.; died October 18, 1980, in Norwich, Conn. Author, photographer, and naturalist. Determined at the age of twelve to become a naturalist and author, Teale eventually spent thirteen years as a feature writer for *Popular Science Monthly*, followed by years as a free-lance writer. In 1966 he won the Pulitzer Prize for general nonfiction with his *Wandering Through the Winter*. This book is one of four in a series chronicling the seasons in America, each the result of more than 19,000 miles of cross-country travel. Another of Teale's particular interests was entomology, and he wrote many books about insects. A number of Teale's works are illustrated with his own photographs, selected from the more than twenty thousand he took of natural history subjects. For young people Teale wrote such books as *The Junior Book of Insects, The Boy's Book of Photography, Insect Friends*, and *The Lost Dog. For More Information See:* Edward H. Dodd, Jr., *Of Nature, Time and Teale*, Dodd, 1960; *Current Biography*, Wilson,

1961; *Contemporary Authors,* Volumes 1-4, revised, Gale, 1967; *Who's Who in America,* 40th edition, Marquis, 1978. *Obituaries: New York Times,* October 21, 1980; *Washington Post,* October 21, 1980; *Newsweek,* November 3, 1980; *Time,* November 3, 1980; *Publishers Weekly,* November 7, 1980; *Contemporary Authors,* Volume 102, Gale, 1981; *AB Bookman's Weekly,* January 5, 1981.

VERNER, Gerald   1897(?)-1980

OBITUARY NOTICE: Born about 1897; died September 16, 1980, in Broadstairs, England. Playwright and author of more than one hundred books, including the popular *The Embankment Murder.* Verner also wrote plays, including "Meet Mr. Callaghan" and "The Urgent Hangman." *For More Information See: Who's Who of Boys' Writers and Illustrators, 1964,* Brian Doyle, 1964; *Who's Who in Spy Fiction,* Elm Tree, 1977. *Obituaries: London Times,* September 16, 1980; *AB Bookman's Weekly,* December 22, 1980; *Contemporary Authors,* Volume 102, Gale, 1981.

WHITNEY, Thomas P(orter)   1917-

PERSONAL: Born January 26, 1917, in Toledo, Ohio; son of Herbert Porter and Louise (Metzger) Whitney; married Tryphena Gray, July 19, 1936 (divorced, 1949); married Julia Zapolskaya, August 3, 1953 (died August, 1965); married Judith Forrestel, October 14, 1966 (divorced June, 1973); married Marguerite Carusone, September 21, 1974; children: (first marriage) John Herbert, Louise; (third marriage) Julia Forrestel. *Education:* Amherst College, A.B. (summa cum laude), 1937; Columbia University, M.A., 1940. *Home:* Roxbury Rd., Washington, Conn. 06793. *Office:* Whitney Book Shops, 59 Elm St., New Canaan, Conn. 06840.

THOMAS P. WHITNEY

CAREER: Bennett College, Millbrook, N.Y., instructor in social sciences, 1940-41; Office of Strategic Services, Washington, D.C., social science analyst, 1941-44; U.S. Embassy, Moscow, attache, chief economic section, 1944-47; Associated Press of America, Moscow, staff correspondent, 1947-53; Associated Press of America, New York City, foreign news analyst, 1953-59; Whitney Enterprises, Inc., New York City, president, 1966-68, chairman of the board, 1966-73. Trustee of Julia A. Whitney Foundation. *Member:* Overseas Press Club (president, 1958-59), P.E.N., American Association for the Advancement of Science, Thoroughbred of America, Turf and Field, Phi Beta Kappa, Alpha Delta Phi. *Awards, honors:* Honorary Litt.D., Amherst College, 1972, and Assumption College, 1975.

WRITINGS—Juveniles: (Translator) Alexander Green, *Scarlet Sails,* Scribner, 1967; *Vasilisa the Beautiful* (ALA Notable Book; illustrated by Nonny Hogrogian), Macmillan, 1970; (editor) *The Young Russians: A Collection of Stories About Them,* Macmillan, 1972; (translator) *The Story of Prince Ivan, the Firebird, and the Gray Wolf* (ALA Notable Book), Scribner, 1968; (translator) *In a Certain Kingdom: Twelve Russian Fairy Tales* (illustrated by Dieter Lange), Macmillan, 1972; (translator) *Marko the Rich and Vasily the Unlucky* (illustrated by Igor Galanin), Macmillan, 1974.

Other: Has Russia Changed?, Foreign Policy Associated-World Affairs Center, 1960; (author of introduction) *The Communist Blueprint for the Future: The Complete Texts of All Four Communist Manifestoes, 1848-1961,* Dutton, 1962; *Russia in My Life,* Reynal, 1962; (editor) Nikita Khrushchev, *Khrushchev Speaks: Selected Speeches, Articles, and Press Conferences, 1949-1961,* University of Michigan Press, 1963.

Translator from the Russian: (Also editor and author of introduction) *The New Writing in Russia,* University of Michigan Press, 1964; Alexander Solzhenitsyn, *First Circle,* Harper, 1968; Vyacheslav Shishkov, *Children of the Street: Life in a Commune of Russia's Besprizorniki,* Strathcona, 1971; A. Solzhenitsyn, *The Nobel Lecture on Literature,* Harper, 1972; Andrei Platonov, *The Foundation Pit,* Ardis, 1972; Vasily Grossman, *Forever Flowing,* Harper, 1973; A. Solzhenitsyn, *The Gulag Archipelago, 1918-1956: An Experiment in Literary Investigation,* Volume I, Harper, 1974; A. Solzhenitsyn, *The Gulag Archipelago,* Volume II, Harper, 1975. Translation of the memoirs and autobiography of former Soviet general, Petro Grigorenes, to be published by W. W. Norton in 1982. Also translator of *One Day in the Life of Ivan Denisovich* by A. Solzhenitsyn. Contributor of articles to periodicals, including *New York Times Magazine, Foreign Policy Bulletin,* and *New Republic.*

SIDELIGHTS: Well known for his translations of Solzhenitsyn's books from Russian, Whitney lives in the quiet, forested village of Washington, Connecticut, where he owns forty acres of land, has five horses, two cats, and two dogs.

His expertise in the Russian language improved after spending nine years in Moscow. "I was six years in Moscow with the AP and then six years in New York; as a foreign news analyst. I was altogether nine years in Moscow—1944 to 1953—before my work with AP, I was with the U.S. Embassy." [Phillip M. Perry, "Thomas P. Whitney Loses Nothing in the Translation," *Writers Digest,* July, 1974.[1]]

Whitney had always wanted to translate a book, although his first book translation did not appear until the 1960's. ". . .I

Out of the woods came Baba Yaga riding in a mortar . . . . ■ (From *Vasilisa the Beautiful*, translated by Thomas P. Whitney. Illustrated by Nonny Hogrogian.)

became very interested in what was happening in Russian literature in the early 1960's. I decided I would write a book about it. In the course of that, I did this anthology, *The New Writing in Russia*. Well, I never finished my own book about Russian writing in the 60's. I got interrupted. I was married to Yulga [Julia Zapolskaya], a Russian singer and composer, whom I'd met in the Soviet Union. She got cancer in 1964 and died in 1965.

"Being with her took a year out of my literary life. When I got back to it, I didn't have the energy to continue. It was an enormous job to do, anyhow.

"I started to do some translating to get back to work. I had done by this time *One Day,* and also an anthology. After that, in 1964 I started out by doing this very interesting and lovely story of Alexander Green, a Russian writer despite his name, called *Scarlet Sails*. I did it for a friend of mine who was an editor at Scribner's. It was successful, and I just went on . . . and on.

"I always say to myself I'm going to go back and do some writing of my own . . . I'm interested in doing some work in history . . . contemporary Russian history, particularly the periods in which I'm most familiar. I have some other projects, so . . . maybe I'll go back and do some writing of my own."[1]

A translator, in general, does not get the recognition which he deserves, according to Whitney. "I think the work of translators is not sufficiently appreciated. I'm talking in general. This is not a personal complaint, because I've had a lot of recognition out of this. As a matter of fact, more than I can handle. I'm wanted on such and such TV show, or to give a lecture here or there, and I do as much as I can within the bounds of time available. . . .

"All too often, book reviews assign reviews on translations to competing translators. I think it's unfortunate, because oftentimes the competing translator will run down the translation of the competitor, so that usually the best thing a translator can hope for in a review of his translation is not to get mentioned at all. Because in that case he knows that nobody has even noticed it was a translation. If the work itself gets praised, he can understand, or anybody can understand by implication, that it's a good translation. Very rarely do any of the reviewers who cover translations mention, and in particular mention positively, the work of the translator.

"There are quite a few people who make a living out of translation. Those most financially successful in translation of Russian are usually involved in technical translating in addition to literary translation. I doubt many people make a living translating literature from Russian. My friends . . . in Ann Arbor, have their own publishing enterprise . . . . It's a husband-and-wife team, and they both know Russian. If you translate as a sideline, that may be the frosting on the cake. It does combine well if you are a professor of Russian literature. If I had any advice to give wiriters interested in doing translating, particularly from Russian, I would say that it combines well with writing of your own. But one shouldn't neglect one's own writing."[1]

Whitney's works are included in the Kerlan Collection at the University of Minnesota.

FOR MORE INFORMATION SEE: Saturday Review, April 28, 1962; *Horn Book,* December, 1970, June, 1972, June, 1974; *Writers Digest,* July, 1974; *Harper's,* July, 1974.

WOODFORD, Peggy   1937-

PERSONAL: Born September 19, 1937, in Assam, India; daughter of Ronald Curtis (an agriculturist) and Ruth (Laine) Woodford; married Walter Aylen (a lawyer), April 1, 1967; children: Alison, Frances, Imogen. *Education:* Attended St. Anne's College, Oxford, 1956-59. *Residence:* London, England. *Agent:* Murray Pollinger, 4 Garrick St., London W.C.2, England.

CAREER: British Broadcasting Corp. (BBC-TV), London, England, research and script assistant, 1961-63; College of Padworth, Reading, England, senior tutor in English, 1963-66; free-lance writer, 1966—. *Awards, honors:* Research scholarship from Italian government, 1960.

WRITINGS—For children: Mozart (biography; illustrated by David Knight), J. Garnet Miller, 1964, Walck, 1966; *Schubert* (biography; illustrated by Barbara Brown), Walck, 1969; *Please Don't Go* (novel), Bodley Head, 1972, Dutton, 1973; *Backwater War* (novel), Bodley Head, 1964, Farrar, Straus, 1975; (editor and contributor) *The Real Thing: Seven Stories of Love* (short stories), Bodley Head, 1977, published as *Looking for Love: Seven Uncommon Love Stories,* Doubleday, 1979; *See You Tomorrow* (novel), Bodley Head, 1979; (editor and contributor) *You Can't Keep Out the Darkness* (short stories), Bodley Head, 1980; *The Girl with a Voice* (novel), Bodley Head, 1981.

For adults: *Abraham's Legacy* (novel), Deutsch, 1963; *Mozart: His Life and Times* (biography), Midas Books, 1977; *Rise of the Raj* (history; introduction by Rumer Godden), Humanities Press, 1978; *Schubert: His Life and Times* (biography), Midas Books, 1978; *New Stories 5,* edited by Susan Hill and Isabel Quigley, Hutchinson, 1980.

WORK IN PROGRESS: Hyenas in Petticoats, a dramatic dialogue about Mary Wollstonecraft, eighteenth century feminist and intellectual, and her daughter, Mary Godwin, who married Percy Bysshe Shelley; *Charity and Gynecology* (projected ti-

PEGGY WOODFORD

tle), a volume of short stories for adults, publication expected in 1982.

SIDELIGHTS: "I love writing, and ever since leaving the university I have always been in the middle of a piece of fiction. To be alone in my study, blank paper before me and pen in hand, is always a time of complete pleasure, however ill the book work in progress is going. I never type; I write at least two drafts of everything in longhand and have always preferred this method to any other.

"I started to write fiction aimed at teenagers almost by accident: a student suggested I try, and since I had a story in my mind which would be admissible, I wrote *Please Don't Go* fairly quickly and very happily. Encouraged by my publishers I wrote three more teenage novels, always planning to return to adult fiction as well. But it is only in the last year that I have begun to write adult fiction again, mainly at the moment, short stories. I love the combination of scope and discipline a series of short stories offers: scope to explore so many different themes and situations within the discipline of a taut frame."

Woodford has definite ideas about the place of young adults in the realm of literature. Far from being merely a re-working of children's themes with a few hard vocabulary words thrown in for spice, Woodford feels "strongly that fiction for teenagers should be adult in every way; the only consideration to be borne always in mind is that the theme and subject matter should appeal to and interest the adolescent."

Woodford's first novel, *Abraham's Legacy,* was written during her year of study in Rome on an Italian government scholarship. Her topic of research was "The Englishwoman in Italy in the Eighteenth Century." She then returned to London and got a job as a research and script assistant for BBC-TV. She worked most often with the late Paul Johnstone, who was connected with the "Chronicle" series.

The next few books Woodford wrote were biographies of the composers Mozart and Schubert. The Midas editions were quite separate books written many years later and for the adult market. In general critical comment about her method of biography, she is praised in her attempt to weave a background of the history and society in which the composers worked. The human rather than the artistic qualities of these men are stressed, an approach that disappointed some critics who thought the musical works should have received greater attention.

Among Woodford's novels are *Please Don't Go,* a story about teenage infatuation and first love, and *Backwater War,* a historical novel about the German occupation of the Channel Islands during World War II. In the latter book Woodford portrays the hardships endured by the Guernsey people. "To outline the simple structure of this novel does no sort of justice to the layers of feeling and experience in it nor to its honesty," wrote Alastair Maclean of the *Times Literary Supplement.* "Miss Woodford is infallible, for example, on the psychology of an occupied countryside. She knows that war brutalizes civilians as well as soldiers and so far from turning her islanders into heroes she makes it clear that self-interest was rampant among them."

Another book, *Looking for Love,* is a collection of short stories that was edited by Woodford, and she is a contributor as well. The stories center on different types of love, be it the love between parent and child, girl and boy, two friends, or the love of infatuation and hero-worship. *You Can't Keep Out the Darkness* is a companion volume to *Looking for Love,* and this time Woodford had another topic in mind. "When I approached the contributors of *You Can't Keep Out the Darkness* they were asked for stories on the theme of a young person's first awareness of good and evil. The resulting stories, and mine too I hope, have been a complete justification of my belief that 'teenage fiction' is adult fiction with the subject matter apt."

FOR MORE INFORMATION SEE: Observer, November 26, 1972, March 30, 1975; *Times Literary Supplement,* December 8, 1972, April 4, 1975; *Washington Post Book World,* May 13, 1973; *Horn Book,* June, 1973, August, 1975, August, 1979; *New York Times Book Review,* December 28, 1975; *New Statesman,* October 14, 1977.

WYMER, Norman George   1911-

PERSONAL: Born June 28, 1911, in London, England; son of George Petre (an army officer) and Margaret (Grogan; a writer) Wymer; married Jean Kinloch (a secretary), June 2, 1934; children: Michael, Graham. *Education:* Attended Charterhouse. *Home:* 11 Grassmer Close, Felpham, Sussex, England.

CAREER: Free-lance reporter and writer. *Evening News,* London, staff reporter, 1931-34; *Daily Telegraph,* London, special correspondent, 1935-46. Consultant and general editor for Odhams, and Oxford University Press.

On 3rd of June, 1668, the expedition set sail. ■ (From *With Mackenzie in Canada* by Norman Wymer. Illustrated by Harry Toothill.)

WRITINGS—Juveniles: *Behind the Scenes at London Airport* (illustrated by H. A. Johns), Phoenix House, 1963; *Behind the Scenes in an Ocean Liner* (illustrated by H. A. Johns), Phoenix House, 1963; *Look at Dogs* (illustrated by Constance Marshall), Hamish Hamilton, 1963; *With Mackenzie in Canada* (illustrated by Harry Toothill), Muller, 1963; *Behind the Scenes on the Oilfield,* Phoenix House, 1964; *Glass,* Baker, 1964, Roy, 1969; *Look at Radio* (illustrated by David Parry), Hamish Hamilton, 1964; *Roads,* Baker, 1964, Roy, 1969; *Behind the Scenes in a Hospital* (illustrated by Laszlo Acs), Phoenix House, 1965; *Behind the Scenes in Parliament* (illustrated by H. A. Johns), Phoenix House, 1966; *From Marconi to Telstar: The Story of Radio,* Longman, 1966; *Pottery,* Roy, 1966; *Timber,* Baker, 1966; *Your Book of Television,* Faber, 1966; *Behind the Scenes in the Police,* Dent, 1970; (editor of simplified version) Charles Dickens, *David Copperfield,* Collins, 1978; (editor of simplified version) R. L. Stevenson, *Dr. Jekyll and Mr. Hyde,* Collins, 1978; (editor of simplified version) Charles Dickens, *Oliver Twist,* Collins, 1979; (editor of simplified version) Jane Austin, *Sense and Sensibility,* Collins, 1979.

Biographies—For young people: *Dr. Arnold of Rugby,* Hale, 1953; *Father of Nobody's Children: A Portrait of Dr. Barnardo,* Hutchinson, 1954; *George Stephenson,* Oxford University Press, 1957; *Louis Braille,* Oxford University Press, 1957; *Medical Scientists and Doctors,* Oxford University Press, 1958; *The Man From the Cape,* Evans, 1959; *Harry Ferguson,* Roy, 1961; *Yehudi Menuhin,* Phoenix House, 1961; *Dr. Barnardo,* Longman, 1962; *Gilbert and Sullivan* (illustrated by Carol Barker), Methuen, 1962, Dutton (illustrated by John Pimlott), 1963; *The True Book About Elizabeth Garrett Anderson,* Muller, 1963; *The Young Helen Keller* (illustrated by William Randell), Roy, 1965.

Other: *English Country Crafts: A Survey of Their Development From Early Times to Present Day,* Batsford, 1946; *A Breath of England* (travel), Lutterworth, 1948; *English Town Crafts: A Survey of Their Development From Early Times to the Present Day,* Batsford, 1949; *Sport in England: A History of Two Thousand Years of Games and Pastimes,* Harrap, 1949; *Companion into Sussex* (travel), Methuen, 1950, Spurbooks, 1972; *Village Life,* Harrap, 1951; *Rural Crafts* (self-illustrated), Oxford University Press, 1952; *Country Folk,* Odhams, 1953; *The Story of Winchester,* Staples, 1955; (editor of abridged version), A. J. Cronin, *The Citadel,* Longman, 1963; *Man Against Nature,* Longman, 1964; (editor of abridged version), Thor Heyerdahl, *The Kon-Tiki Expedition,* Longman, 1965; *The Times Guide to the Sky at Night* (diagrams by B. Weltman), Hamish Hamilton, 1966; *It Happened This Way,* Longman, 1967; *London Today* (photographs by Richard Hamnett), Longman, 1971; *The Dream & the Woman in Grey and Other Pieces for Easy Reading,* University of London Press, 1971; *Oil,* Longman, 1972; (editor of abridged edition), A. J. Cronin,

Hatter's Castle (illustrated by James Cleaver), Longman, 1972; *Man Against Space,* Longman, 1972; (editor of simplified version) Ian Fleming, *For Your Eyes Only: Five James Bond Stories* (illustrated by John Holder), Longman, 1973; *Man and Modern Science,* Longman, 1973; (editor of abridged edition), A. J. Cronin, *The Stars Look Down* (illustrated by Terence Greer), Longman, 1974; (editor of simplified version) Arthur Hailey, *Hotel,* Longman, 1974; *Man on the Move,* Longman, 1976; *Lucky to be Alive,* Longman, 1981; *Inventors,* Hamlyn, 1981.

SIDELIGHTS: Wymer began his career as a journalist and is noted for supplying American newspapers with articles about British life during World War II. He wrote a variety of biographies and science-related books for young people. Among these are the ''Behind the Scenes'' and the ''Lives of Great Men and Women'' series. He is also the author of several English travel books and books about the history of English crafts. In addition, his abridged and simplified versions of other authors' works serve as useful tools for foreign students learning English. He has also written and broadcast many scripts for the BBC. Many of his books have been published in foreign countries, notably Japan.

CUMULATIVE INDEX TO
ILLUSTRATIONS AND AUTHORS

Illustrations Index

(In the following index, the number of the volume in which an illustrator's work appears is given *before* the colon, and the page on which it appears is given *after* the colon. For example, a drawing by Adams, Adrienne appears in Volume 2 on page 6, another drawing by her appears in Volume 3 on page 80, another drawing in Volume 8 on page 1, and another drawing in Volume 15 on page 107.)

YABC

Index citations including this abbreviation refer to listings appearing in *Yesterday's Authors of Books for Children,* also published by the Gale Research Company, which covers authors who died prior to 1960.

Aas, Ulf, *5:* 174
Abbé, S. van. *See* van Abbé, S., *16:* 142
Abel, Raymond, *6:* 122; *7:* 195; *12:* 3; *21:* 86; *25:* 119
Accorsi, William, *11:* 198
Acs, Laszlo, *14:* 156
Adams, Adrienne, *2:* 6; *3:* 80; *8:* 1; *15:* 107; *16:* 180; *20:* 65; *22:* 134-135
Adams, John Wolcott, *17:* 162
Adkins, Alta, *22:* 250
Adkins, Jan, *8:* 3
Adler, Peggy, *22:* 6
Agard, Nadema, *18:* 1
Aichinger, Helga, *4:* 5, 45
Akasaka, Miyoshi, *YABC 2:* 261
Akino, Fuku, *6:* 144
Alajalov, *2:* 226
Albright, Donn, *1:* 91
Alcorn, John, *3:* 159; *7:* 165
Alden, Albert, *11:* 103
Alexander, Martha, *3:* 206; *11:* 103; *13:* 109; *25:* 100
Alexeieff, Alexander, *14:* 6
Aliki. *See* Brandenberg, Aliki
Allamand, Pascale, *12:* 9
Alland, Alexander, *16:* 255
Alland, Alexandra, *16:* 255
Allen, Gertrude, *9:* 6
Almquist, Don, *11:* 8; *12:* 128; *17:* 46; *22:* 110
Aloise, Frank, *5:* 38; *10:* 133
Althea. *See* Braithwaite, Althea
Altschuler, Franz, *11:* 185; *23:* 141
Ambrus, Victor G., *1:* 6-7, 194; *3:* 69; *5:* 15; *6:* 44; *7:* 36; *8:* 210; *12:* 227; *14:* 213; *15:* 213; *22:* 209; *24:* 36
Ames, Lee J., *3:* 12; *9:* 130; *10:* 69; *17:* 214; *22:* 124
Amon, Aline, *9:* 9
Amoss, Berthe, *5:* 5
Amundsen, Dick, *7:* 77

Amundsen, Richard E., *5:* 10; *24:* 122
Ancona, George, *12:* 11
Anderson, Alasdair, *18:* 122
Anderson, C. W. , *11:* 10
Anderson, Carl, *7:* 4
Anderson, Erica, *23:* 65
Anderson, Laurie, *12:* 153, 155
Anderson, Wayne, *23:* 119
Andrew, John, *22:* 4
Andrews, Benny, *14:* 251
Angelo, Valenti, *14:* 8; *18:* 100; *20:* 232
Anglund, Joan Walsh, *2:* 7, 250-251
Anno, Mitsumasa, *5:* 7
Antal, Andrew, *1:* 124
Appleyard, Dev, *2:* 192
Archer, Janet, *16:* 69
Ardizzone, Edward, *1:* 11, 12; *2:* 105; *3:* 258; *4:* 78; *7:* 79; *10:* 100; *15:* 232; *20:* 69, 178; *23:* 223; *24:* 125; *YABC 2:* 25
Arenella, Roy, *14:* 9
Armer, Austin, *13:* 3
Armer, Laura Adams, *13:* 3
Armer, Sidney, *13:* 3
Armitage, Eileen, *4:* 16
Armstrong, George, *10:* 6; *21:* 72
Arno, Enrico, *1:* 217; *2:* 22, 210; *4:* 9; *5:* 43; *6:* 52
Arnosky, Jim, *22:* 20
Arrowood, Clinton, *12:* 193; *19:* 11
Artzybasheff, Boris, *13:* 143; *14:* 15
Aruego, Ariane, *6:* 4
See also Dewey, Ariane
Aruego, Jose, *4:* 140; *6:* 4; *7:* 64
Asch, Frank, *5:* 9
Ashby, Gail, *11:* 135
Ashley, C. W., *19:* 197
Ashmead, Hal, *8:* 70
Atene, Ann, *12:* 18
Atkinson, J. Priestman, *17:* 275

Atwood, Ann, *7:* 9
Augarde, Steve, *25:* 22
Austerman, Miriam, *23:* 107
Austin, Margot, *11:* 16
Austin, Robert, *3:* 44
Averill, Esther, *1:* 17
Axeman, Lois, *2:* 32; *11:* 84; *13:* 165; *22:* 8; *23:* 49
Ayer, Jacqueline, *13:* 7
Ayer, Margaret, *15:* 12

B.T.B. *See* Blackwell, Basil T., *YABC 1:* 68, 69
Babbitt, Natalie, *6:* 6; *8:* 220
Bacon, Bruce, *4:* 74
Bacon, Paul, *7:* 155; *8:* 121
Bacon, Peggy, *2:* 11, 228
Baker, Alan, *22:* 22
Baker, Charlotte, *2:* 12
Baker, Jeannie, *23:* 4
Baker, Jim, *22:* 24
Baldridge, C. LeRoy, *19:* 69
Balet, Jan, *11:* 22
Balian, Lorna, *9:* 16
Ballantyne, R. M., *24:* 34
Ballis, George, *14:* 199
Bang, Molly Garrett, *24:* 37, 38
Banik, Yvette Santiago, *21:* 136
Banner, Angela. *See* Maddison, Angela Mary
Bannerman, Helen, *19:* 13, 14
Bannon, Laura, *6:* 10; *23:* 8
Bare, Arnold Edwin, *16:* 31
Bargery, Geoffrey, *14:* 258
Barkley, James, *4:* 13; *6:* 11; *13:* 112
Barling, Tom, *9:* 23
Barnes, Hiram P., *20:* 28
Barnett, Moneta, *16:* 89; *19:* 142
Barney, Maginel Wright, *YABC 2:* 306
Barnum, Jay Hyde, *11:* 224; *20:* 5

Barrer-Russell, Gertrude, *9:* 65
Barrett, Ron, *14:* 24
Barron, John N., *3:* 261; *5:* 101;
    14: 220
Barrows, Walter, *14:* 268
Barry, Ethelred B., *YABC 1:* 229
Barry, James, *14:* 25
Barry, Katharina, *2:* 159; *4:* 22
Barry, Robert E., *6:* 12
Barth, Ernest Kurt, *2:* 172; *3:* 160;
    8: 26; *10:* 31
Barton, Byron, *8:* 207; *9:* 18;
    23: 66
Bartram, Robert, *10:* 42
Bartsch, Jochen, *8:* 105
Bate, Norman, *5:* 16
Bates, Leo, *24:* 35
Batten, John D., *25:* 161, 162
Bauernschmidt, Marjorie, *15:* 15
Baum, Allyn, *20:* 10
Baum, Willi, *4:* 24-25; *7:* 173
Baumhauer, Hans, *11:* 218;
    15: 163, 165, 167
Baynes, Pauline, *2:* 244; *3:* 149;
    13: 133, 135, 137-141; *19:* 18,
    19, 20
Beame, Rona, *12:* 40
Beard, Dan, *22:* 31, 32
Beard, J. H., *YABC 1:* 158
Bearden, Romare, *9:* 7; *22:* 35
Beardsley, Aubrey, *17:* 14; *23:* 181
Beaton, Cecil, *24:* 208
Beaucé, J. A., *18:* 103
Beck, Charles, *11:* 169
Beck, Ruth, *13:* 11
Becker, Harriet, *12:* 211
Beckett, Sheilah, *25:* 195
Beckhoff, Harry, *1:* 78; *5:* 163
Bedford, F. D., *20:* 118, 122
Bee, Joyce, *19:* 62
Beeby, Betty, *25:* 36
Beech, Carol, *9:* 149
Beek, *25:* 51, 55, 59
Beerbohm, Max, *24:* 208
Behr, Joyce, *15:* 15; *21:* 132;
    23: 161
Behrens, Hans, *5:* 97
Belden, Charles J., *12:* 182
Bell, Corydon, *3:* 20
Bemelmans, Ludwig, *15:* 19, 21
Benda, W. T., *15:* 256
Bendick, Jeanne, *2:* 24
Bennett, F. I., *YABC 1:* 134
Bennett, Rainey, *15:* 26; *23:* 53
Bennett, Richard, *15:* 45; *21:* 11,
    12, 13; *25:* 175
Bennett, Susan, *5:* 55
Benton, Thomas Hart, *2:* 99
Berelson, Howard, *5:* 20; *16:* 58
Berenstain, Jan, *12:* 47
Berenstain, Stan, *12:* 47
Berg, Joan, *1:* 115; *3:* 156; *6:* 26,
    58
Berger, William M., *14:* 143;
    YABC 1: 204
Bering, Claus, *13:* 14

Berkowitz, Jeanette, *3:* 249
Bernadette. *See* Watts, Bernadette
Bernstein, Zena, *23:* 46
Berrill, Jacquelyn, *12:* 50
Berry, Erick. *See* Best, Allena.
Berry, William A., *6:* 219
Berry, William D., *14:* 29; *19:* 48
Berson, Harold, *2:* 17-18; *4:* 28-29,
    220; *9:* 10; *12:* 19; *17:* 45;
    18: 193; *22:* 85
Bertschmann, Harry, *16:* 1
Beskow, Elsa, *20:* 13, 14, 15
Best, Allena, *2:* 26
Bethers, Ray, *6:* 22
Bettina. *See* Ehrlich, Bettina
Betts, Ethel Franklin, *17:* 161,
    164-165; *YABC 2:* 47
Bewick, Thomas, *16:* 40-41, 43-45,
    47; *YABC 1:* 107
Bianco, Pamela, *15:* 31
Bible, Charles, *13:* 15
Bice, Clare, *22:* 40
Biggers, John, *2:* 123
Bileck, Marvin, *3:* 102
Bimen, Levent, *5:* 179
Binks, Robert, *25:* 150
Binzen, Bill, *24:* 47
Birch, Reginald, *15:* 150; *19:* 33,
    34, 35, 36; *YABC 1:* 84;
    YABC 2: 34, 39
Bird, Esther Brock, *1:* 36; *25:* 66
Birmingham, Lloyd, *12:* 51
Biro, Val, *1:* 26
Bjorklund, Lorence, *3:* 188, 252;
    7: 100; *9:* 113; *10:* 66;
    19: 178; *YABC 1:* 242
Blackwell, Basil T., *YABC 1:* 68,
    69
Blades, Ann, *16:* 52
Blaisdell, Elinore, *1:* 121; *3:* 134
Blake, Quentin, *3:* 170; *9:* 21;
    10: 48; *13:* 38; *21:* 180
Blass, Jacqueline, *8:* 215
Blegvad, Erik, *2:* 59; *3:* 98; *5:* 117;
    7: 131; *11:* 149; *14:* 34, 35;
    18: 237; *YABC 1:* 201
Bloch, Lucienne, *10:* 12
Blumenschein, E. L., *YABC 1:* 113,
    115
Boardman, Gwenn, *12:* 60
Bock, Vera, *1:* 187; *21:* 41
Bock, William Sauts, *8:* 7; *14:* 37;
    16: 120; *21:* 141
Bodecker, N. M., *8:* 13; *14:* 2;
    17: 55-57
Bohdal, Susi, *22:* 44
Bolian, Polly, *3:* 270; *4:* 30; *13:* 77
Bolognese, Don, *2:* 147, 231;
    4: 176; *7:* 146; *17:* 43;
    23: 192; *24:* 50
Bond, Arnold, *18:* 116
Bond, Barbara Higgins, *21:* 102
Bonsall, Crosby, *23:* 6
Booth, Franklin, *YABC 2:* 76
Bordier, Georgette, *16:* 54
Borja, Robert, *22:* 48

Bornstein, Ruth, *14:* 44
Borten, Helen, *3:* 54; *5:* 24
Boston, Peter, *19:* 42
Bottner, Barbara, *14:* 46
Bourke-White, Margaret,
    15: 286-287
Bowser, Carolyn Ewing, *22:* 253
Bozzo, Frank, *4:* 154
Bradford, Ron, *7:* 157
Bradley, William, *5:* 164
Brady, Irene, *4:* 31
Braithwaite, Althea, *23:* 12-13
Bramley, Peter, *4:* 3
Brandenberg, Aliki, *2:* 36-37;
    24: 222
Brandon, Brumsic, Jr., *9:* 25
Bransom, Paul, *17:* 121
Brenner, Fred, *22:* 85
Brett, Bernard, *22:* 54
Brick, John, *10:* 15
Bridwell, Norman, *4:* 37
Briggs, Raymond, *10:* 168; *23:* 20,
    21
Bright, Robert, *24:* 55
Brinckloe, Julie, *13:* 18; *24:* 79,
    115
Brisley, Joyce L., *22:* 57
Brock, C. E., *15:* 97; *19:* 247, 249;
    23: 224, 225; *YABC 1:* 194,
    196, 203
Brock, Emma, *7:* 21
Brock, Henry Matthew, *15:* 81;
    16: 141; *19:* 71
Bromhall, Winifred, *5:* 11
Brooke, L. Leslie, *16:* 181-183,
    186; *17:* 15-17; *18:* 194
Brooker, Christopher, *15:* 251
Brotman, Adolph E., *5:* 21
Brown, David, *7:* 47
Brown, Denise, *11:* 213
Brown, Judith Gwyn, *1:* 45; *7:* 5;
    8: 167; *9:* 182, 190; *20:* 16,
    17, 18; *23:* 142
Brown, Marc Tolon, *10:* 17, 197;
    14: 263
Brown, Marcia, *7:* 30; *25:* 203;
    YABC 1: 27
Brown, Margery W., *5:* 32-33;
    10: 3
Brown, Paul, *25:* 26
Browne, Dik, *8:* 212
Browne, Gordon, *16:* 97
Browne, Hablot K., *15:* 80; *21:* 14,
    15, 16, 17, 18, 19, 20; *24:* 25
Browning, Coleen, *4:* 132
Browning, Mary Eleanor, *24:* 84
Bruce, Robert, *23:* 23
Brule, Al, *3:* 135
Brundage, Frances, *19:* 244
Brunhoff, Jean de, *24:* 57, 58
Brunhoff, Laurent de, *24:* 60
Brychta, Alex, *21:* 21
Bryson, Bernarda, *3:* 88, 146
Buba, Joy, *12:* 83
Buchanan, Lilian, *13:* 16

Buck, Margaret Waring, *3:* 30
Buehr, Walter, *3:* 31
Buff, Conrad, *19:* 52, 53, 54
Buff, Mary, *19:* 52, 53
Bull, Charles Livingston, *18:* 207
Bullen, Anne, *3:* 166, 167
Burchard, Peter, *3:* 197; *5:* 35;
    6: 158, 218
Burger, Carl, *3:* 33
Burgeson, Marjorie, *19:* 31
Burkert, Nancy Ekholm, *18:* 186;
    22: 140; *24:* 62, 63, 64, 65;
    YABC 1: 46
Burn, Doris, *6:* 172
Burningham, John, *9:* 68; *16:* 60-61
Burns, Howard M., *12:* 173
Burns, Raymond, *9:* 29
Burns, Robert, *24:* 106
Burr, Dane, *12:* 2
Burra, Edward, *YABC 2:* 68
Burridge, Marge Opitz, *14:* 42
Burris, Burmah, *4:* 81
Burton, Virginia Lee, *2:* 43;
    YABC 1: 24
Busoni, Rafaello, *1:* 186; *3:* 224;
    6: 126; *14:* 5; *16:* 62-63
Butterfield, Ned, *1:* 153
Buzzell, Russ W., *12:* 177
Byfield, Barbara Ninde, *8:* 18
Byrd, Robert, *13:* 218

Caddy, Alice, *6:* 41
Cady, Harrison, *17:* 21, 23; *19:* 57,
    58
Caldecott, Randolph, *16:* 98, 103;
    17: 32-33, 36, 38-39;
    YABC 2: 172
Calder, Alexander, *18:* 168
Calderon, W. Frank, *25:* 160
Caldwell, Doreen, *23:* 77
Callahan, Kevin, *22:* 42
Callahan, Philip S., *25:* 77
Cameron, Julia Margaret, *19:* 203
Campbell, Ann, *11:* 43
Campbell, Walter M., *YABC 2:* 158
Caraway, James, *3:* 200-201
Carigiet, Alois, *24:* 67
Carle, Eric, *4:* 42; *11:* 121; *12:* 29
Carrick, Donald, *5:* 194
Carrick, Valery, *21:* 47
Carroll, Lewis. *See* Dodgson,
    Charles L., *20:* 148;
    YABC 2: 98
Carroll, Ruth, *7:* 41; *10:* 68
Carter, Harry, *22:* 179
Carter, Helene, *15:* 38; *22:* 202,
    203; *YABC 2:* 220-221
Carty, Leo, *4:* 196; *7:* 163
Cary, *4:* 133; *9:* 32; *20:* 2; *21:* 143
Cary, Page, *12:* 41
Case, Sandra E., *16:* 2
Cassel, Lili. *See* Wronker, Lili
    Cassel, *3:* 247; *10:* 204; *21:* 10
Cassels, Jean, *8:* 50

Cassel-Wronker, Lili.
    See also Wronker, Lili Cassel
Castle, Jane, *4:* 80
Cather, Carolyn, *3:* 83; *15:* 203
Cellini, Joseph, *2:* 73; *3:* 35;
    16: 116
Chalmers, Mary, *3:* 145; *13:* 148
Chambers, C. E., *17:* 230
Chambers, Dave, *12:* 151
Chambers, Mary, *4:* 188
Chapman, C. H., *13:* 83, 85, 87
Chapman, Frederick T., *6:* 27
Chappell, Warren, *3:* 172; *21:* 56
Charlip, Remy, *4:* 48
Charlot, Jean, *1:* 137, 138; *8:* 23;
    14: 31
Charmatz, Bill, *7:* 45
Chartier, Normand, *9:* 36
Chase, Lynwood M., *14:* 4
Chastain, Madye Lee, *4:* 50
Chauncy, Francis, *24:* 158
Chen, Tony, *6:* 45; *19:* 131
Cheney, T. A., *11:* 47
Chess, Victoria, *12:* 6
Chew, Ruth, *7:* 46
Cho, Shinta, *8:* 126
Chollick, Jay, *25:* 175
Chorao, Kay, *7:* 200-201; *8:* 25;
    11: 234
Christensen, Gardell Dano, *1:* 57
Christy, Howard Chandler,
    17: 163-165, 168-169; *19:* 186,
    187; *21:* 22, 23, 24, 25
Chronister, Robert, *23:* 138
Church, Frederick, *YABC 1:* 155
Chute, Marchette, *1:* 59
Chwast, Jacqueline, *1:* 63; *2:* 275;
    6: 46-47; *11:* 125; *12:* 202;
    14: 235
Chwast, Seymour, *3:* 128-129;
    18: 43
Cirlin, Edgard, *2:* 168
Clarke, Harry, *23:* 172, 173
Clayton, Robert, *9:* 181
Cleaver, Elizabeth, *8:* 204; *23:* 36
Clement, Charles, *20:* 38
Clevin, Jörgen, *7:* 50
Coalson, Glo, *9:* 72, 85; *25:* 155
Cober, Alan, *17:* 158
Cochran, Bobbye, *11:* 52
CoConis, Ted, *4:* 41
Coerr, Eleanor, *1:* 64
Coggins, Jack, *2:* 69
Cohen, Alix, *7:* 53
Cohen, Vincent O., *19:* 243
Cohen, Vivien, *11:* 112
Colbert, Anthony, *15:* 41; *20:* 193
Colby, C. B., *3:* 47
Cole, Olivia H. H., *1:* 134; *3:* 223;
    9: 111
Collier, David, *13:* 127
Colonna, Bernard, *21:* 50
Connolly, Jerome P., *4:* 128
Cooke, Donald E., *2:* 77
Coombs, Patricia, *2:* 82; *3:* 52;
    22: 119

Cooney, Barbara, *6:* 16-17, 50;
    12: 42; *13:* 92; *15:* 145;
    16: 74, 111; *18:* 189; *23:* 38,
    89, 93; *YABC 2:* 10
Cooper, Mario, *24:* 107
Cooper, Marjorie, *7:* 112
Copelman, Evelyn, *8:* 61; *18:* 25
Corbino, John, *19:* 248
Corcos, Lucille, *2:* 223; *10:* 27
Corey, Robert, *9:* 34
Corlass, Heather, *10:* 7
Cornell, Jeff, *11:* 58
Corrigan, Barbara, *8:* 37
Corwin, Judith Hoffman, *10:* 28
Cory, Fanny Y., *20:* 113
Cosgrove, Margaret, *3:* 100
Costello, David F., *23:* 55
Cox, Charles, *8:* 20
Cox, Palmer, *24:* 76, 77
Craft, Kinuko, *22:* 182
Crane, Alan H., *1:* 217
Crane, H. M., *13:* 111
Crane, Walter, *18:* 46-49, 53-54,
    56-57, 59-61; *22:* 128; *24:* 210,
    217
Credle, Ellis *1:* 69
Crofut, Susan, *23:* 61
Crowell, Pers, *3:* 125
Cruikshank, George, *15:* 76, 83;
    22: 74, 75, 76, 77, 78, 79, 80,
    81, 82, 84, 137; *24:* 22, 23
Crump, Fred H., *11:* 62
Cruz, Ray, *6:* 55
Cuffari, Richard, *4:* 75; *5:* 98;
    6: 56; *7:* 13, 84, 153; *8:* 148,
    155; *9:* 89; *11:* 19; *12:* 55, 96,
    114; *15:* 51, 202; *18:* 5;
    20: 139; *21:* 197; *22:* 14, 192;
    23: 15, 106; *25:* 97
Cugat, Xavier, *19:* 120
Cummings, Richard, *24:* 119
Cunette, Lou, *20:* 93; *22:* 125
Cunningham, Aline, *25:* 180
Cunningham, David, *11:* 13
Cunningham, Imogene, *16:* 122,
    127
Curry, John Steuart, *2:* 5; *19:* 84
Curtis, Bruce, *23:* 96

Dabcovich, Lydia, *25:* 105
D'Amato, Alex, *9:* 48; *20:* 25
D'Amato, Janet, *9:* 48; *20:* 25
Daniel, Alan, *23:* 59
Daniel, Lewis C., *20:* 216
Daniels, Steve, *22:* 16
Danska, Herbert, *24:* 219
Danyell, Alice, *20:* 27
Darley, F.O.C., *16:* 145; *19:* 79,
    86, 88, 185; *21:* 28, 36;
    YABC 2: 175
Darling, Lois, *3:* 59; *23:* 30, 31
Darling, Louis, *1:* 40-41; *2:* 63;
    3: 59; *23:* 30, 31
Darrow, Whitney, Jr., *13:* 25

Darwin, Len, *24:* 82
Dauber, Liz, *1:* 22; *3:* 266
Daugherty, James, *3:* 66; *8:* 178;
    13: 27-28, 161; *18:* 101;
    19: 72; *YABC 1:* 256;
    YABC 2: 174
d'Aulaire, Edgar, *5:* 51
d'Aulaire, Ingri, *5:* 51
David, Jonathan, *19:* 37
Davis, Allan, *20:* 11; *22:* 45
Davis, Bette J., *15:* 53; *23:* 95
Davis, Marguerite, *YABC 1:* 126,
    230
Dawson, Diane, *24:* 127
Dean, Bob, *19:* 211
de Angeli, Marguerite, *1:* 77;
    YABC 1: 166
de Bosschère, Jean, *19:* 252; *21:* 4
De Bruyn, M(onica) G., *13:* 30-31
De Cuir, John F., *1:* 28-29
De Grazia, *14:* 59
de Groat, Diane, *9:* 39; *18:* 7;
    23: 123
de Groot, Lee, *6:* 21
Delaney, A., *21:* 78
de Larrea, Victoria, *6:* 119, 204
Delessert, Etienne, *7:* 140;
    YABC 2: 209
Delulio, John, *15:* 54
Denetsosie, Hoke, *13:* 126
Dennis, Morgan, *18:* 68-69
Dennis, Wesley, *2:* 87; *3:* 111;
    11: 132; *18:* 71-74; *22:* 9;
    24: 196, 200
Denslow, W. W., *16:* 84-87;
    18: 19-20, 24
de Paola, Tomie, *8:* 95; *9:* 93;
    11: 69; *25:* 103
Detmold, Edward J., *22:* 104, 105,
    106, 107; *YABC 2:* 203
Detrich, Susan, *20:* 133
DeVelasco, Joseph E., *21:* 51
de Veyrac, Robert, *YABC 2:* 19
DeVille, Edward A., *4:* 235
Devito, Bert, *12:* 164
Devlin, Harry, *11:* 74
Dewey, Ariane, *7:* 64
    See also Aruego, Ariane
Diamond, Donna, *21:* 200; *23:* 63
Dick, John Henry, *8:* 181
Dickey, Robert L., *15:* 279
DiFiore, Lawrence, *10:* 51; *12:* 190
Dillard, Annie, *10:* 32
Dillon, Corinne B., *1:* 139
Dillon, Diane, *4:* 104, 167; *6:* 23;
    13: 29; *15:* 99
Dillon, Leo, *4:* 104, 167; *6:* 23;
    13: 29; *15:* 99
Dinan, Carol, *25:* 169
Dines, Glen, *7:* 66-67
Dinsdale, Mary, *10:* 65; *11:* 171
Dixon, Maynard, *20:* 165
Doares, Robert G., *20:* 39
Dobias, Frank, *22:* 162
Dobrin, Arnold, *4:* 68
Dodd, Ed, *4:* 69

Dodgson, Charles L., *20:* 148;
    YABC 2: 98
Dodson, Bert, *9:* 138; *14:* 195
Dohanos, Stevan, *16:* 10
Dolson, Hildegarde, *5:* 57
Domanska, Janina, *6:* 66-67;
    YABC 1: 166
Domjan, Joseph, *25:* 93
Donahue, Vic, *2:* 93; *3:* 190; *9:* 44
Donald, Elizabeth, *4:* 18
Donna, Natalie, *9:* 52
Doré, Gustave, *18:* 169, 172, 175;
    19: 93, 94, 95, 96, 97, 98, 99,
    100, 101, 102, 103, 104, 105;
    23: 188; *25:* 197, 199
Doremus, Robert, *6:* 62; *13:* 90
Dorfman, Ronald, *11:* 128
Dougherty, Charles, *16:* 204; *18:* 74
Douglas, Goray, *13:* 151
Dowd, Vic, *3:* 244; *10:* 97
Dowden, Anne Ophelia, *7:* 70-71;
    13: 120
Doyle, Richard, *21:* 31, 32, 33;
    23: 231; *24:* 177
Drawson, Blair, *17:* 53
Drew, Patricia, *15:* 100
Drummond, V. H., *6:* 70
du Bois, William Pene, *4:* 70;
    10: 122
Duchesne, Janet, *6:* 162
Duke, Chris, *8:* 195
Dulac, Edmund, *19:* 108, 109, 110,
    111, 112, 113, 114, 115, 117;
    23: 187; *25:* 152; *YABC 1:* 37;
    YABC 2: 147
Dulac, Jean, *13:* 64
Dunn, Phoebe, *5:* 175
Dunn, Tris, *5:* 175
Dunnington, Tom, *3:* 36; *18:* 281;
    25: 61
Dutz, *6:* 59
Duvoisin, Roger, *2:* 95; *6:* 76-77;
    7: 197
Dypold, Pat, *15:* 37

Eagle, Michael, *11:* 86; *20:* 9;
    23: 18
Earle, Olive L., *7:* 75
Eaton, Tom, *4:* 62; *6:* 64; *22:* 99;
    24: 124
Ebel, Alex, *11:* 89
Ebert, Len, *9:* 191
Edrien, *11:* 53
Edwards, Gunvor, *2:* 71; *25:* 47
Edwards, Linda Strauss, *21:* 134
Eggenhofer, Nicholas, *2:* 81
Egielski, Richard, *11:* 90; *16:* 208
Ehrlich, Bettina, *1:* 83
Eichenberg, Fritz, *1:* 79; *9:* 54;
    19: 248; *23:* 170; *24:* 200;
    YABC 1: 104-105;
    YABC 2: 213
Einsel, Naiad, *10:* 35
Einsel, Walter, *10:* 37

Einzig, Susan, *3:* 77
Eitzen, Allan, *9:* 56; *12:* 212;
    14: 226; *21:* 194
Elgaard, Greta, *19:* 241
Elgin, Kathleen, *9:* 188
Ellacott, S. E., *19:* 118
Elliott, Sarah M., *14:* 58
Emberley, Ed, *8:* 53
Englebert, Victor, *8:* 54
Enos, Randall, *20:* 183
Enright, Maginel Wright, *19:* 240,
    243
Erhard, Walter, *1:* 152
Erickson, Phoebe, *11:* 83
Escourido, Joseph, *4:* 81
Estrada, Ric, *5:* 52, 146; *13:* 174
Ets, Marie Hall, *2:* 102
Eulalie, *YABC 2:* 315
Evans, Katherine, *5:* 64
Ewing, Juliana Horatia, *16:* 92

Falls, C. B., *1:* 19
Farmer, Peter, *24:* 108
Fatigati, Evelyn, *24:* 112
Faul-Jansen, Regina, *22:* 117
Faulkner, Jack, *6:* 169
Fava, Rita, *2:* 29
Fax, Elton C., *1:* 101; *4:* 2; *12:* 77;
    25: 107
Feelings, Tom, *5:* 22; *8:* 56;
    12: 153; *16:* 105
Fehr, Terrence, *21:* 87
Feiffer, Jules, *3:* 91; *8:* 58
Fellows, Muriel H., *10:* 42
Fenton, Carroll Lane, *5:* 66; *21:* 39
Fenton, Mildred Adams, *5:* 66;
    21: 39
Fetz, Ingrid, *11:* 67; *12:* 52;
    16: 205; *17:* 59
Fiammenghi, Gioia, *9:* 66; *11:* 44;
    12: 206; *13:* 57, 59
Field, Rachel, *15:* 113
Fink, Sam, *18:* 119
Finlay, Winifred, *23:* 72
Fiorentino, Al, *3:* 240
Fischer, Hans, *25:* 202
Fisher, Leonard Everett, *3:* 6;
    4: 72, 86; *6:* 197; *9:* 59;
    16: 151, 153; *23:* 44;
    YABC 2: 169
Fisher, Lois, *20:* 62; *21:* 7
Fisk, Nicholas, *25:* 112
Fitschen, Marilyn, *2:* 20-21; *20:* 48
Fitzgerald, F. A., *15:* 116;
    25: 86-87
Fitzhugh, Louise, *1:* 94; *9:* 163
Fitzhugh, Susie, *11:* 117
Fitzsimmons, Arthur, *14:* 128
Flack, Marjorie, *21:* 67;
    YABC 2: 122
Flagg, James Montgomery, *17:* 227
Flax, Zeona, *2:* 245
Fleishman, Seymour, *14:* 232;
    24: 87

Fleming, Guy, *18:* 41
Floethe, Richard, *3:* 131; *4:* 90
Floherty, John J., Jr., *5:* 68
Flora, James, *1:* 96
Florian, Douglas, *19:* 122
Flory, Jane, *22:* 111
Floyd, Gareth, *1:* 74; *17:* 245
Flynn, Barbara, *7:* 31; *9:* 70
Fogarty, Thomas, *15:* 89
Folger, Joseph, *9:* 100
Folkard, Charles, *22:* 132
Forberg, Ati, *12:* 71, 205; *14:* 1;
    22: 113
Ford, George, *24:* 120
Ford, H. J., *16:* 185-186
Foreman, Michael, *2:* 110-111
Fortnum, Peggy, *6:* 29; *20:* 179;
    24: 211; *YABC 1:* 148
Foster, Genevieve, *2:* 112
Foster, Gerald, *7:* 78
Foster, Laura Louise, *6:* 79
Foster, Marian Curtis, *23:* 74
Fox, Charles Phillip, *12:* 84
Fox, Jim, *6:* 187
Fracé, Charles, *15:* 118
Frame, Paul, *2:* 45, 145; *9:* 153;
    10: 124; *21:* 71; *23:* 62;
    24: 123
Francois, André, *25:* 117
Francoise. *See* Seignobosc,
    Francoise, *21:* 145, 146
Frank, Lola Edick, *2:* 199
Frank, Mary, *4:* 54
Frankenberg, Robert, *22:* 116
Franklin, John, *24:* 22
Frascino, Edward, *9:* 133
Frasconi, Antonio, *6:* 80
Fraser, Betty, *2:* 212; *6:* 185;
    8: 103
Fraser, F. A., *22:* 234
Freas, John, *25:* 207
Freeman, Don, *2:* 15; *13:* 249;
    17: 62-63, 65, 67-68; *18:* 243;
    20: 195; *23:* 213, 217
Fregosi, Claudia, *24:* 117
French, Fiona, *6:* 82-83
Friedman, Marvin, *19:* 59
Frith, Michael K., *15:* 138; *18:* 120
Frost, A. B., *17:* 6-7; *19:* 123, 124,
    125, 126, 127, 128, 129, 130;
    YABC 1: 156-157, 160;
    YABC 2: 107
Fry, Guy, *2:* 224
Fry, Rosalie, *3:* 72;
    YABC 2: 180-181
Fry, Rosalind, *21:* 153, 168
Fuchs, Erich, *6:* 84
Fulford, Deborah, *23:* 159
Fuller, Margaret, *25:* 189
Funk, Tom, *7:* 17, 99
Furukawa, Mel, *25:* 42

Gaberell, J., *19:* 236
Gackenbach, Dick, *19:* 168

Gaetano, Nicholas, *23:* 209
Gag, Flavia, *17:* 49, 52
Gág, Wanda, *YABC 1:* 135,
    137-138, 141, 143
Gagnon, Cécile, *11:* 77
Gal, Laszlo, *14:* 127
Galdone, Paul, *1:* 156, 181, 206;
    2: 40, 241; *3:* 42, 144; *4:* 141;
    10: 109, 158; *11:* 21; *12:* 118,
    210; *14:* 12; *16:* 36-37;
    17: 70-74; *18:* 111, 230;
    19: 183; *21:* 154; *22:* 150, 245
Gallagher, Sears, *20:* 112
Galster, Robert, *1:* 66
Gammell, Stephen, *7:* 48; *13:* 149
Gannett, Ruth Chrisman, *3:* 74;
    18: 254
Garbutt, Bernard, *23:* 68
Gardner, Richard. *See* Cummings,
    Richard, *24:* 119
Garnett, Eve, *3:* 75
Garraty, Gail, *4:* 142
Garrett, Edmund H., *20:* 29
Garrison, Barbara, *19:* 133
Gaver, Becky, *20:* 61
Gay, Zhenya, *19:* 135, 136
Geary, Clifford N., *1:* 122; *9:* 104
Geer, Charles, *1:* 91; *3:* 179;
    4: 201; *6:* 168; *7:* 96; *9:* 58;
    10: 72; *12:* 127
Geisel, Theodor Seuss, *1:* 104-105,
    106
Geldart, William, *15:* 121; *21:* 202
Genia, *4:* 84
Gentry, Cyrille R., *12:* 66
George, Jean, *2:* 113
Geritz, Franz, *17:* 135
Gervase, *12:* 27
Gibbons, Gail, *23:* 78
Giguère, George, *20:* 111
Gilbert, John, *19:* 184;
    YABC 2: 287
Gill, Margery, *4:* 57; *7:* 7; *22:* 122;
    25: 166
Gillette, Henry J., *23:* 237
Gilman, Esther, *15:* 124
Giovanopoulos, Paul, *7:* 104
Githens, Elizabeth M., *5:* 47
Gladstone, Gary, *12:* 89; *13:* 190
Gladstone, Lise, *15:* 273
Glanzman, Louis S., *2:* 177; *3:* 182
Glaser, Milton, *3:* 5; *5:* 156;
    11: 107
Glass, Marvin, *9:* 174
Glattauer, Ned, *5:* 84; *13:* 224;
    14: 26
Glauber, Uta, *17:* 76
Gleeson, J. M., *YABC 2:* 207
Gliewe, Unada, *3:* 78-79; *21:* 73
Glovach, Linda, *7:* 105
Gobbato, Imero, *3:* 180-181;
    6: 213; *7:* 58; *9:* 150; *18:* 39;
    21: 167
Goble, Paul, *25:* 121
Godfrey, Michael, *17:* 279
Goffstein, M. B., *8:* 71

Golbin, Andrée, *15:* 125
Goldfeder, Cheryl, *11:* 191
Goldsborough, June, *5:* 154-155;
    8: 92; *14:* 266; *19:* 139
Goldstein, Leslie, *5:* 8; *6:* 60;
    10: 106
Goldstein, Nathan, *1:* 175; *2:* 79;
    11: 41, 232; *16:* 55
Goodall, John S., *4:* 92-93;
    10: 132; *YABC 1:* 198
Goode, Diane, *15:* 126
Goodwin, Harold, *13:* 74
Goodwin, Philip R., *18:* 206
Gordon, Gwen, *12:* 151
Gordon, Margaret, *4:* 147; *5:* 48-49;
    9: 79
Gorecka-Egan, Erica, *18:* 35
Gorey, Edward, *1:* 60-61; *13:* 169;
    18: 192; *20:* 201
Gorsline, Douglas, *1:* 98; *6:* 13;
    11: 113; *13:* 104; *15:* 14;
    YABC 1: 15
Gosner, Kenneth, *5:* 135
Gotlieb, Jules, *6:* 127
Gough, Philip, *23:* 47
Grabianski, *20:* 144
Graham, A. B., *11:* 61
Graham, L., *7:* 108
Graham, Margaret Bloy, *11:* 120;
    18: 305, 307
Grahame-Johnstone, Anne, *13:* 61
Grahame-Johnstone, Janet, *13:* 61
Gramatky, Hardie, *1:* 107
Grant, Gordon, *17:* 230, 234;
    25: 123, 124, 125, 126;
    YABC 1: 164
Grant, (Alice) Leigh, *10:* 52;
    15: 131; *20:* 20
Gray, Reginald, *6:* 69
Green, Eileen, *6:* 97
Greenaway, Kate, *17:* 275; *24:* 180;
    YABC 1: 88-89; *YABC 2:* 131,
    133, 136, 138-139, 141
Greenwald, Sheila, *1:* 34; *3:* 99;
    8: 72
Greiffenhagen, Maurice, *16:* 137
Greifferhager, Maurice,
    YABC 2: 288
Greiner, Robert, *6:* 86
Gretz, Susanna, *7:* 114
Gretzer, John, *1:* 54; *3:* 26; *4:* 162;
    7: 125; *16:* 247; *18:* 117
Grey Owl, *24:* 41
Gri, *25:* 90
Grieder, Walter, *9:* 84
Grifalconi, Ann, *2:* 126; *3:* 248;
    11: 18; *13:* 182
Gringhuis, Dirk, *6:* 98; *9:* 196
Gripe, Harald, *2:* 127
Grisha, *3:* 71
Grose, Helen Mason, *YABC 1:* 260;
    YABC 2: 150
Grossman, Nancy, *24:* 130
Grossman, Robert, *11:* 124
Groth, John, *15:* 79; *21:* 53, 54
Gschwind, William, *11:* 72

Guggenheim, Hans, 2: 10; 3: 37;
  8: 136
Guilbeau, Honoré, 22: 69
Guthrie, Robin, 20: 122

Haas, Irene, 17: 77
Hader, Berta H., 16: 126
Hader, Elmer S., 16: 126
Hafner, Marylin, 22: 196, 216;
  24: 44
Haldane, Roger, 13: 76; 14: 202
Hale, Kathleen, 17: 79
Hall, Douglas, 15: 184
Hall, H. Tom, 1: 227
Hall, Vicki, 20: 24
Halpern, Joan, 10: 25
Hamberger, John, 6: 8; 8: 32;
  14: 79
Hamil, Tom, 14: 80
Hamilton, Helen S., 2: 238
Hamilton, J., 19: 83, 85, 87
Hammond, Chris, 21: 37
Hammond, Elizabeth, 5: 36, 203
Hampshire, Michael, 5: 187;
  7: 110-111
Hampson, Denman, 10: 155;
  15: 130
Handville, Robert, 1: 89
Hane, Roger, 17: 239
Hanley, Catherine, 8: 161
Hann, Jacquie, 19: 144
Hanson, Joan, 8: 76; 11: 139
Hardy, David A., 9: 96
Hardy, Paul, YABC 2: 245
Harlan, Jerry, 3: 96
Harnischfeger, 18: 121
Harper, Arthur, YABC 2: 121
Harrington, Richard, 5: 81
Harrison, Florence, 20: 150, 152
Harrison, Harry, 4: 103
Hart, William, 13: 72
Hartelius, Margaret, 10: 24
Hartshorn, Ruth, 5: 115; 11: 129
Harvey, Gerry, 7: 180
Hassell, Hilton, YABC 1: 187
Hasselriis, Else, 18: 87;
  YABC 1: 96
Hauman, Doris, 2: 184
Hauman, George, 2: 184
Hausherr, Rosmarie, 15: 29
Hawkinson, John, 4: 109; 7: 83;
  21: 64
Hawkinson, Lucy, 21: 64
Haydock, Robert, 4: 95
Haywood, Carolyn, 1: 112
Healy, Daty, 12: 143
Hechtkopf, H., 11: 110
Heigh, James, 22: 98
Heighway, Richard, 25: 160
Henneberger, Robert, 1: 42; 2: 237;
  25: 83
Henry, Thomas, 5: 102
Henstra, Friso, 8: 80
Herbert, Wally, 23: 101

Herbster, Mary Lee, 9: 33
Hergé. See Remi, Georges
Hermanson, Dennis, 10: 55
Herrington, Roger, 3: 161
Heustis, Louise L., 20: 28
Heyduck-Huth, Hilde, 8: 82
Heyer, Hermann, 20: 114, 115
Heyman, Ken, 8: 33
Higginbottom, J. Winslow, 8: 170
Hildebrandt, Greg, 8: 191
Hildebrandt, Tim, 8: 191
Hilder, Rowland, 19: 207
Himler, Ronald, 6: 114; 7: 162;
  8: 17, 84, 125; 14: 76; 19: 145
Hiroshige, 25: 71
Hirsh, Marilyn, 7: 126
Hitz, Demi, 11: 135; 15: 245
Ho, Kwoncjan, 15: 132
Hoban, Lillian, 1: 114; 22: 157
Hoban, Tana, 22: 159
Hoberman, Norman, 5: 82
Hodges, C. Walter, 2: 139; 11: 15;
  12: 25; 23: 34; 25: 96;
  YABC 2: 62-63
Hodges, David, 9: 98
Hofbauer, Imre, 2: 162
Hoff, Syd, 9: 107; 10: 128
Hoffman, Rosekrans, 15: 133
Hoffmann, Felix, 9: 109
Hofsinde, Robert, 21: 70
Hogan, Inez, 2: 141
Hogarth, Paul, YABC 1: 16
Hogenbyl, Jan, 1: 35
Hogner, Nils, 4: 122; 25: 144
Hogrogian, Nonny, 3: 221;
  4: 106-107; 5: 166; 7: 129;
  15: 2; 16: 176; 20: 154;
  22: 146; 25: 217; YABC 2: 84,
  94
Hokusai, 25: 71
Holberg, Richard, 2: 51
Holiday, Henry, YABC 2: 107
Holland, Janice, 18: 118
Holland, Marion, 6: 116
Holling, Holling C., 15: 136-137
Hollinger, Deanne, 12: 116
Holmes, B., 3: 82
Holmes, Bea, 7: 74; 24: 156
Holz, Loretta, 17: 81
Homar, Lorenzo, 6: 2
Homer, Winslow, YABC 2: 87
Honigman, Marian, 3: 2
Hood, Susan, 12: 43
Hook, Jeff, 14: 137
Hoover, Carol A., 21: 77
Hoover, Russell, 12: 95; 17: 2
Horder, Margaret, 2: 108
Horvat, Laurel, 12: 201
Horvath, Ferdinand Kusati, 24: 176
Hotchkiss, De Wolfe, 20: 49
Hough, Charlotte, 9: 112; 13: 98;
  17: 83; 24: 195
Houlihan, Ray, 11: 214
Housman, Laurence, 25: 146, 147
Houston, James, 13: 107
How, W. E., 20: 47

Howard, Alan, 16: 80
Howard, J. N., 15: 234
Howe, Stephen, 1: 232
Howell, Pat, 15: 139
Howell, Troy, 23: 24
Howes, Charles, 22: 17
Hudnut, Robin, 14: 62
Huffaker, Sandy, 10: 56
Huffman, Joan, 13: 33
Huffman, Tom, 13: 180; 17: 212;
  21: 116; 24: 132
Hughes, Arthur, 20: 148, 149, 150
Hughes, Shirley, 1: 20, 21; 7: 3;
  12: 217; 16: 163
Hülsmann, Eva, 16: 166
Hummel, Lisl, YABC 2: 333-334
Humphrey, Henry, 16: 167
Humphreys, Graham, 25: 168
Hunt, James, 2: 143
Hurd, Clement, 2: 148, 149
Hurd, Peter, 24: 30, 31,
  YABC 2: 56
Hustler, Tom, 6: 105
Hutchins, Pat, 15: 142
Hutchinson, William M., 6: 3, 138
Hutchison, Paula, 23: 10
Hutton, Clarke, YABC 2: 335
Hutton, Warwick, 20: 91
Hyman, Trina Schart, 1: 204;
  2: 194; 5: 153; 6: 106; 7: 138,
  145; 8: 22; 10: 196; 13: 96;
  14: 114; 15: 204; 16: 234;
  20: 82; 22: 133; 24: 151;
  25: 79, 82

Ide, Jacqueline, YABC 1: 39
Ilsley, Velma, 3: 1; 7: 55; 12: 109
Inga, 1: 142
Ingraham, Erick, 21: 177
Innocenti, Roberto, 21: 123
Inoue, Yosuke, 24: 118
Ipcar, Dahlov, 1: 124-125
Irvin, Fred, 13: 166; 15: 143-144
Isaac, Joanne, 21: 76
Ishmael, Woodi, 24: 111
Ives, Ruth, 15: 257

Jacobs, Barbara, 9: 136
Jacobs, Lou, Jr., 9: 136; 15: 128
Jacques, Robin, 1: 70; 2: 1; 8: 46;
  9: 20; 15: 187; 19: 253;
  YABC 1: 42
Jagr, Miloslav, 13: 197
Jakubowski, Charles, 14: 192
Jambor, Louis, YABC 1: 11
James, Gilbert, YABC 1: 43
James, Harold, 2: 151; 3: 62; 8: 79
James, Will, 19: 150, 152, 153,
  155, 163
Janosch. See Eckert, Horst
Jansson, Tove, 3: 90

Jaques, Faith, *7:* 11, 132-33;
   21: 83, 84
Jauss, Anne Marie, *1:* 139; *3:* 34;
   10: 57, 119; *11:* 205; *23:* 194
Jeffers, Susan, *17:* 86-87;
   25: 164-165
Jefferson, Louise E., *4:* 160
Jeruchim, Simon, *6:* 173; *15:* 250
Jeschke, Susan, *20:* 89
John, Diana, *12:* 209
John, Helen, *1:* 215
Johns, Jeanne, *24:* 114
Johnson, Bruce, *9:* 47
Johnson, Crockett. *See* Leisk, David
Johnson, D. William, *23:* 104
Johnson, Harper, *1:* 27; *2:* 33;
   18: 302; *19:* 61
Johnson, James David, *12:* 195
Johnson, James Ralph, *1:* 23, 127
Johnson, Milton, *1:* 67; *2:* 71
Johnson, Pamela, *16:* 174
Johnstone, Anne, *8:* 120
Johnstone, Janet Grahame, *8:* 120
Jones, Carol, *5:* 131
Jones, Elizabeth Orton, *18:* 124,
   126, 128-129
Jones, Harold, *14:* 88
Jones, Laurian, *25:* 24, 27
Jones, Robert, *25:* 67
Jones, Wilfred, *YABC 1:* 163
Jucker, Sita, *5:* 93
Jullian, Philippe, *24:* 206; *25:* 203
Jupo, Frank, *7:* 148-149

Kakimoo, Kozo, *11:* 148
Kalmenoff, Matthew, *22:* 191
Kamen, Gloria, *1:* 41; *9:* 119;
   10: 178
Kane, Henry B., *14:* 90;
   18: 219-220
Kane, Robert, *18:* 131
Karlin, Eugene, *10:* 63; *20:* 131
Katona, Robert, *21:* 85; *24:* 126
Kaufman, Angelika, *15:* 156
Kaufman, John, *13:* 158
Kaufmann, John, *1:* 174; *4:* 159;
   8: 43, 192; *10:* 102;
   18: 133-134; *22:* 251
Kaye, Graham, *1:* 9
Keane, Bil, *4:* 135
Keats, Ezra Jack, *3:* 18, 105, 257;
   14: 101, 102
Keegan, Marcia, *9:* 122
Keen, Eliot, *25:* 213
Keeping, Charles, *9:* 124, 185;
   15: 28, 134; *18:* 115
Keith, Eros, *4:* 98; *5:* 138
Kelen, Emery, *13:* 115
Kellogg, Steven, *8:* 96; *11:* 207;
   14: 130; *20:* 58; *YABC 1:* 65,
   73
Kelly, Walt, *18:* 136-141, 144-146,
   148-149
Kemble, E. W., *YABC 2:* 54, 59

Kemp-Welsh, Lucy, *24:* 197
Kennedy, Paul Edward, *6:* 190;
   8: 132
Kennedy, Richard, *3:* 93; *12:* 179;
   YABC 1: 57
Kent, Jack, *24:* 136
Kent, Rockwell, *5:* 166; *6:* 129;
   20: 225, 226, 227, 229
Kepes, Juliet, *13:* 119
Kerr, Judity, *24:* 137
Kessler, Leonard, *1:* 108; *7:* 139;
   14: 107, 227; *22:* 101
Kettelkamp, Larry, *2:* 164
Key, Alexander, *8:* 99
Kiakshuk, *8:* 59
Kiddell-Monroe, Joan, *19:* 201
Kidder, Harvey, *9:* 105
Kimball, Yeffe, *23:* 116
Kindred, Wendy, *7:* 151
King, Robin, *10:* 164-165
Kingman, Dong, *16:* 287
Kingsley, Charles, *YABC 2:* 182
Kipling, John Lockwood,
   YABC 2: 198
Kipling, Rudyard, *YABC 2:* 196
Kirk, Ruth, *5:* 96
Kirmse, Marguerite, *15:* 283;
   18: 153
Kirschner, Ruth, *22:* 154
Klapholz, Mel, *13:* 35
Knight, Christopher, *13:* 125
Knight, Hilary, *1:* 233; *3:* 21;
   15: 92, 158-159; *16:* 258-260;
   18: 235; *19:* 169;
   YABC 1: 168-169, 172
Knotts, Howard, *20:* 4; *25:* 170
Kocsis, J. C. *See* Paul, James
Koering, Ursula, *3:* 28; *4:* 14
Koerner, Henry. *See* Koerner,
   W.H.D.
Koerner, W. H. D., *14:* 216;
   21: 88, 89, 90, 91; *23:* 211
Komoda, Kiyo *9:* 128; *13:* 214
Konashevicha, V., *YABC 1:* 26
Konigsburg, E. L., *4:* 138
Korach, Mimi, *1:* 128-129; *2:* 52;
   4: 39; *5:* 159; *9:* 129; *10:* 21;
   24: 69
Koren, Edward, *5:* 100
Kossin, Sandy, *10:* 71; *23:* 105
Kovacević, Zivojin, *13:* 247
Krahn, Fernando, *2:* 257
Kramer, Frank, *6:* 121
Kraus, Robert, *13:* 217
Kredel, Fritz, *6:* 35; *17:* 93-96;
   22: 147; *24:* 175;
   YABC 2: 166, 300
Krementz, Jill, *17:* 98
Kresin, Robert, *23:* 19
Krush, Beth, *1:* 51, 85; *2:* 233;
   4: 115; *9:* 61; *10:* 191;
   11: 196; *18:* 164-165
Krush, Joe, *2:* 233; *4:* 115; *9:* 61;
   10: 191; *11:* 196; *18:* 164-165
Kubinyi, Laszlo, *4:* 116; *6:* 113;
   16: 118; *17:* 100

Kuhn, Bob, *17:* 91
Künstler, Mort, *10:* 73
Kurelek, William, *8:* 107
Kuriloff, Ron, *13:* 19
Kuskin, Karla, *2:* 170
Kutzer, Ernst, *19:* 249

LaBlanc, André, *24:* 146
La Croix, *YABC 2:* 4
Laimgruber, Monika, *11:* 153
Laite, Gordon, *1:* 130-131; *8:* 209
Lamb, Jim, *10:* 117
Lambert, Saul, *23:* 112
Lambo, Don, *6:* 156
Landa, Peter, *11:* 95; *13:* 177
Landshoff, Ursula, *13:* 124
Lane, John, *15:* 176-177
Lane, John R., *8:* 145
Lang, Jerry, *18:* 295
Langler, Nola, *8:* 110
Lantz, Paul, *1:* 82, 102
Larsen, Suzanne, *1:* 13
Larsson, Karl, *19:* 177
La Rue, Michael D., *13:* 215
Lasker, Joe, *7:* 186-187; *14:* 55
Latham, Barbara, *16:* 188-189
Lathrop, Dorothy, *14:* 117,
   118-119; *15:* 109; *16:* 78-79,
   81; *YABC 2:* 301
Lattimore, Eleanor Frances, *7:* 156
Lauden, Claire, *16:* 173
Lauden, George, Jr., *16:* 173
Laune, Paul, *2:* 235
Lawrence, John, *25:* 131
Lawrence, Stephen, *20:* 195
Lawson, Carol, *6:* 38
Lawson, George, *17:* 280
Lawson, Robert, *5:* 26; *6:* 94;
   13: 39; *16:* 11; *20:* 100, 102,
   103; *YABC 2:* 222,
   224-225, 227-235, 237-241
Lazarevich, Mila, *17:* 118
Lazarus, Keo Felker, *21:* 94
Lazzaro, Victor, *11:* 126
Leacroft, Richard, *6:* 140
Leaf, Munro, *20:* 99
Leander, Patricia, *23:* 27
Lear, Edward, *18:* 183-185
Lebenson, Richard, *6:* 209; *7:* 76;
   23: 145
Le Cain, Errol, *6:* 141; *9:* 3;
   22: 142; *25:* 198
Lee, Doris, *13:* 246
Lee, Manning de V., *2:* 200;
   17: 12; *YABC 2:* 304
Lee, Robert J., *3:* 97
Leech, John, *15:* 59
Lees, Harry, *6:* 112
Legrand, Edy, *18:* 89, 93
Lehrman, Rosalie, *2:* 180
Leichman, Seymour, *5:* 107
Leighton, Clare, *25:* 130
Leisk, David, *1:* 140-141; *11:* 54
Leloir, Maurice, *18:* 77, 80, 83, 99

Lemke, Horst, *14:* 98
Lemon, David Gwynne, *9:* 1
Lenski, Lois, *1:* 144
Lent, Blair, *1:* 116-117; *2:* 174;
    3: 206-207; *7:* 168-169
Lerner, Sharon, *11:* 157; *22:* 56
Leslie, Cecil, *19:* 244
Levin, Ted, *12:* 148
Levit, Herschel, *24:* 223
Levy, Jessica Ann, *19:* 225
Lewin, Ted, *4:* 77; *8:* 168; *20:* 110;
    21: 99, 100
Lewis, Allen, *15:* 112
Leydon, Rita Flodén, *21:* 101
Lieblich, Irene, *22:* 173
Liese, Charles, *4:* 222
Lilly, Charles, *8:* 73; *20:* 127
Lindberg, Howard, *10:* 123;
    16: 190
Linden, Seymour, *18:* 200-201
Linell. *See* Smith, Linell
Lionni, Leo, *8:* 115
Lipinsky, Lino, *2:* 156; *22:* 175
Lippman, Peter, *8:* 31
Lisker, Sonia O., *16:* 274
Lissim, Simon, *17:* 138
Little, Harold, *16:* 72
Livesly, Lorna, *19:* 216
Llerena, Carlos Antonio, *19:* 181
Lloyd, Errol, *11:* 39; *22:* 178
Lo, Koon-chiu, *7:* 134
Lobel, Anita, *6:* 87; *9:* 141; *18:* 248
Lobel, Arnold, *1:* 188-189; *5:* 12;
    6: 147; *7:* 167, 209;
    18: 190-191; *25:* 39, 43
Loefgren, Ulf, *3:* 108
Loescher, Ann, *20:* 108
Loescher, Gil, *20:* 108
Lofting, Hugh, *15:* 182-183
Lonette, Reisie, *11:* 211; *12:* 168;
    13: 56
Longtemps, Ken, *17:* 123
Looser, Heinz, *YABC 2:* 208
Lopshire, Robert, *6:* 149; *21:* 117
Lord, John Vernon, *21:* 104; *23:* 25
Lorraine, Walter H., *3:* 110; *4:* 123;
    16: 192
Loss, Joan, *11:* 163
Louderback, Walt, *YABC 1:* 164
Low, Joseph, *14:* 124, 125; *18:* 68;
    19: 194
Lowenheim, Alfred, *13:* 65-66
Lowitz, Anson, *17:* 124; *18:* 215
Lowrey, Jo, *8:* 133
Lubell, Winifred, *1:* 207; *3:* 15;
    6: 151
Lubin, Leonard B., *19:* 224;
    YABC 2: 96
Luhrs, Henry, *7:* 123; *11:* 120
Lupo, Dom, *4:* 204
Lydecker, Laura, *21:* 113
Lynch, Charles, *16:* 33
Lyon, Elinor, *6:* 154
Lyon, Fred, *14:* 16
Lyons, Oren, *8:* 193

Maas, Dorothy, *6:* 175
Macdonald, Alister, *21:* 55
MacDonald, Norman, *13:* 99
MacDonald, Roberta, *19:* 237
Macguire, Robert Reid, *18:* 67
MacIntyre, Elisabeth, *17:* 127-128
Mack, Stan, *17:* 129
Mackay, Donald, *17:* 60
Mackinstry, Elizabeth, *15:* 110
Maclise, Daniel, *YABC 2:* 257
Madden, Don, *3:* 112-113; *4:* 33,
    108, 155; *7:* 193; *YABC 2:* 211
Maddison, Angela Mary, *10:* 83
Maestro, Giulio, *8:* 124; *12:* 17;
    13: 108; *25:* 182
Mahood, Kenneth, *24:* 141
Maik, Henri, *9:* 102
Maitland, Antony, *1:* 100, 176;
    8: 41; *17:* 246; *24:* 46;
    25: 177, 178
Malvern, Corrine, *2:* 13
Manet, Edouard, *23:* 170
Mangurian, David, *14:* 133
Manning, Samuel F., *5:* 75
Maraja, *15:* 86; *YABC 1:* 28;
    YABC 2: 115
Marcellino, Fred, *20:* 125
Marchiori, Carlos, *14:* 60
Margules, Gabriele, *21:* 120
Mariana. *See* Foster, Marian Curtis
Marino, Dorothy, *6:* 37; *14:* 135
Markham, R. L., *17:* 240
Mars, W. T., *1:* 161; *3:* 115;
    4: 208, 225; *5:* 92, 105, 186;
    8: 214; *9:* 12; *13:* 121
Marsh, Christine, *3:* 164
Marsh, Reginald, *17:* 5; *19:* 89;
    22: 90, 96
Marshall, Anthony D., *18:* 216
Marshall, James, *6:* 160
Martin, David Stone, *23:* 232
Martin, Fletcher, *18:* 213; *23:* 151
Martin, Rene, *7:* 144
Martin, Stefan, *8:* 68
Martinez, John, *6:* 113
Marx, Robert F., *24:* 143
Masefield, Judith, *19:* 208, 209
Mason, George F., *14:* 139
Massie, Diane Redfield, *16:* 194
Matsubara, Naoko, *12:* 121
Matsuda, Shizu, *13:* 167
Matte, L'Enc, *22:* 183
Matthews, F. Leslie, *4:* 216
Matthieu, Joseph, *14:* 33
Matulay, Laszlo, *5:* 18
Matus, Greta, *12:* 142
Mawicke, Tran, *9:* 137; *15:* 191
Maxwell, John Alan, *1:* 148
Mayan, Earl, *7:* 193
Mayer, Mercer, *11:* 192;
    16: 195-196; *20:* 55, 57
Mayhew, Richard, *3:* 106
Mays, Victor, *5:* 127; *8:* 45, 153;
    14: 245; *23:* 50
Mazza, Adriana Saviozzi, *19:* 215

McCann, Gerald, *3:* 50; *4:* 94;
    7: 54
McClary, Nelson, *1:* 111
McClintock, Theodore, *14:* 141
McCloskey, Robert, *1:* 184-185;
    2: 186-187; *17:* 209
McClung, Robert, *2:* 189
McCormick, Dell J., *19:* 216
McCrady, Lady, *16:* 198
McCrea, James, *3:* 122
McCrea, Ruth, *3:* 122
McCully, Emily, *2:* 89; *4:* 120-121,
    146, 197; *5:* 2, 129; *7:* 191;
    11: 122; *15:* 210
McCurdy, Michael, *13:* 153; *24:* 85
McDermott, Beverly Brodsky,
    11: 180
McDermott, Gerald, *16:* 201
McDonald, Jill, *13:* 155
McDonald, Ralph J., *5:* 123, 195
McDonough, Don, *10:* 163
McFall, Christie, *12:* 144
McGee, Barbara, *6:* 165
McGregor, Malcolm, *23:* 27
McHugh, Tom, *23:* 64
McKay, Donald, *2:* 118
McKee, David, *10:* 48; *21:* 9
McKie, Roy, *7:* 44
McLachlan, Edward, *5:* 89
McMillan, Bruce, *22:* 184
McNaught, Harry, *12:* 80
McPhail, David, *14:* 105; *23:* 135
McVay, Tracy, *11:* 68
Meddaugh, Susan, *20:* 42
Melo, John, *16:* 285
Mendelssohn, Felix, *19:* 170
Meng, Heinz, *13:* 158
Merrill, Frank T., *16:* 147; *19:* 71;
    YABC 1: 226, 229, 273
Meryweather, Jack; *10:* 179
Meth, Harold, *24:* 203
Meyer, Herbert, *19:* 189
Meyer, Renate, *6:* 170
Meyers, Bob, *11:* 136
Micale, Albert, *2:* 65; *22:* 185
Middleton-Sandford, Betty, *2:* 125
Mikolaycak, Charles, *9:* 144;
    12: 101; *13:* 212; *21:* 121;
    22: 168
Miles, Jennifer, *17:* 278
Milhous, Katherine, *15:* 193; *17:* 51
Millais, John E., *22:* 230, 231
Millar, H. R., *YABC 1:* 194-195,
    203
Miller, Don, *15:* 195; *16:* 71;
    20: 106
Miller, Frank J., *25:* 94
Miller, Grambs, *18:* 38; *23:* 16
Miller, Jane, *15:* 196
Miller, Marcia, *13:* 233
Miller, Marilyn, *1:* 87
Miller, Shane, *5:* 140
Mizumura Kazue, *10:* 143; *18:* 223
Mochi, Ugo, *8:* 122
Mohr, Nicholasa, *8:* 139
Montresor, Beni, *2:* 91; *3:* 138

Moon, Carl, *25:* 183, 184, 185
Moon, Eliza, *14:* 40
Moon, Ivan, *22:* 39
Mora, Raul Mina, *20:* 41
Mordvinoff, Nicolas, *15:* 179
Morrill, Leslie, *18:* 218
Morrow, Gray, *2:* 64; *5:* 200;
    10: 103, 114; *14:* 175
Morton, Marian, *3:* 185
Moses, Grandma, *18:* 228
Moss, Donald, *11:* 184
Moyers, William, *21:* 65
Mozley, Charles, *9:* 87; *20:* 176,
    192, 193; *22:* 228; *25:* 205;
    YABC 2: 89
Mugnaini, Joseph, *11:* 35
Mullins, Edward S., *10:* 101
Munari, Bruno, *15:* 200
Munowitz, Ken, *14:* 148
Munson, Russell, *13:* 9
Murphy, Bill, *5:* 138
Murr, Karl, *20:* 62
Mutchler, Dwight, *1:* 25
Myers, Bernice, *9:* 147
Myers, Lou, *11:* 2

Nakatani, Chiyoko, *12:* 124
Nason, Thomas W., *14:* 68
Nast, Thomas, *21:* 29
Natti, Susanna, *20:* 146
Navarra, Celeste Scala, *8:* 142
Naylor, Penelope, *10:* 104
Neebe, William, *7:* 93
Needler, Jerry, *12:* 93
Negri, Rocco, *3:* 213; *5:* 67; *6:* 91,
    108; *12:* 159
Neill, John R., *18:* 8, 10-11, 21, 30
Ness, Evaline, *1:* 164-165; *2:* 39;
    3: 8; *10:* 147; *12:* 53
Neville, Vera, *2:* 182
Newberry, Clare Turlay, *1:* 170
Newfeld, Frank, *14:* 121
Nicholson, William, *15:* 33-34;
    16: 48
Nickless, Will, *16:* 139
Nicolas, *17:* 130, 132-133;
    YABC 2: 215
Niebrugge, Jane, *6:* 118
Nielsen, Jon, *6:* 100; *24:* 202
Nielsen, Kay, *15:* 7; *16:* 211-213,
    215, 217; *22:* 143;
    YABC 1: 32-33
Niland, Deborah, *25:* 191
Niland, Kilmeny, *25:* 191
Ninon, *1:* 5
Nixon, K., *14:* 152
Noonan, Julia, *4:* 163; *7:* 207;
    25: 151
Nordenskjold, Birgitta, *2:* 208
Norman, Michael, *12:* 117
Nussbaumer, Paul, *16:* 219
Nyce, Helene, *19:* 219

Oakley, Graham, *8:* 112

Oakley, Thornton, *YABC 2:* 189
Obligado, Lilian, *2:* 28, 66-67;
    6: 30; *14:* 179; *15:* 103; *25:* 84
Obrant, Susan, *11:* 186
Oechsli, Kelly, *5:* 144-145; *7:* 115;
    8: 83, 183; *13:* 117; *20:* 94
Ohlsson, Ib, *4:* 152; *7:* 57; *10:* 20;
    11: 90; *19:* 217
Oliver, Jenni, *23:* 121
Olschewski, Alfred, *7:* 172
Olsen, Ib Spang, *6:* 178-179
Olugebefola, Ademola, *15:* 205
O'Neil, Dan IV, *7:* 176
O'Neill, Jean, *22:* 146
O'Neill, Steve, *21:* 118
Ono, Chiyo, *7:* 97
Orbaan, Albert, *2:* 31; *5:* 65, 171;
    9: 8; *14:* 241; *20:* 109
Orbach, Ruth, *21:* 112
Orfe, Joan, *20:* 81
Ormsby, Virginia H., *11:* 187
Orozco, José Clemente, *9:* 177
Orr, Forrest W., *23:* 9
Orr, N., *19:* 70
Osmond, Edward, *10:* 111
O'Sullivan, Tom, *3:* 176; *4:* 55
Otto, Svend, *22:* 130, 141
Oudry, J. B., *18:* 167
Oughton, Taylor, *5:* 23
Overlie, George, *11:* 156
Owens, Carl, *2:* 35; *23:* 52
Owens, Gail, *10:* 170; *12:* 157;
    19: 16; *22:* 70; *25:* 81
Oxenbury, Helen, *3:* 150-151;
    24: 81

Padgett, Jim, *12:* 165
Page, Homer, *14:* 145
Paget, Sidney, *24:* 90, 91, 93, 95,
    97
Pak, *12:* 76
Palazzo, Tony, *3:* 152-153
Palladini, David, *4:* 113
Palmer, Heidi, *15:* 207
Palmer, Juliette, *6:* 89; *15:* 208
Palmer, Lemuel, *17:* 25, 29
Panesis, Nicholas, *3:* 127
Papas, William, *11:* 223
Papish, Robin Lloyd, *10:* 80
Paraquin, Charles H., *18:* 166
Park, W. B., *22:* 189
Parker, Lewis, *2:* 179
Parker, Nancy Winslow, *10:* 113;
    22: 164
Parker, Robert, *4:* 161; *5:* 74;
    9: 136
Parker, Robert Andrew, *11:* 81
Parnall, Peter, *5:* 137; *16:* 221;
    24: 70
Parrish, Maxfield, *14:* 160, 161,
    164, 165; *16:* 109; *18:* 12-13;
    YABC 1: 149, 152, 267;
    YABC 2: 146, 149
Parry, Marian, *13:* 176; *19:* 179

Pascal, David, *14:* 174
Pasquier, J. A., *16:* 91
Paterson, Diane, *13:* 116
Paterson, Helen, *16:* 93
Paton, Jane, *15:* 271
Patterson, Robert, *25:* 118
Paul, James, *4:* 130; *23:* 161
Paull, Grace, *24:* 157
Payne, Joan Balfour, *1:* 118
Payson, Dale, *7:* 34; *9:* 151;
    20: 140
Payzant, Charles, *21:* 147
Peake, Mervyn, *22:* 136, 149;
    23: 162, 163, 164;
    YABC 2: 307
Peat, Fern B., *16:* 115
Peck, Anne Merriman, *18:* 241;
    24: 155
Pederson, Sharleen, *12:* 92
Pedersen, Vilhelm, *YABC 1:* 40
Peet, Bill, *2:* 203
Peltier, Leslie C., *13:* 178
Pendle, Alexy, *7:* 159; *13:* 34
Peppe, Rodney, *4:* 164-165
Perl, Susan, *2:* 98; *4:* 231;
    5: 44-45, 118; *6:* 199; *8:* 137;
    12: 88; *22:* 193; *YABC 1:* 176
Pesek, Ludek, *15:* 237
Petersham, Maud, *17:* 108, 147-153
Petersham, Miska, *17:* 108,
    147-153
Peterson, R. F., *7:* 101
Peterson, Russell, *7:* 130
Petie, Haris, *2:* 3; *10:* 41, 118;
    11: 227; *12:* 70
Petrides, Heidrun, *19:* 223
Peyton, K. M., *15:* 212
Pfeifer, Herman, *15:* 262
Phillips, Douglas, *1:* 19
Phillips, F. D., *6:* 202
"Phiz." *See* Browne, Hablot K.,
    15: 65; *21:* 14, 15, 16, 17, 18,
    19, 20
Piatti, Celestino, *16:* 223
Picarella, Joseph, *13:* 147
Pickard, Charles, *12:* 38; *18:* 203
Picken, George A., *23:* 150
Pickens, David, *22:* 156
Pienkowski, Jan, *6:* 183
Pimlott, John, *10:* 205
Pincus, Harriet, *4:* 186; *8:* 179;
    22: 148
Pinkney, Jerry, *8:* 218; *10:* 40;
    15: 276; *20:* 66; *24:* 121
Pinkwater, Manus, *8:* 156
Pinto, Ralph, *10:* 131
Pitz, Henry C., *4:* 168; *19:* 165;
    YABC 2: 95, 176
Pogany, Willy, *15:* 46, 49; *19:* 222,
    256; *25:* 214
Polgreen, John, *21:* 44
Politi, Leo, *1:* 178; *4:* 53; *21:* 48
Polseno, Jo, *1:* 53; *3:* 117; *5:* 114;
    17: 154; *20:* 87
Ponter, James, *5:* 204
Poortvliet, Rien, *6:* 212

Portal, Colette, 6: 186; 11: 203
Porter, George, 7: 181
Potter, Beatrix, YABC 1: 208-210, 212, 213
Potter, Miriam Clark, 3: 162
Powers, Richard M., 1: 230; 3: 218; 7: 194
Pratt, Charles, 23: 29
Price, Christine, 2: 247; 3: 163, 253; 8: 166
Price, Garrett, 1: 76; 2: 42
Price, Hattie Longstreet, 17: 13
Price, Norman, YABC 1: 129
Prince, Leonora E., 7: 170
Prittie, Edwin J., YABC 1: 120
Pudlo, 8: 59
Purdy, Susan, 8: 162
Puskas, James, 5: 141
Pyk, Jan, 7: 26
Pyle, Howard, 16: 225-228, 230-232, 235; 24: 27

Quackenbush, Robert, 4: 190; 6: 166; 7: 175, 178; 9: 86; 11: 65, 221
Quidor, John, 19: 82
Quirk, Thomas, 12: 81

Rackham, Arthur, 15: 32, 78, 214-227; 17: 105, 115; 18: 233; 19: 254; 20: 151; 22: 129, 131, 132, 133; 23: 175; 24: 161, 181; YABC 1: 25, 45, 55, 147; YABC 2: 103, 142, 173, 210
Rafilson, Sidney, 11: 172
Raible, Alton, 1: 202-203
Ramsey, James, 16: 41
Ransome, Arthur, 22: 201
Rand, Paul, 6: 188
Raphael, Elaine, 23: 192
Rappaport, Eva, 6: 190
Raskin, Ellen, 2: 208-209; 4: 142; 13: 183; 22: 68
Rau, Margaret, 9: 157
Raverat, Gwen, YABC 1: 152
Ravielli, Anthony, 1: 198; 3: 168; 11: 143
Ray, Deborah, 8: 164
Ray, Ralph, 2: 239; 5: 73
Rayner, Mary, 22: 207
Raynor, Paul, 24: 73
Razzi, James, 10: 127
Read, Alexander D. "Sandy," 20: 45
Reid, Stephen, 19: 213; 22: 89
Reiss, John J., 23: 193
Relf, Douglas, 3: 63
Relyea, C. M., 16: 29
Remi, Georges, 13: 184
Remington, Frederic, 19: 188
Renlie, Frank, 11: 200

Reschofsky, Jean, 7: 118
Rethi, Lili, 2: 153
Reusswig, William, 3: 267
Rey, H. A., 1: 182; YABC 2: 17
Reynolds, Doris, 5: 71
Ribbons, Ian, 3: 10
Rice, Elizabeth, 2: 53, 214
Rice, James, 22: 210
Richards, Henry, YABC 1: 228, 231
Richardson, Ernest, 2: 144
Richardson, Frederick, 18: 27, 31
Richmond, George, 24: 179
Rieniets, Judy King, 14: 28
Riger, Bob, 2: 166
Riley, Kenneth, 22: 230
Ringi, Kjell, 12: 171
Rios, Tere. See Versace, Marie
Ripper, Charles L., 3: 175
Rivkin, Jay, 15: 230
Roach, Marilynne, 9: 158
Roberts, Cliff, 4: 126
Roberts, Doreen, 4: 230
Roberts, Jim, 22: 166; 23: 69
Roberts, W., 22: 2, 3
Robinson, Charles, 3: 53; 5: 14; 6: 193; 7: 150; 7: 183; 8: 38; 9: 81; 13: 188; 14: 248-249; 23: 149
Robinson, Charles [1870-1937], 17: 157, 171-173, 175-176; 24: 207; 25: 204; YABC 2: 308-310, 331
Robinson, Jerry, 3: 262
Robinson, Joan G., 7: 184
Robinson, T. H., 17: 179, 181-183
Robinson, W. Heath, 17: 185, 187, 189, 191, 193, 195, 197, 199, 202; 23: 167; 25: 194; YABC 1: 44; YABC 2: 183
Rocker, Fermin, 7: 34; 13: 21
Rockwell, Anne, 5: 147
Rockwell, Gail, 7: 186
Rockwell, Norman, 23: 39, 196, 197, 199, 200, 203, 204, 207; YABC 2: 60
Rodriguez, Joel, 16: 65
Roever, J. M., 4: 119
Rogers, Carol, 2: 262; 6: 164
Rogers, Frances, 10: 130
Rogers, William A., 15: 151, 153-154
Rojankovsky, Feodor, 6: 134, 136; 10: 183; 21: 128, 129, 130; 25: 110
Rose, Carl, 5: 62
Rosenblum, Richard, 11: 202; 18: 18
Rosier, Lydia, 16: 236; 20: 104; 21: 109; 22: 125
Ross, Clare, 3: 123; 21: 45
Ross, John, 3: 123; 21: 45
Ross, Tony, 17: 204
Rossetti, Dante Gabriel, 20: 151, 153
Roth, Arnold, 4: 238; 21: 133
Rouille, M., 11: 96

Rounds, Glen, 8: 173; 9: 171; 12: 56; YABC 1: 1-3
Rubel, Nicole, 18: 255; 20: 59
Rud, Borghild, 6: 15
Rudolph, Norman Guthrie, 17: 13
Ruffins, Reynold, 10: 134-135
Ruse, Margaret, 24: 155
Russell, E. B., 18: 177, 182
Ruth, Rod, 9: 161
Rutherford, Meg, 25: 174
Ryden, Hope, 8: 176

Sabaka, Donna R., 21: 172
Sacker, Amy, 16: 100
Sagsoorian, Paul, 12: 183; 22: 154
Saint Exupéry, Antoine de, 20: 157
Sale, Morton, YABC 2: 31
Sambourne, Linley, YABC 2: 181
Sampson, Katherine, 9: 197
Samson, Anne S., 2: 216
Sandberg, Lasse, 15: 239, 241
Sanderson, Ruth, 21: 126; 24: 53
Sandin, Joan, 4: 36; 6: 194; 7: 177; 12: 145, 185; 20: 43; 21: 74
Sapieha, Christine, 1: 180
Sarg, Tony, YABC 2: 236
Sargent, Robert, 2: 217
Saris, 1: 33
Sarony, YABC 2: 170
Sasek, Miroslav, 16: 239-242
Sassman, David, 9: 79
Savage, Steele, 10: 203; 20: 77
Savitt, Sam, 8: 66, 182; 15: 278; 20: 96; 24: 192
Scabrini, Janet, 13: 191
Scarry, Richard, 2: 220-221; 18: 20
Schaeffer, Mead, 18: 81, 94; 21: 137, 138, 139
Scharl, Josef, 20: 132; 22: 128
Scheel, Lita, 11: 230
Schick, Joel, 16: 160; 17: 167; 22: 12
Schindelman, Joseph, 1: 74; 4: 101; 12: 49
Schindler, Edith, 7: 22
Schlesinger, Bret, 7: 77
Schmid, Eleanore, 12: 188
Schmiderer, Dorothy, 19: 224
Schmidt, Elizabeth, 15: 242
Schoenherr, John, 1: 146-147, 173; 3: 39, 139; 17: 75
Schomburg, Alex, 13: 23
Schongut, Emanuel, 4: 102; 15: 186
Schoonover, Frank, 17: 107; 19: 81, 190, 233; 22: 88, 129; 24: 189; YABC 2: 282, 316
Schottland, Miriam, 22: 172
Schramm, Ulrik, 2: 16; 14: 112
Schreiber, Elizabeth Anne, 13: 193
Schreiber, Ralph W., 13: 193
Schreiter, Rick, 14: 97; 23: 171
Schroeder, E. Peter, 12: 112
Schroeder, Ted, 11: 160; 15: 189
Schrotter, Gustav, 22: 212

Schulz, Charles M., *10:* 137-142
Schwartz, Charles, *8:* 184
Schwartzberg, Joan, *3:* 208
Schweitzer, Iris, *2:* 137; *6:* 207
Scott, Anita Walker, *7:* 38
Scribner, Joanne, *14:* 236
Searle, Ronald, *24:* 98
Sebree, Charles, *18:* 65
Sedacca, Joseph M., *11:* 25; *22:* 36
Seignobosc, Francoise, *21:* 145, 146
Sejima, Yoshimasa, *8:* 187
Selig, Sylvie, *13:* 199
Seltzer, Isadore, *6:* 18
Seltzer, Meyer, *17:* 214
Sempé, *YABC 2:* 109
Sendak, Maurice, *1:* 135, 190; *3:* 204; *7:* 142; *15:* 199; *17:* 210; *YABC 1:* 167
Sengler, Johanna, *18:* 256
Seredy, Kate, *1:* 192; *14:* 20-21; *17:* 210
Sergeant, John, *6:* 74
Servello, Joe, *10:* 144; *24:* 139
Seton, Ernest Thompson, *18:* 260-269, 271
Seuss, Dr. *See* Geisel, Theodor
Severin, John Powers, *7:* 62
Sewall, Marcia, *15:* 8; *22:* 170
Seward, Prudence, *16:* 243
Sewell, Helen, *3:* 186; *15:* 308
Shanks, Anne Zane, *10:* 149
Sharp, William, *6:* 131; *19:* 241; *20:* 112; *25:* 141
Shaw, Charles G., *13:* 200; *21:* 135
Shecter, Ben, *16:* 244; *25:* 109
Shekerjian, Haig, *16:* 245
Shekerjian, Regina, *16:* 245; *25:* 73
Shenton, Edward, *YABC 1:* 218-219, 221
Shepard, Ernest H., *3:* 193; *4:* 74; *16:* 101; *17:* 109; *25:* 148; *YABC 1:* 148, 153, 174, 176, 180-181
Shepard, Mary, *4:* 210; *22:* 205
Sherwan, Earl, *3:* 196
Shields, Charles, *10:* 150
Shields, Leonard, *13:* 83, 85, 87
Shimin, Symeon, *1:* 93; *2:* 128-129; *3:* 202; *7:* 85; *11:* 177; *12:* 139; *13:* 202-203
Shinn, Everett, *16:* 148; *18:* 229; *21:* 149, 150, 151; *24:* 218
Shore, Robert, *YABC 2:* 200
Shortall, Leonard, *4:* 144; *8:* 196; *10:* 166; *19:* 227, 228-229, 230; *25:* 78
Shulevitz, Uri, *3:* 198-199; *17:* 85; *22:* 204
Sibley, Don, *1:* 39; *12:* 196
Sidjakov, Nicolas, *18:* 274
Siebel, Fritz, *3:* 120; *17:* 145
Siegl, Helen, *12:* 166; *23:* 216
Sills, Joyce, *5:* 199
Silverstein, Alvin, *8:* 189
Silverstein, Virginia, *8:* 189

Simon, Eric M., *7:* 82
Simon, Howard, *2:* 175; *5:* 132; *19:* 199
Simont, Marc, *2:* 119; *4:* 213; *9:* 168; *13:* 238, 240; *14:* 262; *16:* 179; *18:* 221
Singer, Edith G., *2:* 30
Skardinski, Stanley, *23:* 144
Slackman, Charles B., *12:* 201
Slater, Rod, *25:* 167
Sloan, Joseph, *16:* 68
Sloane, Eric, *21:* 3
Slobodkin, Louis, *1:* 200; *3:* 232; *5:* 168; *13:* 251; *15:* 13, 88
Slobodkina, Esphyr, *1:* 201
Smalley, Janet, *1:* 154
Smee, David, *14:* 78
Smith, Alvin, *1:* 31, 229; *13:* 187
Smith, E. Boyd, *19:* 70; *22:* 89; *YABC 1:* 4-5, 240, 248-249
Smith, Edward J., *4:* 224
Smith, Eunice Young, *5:* 170
Smith, Howard, *19:* 196
Smith, Jessie Willcox, *15:* 91; *16:* 95; *18:* 231; *19:* 57, 242; *21:* 29, 156, 157, 158, 159, 160, 161; *YABC 1:* 6; *YABC 2:* 180, 185, 191, 311, 325
Smith, Linell Nash, *2:* 195
Smith, Maggie Kaufman, *13:* 205
Smith, Ralph Crosby, *2:* 267
Smith, Robert D., *5:* 63
Smith, Susan Carlton, *12:* 208
Smith, Terry, *12:* 106
Smith, Virginia, *3:* 157
Smith, William A., *1:* 36; *10:* 154; *25:* 65
Smyth, M. Jane, *12:* 15
Snyder, Jerome, *13:* 207
Sofia, *1:* 62; *5:* 90
Solbert, Ronni, *1:* 159; *2:* 232; *5:* 121; *6:* 34; *17:* 249
Solonevich, George, *15:* 246; *17:* 47
Sommer, Robert, *12:* 211
Sorel, Edward, *4:* 61
Sotomayor, Antonio, *11:* 215
Soyer, Moses, *20:* 177
Spaenkuch, August, *16:* 28
Spanfeller, James, *1:* 72, 149; *2:* 183; *19:* 230, 231, 232; *22:* 66
Sparks, Mary Walker, *15:* 247
Spence, Geraldine, *21:* 163
Spier, Jo, *10:* 30
Spier, Peter, *3:* 155; *4:* 200; *7:* 61; *11:* 78
Spilka, Arnold, *5:* 120; *6:* 204; *8:* 131
Spivak, I. Howard, *8:* 10
Spollen, Christopher J., *12:* 214
Sprattler, Rob, *12:* 176
Spring, Bob, *5:* 60
Spring, Ira, *5:* 60
Staffan, Alvin E., *11:* 56; *12:* 187

Stahl, Ben, *5:* 181; *12:* 91
Stamaty, Mark Alan, *12:* 215
Stanley, Diana, *3:* 45
Steig, William, *18:* 275-276
Stein, Harve, *1:* 109
Steinel, William, *23:* 146
Stephens, Charles H., *YABC 2:* 279
Stephens, William M., *21:* 165
Steptoe, John, *8:* 197
Stern, Simon, *15:* 249-250; *17:* 58
Stevens, Mary, *11:* 193; *13:* 129
Stewart, Charles, *2:* 205
Stirnweis, Shannon, *10:* 164
Stobbs, William, *1:* 48-49; *3:* 68; *6:* 20; *17:* 117, 217; *24:* 150
Stone, David, *9:* 173
Stone, David K., *4:* 38; *6:* 124; *9:* 180
Stone, Helen V., *6:* 209
Stratton-Porter, Gene, *15:* 254, 259, 263-264, 268-269
Streano, Vince, *20:* 173
Strong, Joseph D., Jr., *YABC 2:* 330
Ströyer, Poul, *13:* 221
Stubis, Talivaldis, *5:* 182, 183; *10:* 45; *11:* 9; *18:* 304; *20:* 127
Stubley, Trevor, *14:* 43; *22:* 219; *23:* 37
Stuecklen, Karl W., *8:* 34, 65; *23:* 103
Stull, Betty, *11:* 46
Suba, Susanne, *4:* 202-203; *14:* 261; *23:* 134
Sugarman, Tracy, *3:* 76; *8:* 199
Sullivan, James F., *19:* 280; *20:* 192
Sumichrast, Jözef, *14:* 253
Summers, Leo, *1:* 177; *2:* 273; *13:* 22
Svolinsky, Karel, *17:* 104
Swain, Su Zan Noguchi, *21:* 170
Swan, Susan, *22:* 220-221
Sweat, Lynn, *25:* 206
Sweet, Darryl, *1:* 163; *4:* 136
Sweetland, Robert, *12:* 194
Sylvester, Natalie G., *22:* 222
Szafran, Gene, *24:* 144
Szasz, Susanne, *13:* 55, 226; *14:* 48
Szekeres, Cyndy, *2:* 218; *5:* 185; *8:* 85; *11:* 166; *14:* 19; *16:* 57, 159

Tait, Douglas, *12:* 220
Takakjian, Portia, *15:* 274
Takashima, Shizuye, *13:* 228
Talarczyk, June, *4:* 173
Tallon, Robert, *2:* 228
Tamburine, Jean, *12:* 222
Tandy, H. R., *13:* 69
Tanobe, Miyuki, *23:* 221
Tarkington, Booth, *17:* 224-225
Teale, Edwin Way, *7:* 196
Teason, James, *1:* 14

Illustrations Index

Tee-Van, Helen Damrosch, *10:* 176; *11:* 182
Tempest, Margaret, *3:* 237, 238
Templeton, Owen, *11:* 77
Tenggren, Gustaf, *18:* 277-279; *19:* 15; *YABC 2:* 145
Tenney, Gordon, *24:* 204
Tenniel, John, *YABC 2:* 99
Thackeray, William Makepeace, *23:* 224, 228
Thelwell, Norman, *14:* 201
Thistlethwaite, Miles, *12:* 224
Thollander, Earl, *11:* 47; *18:* 112; *22:* 224
Thomas, Allan, *22:* 13
Thomas, Harold, *20:* 98
Thomas, Martin, *14:* 255
Thompson, George, *22:* 18
Thomson, Arline K., *3:* 264
Thorne, Diana, *25:* 212
Thorvall, Kerstin, *13:* 235
Thurber, James, *13:* 239, 242-245, 248-249
Tichenor, Tom, *14:* 207
Tilney, F. C., *22:* 231
Timmins, Harry, *2:* 171
Tinkelman, Murray, *12:* 225
Tolford, Joshua, *1:* 221
Tolkien, J. R. R., *2:* 243
Tolmie, Ken, *15:* 292
Tomes, Jacqueline, *2:* 117; *12:* 139
Tomes, Margot, *1:* 224; *2:* 120-121; *16:* 207; *18:* 250; *20:* 7; *25:* 62
Toner, Raymond John, *10:* 179
Toothill, Harry, *6:* 54; *7:* 49; *25:* 219
Toothill, Ilse, *6:* 54
Torbert, Floyd James, *22:* 226
Toschik, Larry, *6:* 102
Totten, Bob, *13:* 93
Tremain, Ruthven, *17:* 238
Tresilian, Stuart, *25:* 53
Trez, Alain, *17:* 236
Trier, Walter, *14:* 96
Tripp, F. J., *24:* 167
Tripp, Wallace, *2:* 48; *7:* 28; *8:* 94; *10:* 54, 76; *11:* 92
Trnka, Jiri, *22:* 151; *YABC 1:* 30-31
Troyer, Johannes, *3:* 16; *7:* 18
Tsinajinie, Andy, *2:* 62
Tsugami, Kyuzo, *18:* 198-199
Tuckwell, Jennifer, *17:* 205
Tudor, Bethany, *7:* 103
Tudor, Tasha, *18:* 227; *20:* 185, 186, 187; *YABC 2:* 46, 314
Tulloch, Maurice, *24:* 79
Tunis, Edwin, *1:* 218-219
Turkle, Brinton, *1:* 211, 213; *2:* 249; *3:* 226; *11:* 3; *16:* 209; *20:* 22; *YABC 1:* 79
Turska, Krystyna, *12:* 103
Tusan, Stan, *6:* 58; *22:* 236-237
Tzimoulis, Paul, *12:* 104

Uchida, Yoshiko, *1:* 220

Ulm, Robert, *17:* 238
Unada. *See* Gliewe, Unada, *3:* 78-79; *21:* 73
Ungerer, Tomi, *5:* 188; *9:* 40; *18:* 188
Unwin, Nora S., *3:* 65, 234-235; *4:* 237; *YABC 1:* 59; *YABC 2:* 301
Utpatel, Frank, *18:* 114
Utz, Lois, *5:* 190

Van Abbé, S., *16:* 142; *18:* 282; *YABC 2:* 157, 161
Vandivert, William, *21:* 175
Van Everen, Jay, *13:* 160; *YABC 1:* 121
Van Loon, Hendrik Willem, *18:* 285, 289, 291
Van Stockum, Hilda, *5:* 193
Van Wely, Babs, *16:* 50
Vasiliu, Mircea, *2:* 166, 253; *9:* 166; *13:* 58
Vavra, Robert, *8:* 206
Vawter, Will, *17:* 163
Veeder, Larry, *18:* 4
Ver Beck, Frank, *18:* 16-17
Verney, John, *14:* 225
Verrier, Suzanne, *5:* 20; *23:* 212
Versace, Marie, *2:* 255
Vestal, H. B., *9:* 134; *11:* 101
Viereck, Ellen, *3:* 242; *14:* 229
Vigna, Judith, *15:* 293
Vilato, Gaspar E., *5:* 41
Vimnèra, A., *23:* 154
Vo-Dinh, Mai, *16:* 272
Vogel, Ilse-Margret, *14:* 230
von Schmidt, Eric, *8:* 62
Vosburgh, Leonard, *1:* 161; *7:* 32; *15:* 295-296; *23:* 110
Voter, Thomas W., *19:* 3, 9
Vroman, Tom, *10:* 29

Wagner, John, *8:* 200
Wagner, Ken, *2:* 59
Wainwright, Jerry, *14:* 85
Waldman, Bruce, *15:* 297
Walker, Charles, *1:* 46; *4:* 59; *5:* 177; *11:* 115; *19:* 45
Walker, Dugald Stewart, *15:* 47
Walker, Gil, *8:* 49; *23:* 132
Walker, Jim, *10:* 94
Walker, Mort, *8:* 213
Walker, Stephen, *12:* 229; *21:* 174
Wallace, Beverly Dobrin, *19:* 259
Waller, S. E., *24:* 36
Wallner, Alexandra, *15:* 120
Wallner, John C., *9:* 77; *10:* 188; *11:* 28; *14:* 209
Wallower, Lucille, *11:* 226
Walters, Audrey, *18:* 294
Walton, Tony, *11:* 164; *24:* 209
Waltrip, Lela, *9:* 195

Waltrip, Mildred, *3:* 209
Waltrip, Rufus, *9:* 195
Wan, *12:* 76
Ward, Keith, *2:* 107
Ward, Lynd, *1:* 99, 132, 133, 150; *2:* 108, 158, 196, 259; *18:* 86
Warner, Peter, *14:* 87
Warren, Betsy, *2:* 101
Warren, Marion Cray, *14:* 215
Washington, Nevin, *20:* 123
Washington, Phyllis, *20:* 123
Waterman, Stan, *11:* 76
Watkins-Pitchford, D. J., *6:* 215, 217
Watson, Aldren, *2:* 267; *5:* 94; *13:* 71; *19:* 253; *YABC 2:* 202
Watson, Gary, *19:* 147
Watson, J. D., *22:* 86
Watson, Karen, *11:* 26
Watson, Wendy, *5:* 197; *13:* 101
Watts, Bernadette, *4:* 227
Webber, Helen, *3:* 141
Webber, Irma E., *14:* 238
Weber, William J., *14:* 239
Webster, Jean, *17:* 241
Wegner, Fritz, *14:* 250; *20:* 189
Weidenear, Reynold H., *21:* 122
Weihs, Erika, *4:* 21; *15:* 299
Weil, Lisl, *7:* 203; *10:* 58; *21:* 95; *22:* 188, 217
Weiner, Sandra, *14:* 240
Weisgard, Leonard, *1:* 65; *2:* 191, 197, 204, 264-265; *5:* 108; *21:* 42; *YABC 2:* 13
Weiss, Emil, *1:* 168; *7:* 60
Weiss, Harvey, *1:* 145, 223
Wells, Frances, *1:* 183
Wells, H. G., *20:* 194, 200
Wells, Rosemary, *6:* 49; *18:* 297
Wells, Susan, *22:* 43
Wendelin, Rudolph, *23:* 234
Werenskiold, Erik, *15:* 6
Werner, Honi, *24:* 110
Werth, Kurt, *7:* 122; *14:* 157; *20:* 214
Wetherbee, Margaret, *5:* 3
Wheatley, Arabelle, *11:* 231; *16:* 276
Wheelright, Rowland, *15:* 81; *YABC 2:* 286
Whistler, Rex, *16:* 75
White, David Omar, *5:* 56; *18:* 6
Whithorne, H. S., *7:* 49
Whitney, George Gillett, *3:* 24
Wiese, Kurt, *3:* 255; *4:* 206; *14:* 17; *17:* 18-19; *19:* 47; *24:* 152; *25:* 212
Wiesner, William, *4:* 100; *5:* 200, 201; *14:* 262
Wiggins, George, *6:* 133
Wikland, Ilon, *5:* 113; *8:* 150
Wilde, George, *7:* 139
Wildsmith, Brian, *16:* 281-282; *18:* 170-171
Wilkinson, Gerald, *3:* 40
Williams, Ferelith Eccles, *22:* 238

Williams, Garth, *1:* 197; *2:* 49,
   270; *4:* 205; *15:* 198, 302-304,
   307; *16:* 34; *18:* 283, 298-301;
   YABC 2: 15-16, 19
Williams, Maureen, *12:* 238
Williams, Patrick, *14:* 218
Wilson, Charles Banks, *17:* 92
Wilson, Dagmar, *10:* 47
Wilson, Edward A., *6:* 24; *16:* 149;
   20: 220-221; *22:* 87
Wilson, Jack, *17:* 139
Wilson, John, *22:* 240
Wilson, Peggy, *15:* 4
Wilson, W. N., *22:* 26
Wilwerding, Walter J., *9:* 202
Winchester, Linda, *13:* 231
Windham, Kathryn Tucker, *14:* 260
Winslow, Will, *21:* 124
Winter, Milo, *15:* 97; *19:* 221;
   21: 181, 203, 204, 205;
   YABC 2: 144
Wise, Louis, *13:* 68
Wiseman, B., *4:* 233
Wishnefsky, Phillip, *3:* 14
Wiskur, Darrell, *5:* 72; *10:* 50;
   18: 246

Woehr, Lois, *12:* 5
Wohlberg, Meg, *12:* 100; *14:* 197
Wolf, J., *16:* 91
Wondriska, William, *6:* 220
Wonsetler, John C., *5:* 168
Wood, Grant, *19:* 198
Wood, Myron, *6:* 220
Wood, Owen, *18:* 187
Wood, Ruth, *8:* 11
Woodson, Jack, *10:* 201
Wooten, Vernon, *23:* 70
Worboys, Evelyn, *1:* 166-167
Worth, Wendy, *4:* 133
Wrenn, Charles L., *YABC 1:* 20, 21
Wright, Dare, *21:* 206
Wright, George, *YABC 1:* 268
Wronker, Lili Cassel, *3:* 247;
   10: 204; *21:* 10
Wyeth, Andrew, *13:* 40;
   YABC 1: 133-134
Wyeth, N. C., *13:* 41; *17:* 252-259,
   264-268; *18:* 181; *19:* 80, 191,
   200; *21:* 57, 183; *22:* 91;
   23: 152; *24:* 28, 99;
   YABC 1: 133, 223;
   YABC 2: 53, 75, 171, 187, 317

Yang, Jay, *1:* 8; *12:* 239
Yap, Weda, *6:* 176
Yashima, Taro, *14:* 84
Yohn, F. C., *23:* 128; *YABC 1:* 269
Young, Ed, *7:* 205; *10:* 206;
   YABC 2: 242
Young, Noela, *8:* 221

Zacks, Lewis, *10:* 161
Zalben, Jane Breskin, *7:* 211
Zallinger, Jean, *4:* 192; *8:* 8, 129;
   14: 273
Zallinger, Rudolph F., *3:* 245
Zelinsky, Paul O., *14:* 269
Zemach, Margot, *3:* 270; *8:* 201;
   21: 210-211
Zemsky, Jessica, *10:* 62
Zinkeisen, Anna, *13:* 106
Zonia, Dhimitri, *20:* 234-235
Zweifel, Francis, *14:* 274

Illustrations Index

Author Index

(In the following index, the number of the volume in which an author's sketch appears is given *before* the colon, and the page on which it appears is given *after* the colon. For example, the sketch of Aardema, Verna, appears in Volume 4 on page 1).

YABC

Index citations including this abbreviation refer to listings appearing in *Yesterday's Authors of Books for Children,* also published by the Gale Research Company, which covers authors who died prior to 1960.

Aardema, Verna 1911- , *4:* 1

Aaron, Chester 1923- , *9:* 1

Abbott, Alice. *See* Borland, Kathryn Kilby, *16:* 54

Abbott, Alice. *See* Speicher, Helen Ross (Smith), *8:* 194

Abbott, Jacob 1803-1879, *22:* 1

Abbott, Manager Henry. *See* Stratemeyer, Edward L., *1:* 208

Abdul, Raoul 1929- , *12:* 1

Abel, Raymond 1911- , *12:* 2

Abell, Kathleen 1938- , *9:* 1

Abercrombie, Barbara (Mattes) 1939- , *16:* 1

Abernethy, Robert G. 1935- , *5:* 1

Abisch, Roslyn Kroop 1927- , *9:* 3

Abisch, Roz. *See* Abisch, Roslyn Kroop, *9:* 3

Abodaher, David J. (Naiph) 1919- , *17:* 1

Abrahall, C. H. *See* Hoskyns-Abrahall, Clare, *13:* 105

Abrahall, Clare Hoskyns. *See* Hoskyns-Abrahall, Clare, *13:* 105

Abrahams, Robert D(avid) 1905- , *4:* 3

Abrams, Joy 1941- , *16:* 2

Ackerman, Eugene 1888-1974, *10:* 1

Adair, Margaret Weeks (?)-1971, *10:* 1

Adams, Adrienne 1906- , *8:* 1

Adams, Andy 1859-1935, *YABC 1:* 1

Adams, Dale. *See* Quinn, Elisabeth, *22:* 197

Adams, Harriet S(tratemeyer) 1893(?)- , *1:* 1

Adams, Harrison. *See* Stratemeyer, Edward L., *1:* 208

Adams, Hazard 1926- , *6:* 1

Adams, Richard 1920- , *7:* 1

Adams, Ruth Joyce, *14:* 1

Adamson, Graham. *See* Groom, Arthur William, *10:* 53

Adamson, Joy 1910-1980, *11:* 1; *22:* 5 (Obituary)

Adamson, Wendy Wriston 1942- , *22:* 6

Addona, Angelo F. 1925- , *14:* 1

Addy, Ted. *See* Winterbotham, R(ussell) R(obert), *10:* 198

Adelberg, Doris. *See* Orgel, Doris, *7:* 173

Adelson, Leone 1908- , *11:* 2

Adkins, Jan 1944- , *8:* 2

Adler, David A. 1947- , *14:* 2

Adler, Irene. *See* Storr, Catherine (Cole), *9:* 181

Adler, Irving 1913- , *1:* 2

Adler, Peggy, *22:* 6

Adler, Ruth 1915-1968, *1:* 4

Adoff, Arnold 1935- , *5:* 1

Adorjan, Carol 1934- , *10:* 1

Adshead, Gladys L. 1896- , *3:* 1

Aesop, Abraham. *See* Newbery, John, *20:* 135

Agapida, Fray Antonio. *See* Irving, Washington, *YABC 2:* 164

Agard, Nadema 1948- , *18:* 1

Agle, Nan Hayden 1905- , *3:* 2

Agnew, Edith J(osephine) 1897- , *11:* 3

Ahern, Margaret McCrohan 1921- , *10:* 2

Aichinger, Helga 1937- , *4:* 4

Aiken, Clarissa (Lorenz) 1899- , *12:* 4

Aiken, Conrad 1889- , *3:* 3

Aiken, Joan 1942- , *2:* 1

Ainsworth, Norma, *9:* 4

Ainsworth, Ruth 1908- , *7:* 1

Ainsworth, William Harrison 1805-1882, *24:* 21

Aistrop, Jack 1916- , *14:* 3

Aitken, Dorothy 1916- , *10:* 2

Akers, Floyd. *See* Baum, L(yman) Frank, *18:* 7

Albert, Burton, Jr. 1936- , *22:* 7

Alberts, Frances Jacobs 1907- , *14:* 4

Albrecht, Lillie (Vanderveer) 1894- , *12:* 5

Alcott, Louisa May 1832-1888, *YABC 1:* 7

Alden, Isabella (Macdonald) 1841-1930, *YABC 2:* 1

Alderman, Clifford Lindsey 1902- , *3:* 6

Aldis, Dorothy (Keeley) 1896-1966, *2:* 2

Aldon, Adair. *See* Meigs, Cornelia, *6:* 167

Aldrich, Ann. *See* Meaker, Marijane, *20:* 124

Aldrich, Thomas Bailey 1836-1907, *17:* 2

Aldridge, Josephine Haskell, *14:* 5

Alegria, Ricardo E. 1921- , *6:* 1

Alexander, Anna Cooke 1913- , *1:* 4

Alexander, Frances 1888- , *4:* 6

Alexander, Jocelyn (Anne) Arundel 1930- , *22:* 9

Alexander, Linda 1935- , *2:* 3

Alexander, Lloyd 1924- , *3:* 7

Alexander, Martha 1920- , *11:* 4

Alexander, Rae Pace. *See* Alexander, Raymond Pace, *22:* 10

Alexander, Raymond Pace 1898-1974, *22:* 10

Alexander, Sue 1933- , *12:* 5

Alexander, Vincent Arthur 1925-1980, *23:* 1 (Obituary)

Alexeieff, Alexandre A. 1901- , *14:* 5

Alger, Horatio, Jr. 1832-1899, *16:* 3

Alger, Leclaire (Gowans)
1898-1969, *15:* 1
Aliki. *See* Brandenberg, Aliki,
2: 36
Alkema, Chester Jay 1932- ,
12: 7
Allamand, Pascale 1942- , *12:* 8
Allan, Mabel Esther 1915- , *5:* 2
Allee, Marjorie Hill 1890-1945,
17: 11
Allen, Adam [Joint pseudonym].
See Epstein, Beryl and Samuel,
1: 85
Allen, Allyn. *See* Eberle,
Irmengarde, *2:* 97; *23:* 68
(Obituary)
Allen, Betsy. *See* Cavanna, Betty,
1: 54
Allen, Gertrude E(lizabeth)
1888- , *9:* 5
Allen, Leroy 1912- , *11:* 7
Allen, Marjorie 1931- , *22:* 11
Allen, Merritt Parmelee
1892-1954, *22:* 12
Allen, Nina (Strömgren) 1935- ,
22: 13
Allen, Samuel (Washington)
1917- , *9:* 6
Allerton, Mary. *See* Govan,
Christine Noble, *9:* 80
Alleyn, Ellen. *See* Rossetti,
Christina (Georgina), *20:* 147
Allison, Bob, *14:* 7
Allred, Gordon T. 1930- , *10:* 3
Allsop, Kenneth 1920-1973,
17: 13
Almedingen, E. M. 1898-1971,
3: 9
Almedingen, Martha Edith von. *See*
Almedingen, E. M., *3:* 9
Almquist, Don 1929- , *11:* 8
Alsop, Mary O'Hara 1885-1980,
2: 4; *24:* 26 (Obituary)
Alter, Robert Edmond 1925-1965,
9: 8
Althea. *See* Braithwaite, Althea,
23: 11
Altsheler, Joseph A(lexander)
1862-1919, *YABC 1:* 20
Alvarez, Joseph A. 1930- , *18:* 2
Ambrus, Victor G(tozo) 1935- ,
1: 6
Amerman, Lockhart 1911-1969,
3: 11
Ames, Evelyn 1908- , *13:* 1
Ames, Gerald 1906- , *11:* 9
Ames, Lee J. 1921- , *3:* 11
Ames, Mildred 1919- , *22:* 14
Amon, Aline 1928- , *9:* 8
Amoss, Berthe 1925- , *5:* 4
Anckarsvard, Karin 1915-1969,
6: 2
Ancona, George 1929- , *12:* 10
Andersen, Hans Christian
1805-1875, *YABC 1:* 23

Andersen, Ted. *See* Boyd, Waldo
T., *18:* 35
Anderson, C(larence) W(illiam)
1891-1971, *11:* 9
Anderson, Clifford [Joint
pseudonym]. *See* Gardner,
Richard, *24:* 119
Anderson, Ella. *See* MacLeod,
Ellen Jane (Anderson), *14:* 129
Anderson, Eloise Adell 1927- ,
9: 9
Anderson, George. *See* Groom,
Arthur William, *10:* 53
Anderson, J(ohn) R(ichard) L(ane)
1911- , *15:* 3
Anderson, Joy 1928- , *1:* 8
Anderson, (John) Lonzo 1905- ,
2: 6
Anderson, Lucia (Lewis) 1922- ,
10: 4
Anderson, Mary 1939- , *7:* 4
Anderson, Norman D(ean) 1928- ,
22: 15
Andrews, F(rank) Emerson
1902-1978, *22:* 17
Andrews, J(ames) S(ydney)
1934- , *4:* 7
Andrews, Julie 1935- , *7:* 6
Andrews, Roy Chapman
1884-1960, *19:* 1
Angell, Judie 1937- , *22:* 18
Angell, Madeline 1919- , *18:* 3
Angelo, Valenti 1897- , *14:* 7
Angier, Bradford, *12:* 12
Angle, Paul M(cClelland)
1900-1975, *20:* 1 (Obituary)
Anglund, Joan Walsh 1926- , *2:* 7
Angrist, Stanley W(olff) 1933- ,
4: 9
Anita. *See* Daniel, Anita, *23:* 65
Annett, Cora. *See* Scott, Cora
Annett, *11:* 207
Annixter, Jane. *See* Sturtzel, Jane
Levington, *1:* 212
Annixter, Paul. *See* Sturtzel,
Howard A., *1:* 210
Anno, Mitsumasa 1920- , *5:* 6
Anrooy, Frans van. *See* Van
Anrooy, Francine, *2:* 252
Anthony, C. L. *See* Smith, Dodie,
4: 194
Anthony, Edward 1895-1971,
21: 1
Anticaglia, Elizabeth 1939- ,
12: 13
Anton, Michael (James) 1940- ,
12: 13
Appel, Benjamin 1907-1977,
21: 5 (Obituary)
Appiah, Peggy 1921- , *15:* 3
Appleton, Victor [Collective
pseudonym], *1:* 9
Appleton, Victor II [Collective
pseudonym], *1:* 9
Apsler, Alfred 1907- , *10:* 4

Aquillo, Don. *See* Prince, J(ack)
H(arvey), *17:* 155
Arbuthnot, May Hill 1884-1969,
2: 9
Archer, Frank. *See* O'Connor,
Richard, *21:* 111
Archer, Jules 1915- , *4:* 9
Archer, Marion Fuller 1917- ,
11: 12
Archibald, Joseph S. 1898- ,
3: 12
Arden, Barbie. *See* Stoutenburg,
Adrien, *3:* 217
Ardizzone, Edward 1900-1979,
1: 10; *21:* 5 (Obituary)
Arehart-Treichel, Joan 1942- ,
22: 18
Arenella, Roy 1939- , *14:* 9
Armer, Alberta (Roller) 1904- ,
9: 11
Armer, Laura Adams 1874-1963,
13: 2
Armour, Richard 1906- , *14:* 10
Armstrong, George D. 1927- ,
10: 5
Armstrong, Gerry (Breen) 1929- ,
10: 6
Armstrong, Richard 1903- ,
11: 14
Armstrong, William H. 1914- ,
4: 11
Arnett, Carolyn. *See* Cole, Lois
Dwight, *10:* 26
Arnold, Elliott 1912-1980, *5:* 7;
22: 19 (Obituary)
Arnold, Oren 1900- , *4:* 13
Arnoldy, Julie. *See* Bischoff, Julia
Bristol, *12:* 52
Arnosky, Jim 1946- , *22:* 19
Arnott, Kathleen 1914- , *20:* 1
Arnov, Boris, Jr. 1926- , *12:* 14
Arnstein, Helene S(olomon)
1915- , *12:* 15
Arntson, Herbert E(dward)
1911- , *12:* 16
Aronin, Ben 1904-1980, *25:* 21
(Obituary)
Arora, Shirley (Lease) 1930- ,
2: 10
Arquette, Lois S(teinmetz) 1934- ,
1: 13
Arrowood, (McKendrick Lee)
Clinton 1939- , *19:* 10
Arthur, Ruth M. 1905- , *7:* 6
Artis, Vicki Kimmel 1945- ,
12: 17
Artzybasheff, Boris (Miklailovich)
1899-1965, *14:* 14
Aruego, Ariane. *See* Dewey,
Ariane, *7:* 63
Aruego, Jose 1932- , *6:* 3
Arundel, Honor (Morfydd)
1919-1973, *4:* 15; *24:* 26
(Obituary)
Arundel, Jocelyn. *See* Alexander,
Jocelyn (Anne) Arundel, *22:* 9

Asbjörnsen, Peter Christen
  1812-1885, *15:* 5
Asch, Frank 1946- , *5:* 9
Ashabranner, Brent (Kenneth)
  1921- , *1:* 14
Ashe, Geoffrey (Thomas) 1923- ,
  17: 14
Ashey, Bella. *See* Breinburg,
  Petronella, *11:* 36
Ashford, Daisy. *See* Ashford,
  Margaret Mary, *10:* 6
Ashford, Margaret Mary
  1881-1972, *10:* 6
Ashley, Elizabeth. *See* Salmon,
  Annie Elizabeth, *13:* 188
Asimov, Isaac 1920- , *1:* 15
Asinof, Eliot 1919- , *6:* 5
Aston, James. *See* White, T(erence)
  H(anbury), *12:* 229
Atene, Ann. *See* Atene, (Rita)
  Anna, *12:* 18
Atene, (Rita) Anna 1922- , *12:* 18
Atkinson, M. E. *See* Frankau, Mary
  Evelyn, *4:* 90
Atkinson, Margaret Fleming, *14:* 15
Atticus. *See* Fleming, Ian
  (Lancaster), *9:* 67
Atwater, Florence (Hasseltine
  Carroll), *16:* 11
Atwater, Montgomery Meigs
  1904- , *15:* 10
Atwood, Ann 1913- , *7:* 8
Augarde, Steve 1950- , *25:* 21
Ault, Phillip H. 1914- , *23:* 1
Aung, (Maung) Htin 1910- ,
  21: 5
Aung, U. Htin. *See* Aung, (Maung)
  Htin, *21:* 5
Austin, Elizabeth S. 1907- , *5:* 10
Austin, Margot, *11:* 15
Austin, Oliver L., Jr. 1903- ,
  7: 10
Austin, Tom. *See* Jacobs, Linda C.,
  21: 78
Averill, Esther 1902- , *1:* 16
Avery, Al. *See* Montgomery,
  Rutherford, *3:* 134
Avery, Gillian 1926- , *7:* 10
Avery, Kay 1908- , *5:* 11
Avery, Lynn. *See* Cole, Lois
  Dwight, *10:* 26
Avi. *See* Wortis, Avi, *14:* 269
Ayars, James S(terling) 1898- ,
  4: 17
Ayer, Jacqueline 1930- , *13:* 7
Ayer, Margaret, *15:* 11
Aylesworth, Thomas G(ibbons)
  1927- , *4:* 18
Aymar, Brandt 1911- , *22:* 21

Baastad, Babbis Friis. *See* Friis-
  Baastad, Babbis, *7:* 95
Babbis, Eleanor. *See* Friis-Baastad,
  Babbis, *7:* 95

Babbitt, Natalie 1932- , *6:* 6
Babcock, Dennis Arthur 1948- ,
  22: 21
Bach, Richard David 1936- ,
  13: 7
Bachman, Fred 1949- , *12:* 19
Bacmeister, Rhoda W(arner)
  1893- , *11:* 18
Bacon, Elizabeth 1914- , *3:* 14
Bacon, Margaret Hope 1921- ,
  6: 7
Bacon, Martha Sherman 1917-
  18: 4
Bacon, Peggy 1895- *2:* 11
Baden-Powell, Robert (Stephenson
  Smyth) 1857-1941, *16:* 12
Baerg, Harry J(ohn) 1909- ,
  12: 20
Bagnold, Enid 1889-1981, *1:* 17;
  25: 23
Bailey, Alice Cooper 1890- ,
  12: 22
Bailey, Bernadine Freeman, *14:* 16
Bailey, Carolyn Sherwin
  1875-1961, *14:* 18
Bailey, Jane H(orton) 1916- ,
  12: 22
Bailey, Maralyn Collins (Harrison)
  1941- , *12:* 24
Bailey, Matilda. *See* Radford, Ruby
  L., *6:* 186
Bailey, Maurice Charles 1932- ,
  12: 25
Bailey, Ralph Edgar 1893- ,
  11: 18
Baity, Elizabeth Chesley 1907- ,
  1: 18
Bakeless, John (Edwin) 1894- ,
  9: 12
Bakeless, Katherine Little 1895- ,
  9: 13
Baker, Alan 1951- , *22:* 22
Baker, Augusta 1911- , *3:* 16
Baker, Betty (Lou) 1928- , *5:* 12
Baker, Charlotte 1910- , *2:* 12
Baker, Elizabeth 1923- , *7:* 12
Baker, James W. 1924- , *22:* 23
Baker, Janice E(dla) 1941- ,
  22: 24
Baker, Jeannie 1950- , *23:* 3
Baker, Jeffrey J(ohn) W(heeler)
  1931- , *5:* 13
Baker, Jim. *See* Baker, James W.,
  22: 23
Baker, Laura Nelson 1911- ,
  3: 17
Baker, Margaret 1890- , *4:* 19
Baker, Margaret J(oyce) 1918- ,
  12: 25
Baker, Mary Gladys Steel
  1892-1974, *12:* 27
Baker, (Robert) Michael 1938- ,
  4: 20
Baker, Nina (Brown) 1888-1957,
  15: 12
Baker, Rachel 1904- , *2:* 13

Baker, Samm Sinclair 1909- ,
  12: 27
Balaam. *See* Lamb, G(eoffrey)
  F(rederick), *10:* 74
Balch, Glenn 1902- , *3:* 18
Balducci, Carolyn Feleppa 1946- ,
  5: 13
Baldwin, Anne Norris 1938- ,
  5: 14
Baldwin, Clara, *11:* 20
Baldwin, Gordo. *See* Baldwin,
  Gordon C., *12:* 30
Baldwin, Gordon C. 1908- ,
  12: 30
Baldwin, James 1841-1925,
  24: 26
Baldwin, James (Arthur) 1924- ,
  9: 15
Balet, Jan (Bernard) 1913- ,
  11: 21
Balian, Lorna 1929- , *9:* 16
Ball, Zachary. *See* Masters,
  Kelly R., *3:* 118
Ballantyne, R(obert) M(ichael)
  1825-1894, *24:* 32
Ballard, Lowell Clyne 1904- ,
  12: 30
Ballard, (Charles) Martin 1929- ,
  1: 19
Balogh, Penelope 1916- , *1:* 20
Balow, Tom 1931- , *12:* 31
Bamfylde, Walter. *See* Bevan,
  Tom, *YABC 2:* 8
Bamman, Henry A. 1918- ,
  12: 32
Bancroft, Griffing 1907- , *6:* 8
Bancroft, Laura. *See* Baum,
  L(yman) Frank, *18:* 7
Baner, Skulda V(anadis)
  1897-1964, *10:* 8
Bang, Garrett. *See* Bang, Molly
  Garrett, *24:* 37
Bang, Molly Garrett 1943- ,
  24: 37
Banks, Laura Stockton Voorhees
  1908(?)-1980, *23:* 5 (Obituary)
Banner, Angela. *See* Maddison,
  Angela Mary, *10:* 82
Bannerman, Helen (Brodie Cowan
  Watson) 1863(?)-1946, *19:* 12
Bannon, Laura d. 1963, *6:* 9
Barbary, James. *See* Baumann,
  Amy (Brown), *10:* 9
Barbary, James. *See* Beeching,
  Jack, *14:* 26
Barbour, Ralph Henry 1870-1944,
  16: 27
Barclay, Isabel. *See* Dobell,
  I.M.B., *11:* 77
Bare, Arnold Edwin 1920- ,
  16: 31
Barish, Matthew 1907- , *12:* 32
Barker, Albert W. 1900- , *8:* 3
Barker, Melvern 1907- , *11:* 23
Barker, S. Omar 1894- , *10:* 8
Barker, Will 1908- , *8:* 4

Author Index

Barkley, James Edward 1941- ,
6: 12
Barnaby, Ralph S(tanton) 1893- ,
9: 17
Barnes, (Frank) Eric Wollencott
1907-1962, 22: 25
Barnstone, Willis 1927- , 20: 3
Barnum, Jay Hyde 1888(?)-1962,
20: 4
Barnum, Richard [Collective
pseudonym], 1: 20
Barr, Donald 1921- , 20: 5
Barr, George 1907- , 2: 14
Barr, Jene 1900- , 16: 32
Barrett, Ron 1937- , 14: 23
Barrie, J(ames) M(atthew)
1860-1937, YABC 1: 48
Barry, James P(otvin) 1918- ,
14: 24
Barry, Katharina (Watjen) 1936- ,
4: 22
Barry, Robert 1931- , 6: 12
Barth, Edna 1914-1980, 7: 13;
24: 39 (Obituary)
Barthelme, Donald 1931- , 7: 14
Bartlett, Philip A. [Collective
pseudonym], 1: 21
Bartlett, Robert Merill 1899- ,
12: 33
Barton, Byron 1930- , 9: 17
Barton, May Hollis [Collective
pseudonym], 1: 21
Bartos-Hoeppner, Barbara 1923- ,
5: 15
Baruch, Dorothy W(alter)
1899-1962, 21: 6
Bas, Rutger. See Rutgers van der
Loeff, An(na) Basenau,
22: 211
Bashevis, Isaac. See Singer, Isaac
Bashevis, 3: 203
Bason, Lillian 1913- , 20: 6
Bassett, John Keith. See Keating,
Lawrence A, 23: 107
Bate, Lucy 1939- , 18: 6
Bate, Norman 1916- , 5: 15
Bates, Barbara S(nedeker) 1919- ,
12: 34
Bates, Betty 1921- , 19: 15
Batten, H(arry) Mortimer
1888-1958, 25: 34
Batten, Mary 1937- , 5: 17
Batterberry, Ariane Ruskin
1935- , 13: 10
Battles, Edith 1921- , 7: 15
Baudouy, Michel-Aime 1909- ,
7: 18
Bauer, Helen 1900- , 2: 14
Bauer, Marion Dane 1938- , 20: 8
Bauernschmidt, Marjorie 1926- ,
15: 14
Baum, Allyn Z(elton) 1924- ,
20: 9
Baum, L(yman) Frank 1856-1919,
18: 7
Baum, Willi 1931- , 4: 23

Baumann, Amy (Brown) 1922- ,
10: 9
Baumann, Hans 1914- , 2: 16
Baumann, Kurt 1935- , 21: 8
Bawden, Nina. See Kark, Nina
Mary, 4: 132
Baylor, Byrd 1924- , 16: 33
Baynes, Pauline (Diana) 1922- ,
19: 17
BB. See Watkins-Pitchford, D. J.,
6: 214
Beach, Charles. See Reid, (Thomas)
Mayne, 24: 170
Beach, Charles Amory [Collective
pseudonym], 1: 21
Beach, Edward L(atimer) 1918- ,
12: 35
Beach, Stewart Taft 1899- , 23: 5
Beachcroft, Nina 1931- , 18: 31
Bealer, Alex W(inkler III)
1921-1980, 8: 6; 22: 26
(Obituary)
Beals, Carleton 1893- , 12: 36
Beame, Rona 1934- , 12: 39
Beaney, Jan. See Udall, Jan
Beaney, 10: 182
Beard, Charles Austin 1874-1948,
18: 32
Beard, Dan(iel Carter) 1850-1941,
22: 26
Bearden, Romare (Howard)
1914- , 22: 34
Beardmore, Cedric. See Beardmore,
George, 20: 10
Beardmore, George 1908-1979,
20: 10
Beatty, Hetty Burlingame
1907-1971, 5: 18
Beatty, Jerome, Jr. 1918- , 5: 19
Beatty, John (Louis) 1922-1975,
6: 13; 25: 35 (Obituary)
Beatty, Patricia (Robbins) 1922- ,
1: 21
Bechtel, Louise Seaman 1894- ,
4: 26
Beck, Barbara L. 1927- , 12: 41
Becker, Beril 1901- , 11: 23
Becker, John (Leonard) 1901- ,
12: 41
Beckman, Gunnel 1910- , 6: 14
Bedford, A. N. See Watson, Jane
Werner, 3: 244
Bedford, Annie North. See Watson,
Jane Werner, 3: 244
Beebe, B(urdetta) F(aye) 1920- ,
1: 23
Beebe, (Charles) William
1877-1962, 19: 21
Beeby, Betty 1923- , 25: 37
Beech, Webb. See Butterworth,
W. E., 5: 40
Beeching, Jack 1922- , 14: 26
Beeler, Nelson F(rederick) 1910- ,
13: 11
Beers, Dorothy Sands 1917- ,
9: 18

Beers, Lorna 1897- , 14: 26
Beers, V(ictor) Gilbert 1928- ,
9: 18
Begley, Kathleen A(nne) 1948- ,
21: 9
Behn, Harry 1898- , 2: 17
Behnke, Frances L., 8: 7
Behr, Joyce 1929- , 15: 15
Behrens, June York 1925- ,
19: 30
Behrman, Carol H(elen) 1925- ,
14: 27
Beiser, Arthur 1931- , 22: 36
Beiser, Germaine 1931- , 11: 24
Belaney, Archibald Stansfeld
1888-1938, 24: 39
Belknap, B. H. See Ellis, Edward
S(ylvester), YABC 1: 116
Bell, Corydon 1894- , 3: 19
Bell, Emily Mary. See Cason,
Mabel Earp, 10: 19
Bell, Gertrude (Wood) 1911- ,
12: 42
Bell, Gina. See Iannone, Jeanne,
7: 139
Bell, Janet. See Clymer, Eleanor,
9: 37
Bell, Margaret E(lizabeth) 1898- ,
2: 19
Bell, Norman (Edward) 1899- ,
11: 25
Bell, Raymond Martin 1907- ,
13: 13
Bell, Thelma Harrington 1896- ,
3: 20
Bellairs, John 1938- , 2: 20
Belloc, (Joseph) Hilaire (Pierre)
1870-1953, YABC 1: 62
Bell-Zano, Gina. See Iannone,
Jeanne, 7: 139
Belpré, Pura, 16: 35
Belting, Natalie Maree 1915- ,
6: 16
Belton, John Raynor 1931- ,
22: 37
Belvedere, Lee. See Grayland,
Valerie, 7: 111
Bemelmans, Ludwig 1898-1962,
15: 15
Benary, Margot. See Benary-Isbert,
Margot, 2: 21; 21: 9
Benary-Isbert, Margot 1889-1979,
2: 21; 21: 9 (Obituary)
Benasutti, Marion 1908- , 6: 18
Benchley, Nathaniel 1915- ,
3: 21; 25: 39
Benchley, Peter 1940- , 3: 22
Bender, Lucy Ellen 1942- ,
22: 38
Bendick, Jeanne 1919- , 2: 23
Bendick, Robert L(ouis) 1917- ,
11: 25
Benedict, Dorothy Potter
1889-1979, 11: 26; 23: 5
(Obituary)

Benedict, Lois Trimble
1902-1967, *12:* 44
Benedict, Rex   1920- , *8:* 8
Benét, Laura   1884-1979, *3:* 23;
23: 6 (Obituary)
Benét, Stephen Vincent
1898-1943, *YABC 1:* 75
Benet, Sula   1903- , *21:* 10
Benezra, Barbara   1921- , *10:* 10
Bennett, John   1865-1956,
YABC 1: 84
Bennett, Rainey   1907- , *15:* 27
Bennett, Richard   1899- , *21:* 11
Bennett, Russell H(oradley)
1896- , *25:* 45
Benson, Sally   1900- , *1:* 24
Bently, Nicolas Clerihew
1907-1978, *24:* 43 (Obituary)
Bentley, Phyllis (Eleanor)
1894-1977, *6:* 19; *25:* 45
(Obituary)
Berelson, Howard   1940- , *5:* 20
Berenstain, Janice, *12:* 44
Berenstain, Stan(ley)   1923- ,
12: 45
Beresford, Elisabeth, *25:* 45
Berg, Jean Horton   1913- , *6:* 21
Bergaust, Erik   1925-1978, *20:* 12
Berger, Melvin H.   1927- , *5:* 21
Berger, Terry   1933- , *8:* 10
Berkey, Barry Robert   1935- ,
24: 44
Berkowitz, Freda Pastor   1910- ,
12: 48
Berliner, Franz   1930- , *13:* 13
Berna, Paul   1910- , *15:* 27
Bernadette. *See* Watts, Bernadette,
4: 226
Bernard, Jacqueline (de Sieyes)
1921- , *8:* 11
Bernstein, Joanne E(ckstein)
1943- , *15:* 29
Bernstein, Theodore M(enline)
1904- , *12:* 49
Berrien, Edith Heal. *See* Heal,
Edith, *7:* 123
Berrill, Jacquelyn (Batsel)   1905- ,
12: 50
Berrington, John. *See* Brownjohn,
Alan, *6:* 38
Berry, B. J. *See* Berry, Barbara, J.,
7: 19
Berry, Barbara J.   1937- , *7:* 19
Berry, Erick. *See* Best, Allena
Champlin, *2:* 25; *25:* 48
(Obituary)
Berry, Jane Cobb   1915(?)-1979,
22: 39 (Obituary)
Berry, William D(avid)   1926- ,
14: 28
Berson, Harold   1926- , *4:* 27
Berwick, Jean. *See* Meyer, Jean
Shepherd, *11:* 181
Beskow, Elsa (Maartman)
1874-1953, *20:* 13
Best, (Evangel) Allena Champlin

1892-1974, *2:* 27; *25:* 48
(Obituary)
Best, (Oswald) Herbert   1894- ,
2: 27
Beth, Mary. *See* Miller, Mary Beth,
9: 145
Bethancourt, T. Ernesto   1932- ,
11: 27
Bethell, Jean (Frankenberry)
1922- , *8:* 11
Bethers, Ray   1902- , *6:* 22
Bethune, J. G. *See* Ellis, Edward
S(ylvester), *YABC 1:* 116
Betteridge, Anne. *See* Potter,
Margaret (Newman), *21:* 119
Bettina. *See* Ehrlich, Bettina, *1:* 82
Betz, Eva Kelly   1897-1968,
10: 10
Bevan, Tom   1868-1930(?),
YABC 2: 8
Bewick, Thomas   1753-1828,
16: 38
Beyer, Audrey White   1916- ,
9: 19
Bialk, Elisa, *1:* 25
Bianco, Margery (Williams)
1881-1944, *15:* 29
Bibby, Violet   1908- , *24:* 45
Bible, Charles   1937- , *13:* 14
Bice, Clare   1909-1976, *22:* 39
Bickerstaff, Isaac. *See* Swift,
Jonathan, *19:* 244
Biegel, Paul   1925- , *16:* 49
Biemiller, Carl Ludwig
1912-1979, *21:* 13 (Obituary)
Bierhorst, John   1936- , *6:* 23
Billout, Guy René   1941- , *10:* 11
Binzen, Bill, *24:* 48
Binzen, William. *See* Binzen, Bill,
24: 48
Birch, Reginald B(athurst)
1856-1943, *19:* 31
Birmingham, Lloyd   1924- ,
12: 51
Biro, Val   1921- , *1:* 26
Bischoff, Julia Bristol   1909-1970,
12: 52
Bishop, Claire (Huchet), *14:* 30
Bishop, Curtis   1912-1967, *6:* 24
Bishop, Elizabeth   1911-1979,
24: 49 (Obituary)
Bisset, Donald   1910- , *7:* 20
Bitter, Gary G(len)   1940- , *22:* 41
Bixby, William   1920- , *6:* 24
Black, Algernon David   1900- ,
12: 53
Black, Irma S(imonton)
1906-1972, *2:* 28; *25:* 48
(Obituary)
Blackburn, Claire. *See* Jacobs,
Linda C., *21:* 78
Blackburn, John(ny) Brewton
1952- , *15:* 35
Blackett, Veronica Heath   1927- ,
12: 54
Blades, Ann   1947- , *16:* 51

Bladow, Suzanne Wilson   1937- ,
14: 32
Blaine, John. *See* Goodwin, Harold
Leland, *13:* 73
Blaine, John. *See* Harkins, Philip,
6: 102
Blaine, Margery Kay   1937- ,
11: 28
Blair, Ruth Van Ness   1912- ,
12: 54
Blair, Walter   1900- , *12:* 56
Blake, Olive. *See* Supraner, Robyn,
20: 182
Blake, Quentin   1932- , *9:* 20
Blake, Walker E. *See* Butterworth,
W. E., *5:* 40
Bland, Edith Nesbit. *See* Nesbit,
E(dith), *YABC 1:* 193
Bland, Fabian [Joint pseudonym].
See Nesbit, E(dith),
YABC 1: 193
Blassingame, Wyatt (Rainey)
1909- , *1:* 27
Bleeker, Sonia   1909- , *2:* 30
Blegvad, Erik   1923- , *14:* 33
Blegvad, Lenore   1926- , *14:* 34
Blishen, Edward   1920- , *8:* 12
Bliss, Reginald. *See* Wells,
H(erbert) G(eorge), *20:* 190
Bliss, Ronald G(ene)   1942- ,
12: 57
Bliven, Bruce, Jr.   1916- , *2:* 31
Bloch, Lucienne   1909- , *10:* 11
Bloch, Marie Halun   1910- , *6:* 25
Bloch, Robert   1917- , *12:* 57
Blochman, Lawrence G(oldtree)
1900-1975, *22:* 42
Block, Irvin   1917- , *12:* 59
Blough, Glenn O(rlando)   1907- ,
1: 28
Blue, Rose   1931- , *5:* 22
Blume, Judy (Sussman)   1938- ,
2: 31
Blyton, Carey   1932- , *9:* 22
Blyton, Enid (Mary)   1897-1968,
25: 48
Boardman, Fon Wyman, Jr.
1911- , *6:* 26
Boardman, Gwenn R.   1924- ,
12: 59
Bobbe, Dorothie   1905-1975,
1: 30; *25:* 61 (Obituary)
Bock, Hal. *See* Bock, Harold I.,
10: 13
Bock, Harold I.   1939- , *10:* 13
Bock, William Sauts Netamux'we,
14: 36
Bodecker, N. M.   1922- , *8:* 12
Boden, Hilda. *See* Bodenham, Hilda
Esther, *13:* 16
Bodenham, Hilda Esther   1901- ,
13: 16
Bodie, Idella F(allaw)   1925- ,
12: 60
Bodker, Cecil   1927- , *14:* 39

Boeckman, Charles 1920- , *12:* 61

Boesch, Mark J(oseph) 1917- , *12:* 62

Boesen, Victor 1908- , *16:* 53

Boggs, Ralph Steele 1901- , *7:* 21

Bohdal, Susi 1951- , *22:* 43

Boles, Paul Darcy 1919- , *9:* 23

Bolian, Polly 1925- , *4:* 29

Bolliger, Max 1929- , *7:* 22

Bolognese, Don(ald Alan) 1934- , *24:* 49

Bolton, Carole 1926- , *6:* 27

Bolton, Evelyn. *See* Bunting, Anne Evelyn, *18:* 38

Bond, Gladys Baker 1912- , *14:* 41

Bond, J. Harvey. *See* Winterbotham, R(ussell) R(obert), *10:* 198

Bond, Michael 1926- , *6:* 28

Bond, Nancy (Barbara) 1945- , *22:* 44

Bond, Ruskin 1934- , *14:* 43

Bonehill, Captain Ralph. *See* Stratemeyer, Edward L., *1:* 208

Bonham, Barbara 1926- , *7:* 22

Bonham, Frank 1914- , *1:* 30

Bonner, Mary Graham 1890-1974, *19:* 37

Bonsall, Crosby (Barbara Newell) 1921- , *23:* 6

Bontemps, Arna 1902-1973, *2:* 32; *24:* 51 (Obituary)

Bonzon, Paul-Jacques 1908- , *22:* 46

Boone, Pat 1934- , *7:* 23

Bordier, Georgette 1924- , *16:* 53

Borja, Corinne 1929- , *22:* 47

Borja, Robert 1923- , *22:* 47

Borland, Hal 1900-1978, *5:* 22; *24:* 51 (Obituary)

Borland, Harold Glen. *See* Borland, Hal, *5:* 22; *24:* 51 (Obituary)

Borland, Kathryn Kilby 1916- , *16:* 54

Bornstein, Ruth 1927- , *14:* 44

Borski, Lucia Merecka, *18:* 34

Borten, Helen Jacobson 1930- , *5:* 24

Borton, Elizabeth. *See* Trevino, Elizabeth B. de, *1:* 216

Bortstein, Larry 1942- , *16:* 56

Bosco, Jack. *See* Holliday, Joseph, *11:* 137

Boshell, Gordon 1908- , *15:* 36

Boshinski, Blanche 1922- , *10:* 13

Boston, Lucy Maria (Wood) 1892- , *19:* 38

Bosworth, J. Allan 1925- , *19:* 45

Bothwell, Jean, *2:* 34

Bottner, Barbara 1943- , *14:* 45

Boulle, Pierre (Francois Marie-Louis) 1912- , *22:* 49

Bourne, Leslie. *See* Marshall, Evelyn, *11:* 172

Bourne, Miriam Anne 1931- , *16:* 57

Bova, Ben 1932- , *6:* 29

Bowen, Betty Morgan. *See* West, Betty, *11:* 233

Bowen, Catherine Drinker 1897-1973, *7:* 24

Bowen, David. *See* Bowen, Joshua David, *22:* 51

Bowen, Joshua David 1930- , *22:* 51

Bowen, Robert Sidney 1900(?)-1977, *21:* 13 (Obituary)

Bowie, Jim. *See* Stratemeyer, Edward L., *1:* 208

Bowman, James Cloyd 1880-1961, *23:* 7

Bowman, John S(tewart) 1931- , *16:* 57

Boyce, George A(rthur) 1898- , *19:* 46

Boyd, Waldo T. 1918- , *18:* 35

Boyer, Robert E(rnst) 1929- , *22:* 52

Boyle, Ann (Peters) 1916- , *10:* 13

Boylston, Helen (Dore) 1895- , *23:* 8

Boz. *See* Dickens, Charles, *15:* 55

Bradbury, Bianca 1908- , *3:* 25

Bradbury, Ray (Douglas) 1920- , *11:* 29

Bradley, Virginia 1912- , *23:* 11

Brady, Irene 1943- , *4:* 30

Bragdon, Elspeth 1897- , *6:* 30

Bragdon, Lillian (Jacot), *24:* 51

Bragg, Mabel Caroline 1870-1945, *24:* 52

Braithwaite, Althea 1940- , *23:* 11

Brancato, Robin F(idler) 1936- , *23:* 14

Brandenberg, Aliki Liacouras, *2:* 36

Brandenberg, Franz 1932- , *8:* 14

Brandhorst, Carl T(heodore) 1898- , *23:* 16

Brandon, Brumsic, Jr. 1927- , *9:* 25

Brandon, Curt. *See* Bishop, Curtis, *6:* 24

Branfield, John (Charles) 1931- , *11:* 36

Branley, Franklyn M(ansfield) 1915- , *4:* 32

Branscum, Robbie 1937- , *23:* 17

Bratton, Helen 1899- , *4:* 34

Braude, Michael 1936- , *23:* 18

Braymer, Marjorie 1911- , *6:* 31

Brecht, Edith 1895-1975, *6:* 32; *25:* 61 (Obituary)

Breck, Vivian. *See* Breckenfeld, Vivian Gurney, *1:* 33

Breckenfeld, Vivian Gurney 1895- , *1:* 33

Breda, Tjalmar. *See* DeJong, David C(ornel), *10:* 29

Breinburg, Petronella 1927- , *11:* 36

Breisky, William J(ohn) 1928- , *22:* 53

Brennan, Joseph L. 1903- , *6:* 33

Brennan, Tim. *See* Conroy, Jack (Wesley), *19:* 65

Brenner, Barbara (Johnes) 1925- , *4:* 34

Brent, Stuart, *14:* 47

Brett, Bernard 1925- , *22:* 53

Brett, Grace N(eff) 1900-1975, *23:* 19

Brewster, Benjamin. *See* Folsom, Franklin, *5:* 67

Brewton, John E(dmund) 1898- , *5:* 25

Brick, John 1922-1973, *10:* 14

Bridgers, Sue Ellen 1942- , *22:* 56

Bridges, William (Andrew) 1901- *5:* 27

Bridwell, Norman 1928- , *4:* 36

Brier, Howard M(axwell) 1903-1969, *8:* 15

Briggs, Katharine Mary 1898-1980, *25:* 62 (Obituary)

Briggs, Raymond (Redvers) 1934- , *23:* 19

Bright, Robert 1902- , *24:* 54

Brimberg, Stanlee 1947- , *9:* 25

Brin, Ruth F(irestone) 1921- , *22:* 56

Brinckloe, Julie (Lorraine) 1950- , *13:* 17

Brindel, June (Rachuy) 1919- , *7:* 25

Brindze, Ruth 1903- , *23:* 22

Brink, Carol Ryrie 1895- *1:* 34

Brinsmead, H(esba) F(ay) 1922- , *18:* 36

Brisley, Joyce Lankester 1896- , *22:* 57

Britt, Dell, 1934- *1:* 35

Bro, Margueritte (Harmon) 1894- , *19:* 46

Broadhead, Helen Cross 1913- , *25:* 62

Brock, Betty 1923- , *7:* 27

Brock, Emma L(illian) 1886-1974, *8:* 15

Brockett, Eleanor Hall 1913-1967, *10:* 15

Broderick, Dorothy M. 1929- , *5:* 28

Brokamp, Marilyn 1920- , *10:* 15

Brondfield, Jerome 1913- , *22:* 55

Brondfield, Jerry. *See* Brondfield, Jerome, *22:* 55

Bronson, Lynn. *See* Lampman, Evelyn Sibley, *4:* 140; *23:* 115 (Obituary)

Brooke, L(eonard) Leslie 1862-1940, *17:* 15

Brooke-Haven, P. *See* Wodehouse, P(elham) G(renville), *22:* 241

Brooks, Anita 1914- , *5:* 28

Brooks, Charlotte K., *24:* 56

Brooks, Gwendolyn 1917- , *6:* 33

Brooks, Jerome 1931- , *23:* 23

Brooks, Lester 1924- , *7:* 28

Brooks, Polly Schoyer 1912- , *12:* 63

Brooks, Walter R(ollin) 1886-1958, *17:* 17

Brosnan, James Patrick 1929- , *14:* 47

Brosnan, Jim. *See* Brosnan, James Patrick, *14:* 47

Broun, Emily. *See* Sterne, Emma Gelders, *6:* 205

Brower, Millicent, *8:* 16

Brower, Pauline (York) 1929- , *22:* 59

Browin, Frances Williams 1898- , *5:* 30

Brown, Alexis. *See* Baumann, Amy (Brown), *10:* 9

Brown, Bill. *See* Brown, William L., *5:* 34

Brown, Billye Walker. *See* Cutchen, Billye Walker, *15:* 51

Brown, Bob. *See* Brown, Robert Joseph, *14:* 48

Brown, Dee (Alexander) 1908- , *5:* 30

Brown, Eleanor Frances 1908- , *3:* 26

Brown, George Earl 1883-1964, *11:* 40

Brown, Irene Bennett 1932- , *3:* 27

Brown, Ivor 1891- , *5:* 31

Brown, Judith Gwyn 1933- , *20:* 15

Brown, Marc Tolon 1946- , *10:* 17

Brown, Marcia 1918- , *7:* 29

Brown, Margaret Wise 1910-1952, *YABC 2:* 9

Brown, Margery, *5:* 31

Brown, Marion Marsh 1908- , *6:* 35

Brown, Myra Berry 1918- , *6:* 36

Brown, Pamela 1924- , *5:* 33

Brown, Robert Joseph 1907- , *14:* 48

Brown, Rosalie (Gertrude) Moore 1910- , *9:* 26

Brown, Vinson 1912- , *19:* 48

Brown, Walter R(eed) 1929- , *19:* 50

Brown, Will. *See* Ainsworth, William Harrison, *24:* 21

Brown, William L(ouis) 1910-1964, *5:* 34

Browne, Hablot Knight 1815-1882, *21:* 13

Browne, Matthew. *See* Rands, William Brighty, *17:* 156

Browning, Robert 1812-1889, *YABC 1:* 85

Brownjohn, Alan 1931- *6:* 38

Bruce, Mary 1927- , *1:* 36

Brunhoff, Jean de 1899-1937, *24:* 56

Brunhoff, Laurent de 1925- , *24:* 59

Bryant, Bernice (Morgan) 1908- , *11:* 40

Brychta, Alex 1956- , *21:* 21

Bryson, Bernarda 1905- , *9:* 26

Buchan, John 1875-1940, *YABC 2:* 21

Buchwald, Art(hur) 1925- , *10:* 18

Buchwald, Emilie 1935- , *7:* 31

Buck, Lewis 1925- , *18:* 37

Buck, Margaret Waring 1910- , *3:* 29

Buck, Pearl S(ydenstricker) 1892-1973, *1:* 36; *25:* 63

Buckeridge, Anthony 1912- , *6:* 38

Buckley, Helen E(lizabeth) 1918- , *2:* 38

Buckmaster, Henrietta, *6:* 39

Budd, Lillian 1897- , *7:* 33

Buehr, Walter 1897-1971, *3:* 30

Buff, Conrad 1886-1975, *19:* 51

Buff, Mary Marsh 1890-1970, *19:* 54

Bulla, Clyde Robert 1914- , *2:* 39

Bunting, A. E.. *See* Bunting, Anne Evelyn, *18:* 38

Bunting, Anne Evelyn 1928- , *18:* 38

Bunting, Eve. *See* Bunting, Anne Evelyn, *18:* 38

Bunting, Glenn (Davison) 1957- , *22:* 60

Burch, Robert J(oseph) 1925- , *1:* 38

Burchard, Peter D(uncan), *5:* 34

Burchard, Sue 1937- , *22:* 61

Burchardt, Nellie 1921- , *7:* 33

Burdick, Eugene (Leonard) 1918-1965, *22:* 61

Burford, Eleanor. *See* Hibbert, Eleanor, *2:* 134

Burger, Carl 1888-1967, *9:* 27

Burgess, Anne Marie. *See* Gerson, Noel B(ertram), *22:* 118

Burgess, Em. *See* Burgess, Mary Wyche, *18:* 39

Burgess, Mary Wyche 1916- , *18:* 39

Burgess, Michael. *See* Gerson, Noel B(ertram), *22:* 118

Burgess, Robert F(orrest) 1927- , *4:* 38

Burgess, Thornton W(aldo) 1874-1965, *17:* 19

Burgwyn, Mebane H. 1914- , *7:* 34

Burke, John. *See* O'Connor, Richard, *21:* 111

Burkert, Nancy Ekholm 1933- , *24:* 62

Burland, C. A. *See* Burland, Cottie A., *5:* 36

Burland, Cottie A. 1905- , *5:* 36

Burlingame, (William) Roger 1889-1967, *2:* 40

Burman, Alice Caddy 1896(?)-1977, *24:* 66 (Obituary)

Burman, Ben Lucien 1896- , *6:* 40

Burn, Doris 1923- , *1:* 39

Burnett, Frances (Eliza) Hodgson 1849-1924, *YABC 2:* 32

Burnford, S. D. *See* Burnford, Sheila, *3:* 32

Burnford, Sheila 1918- , *3:* 32

Burningham, John (Mackintosh) 1936- , *16:* 58

Burns, Paul C., *5:* 37

Burns, Raymond (Howard) 1924- , *9:* 28

Burns, William A. 1909- , *5:* 38

Burroughs, Polly 1925- , *2:* 41

Burroway, Janet (Gay) 1936- , *23:* 24

Burt, Jesse Clifton 1921-1976, *20:* 18 (Obituary)

Burt, Olive Woolley 1894- , *4:* 39

Burton, Hester 1913- , *7:* 35

Burton, Maurice 1898- , *23:* 27

Burton, Robert (Wellesley) 1941- , *22:* 62

Burton, Virginia Lee 1909-1968, *2:* 42

Burton, William H(enry) 1890-1964, *11:* 42

Busoni, Rafaello 1900-1962, *16:* 61

Butler, Beverly 1932- , *7:* 37

Butters, Dorothy Gilman 1923- , *5:* 39

Butterworth, Oliver 1915- , *1:* 40

Butterworth, W(illiam) E(dmund III) 1929- , *5:* 40

Byars, Betsy 1928- , *4:* 40

Byfield, Barbara Ninde 1930- , *8:* 19

C.3.3. *See* Wilde, Oscar (Fingal O'Flahertie Wills), *24:* 205

Cable, Mary 1920- , *9:* 29

Caddy, Alice. *See* Burman, Alice Caddy, *24:* 66 (Obituary)

Cadwallader, Sharon 1936- , *7:* 38

Cady, (Walter) Harrison 1877-1970, *19:* 56

Cain, Arthur H. 1913- , *3:* 33

Cain, Christopher. *See* Fleming, Thomas J(ames), *8:* 19

Cairns, Trevor 1922- , *14:* 50
Caldecott, Moyra 1927- , *22:* 63
Caldecott, Randolph (J.)
1846-1886, *17:* 31
Caldwell, John C(ope) 1913- ,
7: 38
Calhoun, Mary (Huiskamp)
1926- , *2:* 44
Calkins, Franklin. *See* Stratemeyer,
Edward L., *1:* 208
Call, Hughie Florence 1890-1969,
1: 41
Callahan, Philip S(erna) 1923- ,
25: 77
Callen, Larry. *See* Callen, Lawrence
Willard, Jr., *19:* 59
Callen, Lawrence Willard, Jr.
1927- , *19:* 59
Calvert, John. *See* Leaf, (Wilbur)
Munro, *20:* 99
Cameron, Edna M. 1905- , *3:* 34
Cameron, Eleanor (Butler) 1912- ,
1: 42; *25:* 78
Cameron, Elizabeth. *See* Nowell,
Elizabeth Cameron, *12:* 160
Cameron, Polly 1928- , *2:* 45
Camp, Walter (Chauncey)
1859-1925, *YABC 1:* 92
Campbell, Ann R. 1925- , *11:* 43
Campbell, Bruce. *See* Epstein,
Samuel, *1:* 87
Campbell, Hope, *20:* 19
Campbell, Jane. *See* Edwards, Jane
Campbell, *10:* 34
Campbell, R. W. *See* Campbell,
Rosemae Wells, *1:* 44
Campbell, Rosemae Wells 1909- ,
1: 44
Campion, Nardi Reeder 1917- ,
22: 64
Candell, Victor 1903-1977, *24:* 66
(Obituary)
Canfield, Dorothy. *See* Fisher,
Dorothy Canfield, *YABC 1:* 122
Canusi, Jose. *See* Barker, S. Omar,
10: 8
Caplin, Alfred Gerald 1909-1979,
21: 22 (Obituary)
Capp, Al. *See* Caplin, Alfred
Gerald, *21:* 22
Cappel, Constance 1936- , *22:* 65
Capps, Benjamin (Franklin)
1922- , *9:* 30
Carafoli, Marci. *See* Ridlon, Marci,
22: 211
Caras, Roger A(ndrew) 1928- ,
12: 65
Carbonnier, Jeanne, *3:* 34
Carey, Bonnie 1941- , *18:* 40
Carey, Ernestine Gilbreth 1908- ,
2: 45
Carigiet, Alois 1902- , *24:* 66
Carini, Edward 1923- , *9:* 30
Carle, Eric 1929- , *4:* 41
Carleton, Captain L. C. *See* Ellis,

Edward S(ylvester),
YABC 1: 116
Carley, V(an Ness) Royal
1906-1976, *20:* 20 (Obituary)
Carlisle, Clark, Jr. *See* Holding,
James, *3:* 85
Carlsen, Ruth C(hristoffer), *2:* 47
Carlson, Bernice Wells 1910- ,
8: 19
Carlson, Dale Bick 1935- , *1:* 44
Carlson, Natalie Savage, *2:* 48
Carlson, Vada F. 1897- , *16:* 64
Carmer, Elizabeth Black 1904- ,
24: 68
Carol, Bill J. *See* Knott, William
Cecil, Jr., *3:* 94
Carpelan, Bo (Gustaf Bertelsson)
1926- , *8:* 20
Carpenter, Allan 1917- , *3:* 35
Carpenter, Frances 1890- , *3:* 36
Carpenter, Patricia (Healy Evans)
1920- , *11:* 43
Carr, Glyn. *See* Styles, Frank
Showell, *10:* 167
Carr, Harriett Helen 1899- , *3:* 37
Carr, Mary Jane, *2:* 50
Carrick, Carol 1935- , *7:* 39
Carrick, Donald 1929- , *7:* 40
Carrighar, Sally, *24:* 69
Carroll, Curt. *See* Bishop, Curtis,
6: 24
Carroll, Latrobe, *7:* 40
Carroll, Laura. *See* Parr, Lucy,
10: 115
Carroll, Lewis. *See* Dodgson,
Charles Lutwidge,
YABC 2: 297
Carse, Robert 1902-1971, *5:* 41
Carson, Captain James. *See*
Stratemeyer, Edward L., *1:* 208
Carson, John F. 1920- , *1:* 46
Carson, Rachel (Louise)
1907-1964, *23:* 28
Carter, Bruce. *See* Hough, Richard
(Alexander), *17:* 83
Carter, Dorothy Sharp 1921- ,
8: 21
Carter, Helene 1887-1960, *15:* 37
Carter, (William) Hodding 1907- ,
2: 51
Carter, Katharine J(ones) 1905- ,
2: 52
Carter, Phyllis Ann. *See* Eberle,
Irmengarde, *2:* 97; *23:* 68
(Obituary)
Carter, William E. 1927- , *1:* 47
Cartner, William Carruthers
1910- , *11:* 44
Carver, John. *See* Gardner, Richard,
24: 119
Cartwright, Sally 1923- , *9:* 30
Cary. *See* Cary, Louis F(avreau),
9: 31
Cary, Louis F(avreau) 1915- ,
9: 31

Caryl, Jean. *See* Kaplan, Jean Caryl
Korn, *10:* 62
Case, Marshal T(aylor) 1941- ,
9: 33
Case, Michael. *See* Howard, Robert
West, *5:* 85
Casewit, Curtis 1922- , *4:* 43
Casey, Brigid 1950- , *9:* 33
Casey, Winifred Rosen. *See* Rosen,
Winifred, *8:* 169
Cason, Mabel Earp 1892-1965,
10: 19
Cass, Joan E(velyn), *1:* 47
Cassel, Lili. *See* Wronker, Lili
Cassell, *10:* 204
Cassel-Wronker, Lili. *See* Wronker,
Lili Cassell, *10:* 204
Castellanos, Jane Mollie (Robinson)
1913- , *9:* 34
Castillo, Edmund L. 1924- , *1:* 50
Castle, Lee. [Joint pseudonym]. *See*
Ogan, George F. and Margaret
E. (Nettles), *13:* 171
Caswell, Helen (Rayburn) 1923- ,
12: 67
Catherall, Arthur 1906- , *3:* 38
Catlin, Wynelle 1930- , *13:* 19
Catton, (Charles) Bruce
1899-1978, *2:* 54; *24:* 71
(Obituary)
Catz, Max. *See* Glaser, Milton,
11: 106
Caudill, Rebecca 1899- , *1:* 50
Causley, Charles 1917- , *3:* 39
Cavallo, Diana 1931- , *7:* 43
Cavanah, Frances 1899- , *1:* 52
Cavanna, Betty 1909- , *1:* 54
Cawley, Winifred 1915- , *13:* 20
Caxton, Pisistratus. *See* Lytton,
Edward G(eorge) E(arle)
L(ytton) Bulwer-Lytton, Baron,
23: 125
Cebulash, Mel 1937- , *10:* 19
Ceder, Georgiana Dorcas, *10:* 21
Cerf, Bennett 1898-1971, *7:* 43
Cerf, Christopher (Bennett)
1941- , *2:* 55
Cervon, Jacqueline. *See* Moussard,
Jacqueline, *24:* 154
Cetin, Frank (Stanley) 1921- ,
2: 55
Chadwick, Lester [Collective
pseudonym], *1:* 55
Chaffee, Allen, *3:* 41
Chaffin, Lillie D(orton) 1925- ,
4: 44
Chaikin, Miriam 1928- , *24:* 71
Challans, Mary 1905- , *23:* 33
Chalmers, Mary 1927- , *6:* 41
Chambers, Aidan 1934- , *1:* 55
Chambers, Margaret Ada Eastwood
1911- , *2:* 56
Chambers, Peggy. *See* Chambers,
Margaret, *2:* 56
Chandler, Caroline A(ugusta)

1906-1979, *22:* 66; *24:* 72
(Obituary)

Chandler, Edna Walker   1908- ,
11: 45

Chandler, Ruth Forbes   1894- ,
2: 56

Channel, A. R. *See* Catherall,
Arthur, *3:* 38

Chapman, Allen [Collective
pseudonym], *1:* 55

Chapman, (Constance) Elizabeth
(Mann)   1919- , *10:* 21

Chapman, Walker. *See* Silverberg,
Robert, *13:* 206

Chappell, Warren   1904- , *6:* 42

Charles, Louis. *See* Stratemeyer,
Edward L., *1:* 208

Charlip, Remy   1929- , *4:* 46

Charlot, Jean   1898- , *8:* 22

Charmatz, Bill   1925- , *7:* 45

Charosh, Mannis   1906- , *5:* 42

Chase, Alice. *See* McHargue,
Georgess, *4:* 152

Chase, Mary (Coyle)   1907- ,
17: 39

Chase, Mary Ellen   1887-1973,
10: 22

Chastain, Madye Lee   1908- ,
4: 48

Chauncy, Nan   1900-1970, *6:* 43

Chaundler, Christine   1887-1972,
1: 56; *25:* 83 (Obituary)

Chen, Tony   1929- , *6:* 44

Chenault, Nell. *See* Smith, Linell
Nash, *2:* 227

Chenery, Janet (Dai)   1923- ,
25: 84

Cheney, Cora   1916- , *3:* 41

Cheney, Ted. *See* Cheney,
Theodore Albert, *11:* 46

Cheney, Theodore Albert   1928- ,
11: 46

Chernoff, Goldie Taub   1909- ,
10: 23

Cherryholmes, Anne. *See* Price,
Olive, *8:* 157

Chetin, Helen   1922- , *6:* 46

Chew, Ruth, *7:* 45

Chidsey, Donald Barr   1902- ,
3: 42

Childress, Alice   1920- , *7:* 46

Childs, (Halla) Fay (Cochrane)
1890-1971, *1:* 56; *25:* 84
(Obituary)

Chimaera. *See* Farjeon, Eleanor,
2: 103

Chipperfield, Joseph E(ugene)
1912- , *2:* 57

Chittenden, Elizabeth F.   1903- ,
9: 35

Chittum, Ida   1918- , *7:* 47

Chorao, (Ann Mc)Kay (Sproat)
1936- , *8:* 24

Chrisman, Arthur Bowie
1889-1953, *YABC 1:* 94

Christensen, Gardell Dano   1907- ,
1: 57

Christgau, Alice Erickson   1902- ,
13: 21

Christian, Mary Blount   1933- ,
9: 35

Christopher, Matt(hew F.)   1917- ,
2: 58

Christy, Howard Chandler
1873-1952, *21:* 22

Chu, Daniel   1933- , *11:* 47

Chukovsky, Kornei (Ivanovich)
1882-1969, *5:* 43

Church, Richard   1893-1972, *3:* 43

Churchill, E. Richard   1937- ,
11: 48

Chute, B(eatrice) J(oy)   1913- ,
2: 59

Chute, Marchette (Gaylord)
1909- , *1:* 58

Chwast, Jacqueline   1932- , *6:* 46

Chwast, Seymour   1931- , *18:* 42

Ciardi, John (Anthony)   1916- ,
1: 59

Clair, Andrée, *19:* 61

Clapp, Patricia   1912- , *4:* 50

Clare, Helen. *See* Hunter Blair,
Pauline, *3:* 87

Clark, Ann Nolan   1898- , *4:* 51

Clark, Frank J(ames)   1922- ,
18: 43

Clark, Garel [Joint pseudonym]. *See*
Garelick, May, *19:* 130

Clark, Margaret Goff   1913- ,
8: 26

Clark, Mavis Thorpe, *8:* 27

Clark, Merle. *See* Gessner, Lynne,
16: 119

Clark, Patricia (Finrow)   1929- ,
11: 48

Clark, Ronald William   1916- ,
2: 60

Clark, Van D(eusen)   1909- ,
2: 61

Clark, Virginia. *See* Gray, Patricia,
7: 110

Clark, Walter Van Tilburg
1909-1971, *8:* 28

Clarke, Arthur C(harles)   1917- ,
13: 22

Clarke, Clorinda   1917- , *7:* 48

Clarke, John. *See* Laklan, Carli,
5: 100

Clarke, Mary Stetson   1911- ,
5: 46

Clarke, Michael. *See* Newlon,
Clarke, *6:* 174

Clarke, Pauline. *See* Hunter Blair,
Pauline, *3:* 87

Clarkson, Ewan   1929- , *9:* 36

Cleary, Beverly (Bunn)   1916- ,
2: 62

Cleaver, Bill, *22:* 66

Cleaver, Carole   1934- , *6:* 48

Cleaver, Elizabeth (Mrazik)
1939- , *23:* 34

Cleaver, Vera, *22:* 67

Cleishbotham, Jebediah. *See* Scott,
Sir Walter, *YABC 2:* 280

Cleland, Mabel. *See* Widdemer,
Mabel Cleland, *5:* 200

Clemens, Samuel Langhorne
1835-1910, *YABC 2:* 51

Clemons, Elizabeth. *See* Nowell,
Elizabeth Cameron, *12:* 160

Clerk, N. W. *See* Lewis, C. S.,
13: 129

Cleven, Cathrine. *See* Cleven,
Kathryn Seward, *2:* 64

Cleven, Kathryn Seward, *2:* 64

Clevin, Jörgen   1920- , *7:* 49

Clewes, Dorothy (Mary)   1907- ,
1: 61

Clifford, Eth. *See* Rosenberg, Ethel,
3: 176

Clifford, Harold B.   1893- ,
10: 24

Clifford, Margaret Cort   1929- ,
1: 63

Clifford, Martin. *See* Hamilton,
Charles Harold St. John, *13:* 77

Clifford, Mary Louise (Beneway)
1926- , *23:* 36

Clifford, Peggy. *See* Clifford,
Margaret Cort, *1:* 63

Clifton, Harry. *See* Hamilton,
Charles Harold St. John, *13:* 77

Clifton, Lucille   1936- , *20:* 20

Clifton, Martin. *See* Hamilton,
Charles Harold St. John, *13:* 77

Clinton, Jon. *See* Prince, J(ack)
H(arvey), *17:* 155

Clive, Clifford. *See* Hamilton,
Charles Harold St. John, *13:* 77

Cloudsley-Thompson, J(ohn)
L(eonard)   1921- , *19:* 61

Clymer, Eleanor   1906- , *9:* 37

Coates, Belle   1896- , *2:* 64

Coates, Ruth Allison   1915- ,
11: 49

Coats, Alice M(argaret)   1905- ,
11: 50

Coatsworth, Elizabeth   1893- ,
2: 65

Cobb, Jane. *See* Berry, Jane Cobb,
22: 39 (Obituary)

Cobb, Vicki   1938- , *8:* 31

Cobbett, Richard. *See* Pluckrose,
Henry (Arthur), *13:* 183

Cober, Alan E.   1935- , *7:* 51

Cobham, Sir Alan. *See* Hamilton,
Charles Harold St. John, *13:* 77

Cocagnac, A(ugustin) M(aurice-
Jean)   1924- , *7:* 52

Cochran, Bobbye A.   1949- ,
11: 51

Cockett, Mary, *3:* 45

Coe, Douglas [Joint pseudonym].
See Epstein, Beryl and Samuel,
1: 87

Coen, Rena Neumann   1925- ,
20: 24

Coerr, Eleanor 1922- , *1:* 64
Coffin, Geoffrey. *See* Mason, F.
    van Wyck, *3:* 117
Coffman, Ramon Peyton 1896- ,
    4: 53
Coggins, Jack (Banham) 1911- ,
    2: 68
Cohen, Barbara 1932- , *10:* 24
Cohen, Daniel 1936- , *8:* 31
Cohen, Joan Lebold 1932- , *4:* 53
Cohen, Peter Zachary 1931- ,
    4: 54
Cohen, Robert Carl 1930- , *8:* 33
Cohn, Angelo 1914- , *19:* 63
Coit, Margaret L(ouise), *2:* 70
Colbert, Anthony 1934- , *15:* 39
Colby, C. B. 1904- , *3:* 46
Colby, Jean Poindexter 1909- ,
    23: 37
Cole, Annette. *See* Steiner, Barbara
    A(nnette), *13:* 213
Cole, Davis, *See* Elting, Mary,
    2: 100
Cole, Jack. *See* Stewart, John
    (William), *14:* 189
Cole, Jackson. *See* Schisgall, Oscar,
    12: 187
Cole, Lois Dwight, *10:* 26
Cole, Sheila R(otenberg) 1939- ,
    24: 73
Cole, William (Rossa) 1919- ,
    9: 40
Coles, Robert (Martin) 1929- ,
    23: 38
Collier, Christopher 1930- ,
    16: 66
Collier, Ethel 1903- , *22:* 68
Collier, James Lincoln 1928- ,
    8: 33
Collier, Jane. *See* Collier, Zena,
    23: 41
Collier, Zena 1926- , *23:* 41
Collins, David 1940- , *7:* 52
Collins, Hunt. *See* Hunter, Evan,
    25: 153
Colman, Hila, *1:* 65
Colman, Morris 1899(?)-1981,
    25: 85 (Obituary)
Colonius, Lillian 1911- , *3:* 48
Colorado (Capella), Antonio J(ulio)
    1903- , *23:* 42
Colt, Martin. *See* Epstein, Samuel,
    1: 87
Colum, Padraic 1881-1972, *15:* 42
Columella. *See* Moore, Clement
    Clarke, *18:* 224
Colver, Anne 1908- , *7:* 54
Colwell, Eileen (Hilda) 1904- ,
    2: 71
Comfort, Jane Levington. *See*
    Sturtzel, Jane Levington,
    1: 212
Comfort, Mildred Houghton
    1886- , *3:* 48
Comins, Ethel M(ae), *11:* 53

Commager, Henry Steele 1902- ,
    23: 43
Comus. *See* Ballantyne, R(obert)
    M(ichael), *24:* 32
Conan Doyle, Arthur. *See* Doyle,
    Arthur Conan, *24:* 89
Cone, Molly (Lamken) 1918- ,
    1: 66
Conford, Ellen 1942- , *6:* 48
Conger, Lesley. *See* Suttles, Shirley
    (Smith), *21:* 166
Conklin, Gladys (Plemon) 1903- ,
    2: 73
Conkling, Hilda 1910- , *23:* 45
Conly, Robert Leslie
    1918(?)-1973, *23:* 45
Connelly, Marc(us Cook)
    1890-1980, *25:* 85 (Obituary)
Connolly, Jerome P(atrick)
    1931- , *8:* 34
Conquest, Owen. *See* Hamilton,
    Charles Harold St. John, *13:* 77
Conroy, Jack (Wesley) 1899- ,
    19: 65
Conroy, John. *See* Conroy, Jack
    (Wesley), *19:* 65
Constant, Alberta Wilson, *22:* 70
Conway, Gordon. *See* Hamilton,
    Charles Harold St. John, *13:* 77
Cook, Bernadine 1924- , *11:* 55
Cook, Fred J(ames) 1911- , *2:* 74
Cook, Joseph J(ay) 1924- , *8:* 35
Cook, Lyn. *See* Waddell, Evelyn
    Margaret, *10:* 186
Cooke, David Coxe 1917- , *2:* 75
Cooke, Donald Ewin 1916- ,
    2: 76
Cookson, Catherine (McMullen)
    1906- , *9:* 42
Coolidge, Olivia E(nsor) 1908- ,
    1: 67
Coombs, Charles 1914- , *3:* 49
Coombs, Chick. *See* Coombs,
    Charles, *3:* 49
Coombs, Patricia 1926- , *3:* 51
Cooney, Barbara 1917- , *6:* 49
Cooper, Gordon 1932- , *23:* 47
Cooper, James Fenimore
    1789-1851, *19:* 68
Cooper, James R. *See* Stratemeyer,
    Edward L., *1:* 208
Cooper, John R. [Collective
    pseudonym], *1:* 68
Cooper, Kay 1941- , *11:* 55
Cooper, Lee (Pelham), *5:* 47
Cooper, Susan 1935- , *4:* 57
Copeland, Helen 1920- , *4:* 57
Copeland, Paul W., *23:* 48
Coppard, A(lfred) E(dgar)
    1878-1957, *YABC 1:* 97
Corbett, Scott 1913- , *2:* 78
Corbin, Sabra Lee. *See* Malvern,
    Gladys, *23:* 133
Corbin, William. *See* McGraw,
    William Corbin, *3:* 124

Corby, Dan. *See* Catherall, Arthur,
    3: 38
Corcoran, Barbara 1911- , *3:* 53
Corcos, Lucille 1908-1973, *10:* 27
Cordell, Alexander. *See* Graber,
    Alexander, *7:* 106
Corey, Dorothy, *23:* 49
Cormack, M(argaret) Grant
    1913- , *11:* 56
Cormier, Robert Edmund 1925- ,
    10: 28
Cornell, J. *See* Cornell, Jeffrey,
    11: 57
Cornell, Jean Gay 1920- , *23:* 50
Cornell, Jeffrey 1945- , *11:* 57
Cornish, Samuel James 1935- ,
    23: 51
Correy, Lee. *See* Stine, G. Harry,
    10: 161
Corrigan, (Helen) Adeline 1909- ,
    23: 53
Corrigan, Barbara 1922- , *8:* 36
Cort, M. C. *See* Clifford, Margaret
    Cort, *1:* 63
Corwin, Judith Hoffman 1946- ,
    10: 28
Cosgrave, John O'Hara II
    1908-1968, *21:* 26 (Obituary)
Coskey, Evelyn 1932- , *7:* 55
Costello, David F(rancis) 1904- ,
    23: 53
Cott, Jonathan 1942- , *23:* 55
Cottam, Clarence 1899-1974,
    25: 85
Cottler, Joseph 1899- , *22:* 71
Cottrell, Leonard 1913-1974,
    24: 74
Courlander, Harold 1908- , *6:* 51
Cousins, Margaret 1905- , *2:* 79
Cowie, Leonard W(allace) 1919- ,
    4: 60
Cowley, Joy 1936- , *4:* 60
Cox, Donald William 1921- ,
    23: 56
Cox, Jack. *See* Cox, John Roberts,
    9: 42
Cox, John Roberts 1915- , *9:* 42
Cox, Palmer 1840-1924, *24:* 75
Cox, Wally 1924-1973, *25:* 86
Coy, Harold 1902- , *3:* 53
Craig, John Eland. *See*
    Chipperfield, Joseph, *2:* 57
Craig, John Ernest 1921- , *23:* 58
Craig, M. Jean, *17:* 45
Craig, Margaret Maze 1911-1964,
    9: 43
Craig, Mary Francis 1923- , *6:* 52
Crane, Caroline 1930- , *11:* 59
Crane, Roy. *See* Crane, Royston
    Campbell, *22:* 72 (Obituary)
Crane, Royston Campbell
    1901-1977, *22:* 72 (Obituary)
Crane, Stephen (Townley)
    1871-1900, *YABC 2:* 94
Crane, Walter 1845-1915, *18:* 44

Crane, William D(wight)   1892- ,
    1: 68
Crary, Margaret (Coleman)
    1906- , *9:* 43
Craven, Thomas   1889-1969,
    22: 72
Crawford, Deborah   1922- , *6:* 53
Crawford, John E.   1904-1971,
    3: 56
Crawford, Phyllis   1899- , *3:* 57
Craz, Albert G.   1926- , *24:* 78
Crayder, Dorothy   1906- , *7:* 55
Crayder, Teresa. *See* Colman, Hila,
    1: 65
Crayon, Geoffrey. *See* Irving,
    Washington, *YABC 2:* 164
Crecy, Jeanne. *See* Williams,
    Jeanne, *5:* 202
Credle, Ellis   1902- , *1:* 68
Cresswell, Helen   1934- , *1:* 70
Cretan, Gladys (Yessayan)
    1921- , *2:* 82
Crew, Helen (Cecilia) Coale
    1866-1941, *YABC 2:* 95
Crichton, (J.) Michael   1942- ,
    9: 44
Crofut, Bill. *See* Crofut, William E.
    III, *23:* 59
Crofut, William E. III   1934- ,
    23: 59
Cromie, Alice Hamilton   1914- ,
    24: 78
Cromie, William J(oseph)   1930- ,
    4: 62
Crompton, Anne Eliot   1930- ,
    23: 61
Crompton, Richmal. *See* Lamburn,
    Richmal Crompton, *5:* 101
Cronbach, Abraham   1882-1965,
    11: 60
Crone, Ruth   1919- , *4:* 63
Cronin, A(rchibald) J(oseph)
    1896-1981, *25:* 89 (Obituary)
Crosby, Alexander L.   1906-1980,
    2: 83; *23:* 62 (Obituary)
Crosher, G(eoffry) R(obins)
    1911- , *14:* 51
Cross, Helen Reeder. *See*
    Broadhead, Helen Cross,
    25: 62
Cross, Wilbur Lucius III   1918- ,
    2: 83
Crossley-Holland, Kevin, *5:* 48
Crouch, Marcus   1913- , *4:* 63
Crout, George C(lement)   1917- ,
    11: 60
Crowe, Bettina Lum   1911- , *6:* 53
Crowell, Pers   1910- , *2:* 84
Crowfield, Christopher. *See* Stowe,
    Harriet (Elizabeth) Beecher,
    YABC 1: 250
Crownfield, Gertrude   1867-1945,
    YABC 1: 103
Crowther, James Gerald   1899- ,
    14: 52

Cruikshank, George   1792-1878,
    22: 73
Crump, Fred H., Jr.   1931- ,
    11: 62
Crump, J(ames) Irving   1887-1979,
    21: 26 (Obituary)
Cruz, Ray   1933- , *6:* 54
Cuffari, Richard   1925-1978,
    6: 54; *25:* 89 (Obituary)
Cullen, Countee   1903-1946,
    18: 64
Culp, Louanna McNary
    1901-1965, *2:* 85
Cumming, Primrose (Amy)
    1915- , *24:* 79
Cummings, Betty Sue   1918- ,
    15: 51
Cummings, Parke   1902- , *2:* 85
Cummings, Richard. *See* Gardner,
    Richard, *24:* 109
Cummins, Maria Susanna
    1827-1866, *YABC 1:* 103
Cunliffe, John Arthur   1933- ,
    11: 62
Cunningham, Captain Frank. *See*
    Glick, Carl (Cannon), *14:* 72
Cunningham, Cathy. *See*
    Cunningham, Chet, *23:* 63
Cunningham, Chet   1928- , *23:* 63
Cunningham, Dale S(peers)   1932- ,
    11: 63
Cunningham, E. V. *See* Fast,
    Howard, *7:* 80
Cunningham, Julia W(oolfolk)
    1916- , *1:* 72
Curiae, Amicus. *See* Fuller,
    Edmund (Maybank), *21:* 45
Curie, Eve   1904- , *1:* 73
Curley, Daniel   1918- , *23:* 63
Curry, Jane L(ouise)   1932- ,
    1: 73
Curry, Peggy Simson   1911- ,
    8: 37
Curtis, Patricia   1921- , *23:* 64
Curtis, Peter. *See* Lofts, Norah
    Robinson, *8:* 119
Cushman, Jerome, *2:* 86
Cutchen, Billye Walker   1930- ,
    15: 51
Cutler, (May) Ebbitt   1923- , *9:* 46
Cutler, Ivor   1923- , *24:* 80
Cutler, Samuel. *See* Folsom,
    Franklin, *5:* 67
Cutt, W(illiam) Towrie   1898- ,
    16: 67
Cuyler, Stephen. *See* Bates, Barbara
    S(nedeker), *12:* 34

Dahl, Borghild   1890- , *7:* 56
Dahl, Roald   1916- , *1:* 74
Dahlstedt, Marden   1921- , *8:* 38
Dale, Jack. *See* Holliday, Joseph,
    11: 137

Dalgliesh, Alice   1893-1979,
    17: 47; *2:* 26 (Obituary)
Daly, Jim. *See* Stratemeyer, Edward
    L., *1:* 208
Daly, Maureen, *2:* 87
D'Amato, Alex   1919- , *20:* 24
D'Amato, Janet   1925- , *9:* 47
Damrosch, Helen Therese. *See* Tee-
    Van, Helen Damrosch, *10:* 176
Dana, Barbara   1940- , *22:* 84
Danachair, Caoimhin O. *See*
    Danaher, Kevin, *22:* 85
Danaher, Kevin   1913- , *22:* 85
D'Andrea, Kate. *See* Steiner,
    Barbara A(nnette), *13:* 213
Dangerfield, Balfour. *See*
    McCloskey, Robert, *2:* 185
Daniel, Anita   1893(?)-1978,
    23: 65; *24:* 81 (Obituary)
Daniel, Anne. *See* Steiner, Barbara
    A(nnette), *13:* 213
Daniel, Hawthorne   1890- , *8:* 39
Daniels, Guy   1919- , *11:* 64
Darby, J. N. *See* Govan, Christine
    Noble, *9:* 80
Darby, Patricia (Paulsen), *14:* 53
Darby, Ray K.   1912- , *7:* 59
Daringer, Helen Fern   1892- ,
    1: 75
Darke, Marjorie   1929- , *16:* 68
Darling, Kathy. *See* Darling, Mary
    Kathleen *1:* 208
Darling, Lois M.   1917- , *3:* 57
Darling, Louis, Jr.   1916-1970,
    3: 59; *23:* 66 (Obituary)
Darling, Mary Kathleen   1943- ,
    9: 48
Darrow, Whitney, Jr.   1909- ,
    13: 24
Darwin, Len. *See* Darwin, Leonard,
    24: 81
Darwin, Leonard   1916- , *24:* 81
Dauer, Rosamond   1934- , *23:* 66
Daugherty, Charles Michael
    1914- , *16:* 70
Daugherty, James (Henry)
    1889-1974, *13:* 26
d'Aulaire, Edgar Parin   1898- ,
    5: 49
d'Aulaire, Ingri (Maartenson Parin)
    1904-1980 *5:* 50; *24:* 82
    (Obituary)
Daveluy, Paule Cloutier   1919- ,
    11: 65
Davenport, Spencer. *See*
    Stratemeyer, Edward L., *1:* 208
David, Jonathan. *See* Ames, Lee J.,
    3: 11
Davidson, Basil   1914- , *13:* 30
Davidson, Jessica   1915- , *5:* 52
Davidson, Margaret   1936- , *5:* 53
Davidson, Marion. *See* Garis,
    Howard R(oger), *13:* 67
Davidson, Mary R.   1885-1973,
    9: 49
Davidson, Rosalie   1921- , *23:* 67

Davis, Bette J. 1923- , *15:* 53
Davis, Burke 1913- , *4:* 64
Davis, Christopher 1928- , *6:* 57
Davis, Daniel S(heldon) 1936- , *12:* 68
Davis, Julia 1904- , *6:* 58
Davis, Louise Littleton 1921- , *25:* 89
Davis, Mary L(ee), 1935- *9:* 49
Davis, Mary Octavia, 1901- *6:* 59
Davis, Paxton 1925- , *16:* 71
Davis, Robert 1881-1949, *YABC 1:* 104
Davis, Russell G. 1922- , *3:* 60
Davis, Verne T. 1889-1973, *6:* 60
Dawson, Elmer A. [Collective pseudonym], *1:* 76
Dawson, Mary 1919- , *11:* 66
Day, Thomas 1748-1789, *YABC 1:* 106
Dazey, Agnes J(ohnston), *2:* 88
Dazey, Frank M., *2:* 88
Deacon, Richard. *See* McCormick, (George) Donald (King), *14:* 141
Dean, Anabel 1915- , *12:* 69
de Angeli, Marguerite 1889- , *1:* 76
DeArmand, Frances Ullmann, *10:* 29
deBanke, Cecile 1889-1965, *11:* 67
De Bruyn, Monica 1952- , *13:* 30
de Camp, Catherine C(rook) 1907- , *12:* 70
DeCamp, L(yon) Sprague 1907- , *9:* 49
Decker, Duane 1910-1964, *5:* 53
Deedy, John 1923- , *24:* 83
Defoe, Daniel 1660(?)-1731, *22:* 86
DeGering, Etta 1898- , *7:* 60
de Grummond, Lena Young, *6:* 61
Deiss, Joseph J. 1915- , *12:* 72
DeJong, David C(ornel) 1905-1967, *10:* 29
de Jong, Dola, *7:* 61
De Jong, Meindert 1906- , *2:* 89
de Kay, Ormonde, Jr. 1923- , *7:* 62
de Kiriline, Louise. *See* Lawrence, Louise de Kirilene, *13:* 126
deKruif, Paul (Henry) 1890-1971 *5:* 54
De Lage, Ida 1918- , *11:* 67
de la Mare, Walter 1873-1956, *16:* 73
Delaney, Harry 1932- , *3:* 61
Delano, Hugh 1933- , *20:* 25
De La Ramée, (Marie) Louise 1839-1908, *20:* 26
Delaune, Lynne, *7:* 63
DeLaurentis, Louise Budde 1920- , *12:* 73

Delderfield, Eric R(aymond) 1909- , *14:* 53
Delderfield, R(onald) F(rederick) 1912-1972, *20:* 34
De Leeuw, Adele Louise 1899- , *1:* 77
Delmar, Roy. *See* Wexler, Jerome (LeRoy), *14:* 243
Deloria, Vine (Victor), Jr. 1933- , *21:* 26
Del Rey, Lester 1915- , *22:* 97
Delton, Judy 1931- , *14:* 54
Delulio, John 1938- , *15:* 54
Delving, Michael. *See* Williams, Jay, *3:* 256; *24:* 221 (Obituary)
Demarest, Doug. *See* Barker, Will, *8:* 4
Demas, Vida 1927- , *9:* 51
Deming, Richard 1915- , *24:* 83
Denney, Diana 1910- , *25:* 90
Dennis, Morgan 1891(?)-1960, *18:* 68
Dennis, Wesley 1903-1966, *18:* 70
Denniston, Elinore 1900-1978, *24:* 85 (Obituary)
Denslow, W(illiam) W(allace) 1856-1915, *16:* 83
de Paola, Thomas Anthony 1934- , *11:* 68
de Paola, Tomie. *See* de Paola, Thomas Anthony, *11:* 68
DePauw, Linda Grant 1940- , *24:* 85
deRegniers, Beatrice Schenk (Freedman) 1914- , *2:* 90
Derleth, August (William) 1909-1971 *5:* 54
Derman, Sarah Audrey 1915- , *11:* 71
de Roo, Anne Louise 1931- , *25:* 91
Derry Down Derry. *See* Lear, Edward, *18:* 182
Derwent, Lavinia, *14:* 56
De Selincourt, Aubrey 1894-1962, *14:* 56
Desmond, Alice Curtis 1897- , *8:* 40
Detine, Padre. *See* Olsen, Ib Spang, *6:* 177
Deutsch, Babette 1895- , *1:* 79
Devaney, John 1926- , *12:* 74
Devereux, Frederick L(eonard), Jr. 1914- , *9:* 51
Devlin, Harry 1918- , *11:* 73
Devlin, (Dorothy) Wende 1918- , *11:* 74
DeWaard, E. John 1935- , *7:* 63
Dewey, Ariane 1937- , *7:* 63
Deyneka, Anita 1943- , *24:* 86
Deyrup, Astrith Johnson 1923- , *24:* 87
Dick, Trella Lamson 1889-1974, *9:* 51

Dickens, Charles 1812-1870, *15:* 55
Dickens, Monica 1915- , *4:* 66
Dickinson, Peter 1927- , *5:* 55
Dickinson, Susan 1931- , *8:* 41
Dickinson, William Croft 1897-1973, *13:* 32
Dickson, Naida 1916- , *8:* 41
Dietz, David H(enry) 1897- , *10:* 30
Dietz, Lew 1907- , *11:* 75
Dillard, Annie 1945- , *10:* 31
Dillard, Polly (Hargis) 1916- , *24:* 88
Dillon, Diane 1933- , *15:* 98
Dillon, Eilis 1920- , *2:* 92
Dillon, Leo 1933- , *15:* 99
Dilson, Jesse 1914- , *24:* 89
Dines, Glen 1925- , *7:* 65
Dinsdale, Tim 1924- , *11:* 76
DiValentin, Maria 1911- , *7:* 68
Dixon, Franklin W. [Collective pseudonym], *1:* 80. *See also* Svenson, Andrew E., *2:* 238; Stratemeyer, Edward, *1:* 208
Dixon, Peter L. 1931- , *6:* 62
Doane, Pelagie 1906-1966, *7:* 68
Dobell, I(sabel) M(arian) B(arclay) 1909- , *11:* 77
Dobler, Lavinia G. 1910- , *6:* 63
Dobrin, Arnold 1928- , *4:* 67
"Dr. A." *See* Silverstein, Alvin, *8:* 188
Dodd, Ed(ward) Benton 1902- , *4:* 68
Dodge, Bertha S(anford) 1902- , *8:* 42
Dodge, Mary (Elizabeth) Mapes 1831-1905, *21:* 27
Dodgson, Charles Lutwidge 1832-1898, *YABC 2:* 97
Dodson, Kenneth M(acKenzie) 1907- , *11:* 77
Doherty, C. H. 1913- , *6:* 65
Dolson, Hildegarde 1908- , *5:* 56
Domanska, Janina, *6:* 65
Domjan, Joseph 1907- , *25:* 92
Donalds, Gordon. *See* Shirreffs, Gordon D., *11:* 207
Donna, Natalie 1934- , *9:* 52
Doob, Leonard W(illiam) 1909- , *8:* 44
Dor, Ana. *See* Ceder, Georgiana Dorcas, *10:* 21
Doré, (Louis Christophe Paul) Gustave 1832-1883, *19:* 92
Dorian, Edith M(cEwen) 1900- *5:* 58
Dorian, Harry. *See* Hamilton, Charles Harold St. John, *13:* 77
Dorian, Marguerite, *7:* 68
Dorman, Michael 1932- , *7:* 68
Doss, Helen (Grigsby) 1918- , *20:* 37
Doss, Margot Patterson, *6:* 68

Dougherty, Charles 1922- ,
18: 74
Douglas, James McM. *See*
Butterworth, W. E., 5: 40
Douglas, Kathryn. *See* Ewing,
Kathryn, 20: 42
Douglas, Marjory Stoneman
1890- , 10: 33
Douty, Esther M(orris) 1911-1978,
8: 44; 23: 68 (Obituary)
Dow, Emily R. 1904- , 10: 33
Dowdell, Dorothy (Florence) Karns
1910- , 12: 75
Dowden, Anne Ophelia 1907- ,
7: 69
Dowdey, Landon Gerald 1923- ,
11: 80
Downer, Marion 1892(?)-1971,
25: 93
Downey, Fairfax 1893- , 3: 61
Downie, Mary Alice 1934- ,
13: 32
Doyle, Arthur Conan 1859-1930,
24: 89
Doyle, Richard 1824-1883, 21: 31
Draco, F. *See* Davis, Julia, 6: 58
Dragonwagon, Crescent 1952- ,
11: 81
Drake, Frank. *See* Hamilton,
Charles Harold St. John, 13: 77
Drapier, M. B.. *See* Swift,
Jonathan, 19: 244
Drawson, Blair 1943- , 17: 52
Dresang, Eliza (Carolyn
Timberlake) 1941- , 19: 106
Drew, Patricia (Mary) 1938- ,
15: 100
Drewery, Mary 1918- , 6: 69
Drummond, V(iolet) H. 1911- ,
6: 71
Drummond, Walter. *See* Silverberg,
Robert, 13: 206
Drury, Roger W(olcott) 1914- ,
15: 101
du Blanc, Daphne. *See* Groom,
Arthur William, 10: 53
Du Bois, Shirley Graham
1907-1977, 24: 105
du Bois, William Pene 1916- ,
4: 69
DuBose, LaRocque (Russ) 1926- ,
2: 93
Ducornet, Erica 1943- , 7: 72
Dudley, Nancy. *See* Cole, Lois
Dwight, 10: 26
Dudley, Robert. *See* Baldwin,
James, 24: 26
Dudley, Ruth H(ubbell) 1905- ,
11: 82
Dugan, Michael (Gray) 1947- ,
15: 101
Duggan, Alfred Leo 1903-1964,
25: 95
du Jardin, Rosamond (Neal)
1902-1963, 2: 94

Dulac, Edmund 1882-1953,
19: 107
Dumas, Alexandre (the elder)
1802-1870, 18: 74
Duncan, Gregory. *See* McClintock,
Marshall, 3: 119
Duncan, Julia K. [Collective
pseudonym], 1: 81
Duncan, Lois. *See* Arquette, Lois
S., 1: 13
Duncan, Norman 1871-1916,
YABC 1: 108
Duncombe, Frances (Riker)
1900- , 25: 97
Dunlop, Agnes M. R., 3: 62
Dunlop, Eileen (Rhona) 1938- ,
24: 108
Dunn, Judy. *See* Spangenberg,
Judith Dunn, 5: 175
Dunn, Mary Lois 1930- , 6: 72
Dunnahoo, Terry 1927- , 7: 73
Dunne, Mary Collins 1914- ,
11: 83
Dupuy, T(revor) N(evitt) 1916- ,
4: 71
Durrell, Gerald (Malcolm) 1925- ,
8: 46
Du Soe, Robert C. 1892-1958,
YABC 2: 121
Dutz. *See* Davis, Mary Octavia,
6: 59
Duvall, Evelyn Millis 1906- ,
9: 52
Duvoisin, Roger (Antoine)
1904-1980, 2: 95; 23: 68
(Obituary)
Dwiggins, Don 1913- , 4: 72
Dwight, Allan. *See* Cole, Lois
Dwight, 10: 26
Dygard, Thomas J. 1931- ,
24: 109

Eagar, Frances 1940- , 11: 85
Eager, Edward (McMaken)
1911-1964, 17: 54
Eagle, Mike 1942- , 11: 86
Earle, Olive L., 7: 75
Earnshaw, Brian 1929- , 17: 57
Eastman, Charles A(lexander)
1858-1939, YABC 1: 110
Eastwick, Ivy O., 3: 64
Eaton, George L. *See* Verral,
Charles Spain, 11: 255
Eaton, Jeanette 1886-1968,
24: 110
Eaton, Tom 1940-, 22: 99
Ebel, Alex 1927- , 11: 88
Eberle, Irmengarde 1898-1979,
2: 97; 23: 68 (Obituary)
Eccles. *See* Williams, Ferelith
Eccles, 22: 237
Eckblad, Edith Berven 1923- ,
23: 68
Eckert, Horst 1931- , 8: 47

Edell, Celeste, 12: 77
Edelman, Lily (Judith) 1915- ,
22: 100
Edey, Maitland A(rmstrong)
1910- , 25: 98
Edgeworth, Maria 1767-1849,
21: 33
Edmonds, I(vy) G(ordon) 1917- ,
8: 48
Edmonds, Walter D(umaux)
1903- , 1: 81
Edmund, Sean. *See* Pringle,
Laurence, 4: 171
Edsall, Marian S(tickney) 1920- ,
8: 50
Edwards, Bertram. *See* Edwards,
Herbert Charles, 12: 77
Edwards, Bronwen Elizabeth. *See*
Rose, Wendy, 12: 180
Edwards, Cecile (Pepin) 1916- ,
25: 99
Edwards, Dorothy, 4: 73
Edwards, Harvey 1929- , 5: 59
Edwards, Herbert Charles 1912- ,
12: 77
Edwards, Jane Campbell 1932- ,
10: 34
Edwards, Julie. *See* Andrews, Julie,
7: 6
Edwards, Julie. *See* Stratemeyer,
Edward L., 1: 208
Edwards, Monica le Doux Newton
1912- , 12: 78
Edwards, Sally 1929- , 7: 75
Edwards, Samuel. *See* Gerson, Noel
B(ertram), 22: 118
Eggenberger, David 1918- , 6: 72
Egielski, Richard 1952- , 11: 89
Egypt, Ophelia Settle 1903- ,
16: 88
Ehrlich, Amy 1942- , 25: 100
Ehrlich, Bettina (Bauer) 1903- ,
1: 82
Eichberg, James Bandman. *See*
Garfield, James B., 6: 85
Eichenberg, Fritz 1901- , 9: 53
Eichner, James A. 1927- , 4: 73
Eifert, Virginia S(nider)
1911-1966, 2: 99
Einsel, Naiad, 10: 34
Einsel, Walter 1926- , 10: 37
Eiseman, Alberta 1925- , 15: 102
Eisenberg, Azriel 1903- , 12: 79
Eitzen, Allan 1928- , 9: 57
Eitzen, Ruth (Carper) 1924- ,
9: 57
Elam, Richard M(ace, Jr.) 1920- ,
9: 57
Elfman, Blossom 1925- , 8: 51
Elia. *See* Lamb, Charles, 17: 101
Eliot, Anne. *See* Cole, Lois
Dwight, 10: 26
Elisofon, Eliot 1911-1973, 21: 38
(Obituary)
Elkin, Benjamin 1911- , 3: 65
Elkins, Dov Peretz 1937- , 5: 61

Ellacott, S(amuel) E(rnest)
1911- , *19:* 117
Elliott, Sarah M(cCarn) 1930- ,
14: 57
Ellis, Edward S(ylvester)
1840-1916, *YABC 1:* 116
Ellis, Ella Thorp 1928- , *7:* 76
Ellis, Harry Bearse 1921- , *9:* 58
Ellis, Mel 1912- , *7:* 77
Ellison, Lucile Watkins
1907(?)-1979, *22:* 102
(Obituary)
Ellison, Virginia Howell 1910- ,
4: 74
Ellsberg, Edward 1891- , *7:* 78
Elspeth. *See* Bragdon, Elspeth,
6: 30
Elting, Mary 1906- , *2:* 100
Elwart, Joan Potter 1927- , *2:* 101
Emberley, Barbara A(nne), *8:* 51
Emberley, Ed(ward Randolph)
1931- , *8:* 52
Embry, Margaret (Jacob) 1919- ,
5: 61
Emerson, Alice B. [Collective
pseudonym], *1:* 84
Emerson, William K(eith) 1925- ,
25: 101
Emery, Anne (McGuigan) 1907- ,
1: 84
Emrich, Duncan (Black Macdonald)
1908- , *11:* 90
Emslie, M. L. *See* Simpson, Myrtle
L(illias), *14:* 181
Engdahl, Sylvia Louise 1933- ,
4: 75
Engle, Eloise Katherine 1923- ,
9: 60
Englebert, Victor 1933- , *8:* 54
Enright, D(ennis) J(oseph) 1920- ,
25: 102
Enright, Elizabeth 1909-1968,
9: 61
Epp, Margaret A(gnes), *20:* 38
Epple, Anne Orth 1927- , *20:* 40
Epstein, Anne Merrick 1931- ,
20: 41
Epstein, Beryl (Williams) 1910- ,
1: 85
Epstein, Samuel 1909- , *1:* 87
Erdman, Loula Grace, *1:* 88
Ericson, Walter. *See* Fast, Howard,
7: 80
Erlich, Lillian (Feldman) 1910- ,
10: 38
Ernst, Kathryn (Fitzgerald)
1942- , *25:* 103
Ervin, Janet Halliday 1923- ,
4: 77
Estep, Irene (Compton), *5:* 62
Estes, Eleanor 1906- , *7:* 79
Estoril, Jean. *See* Allan, Mabel
Esther, *5:* 2
Ets, Marie Hall, *2:* 102
Eunson, Dale 1904- , *5:* 63

Evans, Katherine (Floyd)
1901-1964, *5:* 64
Evans, Mari, *10:* 39
Evans, Mark, *19:* 118
Evans, Patricia Healy. *See*
Carpenter, Patricia, *11:* 43
Evarts, Hal G. (Jr.) 1915- , *6:* 72
Evernden, Margery 1916- , *5:* 65
Ewen, David 1907- , *4:* 78
Ewing, Juliana (Horatia Gatty)
1841-1885, *16:* 90
Ewing, Kathryn 1921- , *20:* 42
Eyerly, Jeannette Hyde 1908- ,
4: 80

Fabe, Maxene 1943- , *15:* 103
Faber, Doris 1924- , *3:* 67
Faber, Harold 1919- , *5:* 65
Fabre, Jean Henri (Casimir)
1823-1915, *22:* 102
Facklam, Margery Metz 1927- ,
20: 43
Fadiman, Clifton (Paul) 1904- ,
11: 91
Fair, Sylvia 1933- , *13:* 33
Fairfax-Lucy, Brian 1898- , *6:* 73
Fairman, Joan A(lexandra)
1935- , *10:* 41
Faithfull, Gail 1936- , *8:* 55
Falconer, James. *See* Kirkup,
James, *12:* 120
Falkner, Leonard 1900- , *12:* 80
Fall, Thomas. *See* Snow, Donald
Clifford, *16:* 246
Fanning, Leonard M(ulliken)
1888-1967, *5:* 65
Faralla, Dana 1909- , *9:* 62
Faralla, Dorothy W. *See* Faralla,
Dana, *9:* 62
Farb, Peter 1929-1980, *12:* 81;
22: 109 (Obituary)
Farber, Norma 1909- , *25:* 104
Farjeon, (Eve) Annabel 1919- ,
11: 93
Farjeon, Eleanor 1881-1965,
2: 103
Farley, Carol 1936- , *4:* 81
Farley, Walter, *2:* 106
Farnham, Burt. *See* Clifford, Harold
B., *10:* 24
Farquhar, Margaret C(utting)
1905- , *13:* 35
Farr, Finis (King) 1904- , *10:* 41
Farrell, Ben. *See* Cebulash, Mel,
10: 19
Farrington, Benjamin 1891-1974,
20: 45 (Obituary)
Farrington, Selwyn Kip, Jr.
1904- , *20:* 45
Fassler, Joan (Grace) 1931- ,
11: 94
Fast, Howard 1914- , *7:* 80
Fatchen, Max 1920- , *20:* 45

Father Xavier. *See* Hurwood,
Bernhardt J., *12:* 107
Fatigati, (Frances) Evelyn de Buhr
1948- , *24:* 112
Fatio, Louise, *6:* 75
Faulhaber, Martha 1926- , *7:* 82
Faulkner, Anne Irvin 1906- ,
23: 70
Faulkner, Nancy. *See* Faulkner,
Anne Irvin, *23:* 70
Fax, Elton Clay 1909- , *25:* 106
Feagles, Anita MacRae, *9:* 63
Feague, Mildred H. 1915- ,
14: 59
Fecher, Constance 1911- , *7:* 83
Feelings, Muriel (Grey) 1938- ,
16: 104
Feelings, Thomas 1933- , *8:* 55
Feelings, Tom. *See* Feelings,
Thomas, *8:* 55
Feiffer, Jules 1929- , *8:* 57
Feil, Hila 1942- , *12:* 81
Feilen, John. *See* May, Julian,
11: 175
Feldman, Anne (Rodgers) 1939- ,
19: 121
Fellows, Muriel H., *10:* 41
Felsen, Henry Gregor 1916- ,
1: 89
Felton, Harold William 1902- ,
1: 90
Felton, Ronald Oliver 1909- ,
3: 67
Fenner, Carol 1929- , *7:* 84
Fenner, Phyllis R(eid) 1899- ,
1: 91
Fenten, D. X. 1932- , *4:* 82
Fenton, Carroll Lane 1900-1969,
5: 66
Fenton, Edward 1917- , *7:* 86
Fenton, Mildred Adams 1899- ,
21: 38
Feravolo, Rocco Vincent 1922- ,
10: 42
Ferber, Edna 1887-1968, *7:* 87
Ferguson, Bob. *See* Ferguson,
Robert Bruce, *13:* 35
Ferguson, Robert Bruce 1927- ,
13: 35
Fergusson, Erna 1888-1964, *5:* 67
Fermi, Laura 1907- , *6:* 78
Fern, Eugene A. 1919- , *10:* 43
Ferris, Helen Josephine
1890-1969, *21:* 39
Ferris, James Cody [Collective
pseudonym], *1:* 92
Fiammenghi, Gioia 1929- , *9:* 64
Fiarotta, Noel 1944- , *15:* 104
Fiarotta, Phyllis 1942- , *15:* 105
Fichter, George S. 1922- , *7:* 92
Fidler, Kathleen, *3:* 68
Fiedler, Jean, *4:* 83
Field, Edward 1924- , *8:* 58
Field, Eugene 1850-1895, *16:* 105
Field, Rachel (Lyman) 1894-1942,
15: 106

Fife, Dale (Odile)   1910- , *18:* 110
Fighter Pilot, A. *See* Johnston,
    H(ugh) A(nthony) S(tephen),
    14: 87
Figueroa, Pablo   1938- , *9:* 66
Fijan, Carol   1918- , *12:* 82
Fillmore, Parker H(oysted)
    1878-1944, *YABC 1:* 121
Finder, Martin. *See* Salzmann,
    Siegmund, *25:* 207
Fink, William B(ertrand)   1916- ,
    22: 109
Finkel, George (Irvine)
    1909-1975, *8:* 59
Finlay, Winifred   1910- , *23:* 71
Finlayson, Ann   1925- , *8:* 61
Firmin, Peter   1928- , *15:* 113
Fischbach, Julius   1894- , *10:* 43
Fisher, Aileen (Lucia)   1906- ,
    1: 92; *25:* 108
Fisher, Clavin C(argill)   1912- ,
    24: 113
Fisher, Dorothy Canfield
    1879-1958, *YABC 1:* 122
Fisher, John (Oswald Hamilton)
    1909- , *15:* 115
Fisher, Laura Harrison   1934- ,
    5: 67
Fisher, Leonard Everett   1924- ,
    4: 84
Fisher, Margery (Turner)   1913- ,
    20: 47
Fisk, Nicholas   1923- , *25:* 111
Fitch, Clarke. *See* Sinclair, Upton
    (Beall), *9:* 168
Fitch, John, IV. *See* Cormier,
    Robert Edmund, *10:* 28
Fitschen, Dale   1937- , *20:* 48
Fitzgerald, Captain Hugh. *See*
    Baum L(yman) Frank, *18:* 7
Fitzgerald, Edward Earl   1919- ,
    20: 49
Fitzgerald, F(rancis) A(nthony)
    1940- , *15:* 115
Fitzgerald, John D(ennis)   1907- ,
    20: 50
Fitzhardinge, Joan Margaret
    1912- , *2:* 107
Fitzhugh, Louise   1928-1974,
    1: 94; *24:* 114 (Obituary)
Flack, Marjorie   1899-1958,
    YABC 2: 123
Flash Flood. *See* Robinson, Jan M.,
    6: 194
Fleischman, (Albert) Sid(ney)
    1920- , *8:* 61
Fleming, Alice Mulcahey   1928- ,
    9: 67
Fleming, Ian (Lancaster)
    1908-1964, *9:* 67
Fleming, Thomas J(ames)   1927- ,
    8: 64
Fletcher, Charlie May   1897- ,
    3: 70
Fletcher, Helen Jill   1911- , *13:* 36

Flexner, James Thomas   1908- ,
    9: 70
Flitner, David P.   1949- , *7:* 92
Floethe, Louise Lee   1913- , *4:* 87
Floethe, Richard   1901- , *4:* 89
Floherty, John Joseph   1882-1964,
    25: 113
Flood, Flash. *See* Robinson, Jan
    M., *6:* 194
Flora, James (Royer)   1914- ,
    1: 95
Florian, Douglas   1950- , *19:* 122
Flory, Jane Trescott   1917- ,
    22: 110
Flynn, Barbara   1928- , *9:* 71
Flynn, Jackson. *See* Shirreffs,
    Gordon D., *11:* 207
Fodor, Ronald V(ictor)   1944- ,
    25: 115
Foley, Rae. *See* Denniston, Elinore,
    24: 85 (Obituary)
Folsom, Franklin (Brewster)
    1907- , *5:* 67
Fooner, Michael, *22:* 112
Forberg, Ati   1925- , *22:* 113
Forbes, Esther   1891-1967, *2:* 108
Forbes, Graham B. [Collective
    pseudonym], *1:* 97
Forbes, Kathryn. *See* McLean,
    Kathryn (Anderson), *9:* 140
Ford, Albert Lee. *See* Stratemeyer,
    Edward L., *1:* 208
Ford, Elbur. *See* Hibbert, Eleanor,
    2: 134
Ford, Hildegarde. *See* Morrison,
    Velma Ford, *21:* 110
Ford, Marcia. *See* Radford, Ruby
    L., *6:* 186
Foreman, Michael   1938- , *2:* 110
Forester, C(ecil) S(cott)
    1899-1966, *13:* 38
Forman, Brenda   1936- , *4:* 90
Forman, James Douglas   1932- ,
    8: 64
Forrest, Sybil. *See* Markun, Patricia
    M(aloney), *15:* 189
Forsee, (Frances) Aylesa, *1:* 97
Foster, Doris Van Liew   1899- ,
    10: 44
Foster, E(lizabeth) C(onnell)
    1902- , *9:* 71
Foster, Elizabeth   1905-1963,
    10: 45
Foster, Elizabeth Vincent   1902- ,
    12: 82
Foster, F. Blanche   1919- , *11:* 95
Foster, Genevieve (Stump)
    1893-1979, *2:* 111; *23:* 73
    (Obituary)
Foster, John T(homas)   1925- ,
    8: 65
Foster, Laura Louise   1918- ,
    6: 78
Foster, Margaret Lesser
    1899-1979, *21:* 43 (Obituary)

Foster, Marian Curtis   1909-1978,
    23: 73
Fourth Brother, The. *See* Aung,
    (Maung) Htin, *21:* 5
Fowke, Edith (Margaret)   1913- ,
    14: 59
Fowles, John   1926- , *22:* 114
Fox, Charles Philip   1913- ,
    12: 83
Fox, Eleanor. *See* St. John, Wylly
    Folk, *10:* 132
Fox, Fontaine Talbot, Jr.
    1884-1964, *23:* 75 (Obituary)
Fox, Freeman. *See* Hamilton,
    Charles Harold St. John, *13:* 77
Fox, Lorraine, *11:* 96
Fox, Michael Wilson   1937- ,
    15: 117
Fox, Paula   1923- , *17:* 59
Frances, Miss. *See* Horwich,
    Frances R., *11:* 142
Franchere, Ruth, *18:* 111
Francis, Dorothy Brenner   1926- ,
    10: 46
Francis, Pamela (Mary)   1926- ,
    11: 97
Francois, André   1915- , *25:* 116
Francoise. *See* Seignobosc,
    Francoise, *21:* 145
Frank, Josette   1893- , *10:* 47
Frankau, Mary Evelyn   1899- ,
    4: 90
Frankel, Bernice, *9:* 72
Frankenberg, Robert   1911- ,
    22: 115
Franklin, Harold   1920- , *13:* 53
Franklin, Max. *See* Deming,
    Richard, *24:* 83
Franklin, Steve. *See* Stevens,
    Franklin, *6:* 206
Franzén, Nils-Olof   1916- , *10:* 47
Frasconi, Antonio   1919- , *6:* 79
Frazier, Neta Lohnes, *7:* 94
Freed, Alvyn M.   1913- , *22:* 117
Freedman, Russell (Bruce)
    1929- , *16:* 115
Freeman, Don   1908-1978, *17:* 60
Freeman, Ira M(aximilian)   1905- ,
    21: 43
Freeman, Lucy (Greenbaum)
    1916- , *24:* 114
Freeman, Mae (Blacker)   1907- ,
    25: 117
Fregosi, Claudia (Anne Marie)
    1946- , *24:* 116
French, Allen   1870-1946,
    YABC 1: 133
French, Dorothy Kayser   1926- ,
    5: 69
French, Fiona   1944- , *6:* 81
French, Kathryn. *See* Mosesson,
    Gloria R(ubin), *24:* 153
French, Paul. *See* Asimov, Isaac,
    1: 15
Frewer, Glyn   1931- , *11:* 98

Frick, C. H. *See* Irwin, Constance
Frick, *6:* 119
Frick, Constance. *See* Irwin,
Constance Frick, *6:* 119
Friedlander, Joanne K(ohn)
1930- , *9:* 73
Friedman, Estelle 1920- , *7:* 95
Friendlich, Dick. *See* Friendlich,
Richard, *11:* 99
Friendlich, Richard J. 1909- ,
11: 99
Friermood, Elisabeth Hamilton
1903- , *5:* 69
Friis, Babbis. *See* Friis-Baastad,
Babbis, *7:* 95
Friis-Baastad, Babbis 1921-1970,
7: 95
Friskey, Margaret Richards
1901- , *5:* 72
Fritz, Jean (Guttery) 1915- , *1:* 98
Froman, Elizabeth Hull
1920-1975, *10:* 49
Froman, Robert (Winslow)
1917- , *8:* 67
Frost, A(rthur) B(urdett)
1851-1928, *19:* 122
Frost, Erica. *See* Supraner, Robyn,
20: 182
Frost, Lesley 1899- , *14:* 61
Frost, Robert (Lee) 1874-1963,
14: 63
Fry, Rosalie 1911- , *3:* 71
Fuchs, Erich 1916- , *6:* 84
Fujita, Tamao 1905- , *7:* 98
Fujiwara, Michiko 1946- ,
15: 120
Fuller, Catherine L(euthold)
1916- , *9:* 73
Fuller, Edmund (Maybank)
1914- , *21:* 45
Fuller, Iola. *See* McCoy, Iola
Fuller, *3:* 120
Fuller, Lois Hamilton 1915- ,
11: 99
Fuller, Margaret. *See* Ossoli, Sarah
Margaret (Fuller) marchesa d',
25: 186
Funk, Thompson. *See* Funk, Tom,
7: 98
Funk, Tom 1911- , *7:* 98
Funke, Lewis 1912- , *11:* 100
Furukawa, Toshi 1924- , *24:* 117
Fyleman, Rose 1877-1957, *21:* 46

Gaeddert, Lou Ann (Bigge)
1931- , *20:* 58
Gàg, Flavia 1907-1979, *24:* 119
(Obituary)
Gág, Wanda (Hazel) 1893-1946,
YABC 1: 135
Gage, Wilson. *See* Steele, Mary Q.,
3: 211
Gagliardo, Ruth Garver

1895(?)-1980, *22:* 118
(Obituary)
Galdone, Paul 1914- , *17:* 69
Galinsky, Ellen 1942- , *23:* 75
Gallant, Roy (Arthur) 1924- ,
4: 91
Gallico, Paul 1897-1976, *13:* 53
Galt, Thomas Franklin, Jr.
1908- , *5:* 72
Galt, Tom. *See* Galt, Thomas
Franklin, Jr., *5:* 72
Gamerman, Martha 1941- ,
15: 121
Gannett, Ruth Stiles 1923- , *3:* 73
Gannon, Robert (Haines) 1931- ,
8: 68
Gantos, Jack. *See* Gantos, John
(Bryan), Jr., *20:* 59
Gantos, John (Bryan), Jr. 1951- ,
20: 59
Gard, Joyce. *See* Reeves, Joyce,
17: 158
Gard, Robert Edward 1910- ,
18: 113
Garden, Nancy 1938- , *12:* 85
Gardner, Dic. *See* Gardner,
Richard, *24:* 119
Gardner, Jeanne LeMonnier, *5:* 73
Gardner, Martin 1914- , *16:* 117
Gardner, Richard 1931- , *24:* 119
Gardner, Richard A. 1931- ,
13: 84
Garelick, May, *19:* 130
Garfield, James B. 1881- , *6:* 85
Garfield, Leon 1921- , *1:* 99
Garis, Howard R(oger)
1873-1962, *13:* 67
Garner, Alan 1934- , *18:* 114
Garnett, Eve C. R., *3:* 75
Garraty, John A. 1920- , *23:* 76
Garrett, Helen 1895- , *21:* 48
Garrigue, Sheila 1931- , *21:* 49
Garrison, Barbara 1931- , *19:* 132
Garrison, Frederick. *See* Sinclair,
Upton (Beall), *9:* 168
Garrison, Webb B(lack) 1919- ,
25: 119
Garst, Doris Shannon 1894- ,
1: 100
Garst, Shannon. *See* Garst, Doris
Shannon, *1:* 100
Garthwaite, Marion H. 1893- ,
7: 100
Gates, Doris 1901- , *1:* 102
Gatty, Juliana Horatia. *See* Ewing,
Juliana (Horatia Gatty), *16:* 90
Gault, William Campbell 1910- ,
8: 69
Gaver, Becky. *See* Gaver, Rebecca,
20: 60
Gaver, Rebecca 1952- , *20:* 60
Gay, Kathlyn 1930- , *9:* 74
Gay, Zhenya 1906-1978, *19:* 134
Geis, Darlene, *7:* 101
Geisel, Theodor Seuss 1904- ,
1: 104

Geldart, William 1936- , *15:* 121
Gelinas, Paul J. 1911- , *10:* 49
Gelman, Steve 1934- , *3:* 75
Gemming, Elizabeth 1932- ,
11: 104
Gentleman, David 1930- , *7:* 102
George, Jean Craighead 1919- ,
2: 112
George, John L(othar) 1916- ,
2: 114
George, S(idney) C(harles)
1898- , *11:* 104
Georgiou, Constantine 1927- ,
7: 102
Geras, Adele (Daphne) 1944- ,
23: 76
Gergely, Tibor 1900-1978, *20:* 61
(Obituary)
Gerson, Noel B(ertram) 1914- ,
22: 118
Gessner, Lynne 1919- , *16:* 119
Gibbons, Gail 1944- , *23:* 77
Gibbs, Alonzo (Lawrence) 1915- ,
5: 74
Gibson, Josephine. *See* Joslin,
Sesyle, *2:* 158
Gidal, Sonia 1922- , *2:* 115
Gidal, Tim N(ahum) 1909- ,
2: 116
Giegling, John A(llan) 1935- ,
17: 75
Gilbert, (Agnes) Joan (Sewell)
1931- , *10:* 50
Gilbert, Nan. *See* Gilbertson,
Mildred, *2:* 116
Gilbert, Sara (Dulaney) 1943- ,
11: 105
Gilbertson, Mildred Geiger
1908- , *2:* 116
Gilbreath, Alice (Thompson)
1921- , *12:* 87
Gilbreth, Frank B., Jr. 1911- ,
2: 117
Gilfond, Henry, *2:* 118
Gilge, Jeanette 1924- , *22:* 121
Gill, Derek L(ewis) T(heodore)
1919- , *9:* 75
Gill, Margery Jean 1925- ,
22: 122
Gillett, Mary, *7:* 103
Gillette, Henry Sampson 1915- ,
14: 71
Gilman, Dorothy. *See* Dorothy
Gilman Butters, *5:* 39
Gilman, Esther 1925- , *15:* 123
Gilmore, Iris 1900- , *22:* 123
Gilson, Barbara. *See* Gilson,
Charles James Louis,
YABC 2: 124
Gilson, Charles James Louis
1878-1943, *YABC 2:* 124
Ginsburg, Mirra, *6:* 86
Giovanni, Nikki 1943- , *24:* 120
Giovanopoulos, Paul 1939- ,
7: 104

Gipson, Frederick B.   1908-1973,
    2: 118; *24:* 121 (Obituary)
Gittings, Jo Manton   1919- , *3:* 76
Gittings, Robert   1911- , *6:* 88
Gladstone, Gary   1935- , *12:* 88
Glaser, Milton   1929- , *11:* 106
Glaspell, Susan   1882-1948,
    YABC 2: 125
Glauber, Uta (Heil)   1936- ,
    17: 75
Glazer, Tom   1914- , *9:* 76
Gleason, Judith   1929- , *24:* 121
Glendinning, Richard   1917- ,
    24: 121
Glendinning, Sally. *See*
    Glendinning, Sara W(ilson),
    24: 122
Glendinning, Sara W(ilson)
    1913- , *24:* 122
Gles, Margaret Breitmaier   1940- ,
    22: 124
Glick, Carl (Cannon)   1890-1971,
    14: 72
Glick, Virginia Kirkus   1893-1980,
    23: 78 (Obituary)
Gliewe, Unada   1927- , *3:* 77
Glines, Carroll V(ane), Jr.   1920- ,
    19: 137
Glovach, Linda   1947- , *7:* 105
Glubok, Shirley, *6:* 89
Gluck, Felix   1924(?)-1981,
    25: 120 (Obituary)
Glynne-Jones, William   1907- ,
    11: 107
Goble, Paul   1933- , *25:* 120
Godden, Rumer   1907- , *3:* 79
Gode, Alexander. *See* Gode von
    Aesch, Alexander (Gottfried
    Friedrich), *14:* 74
Gode von Aesch, Alexander
    (Gottfried Friedrich)
    1906-1970, *14:* 74
Goettel, Elinor   1930- , *12:* 89
Goetz, Delia   1898- , *22:* 125
Goffstein, M(arilyn) B(rooke)
    1940- , *8:* 70
Golann, Cecil Paige   1921- ,
    11: 109
Golbin, Andrée   1923- , *15:* 124
Gold, Phyllis   1941- , *21:* 50
Gold, Sharlya, *9:* 77
Goldberg, Herbert S.   1926- ,
    25: 122
Goldfeder, Cheryl. *See* Pahz,
    Cheryl Suzanne, *11:* 189
Goldfeder, Jim. *See* Pahz, James
    Alon, *11:* 190
Goldfrank, Helen Colodny   1912- ,
    6: 89
Goldin, Augusta   1906- , *13:* 72
Goldsborough, June   1923- ,
    19: 138
Goldsmith, Howard   1943- ,
    24: 123
Goldstein, Philip   1910- , *23:* 79

Goldston, Robert (Conroy)
    1927- , *6:* 90
Gonzalez, Gloria   1940- , *23:* 80
Goodall, John S(trickland)   1908- ,
    4: 92
Goode, Diane   1949- , *15:* 125
Goodman, Elaine   1930- , *9:* 78
Goodman, Walter   1927- , *9:* 78
Goodrich, Samuel Griswold
    1793-1860, *23:* 82
Goodwin, Hal. *See* Goodwin,
    Harold Leland, *13:* 73
Goodwin, Harold Leland   1914- ,
    13: 73
Goossen, Agnes. *See* Epp, Margaret
    A(gnes), *20:* 38
Gordon, Colonel H. R. *See* Ellis,
    Edward S(ylvester),
    YABC 1: 116
Gordon, Dorothy   1893-1970,
    20: 61
Gordon, Esther S(aranga)   1935- ,
    10: 50
Gordon, Frederick [Collective
    pseudonym], *1:* 106
Gordon, Hal. *See* Goodwin, Harold
    Leland, *13:* 73
Gordon, John   1925- , *6:* 90
Gordon, Lew. *See* Baldwin, Gordon
    C., *12:* 30
Gordon, Margaret (Anna)   1939- ,
    9: 79
Gordon, Mildred   1912-1979,
    24: 124 (Obituary)
Gordon, Selma. *See* Lanes, Selma
    G., *3:* 96
Gordon, Sol   1923- , *11:* 111
Gordon, Stewart. *See* Shirreffs,
    Gordon D., *11:* 207
Gordons, The [Joint pseudonym].
    See Gordon, Mildred, *24:* 124
    (Obituary)
Gorelick, Molly C.   1920- , *9:* 80
Gorham, Michael. *See* Folsom,
    Franklin, *5:* 67
Gorsline, Douglas (Warner)
    1913- , *11:* 112
Goryan, Sirak. *See* Saroyan,
    William, *23:* 210; *24:* 181
    (Obituary)
Gottlieb, Bill. *See* Gottlieb, William
    P(aul), *24:* 124
Gottlieb, Gerald   1923- , *7:* 106
Gottlieb, William P(aul), *24:* 124
Goudey, Alice E.   1898- , *20:* 64
Goudge, Elizabeth   1900- , *2:* 119
Gough, Catherine   1931- , *24:* 125
Goulart, Ron   1933- , *6:* 92
Gould, Jean R(osalind)   1919- ,
    11: 114
Gould, Lilian   1920- , *6:* 92
Gould, Marilyn   1923- , *15:* 127
Govan, Christine Noble   1898- ,
    9: 80
Graber, Alexander, *7:* 106

Graff, Polly Anne. *See* Colver,
    Anne, *7:* 54
Graff, (S.) Stewart   1908- , *9:* 82
Graham, Ada   1931- , *11:* 115
Graham, Eleanor   1896- , *18:* 116
Graham, Frank, Jr.   1925- ,
    11: 116
Graham, John   1926- , *11:* 117
Graham, Lorenz B(ell)   1902- ,
    2: 122
Graham, Margaret Bloy   1920- ,
    11: 119
Graham, Robin Lee   1949- ,
    7: 107
Graham, Shirley. *See* Du Bois,
    Shirley Graham, *24:* 105
Grahame, Kenneth   1859-1932,
    YABC 1: 144
Gramatky, Hardie   1907-1979,
    1: 107; *23:* 89 (Obituary)
Grange, Peter. *See* Nicole,
    Christopher Robin, *5:* 141
Granstaff, Bill   1925- , *10:* 51
Grant, Bruce   1893-1977, *5:* 75;
    25: 122 (Obituary)
Grant, Eva   1907- , *7:* 108
Grant, Gordon   1875-1962,
    25: 123
Grant, (Alice) Leigh   1947- ,
    10: 52
Grant, Matthew C. *See* May, Julian,
    11: 175
Grant, Myrna (Lois)   1934- ,
    21: 51
Grant, Neil   1938- , *14:* 75
Gravel, Fern. *See* Hall, James
    Norman, *21:* 54
Graves, Charles Parlin   1911-1972,
    4: 94
Gray, Elizabeth Janet   1902- ,
    6: 93
Gray, Genevieve S.   1920- , *4:* 95
Gray, Jenny. *See* Gray, Genevieve
    S., *4:* 95
Gray, Nicholas Stuart   1922- ,
    4: 96
Gray, Patricia, *7:* 110
Gray, Patsey. *See* Gray, Patricia,
    7: 110
Grayland, V. Merle. *See* Grayland,
    Valerie, *7:* 111
Grayland, Valerie, *7:* 111
Great Comte, The. *See*
    Hawkesworth, Eric, *13:* 94
Greaves, Margaret   1914- , *7:* 113
Green, Adam. *See* Weisgard,
    Leonard, *2:* 263
Green, D. *See* Casewit, Curtis,
    4: 43
Green, Hannah. *See* Greenberg,
    Joanne (Goldenberg), *25:* 127
Green, Jane   1937- , *9:* 82
Green, Mary Moore   1906- ,
    11: 120
Green, Morton   1937- , *8:* 71

Green, Norma B(erger) 1925- ,
  11: 120
Green, Phyllis 1932- , *20:* 65
Green, Roger (Gilbert) Lancelyn
  1918- , *2:* 123
Green, Sheila Ellen 1934- , *8:* 72
Greenaway, Kate 1846-1901,
  YABC 2: 129
Greenberg, Harvey R. 1935- ,
  5: 77
Greenberg, Joanne (Goldenberg)
  1932- , *25:* 127
Greene, Bette 1934- , *8:* 73
Greene, Carla 1916- , *1:* 108
Greene, Constance C(larke)
  1924- , *11:* 121
Greene, Ellin 1927- , *23:* 89
Greene, Graham 1904- , *20:* 66
Greene, Wade 1933- , *11:* 122
Greenfeld, Howard, *19:* 140
Greenfield, Eloise 1929- , *19:* 141
Greening, Hamilton. *See* Hamilton,
  Charles Harold St. John, *13:* 77
Greenleaf, Barbara Kaye 1942- ,
  6: 95
Greenwald, Sheila. *See* Green,
  Sheila Ellen, *8:* 72
Gregg, Walter H(arold) 1919- ,
  20: 75
Gregori, Leon 1919- , *15:* 129
Grendon, Stephen. *See* Derleth,
  August (William), *5:* 54
Grenville, Pelham. *See* Wodehouse,
  P(elham) G(renville), *22:* 241
Gretz, Susanna 1937- , *7:* 114
Gretzer, John, *18:* 117
Grey, Jerry 1926- , *11:* 123
Grey Owl. *See* Belaney, Archibald
  Stansfeld, *24:* 39
Gri. *See* Denney, Diana, *25:* 90
Grice, Frederick 1910- , *6:* 96
Grieder, Walter 1924- , *9:* 83
Griese, Arnold A(lfred) 1921- ,
  9: 84
Grifalconi, Ann 1929- , *2:* 125
Griffith, Jeannette. *See* Eyerly,
  Jeannette, *4:* 80
Griffiths, G(ordon) D(ouglas)
  1910-1973, *20:* 75 (Obituary)
Griffiths, Helen 1939- , *5:* 77
Grimm, Jacob Ludwig Karl
  1785-1863, *22:* 126
Grimm, Wilhelm Karl 1786-1859,
  22: 126
Grimm, William C(arey) 1907- ,
  14: 75
Grimshaw, Nigel (Gilroy) 1925- ,
  23: 91
Grimsley, Gordon. *See* Groom,
  Arthur William, *10:* 53
Gringhuis, Dirk. *See* Gringhuis,
  Richard H. *6:* 97; *25:* 128
  (Obituary)
Gringhuis, Richard H. 1918-1974,
  6: 97; *25:* 128 (Obituary)

Grinnell, George Bird 1849-1938,
  16: 121
Gripe, Maria (Kristina) 1923- ,
  2: 126
Groch, Judith (Goldstein) 1929- ,
  25: 128
Grohskopf, Bernice, *7:* 114
Grol, Lini Richards 1913- , *9:* 85
Grollman, Earl A. 1925- ,
  22: 152
Groom, Arthur William
  1898-1964, *10:* 53
Gross, Sarah Chokla 1906- ,
  9: 86
Grossman, Robert 1940- , *11:* 124
Groth, John 1908- , *21:* 53
Gruenberg, Sidonie M(atsner)
  1881- , *2:* 127
Gugliotta, Bobette 1918- , *7:* 116
Guillaume, Jeanette G. (Flierl)
  1899- , *8:* 74
Guillot, Rene 1900-1969, *7:* 117
Gundrey, Elizabeth 1924- , *23:* 91
Gunston, Bill. *See* Gunston,
  William Tudor, *9:* 88
Gunston, William Tudor 1927- ,
  9: 88
Gunther, John 1901-1970, *2:* 129
Gurko, Leo 1914- , *9:* 88
Gurko, Miriam, *9:* 89
Gustafson, Sarah R. *See* Riedman,
  Sarah R., *1:* 183
Gutman, Naham 1899(?)-1981,
  25: 129 (Obituary)
Guy, Rosa (Cuthbert) 1928- ,
  14: 77

Haas, Irene 1929- , *17:* 76
Habenstreit, Barbara 1937- , *5:* 78
Haber, Louis 1910- , *12:* 90
Hader, Berta (Hoerner)
  1891(?)-1976, *16:* 122
Hader, Elmer (Stanley)
  1889-1973, *16:* 124
Hadley, Franklin. *See*
  Winterbotham, R(ussell)
  R(obert), *10:* 198
Hafner, Marylin 1925- , *7:* 119
Haggard, H(enry) Rider
  1856-1925, *16:* 129
Haggerty, James J(oseph) 1920-
  5: 78
Hagon, Priscilla. *See* Allan, Mabel
  Esther, *5:* 2
Hahn, Emily 1905- , *3:* 81
Hahn, Hannelore 1926- , *8:* 74
Hahn, James (Sage) 1947- , *9:* 90
Hahn, (Mona) Lynn 1949- , *9:* 91
Haig-Brown, Roderick (Langmere)
  1908-1976, *12:* 90
Haines, Gail Kay 1943- , *11:* 124
Haining, Peter 1940- , *14:* 77
Haldane, Roger John 1945- ,
  13: 75

Hale, Edward Everett 1822-1909,
  16: 143
Hale, Helen. *See* Mulcahy, Lucille
  Burnett, *12:* 155
Hale, Kathleen 1898- , *17:* 78
Hale, Linda 1929- , *6:* 99
Hall, Adele 1910- , *7:* 120
Hall, Anna Gertrude 1882-1967,
  8: 75
Hall, Donald (Andrew, Jr.)
  1928- , *23:* 92
Hall, Elvajean, *6:* 100
Hall, James Norman 1887-1951,
  21: 54
Hall, Jesse. *See* Boesen, Victor,
  16: 53
Hall, Lynn 1937- , *2:* 130
Hall, Malcolm 1945- , *7:* 121
Hall, Marjory. *See* Yeakley,
  Marjory Hall, *21:* 207
Hall, Rosalys Haskell 1914- ,
  7: 121
Hallard, Peter. *See* Catherall,
  Arthur, *3:* 38
Hallas, Richard. *See* Knight, Eric
  (Mowbray), *18:* 151
Halliburton, Warren J. 1924- ,
  19: 143
Hallin, Emily Watson 1919- ,
  6: 101
Hall-Quest, Olga W(ilbourne)
  1899- , *11:* 125
Hallstead, William F(inn) III
  1924- , *11:* 126
Hallward, Michael 1889- , *12:* 91
Halsell, Grace 1923- , *13:* 76
Halter, Jon C(harles) 1941- ,
  22: 152
Hamberger, John 1934- , *14:* 79
Hamerstrom, Frances 1907- ,
  24: 125
Hamil, Thomas Arthur 1928- ,
  14: 80
Hamil, Tom. *See* Hamil, Thomas
  Arthur, *14:* 80
Hamilton, Alice. *See* Cromie, Alice
  Hamilton, *24:* 78
Hamilton, Charles Harold St. John
  1875-1961, *13:* 77
Hamilton, Clive. *See* Lewis, C. S.,
  13: 129
Hamilton, Dorothy 1906- , *12:* 92
Hamilton, Edith 1867-1963,
  20: 75
Hamilton, Elizabeth 1906- ,
  23: 94
Hamilton, Robert W. *See*
  Stratemeyer, Edward L., *1:* 208
Hamilton, Virginia 1936- , *4:* 97
Hammer, Richard 1928- , *6:* 102
Hammerman, Gay M(orenus)
  1926- , *9:* 92
Hammontree, Marie (Gertrude)
  1913- , *13:* 89
Hampson, (Richard) Denman
  1929- , *15:* 129

Hamre, Leif 1914- , *5:* 79
Hancock, Sibyl 1940- , *9:* 92
Hane, Roger 1940-1974, *20:* 79
  (Obituary)
Haney, Lynn 1941- , *23:* 95
Hanff, Helene, *11:* 128
Hanlon, Emily 1945- , *15:* 131
Hann, Jacquie 1951- , *19:* 144
Hanna, Paul R(obert) 1902- ,
  9: 93
Hano, Arnold 1922- , *12:* 93
Hanser, Richard (Frederick)
  1909- , *13:* 90
Hanson, Joan 1938- , *8:* 75
Harald, Eric. *See* Boesen, Victor,
  16: 53
Hardwick, Richard Holmes, Jr.
  1923- , *12:* 94
Hardy, Alice Dale [Collective
  pseudonym], *1:* 109
Hardy, David A(ndrews) 1936- ,
  9: 95
Hardy, Stuart. *See* Schisgall, Oscar,
  12: 187
Hardy, Thomas 1840-1928,
  25: 129
Hark, Mildred. *See* McQueen,
  Mildred Hark, *12:* 145
Harkaway, Hal. *See* Stratemeyer,
  Edward L., *1:* 208
Harkins, Philip 1912- , *6:* 102
Harlan, Glen. *See* Cebulash, Mel,
  10: 19
Harmelink, Barbara (Mary), *9:* 97
Harmon, Margaret 1906- , *20:* 80
Harnan, Terry 1920- , *12:* 94
Harnett, Cynthia (Mary), *5:* 79
Harper, Wilhelmina 1884- , *4:* 99
Harrington, Lyn 1911- , *5:* 80
Harris, Christie 1907- , *6:* 103
Harris, Colver. *See* Colver, Anne,
  7: 54
Harris, Dorothy Joan 1931- ,
  13: 91
Harris, Janet 1932-1979, *4:* 100;
  23: 97 (Obituary)
Harris, Joel Chandler 1848-1908,
  YABC 1: 154
Harris, Leon A., Jr. 1926- ,
  4: 101
Harris, Lorle K(empe) 1912- ,
  22: 153
Harris, Rosemary (Jeanne), *4:* 101
Harris, Sherwood 1932- , *25:* 139
Harrison, Deloris 1938- , *9:* 97
Harrison, Harry 1925- , *4:* 102
Hartley, Ellen (Raphael) 1915- ,
  23: 97
Hartley, William B(rown) 1913- ,
  23: 98
Hartman, Louis F(rancis)
  1901-1970, *22:* 154
Hartshorn, Ruth M. 1928- ,
  11: 129
Harwin, Brian. *See* Henderson,
  LeGrand, *9:* 104

Harwood, Pearl Augusta (Bragdon)
  1903- , *9:* 98
Haskell, Arnold 1903- , *6:* 104
Haskins, James 1941- , *9:* 100
Haskins, Jim. *See* Haskins, James,
  9: 100
Hassler, Jon (Francis) 1933- ,
  19: 145
Hatlo, Jimmy 1898-1963, *23:* 100
  (Obituary)
Haugaard, Erik Christian 1923- ,
  4: 104
Hauser, Margaret L(ouise) 1909- ,
  10: 54
Hausman, Gerald 1945- , *13:* 93
Hausman, Gerry. *See* Hausman,
  Gerald, *13:* 93
Hautzig, Esther 1930- , *4:* 105
Havenhand, John. *See* Cox, John
  Roberts, *9:* 42
Havighurst, Walter (Edwin)
  1901- , *1:* 109
Haviland, Virginia 1911- , *6:* 105
Hawes, Judy 1913- , *4:* 107
Hawk, Virginia Driving. *See* Sneve,
  Virginia Driving Hawk, *8:* 193
Hawkesworth, Eric 1921- , *13:* 94
Hawkins, Arthur 1903- , *19:* 146
Hawkins, Quail 1905- , *6:* 107
Hawkinson, John 1912- , *4:* 108
Hawkinson, Lucy (Ozone)
  1924-1971, *21:* 63
Hawley, Mable C. [Collective
  pseudonym], *1:* 110
Hawthorne, Captain R. M. *See*
  Ellis, Edward S(ylvester),
  YABC 1: 116
Hawthorne, Nathaniel 1804-1864,
  YABC 2: 143
Hay, John 1915- , *13:* 95
Hay, Timothy. *See* Brown,
  Margaret Wise, *YABC 2:* 9
Haycraft, Howard 1905- , *6:* 108
Haycraft, Molly Costain 1911- ,
  6: 110
Hayden, Robert E(arl) 1913- ,
  19: 147
Hayes, Carlton J. H. 1882-1964,
  11: 129
Hayes, John F. 1904- , *11:* 129
Hayes, Will, *7:* 122
Hayes, William D(imitt) 1913- ,
  8: 76
Hays, Wilma Pitchford 1909- ,
  1: 110
Haywood, Carolyn 1898- , *1:* 111
Head, Gay. *See* Hauser, Margaret
  L(ouise), *10:* 54
Headley, Elizabeth. *See* Cavanna,
  Betty, *1:* 54
Headstrom, Richard 1902- , *8:* 77
Heady, Eleanor B(utler) 1917- ,
  8: 78
Heal, Edith 1903- , *7:* 123
Healey, Brooks. *See* Albert, Burton,
  Jr., *22:* 7

Heath, Veronica. *See* Blackett,
  Veronica Heath, *12:* 54
Heaven, Constance. *See* Fecher,
  Constance, *7:* 83
Hecht, George J(oseph)
  1895-1980, *22:* 155 (Obituary)
Hecht, Henri Joseph 1922- ,
  9: 101
Hechtkopf, Henryk 1910- , *17:* 79
Hegarty, Reginald Beaton
  1906-1973, *10:* 54
Heiderstadt, Dorothy 1907- ,
  6: 111
Hein, Lucille Eleanor 1915- ,
  20: 80
Heinlein, Robert A(nson) 1907- ,
  9: 102
Heins, Paul 1909- , *13:* 96
Helfman, Elizabeth S(eaver)
  1911- ., *3:* 83
Helfman, Harry 1910- , *3:* 84
Hellman, Hal. *See* Hellman,
  Harold, *4:* 109
Hellman, Harold 1927- , *4:* 109
Helps, Racey 1913-1971, *2:* 131;
  25: 139 (Obituary)
Hemming, Roy 1928- , *11:* 130
Henderley, Brooks [Collective
  pseudonym], *1:* 113
Henderson, LeGrand 1901-1965,
  9: 104
Henderson, Nancy Wallace
  1916- , *22:* 155
Henderson, Zenna (Chlarson)
  1917- *5:* 81
Hendrickson, Walter Brookfield, Jr.
  1936- , *9:* 104
Henry, Joanne Landers 1927- ,
  6: 112
Henry, Marguerite, *11:* 131
Henry, O. *See* Porter, William
  Sydney, *YABC 2:* 259
Henry, Oliver. *See* Porter, William
  Sydney, *YABC 2:* 259
Henstra, Friso 1928- , *8:* 80
Herald, Kathleen. *See* Peyton,
  Kathleen (Wendy), *15:* 211
Herbert, Cecil. *See* Hamilton,
  Charles Harold St. John, *13:* 77
Herbert, Don 1917- , *2:* 131
Herbert, Frank (Patrick) 1920- ,
  9: 105
Herbert, Wally. *See* Herbert, Walter
  William, *23:* 101
Herbert, Walter William 1934- ,
  23: 101
Hergé. *See* Remi, Georges, *13:* 183
Herman, Charlotte 1937- , *20:* 81
Hermanson, Dennis (Everett)
  1947- , *10:* 55
Herrmanns, Ralph 1933- ,
  11: 133
Herron, Edward A(lbert) 1912- ,
  4: 110

Hersey, John (Richard) 1914- ,
    25: 139
Hertz, Grete Janus 1915- ,
    23: 102
Hess, Lilo 1916- , *4:* 111
Heuman, William 1912-1971,
    21: 64
Hewett, Anita 1918- , *13:* 97
Hext, Harrington. *See* Phillpotts,
    Eden, *24:* 159
Hey, Nigel S(tewart) 1936- ,
    20: 83
Heyduck-Huth, Hilde 1929- ,
    8: 81
Heyerdahl, Thor 1914- , *2:* 132
Heyliger, William 1884-1955,
    YABC 1: 163
Heyward, Du Bose 1885-1940,
    21: 66
Hibbert, Christopher 1924- ,
    4: 112
Hibbert, Eleanor Burford 1906- ,
    2: 134
Hickman, Janet 1940- , *12:* 97
Hickok, Lorena A. 1892(?)-1968,
    20: 83
Hicks, Eleanor B. *See* Coerr,
    Eleanor, *1:* 64
Hicks, Harvey. *See* Stratemeyer,
    Edward L., *1:* 208
Hieatt, Constance B(artlett)
    1928- , *4:* 113
Hiebert, Ray Eldon 1932- ,
    13: 98
Higdon, Hal 1931- , *4:* 115
Highet, Helen. *See* MacInnes,
    Helen, *22:* 181
Hightower, Florence 1916- ,
    4: 115
Hildick, E. W. *See* Hildick,
    Wallace, *2:* 135
Hildick, (Edmund) Wallace
    1925- , *2:* 135
Hill, Donna (Marie), *24:* 127
Hill, Elizabeth Starr 1925- ,
    24: 129
Hill, Grace Brooks [Collective
    pseudonym], *1:* 113
Hill, Grace Livingston 1865-1947,
    YABC 2: 162
Hill, Kathleen Louise 1917- ,
    4: 116
Hill, Kay. *See* Hill, Kathleen
    Louise, *4:* 116
Hill, Lorna 1902- , *12:* 97
Hill, Monica. *See* Watson, Jane
    Werner, *3:* 244
Hill, Robert W(hite) 1919- ,
    12: 98
Hill, Ruth A. *See* Viguers, Ruth
    Hill, *6:* 214
Hill, Ruth Livingston. *See* Munce,
    Ruth Hill, *12:* 156
Hillerman, Tony 1925- , *6:* 113
Hillert, Margaret 1920- , *8:* 82
Hilton, Irene (P.) 1912- , *7:* 124

Hilton, Ralph 1907- , *8:* 83
Hilton, Suzanne 1922- , *4:* 117
Himler, Ann 1946- , *8:* 84
Himler, Ronald 1937- , *6:* 114
Hinton, S(usan) E(loise) 1950- ,
    19: 147
Hirsch, S. Carl 1913- , *2:* 137
Hirsh, Marilyn 1944- , *7:* 126
Hiser, Iona Seibert 1901- , *4:* 118
Hitchcock, Alfred (Joseph)
    1899-1980, *24:* 131 (Obituary)
Hitte, Kathryn 1919- , *16:* 158
Hitz, Demi 1942- , *11:* 134
Ho, Minfong 1951- , *15:* 131
Hoban, Lillian 1925- , *22:* 157
Hoban, Russell C(onwell) 1925- ,
    1: 113
Hoban, Tana, *22:* 158
Hobart, Lois, *7:* 127
Hoberman, Mary Ann 1930- ,
    5: 82
Hochschild, Arlie Russell 1940- ,
    11: 135
Hockenberry, Hope. *See* Newell,
    Hope (Hockenberry), *24:* 154
Hodge, P(aul) W(illiam) 1934- ,
    12: 99
Hodges, C(yril) Walter 1909- ,
    2: 138
Hodges, Carl G. 1902-1964,
    10: 56
Hodges, Elizabeth Jamison, *1:* 114
Hodges, Margaret Moore 1911- ,
    1: 116
Hoexter, Corinne K. 1927- ,
    6: 115
Hoff, Carol 1900- , *11:* 136
Hoff, Syd(ney) 1912- , *9:* 106
Hoffman, Phyllis M. 1944- ,
    4: 120
Hoffman, Rosekrans 1926- ,
    15: 133
Hoffmann, Felix 1911-1975,
    9: 108
Hofsinde, Robert 1902-1973,
    21: 69
Hogan, Bernice Harris 1929- ,
    12: 99
Hogan, Inez 1895- , *2:* 140
Hogarth, Jr. *See* Kent, Rockwell,
    6: 128
Hogg, Garry 1902- , *2:* 142
Hogner, Dorothy Childs, *4:* 121
Hogner, Nils 1893-1970, *25:* 142
Hogrogian, Nonny 1932- , *7:* 128
Hoke, Helen (L.) 1903- , *15:* 133
Hoke, John 1925- , *7:* 129
Holbeach, Henry. *See* Rands,
    William Brighty, *17:* 156
Holberg, Ruth Langland 1889- ,
    1: 117
Holbrook, Peter. *See* Glick, Carl
    (Cannon), *14:* 72
Holbrook, Stewart Hall
    1893-1964, *2:* 143
Holding, James 1907- , *3:* 85

Holisher, Desider 1901-1972,
    6: 115
Holl, Adelaide (Hinkle), *8:* 84
Holland, Isabelle 1920- , *8:* 86
Holland, Janice 1913-1962,
    18: 117
Holland, John L(ewis) 1919- ,
    20: 87
Holland, Marion 1908- , *6:* 116
Hollander, John 1929- , *13:* 99
Holliday, Joe. *See* Holliday, Joseph,
    11: 137
Holliday, Joseph 1910- , *11:* 137
Holling, Holling C(lancy) 1900- ,
    15: 135
Holm, (Else) Anne (Lise) 1922- ,
    1: 118
Holman, Felice 1919- , *7:* 131
Holmes, Rick. *See* Hardwick,
    Richard Holmes, Jr., *12:* 94
Holmquist, Eve 1921- , *11:* 138
Holt, Margaret 1937- , *4:* 122
Holt, Michael (Paul) 1929- ,
    13: 100
Holt, Stephen. *See* Thompson,
    Harlan H., *10:* 177
Holt, Victoria. *See* Hibbert,
    Eleanor, *2:* 134
Holton, Leonard. *See* Wibberley,
    Leonard, *2:* 271
Holyer, Erna Maria 1925- ,
    22: 159
Holyer, Ernie. *See* Holyer, Erna
    Maria, *22:* 159
Holz, Loretta (Marie) 1943- ,
    17: 81
Homze, Alma C. 1932- , *17:* 82
Honig, Donald 1931- , *18:* 119
Honness, Elizabeth H. 1904- ,
    2: 145
Hood, Joseph F. 1925- , *4:* 123
Hood, Robert E. 1926- , *21:* 70
Hooker, Ruth 1920- , *21:* 71
Hooks, William H(arris) 1921- ,
    16: 159
Hoopes, Ned E(dward) 1932- ,
    21: 73
Hoopes, Roy 1922- , *11:* 140
Hoover, Helen (Drusilla Blackburn)
    1910- , *12:* 100
Hope, Laura Lee [Collective
    pseudonym], *1:* 119
Hope Simpson, Jacynth 1930- ,
    12: 102
Hopf, Alice L(ightner) 1904- ,
    5: 82
Hopkins, A. T. *See* Turngren,
    Annette, *23:* 233 (Obituary)
Hopkins, Joseph G(erard) E(dward)
    1909- , *11:* 141
Hopkins, Lee Bennett 1938- ,
    3: 85
Hopkins, Lyman. *See* Folsom,
    Franklin, *5:* 67
Hopkins, Marjorie 1911- , *9:* 110
Horgan, Paul 1903- , *13:* 102

Hornblow, Arthur, (Jr.)
    1893-1976, *15:* 138
Hornblow, Leonora (Schinasi)
    1920- , *18:* 120
Horner, Dave 1934- , *12:* 104
Hornos, Axel 1907- , *20:* 88
Horvath, Betty 1927- , *4:* 125
Horwich, Frances R(appaport)
    1908- , *11:* 142
Hosford, Dorothy (Grant)
    1900-1952, *22:* 161
Hosford, Jessie 1892- , *5:* 83
Hoskyns-Abrahall, Clare, *13:* 105
Houck, Carter 1924- , *22:* 164
Hough, (Helen) Charlotte 1924- ,
    9: 110
Hough, Richard (Alexander)
    1922- , *17:* 83
Houghton, Eric 1930- , *7:* 132
Houlehen, Robert J. 1918- ,
    18: 121
Household, Geoffrey (Edward West)
    1900- , *14:* 81
Housman, Laurence 1865-1959,
    25: 144
Houston, James A(rchibald)
    1921- , *13:* 106
Howard, Prosper. *See* Hamilton,
    Charles Harold St. John, *13:* 77
Howard, Robert West 1908- ,
    5: 85
Howarth, David 1912- , *6:* 117
Howell, Pat 1947- , *15:* 139
Howell, S. *See* Styles, Frank
    Showell, *10:* 167
Howell, Virginia Tier. *See* Ellison,
    Virginia Howell, *4:* 74
Howes, Barbara 1914- , *5:* 87
Hoyle, Geoffrey 1942- , *18:* 121
Hoyt, Olga (Gruhzit) 1922- ,
    16: 161
Hubbell, Patricia 1928- , *8:* 86
Hubley, John 1914-1977, *24:* 131
    (Obituary)
Hudson, Jeffrey. *See* Crichton, (J.)
    Michael, *9:* 44
Huffaker, Sandy 1943- , *10:* 56
Huffman, Tom, *24:* 131
Hughes, Langston 1902-1967,
    4: 125
Hughes, Monica 1925- , *15:* 140
Hughes, Richard (Arthur Warren)
    1900-1976, *8:* 87; *25:* 153
    (Obituary)
Hughes, Shirley 1929- , *16:* 162
Hull, Eleanor (Means) 1913- ,
    21: 74
Hull, Eric Traviss. *See* Harnan,
    Terry, *12:* 94
Hull, H. Braxton. *See* Jacobs,
    Helen Hull, *12:* 112
Hull, Katharine 1921-1977,
    23: 103
Hülsmann, Eva 1928- , *16:* 165
Hults, Dorothy Niebrugge 1898- ,
    6: 117

Hume, Lotta Carswell, *7:* 133
Hume, Ruth Fox 1922-1980,
    22: 165 (Obituary)
Humphrey, Henry (III) 1930- ,
    16: 167
Hungerford, Pixie. *See* Brinsmead,
    H(esba) F(ay), *18:* 36
Hunt, Francis. *See* Stratemeyer,
    Edward L., *1:* 208
Hunt, Irene 1907- , *2:* 146
Hunt, Mabel Leigh 1892- , *1:* 120
Hunt, Morton 1920- , *22:* 165
Hunter, Dawe. *See* Downie, Mary
    Alice, *13:* 32
Hunter, Evan 1926- , *25:* 153
Hunter, Hilda 1921- , *7:* 135
Hunter, Kristin (Eggleston)
    1931- , *12:* 105
Hunter, Mollie. *See* McIllwraith,
    Maureen, *2:* 193
Hunter Blair, Pauline 1921- ,
    3: 87
Huntington, Harriet E(lizabeth)
    1909- , *1:* 121
Huntsberry, William E(mery)
    1916- , *5:* 87
Hurd, Clement 1908- , *2:* 147
Hurd, Edith Thacher 1910- ,
    2: 150
Hurwitz, Johanna 1937- , *20:* 88
Hurwood, Bernhardt J. 1926- ,
    12: 107
Hutchins, Carleen Maley 1911- ,
    9: 112
Hutchins, Pat 1942- , *15:* 141
Hutchins, Ross E(lliott) 1906- ,
    4: 127
Hutchmacher, J. Joseph 1929- ,
    5: 88
Hutto, Nelson (Allen) 1904- ,
    20: 90
Hutton, Warwick 1939- , *20:* 90
Hyde, Dayton O(gden), *9:* 113
Hyde, Hawk. *See* Hyde, Dayton
    O(gden), *9:* 113
Hyde, Margaret Oldroyd 1917- ,
    1: 122
Hyde, Wayne F. 1922- , *7:* 135
Hylander, Clarence J. 1897-1964,
    7: 137
Hyman, Robin P(hilip) 1931- ,
    12: 108
Hyman, Trina Schart 1939- ,
    7: 137
Hymes, Lucia M. 1907- , *7:* 139
Hyndman, Jane Andrews
    1912-1978, *1:* 122; *23:* 103
    (Obituary)
Hyndman, Robert Utley
    1906(?)-1973, *18:* 123

Iannone, Jeanne, *7:* 139
Ibbotson, Eva 1925- , *13:* 108

Ibbotson, M. C(hristine) 1930- ,
    5: 89
Ilsley, Velma (Elizabeth) 1918- ,
    12: 109
Ingham, Colonel Frederic. *See*
    Hale, Edward Everett, *16:* 143
Ingraham, Leonard W(illiam)
    1913- , *4:* 129
Ingrams, Doreen 1906- , *20:* 92
Inyart, Gene, 1927- *6:* 119
Ionesco, Eugene, 1912- *7:* 140
Ipcar, Dahlov (Zorach) 1917- ,
    1: 125
Irvin, Fred 1914- , *15:* 143
Irving, Robert. *See* Adler, Irving,
    1: 2
Irving, Washington 1783-1859,
    YABC 2: 164
Irwin, Constance Frick 1913- ,
    6: 119
Irwin, Keith Gordon 1885-1964,
    11: 143
Isaac, Joanne 1934- , *21:* 75
Isham, Charlotte H(ickox) 1912- ,
    21: 76
Ish-Kishor, Judith 1892-1972,
    11: 144
Ish-Kishor, Sulamith 1896-1977,
    17: 84
Israel, Elaine 1945- , *12:* 110
Iwamatsu, Jun Atsushi 1908- ,
    14: 83

Jackson, C. Paul 1902- , *6:* 120
Jackson, Caary. *See* Jackson, C.
    Paul, *6:* 120
Jackson, Jesse 1908- , *2:* 150
Jackson, O. B. *See* Jackson, C.
    Paul, *6:* 120
Jackson, Robert B(lake) 1926- ,
    8: 89
Jackson, Sally. *See* Kellogg, Jean,
    10: 66
Jackson, Shirley 1919-1965,
    2: 152
Jacob, Helen Pierce 1927- ,
    21: 77
Jacobs, Flora Gill 1918- , *5:* 90
Jacobs, Helen Hull 1908- ,
    12: 112
Jacobs, Joseph 1854-1916,
    25: 159
Jacobs, Leland Blair 1907- ,
    20: 93
Jacobs, Linda C. 1943- , *21:* 78
Jacobs, Lou(is), Jr. 1921- ,
    2: 155
Jacobson, Daniel 1923- , *12:* 113
Jacobson, Morris K(arl) 1906- ,
    21: 79
Jacopetti, Alexandra 1939- ,
    14: 85
Jagendorf, Moritz (Adolf)

1888-1981, *2:* 155; *24:* 132
(Obituary)
James, Andrew. *See* Kirkup, James,
12: 120
James, Dynely. *See* Mayne,
William, *6:* 162
James, Harry Clebourne   1896- ,
11: 144
James, Josephine. *See* Sterne,
Emma Gelders, *6:* 205
James, T. F. *See* Fleming, Thomas
J(ames), *8:* 64
James, Will(iam Roderick)
1892-1942, *19:* 148
Jane, Mary Childs   1909- , *6:* 122
Janes, Edward C.   1908- , *25:* 167
Janeway, Elizabeth (Hall)   1913- ,
19: 165
Janosch. *See* Eckert, Horst, *8:* 47
Jansen, Jared. *See* Cebulash, Mel,
10: 19
Janson, H(orst) W(oldemar)
1913- , *9:* 114
Jansson, Tove   1914- , *3:* 88
Janus, Grete. *See* Hertz, Grete
Janus, *23:* 102
Jaques, Faith   1923- , *21:* 81
Jarman, Rosemary Hawley
1935- , *7:* 141
Jarrell, Randall   1914-1965, *7:* 141
Jauss, Anne Marie   1907- , *10:* 57
Jayne, Lieutenant R. H.. *See* Ellis,
Edward S(ylvester),
YABC 1: 116
Jeake, Samuel, Jr. *See* Aiken,
Conrad, *3:* 3
Jefferies, (John) Richard
1848-1887, *16:* 168
Jeffers, Susan, *17:* 86
Jefferson, Sarah. *See* Farjeon,
Annabel, *11:* 93
Jeffries, Roderic   1926- , *4:* 129
Jenkins, Marie M.   1909- , *7:* 143
Jenkins, William A(twell)   1922- ,
9: 115
Jennings, Gary (Gayne)   1928- ,
9: 115
Jennings, Robert. *See* Hamilton,
Charles Harold St. John, *13:* 77
Jennings, S. M. *See* Meyer, Jerome
Sydney, *3:* 129; *25:* 181
(Obituary)
Jennison, C. S. *See* Starbird, Kaye,
6: 204
Jennison, Keith Warren   1911- ,
14: 86
Jensen, Niels   1927- , *25:* 168
Jensen, Virginia Allen   1927- ,
8: 90
Jewett, Eleanore Myers
1890-1967, *5:* 90
Jewett, Sarah Orne   1849-1909,
15: 144
Johns, Avery. *See* Cousins,
Margaret, *2:* 79
Johnson, A. E.

[Joint pseudonym] *See* Johnson,
Annabell and Edgar, *2:* 156,
157
Johnson, Annabell Jones   1921- ,
2: 156
Johnson, Charles R.   1925- ,
11: 146
Johnson, Chuck. *See* Johnson,
Charles R., *11:* 146
Johnson, Crockett. *See* Leisk, David
Johnson, *1:* 141
Johnson, D(ana) William   1945- ,
23: 103
Johnson, Dorothy M.   1905- ,
6: 123
Johnson, Edgar Raymond   1912- ,
2: 157
Johnson, Elizabeth   1911- , *7:* 144
Johnson, Eric W(arner)   1918- ,
8: 91
Johnson, Evelyne   1932- , *20:* 95
Johnson, Gaylord   1884- , *7:* 146
Johnson, Gerald White   1890- ,
19: 166
Johnson, James Ralph   1922- ,
1: 126
Johnson, LaVerne B(ravo)   1925- ,
13: 108
Johnson, Lois S(mith), *6:* 123
Johnson, Lois W(alfrid)   1936- ,
22: 165
Johnson, Benj. F., of Boone. *See*
Riley, James Whitcomb,
17: 159
Johnson, (Walter) Ryerson
1901- , *10:* 58
Johnson, Shirley K(ing)   1927- ,
10: 59
Johnson, Siddie Joe   1905-1977,
20: 95 (Obituary)
Johnson, William Weber   1909- ,
7: 147
Johnston, Agnes Christine. *See*
Dazey, Agnes J., *2:* 88
Johnston, H(ugh) A(nthony)
S(tephen)   1913-1967, *14:* 87
Johnston, Johanna, *12:* 115
Johnston, Portia. *See* Takakjian,
Portia, *15:* 273
Johnston, Tony   1942- , *8:* 94
Jones, Adrienne   1915- , *7:* 147
Jones, Diana Wynne   1934- ,
9: 116
Jones, Elizabeth Orton   1910- ,
18: 123
Jones, Evan,   1915-   *3:* 90
Jones, Gillingham. *See* Hamilton,
Charles Harold St. John, *13:* 77
Jones, Harold   1904- , *14:* 87
Jones, Helen L.1904(?)-1973,
22: 167 (Obituary)
Jones, Hortense P.   1918- , *9:* 118
Jones, Mary Alice, *6:* 125
Jones, Weyman   1928- , *4:* 130
Jonk, Clarence   1906- , *10:* 59

Jordan, Hope (Dahle)   1905- ,
15: 150
Jordan, June   1936- , *4:* 131
Jordan, Mildred   1901- , *5:* 91
Jorgenson, Ivar. *See* Silverberg,
Robert, *13:* 206
Joseph, Joseph M(aron)
1903-1979, *22:* 167
Joslin, Sesyle   1929- , *2:* 158
Joyce, J(ames) Avery, *11:* 147
Jucker, Sita   1921- , *5:* 92
Judd, Frances K. [Collective
pseudonym], *1:* 127
Jumpp, Hugo. *See* MacPeek, Walter
G., *4:* 148; *25:* 177 (Obituary)
Jupo, Frank J.   1904- , *7:* 148
Juster, Norton   1929- , *3:* 91
Justus, May,   1898- *1:* 127

Kabdebo, Tamas. *See* Kabdebo,
Thomas, *10:* 60
Kabdebo, Thomas   1934- , *10:* 60
Kakimoto, Kozo   1915- , *11:* 147
Kalashnikoff, Nicholas   1888-1961,
16: 173
Kalb, Jonah   1926- , *23:* 105
Kaler, James Otis   1848-1912,
15: 151
Kalnay, Francis   1899- , *7:* 149
Kamen, Gloria   1923- , *9:* 118
Kamm, Josephine (Hart)   1905- ,
24: 133
Kane, Henry Bugbee   1902-1971,
14: 91
Kane, Robert W.   1910- , *18:* 131
Kanzawa, Toshiko. *See* Furukawa,
Toshi, *24:* 117
Kaplan, Bess   1927- , *22:* 168
Kaplan, Boche   1926- , *24:* 134
Kaplan, Irma   1900- , *10:* 61
Kaplan, Jean Caryl Korn   1926- ,
10: 62
Karen, Ruth   1922- , *9:* 120
Kark, Nina Mary   1925- , *4:* 132
Karlin, Eugene   1918- , *10:* 62
Karp, Naomi J.   1926- , *16:* 174
Kashiwagi, Isami   1925- , *10:* 64
Kästner, Erich   1899-1974, *14:* 91
Katchen, Carole   1944- , *9:* 122
Kathryn. *See* Searle, Kathryn
Adrienne, *10:* 143
Katona, Robert   1949- , *21:* 84
Katz, Bobbi   1933- , *12:* 116
Katz, Fred   1938- , *6:* 126
Katz, William Loren   1927- ,
13: 109
Kaufman, Mervyn D.   1932- ,
4: 133
Kaufmann, Angelika   1935- ,
15: 155
Kaufmann, John   1931- , *18:* 132
Kaula, Edna Mason   1906- ,
13: 110
Kavaler, Lucy   1930- , *23:* 106

Kay, Helen. *See* Goldfrank, Helen
   Colodny, *6:* 89
Kay, Mara, *13:* 111
Kaye, Geraldine 1925- , *10:* 64
Keane, Bil 1922- , *4:* 134
Keating, Bern. *See* Keating, Leo
   Bernard, *10:* 65
Keating, Lawrence A. 1903-1966,
   23: 107
Keating, Leo Bernard 1915- ,
   10: 65
Keats, Ezra Jack 1916- , *14:* 99
Keegan, Marcia 1943- , *9:* 121
Keen, Martin L. 1913- , *4:* 135
Keene, Carolyn. *See* Adams,
   Harriet S., *1:* 1
Keeping, Charles (William James)
   1924- , *9:* 123
Keir, Christine. *See* Pullein-
   Thompson, Christine, *3:* 164
Keith, Carlton. *See* Robertson,
   Keith, *1:* 184
Keith, Harold (Verne) 1903- ,
   2: 159
Kelen, Emery 1896- , *13:* 114
Keller, B(everly) L(ou), *13:* 115
Keller, Charles 1942- , *8:* 94
Keller, Gail Faithfull. *See* Faithfull,
   Gail, *8:* 55
Kellin, Sally Moffet 1932- ,
   9: 125
Kellogg, Gene. *See* Kellogg, Jean,
   10: 66
Kellogg, Jean 1916- , *10:* 66
Kellogg, Steven 1941- , *8:* 95
Kellow, Kathleen. *See* Hibbert,
   Eleanor, *2:* 134
Kelly, Eric P(hilbrook)
   1884-1960, *YABC 1:* 165
Kelly, Ralph. *See* Geis, Darlene,
   7: 101
Kelly, Regina Z., *5:* 94
Kelly, Walt(er Crawford)
   1913-1973, *18:* 135
Kelsey, Alice Geer 1896- , *1:* 129
Kemp, Gene 1926- , *25:* 169
Kempner, Mary Jean 1913-1969,
   10: 67
Kempton, Jean Welch 1914- ,
   10: 67
Kendall, Carol (Seeger) 1917- ,
   11: 148
Kendall, Lace. *See* Stoutenburg,
   Adrien, *3:* 217
Kennedy, John Fitzgerald
   1917-1963, *11:* 150
Kennedy, Joseph 1929- , *14:* 104
Kennedy, (Jerome) Richard
   1932- , *22:* 169
Kennedy, X. J. *See* Kennedy,
   Joseph, *14:* 104
Kennell, Ruth E(pperson)
   1893-1977, *6:* 127; *25:* 170
   (Obituary)
Kenny, Herbert A(ndrew) 1912- ,
   13: 117

Kent, Jack. *See* Kent, John
   Wellington, *24:* 135
Kent, John Wellington 1920- ,
   24: 135
Kent, Margaret 1894- , *2:* 161
Kent, Rockwell 1882-1971, *6:* 128
Kent, Sherman 1903- , *20:* 96
Kenworthy, Leonard S. 1912- ,
   6: 131
Kenyon, Ley 1913- , *6:* 131
Kepes, Juliet A(ppleby) 1919- ,
   13: 118
Kerigan, Florence 1896- , *12:* 117
Kerman, Gertrude Lerner 1909- ,
   21: 85
Kerr, Jessica 1901- , *13:* 119
Kerr, (Anne) Judith 1923- ,
   24: 137
Kerr, M. E. *See* Meaker, Marijane,
   20: 124
Kerry, Frances. *See* Kerigan,
   Florence, *12:* 117
Kerry, Lois. *See* Arquette, Lois S.,
   1: 13
Ker Wilson, Barbara 1929- ,
   20: 97
Kessler, Leonard P. 1921- ,
   14: 106
Kesteven, G. R. *See* Crosher,
   G(eoffry) R(obins), *14:* 51
Kettelkamp, Larry 1933- , *2:* 163
Kevles, Bettyann 1938- , *23:* 107
Key, Alexander (Hill) 1904-1979,
   8: 98; *23:* 108 (Obituary)
Khanshendel, Chiron. *See* Rose,
   Wendy, *12:* 180
Kherdian, David 1931- , *16:* 175
Kiddell, John 1922- , *3:* 93
Kiefer, Irene 1926- , *21:* 87
Killilea, Marie (Lyons) 1913- ,
   2: 165
Kilreon, Beth. *See* Walker, Barbara
   K., *4:* 219
Kimbrough, Emily 1899- , *2:* 166
Kimmel, Eric A. 1946- , *13:* 120
Kindred, Wendy 1937- , *7:* 150
Kines, Pat Decker 1937- ,
   12: 118
King, Arthur. *See* Cain, Arthur H.,
   3: 33
King, Billie Jean 1943- , *12:* 119
King, Cynthia 1925- , *7:* 152
King, Frank O. 1883-1969,
   22: 170 (Obituary)
King, Marian, *23:* 108
King, Martin. *See* Marks, Stan(ley),
   14: 136
King, Martin Luther, Jr.
   1929-1968, *14:* 108
King, Reefe. *See* Barker, Albert
   W., *8:* 3
King, Stephen 1947- , *9:* 126
Kingman, (Mary) Lee 1919- ,
   1: 133
Kingsland, Leslie William 1912- ,
   13: 121

Kingsley, Charles 1819-1875,
   YABC 2: 179
Kinney, C. Cle 1915- , *6:* 132
Kinney, Harrison 1921- , *13:* 122
Kinney, Jean Stout 1912- ,
   12: 120
Kinsey, Elizabeth. *See* Clymer,
   Eleanor, *9:* 37
Kipling, (Joseph) Rudyard
   1865-1936, *YABC 2:* 193
Kirk, Ruth (Kratz) 1925- , *5:* 95
Kirkup, James 1927- , *12:* 120
Kirkus, Virginia. *See* Glick,
   Virginia Kirkus, *23:* 78
   (Obituary)
Kirtland, G. B. *See* Joslin, Sesyle,
   2: 158
Kishida, Eriko 1929- , *12:* 123
Kisinger, Grace Gelvin
   1913-1965, *10:* 68
Kissin, Eva H. 1923- , *10:* 68
Kjelgaard, James Arthur
   1910-1959, *17:* 88
Kjelgaard, Jim. *See* Kjelgaard,
   James Arthur, *17:* 88
Klass, Morton 1927- , *11:* 152
Kleberger, Ilse 1921- , *5:* 96
Klein, H. Arthur, *8:* 99
Klein, Leonore 1916- , *6:* 132
Klein, Mina C(ooper), *8:* 100
Klein, Norma 1938- , *7:* 152
Klimowicz, Barbara 1927- ,
   10: 69
Knickerbocker, Diedrich. *See*
   Irving, Washington,
   YABC 2: 164
Knifesmith. *See* Cutler, Ivor, *24:* 80
Knight, Damon 1922- , *9:* 126
Knight, David C(arpenter), *14:* 111
Knight, Eric (Mowbray)
   1897-1943, *18:* 151
Knight, Francis Edgar, *14:* 112
Knight, Frank. *See* Knight, Francis
   Edgar, *14:* 112
Knight, Hilary 1926- , *15:* 157
Knight, Mallory T. *See* Hurwood,
   Bernhardt J., *12:* 107
Knight, Ruth Adams 1898-1974,
   20: 98 (Obituary)
Knott, Bill. *See* Knott, William
   Cecil, Jr., *3:* 94
Knott, William Cecil, Jr. 1927- ,
   3: 94
Knotts, Howard (Clayton, Jr.)
   1922- , *25:* 170
Knowles, John 1926- , *8:* 101
Knox, Calvin. *See* Silverberg,
   Robert, *13:* 206
Knudson, R. R. *See* Knudson,
   Rozanne, *7:* 154
Knudson, Rozanne 1932- , *7:* 154
Koch, Dorothy Clarke 1924- ,
   6: 133
Kocsis, J. C. *See* Paul, James,
   23: 161

Koerner, W(illiam) H(enry) D(avid)
1878-1938, *21:* 88
Kohler, Julilly H(ouse)
1908-1976, *20:* 99 (Obituary)
Kohn, Bernice (Herstein) 1920- ,
4: 136
Kohner, Frederick 1905- , *10:* 70
Kolba, Tamara, *22:* 171
Komisar, Lucy 1942- , *9:* 127
Komoda, Beverly 1939- , *25:* 171
Komoda, Kiyo 1937- , *9:* 127
Komroff, Manuel 1890-1974,
2: 168; *20:* 99 (Obituary)
Konigsburg, E(laine) L(obl)
1930- , *4:* 137
Koning, Hans. *See* Koningsberger,
Hans, *5:* 97
Koningsberger, Hans 1921- ,
5: 97
Konkle, Janet Everest 1917- ,
12: 124
Koob, Theodora (Johanna Foth)
1918- , *23:* 110
Korach, Mimi 1922- , *9:* 128
Koren, Edward 1935- , *5:* 98
Korinetz, Yuri (Iosifovich)
1923- , *9:* 129
Korty, Carol 1937- , *15:* 159
Kossin, Sandy (Sanford) 1926- ,
10: 71
Kotzwinkle, William 1938- ,
24: 138
Koutoukas, H. M. *See* Rivoli,
Mario, *10:* 129
Kouts, Anne 1945- , *8:* 103
Kramer, George. *See* Heuman,
William, *21:* 64
Krantz, Hazel (Newman) 1920- ,
12: 126
Krasilovsky, Phyllis 1926- ,
1: 134
Kraus, Robert 1925- , *4:* 139
Krauss, Ruth, *1:* 135
Krautter, Elisa. *See* Bialk, Elisa,
1: 25
Kredel, Fritz 1900-1973, *17:* 92
Krementz, Jill 1940- , *17:* 96
Kristof, Jane 1932- , *8:* 104
Kroeber, Theodora (Kracaw)
1897- , *1:* 136
Kroll, Francis Lynde 1904-1973,
10: 72
Kroll, Steven 1941- , *19:* 168
Krumgold, Joseph 1908-1980,
1: 136; *23:* 111 (Obituary)
Krush, Beth 1918- , *18:* 162
Krush, Joe 1918- , *18:* 163
Krüss, James 1926- , *8:* 104
Kubinyi, Laszlo 1937- , *17:* 99
Kumin, Maxine (Winokur)
1925- , *12:* 127
Kunhardt, Dorothy Meserve
1901(?)-1979, *22:* 172
(Obituary)
Künstler, Morton 1927- , *10:* 73

Kupferberg, Herbert 1918- ,
19: 169
Kuratomi, Chizuko 1939- ,
12: 128
Kurelek, William 1927- , *8:* 106
Kurland, Gerald 1942- , *13:* 123
Kuskin, Karla (Seidman) 1932- ,
2: 169
Kuttner, Paul 1931- , *18:* 165
Kvale, Velma R(uth) 1898- ,
8: 108
Kyle, Elisabeth. *See* Dunlop, Agnes
M. R., *3:* 62

Lacy, Leslie Alexander 1937- ,
6: 135
Lader, Lawrence 1919- , *6:* 135
Lady of Quality, A. *See* Bagnold,
Enid, *1:* 17; *25:* 23
La Farge, Oliver (Hazard Perry)
1901-1963, *19:* 170
La Farge, Phyllis, *14:* 113
La Fontaine, Jean de 1621-1695,
18: 166
Lagerlöf, Selma (Ottiliana Lovisa)
1858-1940, *15:* 160
Laimgruber, Monika 1946- ,
11: 153
Laklan, Carli 1907- , *5:* 100
la Mare, Walter de. *See* de la Mare,
Walter, *16:* 73
Lamb, Beatrice Pitney 1904- ,
21: 92
Lamb, Charles 1775-1834,
17: 101
Lamb, G(eoffrey) F(rederick),
10: 74
Lamb, Lynton 1907- , *10:* 75
Lamb, Mary Ann 1764-1847,
17: 112
Lamb, Robert (Boyden) 1941- ,
13: 123
Lambert, Janet (Snyder)
1894-1973, *25:* 172
Lambert, Saul 1928- , *23:* 111
Lamburn, Richmal Crompton
1890-1969, *5:* 101
Lamorisse, Albert (Emmanuel)
1922-1970, *23:* 112
Lamplugh, Lois 1921- , *17:* 116
Lampman, Evelyn Sibley
1907-1980, *4:* 140; *23:* 115
(Obituary)
Lamprey, Louise 1869-1951,
YABC 2: 221
Lancaster, Bruce 1896-1963,
9: 130
Land, Barbara (Neblett) 1923- ,
16: 177
Land, Jane [Joint pseudonym]. *See*
Borland, Kathryn Kilby,
16: 54. *See* Speicher, Helen
Ross (Smith), *8:* 194

Land, Myrick (Ebben) 1922- ,
15: 174
Land, Ross [Joint pseudonym]. *See*
Borland, Kathryn Kilby,
16: 54. *See* Speicher, Helen
Ross (Smith), *8:* 194
Landau, Elaine 1948- , *10:* 75
Landeck, Beatrice 1904- , *15:* 175
Landin, Les(lie) 1923- , *2:* 171
Landshoff, Ursula 1908- , *13:* 124
Lane, Carolyn 1926- , *10:* 76
Lane, John 1932- , *15:* 175
Lanes, Selma G. 1929- , *3:* 96
Lang, Andrew 1844-1912, *16:* 178
Lange, John. *See* Crichton, (J.)
Michael, *9:*
Lange, Suzanne 1945- , *5:* 103
Langley, Noel 1911-1980, *25:* 173
(Obituary)
Langner, Nola 1930- , *8:* 110
Langstaff, John 1920- , *6:* 135
Langstaff, Launcelot. *See* Irving,
Washington, *YABC 2:* 164
Langton, Jane 1922- , *3:* 97
Lanier, Sidney 1842-1881,
18: 176
Larrecq, John M(aurice)
1926-1980, *25:* 173 (Obituary)
Larrick, Nancy G. 1910- , *4:* 141
Larsen, Egon 1904- , *14:* 115
Larson, Eve. *See* St. John, Wylly
Folk, *10:* 132
Larson, William H. 1938- ,
10: 77
Lasell, Elinor H. 1929- , *19:* 178
Lasell, Fen H. *See* Lasell, Elinor
H., *19:* 178
Lasher, Faith B. 1921- , *12:* 129
Lasker, Joe 1919- , *9:* 131
Lasky, Kathryn 1944- , *13:* 124
Lassalle, C. E. *See* Ellis, Edward
S(ylvester), *YABC 1:* 116
Latham, Barbara 1896- , *16:* 187
Latham, Frank B. 1910- , *6:* 137
Latham, Jean Lee 1902- , *2:* 171
Latham, Mavis. *See* Clark, Mavis
Thorpe, *8:* 27
Latham, Philip. *See* Richardson,
Robert S(hirley), *8:* 164
Lathrop, Dorothy P(ulis)
1891-1980, *14:* 116; *24:* 140
(Obituary)
Lattimore, Eleanor Frances
1904- , *7:* 155
Lauber, Patricia (Grace) 1924- ,
1: 138
Laugesen, Mary E(akin) 1906- ,
5: 104
Laughbaum, Steve 1945- ,
12: 131
Laughlin, Florence 1910- , *3:* 98
Laurence, Ester Hauser 1935- ,
7: 156
Lauritzen, Jonreed 1902- ,
13: 125

Lavine, Sigmund A. 1908- ,
3: 100
Lawrence, Josephine
1890(?)-1978; 24: 140
(Obituary)
Lawrence, Louise de Kiriline
1894- , 13: 126
Lawrence, Mildred 1907- , 3: 101
Lawson, Don(ald Elmer) 1917- ,
9: 132
Lawson, Marion Tubbs 1896- ,
22: 172
Lawson, Robert 1892-1957,
YABC 2: 222
Laycock, George (Edwin) 1921-
5: 105
Lazarevich, Mila 1942- , 17: 118
Lazarus, Keo Felker 1913- ,
21: 94
Lea, Alec 1907- , 19: 179
Lea, Richard. See Lea, Alec,
19: 179
Leacroft, Helen 1919- , 6: 139
Leacroft, Richard 1914- , 6: 139
Leaf, (Wilbur) Munro 1905-1976,
20: 99
Lear, Edward 1812-1888, 18: 182
Leavitt, Jerome E(dward) 1916- ,
23: 115
LeCain, Errol 1941- , 6: 141
Lee, Carol. See Fletcher, Helen Jill,
13: 36
Lee, Dennis (Beynon) 1939- ,
14: 120
Lee, (Nelle) Harper 1926- ,
11: 154
Lee, Manning de V(illeneuve)
1894-1980, 22: 173 (Obituary)
Lee, Mary Price 1934- , 8: 111
Lee, Mildred 1908- , 6: 142
Lee, Robert C. 1931- , 20: 104
Lee, Robert J. 1921- , 10: 77
Lee, Tanith 1947- , 8: 112
Leekley, Thomas B(riggs) 1910- ,
23: 117
Lefler, Irene (Whitney) 1917- ,
12: 131
Le Gallienne, Eva 1899- , 9: 133
LeGrand. See Henderson, LeGrand,
9: 104
Le Guin, Ursula K(roeber)
1929- , 4: 142
Legum, Colin 1919- , 10: 78
Lehr, Delores 1920- , 10: 79
Leichman, Seymour 1933- ,
5: 106
Leighton, Margaret 1896- , 1: 140
Leipold, L. Edmond 1902- ,
16: 189
Leisk, David Johnson 1906-1975,
1: 141
Leitch, Patricia 1933- , 11: 155
Lenard, Alexander 1910-1972,
21: 95 (Obituary)
L'Engle, Madeleine 1918- ,
1: 141

Lengyel, Emil 1895- , 3: 102
Lens, Sidney 1912- , 13: 127
Lenski, Lois 1893-1974, 1: 142
Lent, Blair 1930- , 2: 172
Lent, Henry Bolles 1901-1973,
17: 119
Leodhas, Sorche Nic. See Alger,
Leclaire (Gowans), 15: 1
Leong Gor Yun. See Ellison,
Virginia Howell, 4: 74
Lerner, Marguerite Rush 1924- ,
11: 156
Lerner, Sharon (Ruth) 1938- ,
11: 157
LeShan, Eda J(oan) 1922- ,
21: 95
LeSieg, Theo. See Geisel, Theodor
Seuss, 1: 104
Leslie, Robert Franklin 1911- ,
7: 158
Lesser, Margaret 1899(?)-1979,
22: 173 (Obituary)
Lester, Julius B. 1939- , 12: 132
Le Sueur, Meridel 1900- , 6: 143
Leutscher, Alfred (George)
1913- , 23: 117
Levin, Betty 1927- , 19: 179
Levin, Marcia Obrasky 1918- ,
13: 128
Levin, Meyer 1905- , 21: 96
Levine, I(srael) E. 1923- ,
12: 134
Levine, Joan Goldman, 11: 157
Levine, Rhoda, 14: 122
Levitin, Sonia 1934- , 4: 144
Lewin, Ted 1935- , 21: 98
Lewis, C(live) S(taples)
1898-1963, 13: 129
Lewis, Claudia (Louise) 1907- ,
5: 107
Lewis, E. M., 20: 105
Lewis, Elizabeth Foreman
1892-1958, YABC 2: 243
Lewis, Francine. See Wells, Helen,
2: 266
Lewis, Hilda (Winifred)
1896-1974, 20: 105 (Obituary)
Lewis, Lucia Z. See Anderson,
Lucia (Lewis), 10: 4
Lewis, Paul. See Gerson, Noel
B(ertram), 22: 118
Lewis, Richard 1935- , 3: 104
Lewiton, Mina 1904-1970, 2: 174
Lexau, Joan M., 1: 144
Ley, Willy 1906-1969, 2: 175
Leydon, Rita (Flodén) 1949- ,
21: 100
Libby, Bill. See Libby, William
M., 5: 109
Libby, William M. 1927- , 5: 109
Liberty, Gene 1924- , 3: 106
Liebers, Arthur 1913- , 12: 134
Lieblich, Irene 1923- , 22: 173
Lietz, Gerald S. 1918- , 11: 159
Lifton, Betty Jean, 6: 143

Lightner, A. M. See Hopf, Alice L.
5: 82
Liman, Ellen (Fogelson) 1936- ,
22: 174
Limburg, Peter R(ichard) 1929- ,
13: 147
Lincoln, C(harles) Eric 1924- ,
5: 111
Linde, Gunnel 1924- , 5: 112
Lindgren, Astrid 1907- , 2: 177
Lindop, Edmund 1925- , 5: 113
Lindquist, Jennie Dorothea
1899-1977, 13: 148
Lindquist, Willis 1908- , 20: 105
Lingard, Joan, 8: 113
Lionni, Leo 1910- , 8: 114
Lipinsky de Orlov, Lino S.
1908- , 22: 174
Lipkind, William 1904-1974,
15: 178
Lipman, David 1931- , 21: 101
Lipman, Matthew 1923- , 14: 122
Lippincott, Joseph Wharton
1887-1976, 17: 120
Lippincott, Sarah Lee 1920- ,
22: 177
Lipsyte, Robert 1938- , 5: 114
Lisle, Seward D. See Ellis, Edward
S(ylvester), YABC 1: 116
Liss, Howard 1922- , 4: 145
List, Ilka Katherine 1935- ,
6: 145
Liston, Robert A. 1927- , 5: 114
Litchfield, Ada B(assett) 1916- ,
5: 115
Little, (Flora) Jean 1932- , 2: 178
Littledale, Freya (Lota), 2: 179
Lively, Penelope 1933- , 7: 159
Liversidge, (Henry) Douglas
1913- , 8: 116
Livingston, Myra Cohn 1926- ,
5: 116
Livingston, Richard R(oland)
1922- , 8: 118
Llerena-Aguirre, Carlos Antonio
1952- , 19: 180
Llewellyn, Richard. See Llewellyn
Lloyd, Richard Dafydd
Vyvyan, 11: 160
Llewellyn, T. Harcourt. See
Hamilton, Charles Harold St.
John, 13: 77
Llewellyn Lloyd, Richard Dafydd
Vyvyan 1906- , 11: 160
Lloyd, Errol 1943- , 22: 178
Lloyd, Norman 1909-1980,
23: 118 (Obituary)
Lloyd, (Mary) Norris 1908- ,
10: 79
Lobel, Anita 1934- , 6: 146
Lobel, Arnold 1933- , 6: 147
Lobsenz, Amelia, 12: 135
Lobsenz, Norman M. 1919- ,
6: 148
Lochlons, Colin. See Jackson, C.
Paul, 6: 120

Author Index

Locke, Clinton W. [Collective pseudonym], *1:* 145

Locke, Lucie 1904- , *10:* 81

Loeb, Robert H., Jr. 1917- , *21:* 102

Loeper, John J(oseph) 1929- , *10:* 81

Loescher, Ann Dull 1942- , *20:* 107

Loescher, Gil(burt Damian) 1945- , *20:* 107

Löfgren, Ulf 1931- , *3:* 106

Lofting, Hugh 1886-1947, *15:* 180

Lofts, Norah (Robinson) 1904- , *8:* 119

Logue, Christopher 1926- , *23:* 119

Lomas, Steve. *See* Brennan, Joseph L., *6:* 33

Lomask, Milton 1909- , *20:* 109

London, Jack 1876-1916, *18:* 195

London, Jane. *See* Geis, Darlene, *7:* 101

London, John Griffith. *See* London, Jack, *18:* 195

Lonergan, (Pauline) Joy (Maclean) 1909- , *10:* 82

Long, Helen Beecher [Collective pseudonym], *1:* 146

Long, Judith Elaine 1953- , *20:* 110

Long, Judy. *See* Long, Judith Elaine, *20:* 110

Longfellow, Henry Wadsworth 1807-1882, *19:* 181

Longman, Harold S. 1919- , *5:* 117

Longtemps, Kenneth 1933- , *17:* 123

Longway, A. Hugh. *See* Lang, Andrew, *16:* 178

Loomis, Robert D., *5:* 119

Lopshire, Robert 1927- , *6:* 149

Lord, Beman 1924- , *5:* 119

Lord, (Doreen Mildred) Douglas 1904- , *12:* 136

Lord, John Vernon 1939- , *21:* 103

Lord, Nancy. *See* Titus, Eve, *2:* 240

Lord, Walter 1917- , *3:* 109

Lorraine, Walter (Henry) 1929- , *16:* 191

Loss, Joan 1933- , *11:* 162

Lot, Parson. *See* Kingsley, Charles, *YABC 2:* 179

Lothrop, Harriet Mulford Stone 1844-1924, *20:* 110

Lourie, Helen. *See* Storr, Catherine (Cole), *9:* 181

Love, Katherine 1907- , *3:* 109

Lovelace, Delos Wheeler 1894-1967, *7:* 160

Lovelace, Maud Hart 1892-1980, *2:* 181; *23:* 120 (Obituary)

Lovett, Margaret (Rose) 1915- , *22:* 179

Low, Alice 1926- , *11:* 163

Low, Elizabeth Hammond 1898- , *5:* 120

Low, Joseph 1911- , *14:* 123

Lowe, Jay, Jr.. *See* Loper, John J(oseph), *10:* 81

Lowenstein, Dyno 1914- , *6:* 150

Lowitz, Anson C. 1901(?)-1978, *18:* 214

Lowitz, Sadyebeth (Heath) 1901-1969, *17:* 125

Lowry, Lois 1937- , *23:* 120

Lowry, Peter 1953- , *7:* 160

Lubell, Cecil 1912- , *6:* 150

Lubell, Winifred 1914- , *6:* 151

Lucas, E(dward) V(errall) 1868-1938, *20:* 117

Luckhardt, Mildred Corell 1898- , *5:* 122

Ludlum, Mabel Cleland. *See* Widdemer, Mabel Cleland, *5:* 200

Lueders, Edward (George) 1923- , *14:* 125

Lugard, Flora Louisa Shaw 1852-1929, *21:* 104

Luger, Harriett M(andelay) 1914- , *23:* 122

Luhrmann, Winifred B(ruce) 1934- , *11:* 165

Luis, Earlene W. 1929- , *11:* 165

Lum, Peter. *See* Crowe, Bettina Lum, *6:* 53

Lund, Doris (Herold) 1919- , *12:* 137

Lunn, Janet 1928- , *4:* 146

Luther, Frank 1905-1980, *25:* 173 (Obituary)

Luttrell, Guy L. 1938- , *22:* 180

Lutzker, Edythe 1904- , *5:* 124

Luzzati, Emanuele 1912- , *7:* 161

Lydon, Michael 1942- , *11:* 165

Lyle, Katie Letcher 1938- , *8:* 121

Lynch, Lorenzo 1932- , *7:* 161

Lynch, Patricia (Nora) 1898-1972, *9:* 134

Lynn, Mary. *See* Brokamp, Marilyn, *10:* 15

Lynn, Patricia. *See* Watts, Mabel Pizzey, *11:* 227

Lyon, Elinor 1921- , *6:* 154

Lyon, Lyman R. *See* De Camp, L(yon) Sprague, *9:* 49

Lyons, Dorothy 1907- , *3:* 110

Lystad, Mary (Hanemann) 1928- , *11:* 166

Lyttle, Richard B(ard) 1927- , *23:* 123

Lytton, Edward G(eorge) E(arle) L(ytton) Bulwer-Lytton, Baron 1803-1873, *23:* 125

Maas, Selve, *14:* 127

Mac. *See* MacManus, Seumas, *25:* 175

MacBeth, George 1932- , *4:* 146

MacClintock, Dorcas 1932- , *8:* 122

MacDonald, Anson. *See* Heinlein, Robert A(nson), *9:* 102

MacDonald, Betty (Campbell Bard) 1908-1958, *YABC 1:* 167

Macdonald, Blackie. *See* Emrich, Duncan, *11:* 90

Mac Donald, Golden. *See* Brown, Margaret Wise, *YABC 2:* 9

Macdonald, Marcia. *See* Hill, Grace Livingston, *YABC 2:* 162

Macdonald, Shelagh 1937- , *25:* 174

Macdonald, Zillah K(atherine) 1885- , *11:* 167

MacFarlane, Iris 1922- , *11:* 170

MacGregor-Hastie, Roy 1929- , *3:* 111

MacInnes, Helen 1907- , *22:* 181

MacIntyre, Elisabeth 1916- , *17:* 125

Mack, Stan(ley), *17:* 128

MacKellar, William 1914- , *4:* 148

Mackenzie, Dr. Willard. *See* Stratemeyer, Edward L., *1:* 208

MacLean, Alistair (Stuart) 1923- , *23:* 131

MacLeod, Beatrice (Beach) 1910- , *10:* 82

MacLeod, Ellen Jane (Anderson) 1916- , *14:* 129

MacManus, James. *See* MacManus, Seumas, *25:* 175

MacManus, Seumas 1869-1960, *25:* 175

MacMillan, Annabelle. *See* Quick, Annabelle, *2:* 207

MacPeek, Walter G. 1902-1973, *4:* 148; *25:* 177 (Obituary)

MacPherson, Margaret 1908- , *9:* 135

Macrae, Hawk. *See* Barker, Albert W., *8:* 3

MacRae, Travis. *See* Feagles, Anita (MacRae), *9:* 63

Macumber, Mari. *See* Sandoz, Mari, *5:* 159

Madden, Don 1927- , *3:* 112

Maddison, Angela Mary 1923- , *10:* 82

Maddock, Reginald 1912- , *15:* 184

Madian, Jon 1941- , *9:* 136

Madison, Arnold 1937- , *6:* 155

Madison, Winifred, *5:* 125

Maestro, Giulio 1942- , *8:* 123

Maher, Ramona 1934- , *13:* 149

Mahon, Julia C(unha) 1916- , *11:* 171

Mahony, Elizabeth Winthrop 1948- , *8:* 125

Mahood, Kenneth 1930- , *24:* 140

Mahy, Margaret 1936- , *14:* 129

Maidoff, Ilka List. *See* List, Ilka Katherine, *6:* 145

Maik, Henri. *See* Hecht, Henri Joseph, *9:* 101

Maitland, Antony (Jasper) 1935- , *25:* 177

Malcolmson, Anne. *See* Storch, Anne B. von, *1:* 221

Malcolmson, David 1899- , *6:* 157

Malmberg, Carl 1904- , *9:* 136

Malo, John 1911- , *4:* 149

Maltese, Michael 1908(?)-1981, *24:* 141(Obituary

Malvern, Gladys (?)-1962, *23:* 133

Manchel, Frank 1935- , *10:* 83

Mangione, Jerre 1909- , *6:* 157

Mangurian, David 1938- , *14:* 131

Maniscalco, Joseph 1926- , *10:* 85

Manley, Seon, *15:* 185

Mann, Peggy, *6:* 157

Mannheim, Grete (Salomon) 1909- , *10:* 85

Manning, Rosemary 1911- , *10:* 87

Manning-Sanders, Ruth 1895- , *15:* 186

Manton, Jo. *See* Gittings, Jo Manton, *3:* 76

Manushkin, Fran 1942- , *7:* 161

Mapes, Mary A. *See* Ellison, Virginia Howell, *4:* 74

Mara, Jeanette. *See* Cebulash, Mel, *10:* 19

Marais, Josef 1905-1978, *24:* 141 (Obituary)

Marasmus, Seymour. *See* Rivoli, Mario, *10:* 129

Marcellino. *See* Agnew, Edith J., *11:* 3

Marchant, Bessie 1862-1941, *YABC 2:* 245

Marchant, Catherine. *See* Cookson, Catherine (McMulen), *9:* 42

Marcher, Marion Walden 1890- , *10:* 87

Marcus, Rebecca B(rian) 1907- , *9:* 138

Margolis, Richard J(ules) 1929- , *4:* 150

Mariana. *See* Foster, Marian Curtis, *23:* 73

Marino, Dorothy Bronson 1912- , *14:* 134

Mark, Jan 1943- , *22:* 182

Mark, Pauline (Dahlin) 1913- , *14:* 136

Mark, Polly. *See* Mark, Pauline (Dahlin), *14:* 136

Markins, W. S. *See* Jenkins, Marie M., *7:* 143

Marks, J(ames) M(acdonald) 1921- , *13:* 150

Marks, Margaret L. 1911(?)-1980, *23:* 134 (Obituary)

Marks, Mickey Klar, *12:* 139

Marks, Peter. *See* Smith, Robert Kimmel, *12:* 205

Marks, Stan(ley) 1929- , *14:* 136

Markun, Patricia M(aloney) 1924- , *15:* 189

Marlowe, Amy Bell [Collective pseudonym], *1:* 146

Marokvia, Mireille (Journet) 1918- , *5:* 126

Mars, W. T. *See* Mars, Witold Tadeusz J., *3:* 114

Mars, Witold Tadeusz, J. 1912- , *3:* 114

Marsh, J. E. *See* Marshall, Evelyn, *11:* 172

Marsh, Jean. *See* Marshall, Evelyn, *11:* 172

Marshall, Anthony D(ryden) 1924- , *18:* 215

Marshall, (Sarah) Catherine 1914- , *2:* 182

Marshall, Douglas. *See* McClintock, Marshall, *3:* 119

Marshall, Evelyn 1897- , *11:* 172

Marshall, James 1942- , *6:* 161

Marshall, S(amuel) L(yman) A(twood) 1900-1977, *21:* 107

Marsten, Richard. *See* Hunter, Evan, *25:* 153

Martin, Eugene [Collective pseudonym], *1:* 146

Martin, Fredric. *See* Christopher, Matt, *2:* 58

Martin, J(ohn) P(ercival) 1880(?)-1966, *15:* 190

Martin, Jeremy. *See* Levin, Marcia Obransky, *13:* 128

Martin, Lynne 1923- , *21:* 109

Martin, Marcia. *See* Levin, Marcia Obransky, *13:* 128

Martin, Nancy. *See* Salmon, Annie Elizabeth, *13:* 188

Martin, Patricia Miles 1899- , *1:* 146

Martin, Peter. *See* Chaundler, Christine, *1:* 56; *25:* 83 (Obituary)

Martin, Rene (?)-1977, *20:* 123 (Obituary)

Martin, Vicky. *See* Storey, Victoria Carolyn, *16:* 248

Martineau, Harriet 1802-1876, *YABC 2:* 247

Martini, Teri 1930- , *3:* 116

Marx, Robert F(rank) 1936- , *24:* 142

Marzani, Carl (Aldo) 1912- , *12:* 140

Masefield, John 1878-1967, *19:* 204

Mason, F. van Wyck 1901- , *3:* 117

Mason, Frank W. *See* Mason, F. van Wyck, *3:* 117

Mason, George Frederick 1904- , *14:* 138

Mason, Miriam E(vangeline) 1900- , *2:* 183

Mason, Tally. *See* Derleth, August (William), *5:* 54

Mason, Van Wyck. *See* Mason, F. van Wyck, *3:* 117

Masselman, George 1897-1971, *19:* 214

Massie, Diane Redfield, *16:* 193

Masters, Kelly R. 1897- , *3:* 118

Masters, William. *See* Cousins, Margaret, *2:* 79

Mathis, Sharon Bell 1937- , *7:* 162

Matson, Emerson N(els) 1926- , *12:* 141

Matsui, Tadashi 1926- , *8:* 126

Matsuno, Masako 1935- , *6:* 161

Matte, (Encarnacion) L'Enc 1936- , *22:* 182

Matus, Greta 1938- , *12:* 142

Maves, Mary Carolyn 1916- , *10:* 88

Maves, Paul B(enjamin) 1913- , *10:* 88

Mawicke, Tran 1911- , *15:* 190

Maxon, Anne. *See* Best, Allena Champlin, *2:* 25; *25:* 48 (Obituary)

Maxwell, Arthur S. 1896-1970, *11:* 173

Maxwell, Edith 1923- , *7:* 164

May, Charles Paul 1920- , *4:* 151

May, Julian 1931- , *11:* 175

Mayberry, Florence V(irginia Wilson), *10:* 89

Mayer, Ann M(argaret) 1938- , *14:* 140

Mayer, Mercer 1943- , *16:* 195

Mayne, William 1928- , *6:* 162

Mays, (Lewis) Victor, (Jr.) 1927- , *5:* 126

Mazer, Norma Fox 1931- , *24:* 144

Mazza, Adriana 1928- , *19:* 215

McBain, Ed. *See* Hunter, Evan, *25:* 153

McCaffrey, Anne 1926- , *8:* 127

McCain, Murray 1926- , *7:* 165

McCall, Edith S. 1911- , *6:* 163

McCall, Virginia Nielsen 1909- , *13:* 151

McCallum, Phyllis 1911- , *10:* 90

McCarthy, Agnes 1933- , *4:* 152

McCarty, Rega Kramer 1904- , *10:* 91

McCaslin, Nellie 1914- , *12:* 143

McClintock, Marshall   1906-1967, *3:* 119
McClintock, Mike. *See* McClintock, Marshall, *3:* 119
McClintock, Theodore   1902-1971, *14:* 140
McClinton, Leon   1933- , *11:* 178
McCloskey, Robert   1914- , *2:* 185
McClung, Robert M.   1916- , *2:* 188
McCord, David (Thompson Watson) 1897- , *18:* 217
McCormick, Dell J.   1892-1949, *19:* 216
McCormick, (George) Donald (King)   1911- , *14:* 141
McCoy, Iola Fuller, *3:* 120
McCoy, J(oseph) J(erome)   1917- , *8:* 127
McCrady, Lady   1951- , *16:* 197
McCrea, James   1920- , *3:* 121
McCrea, Ruth   1921- , *3:* 121
McCullough, Frances Monson 1938- , *8:* 129
McCully, Emily Arnold   1939- , *5:* 128
McCurdy, Michael   1942- , *13:* 153
McDearmon, Kay, *20:* 123
McDermott, Beverly Brodsky 1941- , *11:* 179
McDermott, Gerald   1941- , *16:* 199
McDole, Carol. *See* Farley, Carol, *4:* 81
McDonald, Gerald D.   1905-1970, *3:* 123
McDonald, Jill (Masefield) 1927- , *13:* 154
McDonald, Lucile Saunders 1898- , *10:* 92
McDonnell, Lois Eddy   1914- , *10:* 94
McEwen, Robert (Lindley) 1926-1980, *23:* 134 (Obituary)
McFall, Christie   1918- , *12:* 144
McFarland, Kenton D(ean) 1920- , *11:* 180
McGaw, Jessie Brewer   1913- , *10:* 95
McGee, Barbara   1943- , *6:* 165
McGiffin, (Lewis) Lee (Shaffer) 1908- , *1:* 148
McGill, Marci. *See* Ridlon, Marci, *22:* 211
McGinley, Phyllis   1905-1978, *2:* 190; *24:* 145 (Obituary)
McGovern, Ann, *8:* 130
McGowen, Thomas E.   1927- , *2:* 192
McGowen, Tom. *See* McGowen, Thomas, *2:* 192
McGrady, Mike   1933- , *6:* 166
McGraw, Eloise Jarvis   1915- , *1:* 149

McGraw, William Corbin   1916- , *3:* 124
McGregor, Craig   1933- , *8:* 131
McGregor, Iona   1929- , *25:* 179
McGuire, Edna   1899- , *13:* 155
McHargue, Georgess, *4:* 152
McIlwraith, Maureen   1922- , *2:* 193
McKay, Robert W.   1921- ., *15:* 192
McKown, Robin, *6:* 166
McLean, Kathryn (Anderson) 1909-1966, *9:* 140
McLeod, Emilie Warren   1926- , *23:* 135
McMeekin, Clark. *See* McMeekin, Isabel McLennan, *3:* 126
McMeekin, Isabel McLennan 1895- , *3:* 126
McMillan, Bruce   1947- , *22:* 183
McMullen, Catherine. *See* Cookson, Catherine (McMullen), *9:* 42
McMurtrey, Martin A(loysius) 1921- , *21:* 110
McNair, Kate, *3:* 127
McNamara, Margaret C(raig) 1915-1981, *24:* 145 (Obituary)
McNeely, Jeannette   1918- , *25:* 180
McNeer, May, *1:* 150
McNeill, Janet   1907- , *1:* 151
McNickle, (William) D'Arcy 1904-1977, *22:* 185 (Obituary)
McNulty, Faith   1918- , *12:* 144
McPherson, James M.   1936- , *16:* 202
McQueen, Mildred Hark   1908- , *12:* 145
McSwigan, Marie   1907-1962, *24:* 146
Mead, Margaret   1901-1978, *20:* 123 (Obituary)
Mead, Russell (M., Jr.)   1935- , *10:* 96
Meade, Ellen (Roddick)   1936- , *5:* 130
Meade, Marion   1934- , *23:* 136
Meader, Stephen W(arren)   1892- , *1:* 153
Meadow, Charles T(roub)   1929- , *23:* 136
Meadowcroft, Enid LaMonte. *See* Wright, Enid Meadowcroft, *3:* 267
Meaker, M. J. *See* Meaker, Marijane, *20:* 124
Meaker, Marijane   1927- , *20:* 124
Means, Florence Crannell 1891-1980, *1:* 154; *25:* 181 (Obituary)
Medary, Marjorie   1890- , *14:* 143
Medearis, Mary   1915- , *5:* 130
Mee, Charles L., Jr.   1938- , *8:* 132
Meeker, Oden   1918(?)-1976, *14:* 144

Meeks, Esther MacBain, *1:* 155
Mehdevi, Alexander   1947- , *7:* 166
Mehdevi, Anne (Marie) Sinclair, *8:* 132
Meigs, Cornelia Lynde 1884-1973, *6:* 167
Melcher, Frederic Gershom 1879-1963, *22:* 185 (Obituary)
Melcher, Marguerite Fellows 1879-1969, *10:* 96
Melin, Grace Hathaway 1892-1973, *10:* 96
Mellersh, H(arold) E(dward) L(eslie)   1897- , *10:* 97
Meltzer, Milton   1915- , *1:* 156
Melville, Anne. *See* Potter, Margaret (Newman), *21:* 119
Melwood, Mary. *See* Lewis, E. M., *20:* 105
Melzack, Ronald   1929- , *5:* 130
Memling, Carl   1918-1969, *6:* 169
Mendel, Jo [House pseudonym]. *See* Bond, Gladys Baker, *14:* 41
Meng, Heinz (Karl)   1924- , *13:* 157
Mercer, Charles (Edward)   1917- , *16:* 203
Meredith, David William. *See* Miers, Earl Schenck, *1:* 160
Merriam, Eve   1916- , *3:* 128
Merrill, Jean (Fairbanks)   1923- , *1:* 158
Metcalf, Suzanne. *See* Baum, L(yman) Frank, *18:* 7
Meyer, Carolyn   1935- , *9:* 140
Meyer, Edith Patterson   1895- , *5:* 131
Meyer, F(ranklyn) E(dward) 1932- , *9:* 142
Meyer, Jean Shepherd   1929- , *11:* 181
Meyer, Jerome Sydney 1895-1975, *3:* 129; *25:* 181 (Obituary)
Meyer, June. *See* Jordan, June, *4:* 131
Meyer, Louis A(lbert)   1942- , *12:* 147
Meyer, Renate   1930- , *6:* 170
Meyers, Susan   1942- , *19:* 216
Meynier, Yvonne (Pollet)   1908- , *14:* 146
Micale, Albert   1913- , *22:* 185
Micklish, Rita   1931- , *12:* 147
Miers, Earl Schenck   1910- , *1:* 160
Miklowitz, Gloria D.   1927- , *4:* 154
Mikolaycak, Charles   1937- , *9:* 143
Miles, Betty   1928- , *8:* 132
Miles, Miska. *See* Martin, Patricia Miles, *1:* 146
Milgrom, Harry   1912- , *25:* 181

Milhous, Katherine 1894-1977, *15:* 192

Militant. *See* Sandburg, Carl (August), *8:* 177

Millar, Barbara F. 1924- , *12:* 149

Miller, Albert G(riffith) 1905- , *12:* 150

Miller, Alice P(atricia McCarthy), *22:* 187

Miller, Don 1923- , *15:* 194

Miller, Doris R. *See* Mosesson, Gloria R(ubin), *24:* 153

Miller, Eddie. *See* Miller, Edward, *8:* 134

Miller, Edward 1905-1974, *8:* 134

Miller, Helen M(arkley), *5:* 133

Miller, Jane (Judith) 1925- , *15:* 196

Miller, John. *See* Samachson, Joseph, *3:* 182

Miller, Mary Beth 1942- , *9:* 145

Milne, A(lan) A(lexander) 1882-1956, *YABC 1:* 174

Milne, Lorus J., *5:* 133

Milne, Margery, *5:* 134

Milotte, Alfred G(eorge) 1904- , *11:* 181

Milton, Hilary (Herbert) 1920- , *23:* 137

Milton, John R(onald) 1924- , *24:* 147

Minarik, Else Holmelund 1920- , *15:* 197

Miner, Lewis S. 1909- , *11:* 183

Minier, Nelson. *See* Stoutenburg, Adrien, *3:* 217

Mintonye, Grace, *4:* 156

Mirsky, Jeannette 1903- , *8:* 135

Mirsky, Reba Paeff 1902-1966, *1:* 161

Miskovits, Christine 1939- , *10:* 98

Miss Francis. *See* Horwich, Francis R., *11:* 142

Miss Read. *See* Saint, Dora Jessie, *10:* 132

Mitchell, (Sibyl) Elyne (Keith) 1913- , *10:* 98

Mitchell, Yvonne 1925-1979, *24:* 148 (Obituary)

Mitchison, Naomi Margaret (Haldane) 1897- , *24:* 148

Mizumura, Kazue, *18:* 222

Moe, Barbara 1937- , *20:* 126

Moeri, Louise 1924- , *24:* 151

Moffett, Martha (Leatherwood) 1934- , *8:* 136

Mohn, Viola Kohl 1914- , *8:* 138

Mohr, Nicholasa 1935- , *8:* 138

Molarsky, Osmond 1909- , *16:* 204

Molloy, Paul 1920- , *5:* 135

Moncure, Jane Belk, *23:* 139

Monjo, F(erdinand) N. 1924-1978, *16:* 206

Monroe, Lyle. *See* Heinlein, Robert A(nson), *9:* 102

Monsell, Helen (Albee) 1895-1971, *24:* 152

Montana, Bob 1920-1975, *21:* 110(Obituary)

Montgomery, Constance. *See* Cappell, Constance, *22:* 65

Montgomery, Elizabeth Rider, *3:* 132

Montgomery, L(ucy) M(aud) 1874-1942, *YABC 1:* 182

Montgomery, Rutherford George 1894- , *3:* 134

Montresor, Beni 1926- , *3:* 136

Moody, Ralph Owen 1898- , *1:* 162

Moon, Carl 1879-1948, *25:* 182

Moon, Grace 1877(?)-1947, *25:* 185

Moon, Sheila (Elizabeth) 1910- , *5:* 136

Moor, Emily. *See* Deming, Richard, *24:* 83

Moore, Anne Carroll 1871-1961, *13:* 158

Moore, Clement Clarke 1779-1863, *18:* 224

Moore, Eva 1942- , *20:* 127

Moore, Fenworth. *See* Stratemeyer, Edward L., *1:* 208

Moore, Janet Gaylord 1905- , *18:* 236

Moore, John Travers 1908- , *12:* 151

Moore, Margaret Rumberger 1903- , *12:* 154

Moore, Marianne (Craig) 1887-1972, *20:* 128

Moore, Regina. *See* Dunne, Mary Collins, *11:* 83

Moore, Rosalie. *See* Brown, Rosalie (Gertrude) Moore, *9:* 26

Moore, Ruth, *23:* 142

Moore, S. E., *23:* 142

Mordvinoff, Nicolas 1911-1973, *17:* 129

More, Caroline. *See* Cone, Molly Lamken, *1:* 66

More, Caroline. *See* Strachan, Margaret Pitcairn, *14:* 193

Morey, Charles. *See* Fletcher, Helen Jill, *13:* 36

Morey, Walt 1907- , *3:* 139

Morgan, Jane. *See* Cooper, James Fenimore, *19:* 68

Morgan, Lenore 1908- , *8:* 139

Morgan, Shirley 1933- , *10:* 99

Morrah, Dave. *See* Morrah, David Wardlaw, Jr., *10:* 100

Morrah, David Wardlaw, Jr. 1914- , *10:* 100

Morressy, John 1930- , *23:* 143

Morris, Desmond (John) 1928- , *14:* 146

Morris, Robert A. 1933- , *7:* 166

Morrison, Gert W. *See* Stratemeyer, Edward L., *1:* 208

Morrison, Lillian 1917- , *3:* 140

Morrison, Lucile Phillips 1896- , *17:* 134

Morrison, Velma Ford 1909- , *21:* 110

Morrison, William. *See* Samachson, Joseph, *3:* 182

Morriss, James E(dward) 1932- , *8:* 139

Morrow, Betty. *See* Bacon, Elizabeth, *3:* 14

Morse, Carol. *See* Yeakley, Marjory Hall, *21:* 207

Morse, Dorothy B(ayley) 1906-1979, *24:* 153 (Obituary)

Mort, Vivian. *See* Cromie, Alice Hamilton, *24:* 78

Morton, Miriam 1918- , *9:* 145

Moscow, Alvin 1925- , *3:* 142

Mosel, Arlene 1921- , *7:* 167

Mosesson, Gloria R(ubin), *24:* 153

Moskin, Marietta D(unston) 1928- , *23:* 150

Moss, Don(ald) 1920- , *11:* 183

Motz, Lloyd, *20:* 133

Mountfield, David. *See* Grant, Neil, *14:* 75

Moussard, Jacqueline 1924- , *24:* 154

Mowat, Farley 1921- , *3:* 142

Mulcahy, Lucille Burnett, *12:* 155

Mulgan, Catherine. *See* Gough, Catherine, *24:* 125

Muller, Billex. *See* Ellis, Edward S(ylvester), *YABC 1:* 116

Mullins, Edward S(wift) 1922- , *10:* 101

Mulvihill, William Patrick 1923- , *8:* 140

Mun. *See* Leaf, (Wilbur) Munro, *20:* 99

Munari, Bruno 1907- , *15:* 199

Munce, Ruth Hill 1898- , *12:* 156

Munowitz, Ken 1935-1977, *14:* 149

Munson(-Benson), Tunie 1946- , *15:* 201

Munzer, Martha E. 1899- , *4:* 157

Murphy, Barbara Beasley 1933- , *5:* 137

Murphy, E(mmett) Jefferson 1926- , *4:* 159

Murphy, Pat. *See* Murphy, E(mmett) Jefferson, *4:* 159

Murphy, Robert (William) 1902-1971, *10:* 102

Murray, Marian, *5:* 138

Murray, Michele 1933-1974, *7:* 170

Musgrave, Florence 1902- , *3:* 144

Mussey, Virginia T. H. *See* Ellison, Virginia Howell, *4:* 74

Mutz. *See* Kunstler, Morton, *10:* 73

Myers, Bernice, *9:* 146
Myers, Hortense (Powner) 1913- ,
  10: 102
Myrus, Donald (Richard) 1927- ,
  23: 147

Nash, Linell. *See* Smith, Linell
  Nash, *2:* 227
Nash, (Frediric) Ogden
  1902-1971, *2:* 194
Nast, Elsa Ruth. *See* Watson, Jane
  Werner, *3:* 244
Nathan, Dorothy (Goldeen)
  (?)-1966, *15:* 202
Nathan, Robert 1894- , *6:* 171
Navarra, John Gabriel 1927- ,
  8: 141
Naylor, Penelope 1941- , *10:* 104
Naylor, Phyllis Reynolds 1933- ,
  12: 156
Nazaroff, Alexander I. 1898- ,
  4: 160
Neal, Harry Edward 1906- ,
  5: 139
Nee, Kay Bonner, *10:* 104
Needleman, Jacob 1934- , *6:* 172
Negri, Rocco 1932- , *12:* 157
Neigoff, Anne, *13:* 165
Neigoff, Mike 1920- , *13:* 166
Neilson, Frances Fullerton (Jones)
  1910- , *14:* 149
Neimark, Anne E. 1935- , *4:* 160
Nelson, Esther L. 1928- , *13:* 167
Nelson, Mary Carroll 1929- ,
  23: 147
Nesbit, E(dith) 1858-1924,
  YABC 1: 193
Nesbit, Troy. *See* Folsom, Franklin,
  5: 67
Nespojohn, Katherine V. 1912- ,
  7: 170
Ness, Evaline (Michelow) 1911- ,
  1: 165
Neufeld, John 1938- , *6:* 173
Neumeyer, Peter F(lorian) 1929- ,
  13: 168
Neurath, Marie (Reidemeister)
  1898- , *1:* 166
Neville, Emily Cheney 1919- ,
  1: 169
Neville, Mary. *See* Woodrich, Mary
  Neville, *2:* 274
Nevins, Albert J. 1915- , *20:* 134
Newberry, Clare Turlay 1903- ,
  1: 170
Newbery, John 1713-1767,
  20: 135
Newell, Crosby. *See* Bonsall,
  Crosby (Barbara Newell), *23:* 6
Newell, Edythe W. 1910- ,
  11: 185
Newell, Hope (Hockenberry)
  1896-1965, *24:* 154
Newlon, Clarke, *6:* 174

Newman, Robert (Howard)
  1909- , *4:* 161
Newman, Shirlee Petkin 1924- ,
  10: 105
Newton, James R(obert) 1935- ,
  23: 149
Newton, Suzanne 1936- , *5:* 140
Nic Leodhas, Sorche. *See* Alger,
  Leclaire (Gowans), *15:* 1
Nichols, Cecilia Fawn 1906- ,
  12: 159
Nichols, (Joanna) Ruth 1948- ,
  15: 204
Nickelsburg, Janet 1893- ,
  11: 185
Nickerson, Betty. *See* Nickerson,
  Elizabeth, *14:* 150
Nickerson, Elizabeth 1922- ,
  14: 150
Nicol, Ann. *See* Turnbull, Ann
  (Christine), *18:* 281
Nicolas. *See* Mordvinoff, Nicolas,
  17: 129
Nicolay, Helen 1866-1954,
  YABC 1: 204
Nicole, Christopher Robin 1930- ,
  5: 141
Nielsen, Kay (Rasmus)
  1886-1957, *16:* 210
Nielsen, Virginia. *See* McCall,
  Virginia Nielsen, *13:* 151
Nixon, Joan Lowery 1927- ,
  8: 143
Nixon, K. *See* Nixon, Kathleen
  Irene (Blundell), *14:* 152
Nixon, Kathleen Irene (Blundell),
  14: 152
Noble, Iris 1922- , *5:* 142
Nodset, Joan M. *See* Lexau, Joan
  M., *1:* 144
Nolan, Jeannette Covert 1897- ,
  2: 196
Noonan, Julia 1946- , *4:* 163
Norcross, John. *See* Conroy, Jack
  (Wesley), *19:* 65
Nordhoff, Charles (Bernard)
  1887-1947, *23:* 150
Nordstrom, Ursula, *3:* 144
Norman, James. *See* Schmidt,
  James Norman, *21:* 141
Norris, Gunilla B(rodde) 1939- ,
  20: 139
North, Andrew. *See* Norton, Alice
  Mary, *1:* 173
North, Captain George. *See*
  Stevenson, Robert Louis,
  YABC 2: 307
North, Joan 1920- , *16:* 218
North, Robert. *See* Withers, Carl
  A., *14:* 261
North, Sterling 1906-1974, *1:* 171
Norton, Alice Mary 1912- ,
  1: 173
Norton, Andre. *See* Norton, Alice
  Mary, *1:* 173
Norton, Browning. *See* Norton,

Frank R(owland) B(rowning),
  10: 107
Norton, Frank R(owland)
  B(rowning) 1909- , *10:* 107
Norton, Mary 1903- , *18:* 236
Nowell, Elizabeth Cameron,
  12: 160
Nussbaumer, Paul (Edmond)
  1934- , *16:* 218
Nyce, (Nellie) Helene von Strecker
  1885-1969, *19:* 218
Nyce, Vera 1862-1925, *19:* 219
Nye, Robert 1939- , *6:* 174

Oakes, Vanya 1909- , *6:* 175
Oakley, Don(ald G.) 1927- ,
  8: 144
Oakley, Helen 1906- , *10:* 107
Obrant, Susan 1946- , *11:* 186
O'Brien, Robert C. *See* Conly,
  Robert Leslie, *23:* 45
O'Carroll, Ryan. *See* Markun,
  Patricia M(aloney), *15:* 189
O'Connell, Peg. *See* Ahern,
  Margaret McCrohan, *10:* 2
O'Connor, Patrick. *See* Wibberley,
  Leonard, *2:* 271
O'Connor, Richard 1915-1975,
  21: 111 (Obituary)
O'Daniel, Janet 1921- , *24:* 155
O'Dell, Scott 1903- , *12:* 161
Odenwald, Robert P(aul)
  1899-1965, *11:* 187
Oechsli, Kelly 1918- , *5:* 143
Offit, Sidney 1928- , *10:* 108
Ofosu-Appiah, L(awrence) H(enry)
  1920- , *13:* 170
Ogan, George F. 1912- , *13:* 171
Ogan, M. G. [Joint pseudonym].
  See Ogan, George F. and
  Margaret E. (Nettles), *13:* 171
Ogan, Margaret E. (Nettles)
  1923- , *13:* 171
Ogburn, Charlton, Jr. 1911- ,
  3: 145
O'Hara, Mary. *See* Alsop, Mary
  O'Hara, *2:* 4; *24:* 26 (Obituary)
Ohlsson, Ib 1935- , *7:* 171
Olcott, Frances Jenkins
  1872(?)-1963, *19:* 220
Olds, Elizabeth 1896- , *3:* 146
Olds, Helen Diehl 1895-1981,
  9: 148; *25:* 186 (Obituary)
Oldstyle, Jonathan. *See* Irving,
  Washington, *YABC 2:* 164
O'Leary, Brian 1940- , *6:* 176
Oliver, John Edward 1933- ,
  21: 112
Olmstead, Lorena Ann 1890- ,
  13: 172
Olney, Ross R. 1929- , *13:* 173
Olschewski, Alfred 1920- , *7:* 172
Olsen, Ib Spang 1921- , *6:* 177

Olugebefola, Ademole 1941- ,
    15: 204
Ommanney, F(rancis) D(ownes)
    1903-1980, 23: 159
O'Neill, Mary L(e Duc) 1908- ,
    2: 197
Opie, Iona 1923- , 3: 148
Opie, Peter 1918- , 3: 149
Oppenheim, Joanne 1934- ,
    5: 146
Orbach, Ruth Gary 1941- ,
    21: 112
Orgel, Doris 1929- , 7: 173
Orleans, Ilo 1897-1962, 10: 110
Ormondroyd, Edward 1925- ,
    14: 153
Ormsby, Virginia H(aire), 11: 187
Orth, Richard. See Gardner,
    Richard, 24: 119
Osborne, Chester G. 1915- ,
    11: 188
Osborne, David. See Silverberg,
    Robert, 13: 206
Osborne, Leone Neal 1914- ,
    2: 198
Osmond, Edward 1900- , 10: 110
Ossoli, Sarah Margaret (Fuller)
    marchesa d' 1810-1850,
    25: 186
Otis, James. See Kaler, James Otis,
    15: 151
Ouida. See De La Ramée, (Marie)
    Louise, 20: 26
Ousley, Odille 1896- , 10: 111
Owen, Caroline Dale. See
    Snedecker, Caroline Dale
    (Parke), YABC 2: 296
Owen, Clifford. See Hamilton,
    Charles Harold St. John, 13: 77
Oxenbury, Helen 1938- , 3: 151

Packer, Vin. See Meaker, Marijane,
    20: 124
Page, Eileen. See Heal, Edith,
    7: 123
Page, Eleanor. See Coerr, Eleanor,
    1: 64
Pahz, (Anne) Cheryl Suzanne
    1949- , 11: 189
Pahz, James Alon 1943- , 11: 190
Paice, Margaret 1920- , 10: 111
Paine, Roberta M. 1925- ,
    13: 174
Paisley, Tom. See Bethancourt, T.
    Ernesto, 11: 27
Palazzo, Anthony D. 1905-1970,
    3: 152
Palazzo, Tony. See Palazzo,
    Anthony D., 3: 152
Palder, Edward L. 1922- , 5: 146
Pallas, Norvin 1918- , 23: 160
Palmer, C(yril) Everard 1930- ,
    14: 153

Palmer, (Ruth) Candida 1926- ,
    11: 191
Palmer, Heidi 1948- , 15: 206
Palmer, Juliette 1930- , 15: 208
Panetta, George 1915-1969,
    15: 210
Pansy. See Alden, Isabella
    (Macdonald), YABC 2: 1
Panter, Carol 1936- , 9: 150
Papashvily, George 1898-1978,
    17: 135
Papashvily, Helen (Waite) 1906- ,
    17: 141
Pape, D(onna) L(ugg) 1930- ,
    2: 198
Paradis, Adrian A(lexis) 1912- ,
    1: 175
Paradis, Marjorie (Bartholomew)
    1886(?)-1970, 17: 143
Parish, Peggy 1927- , 17: 144
Park, Bill. See Park, W(illiam)
    B(ryan), 22: 188
Park, Ruth, 25: 190
Park, W(illiam) B(ryan) 1936- ,
    22: 188
Parker, Elinor 1906- , 3: 155
Parker, Nancy Winslow 1930- ,
    10: 113
Parker, Richard 1915- , 14: 156
Parker, Robert. See Boyd, Waldo
    T., 18: 35
Parkinson, Ethelyn M(inerva)
    1906- , 11: 192
Parks, Edd Winfield 1906-1968,
    10: 114
Parks, Gordon (Alexander
    Buchanan) 1912- , 8: 145
Parley, Peter. See Goodrich, Samuel
    Griswold, 23: 82
Parlin, John. See Graves, Charles
    Parlin, 4: 94
Parnall, Peter 1936- , 16: 220
Parr, Lucy 1924- , 10: 115
Parrish, Mary. See Cousins,
    Margaret, 2: 79
Parrish, (Frederick) Maxfield
    1870-1966, 14: 158
Parry, Marian 1924- , 13: 175
Pascal, David 1918- , 14: 174
Paschal, Nancy. See Trotter, Grace
    V(iolet), 10: 180
Patent, Dorothy Hinshaw 1940- ,
    22: 190
Paterson, Katherine (Womeldorf)
    1932- , 13: 176
Paton, Alan (Stewart) 1903- ,
    11: 194
Paton Walsh, Gillian 1939- ,
    4: 164
Patterson, Lillie G., 14: 174
Paul, Aileen 1917- , 12: 164
Paul, James 1936- , 23: 161
Pauli, Hertha 1909- , 3: 155
Paull, Grace A. 1898- , 24: 156
Paulsen, Gary 1939- , 22: 192

Paulson, Jack. See Jackson, C.
    Paul, 6: 120
Pavel, Frances 1907- , 10: 116
Payson, Dale 1943- , 9: 150
Payzant, Charles, 18: 239
Payzant, Jessie Mercer Knechtel.
    See Shannon, Terry, 21: 147
Paz, A. See Pahz, James Alon,
    11: 190
Paz, Zan. See Pahz, Cheryl
    Suzanne, 11: 189
Peake, Mervyn 1911-1968,
    23: 162
Peale, Norman Vincent 1898- ,
    20: 140
Pearce, (Ann) Philippa, 1: 176
Peare, Catherine Owens 1911- ,
    9: 152
Pease, Howard 1894-1974, 2: 199;
    25: 191 (Obituary)
Peck, Anne Merriman 1884- ,
    18: 240
Peck, Richard 1934- , 18: 242
Peck, Robert Newton III 1928- ,
    21: 113
Peeples, Edwin A. 1915- , 6: 181
Peet, Bill. See Peet, William B.,
    2: 201
Peet, William Bartlett 1915- ,
    2: 201
Pelaez, Jill 1924- , 12: 165
Pellowski, Anne 1933- , 20: 145
Pelta, Kathy 1928- , 18: 245
Peltier, Leslie C(opus) 1900- ,
    13: 177
Pembury, Bill. See Groom, Arthur
    William, 10: 53
Pendennis, Arthur, Esquire. See
    Thackeray, William
    Makepeace, 23: 223
Pender, Lydia 1907- , 3: 157
Pendery, Rosemary, 7: 174
Penn, Ruth Bonn. See Rosenberg,
    Ethel, 3: 176
Pennage, E. M. See Finkel, George
    (Irvine), 8: 59
Penrose, Margaret. See Stratemeyer,
    Edward L., 1: 208
Pepe, Phil(ip) 1935- , 20: 145
Peppe, Rodney 1934- , 4: 164
Percy, Charles Henry. See Smith,
    Dodie, 4: 194
Perera, Thomas Biddle 1938- ,
    13: 179
Perkins, Marlin 1905- , 21: 114
Perl, Lila, 6: 182
Perl, Susan 1922- , 22: 193
Perlmutter, O(scar) William
    1920-1975, 8: 149
Perrault, Charles 1628-1703,
    25: 192
Perrine, Mary 1913- , 2: 203
Pershing, Marie. See Schultz, Pearle
    Henriksen, 21: 142
Peters, Caroline. See Betz, Eva
    Kelly, 10: 10

Peters, S. H. See Porter, William
Sydney, YABC 2: 259
Petersham, Maud (Fuller)
1890-1971, 17: 146
Petersham, Miska 1888-1960,
17: 149
Peterson, Hans 1922- , 8: 149
Peterson, Harold L(eslie) 1922- ,
8: 151
Peterson, Helen Stone 1910- ,
8: 152
Petie, Haris 1915- , 10: 118
Petrides, Heidrun 1944- , 19: 222
Petrovskaya, Kyra. See Wayne,
Kyra Petrovskaya, 8: 213
Petry, Ann (Lane), 5: 148
Pevsner, Stella, 8: 154
Peyton, K. M. See Peyton,
Kathleen (Wendy), 15: 211
Peyton, Kathleen (Wendy) 1929- ,
15: 211
Pfeffer, Susan Beth 1948- ,
4: 166
Phelan, Mary Kay 1914- , 3: 158
Philbrook, Clem(ent E.) 1917- ,
24: 158
Phillips, Irv. See Phillips, Irving
W., 11: 196
Phillips, Irving W. 1908- ,
11: 196
Phillips, Jack. See Sandburg, Carl
(August), 8: 177
Phillips, Leon. See Gerson, Noel
B(ertram), 22: 118
Phillips, Loretta (Hosey) 1893- ,
10: 119
Phillips, Louis 1942- , 8: 155
Phillips, Mary Geisler 1881-1964,
10: 119
Phillips, Prentice 1894- , 10: 119
Phillpotts, Eden 1862-1960,
24: 159
Phipson, Joan. See Fitzhardinge,
Joan M., 2: 107
Phiz. See Browne, Hablot Knight,
21: 13
Phleger, Marjorie Temple, 1: 176
Piaget, Jean 1896-1980, 23: 166
(Obituary)
Piatti, Celestino 1922- , 16: 222
Picard, Barbara Leonie 1917- ,
2: 205
Pienkowski, Jan 1936- , 6: 182
Pierce, Katherine. See St. John,
Wylly Folk, 10: 132
Pierce, Ruth (Ireland) 1936- ,
5: 148
Pierik, Robert 1921- , 13: 180
Pike, E(dgar) Royston 1896- ,
22: 194
Pilarski, Laura 1926- , 13: 181
Pilgrim, Anne. See Allan, Mabel
Esther, 5: 2
Pilkington, Francis Meredyth
1907- , 4: 166

Pilkington, Roger (Windle)
1915- , 10: 120
Pine, Tillie S(chloss) 1897- ,
13: 182
Pinkwater, Manus 1941- , 8: 156
Piper, Roger. See Fisher, John
(Oswald Hamilton), 15: 115
Piper, Watty. See Bragg, Mabel
Caroline, 24: 52
Piro, Richard 1934- , 7: 176
Pitrone, Jean Maddern 1920- ,
4: 167
Pitz, Henry C(larence) 1895-1976,
4: 167; 24: 162 (Obituary)
Pizer, Vernon 1918- , 21: 116
Place, Marian T. 1910- , 3: 160
Plaidy, Jean. See Hibbert, Eleanor,
2: 134
Platt, Kin 1911- , 21: 117
Plimpton, George (Ames) 1927- ,
10: 121
Plomer, William (Charles Franklin)
1903-1973, 24: 163
Plowman, Stephanie 1922- ,
6: 184
Pluckrose, Henry (Arthur) 1931- ,
13: 183
Plum, J. See Wodehouse, P(elham)
G(renville), 22: 241
Plummer, Margaret 1911- ,
2: 206
Podendorf, Illa E., 18: 247
Poe, Edgar Allan 1809-1849,
23: 167
Pohl, Frederik 1919- , 24: 165
Pohlmann, Lillian (Grenfell)
1902- , 11: 196
Pointon, Robert. See Rooke,
Daphne (Marie), 12: 178
Pola. See Watson, Pauline, 14: 235
Polatnick, Florence T. 1923- ,
5: 149
Polder, Markus. See Krüss, James,
8: 104
Polhamus, Jean Burt 1928- ,
21: 118
Politi, Leo 1908- , 1: 177
Polking, Kirk 1925- , 5: 149
Polland, Madeleine A. 1918- ,
6: 185
Pollock, Mary. See Blyton, Enid
(Mary), 25: 48
Polseno, Jo, 17: 153
Pomerantz, Charlotte, 20: 146
Pond, Alonzo W(illiam) 1894- ,
5: 150
Poole, Gray Johnson 1906- ,
1: 179
Poole, Josephine 1933- , 5: 152
Poole, Lynn 1910-1969, 1: 179
Portal, Colette 1936- , 6: 186
Porter, Katherine Anne
1890-1980, 23: 192 (Obituary)
Porter, Sheena 1935- , 24: 166
Porter, William Sydney
1862-1910, YABC 2: 259

Posell, Elsa Z., 3: 160
Posten, Margaret L(ois) 1915- ,
10: 123
Potter, (Helen) Beatrix 1866-1943,
YABC 1: 205
Potter, Margaret (Newman)
1926- , 21: 119
Potter, Marian 1915- , 9: 153
Potter, Miriam Clark 1886-1965,
3: 161
Powell, Richard Stillman. See
Barbour, Ralph Henry, 16: 27
Powers, Anne. See Schwartz, Anne
Powers, 10: 142
Powers, Margaret. See Heal, Edith,
7: 123
Prelutsky, Jack, 22: 195
Preussler, Otfried 1923- , 24: 167
Price, Christine 1928-1980,
3: 162; 23: 192 (Obituary)
Price, Garrett 1896-1979, 22: 197
(Obituary)
Price, Jennifer. See Hoover, Helen
(Drusilla Blackburn), 12: 100
Price, Lucie Locke. See Locke,
Lucie, 10: 81
Price, Olive 1903- , 8: 157
Price, Susan 1955- , 25: 206
Prieto, Mariana B(eeching)
1912- , 8: 160
Prince, J(ack) H(arvey) 1908- ,
17: 155
Pringle, Laurence 1935- , 4: 171
Proctor, Everitt. See Montgomery,
Rutherford, 3: 134
Provensen, Alice 1918- , 9: 154
Provensen, Martin 1916- , 9: 155
Pryor, Helen Brenton 1897-1972,
4: 172
Pudney, John (Sleigh) 1909-1977,
24: 168
Pugh, Ellen T. 1920- , 7: 176
Pullein-Thompson, Christine
1930- , 3: 164
Pullein-Thompson, Diana, 3: 165
Pullein-Thompson, Josephine,
3: 166
Purdy, Susan Gold 1939- , 8: 161
Purscell, Phyllis 1934- , 7: 177
Putnam, Arthur Lee. See Alger,
Horatio, Jr., 16: 3
Pyle, Howard 1853-1911, 16: 224
Pyne, Mable Mandeville
1903-1969, 9: 155

Quackenbush, Robert M. 1929- ,
7: 177
Quammen, David 1948- , 7: 179
Quarles, Benjamin 1904- ,
12: 166
Queen, Ellery, Jr. See Holding,
James, 3: 85
Quick, Annabelle 1922- , 2: 207

Quin-Harkin, Janet 1941- ,
  18: 247
Quinn, Elisabeth 1881-1962,
  22: 197
Quinn, Vernon. *See* Quinn,
  Elisabeth, *22:* 197

Rabe, Berniece 1928- , *7:* 179
Rabe, Olive H(anson) 1887-1968,
  13: 183
Rackham, Arthur 1867-1939,
  15: 213
Radford, Ruby L(orraine)
  1891-1971, *6:* 186
Radlauer, Edward 1921- , *15:* 227
Radlauer, Ruth (Shaw) 1926- ,
  15: 229
Radley, Gail 1951- , *25:* 206
Raebeck, Lois 1921- , *5:* 153
Raftery, Gerald (Bransfield)
  1905- , *11:* 197
Raiff, Stan 1930- , *11:* 197
Ralston, Jan. *See* Dunlop, Agnes
  M. R., *3:* 62
Ramal, Walter. *See* de la Mare,
  Walter, *16:* 73
Ranadive, Gail 1944- , *10:* 123
Rand, Paul 1914- , *6:* 188
Randall, Florence Engel 1917- ,
  5: 154
Randall, Janet. *See* Young, Janet
  Randall and Young, Robert
  W., *3:* 268-269
Randall, Robert. *See* Silverberg,
  Robert, *13:* 206
Randall, Ruth Painter 1892-1971,
  3: 167
Randolph, Lieutenant J. H. *See*
  Ellis, Edward S(ylvester),
  YABC 1: 116
Rands, William Brighty
  1823-1882, *17:* 156
Ranney, Agnes V. 1916- , *6:* 189
Ransome, Arthur (Michell)
  1884-1967, *22:* 198
Rapaport, Stella F(read), *10:* 126
Raphael, Elaine (Chionchio)
  1933- , *23:* 192
Rappaport, Eva 1924- , *6:* 189
Raskin, Edith (Lefkowitz) 1908- ,
  9: 156
Raskin, Ellen 1928- , *2:* 209
Raskin, Joseph 1897- , *12:* 166
Rathjen, Carl H(enry) 1909- ,
  11: 198
Rau, Margaret 1913- , *9:* 157
Raucher, Herman 1928- , *8:* 162
Ravielli, Anthony 1916- , *3:* 169
Rawlings, Marjorie Kinnan
  1896-1953, *YABC 1:* 218
Rawls, (Woodrow) Wilson
  1913- , *22:* 205
Ray, Deborah 1940- , *8:* 163

Ray, Irene. *See* Sutton, Margaret
  Beebe, *1:* 213
Ray, JoAnne 1935- , *9:* 157
Ray, Mary (Eva Pedder) 1932- ,
  2: 210
Raymond, Robert. *See* Alter, Robert
  Edmond, *9:* 8
Rayner, Mary 1933- , *22:* 207
Razzell, Arthur (George) 1925- ,
  11: 199
Razzi, James 1931- , *10:* 126
Read, Elfreida 1920- , *2:* 211
Read, Piers Paul 1941- , *21:* 119
Redding, Robert Hull 1919- ,
  2: 212
Redway, Ralph. *See* Hamilton,
  Charles Harold St. John, *13:* 77
Redway, Ridley. *See* Hamilton,
  Charles Harold St. John, *13:* 77
Reed, Betty Jane 1921- , *4:* 172
Reed, Gwendolyn E(lizabeth)
  1932- , *21:* 120
Reed, William Maxwell
  1871-1962, *15:* 230
Reeder, Colonel Red. *See* Reeder,
  Russell P., Jr., *4:* 174
Reeder, Russell P., Jr. 1902- ,
  4: 174
Rees, Ennis 1925- , *3:* 169
Reeves, James 1909- , *15:* 231
Reeves, Joyce 1911- , *17:* 158
Reeves, Ruth Ellen. *See* Ranney,
  Agnes V., *6:* 189
Reggiani, Renée, *18:* 248
Reid, Barbara 1922- , *21:* 121
Reid, Eugenie Chazal 1924- ,
  12: 167
Reid, John Calvin, *21:* 122
Reid,, (Thomas) Mayne
  1818-1883, *24:* 170
Reid Banks, Lynne 1929- ,
  22: 208
Reinfeld, Fred 1910-1964, *3:* 170
Reiss, Johanna de Leeuw 1932- ,
  18: 250
Reiss, John J., *23:* 193
Reit, Seymour, *21:* 123
Reit, Sy. *See* Reit, Seymour,
  21: 123
Remi, Georges 1907- , *13:* 183
Renault, Mary. *See* Challans, Mary,
  23: 33
Rendina, Laura Cooper 1902- ,
  10: 127
Renick, Marion (Lewis) 1905- ,
  1: 180
Renlie, Frank H. 1936- , *11:* 200
Renvoize, Jean 1930- , *5:* 157
Resnick, Seymour 1920- ,
  23: 193
Retla, Robert. *See* Alter, Robert
  Edmond, *9:* 8
Reuter, Carol (Joan) 1931- ,
  2: 213
Rey, H(ans) A(ugusto) 1898-1977,
  1: 181

Reyher, Becky. *See* Reyher,
  Rebecca Hourwich, *18:* 253
Reyher, Rebecca Hourwich
  1897- , *18:* 253
Reynolds, Malvina 1900-1978,
  24: 173 (Obituary)
Rhys, Megan. *See* Williams,
  Jeanne, *5:* 202
Ricciuti, Edward R(aphael)
  1938- , *10:* 110
Rice, Elizabeth 1913- , *2:* 213
Rice, Inez 1907- , *13:* 186
Rice, James 1934- , *22:* 210
Rich, Elaine Sommers 1926- ,
  6: 190
Rich, Josephine 1912- , *10:* 129
Richard, Adrienne 1921- , *5:* 157
Richards, Frank. *See* Hamilton,
  Charles Howard St. John,
  13: 77
Richards, Hilda. *See* Hamilton,
  Charles Howard St. John,
  13: 77
Richards, Laura E(lizabeth Howe)
  1850-1943, *YABC 1:* 224
Richardson, Grace Lee. *See*
  Dickson, Naida, *8:* 41
Richardson, Robert S(hirley)
  1902- , *8:* 164
Richoux, Pat 1927- , *7:* 180
Richter, Conrad 1890-1968,
  3: 171
Richter, Hans Peter 1925- ,
  6: 191
Ridge, Antonia, *7:* 181
Ridley, Nat, Jr. *See* Stratemeyer,
  Edward L., *1:* 208
Ridlon, Marci 1942- , *22:* 211
Riedman, Sarah R(egal) 1902- ,
  1: 183
Riesenberg, Felix, Jr. 1913-1962,
  23: 194
Rikhoff, Jean 1928- , *9:* 158
Riley, James Whitcomb
  1849-1916, *17:* 159
Ringi, Kjell Arne Sörensen
  1939- , *12:* 168
Rinkoff, Barbara (Jean) 1923- ,
  4: 174
Rios, Tere. *See* Versace, Marie
  Teresa, *2:* 254
Ripley, Elizabeth Blake
  1906-1969, *5:* 158
Ripper, Charles L. 1929- , *3:* 174
Ritchie, Barbara (Gibbons), *14:* 176
Ritts, Paul 1920(?)-1980, *25:* 207
  (Obituary)
Riverside, John. *See* Heinlein,
  Robert A(nson), *9:* 102
Rivoli, Mario 1943- , *10:* 129
Roach, Marilynne K(athleen)
  1946- , *9:* 158
Roach, Portia. *See* Takakjian,
  Portia, *15:* 273
Robbins, Raleigh. *See* Hamilton,
  Charles Harold St. John, *13:* 77

Robbins, Ruth   1917(?)- , *14:* 177
Roberts, David. *See* Cox, John
    Roberts, *9:* 42
Roberts, Jim. *See* Bates, Barbara
    S(nedeker), *12:* 34
Roberts, Terence. *See* Sanderson,
    Ivan T., *6:* 195
Roberts, Willo Davis   1928- ,
    21: 125
Robertson, Barbara (Anne)
    1931- , *12:* 172
Robertson, Don   1929- , *8:* 165
Robertson, Dorothy Lewis   1912- ,
    12: 173
Robertson, Jennifer (Sinclair)
    1942- , *12:* 174
Robertson, Keith   1914- , *1:* 184
Robins, Seelin. *See* Ellis, Edward
    S(ylvester), *YABC 1:* 116
Robinson, Adjai   1932- , *8:* 165
Robinson, Barbara (Webb)
    1927- , *8:* 166
Robinson, Charles   1870-1937,
    17: 171
Robinson, Charles   1931- , *6:* 192
Robinson, Jan M.   1933- , *6:* 194
Robinson, Jean O.   1934- , *7:* 182
Robinson, Joan (Mary) G(ale
    Thomas)   1910- , *7:* 183
Robinson, Maudie (Millian Oller)
    1914- , *11:* 200
Robinson, Ray(mond Kenneth)
    1920- , *23:* 194
Robinson, T(homas) H(eath)
    1869-1950, *17:* 178
Robinson, W(illiam) Heath
    1872-1944, *17:* 184
Robison, Bonnie   1924- , *12:* 175
Robottom, John   1934- , *7:* 185
Roche, A. K. [Joint pseudonym].
    See Abisch, Roslyn Kroop,
    9: 3. *See* Kaplan, Boche,
    24: 134
Rockwell, Norman (Percevel)
    1894-1978, *23:* 195
Rockwell, Thomas   1933- , *7:* 185
Rockwood, Roy [Collective
    pseudonym], *1:* 185
Rodgers, Mary   1931- , *8:* 167
Rodman, Emerson. *See* Ellis,
    Edward S(ylvester),
    YABC 1: 116
Rodman, Maia. *See*
    Wojciechowska, Maia, *1:* 228
Rodman, Selden   1909- , *9:* 159
Rodowsky, Colby   1932- , *21:* 126
Roe, Harry Mason. *See*
    Stratemeyer, Edward L., *1:* 208
Rogers, (Thomas) Alan
    (Stinchcombe)   1937- , *2:* 215
Rogers, Frances   1888-1974,
    10: 130
Rogers, Matilda   1894- , *5:* 158
Rogers, Pamela   1927- , *9:* 160
Rogers, Robert. *See* Hamilton,
    Charles Harold St. John, *13:* 77

Rogers, W(illiam) G(arland)
    1896-1978, *23:* 208
Rojan. *See* Rojankovsky, Feodor
    (Stepanovich), *21:* 127
Rojankovsky, Feodor (Stepanovich)
    1891-1970, *21:* 127
Rokeby-Thomas, Anna E(lma)
    1911- , *15:* 233
Roland, Albert   1925- , *11:* 201
Rolerson, Darrell A(llen)   1946- ,
    8: 168
Roll, Winifred   1909- , *6:* 194
Rollins, Charlemae Hill   1897- ,
    3: 175
Rongen, Björn   1906- , *10:* 131
Rood, Ronald (N.)   1920- ,
    12: 177
Rooke, Daphne (Marie)   1914- ,
    12: 178
Rose, Anne, *8:* 168
Rose, Florella. *See* Carlson, Vada
    F., *16:* 64
Rose, Wendy   1948- , *12:* 180
Rosen, Sidney   1916- , *1:* 185
Rosen, Winifred   1943- , *8:* 169
Rosenbaum, Maurice   1907- ,
    6: 195
Rosenberg, Ethel, *3:* 176
Rosenberg, Nancy Sherman
    1931- , *4:* 177
Rosenberg, Sharon   1942- , *8:* 171
Rosenbloom, Joseph   1928- ,
    21: 131
Rosenblum, Richard   1928- ,
    11: 202
Rosenburg, John M.   1918- ,
    6: 195
Ross, David   1896-1975, *20:* 147
    (Obituary)
Ross, Diana. *See* Denney, Diana,
    25: 90
Ross, Tony   1938- , *17:* 203
Rossetti, Christiana (Georgina)
    1830-1894, *20:* 147
Roth, Arnold   1929- , *21:* 133
Rothkopf, Carol Z.   1929- , *4:* 177
Rothman, Joel   1938- , *7:* 186
Rounds, Glen (Harold)   1906- ,
    8: 171
Rourke, Constance (Mayfield)
    1885-1941, *YABC 1:* 232
Rowland, Florence Wightman
    1900- , *8:* 173
Roy, Liam. *See* Scarry, Patricia,
    2: 218
Rubel, Nicole   1953- , *18:* 255
Ruchlis, Hy   1913- , *3:* 177
Rudolph, Marguerita   1908- ,
    21: 133
Rudomin, Esther. *See* Hautzig,
    Esther, *4:* 105
Ruedi, Norma Paul. *See* Ainsworth,
    Norma, *9:* 4
Ruhen, Olaf   1911- , *17:* 204
Rukeyser, Muriel   1913-1980,
    22: 211 (Obituary)

Rumsey, Marian (Barritt)   1928- ,
    16: 236
Rushmore, Helen   1898- , *3:* 178
Rushmore, Robert (William)
    1926- , *8:* 174
Ruskin, Ariane   1935- , *7:* 187
Ruskin, John   1819-1900, *24:* 173
Russell, Charlotte. *See* Rathjen,
    Carl H(enry), *11:* 198
Russell, Franklin   1926- , *11:* 203
Russell, Helen Ross   1915- ,
    8: 175
Russell, Patrick. *See* Sammis, John,
    4: 178
Russell, Solveig Paulson   1904- ,
    3: 179
Ruth, Rod   1912- , *9:* 160
Ruthin, Margaret, *4:* 178
Rutgers van der Loeff, An(na)
    Basenau   1910- , *22:* 211
Rutz, Viola Larkin   1932- ,
    12: 181
Ruzicka, Rudolph   1883-1978,
    24: 181 (Obituary)
Ryan, Cheli Durán, *20:* 154
Ryan, John (Gerald Christopher)
    1921- , *22:* 214
Ryan, Peter (Charles)   1939- ,
    15: 235
Rydberg, Ernest E(mil)   1901- ,
    21: 135
Rydell, Wendell. *See* Rydell,
    Wendy, *4:* 178
Rydell, Wendy, *4:* 178
Ryden, Hope, *8:* 176

Sabin, Edwin Legrand   1870-1952,
    YABC 2: 277
Sabuso. *See* Phillips, Irving W.,
    11: 196
Sachs, Marilyn   1927- , *3:* 180
Sackett, S(amuel) J(ohn)   1928- ,
    12: 181
Sackson, Sid   1920- , *16:* 237
Sadie, Stanley (John)   1930- ,
    14: 177
Sage, Juniper [Joint pseudonym].
    See Brown, Margaret Wise,
    YABC 2: 9
Sage, Juniper. *See* Hurd, Edith,
    2: 150
Sagsoorian, Paul   1923- , *12:* 183
Saint, Dora Jessie   1913- , *10:* 132
St. Briavels, James. *See* Wood,
    James Playsted, *1:* 229
Saint Exupéry, Antoine de
    1900-1944, *20:* 154
St. George, Judith   1931- ,
    13: 187
St. John, Philip. *See* Del Rey,
    Lester, *22:* 97
St. John, Wylly Folk   1908- ,
    10: 132

St. Meyer, Ned. *See* Stratemeyer, Edward L., *1:* 208

St. Tamara. *See* Kolba, Tamara, *22:* 171

Saito, Michiko. *See* Fujiwara, Michiko, *15:* 120

Salmon, Annie Elizabeth 1899- , *13:* 188

Salten, Felix. *See* Salzmann, Siegmund, *25:* 207

Salter, Cedric. *See* Knight, Francis Edgar, *14:* 112

Salzmann, Siegmund 1869-1945, *25:* 207

Samachson, Dorothy 1914- , *3:* 182

Samachson, Joseph 1906- , *3:* 182

Sammis, John 1942- , *4:* 178

Samson, Anne S(tringer) 1933- , *2:* 216

Samson, Joan 1937-1976, *13:* 189

Samuels, Charles 1902- , *12:* 183

Samuels, Gertrude, *17:* 206

Sanchez, Sonia 1934- , *22:* 214

Sanchez-Silva, Jose Maria 1911- , *16:* 237

Sandberg, (Karin) Inger 1930- , *15:* 238

Sandberg, Lasse (E. M.) 1924- , *15:* 239

Sandburg, Carl (August) 1878-1967, *8:* 177

Sandburg, Charles A. *See* Sandburg, Carl (August), *8:* 177

Sandburg, Helga 1918- , *3:* 184

Sanderlin, George 1915- , *4:* 180

Sanderlin, Owenita (Harrah) 1916- , *11:* 204

Sanderson, Ivan T. 1911-1973, *6:* 195

Sandin, Joan 1942- , *12:* 185

Sandoz, Mari (Susette) 1901-1966, *5:* 159

Sanger, Marjory Bartlett 1920- , *8:* 181

Sarac, Roger. *See* Caras, Roger A(ndrew), *12:* 65

Sarg, Anthony Fredrick. *See* Sarg, Tony, *YABC 1:* 233

Sarg, Tony 1880-1942, *YABC 1:* 233

Sargent, Robert 1933- , *2:* 216

Sargent, Shirley 1927- , *11:* 205

Sarnoff, Jane 1937- , *10:* 133

Saroyan, William 1908-1981, *23:* 210; *24:* 181 (Obituary)

Sasek, Miroslav 1916-1980, *16:* 239; *23:* 218 (Obituary)

Sattler, Helen Roney 1921- , *4:* 181

Saunders, Caleb. *See* Heinlein, Robert A(nson), *9:* 102

Saunders, Keith 1910- , *12:* 186

Saunders, Rubie (Agnes) 1929- , *21:* 136

Savage, Blake. *See* Goodwin, Harold Leland, *13:* 73

Savery, Constance (Winifred) 1897- , *1:* 186

Saville, (Leonard) Malcolm 1901- , *23:* 218

Saviozzi, Adriana. *See* Mazza, Adriana, *19:* 215

Savitt, Sam, *8:* 181

Savitz, Harriet May 1933- , *5:* 161

Sawyer, Ruth 1880-1970, *17:* 207

Sayers, Frances Clarke 1897- , *3:* 185

Sazer, Nina 1949- , *13:* 191

Scabrini, Janet 1953- , *13:* 191

Scagnetti, Jack 1924- , *7:* 188

Scanlon, Marion Stephany, *11:* 206

Scarf, Maggi. *See* Scarf, Maggie, *5:* 162

Scarf, Maggie 1932- , *5:* 162

Scarry, Patricia (Murphy) 1924- , *2:* 218

Scarry, Patsy. *See* Scarry, Patricia, *2:* 218

Scarry, Richard (McClure) 1919- , *2:* 218

Schaefer, Jack 1907- , *3:* 186

Schaeffer, Mead 1898- , *21:* 137

Schechter, Betty (Goodstein) 1921- , *5:* 163

Scheer, Julian (Weisel) 1926- , *8:* 183

Scheffer, Victor B. 1906- , *6:* 197

Schell, Orville H. 1940- , *10:* 136

Schemm, Mildred Walker 1905- , *21:* 139

Scherf, Margaret 1908- , *10:* 136

Schick, Eleanor 1942- , *9:* 161

Schiff, Ken 1942- , *7:* 189

Schiller, Andrew 1919- , *21:* 139

Schiller, Barbara (Heyman) 1928- , *21:* 140

Schisgall, Oscar 1901- , *12:* 187

Schlein, Miriam 1926- , *2:* 222

Schloat, G. Warren, Jr. 1914- , *4:* 181

Schmid, Eleonore 1939- , *12:* 188

Schmiderer, Dorothy 1940- , *19:* 223

Schmidt, Elizabeth 1915- , *15:* 242

Schmidt, James Norman 1912- , *21:* 141

Schneider, Herman 1905- , *7:* 189

Schneider, Nina 1913- , *2:* 222

Schnirel, James R(einhold) 1931- , *14:* 178

Schoen, Barbara 1924- , *13:* 192

Scholastica, Sister Mary. *See* Jenkins, Marie M., *7:* 143

Scholefield, Edmund O. *See* Butterworth, W. E., *5:* 40

Schone, Virginia, *22:* 215

Schoonover, Frank (Earle) 1877-1972, *24:* 182

Schoor, Gene 1921- , *3:* 188

Schreiber, Elizabeth Anne (Ferguson) 1947- , *13:* 192

Schreiber, Ralph W(alter) 1942- , *13:* 194

Schroeder, Ted 1931(?)-1973, *20:* 163 (Obituary)

Schulman, Janet 1933- , *22:* 216

Schulman, L(ester) M(artin) 1934- , *13:* 194

Schultz, Gwendolyn, *21:* 142

Schultz, James Willard 1859-1947, *YABC 1:* 238

Schultz, Pearle Henriksen 1918- , *21:* 142

Schulz, Charles M(onroe) 1922- , *10:* 137

Schurfranz, Vivian 1925- , *13:* 194

Schutzer, A. I. 1922- , *13:* 195

Schwartz, Alvin 1927- , *4:* 183

Schwartz, Anne Powers 1913- , *10:* 142

Schwartz, Charles W(alsh) 1914- , *8:* 184

Schwartz, Elizabeth Reeder 1912- , *8:* 184

Schwartz, Stephen (Lawrence) 1948- , *19:* 224

Scoppettone, Sandra 1936- , *9:* 162

Scott, Cora Annett (Pipitone) 1931- , *11:* 207

Scott, Dan [House pseudonym]. *See* Barker, S. Omar, *10:* 8

Scott, Dan. *See* Stratemeyer, Edward L., *1:* 208

Scott, John 1912-1976, *14:* 178

Scott, John Anthony 1916- , *23:* 219

Scott, John M(artin) 1913- , *12:* 188

Scott, Tony. *See* Scott, John Anthony, *23:* 219

Scott, Sir Walter 1771-1832, *YABC 2:* 280

Scribner, Charles, Jr. 1921- , *13:* 195

Scuro, Vincent 1951- , *21:* 144

Seamands, Ruth (Childers) 1916- , *9:* 163

Searight, Mary W(illiams) 1918- , *17:* 211

Searle, Kathryn Adrienne 1942- , *10:* 143

Sears, Stephen W. 1932- , *4:* 184

Sebastian, Lee. *See* Silverberg, Robert, *13:* 206

Sechrist, Elizabeth Hough 1903- , *2:* 224

Sedges, John. *See* Buck, Pearl S., *1:* 36; *25:* 63

Seed, Jenny 1930- , *8:* 186

Seed, Sheila Turner 1937(?)-1979, *23:* 220 (Obituary)

Author Index

Seeger, Elizabeth 1889-1973,
20: 163 (Obituary)
Seeger, Pete(r) 1919- , 13: 196
Segal, Lore 1928- , 4: 186
Seidelman, James Edward 1926- ,
6: 197
Seidman, Laurence (Ivan) 1925- ,
15: 244
Seigal, Kalman 1917- , 12: 190
Seignobosc, Francoise 1897-1961,
21: 145
Seixas, Judith S. 1922- , 17: 212
Sejima, Yoshimasa 1913- , 8: 186
Selden, George. See Thompson,
George Selden, 4: 204
Self, Margaret Cabell 1902- ,
24: 191
Selig, Sylvie 1942- , 13: 199
Selsam, Millicent E(llis) 1912- ,
1: 188
Seltzer, Meyer 1932- , 17: 213
Sendak, Maurice (Bernard)
1928- , 1: 190
Sengler, Johanna 1924- , 18: 255
Serage, Nancy 1924- , 10: 143
Seredy, Kate 1899-1975, 1: 193;
24: 193 (Obituary)
Seroff, Victor I(lyitch) 1902- ,
12: 190
Serraillier, Ian (Lucien) 1912- ,
1: 193
Servello, Joe 1932- , 10: 143
Service, Robert W(illiam)
1874(?)-1958, 20: 163
Serwer, Blanche L. 1910- ,
10: 144
Seton, Anya, 3: 188
Seton, Ernest Thompson
1860-1946, 18: 257
Seuling, Barbara 1937- , 10: 145
Seuss, Dr. See Geisel, Theodor
Seuss, 1: 104
Severn, Bill. See Severn, William
Irving, 1: 195
Severn, David. See Unwin, David
S(torr), 14: 217
Severn, William Irving 1914- ,
1: 195
Seward, Prudence 1926- , 16: 242
Sewell, Anna 1820-1878, 24: 193
Sexton, Anne (Harvey)
1928-1974, 10: 146
Seymour, Alta Halverson, 10: 147
Shafer, Robert E(ugene) 1925- ,
9: 164
Shahn, Ben(jamin) 1898-1969,
21: 146 (Obituary)
Shahn, Bernarda Bryson. See
Bryson, Bernarda, 9: 26
Shanks, Ann Zane (Kushner),
10: 148
Shannon, Terry, 21: 147
Shapp, Martha 1910- , 3: 189
Sharfman, Amalie, 14: 179
Sharma, Partap 1939- , 15: 244

Sharmat, Marjorie Weinman
1928- , 4: 187
Sharp, Margery 1905- , 1: 196
Sharpe, Mitchell R(aymond)
1924- , 12: 191
Shaw, Arnold 1909- , 4: 189
Shaw, Charles (Green) 1892-1974,
13: 200
Shaw, Flora Louisa. See Lugard,
Flora Louisa Shaw, 21: 104
Shaw, Ray, 7: 190
Shaw, Richard 1923- , 12: 192
Shay, Arthur 1922- , 4: 189
Shecter, Ben 1935- , 16: 243
Sheedy, Alexandra Elizabeth
1962- , 19: 225
Sheehan, Ethna 1908- , 9: 165
Shekerjian, Regina Tor, 16: 244
Sheldon, Ann [Collective
pseudonym], 1: 198
Sheldon, Aure 1917-1976, 12: 194
Shelton, William Roy 1919- ,
5: 164
Shemin, Margaretha 1928- ,
4: 190
Shepard, Ernest Howard
1879-1976, 3: 191; 24: 201
(Obituary)
Shephard, Esther 1891- , 5: 165
Shepherd, Elizabeth, 4: 191
Sherburne, Zoa 1912- , 3: 194
Sherman, Diane (Finn) 1928- ,
12: 194
Sherman, Elizabeth. See Friskey,
Margaret Richards, 5: 72
Sherman, Nancy. See Rosenberg,
Nancy Sherman, 4: 177
Sherrod, Jane. See Singer, Jane
Sherrod, 4: 192
Sherry, (Dulcie) Sylvia 1932- ,
8: 187
Sherwan, Earl 1917- , 3: 195
Shiefman, Vicky, 22: 217
Shields, Charles 1944- , 10: 149
Shimin, Symeon 1902- , 13: 201
Shinn, Everett 1876-1953, 21: 148
Shippen, Katherine B(inney)
1892-1980, 1: 198; 23: 221
(Obituary)
Shipton, Eric 1907- , 10: 151
Shirreffs, Gordon D(onald)
1914- , 11: 207
Shortall, Leonard W., 19: 226
Shotwell, Louisa R. 1902- ,
3: 196
Showalter, Jean B(reckinridge),
12: 195
Showers, Paul C. 1910- , 21: 152
Shub, Elizabeth, 5: 166
Shulevitz, Uri 1935- , 3: 197
Shulman, Alix Kates 1932- ,
7: 191
Shulman, Irving 1913- , 13: 204
Shumsky, Zena. See Collier, Zena,
23: 41

Shura, Mary Francis. See Craig,
Mary Francis, 6: 52
Shuttlesworth, Dorothy, 3: 200
Shyer, Marlene Fanta, 13: 205
Sibley, Don 1922- , 12: 195
Siculan, Daniel 1922- , 12: 197
Sidjakov, Nicolas 1924- , 18: 272
Sidney, Margaret. See Lothrop,
Harriet Mulford Stone, 20: 110
Silcock, Sara Lesley 1947- ,
12: 199
Silver, Ruth. See Chew, Ruth,
7: 45
Silverberg, Robert, 13: 206
Silverman, Mel(vin Frank)
1931-1966, 9: 166
Silverstein, Alvin 1933- , 8: 188
Silverstein, Virginia B(arbara
Opshelor) 1937- , 8: 190
Simon, Charlie May. See Fletcher,
Charlie May, 3: 70
Simon, Howard 1903-1979,
21: 154 (Obituary)
Simon, Joe. See Simon, Joseph H.,
7: 192
Simon, Joseph H. 1913- , 7: 192
Simon, Martin P(aul William)
1903-1969, 12: 200
Simon, Mina Lewiton. See Lewiton,
Mina, 2: 174
Simon, Norma 1927- , 3: 201
Simon, Seymour 1931- , 4: 191
Simon, Shirley (Schwartz) 1921- ,
11: 210
Simonetta, Linda 1948- , 14: 179
Simonetta, Sam 1936- , 14: 180
Simont, Marc 1915- , 9: 167
Simpson, Colin 1908- , 14: 181
Simpson, Myrtle L(illias) 1931- ,
14: 181
Sinclair, Upton (Beall) 1878-1968,
9: 168
Singer, Isaac. See Singer, Isaac
Bashevis, 3: 203
Singer, Isaac Bashevis 1904- ,
3: 203
Singer, Jane Sherrod 1917- ,
4: 192
Singer, Susan (Mahler) 1941- ,
9: 170
Sisson, Rosemary Anne 1923- ,
11: 211
Sivulich, Sandra (Jeanne) Stroner
1941- , 9: 171
Skelly, James R(ichard) 1927- ,
17: 215
Skinner, Constance Lindsay
1882-1939, YABC 1: 247
Skinner, Cornelia Otis 1901- ,
2: 225
Skorpen, Liesel Moak 1935- ,
3: 206
Skurzynski, Gloria (Joan) 1930- ,
8: 190
Slackman, Charles B. 1934- ,
12: 200

Slade, Richard 1910-1971, *9:* 171

Sleator, William 1945- , *3:* 207

Sleigh, Barbara 1906- , *3:* 208

Slicer, Margaret O. 1920- ,
    4: 193

Slobodkin, Florence (Gersh)
    1905- , *5:* 167

Slobodkin, Louis 1903- , *1:* 199

Slobodkina, Esphyr 1909- ,
    1: 201

Slote, Alfred 1926- , *8:* 192

Small, Ernest. *See* Lent, Blair,
    2: 172

Smaridge, Norah 1903- , *6:* 198

Smiley, Virginia Kester 1923- ,
    2: 227

Smith, Beatrice S(chillinger),
    12: 201

Smith, Betty 1896-1972, *6:* 199

Smith, Bradford 1909-1964,
    5: 168

Smith, Datus C(lifford), Jr.
    1907- , *13:* 208

Smith, Dodie, *4:* 194

Smith, Dorothy Stafford 1905- ,
    6: 201

Smith, E(lmer) Boyd
    1860-1943- , *YABC 1:* 248

Smith, Eunice Young 1902- ,
    5: 169

Smith, Frances C. 1904- , *3:* 209

Smith, Gary R(ichard) 1932- ,
    14: 182

Smith, George Harmon 1920- ,
    5: 171

Smith, H(arry) Allen 1907-1976,
    20: 171 (Obituary)

Smith, Howard Everett, Jr.
    1927- , *12:* 201

Smith, Hugh L(etcher) 1921-1968,
    5: 172

Smith, Imogene Henderson
    1922- , *12:* 203

Smith, Jean. *See* Smith, Frances C.,
    3: 209

Smith, Jean Pajot 1945- , *10:* 151

Smith, Jessie Willcox 1863-1935,
    21: 155

Smith, Johnston. *See* Crane,
    Stephen (Townley),
    YABC 2: 84

Smith, Lafayette. *See* Higdon, Hal,
    4: 115

Smith, Linell Nash 1932- , *2:* 227

Smith, Marion Hagens 1913- ,
    12: 204

Smith, Marion Jaques 1899- ,
    13: 209

Smith, Mary Ellen, *10:* 152

Smith, Mike. *See* Smith, Mary
    Ellen, *10:* 152

Smith, Nancy Covert 1935- ,
    12: 204

Smith, Norman F. 1920- , *5:* 172

Smith, Robert Kimmel 1930- ,
    12: 205

Smith, Ruth Leslie 1902- , *2:* 228

Smith, Sarah Stafford. *See* Smith,
    Dorothy Stafford, *6:* 201

Smith, Susan Carlton 1923- ,
    12: 207

Smith, Vian (Crocker) 1919-1969,
    11: 213

Smith, Ward. *See* Goldsmith,
    Howard, *24:* 123

Smith, William A., *10:* 153

Smith, William Jay 1918- ,
    2: 229

Smith, Z. Z. *See* Westheimer,
    David, *14:* 242

Snedeker, Caroline Dale (Parke)
    1871-1956, *YABC 2:* 296

Sneve, Virginia Driving Hawk
    1933- , *8:* 193

Sniff, Mr. *See* Abisch, Roslyn
    Kroop, *9:* 3

Snodgrass, Thomas Jefferson. *See*
    Clemens, Samuel Langhorne,
    YABC 2: 51

Snow, Donald Clifford 1917- ,
    16: 246

Snow, Dorothea J(ohnston)
    1909- , *9:* 172

Snyder, Anne 1922- , *4:* 195

Snyder, Jerome 1916-1976,
    20: 171 (Obituary)

Snyder, Zilpha Keatley 1927- ,
    1: 202

Snyderman, Reuven K. 1922- ,
    5: 173

Sobol, Donald J. 1924- , *1:* 203

Soderlind, Arthur E(dwin) 1920- ,
    14: 183

Softly, Barbara (Frewin) 1924- ,
    12: 209

Sohl, Frederic J(ohn) 1916- ,
    10: 154

Solbert, Romaine G. 1925- ,
    2: 232

Solbert, Ronni. *See* Solbert,
    Romaine G., *2:* 232

Solomons, Ikey, Esquire, Jr.. *See*
    Thackeray, William
    Makepeace, *23:* 223

Solonevich, George 1915- ,
    15: 245

Solot, Mary Lynn 1939- , *12:* 210

Sommer, Elyse 1929- , *7:* 192

Sommer, Robert 1929- , *12:* 211

Sommerfelt, Aimee 1892- ,
    5: 173

Sonneborn, Ruth 1899- , *4:* 196

Sorche, Nic Leodhas. *See* Alger,
    Leclaire (Gowans), *15:* 1

Sorensen, Virginia 1912- , *2:* 233

Sorrentino, Joseph N., *6:* 203

Sortor, June Elizabeth 1939- ,
    12: 212

Sortor, Toni. *See* Sortor, June
    Elizabeth, *12:* 212

Soskin, V. H. *See* Ellison, Virginia
    Howell, *4:* 74

Sotomayor, Antonio 1902- ,
    11: 214

Soudley, Henry. *See* Wood, James
    Playsted, *1:* 229

Soule, Gardner (Bosworth)
    1913- , *14:* 183

Soule, Jean Conder 1919- ,
    10: 154

Southall, Ivan 1921- , *3:* 210

Spanfeller, James J(ohn) 1930- ,
    19: 230

Spangenberg, Judith Dunn 1942- ,
    5: 175

Spar, Jerome 1918- , *10:* 156

Sparks, Mary W. 1920- , *15:* 247

Spaulding, Leonard. *See* Bradbury,
    Ray, *11:* 29

Speare, Elizabeth George 1908- ,
    5: 176

Spearing, Judith (Mary Harlow)
    1922- , *9:* 173

Specking, Inez 1890-196(?),
    11: 217

Speicher, Helen Ross (Smith)
    1915- , *8:* 194

Spellman, John W(illard) 1934- ,
    14: 186

Spence, Eleanor (Rachel) 1927- ,
    21: 163

Spencer, Ann 1918- , *10:* 156

Spencer, Cornelia. *See* Yaukey,
    Grace S. *5:* 203

Spencer, Elizabeth 1921- ,
    14: 186

Spencer, William 1922- , *9:* 175

Sperry, Armstrong W. 1897- ,
    1: 204

Sperry, Raymond, Jr. [Collective
    pseudonym], *1:* 205

Spiegelman, Judith M., *5:* 179

Spier, Peter (Edward) 1927- ,
    4: 198

Spilhaus, Athelstan 1911- ,
    13: 209

Spilka, Arnold 1917- , *6:* 203

Spink, Reginald (William) 1905- ,
    11: 217

Spinossimus. *See* White, William,
    16: 276

Spollen, Christopher 1952- ,
    12: 213

Sprigge, Elizabeth 1900-1974,
    10: 157

Spykman, E(lizabeth) C.
    19(?)-1965, *10:* 157

Spyri, Johanna (Heusser)
    1827-1901, *19:* 232

Squire, Miriam. *See* Sprigge,
    Elizabeth, *10:* 157

Squires, Phil. *See* Barker, S. Omar,
    10: 8

S-Ringi, Kjell. *See* Ringi, Kjell,
    12: 168

Stadtler, Bea 1921- , *17:* 215

Stafford, Jean 1915-1979, *22:* 218
    (Obituary)

Stahl, Ben(jamin)   1910- , *5:* 179
Stamaty, Mark Alan   1947- ,
    12: 214
Stambler, Irwin   1924- , *5:* 181
Stanhope, Eric. *See* Hamilton,
    Charles Harold St. John, *13:* 77
Stankevich, Boris   1928- , *2:* 234
Stanley, Robert. *See* Hamilton,
    Charles Harold St. John, *13:* 77
Stanstead, John. *See* Groom, Arthur
    William, *10:* 53
Stapp, Arthur D(onald)
    1906-1972, *4:* 201
Starbird, Kaye   1916- , *6:* 204
Stark, James. *See* Goldston, Robert,
    6: 90
Starkey, Marion L.   1901- ,
    13: 211
Starret, William. *See* McClintock,
    Marshall, *3:* 119
Staunton, Schuyler. *See* Baum,
    L(yman) Frank, *18:* 7
Stearns, Monroe (Mather)   1913- ,
    5: 182
Steele, Chester K. *See* Stratemeyer,
    Edward L., *1:* 208
Steele, Mary Q., *3:* 211
Steele, (Henry) Max(well)   1922- ,
    10: 159
Steele, William O(wen)   1917- ,
    1: 205
Steig, William   1907- , *18:* 275
Stein, M(eyer) L(ewis), *6:* 205
Stein, Mini, *2:* 234
Steinbeck, John (Ernst)
    1902-1968, *9:* 176
Steinberg, Alfred   1917- , *9:* 178
Steinberg, Fred J.   1933- , *4:* 201
Steiner, Barbara A(nnette)   1934- ,
    13: 213
Steiner, Stan(ley)   1925- , *14:* 187
Stephens, Mary Jo   1935- , *8:* 196
Stephens, William M(cLain)
    1925- , *21:* 165
Steptoe, John (Lewis)   1950- ,
    8: 198
Sterling, Dorothy   1913- , *1:* 206
Sterling, Helen. *See* Hoke, Helen
    (L.), *15:* 133
Sterling, Philip   1907- , *8:* 198
Stern, Madeleine B(ettina)   1912- ,
    14: 188
Stern, Philip Van Doren   1900- ,
    13: 215
Stern, Simon   1943- , *15:* 248
Sterne, Emma Gelders   1894-1971,
    6: 205
Steurt, Marjorie Rankin   1888- ,
    10: 159
Stevens, Carla M(cBride)   1928- ,
    13: 217
Stevens, Franklin   1933- , *6:* 206
Stevens, Peter. *See* Geis, Darlene,
    7: 101
Stevenson, Anna (M.)   1905- ,
    12: 216

Stevenson, Augusta, *2:* 235
Stevenson, Burton E(gbert)
    1872-1962, *25:* 213
Stevenson, Janet   1913- , *8:* 199
Stevenson, Robert Louis
    1850-1894, *YABC 2:* 307
Stewart, A(gnes) C(harlotte),
    15: 250
Stewart, Charles. *See* Zurhorst,
    Charles (Stewart, Jr.), *12:* 240
Stewart, Elizabeth Laing   1907- ,
    6: 206
Stewart, John (William)   1920- ,
    14: 189
Stewart, George Rippey
    1895-1980, *3:* 213; *23:* 221
    (Obituary)
Stewart, Mary (Florence Elinor)
    1916- , *12:* 217
Stewart, Robert Neil   1891-1972,
    7: 192
Stiles, Martha Bennett, *6:* 207
Stillerman, Robbie   1947- ,
    12: 219
Stine, G(eorge) Harry   1928- ,
    10: 161
Stinetorf, Louise   1900- , *10:* 162
Stirling, Arthur. *See* Sinclair, Upton
    (Beall), *9:* 168
Stirling, Nora B., *3:* 214
Stirnweis, Shannon   1931- ,
    10: 163
Stobbs, William   1914- , *17:* 216
Stoddard, Edward G.   1923- ,
    10: 164
Stoddard, Hope   1900- , *6:* 207
Stoddard, Sandol. *See* Warburg,
    Sandol Stoddard, *14:* 234
Stoiko, Michael   1919- , *14:* 190
Stokes, Cedric. *See* Beardmore,
    George, *20:* 10
Stokes, Jack (Tilden)   1923- ,
    13: 218
Stolz, Mary (Slattery)   1920- ,
    10: 165
Stone, Alan [Collective
    pseudonym], *1:* 208. *See also*
    Svenson, Andrew E., *2:* 238
Stone, D(avid) K(arl)   1922- ,
    9: 179
Stone, Eugenia   1879-1971, *7:* 193
Stone, Gene. *See* Stone, Eugenia,
    7: 193
Stone, Helen V., *6:* 208
Stone, Irving   1903- , *3:* 215
Stone, Raymond [Collective
    pseudonym], *1:* 208
Stone, Richard A. *See* Stratemeyer,
    Edward L., *1:* 208
Stonehouse, Bernard   1926- ,
    13: 219
Storch, Anne B. von. *See* von
    Storch, Anne B., *1:* 221
Storey, (Elizabeth) Margaret
    (Carlton)   1926- , *9:* 180

Storey, Victoria Carolyn   1945- ,
    16: 248
Storme, Peter. *See* Stern, Philip
    Van Doren, *13:* 215
Storr, Catherine (Cole)   1913- ,
    9: 181
Stoutenburg, Adrien   1916- ,
    3: 217
Stover, Allan C(arl)   1938- ,
    14: 191
Stover, Marjorie Filley   1914- ,
    9: 182
Stowe, Harriet (Elizabeth) Beecher
    1811-1896, *YABC 1:* 250
Strachan, Margaret Pitcairn
    1908- , *14:* 193
Stranger, Joyce. *See* Wilson, Joyce
    M(uriel Judson), *21:* 201
Stratemeyer, Edward L.
    1862-1930, *1:* 208
Stratton-Porter, Gene   1863-1924,
    15: 251
Strayer, E. Ward. *See* Stratemeyer,
    Edward L., *1:* 208
Streano, Vince(nt Catello)   1945- ,
    20: 172
Streatfeild, Noel   1897- , *20:* 173
Street, Julia Montgomery   1898- ,
    11: 218
Strong, Charles. *See* Epstein,
    Samuel, *1:* 87
Ströyer, Poul   1923- , *13:* 221
Stuart, Forbes   1924- , *13:* 222
Stuart, Ian. *See* MacLean, Alistair
    (Stuart), *23:* 131
Stuart, (Hilton) Jesse   1907- ,
    2: 236
Stuart, Sheila. *See* Baker, Mary
    Gladys Steel, *12:* 27
Stubis, Talivaldis   1926- , *5:* 183
Stubley, Trevor (Hugh)   1932- ,
    22: 218
Sture-Vasa, Mary. *See* Alsop,
    Mary, *2:* 4
Sturton, Hugh. *See* Johnston,
    H(ugh) A(nthony) S(tephen),
    14: 87
Sturtzel, Howard A(llison)   1894- ,
    1: 210
Sturtzel, Jane Levington   1903- ,
    1: 212
Styles, Frank Showell   1908- ,
    10: 167
Suba, Susanne, *4:* 202
Subond, Valerie. *See* Grayland,
    Valerie, *7:* 111
Suhl, Yuri   1908- , *8:* 200
Sullivan, George E(dward)
    1927- , *4:* 202
Sullivan, Mary W(ilson)   1907- ,
    13: 224
Sullivan, Thomas Joseph, Jr.
    1947- , *16:* 248
Sullivan, Tom. *See* Sullivan,
    Thomas Joseph, Jr., *16:* 248
Supraner, Robyn   1930- , *20:* 182

Surge, Frank   1931- , *13:* 225
Susac, Andrew   1929- , *5:* 184
Sutcliff, Rosemary   1920- , *6:* 209
Sutherland, Efua (Theodora
    Morgue)   1924- , *25:* 215
Sutherland, Margaret   1941- ,
    15: 271
Suttles, Shirley (Smith)   1922- ,
    21: 166
Sutton, Margaret (Beebe)   1903- ,
    1: 213
Svenson, Andrew E.   1910- ,
    2: 238
Swain, Su Zan (Noguchi)   1916- ,
    21: 169
Swan, Susan   1944- , *22:* 219
Swarthout, Kathryn   1919- ,
    7: 194
Sweeney, James B(artholomew)
    1910- , *21:* 170
Swenson, Allan A(rmstrong)
    1933- , *21:* 172
Swenson, May   1919- , *15:* 271
Swift, David. *See* Kaufmann, John,
    18: 132
Swift, Hildegarde Hoyt
    1890(?)-1977, *20:* 184
    (Obituary)
Swift, Jonathan   1667-1745,
    19: 244
Swiger, Elinor Porter   1927- ,
    8: 202
Swinburne, Laurence   1924- ,
    9: 183
Sylvester, Natalie G(abry)   1922- ,
    22: 222
Syme, (Neville) Ronald   1913- ,
    2: 239
Synge, (Phyllis) Ursula   1930- ,
    9: 184
Sypher, Lucy Johnston   1907- ,
    7: 195
Szasz, Suzanne Shorr   1919- ,
    13: 226
Szekeres, Cyndy   1933- , *5:* 184

Taber, Gladys (Bagg)   1899-1980,
    22: 223 (Obituary)
Tabrah, Ruth Milander   1921- ,
    14: 194
Tait, Douglas   1944- , *12:* 220
Takakjian, Portia   1930- , *15:* 273
Takashima, Shizuye   1928- ,
    13: 227
Talbot, Charlene Joy   1928- ,
    10: 169
Talbot, Toby   1928- , *14:* 195
Talker, T. *See* Rands, William
    Brighty, *17:* 156
Tallcott, Emogene, *10:* 170
Talmadge, Marian, *14:* 196
Tamarin, Alfred, *13:* 229
Tamburine, Jean   1930- , *12:* 221

Tannenbaum, Beulah   1916- ,
    3: 219
Tanner, Louise S(tickney)   1922- ,
    9: 185
Tanobe, Miyuki   1937- , *23:* 222
Tapio, Pat Decker. *See* Kines, Pat
    Decker, *12:* 118
Tarkington, (Newton) Booth
    1869-1946, *17:* 218
Tarry, Ellen   1906- , *16:* 250
Tarshis, Jerome   1936- , *9:* 186
Tashjian, Virginia A.   1921- ,
    3: 220
Tasker, James, *9:* 187
Tate, Ellalice. *See* Hibbert, Eleanor,
    2: 134
Tate, Joan   1922- , *9:* 188
Tatham, Campbell. *See* Elting,
    Mary, *2:* 100
Taylor, Barbara J.   1927- ,
    10: 171
Taylor, Carl   1937- , *14:* 196
Taylor, David   1900-1965, *10:* 172
Taylor, Elizabeth   1912-1975,
    13: 230
Taylor, Florance Walton, *9:* 190
Taylor, Florence M(arion
    Tompkins)   1892- , *9:* 191
Taylor, Herb(ert Norman, Jr.)
    1942- , *22:* 223
Taylor, Mildred D., *15:* 275
Taylor, Robert Lewis   1912- ,
    10: 172
Taylor, Sydney (Brenner), *1:* 214
Taylor, Theodore   1924- , *5:* 185
Teal, Val   1903- , *10:* 174
Teale, Edwin Way   1899-1980,
    7: 196; *25:* 215 (Obituary)
Tee-Van, Helen Damrosch
    1893- , *10:* 176
Telescope, Tom. *See* Newbery,
    John, *20:* 135
Temko, Florence, *13:* 231
Templar, Maurice. *See* Groom,
    Arthur William, *10:* 53
Tenggren, Gustaf   1896- , *18:* 277
Tennant, Kylie   1912- , *6:* 210
ter Haar, Jaap   1922- , *6:* 211
Terhune, Albert Payson
    1872-1942, *15:* 277
Terris, Susan   1937- , *3:* 221
Terry, Luther L(eonidas)   1911- ,
    11: 220
Terry, Walter   1913- , *14:* 198
Terzian, James P.   1915- , *14:* 199
Thacher, Mary McGrath   1933- ,
    9: 192
Thackeray, William Makepeace
    1811-1863, *23:* 223
Tharp, Louise Hall   1898- , *3:* 223
Thayer, Jane. *See* Woolley,
    Catherine, *3:* 265
Thayer, Peter. *See* Wyler, Rose,
    18: 303
Thelwell, Norman   1923- ,
    14: 200

Thieda, Shirley Ann   1943- ,
    13: 233
Thiele, Colin (Milton)   1920- ,
    14: 201
Thistlethwaite, Miles   1945- ,
    12: 223
Thollander, Earl   1922- , *22:* 224
Thomas, H. C.. *See* Keating,
    Lawrence A., *23:* 107
Thomas, J. F. *See* Fleming, Thomas
    J(ames), *8:* 64
Thomas, Joan Gale. *See* Robinson,
    Joan G., *7:* 183
Thomas, Lowell (Jackson), Jr.
    1923- , *15:* 290
Thompson, Christine Pullein. *See*
    Pullein-Thompson, Christine,
    3: 164
Thompson, David H(ugh)   1941- ,
    17: 236
Thompson, Diana Pullein. *See*
    Pullein-Thompson, Diana,
    3: 165
Thompson, George Selden   1929- ,
    4: 204
Thompson, Harlan H.   1894- ,
    10: 177
Thompson, Josephine Pullein. *See*
    Pullein-Thompson, Josephine,
    3: 166
Thompson, Kay   1912- , *16:* 257
Thompson, Stith   1885-1976,
    20: 184 (Obituary)
Thompson, Vivian L.   1911- ,
    3: 224
Thorndyke, Helen Louise
    [Collective pseudonym], *1:* 216
Thorne, Ian. *See* May, Julian,
    11: 175
Thornton, W. B. *See* Burgess,
    Thornton Waldo, *17:* 19
Thorpe, E(ustace) G(eorge)
    1916- , *21:* 173
Thorvall, Kerstin   1925- , *13:* 233
Thum, Marcella, *3:* 226
Thundercloud, Katherine. *See* Witt,
    Shirley Hill, *17:* 247
Thurber, James (Grover)
    1894-1961, *13:* 235
Thwaite, Ann (Barbara Harrop)
    1932- , *14:* 206
Ticheburn, Cheviot. *See* Ainsworth,
    William Harrison, *24:* 21
Tichenor, Tom   1923- , *14:* 206
Timmins, William F., *10:* 177
Tinkelman, Murray   1933- ,
    12: 224
Titmarsh, Michael Angelo. *See*
    Thackeray, William
    Makepeace, *23:* 223
Titus, Eve   1922- , *2:* 240
Tobias, Tobi   1938- , *5:* 187
Todd, Anne Ophelia. *See* Dowden,
    Anne Ophelia, *7:* 69
Todd, Barbara K.   1917- , *10:* 178

Todd, H(erbert) E(atton) 1908- ,
11: 221
Tolkien, J(ohn) R(onald) R(euel)
1892-1973, 2: 242; 24: 201
(Obituary)
Tolles, Martha 1921- , 8: 203
Tolmie, Ken(neth Donald) 1941- ,
15: 291
Tomfool. See Farjeon, Eleanor,
2: 103
Tomlinson, Jill 1931-1976,
3: 227; 24: 201 (Obituary)
Tompert, Ann 1918- , 14: 208
Toner, Raymond John 1908- ,
10: 179
Toonder, Martin. See Groom,
Arthur William, 10: 53
Toothaker, Roy Eugene 1928- ,
18: 280
Tooze, Ruth 1892-1972, 4: 205
Topping, Audrey R(onning)
1928- , 14: 209
Tor, Regina. See Shekerjian, Regina
Tor, 16: 244
Torbert, Floyd James 1922- ,
22: 226
Totham, Mary. See Breinburg,
Petronella, 11: 36
Tournier, Michel 1924- , 23: 232
Townsend, John Rowe 1922- ,
4: 206
Toye, William E(ldred) 1926- ,
8: 203
Traherne, Michael. See Watkins-
Pitchford, D. J., 6: 214
Trapp, Maria (Augusta) von
1905- , 16: 260
Travers, P(amela) L(yndon)
1906- , 4: 208
Trease, (Robert) Geoffrey 1909- ,
2: 244
Tredez, Alain 1926- , 17: 236
Treece, Henry 1911-1966, 2: 246
Tregaskis, Richard 1916- , 3: 228
Trell, Max 1900- , 14: 211
Tremain, Ruthven 1922- , 17: 237
Trent, Timothy. See Malmberg,
Carl, 9: 136
Tresselt, Alvin 1916- , 7: 197
Trevino, Elizabeth B(orton) de
1904- , 1: 216
Trevor, (Lucy) Meriol 1919- ,
10: 180
Trez, Alain. See Tredez, Alain,
17: 236
Tripp, Eleanor B. 1936- , 4: 210
Tripp, Paul, 8: 204
Trivett, Daphne (Harwood)
1940- , 22: 227
Trollope, Anthony 1815-1882,
22: 229
Trost, Lucille Wood 1938- ,
12: 226
Trotter, Grace V(iolet) 1900- ,
10: 180

Tucker, Caroline. See Nolan,
Jeannette, 2: 196
Tudor, Tasha, 20: 184
Tully, John (Kimberley) 1923- ,
14: 212
Tunis, Edwin (Burdett)
1897-1973, 1: 217; 24: 201
(Obituary)
Turkle, Brinton 1915- , 2: 248
Turlington, Bayly 1919- , 5: 187
Turnbull, Agnes Sligh, 14: 213
Turnbull, Ann (Christine) 1943- ,
18: 281
Turner, Alice K. 1940- , 10: 181
Turner, Ann W(arren) 1945- ,
14: 214
Turner, Elizabeth 1774-1846,
YABC 2: 332
Turner, Josie. See Crawford,
Phyllis, 3: 57
Turner, Philip 1925- , 11: 222
Turner, Sheila R.. See Seed, Sheila
Turner, 23: 220 (Obituary)
Turngren, Annette 1902(?)-1980,
23: 233 (Obituary)
Turngren, Ellen (?)-1964, 3: 230
Tusan, Stan 1936- , 22: 236
Twain, Mark. See Clemens, Samuel
Langhorne, YABC 2: 51
Tweedsmuir, Baron. See Buchan,
John, YABC 2: 21
Tyler, Anne 1941- , 7: 198

Ubell, Earl 1926- , 4: 210
Uchida, Yoshiko 1921- , 1: 219
Udall, Jan Beaney 1938- ,
10: 182
Udry, Janice May 1928- , 4: 212
Ullman, James Ramsey
1907-1971, 7: 199
Ulm, Robert 1934-1977, 17: 238
Ulyatt, Kenneth 1920- , 14: 216
Unada. See Gliewe, Unada, 3: 77
Uncle Gus. See Rey, H. A., 1: 181
Uncle Ray. See Coffman, Ramon
Peyton, 4: 53
Underhill, Alice Mertie
1900-1971, 10: 182
Ungerer, Jean Thomas 1931- ,
5: 187
Ungerer, Tomi. See Ungerer, Jean
Thomas, 5: 187
Unkelbach, Kurt 1913- , 4: 213
Unnerstad, Edith 1900- , 3: 230
Unrau, Ruth 1922- , 9: 192
Unstead R(obert) J(ohn) 1915- ,
12: 226
Unsworth, Walt 1928- , 4: 215
Untermeyer, Louis 1885- , 2: 250
Unwin, David S(torr) 1918- ,
14: 217
Unwin, Nora S. 1907- , 3: 233
Usher, Margo Scegge. See
McHargue, Georgess, 4: 152

Uttley, Alice Jane 1884- , 3: 235
Uttley, Alison. See Uttley, Alice
Jane, 3: 235
Utz, Lois 1932- , 5: 189

Vaeth, J(oseph) Gordon 1921- ,
17: 239
Valen, Nanine 1950- , 21: 173
Valens, Evans G., Jr. 1920- ,
1: 220
Van Abbé, Salaman 1883-1955,
18: 282
Van Anrooy, Francine 1924- ,
2: 252
Van Anrooy, Frans. See Van
Anrooy, Francine, 2: 252
Vance, Eleanor Graham 1908- ,
11: 223
Vandenburg, Mary Lou 1943- ,
17: 240
Vander Boom, Mae M., 14: 219
Van der Veer, Judy 1912- ,
4: 216
Vandivert, Rita (Andre) 1905- ,
21: 174
Van Duyn, Janet 1910- , 18: 283
Van Dyne, Edith. See Baum,
L(yman) Frank, 18: 7
Van Leeuwen, Jean 1937- ,
6: 212
Van Lhin, Erik. See Del Rey,
Lester, 22: 97
Van Loon, Hendrik Willem
1882-1944, 18: 284
Van Orden, M(erton) D(ick)
1921- , 4: 218
Van Rensselaer, Alexander (Taylor
Mason) 1892-1962, 14: 219
Van Riper, Guernsey, Jr. 1909- ,
3: 239
Van Stockum, Hilda 1908- ,
5: 191
Van Tuyl, Barbara 1940- ,
11: 224
Van Vogt, A(lfred) E(lton)
1912- , 14: 220
Van Woerkom, Dorothy (O'Brien)
1924- , 21: 176
Van Wyck Mason. See Mason, F.
van Wyck, 3: 117
Van-Wyck Mason, F. See Mason,
F. van Wyck, 3: 117
Varley, Dimitry V. 1906- ,
10: 183
Vasiliu, Mircea 1920- , 2: 254
Vaughan, Carter A. See Gerson,
Noel B(ertram), 22: 118
Vaughan, Harold Cecil 1923- ,
14: 221
Vaughan, Sam(uel) S. 1928- ,
14: 222
Vaughn, Ruth 1935- , 14: 223
Vavra, Robert James 1944- ,
8: 206

Vecsey, George   1939- , *9:* 192

Veglahn, Nancy (Crary)   1937- , *5:* 194

Venable, Alan (Hudson)   1944- , *8:* 206

Vequin, Capini. *See* Quinn, Elisabeth, *22:* 197

Verne, Jules   1828-1905, *21:* 178

Verner, Gerald   1897(?)-1980, *25:* 216 (Obituary)

Verney, John   1913- , *14:* 224

Vernon, (Elda) Louise A(nderson)   1914- , *14:* 225

Vernor, D. *See* Casewit, Curtis, *4:* 43

Verral, Charles Spain   1904- , *11:* 225

Versace, Marie Teresa Rios   1917- , *2:* 254

Vesey, Paul. *See* Allen, Samuel (Washington), *9:* 6

Vestly, Anne-Cath(arina)   1920- , *14:* 228

Vicarion, Count Palmiro. *See* Logue, Christopher, *23:* 119

Vicker, Angus. *See* Felsen, Henry Gregor, *1:* 89

Victor, Edward   1914- , *3:* 240

Viereck, Ellen K.   1928- , *14:* 229

Viereck, Phillip   1925- , *3:* 241

Viertel, Janet   1915- , *10:* 183

Vigna, Judith   1936- , *15:* 292

Viguers, Ruth Hill   1903-1971, *6:* 214

Villiard, Paul   1910-1974, *20:* 188 (Obituary)

Villiers, Alan (John)   1903- , *10:* 184

Vincent, Mary Keith. *See* St. John, Wylly Folk, *10:* 132

Vining, Elizabeth Gray. *See* Gray, Elizabeth Janet, *6:* 93

Vinson, Kathryn   1911- , *21:* 193

Vinton, Iris, *24:* 202

Viorst, Judith, *7:* 200

Visser, W(illiam) F(rederick) H(endrik)   1900-1968, *10:* 186

Vo-Dinh, Mai   1933- , *16:* 271

Vogel, Ilse-Margret   1914- , *14:* 231

Vogel, John H(ollister), Jr.   1950- , *18:* 292

Vogt, Esther Loewen   1915- , *14:* 231

Voight, Virginia Frances   1909- , *8:* 208

von Almedingen, Martha Edith. *See* Almedingen, E. M., *3:* 9

von Klopp, Vahrah. *See* Malvern, Gladys, *23:* 133

von Storch, Anne B.   1910- , *1:* 221

Vosburgh, Leonard (W.)   1912- , *15:* 294

Voyle, Mary. *See* Manning, Rosemary, *10:* 87

Waddell, Evelyn Margaret   1918- , *10:* 186

Wagenheim, Kal   1935- , *21:* 196

Wagner, Sharon B.   1936- , *4:* 218

Wagoner, David (Russell)   1926- , *14:* 232

Wahl, Jan   1933- , *2:* 256

Walden, Amelia Elizabeth, *3:* 242

Waldman, Bruce   1949- , *15:* 297

Waldron, Ann Wood   1924- , *16:* 273

Walker, Barbara K.   1921- , *4:* 219

Walker, David Harry   1911- , *8:* 210

Walker, Diana   1925- , *9:* 193

Walker, Holly Beth. *See* Bond, Gladys Baker, *14:* 41

Walker, Mildred. *See* Schemm, Mildred Walker, *21:* 139

Walker, (Addison) Mort   1923- , *8:* 211

Walker, Pamela   1948- , *24:* 203

Walker, Stephen J.   1951- , *12:* 228

Wallace, Barbara Brooks, *4:* 221

Wallace, Beverly Dobrin   1921- , *19:* 258

Wallace, John A.   1915- , *3:* 243

Wallace, Nigel. *See* Hamilton, Charles Harold St. John, *13:* 77

Waller, Leslie   1923- , *20:* 188

Wallis, G. McDonald. *See* Campbell, Hope, *20:* 19

Wallner, John C.   1945- , *10:* 189

Wallower, Lucille, *11:* 226

Walsh, Jill Paton. *See* Paton Walsh, Gillian, *4:* 164

Walter, Villiam Christian. *See* Andersen, Hans Christian, *YABC 1:* 23

Walters, Audrey   1929- , *18:* 293

Walton, Richard J.   1928- , *4:* 223

Waltrip, Lela (Kingston)   1904- , *9:* 194

Waltrip, Rufus (Charles)   1898- , *9:* 195

Walworth, Nancy Zinsser   1917- , *14:* 233

Wannamaker, Bruce. *See* Moncure, Jane Belk, *23:* 139

Warbler, J. M. *See* Cocagnac, A. M., *7:* 52

Warburg, Sandol Stoddard   1927- , *14:* 234

Ward, Lynd (Kendall)   1905- , *2:* 257

Ward, Martha (Eads)   1921- , *5:* 195

Wardell, Dean. *See* Prince, J(ack) H(arvey), *17:* 155

Ware, Leon (Vernon)   1909- , *4:* 224

Warner, Frank A. [Collective pseudonym], *1:* 222

Warner, Gertrude Chandler   1890- , *9:* 195

Warren, Billy. *See* Warren, William Stephen, *9:* 196

Warren, Elizabeth. *See* Supraner, Robyn, *20:* 182

Warren, Joyce W(illiams)   1935- , *18:* 294

Warren, Mary Phraner   1929- , *10:* 190

Warren, William Stephen   1882-1968, *9:* 196

Warshofsky, Fred   1931- , *24:* 203

Warshofsky, Isaac. *See* Singer, Isaac Bashevis, *3:* 203

Wa-sha-quon-asin. *See* Belaney, Archibald Stansfeld, *24:* 39

Washburne, Heluiz Chandler   1892- , *10:* 192

Waters, John F(rederick)   1930- , *4:* 225

Watkins-Pitchford, D. J.   1905- , *6:* 214

Watson, Clyde   1947- , *5:* 196

Watson, Helen Orr   1892-1978, *24:* 205 (Obituary)

Watson, James   1936- , *10:* 192

Watson, Jane Werner   1915- , *3:* 244

Watson, Pauline   1925- , *14:* 235

Watson, Sally   1924- , *3:* 245

Watson, Wendy (McLeod)   1942- , *5:* 198

Watt, Thomas   1935- , *4:* 226

Watts, Bernadette   1942- , *4:* 226

Watts, Franklin (Mowry)   1904-1978, *21:* 196 (Obituary)

Watts, Mabel Pizzey   1906- , *11:* 227

Waugh, Dorothy, *11:* 228

Wayland, Patrick. *See* O'Connor, Richard, *21:* 111

Wayne, Kyra Petrovskaya   1918- , *8:* 213

Wayne, Richard. *See* Decker, Duane, *5:* 53

Waystaff, Simon. *See* Swift, Jonathan, *19:* 244

Weales, Gerald (Clifford)   1925- , *11:* 229

Weaver, Ward. *See* Mason, F. van Wyck, *3:* 117

Webb, Christopher. *See* Wibberley, Leonard, *2:* 271

Webber, Irma E(leanor Schmidt)   1904- , *14:* 237

Weber, Alfons   1921- , *8:* 215

Weber, Lenora Mattingly   1895-1971, *2:* 260

Weber, William John   1927- , *14:* 239

Webster, Alice (Jane Chandler)   1876-1916, *17:* 241

Webster, David   1930- , *11:* 230

Webster, Frank V. [Collective pseudonym], *1:* 222

Webster, Gary. *See* Garrison, Webb
B(lack), *25:* 119
Webster, James 1925- , *17:* 242
Webster, Jean. *See* Webster, Alice
(Jane Chandler), *17:* 241
Wechsler, Herman 1904-1976,
20: 189 (Obituary)
Weddle, Ethel H(arshbarger)
1897- , *11:* 231
Wegner, Fritz 1924- , *20:* 189
Weihs, Erika 1917- , *15:* 297
Weik, Mary Hays 1898(?)-1979,
3: 247; *23:* 233 (Obituary)
Weil, Ann Yezner 1908-1969,
9: 197
Weil, Lisl, *7:* 202
Weilerstein, Sadie Rose 1894- ,
3: 248
Weiner, Sandra 1922- , *14:* 240
Weingarten, Violet 1915- , *3:* 250
Weingartner, Charles 1922- ,
5: 199
Weir, LaVada, *2:* 261
Weir, Rosemary (Green) 1905- ,
21: 196
Weisberger, Bernard A(llen)
1922- , *21:* 198
Weisgard, Leonard (Joseph)
1916- , *2:* 263
Weiss, Adelle 1920- , *18:* 296
Weiss, Harvey 1922- , *1:* 222
Weiss, Malcolm E. 1928- ,
3: 251
Weiss, Miriam. *See* Schlein,
Miriam, *2:* 222
Weiss, Renee Karol 1923- ,
5: 199
Welch, Jean-Louise. *See* Kempton,
Jean Welch, *10:* 67
Welch, Pauline. *See* Bodenham,
Hilda Esther, *13:* 16
Welch, Ronald. *See* Felton, Ronald
Oliver, *3:* 67
Wellman, Manly Wade 1903- ,
6: 217
Wellman, Paul I. 1898-1966,
3: 251
Wells, H(erbert) G(eorge)
1866-1946, *20:* 190
Wells, Helen 1910- , *2:* 266
Wells, J. Wellington. *See* DeCamp,
L(yon) Sprague, *9:* 49
Wells, Rosemary, *18:* 296
Wels, Byron G(erald) 1924- ,
9: 197
Welty, S. F. *See* Welty, Susan F.,
9: 198
Welty, Susan F. 1905- , *9:* 198
Wendelin, Rudolph 1910- ,
23: 233
Werner, Jane. *See* Watson, Jane
Werner, *3:* 244
Werner, K. *See* Casewit, Curtis,
4: 43
Wersba, Barbara 1932- , *1:* 224

Werstein, Irving 1914-1971,
14: 240
Werth, Kurt 1896- , *20:* 213
West, Barbara. *See* Price, Olive,
8: 157
West, Betty 1921- , *11:* 233
West, C. P. *See* Wodehouse,
P(elham) G(renville), *22:* 241
West, James. *See* Withers, Carl A.,
14: 261
West, Jerry. *See* Stratemeyer,
Edward L., *1:* 208
West, Jerry. *See* Svenson, Andrew
E., *2:* 238
West, Ward. *See* Borland, Hal,
5: 22; *24:* 51 (Obituary)
Westall, Robert (Atkinson)
1929- , *23:* 235
Westervelt, Virginia (Veeder)
1914- , *10:* 193
Westheimer, David 1917- ,
14: 242
Weston, John (Harrison) 1932- ,
21: 199
Westwood, Jennifer 1940- ,
10: 194
Wexler, Jerome (LeRoy) 1923- ,
14: 243
Wheatley, Arabelle 1921- ,
16: 275
Wheeler, Captain. *See* Ellis,
Edward S(ylvester),
YABC 1: 116
Wheeler, Janet D. [Collective
pseudonym], *1:* 225
Wheeler, Opal 1898- , *23:* 236
Whelan, Elizabeth M(urphy)
1943- , *14:* 244
Whitcomb, Jon 1906- , *10:* 195
White, Anne Terry 1896- , *2:* 267
White, Dale. *See* Place, Marian T.,
3: 160
White, Dori 1919- , *10:* 195
White, E(lwyn) B(rooks) 1899- ,
2: 268
White, Eliza Orne 1856-1947,
YABC 2: 333
White, Florence M(eiman) 1910- ,
14: 244
White, Laurence B., Jr. 1935- ,
10: 196
White, Ramy Allison [Collective
pseudonym], *1:* 225
White, Robb 1909- , *1:* 225
White, T(erence) H(anbury)
1906-1964, *12:* 229
White, William, Jr. 1934- ,
16: 276
Whitehead, Don(ald) F. 1908- ,
4: 227
Whitehouse, Arch. *See* Whitehouse,
Arthur George, *14:* 246;
23: 238 (Obituary)
Whitehouse, Arthur George
1895-1979, *14:* 246; *23:* 238
(Obituary)

Whitinger, R. D. *See* Place, Marian
T., *3:* 160
Whitman, Walt(er) 1819-1892,
20: 215
Whitney, Alex(andra) 1922- ,
14: 249
Whitney, Phyllis A(yame) 1903- ,
1: 226
Whitney, Thomas P(orter) 1917- ,
25: 216
Wibberley, Leonard 1915- ,
2: 271
Widdemer, Mabel Cleland
1902-1964, *5:* 200
Widenberg, Siv 1931- , *10:* 197
Wier, Ester 1910- , *3:* 252
Wiese, Kurt 1887-1974, *3:* 254;
24: 205 (Obituary)
Wiesner, Portia. *See* Takakjian,
Portia, *15:* 273
Wiesner, William 1899- , *5:* 200
Wiggin, Kate Douglas (Smith)
1856-1923, *YABC 1:* 258
Wilbur, Richard (Purdy) 1921- ,
9: 200
Wilde, Gunther. *See* Hurwood,
Bernhardt J., *12:* 107
Wilde, Oscar (Fingal O'Flahertie
Wills) 1854-1900, *24:* 205
Wilder, Laura Ingalls 1867-1957,
15: 300
Wildsmith, Brian 1930- , *16:* 277
Wilkins, Frances 1923- , *14:* 249
Wilkinson, Brenda 1946- ,
14: 250
Wilkinson, Burke 1913- , *4:* 229
Will. *See* Lipkind, William, *15:* 178
Willard, Barbara (Mary) 1909- ,
17: 243
Willard, Mildred Wilds 1911- ,
14: 252
Willey, Robert. *See* Ley, Willy,
2: 175
Williams, Barbara 1925- ,
11: 233
Williams, Beryl. *See* Epstein,
Beryl, *1:* 85
Williams, Charles. *See* Collier,
James Lincoln, *8:* 33
Williams, Clyde C. 1881- ,
8: 216
Williams, Eric (Ernest) 1911- ,
14: 253
Williams, Ferelith Eccles 1920- ,
22: 237
Williams, Frances B. *See* Browin,
Frances Williams, *5:* 30
Williams, Garth (Montgomery)
1912- , *18:* 298
Williams, Guy R. 1920- , *11:* 235
Williams, Hawley. *See* Heyliger,
William, *YABC 1:* 163
Williams, J. R. *See* Williams,
Jeanne, *5:* 202
Williams, J. Walker. *See*

Wodehouse, P(elham) G(renville), *22:* 241

Williams, Jay   1914-1978, *3:* 256; *24:* 221 (Obituary)

Williams, Jeanne   1930- , *5:* 202

Williams, Maureen   1951- , *12:* 238

Williams, Michael. *See* St. John, Wylly Folk, *10:* 132

Williams, Patrick J. *See* Butterworth, W. E., *5:* 40

Williams, Selma R(uth)   1925- , *14:* 256

Williams, Slim. *See* Williams, Clyde C., *8:* 216

Williams, Ursula Moray   1911- , *3:* 257

Williamson, Joanne Small   1926- , *3:* 259

Wilma, Dana. *See* Faralla, Dana, *9:* 62

Wilson, Beth P(ierre), *8:* 218

Wilson, Carter   1941- , *6:* 218

Wilson, Dorothy Clarke   1904- , *16:* 283

Wilson, Ellen (Janet Cameron), *9:* 200

Wilson, (Leslie) Granville   1912- , *14:* 257

Wilson, Hazel   1898- , *3:* 260

Wilson, John   1922- , *22:* 239

Wilson, Joyce M(uriel Judson), *21:* 201

Wilson, Walt(er N.)   1939- , *14:* 258

Wilton, Elizabeth   1937- , *14:* 259

Wilwerding, Walter Joseph   1891-1966, *9:* 201

Winders, Gertrude Hecker, *3:* 261

Windham, Basil. *See* Wodehouse, P(elham) G(renville), *22:* 241

Windham, Kathryn T(ucker)   1918- , *14:* 259

Windsor, Claire. *See* Hamerstrom, Frances, *24:* 125

Winfield, Arthur M. *See* Stratemeyer, Edward L., *1:* 208

Winfield, Edna. *See* Stratemeyer, Edward L., *1:* 208

Winter, Milo (Kendall)   1888-1956, *21:* 202

Winter, R. R.. *See* Winterbotham, R(ussell) R(obert), *10:* 198

Winterbotham, R(ussell) R(obert)   1904-1971, *10:* 198

Winthrop, Elizabeth. *See* Mahony, Elizabeth Winthrop, *8:* 125

Wirtenberg, Patricia Z.   1932- , *10:* 199

Wise, William   1923- , *4:* 230

Wise, Winifred E., *2:* 273

Wiseman, B(ernard)   1922- , *4:* 232

Withers, Carl A.   1900-1970, *14:* 261

Witt, Shirley Hill   1934- , *17:* 247

Wizard, Mr. *See* Herbert, Don, *2:* 131

Wodehouse, P(elham) G(renville)   1881-1975, *22:* 241

Wohlrabe, Raymond A.   1900- , *4:* 234

Wojciechowska, Maia   1927- , *1:* 228

Wolcott, Patty   1929- , *14:* 264

Wolfe, Burton H.   1932- , *5:* 202

Wolfe, Louis   1905- , *8:* 219

Wolfenden, George. *See* Beardmore, George, *20:* 10

Wolff, Robert Jay   1905- , *10:* 199

Wolkstein, Diane   1942- , *7:* 204

Wondriska, William   1931- , *6:* 219

Wood, Edgar A(llardyce)   1907- , *14:* 264

Wood, James Playsted   1905- , *1:* 229

Wood, Kerry. *See* Wood, Edgar A(llardyce), *14:* 264

Wood, Nancy   1936- , *6:* 220

Woodard, Carol   1929- , *14:* 266

Woodburn, John Henry   1914- , *11:* 236

Woodford, Peggy   1937- , *25:* 218

Woodrich, Mary Neville   1915- , *2:* 274

Woods, Margaret   1921- , *2:* 275

Woods, Nat. *See* Stratemeyer, Edward L., *1:* 208

Woodson, Jack. *See* Woodson, John Waddie, Jr., *10:* 200

Woodson, John Waddie, Jr., *10:* 200

Woodward, Cleveland   1900- , *10:* 201

Woody, Regina Jones   1894- , *3:* 263

Wooldridge, Rhoda   1906- , *22:* 249

Woolley, Catherine   1904- , *3:* 265

Woolsey, Janette   1904- , *3:* 266

Worcester, Donald Emmet   1915- , *18:* 301

Worline, Bonnie Bess   1914- , *14:* 267

Wormser, Sophie   1896- , *22:* 250

Worth, Valerie   1933- , *8:* 220

Wortis, Avi   1937- , *14:* 269

Wriggins, Sally Hovey   1922- , *17:* 248

Wright, Dare   1926(?)- , *21:* 206

Wright, Enid Meadowcroft   1898-1966, *3:* 267

Wright, Esmond   1915- , *10:* 202

Wright, Frances Fitzpatrick   1897- , *10:* 202

Wright, Judith   1915- , *14:* 270

Wright, Kenneth. *See* Del Rey, Lester, *22:* 97

Wright, R(obert) H.   1906- , *6:* 220

Wrightson, Patricia   1921- , *8:* 220

Wronker, Lili Cassel   1924- , *10:* 204

Wyeth, N(ewell) C(onvers)   1882-1945, *17:* 249

Wyler, Rose   1909- , *18:* 303

Wymer, Norman George   1911- , *25:* 219

Wyndham, Lee. *See* Hyndman, Jane Andrews, *1:* 122; *23:* 103 (Obituary)

Wyndham, Robert. *See* Hyndman, Robert Utley, *18:* 123

Wynter, Edward (John)   1914- , *14:* 271

Wynyard, Talbot. *See* Hamilton, Charles Harold St. John, *13:* 77

Wyss, Thelma Hatch   1934- , *10:* 205

Yamaguchi, Marianne   1936- , *7:* 205

Yang, Jay   1941- , *12:* 239

Yashima, Taro. *See* Iwamatsu, Jun Atsushi, *14:* 83

Yates, Elizabeth   1905- , *4:* 235

Yaukey, Grace S(ydenstricker)   1899- , *5:* 203

Yeakley, Marjory Hall   1908- , *21:* 207

Yeo, Wilma (Lethem)   1918-, *24:* 221

Yep, Laurence M.   1948- , *7:* 206

Yerian, Cameron John, *21:* 208

Yerian, Margaret A., *21:* 209

Yolen, Jane H.   1939- , *4:* 237

York, Andrew. *See* Nicole, Christopher Robin, *5:* 141

Yonge, Charlotte Mary   1823-1901, *17:* 272

York, Carol Beach   1928- , *6:* 221

Young, Bob. *See* Young, Robert W., *3:* 269

Young, Clarence [Collective pseudonym], *1:* 231

Young, Ed   1931- , *10:* 205

Young, Edward. *See* Reinfeld, Fred, *3:* 170

Young, Jan. *See* Young, Janet Randall, *3:* 268

Young, Janet Randall   1919- , *3:* 268

Young, Margaret B(uckner)   1922- , *2:* 275

Young, Miriam   1913-1934, *7:* 208

Young, (Rodney Lee) Patrick (Jr.)   1937- , *22:* 251

Young, Robert W.   1916-1969, *3:* 269

Young, Scott A(lexander)   1918- , *5:* 204

Zalben, Jane Breskin   1950- , *7:* 211

Author Index

Zallinger, Jean (Day)   1918- ,
   14: 272
Zappler, Lisbeth   1930- , *10:* 206
Zei, Alki, *24:* 223
Zellan, Audrey Penn   1950- ,
   22: 252
Zemach, Harve   1933- , *3:* 270
Zemach, Margot   1931- , *21:* 209
Ziemienski, Dennis   1947- ,
   10: 206
Zillah. *See* Macdonald, Zillah K.,
   11: 167
Zim, Herbert S(pencer)   1909- ,
   1: 231
Zimmerman, Naoma   1914- ,
   10: 207
Zindel, Paul   1936- , *16:* 283
Ziner, (Florence) Feenie   1921- ,
   5: 204
Zion, (Eu)Gene   1913-1975,
   18: 305
Zolotow, Charlotte S.   1915- ,
   1: 233
Zonia, Dhimitri   1921- , *20:* 233
Zurhorst, Charles (Stewart, Jr.)
   1913- , *12:* 240
Zweifel, Frances   1931- , *14:* 273